Historical Morphology

Trends in Linguistics
Studies and Monographs 17

Editor

Werner Winter

Mouton Publishers
The Hague · Paris · New York

Historical Morphology

edited by

Jacek Fisiak

Mouton Publishers
The Hague · Paris · New York

Professor Jacek Fisiak
Institute of English
Adam Mickiewicz University
Poznań, Poland

Papers prepared for the
International Conference on Historical Morphology
held at Boszkowo, Poland, 15–18 March 1978.

ISBN 90 279 3038 4

Preface

The present volume contains twenty-three papers prepared for presentation at the International Conference on Historical Morphology held at Boszkowo (Poland) between the 15th and 18th of March, 1978.

The conference, organized by the Institute of English, Adam Mickiewicz University, Poznań, brought together 62 linguists from 15 countries working within a number of different theoretical paradigms and using a wide range of Indo-European and non-Indo-European languages in their analyses.

Not all the papers presented at the conference have been included in this collection. Some had been committed for publication in other places, others were only loosely connected with the topic of the conference and will also appear elsewhere. One paper (R. Lass), although not read and discussed at Boszkowo, has been included here with the permission of the author who was prevented from coming to the conference at the last moment.

The papers as well as the discussion at the conference fairly adequately reflect the present situation in historical morphology. The nature of morphological change is far from being fully understood, as is linguistic change in general, although numerous successful attempts have been made to clarify certain of its aspects in more remote and recent times. Both synchronic, and consequently, diachronic morphology still lack a workable theory which further complicates the understanding of relations on the border of phonology, morphology and syntax.

Several of the papers in this volume address themselves to these fundamental issues. Some deal with explanations of particular processes or changes in one or more languages. A few of the papers may look on the face of it only vaguely connected with historical morphology. It seems, however, that as a whole, the present collection is at least a small step towards a better understanding of morphological change in general as well as various morphological processes in particular. Furthermore, by formulating questions to which no satisfactory answers are currently available, it also indicates potential areas of fruitful research in the future.

The organizers of the Boszkowo conference would like to take this opportunity and thank all the conference members for their active participation. Long and lively discussions have often contributed to the numerous changes in final versions of papers submitted for publication.

Words of thanks are due to the Vice Rector of Adam Mickiewicz University for Research and Foreign Exchanges, Professor Stefan Kozarski, for providing a substantial contribution to the conference, i.e. ample funding. Thanks are also due to the administration of the Boszkowo conference centre, to Miss Barbara Płocińska, M.A. and Dr. Ewa Siarkiewicz-Bivand for skilful handling of all the administrative details.

Poznań, July 1978   Jacek Fisiak

Table of contents

Contents

List of participants

at the International Conference on Historical Morphology held at Boszkowo, Poland, March 15–18, 1978

Director
Professor Jacek Fisiak   Adam Mickiewicz University, Poznań

Participants

Professor Henning Andersen	University of Copenhagen
Professor Stephen R. Anderson	U.C.L.A
Professor Mark Aronoff	S.U.N.Y. Stony Brook
Docent Wiesław Awedyk	Adam Mickiewicz University, Poznań
Professor John Beatty	C.U.N.Y.
Professor Rolf Berndt	University of Rostock
Dr. Robert Borsley	Adam Mickiewicz University, Poznań
Professor Lyle Campbell	S.U.N.Y. Albany
Professor Broder Carstensen	Gesamthochschule Paderborn
Mr. David Clement	University of Edinburgh
Dr. Bernard Comrie	University of Cambridge
Docent James Critz	University of Warsaw
Professor Jan Cygan	University of Wrocław
Professor Xavier Dekeyser	University of Antwerp
Mr. James Dingley	University of Reading
Dr. Grzegorz Dogil	Adam Mickiewicz University, Poznań
Docent Stig Eliasson	University of Uppsala
Professor Peter Erdmann	University of Saarbrücken
Docent James Fidelholtz	Maria Skłodowska-Curie University, Lublin
Professor Udo Fries	University of Zürich

Mr. Christopher Greene	Adam Mickiewicz University, Poznań
Docent Edmund Gussman	Maria Skłodowska-Curie University, Lublin
Professor Martin B. Harris	University of Salford
Dr. Frank Heny	University of Groningen
Professor Joan Bybee Hooper	S.U.N.Y. Buffalo
Professor George Horn	Adam Mickiewicz University, Poznań
Professor David G. Huntley	University of Toronto
Professor Charles Jones	University of Durham
Docent Piotr Kakietek	University of Silesia, Katowice
Professor Dieter Kastovsky	University of Wuppertal
Professor Jonathan Kaye	University of Montreal
Dr. Veronica Kniezsa	Lorand Eötvös University, Budapest
Professor Frederik H. H. Kortlandt	University of Leiden
Docent Roman Laskowski	Polish Academy of Science, Cracow
Professor Helmut Lüdtke	University of Kiel
Professor Witold Mańczak	Jagiellonian University of Cracow
Dr. Bogusław Marek	Maria Skłodowska-Curie University, Lublin
Mrs. Hanna Mausch	Adam Mickiewicz University, Poznań
Ms. Donka Minkova	University of Sofia
Mr. Paul Neubauer	Adam Mickiewicz University, Poznań
Ms. Barbara Nykiel	Pedagogical University, Bydgoszcz
Dr. Adam Pasicki	Catholic University of Lublin
Dr. Frans Plank	University of Hannover
Ms. Barbara Płocińska	Adam Mickiewicz University, Poznań
Professor Kazimierz Polański	University of Silesia, Katowice
Docent Elisabeth Riddle	Adam Mickiewicz University, Poznań
Professor Sandor Rot	Lorand Eötvös University, Budapest
Dr. Jerzy Rubach	University of Warsaw
Professor Blair A. Rudes	University of Bucharest
Mr. Władysław Rybarkiewicz	University of Łódź
Professor Russel G. Schuh	U.C.L.A.
Dr. Ewa Siarkiewicz-Bivand	Adam Mickiewicz University, Poznań
Dr. Wojciech Smoczyński	Jagiellonian University of Cracow
Professor Jürgen Strauß	University of Trier

Professor Sarah G. Thomason	University of Pittsburgh
Professor Josef Vachek	Charles University, Prague
Professor Nigel Vincent	University of Hull
Dr. Jerzy Wełna	University of Warsaw
Professor Werner Winter	University of Kiel
Dr. Wolfgang U. Wurzel	Academy of Science, Berlin, G.D.R.

HENNING ANDERSEN

Morphological change:
towards a typology

1.0   There may not be any need to argue for the utility of a typology of innovations in morphology. Linguists concerned with historical morphology know that the various attempts that have been made to explain morphological change by means of half a dozen "laws of analogy" have met with very little success mainly because of the immense variety of kinds of change that need to be explained. And it stands to reason that it is premature to seek explanations of a class of phenomena before the full range and the diversity of the phenomena to be explained have been established. Still, at a time when taxonomies are in disfavour, it seems reasonable to begin a paper on the typology of change by clarifying the relationship between explanation and taxonomy in historical linguistics.

There can be no quarrel that historical linguistics is a nomothetic discipline, and that its ultimate aim is to understand language change by uncovering the lawlike connections between language states and the innovations they give rise to, to formulate generalizations which to the greatest possible extent explain linguistic innovations as necessary consequences of given linguistic facts.

This endeavour can only be based on a body of accurate accounts of actual linguistic innovations. This means, on the one hand, that data from languages whose history is known should be given preference over unattested changes between reconstructed language states. On the other hand, it means that the diachronic correspondences that can be defined between consecutive states of a language must be analysed and understood as the results of sequences of quite different — and quite differently motivated — innovations. One cannot hope to form valid generalizations except on the basis of innovations described and interpreted as real events.

Description and interpretation presuppose experience in the sense that they always, implicitly or explicitly, involve a comparison between the phenomenon to be interpreted and other known phenomena. To give a plausible account of some linguistic change one must know what innovations are possible under given circumstances. The aim of a typology of linguistic innovations is to give a systematic presentation of our experience with kinds of innovation, a categorization of the possible which can be used both as a heuristic tool in investigating individual changes and as a framework for that sorting of our data which must precede any attempt to formulate laws of change.

1.0.1   The present paper is intended as a continuation of my report to the First International Conference on Historical Linguistics, Edinburgh 1974, "Towards a typology of change: Bifurcating changes and binary relations". In that report I defined a set of general criteria for a typology of linguistic change and showed that these are equally applicable to lexical innovations and phonological innovations. Incidentally it turned out that also specific classes of innovations in phonology correspond point by point to the classification of semantic changes proposed on entirely different grounds by Stern (1931).

As one turns from innovations in phonology and semantics to inflectional morphology, one might look to traditional surveys of analogical change in the hope of finding reflected in them some important criteria which could guide us towards a systematic understanding of morphological change. Unfortunately, neither in the work of the neogrammarians nor in more recent contributions to the study of analogy do we find important types of innovation defined with sufficient clarity to be helpful in this regard. The traditional distinctions between material and formal analogy (Osthoff 1879), neologism and remodelling (Brugmann 1906), expression changed to fit content and content changed to fit expression (Wheeler 1887), or proportional and non-proportional analogy (Hermann 1931) are of little or no value, for they are much too general.

An attentive reading of such detailed surveys of analogical change as Paul's (1920), von der Gabelentz's (1901), or Hermann's (1931), or of the more specialized studies of Kuryłowicz (1949) or Mańczak (1957, 1958, 1963) will convince anyone that there are a great many quite diverse types of innovation in morphology. Individual examples discussed in these works illustrate important aspects of morphological change, but the discussions consistently lack analytic depth in essential respects, important distinctions are often overlooked or, where they are drawn in one example, their relevance for other examples is not recognized. A weakness shared by all surveys of analogical change to date has been a failure to define different types of development relative to one another. If one asks why this might be so, the answer will have to point to two major theoretical deficiencies in this area of investigation: the discipline has so far worked without an explicit theory of change and without an articulate theory of morphology.

1.1   The lack of a workable theory of synchronic morphology is undoubtedly the greatest obstacle for the student of historical morphology,
for without an explicit conception of the nature of morphological structure, one cannot even adequately define the correspondences between
successive states of a morphological system which are the raw material
the language historian has to interpret. Without such a theory, of course,
also an attempt to classify innovations in morphology may seem a doubtful undertaking. Still it is possible precisely through an attempt to define
different types of innovation to gain some insight into the structure of a
morphological system — or at least into some of the constitutive features
of such a system.

   In order to facilitate the discussion of the various types of innovation to
be surveyed below, I will briefly mention some of the notions that I
assume to be essential for the investigation of morphological change.

1.1.1   First a distinction must be made between change in morphology
and change in morphophonemics. The term morphological change
should be limited to changes in the relations among linguistic signs,
whether relations among signata or among signantia. Morphophonemic
change, by contrast, is change in the relations among variants of signantia
(allomorphs) (Andersen 1969). Traditionally changes of both kinds have
been referred to indiscriminately as analogical. This term is better
avoided, for its meaning is so general as to make it applicable to the most
various types of morphological and morphophonemic change and of no
particular value in the discussion of most.

1.1.2   A central notion in a theory of morphology is that of the content
sign, or morpheme, which can be understood as consisting of a signans
(sign vehicle or means), a signatum (sign value or object), and a sign rule
(cf. 1.1.5) establishing the relation between the two (cf. 1.1.4). Morphemes vary greatly according to the kinds of signantia, the kinds of
signata, and the kinds of signatum–signans relations they comprise.

   Different types of absolute signantia are to be distinguished. The
distinction between zero and real signantia is traditional, but it seems
likely that the historical linguist will have to recognize zero signantia
under various circumstances where traditionally descriptivists would not
postulate them (cf. 5.2.2). Real signantia can be direct (e.g. sentence
intonation marking subordination or interrogative status), but typically
involve both articulations of language being mediate, i.e. consisting of
(combinations of) distinctive feature values or, as they will be called here,
diacritic signs. Traditionally morphological analysis has operated with
whole phonemes and phoneme sequences and has overlooked that

grammatical meaning can be expressed by single diacritic signs. The study
of morphological innovations shows that the synchronic analysis must
operate with the ultimate constituents of the expression systems, which
are the diacritic signs (cf. Jakobson 1958, 1966; Huntley 1968; Leed
1970).

Furthermore, signantia can be relative, i.e. consist in the modification
of a real signans (Isačenko 1975). Consonant gradation, apophony,
accentual alternations, reduplication, and element inversion are typical
examples. In synchronic analysis it may be difficult to determine whether
an alternation is to be interpreted as morphophonemic (the alternants are
co-variants of absolute signantia) or morphological (the modification of
the signans is in itself a signans). Morphological innovations show that
this dilemma may exist also for learners of a language.

1.1.3   Signata may be absolute. A distinction must be made between
asynthetic signata, consisting of a single content element (e.g. '3rd person' expressed by *-t* in Russ. *s,id,-í-t* '(one) sits', *s,id,-á-t* '(some) sit') and
synthetic signata, combinations of content elements (e.g. 'non-3rd person, speaker, singular' expressed by *-u* in Russ. *s,iž-ú* 'I sit'). Here, as in
the case of signantia, the analysis must be pushed to its conclusion, and
traditionally recognized content units such as cases and tenses must be
analysed into features of grammatical meaning, that is, as synthetic
signata. Otherwise the specialization of signans elements for classes of
signata — such as, in the Russian declensions, *-m(,)-* as a marker of
peripheral cases (locative, dative, and instrumental) — cannot be
described. Furthermore, only when such more general elements of
grammatical meaning are recognized is it possible to understand
similarities of expression between different specific categories as motivated, e.g. Engl. *-z* 'plural' (a quantifier descriptor, in Jakobson's (1957)
terminology) and *-z* 'possessive' (a quantifier connector).

Besides absolute signata one must recognize relative signata. In Russian, the nominal desinence *-u* is found in ascriptive non-quantifier cases
(accusative and dative) and in non-ascriptive quantifier cases (genitive II
and locative II). The historical development of this desinence makes it
difficult to view this as an instance of accidental homonymy and reasonable to hypothesize here a syncretism among the cases sharing the value
of 'marked ascriptivity'. Similar considerations suggest that the identity
of the signantia of the English *-z* '(substantival) plural' and *-z* '(verbal)
singular — again the result of a morphological innovation — may be
motivated by their similar value of 'marked quantifier descriptor'.

1.1.4   Morphological analysis must distinguish different types of signatum–signans relations. Linguistic signs are primarily symbolic (conventional, arbitrary), shifters (e.g. mood, tense, person, cf. Jakobson 1957) being symbolic-indexical (their signata include reference to the speech acts in which they are used) and onomatopoeia being symbolic-iconic (their signantia are similar to aspects of their referents). But to understand the relations among signs — in paradigms as well as in syntagms — purely iconic and purely indexical signatum–signans relations must be considered as well.

Relations of similarity among signantia may reflect relations of similarity among their signata. In the lexicon such correspondences between sound and meaning are exemplified by the so-called phonaesthemes (Samuels 1972). Such diagrammatic relations are typically more or less sporadic in the lexicon, but in a morphological system they may be paramount. Typical examples of diagrammatic patterns are the specialization of certain phonemes or diacritic signs as (parts of) signantia for classes of signata, e.g. consonants for past tense morphemes (*-l-, -f-*), but vowels for present tense morphemes (*-i-, -a-, -o-, -u-*) in Russian, the specialization of certain morpheme structures for specific signatum classes, e.g. zero desinences for the unmarked term of diverse grammatical categories or the distinction between longer and shorter desinences as an expression for such quantifier oppositions as plural vs. singular number or imperfective vs. perfective aspect (cf. Greenberg 1963; Jakobson 1957, 1958, 1966).

The importance of diagrammatic relations for the cohesion of syntagms will be touched on in 4.1.2. Here I will mention the need to distinguish symbolic and indexical signatum-signans relations in syntagms. The signans of one sign may be an index of the signatum of another morpheme. Thus Engl. *geese* means 'goose' and 'plural', but it means 'plural' only by virtue of occurring before (the zero allomorph of) the plural morpheme.

The notions of "cumulative" and "overlapping" exponence (Matthews 1974), which seem motivated at a preliminary stage of morphological analysis, lose their justification as soon as such complexes of symbolized ('goose') and indexed ('plural') signata are properly analysed. Which is not to say that the real problems of analysis disappear which are posed by cases like Engl. *-z* (*fail-s*), which likely symbolically represents 'singular' and indexically '3rd person, present, indicative', all represented by zero (as implied above), but allows of several other interpretations, including that of a synthetic signatum (cf. Anttila 1975).

1.1.5 Finally, while the relation between a signatum and its signans in a grammar is an entailment relation of the form "If content 'x', then expression *x*," it is important to recognize that for the language learner, who has to formulate such deductive rules, the signans is primary and the signatum has to be inferred abductively. Very commonly morphological innovations involve the formulation, as an unwarranted deductive rule, of a signans-signatum relation which is warranted as an inductive inference. In the analysis of morphological innovations, it is therefore essential that both the deductive and the inductive orientations of signatum-signans relations be established.

1.1.6   These informal remarks on some of the elementary notions in a theory of morphology are very far from reflecting the complexity of the conceptual apparatus such a theory must comprise. They are intended only to describe, however superficially, some of the aspects of morphology that have often been overlooked — in synchronic as well as in diachronic studies — but which cannot be disregarded in a systematic study of morphological innovations if valid generalizations are to be hoped for.

It would be desirable to add here some remarks on morphophonemics. It is clear that the traditional way of presenting morphophonemic alternations as an assemblage of mechanical, ad hoc rules is inadequate, and that morphophonemic systems present diagrammatic patterns, of greater or lesser transparency, which must be grasped if innovations in morphophonemics are to be fully understood (Shapiro 1969). In the survey below, however, the focus will be on morphological innovations, and morphophonemic innovations will be discussed mainly en passant in order to emphasize the contrast between these two domains of language structure.

1.2   A second reason for the lack of success of previous attempts at a synthetic view of historical morphology is, as I mentioned above (1.0.1), the lack of an explicit theory of language change. This is not to say that individual kinds of change have not been described explicitly. For instance, quite an adequate account of the process of language transmission as a locus of linguistic innovation can be found as early as in Osthoff's work (1879). Paul gives very detailed accounts of such aspects of change as the creation of analogical neologisms and the gradual acceptance of neologisms by a speech community (1920). Stern, again, achieved a typology of semantic innovations which in its essentials is valid, and in the process he described in detail how several different kinds of change may come about (1931). But these early accounts did not succeed in defining a minimal set of functional and structural factors which determine all possible types of innovations, and hence they could not analyse individual instances of change consistently or in commensurate terms.

Later investigators, such as Kuryłowicz and Mańczak, have conformed to the pattern, so prevalent in the early phase of structuralism, of viewing language as detached from the real life contexts in which it functions and is transmitted and have thereby restricted themselves to investigations of diachronic correspondences. Since correspondences can arise by many different types of innovation, such an approach can only lead to valid generalizations of a statistical nature, as Mańczak realized from the outset. The search for laws of morphological and morphophonemic change, in the sense given this notion by Kuryłowicz, is an important task for the future. But it stands to reason that it must be based on an analysis of innovations, adequately described in comparable terms, and not on correspondences which are results of sequences of innovations.

1.2.1   In the following survey I will presuppose as reasonably realistic the theory of change put forward in Andersen 1973. This theory distinguishes two modes of innovation, abductive and deductive. Abductive innovations are innovations that arise in the process of (abductively) inferring elements of a grammar from speech. Abductive innovations result in correspondences between elements of a grammar (G-2) and homologous elements of the grammar (G-1) from whose output G-2 was inferred. Deductive innovations are innovations that arise in the (deductive) process of deriving a phonetic output from a semantic representation (which in turn can be viewed as the output of a pragmatic competence) by means of a grammar. Deductive innovations are observable as correspondences between the output (O-2) of one grammar (G-2) and the output from which G-2 was inferred.

1.2.2   Further, two categories of innovations are distinguished, termed adaptive and evolutive. Adaptive innovations arise as purposeful modifications of a grammar, aimed at making it better suited to serve one or another of the functions of language in communication. In explanations of adaptive innovations, the grammar is seen as a constituent part of a communicative system, and reference to the other constitutents of this system, the speech situation, is necessary; in deductive innovations, to the speaker himself, the addressee, the referential content, the character of the message, or the channel of communication; in abductive innovations, to the interlocutor's grammar and its output (cf. Jakobson 1964).

Evolutive innovations lack any such specific motivation. Abductive evolutive innovations are explained by the surface forms and referential content from which the innovative elements of the grammar are inferred and by the strategies used in the abductive process. Deductive evolutive innovations are typically explained wholly by the underlying representations and the rules operating on them in the grammar that produces the innovations. Only to a limited extent do other factors enter the picture (cf. 4.1).

1.2.3   Finally, the theory includes an account of the functions of different types of innovations, formulated in such general terms that it is uniformly applicable to innovations in all parts of linguistic structure (Andersen 1973). Since questions of causality are not of principal concern in the survey below, an application of this part of the theory to the data of historical morphology and morphophonemics must be deferred to a later occasion.

1.2.4   With the help of the two dichotomies abductive/deductive and adaptive/evolutive, all instances of change can be analysed as sequential complexes of innovations. For instance, a neologism may arise as an individual adaptive (deductive) innovation serving a specific purpose in communication. But only through numerous (abductive) contact innovations can it gain the acceptance of a speech community, and only through subsequent collective (deductive) innovations does it gain currency. In a language contact situation, the primary grammar may interfere with the secondary grammar both when this is (abductively) acquired and when it is (deductively) used to produce utterances in the secondary language. The secondary grammar may interfere with the primary grammar in the (deductive) production of utterances in the secondary language. But it is only when this novel output serves as basis for collective (abductive) contact innovations or for (abductive) first language acquisition within the speech community that the result of the interference comes to be more than individual deviations from the received norms of one or the other language and acquires the status of a social fact.

    In the survey below, I will generally abstract from the various mechanisms of change involved in the codification of different types of innovations and will concentrate on the initial innovations. This is an unavoidable simplification, which is made with the understanding that in the proper place, each of the examples adduced below would be expanded into a full scale account of the sequence of differently motivated innovations by which it was followed.

2.0   Adaptive innovations: The deductive innovations which arise in response to a perceived inadequacy of a grammar to carry the semantic content the speakers wish it to express can be categorized according to the communicative function they are intended to serve — the emotive, the conative, the referential, the poetic (or aesthetic), and the phatic (cf. Jakobson 1964). More important from the point of view chosen here, innovations can be made at different levels of the grammar.

2.1   Accommodative innovations in inflectional morphology consist in the novel selection or combination of features of grammatical meaning to correspond to freshly perceived communicative needs. They parallel the types of lexical innovation Stern termed substitution and nomination.

Innovations in selection are the origin of grammatical transposition (or grammatical metaphor). The Russian use of the plural to express great extent, quantity or degree may be emotive in origin (e.g. *morózi* 'severe cold', lit.: 'frosts'); the ironic, archaizing *t,el,esá*, lit.: 'bodies' or 'corpora', used about a fat person's body, being jocular, serves an aesthetic function. The widespread replacement of the imperative with other moods, substitutions aimed at obtaining the cooperation of the addressee, evidently serves the conative function. The eventual replacement of the inherited imperative by the optative in prehistoric Slavic undoubtedly had its origin in such a transposition (cf. Kuryłowicz 1964:136).

While innovations in selection are observable only as modifications in the referential value of existing morphological means, innovations in the combination of features of grammatical meaning directly affect inflectional paradigms. As an example, consider the Russian affixation of the '2nd person, plural' desinence *-t,e* to the '1st person, plural' forms used for the inclusive imperative of perfective verbs to signal plural addressee or politeness (e.g. *po-govor,-i-m* 'let us talk', *po-govor,-i-m-t,e* 'let us talk'), and not only to these verb forms, but also to indeclinables with conative function, e.g. *na, na-t,e* 'there you are', *nu, nu-t,e* 'well', *polno, polno-t,e* 'enough!' (Obnorskij 1953:147).

Another example is the extension of the narrative paradigm in the history of Bulgarian (see example (1)). Originally developed as a counterpart of the aorist (paradigm A) — I will return to this below (3.1) — the narrative was needed also in conjunction with other tenses. A new

(1)

	A		B	
	'vouched for'	'narrative'	'vouched for'	'narrative'
Pres.	*piše*		*piše* ⎱	*pišel*
Impf.	*pišeše*		*pišeše* ⎰	
Aor.	*pisa*	*pisal*	*pisa*	*pisal*
Perf.	*pisal e*		*pisal e* ⎱	*bil pisal*
Plup.	*beše pisal*		*beše pisal* ⎰	

compound preterite was formed to carry the meaning of 'narrative' plus 'retrospective', corresponding to the "vouched for" perfect and pluperfect, and another, based on a new *l*-participle formed from the imperfect tense stem, was created to correspond to the "vouched for" present and imperfect (paradigm B; the verb 'to write') (Mirčev 1963:208f., Gołąb 1959).

Innovations such as this, motivated by the referential function, seem relatively rare in inflectional morphology — they are also difficult to distinguish from the deductive evolutive innovations discussed in 3.5. Accommodative innovations are more frequently motivated by the aesthetic function, as deliberately jocular, or at least attention-focusing, formations. As a striking example one can note the use of participial suffixes with hyperbolic value in adjectives in Russian, e.g. (with the present active participle suffix) *bol,š-ušč-ij* 'hugeous', *tolst-ušč-ij* 'fat' *zl,-ušč-ij* 'wicked' (Obnorskij 1953:195f., Al'muxamedova 1976).

2.2   Remedial innovations are innovations in signantia, innovations that serve to reestablish distinctions between signantia which have become identical (have become homonymous) or have come to have identical realizations (have become homophonous) through sound change.

2.2.1   Homonymy can be eliminated in various ways, e.g. (a) lexico-syntactically by periphrasis, (b) morphologically by syncretism, one (or several) of the homonymous desinences being replaced with another (others) from the same paradigm, or (c) morphophonemically by an innovation in the selection of desinence allomorphs.

To suggest the character of an innovation of type (b), one can take the well known replacement of accusative desinences with genitive desinences with nominal stems denoting animates in the Slavic languages. The innovation is limited to those paradigms in which the accusative is otherwise identical with the nominative and is thus clearly morphological and not syntactical. It seems likely, though, that this innovation should be interpreted in a different way (see 5.1).

As an example of (c), consider the early Russian development by which the genitive plural allomorphs *-ŭ*, *-ĭ* in original *o*-stem masculines — where they had become identical to the nominative singular desinences *ŭ*, *-ĭ* by sound change — were replaced by the allomorphs *-ovŭ*, *-evŭ* characteristic of original *u*-stems (cf. Borkovskij — Kuznecov 1965:200).

2.2.2   Homophony, too, can be eliminated in various ways, at least by morphophonemic and phonological innovation.

In large parts of the Russian language area, neutralization rules produce identical realizations of unstressed /o a e i/ and after a palatalized consonant: the nom.sg. forms [s,istrá p,itnó st,iná pl,itá] have the same underlying stem vowel as the corresponding plurals [s,óstri p,átna st,éni pl,íti] 'sister, spot, wall, hearth'. In the second conjugation, the neutralization leads to the homophony of the 3rd sg. and 3rd pl. forms of stem-stressed and mobile-stressed verbs (see (2)). Many dialects (including the old Moscow city dialect; cf. Jakobson 1948) have replaced the 3rd pl. desinence of these verbs with the corresponding desinence of the first conjugation (see (2), dialect A), thus maintaining the morphological distinction between 3rd sg. and 3rd pl. by merging the two (morphophonemic) conjugation classes after accented stems.

(2) First and second conjugation end-stressed and mobile-stressed verbs in Russan dialects

	End-stressed Dialect A and B		Mobile-stressed Dialect A		Dialect B	
	I conj.	II conj.	I conj.	II conj.	I conj.	II conj.
3rd sg.	*živ,-ó-t*	*s,id,-í-t*	*kól,-i-t*	*xód,-i-t*	*kól,-i-t*	*xód,-i-t*
3rd pl.	*živ,-ú-t*	*s,id,-á-t*	*kól,-u-t*	*xód,-u-t*	*kól,-u-t*	*xód,-ə-t*

Other dialects (see (2), dialect B) (including those on which the current orthoepic norms are based) exempt the 3rd pl. desinence (and a number of other desinences as well) from one of the neutralization rules, thereby maintaining the morphological distinction and keeping the conjugation classes clear-cut at the cost of constraining a phonological rule (Obnorskij 1953:147f.; Avanesov — Orlova 1965:150; Halle 1959:50, 70; Shapiro 1968:18f.).

The morphophonemic and the phonological innovation described here are a clear instance of a bifurcation, two logically alternative innovations which, as far as one can judge, are equally possible. It shows that bifurcations are not limited to abductive innovations (illustrated in Andersen 1975), but can also arise in the deductive modification of a grammatical system where the typological properties of the language leave a choice between several options.

3.0 Contact innovations arise when speakers adjust their speech to the usage of others. As suggested in 1.2.4, it is through contact innovations that members of a speech community continually adapt their usage to what they perceive to be the current norms of their speech community. Second language learning, too, is a kind of contact innovation, only of a different order of magnitude. Contact innovations can only consist in an elaboration of a grammar, but their ultimate consequences as contact changes may be describable either as simplifications or as elaborations. In inflectional morphology, contact innovations may affect the system of signata and/or the system of signantia or the morphophonemic system.

3.1   It is not difficult to give examples of morphological calques, i.e. instances in which a grammatical category appears to have been borrowed and given expression with native morphological means. In prehistoric Baltic, for instance, the local cases (illative, allative, and adessive) of a contiguous Finnic language were adopted, expressed with combinations of a native grammatical case plus a postposition, and made subject to agreement just like the inherited cases (cf. Senn 1966:92f.; Stang 1966:228f.). Middle Bulgarian and Macedonian apparently adopted from Turkish the category of narrative, employing inherited perfect forms in the novel function of aorist plus narrative, and making use of the formerly stylistic difference between presence and absence of the auxiliary in the third person to express the opposition non-narrative perfect vs. narrative aorist (cf. 2.1).

It seems likely, though, that such innovations are best understood not as parallels to lexical calques, that is, as purposeful modifications of the speakers' primary grammars, but as results of interference in the deductive production of utterances by speakers with a composite linguistic competence. I will return to them in 3.5.

3.2   Morphological borrowing proper is probably most common where the secondary grammar is closely related to the primary one. The acquisition of the Standard German opposition simple preterite vs. perfect by speakers of southern varieties of German, or of the Standard Danish three-gender system by speakers of genderless Jutish dialects, or of the case system of Standard Serbocroatian by speakers of southern varieties of Serbian are examples involving a restructuring of the system of signata as well as the adoption of new signantia. To take another example, Russian, which early abandoned the use of participles — reinterpreting nominatives of participles as verbal adverbs and retaining only a small number of inflected participial forms lexicalized as adjectives — has adopted participial constructions with the value of reduced relative clauses from Russian Church Slavonic, borrowing the appropriate participial suffices from this language (Bulaxovskij 1958:234f.).

The converse type of innovation can be exemplified from those Russian dialects in which two preterites are distinguished, a simple (e.g., *on u-jéxa-l* 'he left') and a retrospective (e.g. *on u-jéxa-vši* 'he has/had left') (Obnorskij 1953:153f.; Veyrenc 1962:97f.). Adapting their speech to the norms of the standard language, speakers having this distinction suppress it, using the forms of the simple preterite, which is over'ly similar to the single past tense of Standard Russian, for both their native preterites. See also Kuz'mina–Nemčenko 1971:116f.

3.3 The replacement of native inflectional signantia with borrowed ones is a commonplace phenomenon where dialect speakers acquire and use the desinences of a prestige dialect such as a standard language. A simple example is the replacement in various Russian dialects of different shapes of the adjectival desinence for 'gen.sg., masc.-neut.' (*-ogo, -oγo, -oo*) by the standard desinence *-ovo* (Avanesov–Orlova 1965:120).

3.4 As an example of a contact innovation in morphophonemics one can take the reintroduction of consonant alternations in 2nd conjugation verbs in Russian dialects which have long since abandoned alternations preserved in the standard language. By this innovation, the alternations listed under (A) in (3) are introduced in the paradigms of verbs with stems in *-i* or *-e* (infinitives listed under (B)), so that 1st person sg. present tense forms (C) become identical with those of the standard language (D). Actually the dialects in question have these alternations in the inflection of other verb types and accompanying derivational suffixation. Still the alternations are extended to verbs in *-i* and *-e* gradually, usually first to stems in *-d*, and last to stems with a final labial, as indicated by the numbers under (E). Other dialects show a different progression, reintroducing the alternations first in verbs with end stress in the 1st person sg. and only later in verbs with stem stress (Bromlej–Bulatova 1972:225f.).

(3)	A	B	C	D	E
	d, ~ž	*xod,í-t,*	*xod,-ú*	*xož-ú*	1
	t, ~č	*krut,í-t,*	*krut,-ú*	*kruč-ú*	2
	s, ~š	*nos,í-t,*	*nos,-ú*	*noš-ú*	2
	z, ~ž	*voz,í-t,*	*voz,-ú*	*vož-ú*	2
	p, ~pl,	*top,í-t,*	*top,-ú*	*topl,-ú*	3
	b, ~bl,	*l,ub,í-t,*	*l,ub,-ú*	*l,ubl,-ú*	3
	m, ~ml,	*tom,í-t,*	*tom,-ú*	*toml,-ú*	3
	v, ~vl,	*lov,í-t,*	*lov,-ú*	*lovl,-ú*	3

3.5 Just as the preceding examples, the last one is motivated by the greater prestige of the imitated usage. There are, however, innovations in contact situations for which it seems hazardous to posit such a motivation, and which are more naturally accounted for simply by reference to the greater simplicity of the grammar whose usage is generalized. Consider the Polish *dobëtk*//*dobytek* isogloss, which since it arose some 900 years ago has been slowly shifting northward. The *dobëtk* dialects north of the isogloss break up stem final consonant clusters before zero desinences according to the following general rule (which has lexical exceptions): if the stem final segment is a voiced obstruent or a sonorant, and the preceding segment is not a vowel, an *e* or *ë* is inserted before the last segment; if the last segment is a voiceless obstruent, and it is preceded by two non-vowels, an *e* or *ë* is inserted before the penultimate segment. The *dobytek* dialects south of the isogloss insert an *e* before any stem final consonant if it is preceded by a consonant (again with lexically marked exceptions). Each of these vowel insertion patterns has been productive and perfectly stable — except along the isogloss, where the *dobëtk* pattern has proved recessive and the *dobytek* pattern dominant. It seems evident that in interdialectal communication, it must have been easier for *dobëtk* speakers to adapt their speech to that of their *dobytek* inter-locutors than vice versa. But it must also be recognized that wherever the two patterns have coexisted in a speech community, learners have more easily learnt to produce acceptable forms with the *dobytek* rule and may hence have tended to acquire only this simpler rule (Andersen 1970).

Besides contact innovations, then, it seems necessary to recognize two categories of interference innovations which are not motivated by specific communicative functions: the deductive ones discussed in 3.1, which arise in the speech of speakers with a composite grammar, and abductive ones originating when grammars are inferred from speech data reflecting heterogeneous norms of usage. In the survey of evolutive innovations below I will bypass these types of complex innovations and limit myself to the types of innovations that can be explained on the basis of a single grammar or speech data reflecting unified norms of usage.

4.0   Evolutive innovations: These are, as mentioned in 1.2.2, the innova-tions that arise when a linguistic system is transmitted within a speech community, and which are explained entirely by relations within the grammar and the general strategies speakers use when they infer a grammar from the speech of their models and when they use their grammatical competence to produce speech themselves. The typical evolutive change in morphology or morphophonemics involves both abductive and deductive innovations. In the model of change applied here, abductive innovations are assigned principal importance, for it is in these, covert innovations that new relations among signata and signantia or among variants of signantia are formulated. Deductive innovations, on the other hand, typically merely bring out into the open, as observable innovations in usage, the consequences of previous abductions.

In analysing an evolutive change such as the redistribution of desinences between Old Russian and Modern Russian described in (4), we can therefore concentrate on positing the abductive innovation, made by generations of speakers, without which the present distribution of the desinences -*u* and -*e* would not have come about: the two allomorphs of the Old Russian locative desinence were interpreted as distinct morphemes embodying the case opposition non-ascriptive vs. ascriptive (cf. Jakobson 1958/1971:173f.).

(4)   (a)   In Old Russian, two or three dozen masculine 1st declension nouns (original *u*-stems) have the locative singular desinence -*u*. All other masculine 1st declension nouns (original *o*-stems) have the locative singular desinence -*ĕ*.

(b)   In Modern Russian, over 100 masculine 1st declension nouns distinguish two locatives in the singular, one in -*u*, governed by the prepositions *v* 'in' and *na* 'on' denoting concrete location in space or time, the other in -*e*, governed by *v* and *na* in other senses and by other prepositions.

We can simplify our account in one more respect. Just as "el cambio fónico no termina, sine que empieza con la 'ley fonética'" (Coseriu 1958:57), so we may assume — where there is no evidence to the contrary — that from the very beginning of a morphological or morphophonemic development such as the one illustrated by the correspondence in (4), significant numbers of speakers in inferring their grammars formulate as a primary generalization about the observed speech data what eventually appears as the outcome of the development (cf. Andersen 1969:825f., 1973:587). At any point during the development, speakers have to supplement this primary generalization with adaptive rules and lexical exception features in order to conform to contemporary norms. But the primary generalization limits their ability to do this effectively, predisposes them to accept only some deviations from the norms in the speech of others as being in accordance with the system of the language, and in this way contributes to steering the development towards its conclusion. An observable morphological or morphophonemic development, then, can be seen as a process of making the norms of usage fit the relations and rules that constitute the core of the grammar, its functional system

(Coseriu 1962:106f.). On the basis of this view of evolutive change, it is legitimate in the kind of survey to be given below not only to limit the account of the individual example to the crucial abductive innovation, but also to restrict it to the primary generalization.

4.1   The merely accessory role assigned to the deductive innovations in most types of evolutive change agrees well with the axiom that "nihil est in sermone, quod non prius fuit in grammatica". There are, however, several types of innovation in morphology which can only be understood as originating in the production of speech, and which for their explanation require reference to the grammar and to strategies of speech production.

In section 3.5 I mentioned interference innovations in the speech of speakers with composite grammars as an example of deductive evolutive innovations. The types to be considered here are similar inasmuch as they can be viewed as interference phenomena, albeit intragrammatical.

4.1.1.   Paradigmatic assimilation: Lexical blends are a well known example of assimilation between members of a lexical paradigm. Ger. *Gemäldnis*, a portmanteau formation of *Bildnis* and its hyponym *Gemälde*, Engl. *irregardless*, based on the synonyms *irrespective* and *regardless*, are familiar examples involving whole morphemes. Signans parts smaller than morphemes are involved in the creation of such standard examples as Late Latin *sinexter* from *sinister* and its antonym *dexter* or of early dialectal Romance *grevis* from *gravis* and its antonym *levis* (cf. Hermann 1931:78f.). In the case of synonyms, the identity of meaning may be reflected in a single new signans. Antonyms remain distinct, but the near identity of their signata is diagrammed by the greatest possible similarity of their signantia.

Purely deductive innovations like these are difficult to instantiate in inflectional morphology. Superficially, the desinence of Russ. *dv-um,á* 'two; instr.', *tr,-om,á* 'three; instr.', *četir,-m,á* 'four; instr.' might look like blends of the earlier, well attested desinences of *dv-umá, tr,-em,í, četir,-m,í*. But in this and other similar cases it seems more appropriate to analyse the desences into their constituent elements and interpret the changes as results of abductive innovations (see 5.3.3 and 5.5.2 for parallels).

4.1.2.   Syntagmatic assimilation: The well-established characteristic mutual rapprochement of the members of irreversible binomials (such as in (5)) arises typically as a result of semantic solidarity plus syntactic vicinity (Malkiel 1968:319).

(5)   Old Fr. *au feur et mesure*; 17th c. *au fur et mesure*; Mod. Fr. *au fur et à mesure*.

Where the semantic solidarity is based on a similarity relation and the constituents of the binomial are at the same time members of one paradigm — as in *grevis aut levis* (cf. Hermann 1931:79) — one may speak of paradigmatic assimilation. But semantic solidarity may be based on other relations and may bind together members of different paradigms. A morphological assimilation in such cases may be termed syntagmatic.

As an example, consider the change of conjugation in the aorist of the verb 'to see' in areas of Western Bulgaria, Macedonia, and Southern Serbia ((6), dialects A, B, C) (Alexander 1976:344f., 471f.).

(6)		Dialect A	Dialect B	Dialect C
	Aor. 1sg	*vide-x*	*vid-ox*	*vid-ox*
	2-3sg.	*vide-Ø*	*vid-e*	*vid-e*
	1pl.	*vide-xme*	*vid-oxme*	*vid-oxme*
	2pl.	*vide-xte*	*vid-oxte*	*vid-oxte*
	3pl.	*vide-xa*	*vid-oxa*	*vid-oxa*

The change, by which the verb 'to see' becomes exceptional among *e*-stem verbs by forming its aorist like verbs ending in an obstruent, is enigmatic and appears unmotivated in dialects of the B type. But in some smaller areas, the conjugation of 'to see' has changed not only in the aorist, but also in the participle used to make periphrastic forms ((7), dialect C).

(7)		Dialect A	Dialect B	Dialect C
	Pcpl. masc.	*vide-l-Ø*	*vide-l-Ø*	*višel-Ø*
	fem.	*vide-l-a*	*vide-l-a*	*višl-a*

This is a startling innovation, for by it the verb 'to see' comes to have a suppletive paradigm. It is a paradigm that is otherwise unique to the verb 'to go', *id-*, and its prefixal derivatives (e.g. *ot-id-* 'leave', *prid-* 'to come') (see (8)). A semantic solidarity between these verbs exists only in syntagms such as *idoxme i vidoxme* 'we went and saw', *prišel e i višel* 'he has come and seen', which are likely the source of the innovations in dialects of both the B and the C type.

(8)		Dialects A, B, C		
	Aor. 1sg.	*id-ox*	Pcpl. masc.	*išel-Ø*
	2-3sg.	*id-e*	fem.	*išl-a*
	1pl.	*id-oxme*		
	2pl.	*id-oxte*		
	3pl.	*id-oxa*		

Semantic solidarity and syntactic vicinity are characteristic also of
hypotactic and appositive syntagms. The widespread, though irregular,
iteration of prepositions in such syntagms in Old Russian illustrates the
strong tendency to supplement the contiguity relations in syntagms with
similarity relations (9). It is this tendency — which can only be understood as a production strategy — which must be universally responsible
for the development of grammatical concord.

(9) *Se jaz, knjaz' velikij Semen Ivanovič vseja Rusi, s svojeju brat'eju
     molodšeju so knjazem s Ivanom i s knjazem Andreem.* . . .

     Literally: 'I, Grand Prince of All Russia Semën Ivanovič with my
     younger brothers with Prince with Ivan and with Prince Andrej', i.e.
     with my younger brothers Prince Ivan and Prince Andrej (Treaty
     1341; cf. Bulaxovskij 1958:404f., Borkovskij — Kuznecov
     1965:449f., 453f.).

5.0   Abductive evolutive innovations: These are the chief source of
change in the internal history of a language, arising as they do in the
process of grammar formation, in which every speaker of the language
grasps its over-all design and formulates extensive, detailed systems of
rules to account for both the norms of usage he himself acquires
actively and for others which may be current in his speech community.
The way in which the language learner accomplishes this task can be
studied systematically through an analysis of abductive innovations, for
each kind of strategy used, each level of analysis, holds its peculiar
possibilities of innovation where the data the language learner has
to analyse do not univocally point to a single resolution. In Andersen
1975 I showed that the most fertile method one can use in the investigation of the abductive process is the comparison of pairs of alternative innovations, bifurcations, and argued that a definitive typology
of abductive innovations must enumerate all the possible kinds of
decisions the learner must make in abducing a linguistic structure.
The extreme complexity of inflectional morphology — and the data
I have at my disposal — make it impossible to apply this method
consistently here. But enough examples of alternative innovations will
be given below, I hope, to suggest that this research programme is
reasonable.

5.0.1   In a language learner's analysis, several kinds of decisions can be
discerned. One of these results in a segmentation of the surface forms into
signantia. The term 'segmentation' is somewhat awkward when one

considers that some signantia are not composed of whole segments, but of single diacritic signs or combinations of diacritic signs smaller than phonemes. The term seems quite inappropriate once one accepts that some morphological signs have relative signantia (cf. 1.1.2). But the term is traditional and may stay.

By another kind of decisions, the valuation of signantia, the phonological composition of signantia is determined.

In yet another decision process, signantia with similar reference are matched. It is in this operation that alternations may be identified. This may be termed the valuation of signata, for it consists in assigning symbolic signata to individual signantia and, when an alternation has been identified, in assigning different relative value to the alternants, some alternant(s) (or class(es) of alternants) being valuated as marked — and characterized by some positively defined privileges of occurrence — and one alternant (or class of alternants) being valuated as unmarked — occurring "elsewhere". The privileges of occurrence of a signans are tantamount to its indexical signatum (cf. 1.1.4).

Both kinds of operation, segmentation and valuation, are to a more or less evident extent governed by higher order hypotheses about the design of the language, about — among other things — how the system of morphological categories is structured and individual categories ranked, and what morphological techniques and processes of synthesis (Sapir 1921:120f.) are to be given preference (cf. Coseriu 1968:99f.), and about real and virtual diagrammatic relations between the system of morphological categories and the corresponding systems of signantia (Jakobson 1965).

This whole complex of operations comprises thousands of decisions, each of which in principle involves a potential innovation. To resolve it into an ordered series of discrete steps, each with its decision procedure, is impossible. It is clear, for example, that the valuation of a string of signata both precedes the segmentation — it is the complex nature of the content side that motivates the analysis of the expression side – and in the end results from it. In other words, the processes of valuation and segmentation are concurrent. But one can still define the types of abductive innovation that are possible in morphology and morphophonemics and hope, thereby, to gain some insight into the strategies learners use.

5.0.2   The exposition in the following sections will deal first with innovations in the system of morphological categories (5.1) and then with innovations involving individual morphemes (5.2). Morphophonemic alternations in grammatical morphemes will be discussed in 5.3 and stem

alternations in 5.4. Section 5.5 will be devoted to innovations which are
motivated by the morphological or morphophonemic system.

5.1.1 Innovations in morphological categories can arise apparently
spontaneously, that is, without any evident motivation in the abductive
process.

As an example one can mention the radical reduction of the Old
Russian system of finite preterite tenses (imperfect, aorist, and maybe
half a dozen periphrastic tenses; cf. van Schooneveld 1959) to a single
preterite (the original perfect) which takes place within three or four
centuries in almost all East Slavic dialects in the Middle Ages (Borkovskij
— Kuznecov 1965:292f.).

A converse development is the rise of the morphological category of
animacy in the Slavic languages. In prehistoric Slavic, sound changes
make the accusative homonymous with the nominative in several nominal declensions. In other declensions, it has a discrete desinence. Only in
one paradigm, the animate interrogative (indefinite) pronoun *kŭto* 'who',
is the accusative homonymous (or syncretic) with the genitive. By the
beginning of the attested period, genitive desinences are used fairly
regularly instead of accusative desinences with singular nouns (and adjectives) of the first mentioned declensions when they denote (or modify
nouns denoting) free, healthy, adult male persons. In Russian, "genitival" accusatives are regular with singular nouns denoting any male person by the 1300's, with plural nouns denoting male persons from the
13–1400's, with plurals denoting female persons from the 14–1500's;
masculine singular nouns denoting animals have genitival accusatives
from the 1300's on, plurals (regardless of gender) from the 1600's.

These are examples of a kind of morphological innovation which is not
adaptive: there is no basis for viewing them as contact innovations, and
although the outcome of the latter development — a consistent morphological marking of the subject and object cases of animate nouns —
can be said to be desirable, it can hardly be interpreted as a remedial
innovation (cf. 2.2.1), that is, as an active, purposeful modification of the
system for the sake of avoiding "pernicious homonymy". The very slow
process by which the norms of usage have changed indicates rather that it
has been motivated from within. Such an interpretation seems attractive
in the case of the reduction of the preterite system, which can be seen as
connected with the ascendancy of the category of aspect, which comes to
dominate the Russian verb in the same period: the system of shifter
categories in the verb (the old tenses) is reduced as the role of non-shifter
event designators (the aspects and subaspects) is strengthened. (For the
theory of morphological categories used here, see Jakobson 1957.)

One possible way of understanding such instances of long term drift involves the assumption that apart from hypotheses about the actual system of morphological categories of his language, a language learner formulates higher order hypotheses about its typological properties, and that these hypotheses, which may involve a ranking of different generic and specific morphological categories, determine which categories will be exposed to reduction and loss — as here the verbal shifters — and which may be further elaborated (cf. Coseriu 1968:99f.) — here, the generic categories of aspect (event designators) and gender (participant designators). This is a plausible way of accounting for long term drift in phonological systems (cf. Isačenko 1939; Andersen 1978), but before explanations of this kind proposed for innovations in morphological type can be evaluated, we obviously need to know more about the typology of systems of morphological categories (cf. Hjelmslev 1963:92f.).

5.1.2   Other innovations in morphological categories appear to arise out of indeterminacies in the speech data from which the morphological system is inferred. One can distinguish instances of indeterminacy in the relation between the system of signata and the norms of reference and in the relation between the system of signata and the system of signantia.

5.1.2.1   In prehistoric Slavic, the inherited optative is reinterpreted as an imperative, undoubtedly because it was used to express commands, requests, and advice; it ceased to function as a grammatical transposition (cf. 2.1); cf. Stern's category of "fading" (1931). The consequences of this innovation — from which we can infer it — were that the optative was lost as a morphological category, being renewed by periphrastic means (a remedial innovation, cf. 2.2); the forms of the original imperative fell into disuse and disappeared; and the inflection for person in the original optative was lost: it is still attested in Old Church Slavonic, but in Modern Russian, for instance, only the 2nd person singular survives from which a new 2nd person plural is derived by the addition of the morpheme *-t,e* 'plural' (mentioned in 2.1), e.g. *živ,-í, živ,-í-t,e* 'live!' (ORuss. *živ-i, živ-ě-te*).

The example shows how the content of a morphological category can change through an innovation in valuation — made possible by the category's referential value and independent of its expression.

5.1.2.2   When the signantia of distinct morphological categories become homonymous through sound change, a category may be lost. A typical example is the reduction and loss of gender distinctions in English and in Danish dialects, where sound change has obliterated distinctions in

agreement and gendered pronouns have been restricted to express
natural gender (with few exceptions in English).

Homonymy of signantia, as in these developments, is not the only kind
of indeterminacy in the relation between signata and signantia which may
give rise to innovations in a system of morphological categories. There is a
logical converse in cases where the existence of allomorphs for a single
signatum motivates the innovation of a new morphological distinction. In
Old Russian, two declensions which had become partially similar through
sound change (the earlier *o*-stem and *u*-stem declensions) could not be
kept distinct and were amalgamated. The resulting two variants of the
locative desinence, -*e* and -*u*, which originally occurred each with its set of
lexemes, were differentiated grammatically, -*ú* (locative II) being specialized for concrete location (governed by *v* 'in' and *na* 'on'), -*e* (locative I)
being used with these prepositions in other senses and with other prepositions governing the locative. The distinction is now made with well over a
hundred substantives of the first declension (plus their diminutives). At
the same time, stress levelling in third declension nouns had created
locatives with alternative stress. These were harnessed to the same distinction, so that now some 20 third declension nouns have a locative I in -*i*
and a locative II in -*í* (Bulaxovskij 1958:135f.; Kiparsky 1967:34f.).

There is a difference worth noting between this innovation and the
previous one in that the development of the two locatives and the similar
development of a morphological distinction between two genitives, genitive II (with the original *u*-stem desinence -*u*) for purely quantitative
determination and genitive I (with the original *o*-stem desinence -*a*) for
the other functions of the genitive — do not involve the rise of new
morphological categories, but only the creation of new combinations of
existing features of case meaning (cf. Jakobson 1958/1971:173f.);
whereas in the development of English and the Danish dialects mentioned, genders are lost as morphological categories. Viewed as diachronic correspondences, therefore, these changes are quite different.
But as innovations they are comparable: both types of innovation arise
due to an indeterminacy in the relation between signantia and morphological signata, and the two kinds of indeterminacy involved are truly
converse.

5.1.3   It is far from certain that a strict distinction should be made
between the apparently spontaneous innovations (5.1.1) and the innovations that appear to be motivated by indeterminacies in speech data
(5.1.2). It is hardly possible to maintain that morphological distinctions
arise just because there are signantia available to carry them, or that
morphological distinctions should disappear just because sound changes

whittle away at certain desinences. It seems reasonable to assume that the apparently motivated innovations are in part determined by the typological properties of the language in question and that the apparently spon-
·taneous innovations are in fact set off by kinds of indeterminacy which are merely difficult to establish.

5.2 Morphological innovations in the narrow sense comprise innovations in the valuation of individual morphological signs, innovations in the segmentation of signantia, and innovations in segmentation involving a new valuation of signata. Finally we will consider morphic innovations.

5.2.1 Innovations in valuation can be motivated by indeterminacies in the referential value of a signatum or in the relation between signantia and signata. Indeterminacies of the latter kind can be of a morphological or of a phonological kind.

As an example of a morphologically conditioned indeterminacy (homonymy) giving rise to an innovation in valuation, one can mention the re-interpretation of the Old Russian feminine singular collective nouns such as *gospoda* 'lords, gentlemen', *bratíja* 'brothers' as plurals. The singular collectives required a plural predicate but singular modifiers, and were in their declension quite distinct from plurals. The loss of the dual, however, gave rise to a new nominative plural ending in *-á* (e.g. *boká* 'sides', *b,er,egá* 'river banks', *rogá* 'horns') and made the nominative singular of these collectives ambiguous. They were reinterpreted and combined with plural modifiers and, subsequently, with regular plural desinences in the oblique cases (cf. Borkovskij — Kuznecov 1965:212f.).

A similar innovation, but conditioned by a phonological ambiguity (homophony), affected Russian stem-stressed neuter collectives, whose nominative singular desinence, as a consequence of vowel reduction, became indistinguishable from the nominative plural of non-collectives: *kam,én,jo* 'stones', *kolós,jo* 'ears (of grain)', *zúb,jo* 'teeth', *súčjo* 'branches' were reinterpreted as *kam,én,ja, kolós,ja, zúb,ja, súčja* (to mention only a few examples). As in the preceding example, the consequences of this abductive innovation were first syntactic — as plurals they require plural modifiers (e.g. 17th c. Russ. *gruda bol'six kamen'ja* 'a heap of large (gen.pl. desinence) rocks (gen.sg. desinence)') — and then morphological: in the oblique cases their singular desinences were replaced with plural desinences (cf. Borkovskij — Kuznecov 1965:213f.).

In a number of nouns, the individualizing and collective plurals are semantically distinct: *zúb* 'tooth' has the plurals *zúbi* 'teeth' and *zúb,ja* 'cogs', *l,íst* 'leaf' distinguishes *l,istí* 'leaves, sheets' and *l,íst,ja* 'foliage'. But in several nouns, the collective has simply replaced the original plural, e.g. *brát,ja, kolós,ja, mužjá* 'husbands', *kn,az,já* 'princes'. This is the result of an innovation in valuation motivated by referential ambiguity, the first subtype mentioned at the beginning of this section.

5.2.2   Innovations in the segmentation of signantia are typically motivated by ambiguities in the signantia.

A simple example is the metanalysis of the past passive participle of the Russian verb *dat*, 'to give', *dád,onnij*. It was irregular by being formed (in synchronic terms) from the present tense stem alternant (i.e. *dad,-onn-ij*) or — if interpreted as formed from the past tense stem — by having a unique participial suffix (*da-d,onn-ij*). Most Russian dialects have evidently preferred the latter segmentation and form a regular past passive participle from this stem, *dá-nn-ij*, having eliminated the unique suffix alternant. But some dialects have retained the anomalous suffix and have extended its occurrence to the antonyms of 'to give': *brád,onnij* 'taken (imperfective)', *vz,ád,onnij* 'taken (perfective)' (Avanesov — Orlova 1965:170); cf. (10).

(10)

	Middle Russian		Standard Russian		Russian dialects	
Inf.	*dá-t,*	*brá-t,*	*dá-t,*	*brá-t,*	*dá-t,*	*brá-t,*
Past	*dá-l*	*brá-l*	*dá-l*	*brá-l*	*dá-l*	*brá-l*
Pres. 3pl.	*dad-út*	*b,or-út*	*dad-út*	*b,or-út*	*dad-út*	*b,or-út*
P. p. p.	*dád,-onnij*	*brá-nnij*	*dá-nnij*	*brá-nnij*	*dá-d,onnij*	*brá-d,onnij*

A particularly frequent type of innovation in segmentation involves zero signantia.

In Middle English, the plural of *child, child-er* (i.e. 'child' plus 'plural') was reinterpreted as an allomorph of *child* plus a zero plural marker, *childer-Ø*. The deductive consequence of this innovation was that the zero allomorph for 'plural' could be replaced by the more productive *-en*, hence Modern Engl. *children*.

The example is well worth noting, for it shows that the qualms of some descriptivists (e.g. Haas 1954, Matthews 1974) against positing zero allomorphs find no justification in the history of languages. Of course Middle English *childer* never ceased to mean both 'child' and 'plural'. But there is no reason why it would need a new plural desinence if a resegmentation had not occurred. Such a resegmentation was motivated, one may assume, by a reduction of the plural value of *childer* from symbolic to indexical, which, as well, motivated the addition of an explicit, i.e. real, symbolic plural sign (cf. 1.4).

5.2.3 Innovations in the segmentation of signata: In the examples discussed in 5.2.2, the number of signantia and the symbolic signata assigned to them remained constant through the innovation. Innovations in the segmentation of signata, by contrast, involve the creation of new symbolic signs. When they accompany innovations in the segmentation of signantia, they yield either fewer signantia with more complex symbolic signata or more signantia of lesser complexity. We will look at some examples of the latter type.

In the paradigm of the Russian numeral 'two', the nominative is difficult to analyse (cf. (11)). Most linguists would probably identify the desinences *-a* and *-e* as carriers of both case and gender meaning. The stem of the nominative feminine would then be considered an allomorph conditioned by the *-e* desinence. Russianists who believe that (paired) consonants are always palatalized before *e* in Russian — it once was so — would consider the allomorph *dv,-* automatically conditioned; those who take seriously the fact that plain consonants occur before *e* in a large number of loan words would at least recognize that (paired) consonants are always palatalized before desinence initial *e* and would define the stem alternation as a phonologically conditioned morphophonemic alteration.

(11)

	Standard Russian		Dialects	
	M, N	F	M, N	F
Nom.	*dva*	*dv,é*	*dvá*	*dv,é*
Acc.	=N/G		=N/G	
Gen.	*dvúx*		*dvúx*	*dv,úx*
Loc.	*dvúx*		*dvúx*	*dv,úx*
Dat.	*dvúm*		*dvúm*	*dv,úm*
Instr.	*dvum,á*		*dvum,á*	*dv,um,á*

Judging by the dialectal innovation shown in (11) (which is not limited to Russian dialects, but has taken place also in Belorussian), learners of this language have analysed these forms differently (cf. Avanesov — Orlova 1965:135; Bulatova 1973; Avanesaw 1964:210). They have recognized signata of three kinds in these forms: 'two', gender, and case, and have segmented the signantia accordingly, thus the nominative feminine, for instance, *dv-,-é*, the genitive feminine, by implication, *dv-Ø-ux*, and so forth. This abductive innovation has had two consequences:

(1) the signans of 'feminine' presented an unmotivated alternation between palatalization in the nominative and lack of it in the oblique cases;
in deductive innovations, this alternation has been eliminated, palatalization being generalized; and (2) the nominative desinence presents an
unmotivated alternation; one cannot tell whether -*a* or -*e* is the marked
alternant; nor can one tell whether they are conditioned by the different
genders of the stems or by the phonological difference between the stems,
that is, their indexical value is ambiguous.

The innovation is interesting as an argument against the sceptics who
object to morphological analysis as a method that "sets up a fictitious
agglutinating analog" (Lounsbury 1953:13) and prefer to dispense with
"the nonsense of zeros" and deal with whole words (Matthews
1974:116f.).

This is not an isolated example, as a return to the collective plurals
mentioned in 5.2.1 will show. In Russian, generally speaking, the nominal
plural desinences denote 'plural' plus case. In all Russian dialects there
are some nouns with a special stem allomorph that occurs only before
plural desinences and therefore has the indexical value of 'plural', e.g.
sos,éd- 'neighbour', whose plural stem is *sos,éd,-*. In the original collectives, the plural stem contains a morph -*j*- with only this indexical signatum. In some Russian dialects, the original collectives have apparently
been reinterpreted: the -*j*- morph has been valuated as a symbolic sign
for 'plural', and the plural desinences correspondingly reduced to symbolic signs only for case and indexical signs for 'plural'. As a consequence, inherited plurals like *stakáni* 'glasses', *b,er,ázi* 'birches', *lósad,i*
'horses' and many others are being replaced by a productive plural
formation, with a real, symbolic sign for 'plural', *stakán,ja, b,er,óz,ja,
losad,já*, etc. (Avanesov — Orlova 1965:114; Bromlej — Bulatova
1972:95f.).

5.2.4 Morphic innovations: While the signata of morphological signs
are established by a valuation based on their reference or function, the
signantia are defined on the basis of their pronunciation. The identification of the diacritic signs that make up a morph is an operation that may
give rise to morphic innovations.

Every dialect survey, every etymological dictionary provides examples
of sporadic morphic changes in lexemes. The widespread pronunciation
[blaus] for [blauz] *blouse*, or the New England dialectal [trɔθ] for [trɔf]
trough, are such examples, where neither regular sound change nor
paradigmatic or syntagmatic assimilation (cf. 4.1) can be appealed to for
an explanation, and the only plausible source of the change seems to be an
idiolectal deviation from the norm — based on a mishearing — a devia-

tion which for no linguistic reasons has come to be codified in the norms of a whole speech community.

Such apparently haphazard morphic innovations occur in inflectional morphology as well. Since these are in principle unmotivated alterations of signantia, one hesitates to cite examples, for what seems unmotivated today may be explained tomorrow. But perhaps such puzzles as the Indoeuropean desinences with *-bh-* in some dialects and *-m-* in others are in origin of this type. Another likely example is the Lithuanian frequentative preterite formed with the suffix -*dav*- (e.g. *dúodavo* 'used to give' from *dúoti* 'give'), but in some dialects with a suffix -*lav*- (e.g. *dúolavo*) (cf. Stang 1942:173).

Apart from these apparently haphazard morphic innovations, two types of motivated ones can be defined, syntagmatic and paradigmatic reduction, to which I will return below (5.5.1.2, 5.5.1.3).

5.3   Innovations in indexical signata: When different morphological signantia have been defined through segmentation (cf. 5.2.2) and identification of their constituent diacritic signs (cf. 5.2.4) and are to be valuated,
the logically first decision to be made is whether differences in reference
between similar signata reflect (a) a grammatical opposition or (b) contextual variation based on an identity of grammatical content.

In case the former kind of decision is made, the difference is thereby interpreted as a grammatical opposition. This is the way existing grammatical oppositions are preserved from generation to generation. It is also the way in which new oppositions arise, as we saw in the grammatical differentiation of the Russian locative (5.1.2.2). Finally, by decisions of this kind an existing grammatical opposition may be reinterpreted in the morphological system as a whole (5.1.2.1) or in individual morphemes (5.2.1).

On the other hand, if different signantia are judged to have identical grammatical content, they are thereby interpreted as covariants, and further decisions must be made to determine their distribution. The alternation they present may be interpreted as (a) phonological or (b) non-phonological.

Phonological (alias automatic) alternations — the results of neutralization rules — do not concern the morphology as such. But it is possible for alternants that can be described as automatic to be valuated as (parts of) morphological signantia, as was seen in 5.2.3.

If an alternation is judged to be non-phonological, it must be interpreted either as morphophonemic — the covariants (or all but one of them) being assigned indexical signata (see 5.3.1–5.4.3) — or as morphological, i.e. as a relative signans with a symbolic signatum (5.4.4).

5.3.1   An alternant may be valuated as a phonological index pointing to the signans of a contiguous grammatical or lexical morpheme.

When in primitive Slavic IE*k merged with part of the reflexes of IE*s, the aorist morpheme had two allomorphs, -x- occurring before a vowel after a stem final *i, u, r*, or *k* and -s- occurring elsewhere. -x- was interpreted as the basic alternant (cf. Andersen 1968) and -s- was valuated as an index of a preceding or following non-compact consonant. Consequently Old Church Slavonic preserves -s- in *ně-s-ŭ* 'I carried' (cf. *nes-ǫ* 'I carry'), *vě-s-ŭ* 'I led' (cf. *ved-ǫ*), *grě-s-ŭ* 'I rowed' (cf. *greb-ǫ*), *na-čę-s-ŭ* 'I began' (cf. *na-čĭn-ǫ*), *ę-s-ŭ* 'I took' (cf. *im-ǫ*), but has -x- not only in *bi-x-ŭ* 'I beat', *by-x-ŭ* 'I was', *plu-x-ŭ* 'I sailed', *trĭ-x-ŭ* 'I rubbed' (cf. *tĭr-ǫ*), but also in *zna-x-ŭ* 'I knew', *vidě-x-ŭ* 'I saw', *kla-x-ŭ* 'I pierced' (cf. *kol´-ǫ*), the last of which show the extension of -x- which was the deductive consequence of the limited privileges of occurrence accorded -s-.

It is in principle irrelevant whether the alternation is in origin a phonological alternation (as the preceding one) or a morphophonemic alternation. Thus, in Middle Russian, when the several substantival declensions began to merge in the plural, the productive genitive plural desinence for masculines was -*ov*. A tiny number of masculines had the genitive plural desinence -*ej* (viz. the original *i*- stems). While -*ov* occurred without phonological restrictions, -*ej* was found only after stems ending in a palatalized or palatal consonant. This made it interpretable as a phonological index, and it has been generalized for masculines ending in a palatalized or palatal consonant at the expense of -*ov*, which has been restricted to stems ending in a plain (paired) consonant, or *c*, or *j* (Borkovskij — Kuznecov 1965:200, 203f.).

5.3.2   An alternant may be valuated as an index of morphological signata.

The Middle Russian change of $e > o$ produced an alternation in the present tense marker of 1st conjugation verbs, apparently preserved in some dialects (cf. (12), paradigm A)

(12)	A	B	C	D
2nd sg.	-*e*-	-*e*-	-*e*-	-*o*-
3rd sg.	-*e*-	-*e*-	-*o*-	-*o*-
1st pl.	-*o*-	-*o*-	-*o*-	-*o*-
2nd pl.	-*e*-	-*o*-	-*e*-	-*o*-

The fact that -*o*- occurred in the first person plural made it possible to interpret -*o*- as a plural index, a possibility that has been realized in some dialects (B). While in these dialects the basic (unmarked) present tense allomorph is *-e-*, in most Russian dialects it is *-o-*. Some of these have interpreted *-e-* as a 2nd person marker (C), but in most dialects the alternation has been eliminated, *-o-* being generalized, as in the standard language (D) (cf. Avanesov — Orlova 1965:163f.).

The morphological signatum indexed by an allomorph may be (part of) the content of a grammatical morpheme, as in the preceding example, or of a lexical morpheme: in early Czech, when the morphophonemic distinction between the original *o*-stem and *u*-stem declensions was abandoned, the dative singular of the new 1st declension had two allomorphs, *ov,i* — occurring with a small number of masculine stems (the original *u*-stems) — and *-u*, occurring with the vast majority of masculines and all neuters. While strictly speaking the stems taking *-ov,i* had no lexical or grammatical features in common, two of the most frequent of them, *sin* 'son' and *vōl* 'ox' were animate. The allomorph *-ov,i* was interpreted as an index of animacy, which already had obligatory, morphological expression in the accusative of masculine nouns (cf. the example in 5.1.1), and accordingly extended to all animate masculines (with a few lexical and stylistic exceptions) (cf. Vážný 1963:26f.).

5.3.3   An alternant may be valuated as an index of lexical signata.

The Middle Russian first declension, just like the Czech one, had two allomorphs for the dative singular, *-ov,i*, occurring with a small number of masculines, and *-u*, occurring with the vast majority of masculines and all neuters. The allomorph *-ov,i* has been completely superseded by *-u*, most likely because it was restricted to specific lexical items which defied generalization (cf. Kiparsky 1967:30f.).

The valuation of an allomorph as an index of lexical content may lead, as well, to its extension. For instance, in Middle Ukrainian, as the distinction between dual and plural number was abandoned, the instrumental plural desinence had two sets of allomorphs, the original dual desinences, of the form *-(V)ma* — preserved in Modern Ukrainian *očyma* 'eyes', *ušyma* 'ears', *plečyma* 'shoulders', *dvoma* 'two', *oboma* 'both' — and desinences of the form *-(V)(m)y*, which occurred with all adjectives and pronouns, and all types of substantives. The allomorph *-(V)ma* was apparently interpreted as an index of 'lexical quantifier', for it has been extended to all cardinal numerals (e.g. *tr-y, tr,-omá* 'three ,*pjat,, pjat,-má* 'five') and pro-numerals (*kil'k-y, kil'k-omá* 'some', *bahát-o, bahat,-má*) and to the totalizing determinative pronoun *ves,* 'all' (*us,-imá*) (cf. Samijlenko 1964:139f., 172f., 1970:161; Kernyc'kyj 1967:162f.).

5.3.4   The preceding three sections have given examples of innovations giving rise to indexical signata which are absolute (cf. 1.2.3): the -*s*-allomorph of the aorist morpheme in primitive Slavic pointed to a contiguous non-compact consonant (5.3.1), the -*o*- allomorph of the present tense morpheme in one group of Russian dialects points to the plural meaning of the following person affix (5.3.2), and the -(*V*)*ma* allomorph of the instrumental plural desinence in Ukrainian points to a specific content feature of the preceding stem (5.3.3). But indexical signata may also be relative.

In early East Slavic, the 3rd person desinence had two alternants, -*tǐ* and -∅, with a distribution between singular and plural and between the two present tense conjugations which so far has defied reconstruction. In modern Russian dialects, several patterns are found, which are being replaced by that of the standard language (see (13), A), but can still be discerned.

(13)		A		B		C		D	
		I conj.	II conj.	I	II	I	II	I	II
3rd sg.		*pad,-ó-t*	*s,id,-í-t*	-∅	-*t*	-∅	-*t*	-∅	-∅
3rd pl.		*pad -ú-t*	*s,id,-á-t*	-*t*	-*t*	-*t*	-∅	-*t*	-∅

Pattern (C) is a clear example of a relative index: the 3rd person morpheme has two allomorphs with the same symbolic signatum ('3rd person'); but each of them is an index of the singular in one conjugation, but of the plural in the other (cf. Avanesov — Orlova 1965:162).

It may be added that this pattern, which undoubtedly is an innovation, is quite germane to the inherited alternation in the present tense morpheme, which also provides a relative index of the plural in the 3rd person: where the tense morpheme's basic shape is a non-high vowel (the 1st conjugation), an allomorph with a high vowel signals 'plural' in the 3rd person; where the basic shape is a high vowel (the 2nd conjugation), an allomorph with a low vowel signals 'plural' in the 3rd person (cf. the formulation in Jakobson 1948/1971:123). Number, then, is not expressed symbolically in the 3rd person of the present tense, but in all varieties of Russian merely indexed by allomorphs of the present tense morpheme and, in some dialects, by allomorphs of the 3rd person morpheme as well.

5.4 Innovations in stem alternations: A typology of innovations in inflectional morphology must include some types of innovations in the morphophonemics of stems, for alternations in stems may either directly (come to) carry grammatical meaning (as relative signantia with symbolic signata), or they may point to the signantia or signata of grammatical morphemes (as relative signantia with indexical signata) (cf. 1.1.2, 1.1.4). On the other hand, there are several types of morphophonemic innovations which are at most of marginal interest to morphology. In the survey to follow, some of these will be mentioned, but interest will be centred around the types that involve grammatical categories.

When different lexemic signantia have been defined through segmentation (cf. 5.2.2) and identification of their diacritic signs (cf. 5.2.4), and are to be valuated, the logically first decision to be made is whether differences of reference between them reflect a semantic opposition or contextual variation based on an identity of semantic content. The decision may be illustrated simply with the development of the two lexemes *shade* and *shadow* from the stem allomorphs of Old English *sceadu* (~*sceadw-*) 'shade, shadow' on the one hand and of *meadow* from OE *mǣd* (~*mǣdw-*) 'meadow'.

5.4.1 Innovations in the locus of an alternation. When an alternation between two (or more) stems has been identified, a decision must be made whether it is a singular alternation or a general alternation. Singular alternations include cases of (total or partial) suppletion — e.g. Engl. *die*, pl. *dice; man*, pl. *men*. General alternations are amenable to generalization — the alternations of tense and lax obstruents in Engl. *knife*, pl. *knives; bath*, pl. *baths; house*, pl. *houses*. It does not seem possible at present to establish a principled line of demarcation between these two alternatives.

When an alternation is judged to be general, it must be decided whether it is a property of individual lexemes or characteristic of a class of lexemes — and in the latter case, the class must be defined by (some combination of) content features (semantic or grammatical) and/or signans features (morphophonemic or phonological). As an example one can take the alternation of plain with palatalized consonants before the nominative plural desinence -*i* in 1st declension nouns in Middle Russian and Middle Polish. In Russian this alternation was apparently treated as a property of individual lexemes: it was early restricted to animates and then gradually curtailed; now only two nouns have it, *córt*, pl. *cért,-i* 'devil' and *sos,éd*, pl. *sos,éd,-i* 'neighbour'. In Polish, this alternation was interpreted as a property of masculines denoting male persons (i.e. its locus was defined by a combination of grammatical and semantic features); the alternation was not only maintained in first declension nouns (e.g. *sǫsad*, pl. *sǫseʒ-i* 'neighbour'), but in conformity with this interpretation extended to second declension nouns (e.g. *sług-a*, pl. *słuʒ-y* 'servant', *poet-a*, pl. *poeć-i* 'poet') (cf. Borkovskij — Kuznecov 1965:215f.; Kiparsky 1967:42f.; Klemensiewicz et al. 1965:308).

5.4.2   Innovations in the alternating elements: When an alternation has been interpreted as general, a decision must be made as to the direction of the alternation, i.e. which alternant(s) is/are basic and which, derived (see further 5.4.3).

The class of phonological elements (diacritic signs, segments) subject to alternation must be defined. If an innovation is made, the class of basic alternants will be expanded or restricted. An example of expansion: in Latvian, the alternation of dentals with palatals ($t \sim š$, $d \sim ž$, $s \sim š$, $z \sim ž$) has been expanded to include the dental affricates, reflexes of the velar palatalization, $c \sim č$, $ʒ \sim ǯ$), in certain loci (cf. Endzelīns 1971:59). An example of restriction: in Russian, in certain loci where s alternates with $š$, the cluster *sl*, formerly alternated with *šl*,; but Modern Russian has *mísl,-u* 'I think' corresponding to Middle Russian *mísl,-u* (infinitive *misl,i-t,*).

The class of derived alternants that occurs in a given locus must be defined. If an innovative definition is made, the class of derived alternants may be differentiated (a reductive alternation becoming less reductive) or reduced (an alternation becoming (more) reductive), or it may be replaced — partly or completely — by another class of alternants. An example of differentiation: in Early Ukrainian, stem-final dentals alternated with palatals in second conjugation verbs before the 1st person singular desinence (as in (14) (A)).

(14)

	A	B
basic	t d s z	t d s z
derived	č ž š ž	č ʒ š ž

In part of the Ukrainian language area, *d* has come to alternate with *ʒ*, whereby the alternation has become less reductive. An example of the replacement of one class of derived alternants with another: in Early Ukrainian, stem final consonants alternated with one class of derived alternants in the 1st person singular and with another class of derived alternants in the 3rd person plural of second conjugation verbs (see (15) (A)).

(15)

(A)	basic	t	d	s	z	č	š	ž	p	b	f	m	v	n	l	r
	1st sg.	č	ʒ	š	ž	č	š	ž	pl,	bl,	fl,	ml,	vl,	n,	l,	r,
	3rd pl.	t,	d,	s,	z,	č	š	ž	pj	bj	fj	mj	vj	n,	l,	r,
(B)	3rd pl.	t,	d,	s,	z,	č	š	ž	pl,	bl,	fl,	ml,	vl,	n,	l,	r,
(C)	1st sg.	t,	d,	s,	z,	č	š	ž	pj	bj	fj	mj	vj	n,	l,	r,

In some dialects, including the ones on which the standard language is based, part of the latter class of alternants has been replaced with part of the former (see (15) (B). In many dialects, the former class has been replaced in its entirety by the latter (see (15) (C); cf. the examples in (16)). All varieties of Ukrainian maintain the classes of alternants of (15)(A) unchanged in other loci (cf. Žylko 1966:94f.).

(16)	A	B	C
Inf.	*l,ubý-ty*	*l,úby-ty*	*l,ubý-ty*
1st sg.	*l,ubl,-ú*	*l,ubl,-ú*	*l,ubj-ú*
3rd pl.	*l,úbj-a-t,*	*l,úbl,-a-t,*	*l,úbj-a-t,*

5.4.3 Innovations in indexical value: As mentioned in 5.4.2, when an alternation has been defined as general in a certain locus, a decision must be made as to which class of alternants is basic and which derived. It is characteristic that what is materially one and the same alternation may be given different direction in different loci. This can be inferred from the different directions in which alternations are levelled when they lapse, for when an alternation is abandoned, it is the basic alternant that is generalized. Consider, for instance the $e \sim o$ alternation in Polish, which is generally levelled in favor of o in nouns (i.e. *vosna* 'spring; nom.sg.', *vośn-e* 'loc.sg.', earlier *veśń-e*), but in favour of e in the present tense of verbs (e.g. dialectal *ńes-ę* 'carry; 1st sg.', *ńeś-e-s* '2nd sg.', earlier, and Standard Polish, *ńos-ę, ńeś-e-s*) (cf. Dejna 1973:184; Klemensiewicz et al. 1965:79).

The decision as to the direction of an alternation depends entirely on the indexical signata assigned to the class of derived alternants. These may be morphophonemic (5.4.3.1) or morphological (5.4.3.2).

5.4.3.1 In some Russian dialects, the alternation $\gamma \sim \check{z}$ in the present tense of verbs with stems in γ — originally occurring as in (17) (A) — has been correlated with the stress, so that $\gamma \sim \check{z}$ before unstressed vocalic desinences. There are three accentual paradigms, fixed stem stress (B), fixed end stress (C), and mobile stress (D), and correspondingly three reflexes of the original consonant alternation (cf. Avanesov — Orlova 1965:156).

(17)	A	B	C	D
1st sg.	γ	*l,áž-u*	*str,iγ-ú*	*moγ-ú*
2nd sg.	$\check{z}$	*l,áž-oš*	*str,iγ-óš*	*móž-oš*
3rd sg.	$\check{z}$	*l,áž-ot*	*str,iγ-ót*	*móž-ot*
1st pl.	$\check{z}$	*l,áž-om*	*str,iγ-óm*	*móž-om*
2nd pl.	$\check{z}$	*l,áž-ot,o*	*str,iγ-ót,o*	*móž-ot,o*
3rd pl.	γ	*l,áž-ut*	*str,iγ-út*	*móž-ut*

Patterns like this, where one morphophonemic alternation mirrors another so that they together form what may be called an automorphic structure in the paradigm, were first described explicitly by Shapiro, who gives several examples of existing or emerging patterns of this kind from contemporary Russian (1969). They can also be undone by morphophonemic innovation, as the next example suggests.

In many Russian dialects, verbs with stems in k present two parallel alternations in the present tense paradigm, $k \sim \check{c}$ and $o \sim e$ (cf. (18) (A)). Historically speaking, the latter alternation is the younger of the two; it has its origin in a change of $e > o$, which did not take place before (inter alia) $\check{c}$. In some dialects, the consonant alternation has been eliminated, but the $o \sim e$ alternation is maintained — undoubtedly with morphological indexical value (cf. Avanesov — Orlova 1965:155); see (18) (B).

(18)	A	B
1st sg.	p,ok-ú	p,ok-ú
2nd sg.	p,eč-óš	p,ek-óš
3rd sg.	p,eč-ót	p,ek-ót
1st pl.	p,eč-óm	p,ek-óm
2nd pl.	p,eč-ót,o	p,ek-ót,o
3rd pl.	p,ok-út	p,ok-út

5.4.3.2   An alternation may be valuated as having morphological indexical value. In this case there are two possibilities: the derived alternant(s) may index morphological signantia or they may index morphological signata.

In Polish, the inherited alternation of stem final consonants (see (19) (A)) in original class IV verbs before the desinence of the first person singular -ę (B) has been extended so that it occurs also before 3rd person plural desinence -ǫ (C). It appears that the derived alternants index desinences that begin with a nasal vowel. (In other loci, the same alternants have other indexical values.) (Cf. Klemensiewicz et al. 1965: 364.)

(19)	A	B	C	D
	ć~c	1st sg.	noš-ę	noš-ę
	ʒ́~ʒ	2nd sg.	noś-is	noś-is
	ś~š	3rd sg.	noś-i	noś-i
	ź~ž	1st pl.	noś-imy	noś-imy
		2nd pl.	noś-iće	noś-iće
		3rd pl.	*noś-ǫ	noš-ǫ

In Russian, the inherited alternation of stem final plain consonants with palatalized consonants before the nom. pl. desinence *-i* — whose locus has been restricted to two nouns (cf. 5.4.1) — has changed: the derived alternants have been valuated as indexes of 'plural', and stem final palatalized consonants correspondingly extended to all plural forms. Thus Modern Russian has such plural forms as *sos,éd,-i* 'nom.', *sos,éd,-ej* 'gen.', *sos,éd,-am* 'dat.' corresponding to Middle Russian *sos,éd,-i, sos,éd-ov, sos,éd-am.*

5.4.4 Morphological alternations: In 5.2.3 we saw how the *-j-* suffix which in most Russian dialects probably is a mere index of 'plural', in some dialects apparently has been valuated as symbolic and hence is being generalized as an absolute, real signans with an asynthetic signatum.

When an alternation is general (5.4) and the derived alternant(s) can be interpreted as a relative index of a grammatical signatum, as in the Russian example we have just seen (5.4.3.2), there exists in principle the alternative possibility that the derived alternant(s) be valuated as a relative signans with the grammatical content in question as symbolic signatum. Such an interpretation is particularly likely, one may suppose, when the grammatical signatum lacks a stable, real signans — either because the given signans comprises diverse allomorphs, or because it is zero.

A clear example from the derivational morphology of Russian is the non-suffixal formation of abstract nouns from adjectives, where the change in part of speech is symbolized by the derived alternants of stem final consonants, e.g. *d,ik-* 'wild', *d,ič-* 'game (animals)'; *t,ix-* 'quiet; adj.', *t,iš-* 'quiet; subst.'; *nov-* 'new', *nov,-* 'virgin soil'; *krut-* 'steep', *krut,-* 'sheer cliff side' (cf. Isačenko 1975:336f.).

In Western Jutish, the apocope of *ə*, which affected various desinences, apparently prompted a transfer of grammatical signata to derived stem alternants. Now the plural of substantives is formed in part by a complex of alternations involving the prosodic features of stød (20) (A) and quantity (B) and the inherent feature of protensity, realized as length in sonorants (C) and preglottalization in stops (D). The same alternations serve to signal 'plural' and 'definite' in adjectives, and to differentiate the infinitive from the bare stem of the imperative and the preterite from the past passive participle. In addition, they accompany various suffixes, inflectional and derivational (cf. Ringgård 1960:14f.).

In cases like this, where a class of derived alternants alone functions as a relative signans for a grammatical signatum, it is appropriate to speak of a morphological alternation, as distinct from the morphophonemic alter-

nations which merely accompany inflection, and whose derived alternants, having only indexical value, serve to support and sharpen the
expression of independently symbolized grammatical signata.

(20)		Sg.	Pl.	
	(A)	*hu:ʔs*	*hu:s*	'house'
		go:ʔə	*go:ə*	'farm'
	(B)	*fað*	*få:ð*	'platter'
		præsd	*præ:sd*	'minister'
	(C)	*føl*	*føl·*	'foal'
		heŋsd	*heŋ·sd*	'stallion'
	(D)	*bæŋk*	*bæŋ'k*	'bench'
		stɔrk	*stɔr'k*	'stork'
		hat	*ha't*	'hat'

5.5   System-motivated innovations: The preceding survey of abductive
innovations began with a discussion of the difference between apparently
spontaneous innovations in morphological categories and the types of
innovation which can be understood as motivated by indeterminacies in
the speech data language learners have to analyse — indeterminacies
which allow of alternative resolutions, one of which is an innovation
(5.1.1–5.1.3). In the intervening sections, a number of types of innovation of the latter kind has been described — in morphology proper (5.2)
and in morphophonemics (5.3 and 5.4). Here I should like to exemplify
some types of innovation which cannot be understood simply as possible
resolutions of indeterminate speech data, but to be explained require
reference to the system into which the innovated elements are integrated.
  In 5.2–5.4 we saw that the analysis of innovations motivated by indeterminacies in speech data requires constant attention to the indexical
relations which make grammatical morphemes cohere with one another
and with lexical morphemes. Diagrammatic relations hold a comparable
place of importance in the explication of system-motivated innovations,
for a linguistic system, one may maintain, is a structure constituted chiefly
by diagrammatic relations. Although this insight is old and probably can
be traced through the history of linguistics, it has not been stated in
explicit terms until recent times (cf. Paul 1920:26f., 106f., 189f.), and it is
only in Jakobson's "Quest for the essence of language" (1965) that a first
attempt has been made to formulate it in semiotic terms. As a consequence, there is as yet no answer to such questions as how extensive is the
"compulsory diagrammatization" in language, or what kinds of diagrams
can reasonably be posited as real, constitutive features of language structure.
Historical morphology is likely to be able to help answer these questions.

Generally speaking, any change which leads to a simple mapping relation between content and expression can be viewed as a manifestation of the diagrammatic character of language structure. Several of the examples that have been examined above can be viewed as system motivated in this general way and could be categorized in terms of the formulaic representations used by Anttila (1972), e.g. the innovation by which the allomorphs of the Middle Russian genitive singular *-a* and *-u* were invested with distinct grammatical meaning (5.2.1.2): $\wedge > ||$; the one by which the allomorphy of the Middle Russian dative singular was reduced (5.3.3): $\wedge > |$; the morphological differentiation of animate and inanimate nouns in the accusative in the Slavic languages (5.1.1): $\vee > ||$; the loss of gender distinctions following the reduction of desinences in English (5.1.2): $\vee > |$. No doubt such diachronic correspondences, by whatever innovations they come about, indirectly reflect the diagrammatic character of language because they invariably involve deductive innovations, and these directly manifest the diagrammatic relations of the system.

Here, however, we will be concerned with abductive innovations that create new mapping relations among signata, between signata and signantia, and among signantia. We will consider first some types of innovations in morphology (5.5.1.1–5.5.1.4), then some morphophonemic innovations (5.5.2–5.5.2.3).

5.5.1.1   Innovations in valuation: In Old Russian, the numeral 'two' distinguished gender in the nominative (and accusative) — *dŭv-a* 'masc.' vs. *dŭv-ě* 'neut., fem.'. Texts from the late 1200's on show a new valuation of the desinences — *dv-a* 'masc., neut.' vs. *dv,-e* 'fem.' (cf. Kiparsky 1967:174).

One cannot assume that this innovation arose due to any indeterminacy in the use of the inherited forms. To understand it, it is necessary to take into account at least two circumstances. First, after the loss of the dual, a number of masculine nouns had retained the dual desinence *-a* as a nominative plural desinence; *-a* was the original desinence in the nominative plural of neuters; no feminines had a nominative plural in *-a*; in the nominative plural, then, *-a* had the inductive signatum 'non-feminine'. Secondly, in the singular — in pronouns and adjectives, and in the 1st declension of substantives — the neuter shared all the desinences of the oblique cases with the masculine, so that in pronouns and adjectives, two paradigms were distinguished, one 'feminine', the other, 'non-feminine'.

The new valuation, in other words, consisted in the primary gender opposition of the Russian nominal system — 'feminine' vs. 'non-feminine' — being projected onto the desinences of *dv-a* and *dv,-e*, so that the relation between their signata reflected the relation between the gender signata of pronouns and adjectives. At the same time, the inductive entailment -*a* ⊃ 'non-feminine' of the substantival nominative plural was imposed on *dv-a* as a deductive entailment, 'non-feminine' ⊃ -*a*.

The innovation can hardly be understood otherwise than as motivated by the structure of the gender system.

5.5.1.2   Paradigmatic reduction is a type of morphic innovation by which the paradigmatic diversity of desinences with similar signata is reduced in such a way that similarity of content comes to be reflected in a similarity of signantia.

Independently of each other, Slovincian and Russian dialects have changed the pronominal and adjectival desinence -*ogo* 'gen.sg., masc.-neut.' to -*ovo*. The changes cannot be understood as results of regular phonetic change, but Russian dialect forms of the desinence (-*oho*, -*oo*) suggest that the new shape of the desinence has been inferred from allegro forms (Borkovskij — Kuznecov 1965:250f.). The *v*, however, cannot be understood except on the basis of the morphological system. These languages employed only six consonants in nominal desinences. Several of these were clearly correlated with specific features of case meaning — *m* and *m*, with the peripheral cases (locative, dative, instrumental), *x* with the quantifier cases (genitive, locative). *g* occurred only in the genitive singular desinence -*ogo*. *v* occurred only in the desinence -*ov* 'gen.pl.'. This seems to explain how *v* could be imposed beside the *g*, which presumably continued to occur in lento forms of the desinence, and could subsequently be generalized. One more factor in the morphology of these languages which may be relevant is the fact that *v* occurred also in the derivational suffix -*ov*- which forms possessive adjectives.

By the innovation, then, the diversity of signantia for the genitive was reduced through the imposition of a familiar signans element — in defiance of the observable speech data, but with sufficient support in the identity of content of the relevant morphemes. Understood in this way, paradigmatic reduction has an exact counterpart in the kind of lexical signans change termed folk etymology (*sparrow grass* for *asparagus*). Both kinds of innovation can be viewed as the result of a learner's strategy, a tendency to perceive as similar signantia with similar content.

Paradigmatic reduction can be contrasted with the innovations in indexical signata discussed in 5.3.2. Both kinds of innovation lead to a redistribution of allomorphs (here a levelling). In reality, however, there may be an important difference between the alternations in inflectional paradigms whose forms can be reasonably thought of as produced by morphological rules, and allomorphy in a repertoire of desinences which are probably learnt and produced as units. The former allow of innovations in the formulation of indexical relations, the latter probably do not.

5.5.1.3   Syntagmatic reduction is a simplification of signantia consisting in the omission either of individual diacritic signs or of whole segments.

All Russian dialects have lost the distinction between desinence final *m*, (as in the original shapes of the desinences -*om*, -*im*, -*em*, 'instr.sg.', *om* 'loc.sg.') and -*m* (as in the original shapes of the desinences -*am*, -*im*, *em*, -*um*, -*om* 'dat.pl.'), omitting the diacritic sign "+sharped" (palatalized) from the former set of desinences. Similarly, North Russian dialects have reduced the 3rd person desinence from a palatalized -*t*, to a plain -*t* (Borkovskij — Kuznecov 1965:119f., 312).

Reduction by whole segments is involved in the shortening of a number of desinences in Russian: the nominal desinences ORuss. -*ojě* 'gen.sg.', -*oji* 'dat.loc.sg.', -*oju* 'instr.sg.' have become -*oj*; the verbal desinences -*ši* '2nd sg.', and the unstressed infinitive -*t,i* and imperative -*i* have become *š*, -*t,*, and -∅ respectively (Borkovskij — Kuznecov 1965:157f.).

Syntagmatic reduction can be understood as the result of a learner's strategy not to recognize more diacritic signs in morphological signantia than are necessary for their differentiation. Since syntagmatic reduction may lead to syncretism — e.g. the adjectival desinence -*oj* 'gen.loc.dat.instr., fem.' — this is clearly a system-motivated type of innovation through which relations among signata come to be reflected in relations among signantia.

5.5.1.4   Diagrams with relative signantia: Besides innovations in which a signatum — signans relation comes to mirror another (as in 5.5.1.1) or a relation among signata comes to be reflected by a corresponding relation between signantia — an opposition by distinct desinences, as in *dv-a* vs. *dv,-e* (5.5.1.1), similarity of content, by similar desinences, as in the case of -*ovo* (5.5.1.2), or by a syncretism, as in the case of -*oj* (5.5.1.3) — there are innovations in which a relation between signata comes to be reflected in a similar relation between the phonological shapes of the corresponding signantia.

An example — which at the same time illustrates the abstract sort of motivation that produces such diagrams — is the development of the Russian substantival declensions. Here a number of separate innovations, each with its independent motivation, and exemplifying quite different types — have produced dative and instrumental singular desinences just one segment shorter than the corresponding plural desinences and nominative, genitive and instrumental plural desinences at most one segment longer than the corresponding singular desinences. It is difficult not to see here a drift towards a diagram in which the opposition plural vs. singular ('more than one' vs. 'unspecified number') is reflected by a difference in number of segments (n + 1 vs. n) in the corresponding desinences (cf. Jakobson 1966/1971:202); see (21).

(21)   Number of segments in the substantival desinences of Middle Russian and Modern Russian. Innovated desinences are starred.

	Middle Russian			Modern Russian		
	I decl.	II decl.	III decl.	I decl.	II decl.	III decl.
nom. sg.	0/1	1	0	0/1	1	0
acc.	0/1	1	0	0/1	1	0
gen.	1	1	1	1	1	1
loc.	1	1	1	1	1	1
dat.	1/3	1	1	*1	1	1
instr.	2	3	2	2	*2	2
nom.pl.	1/2/3	1	1	*1	1	1
acc.	1	1	1	1	1	1
gen.	0/2	0	2	0/2	*0/2	2
loc.	2	2	2	2	2	2
dat.	2	2	2	2	2	2
instr.	1/2	3	2	*3	3	*3

5.5.2   Innovations in alternations are more obviously system-motivated than are innovations in morphological sign relations. For the latter are paradigmatic relations, relations to entities in absentia, but alternations involve the palpable indexical relations on the syntagmatic axis between signantia and the signata of neighbouring morphemes and among the signantia of contiguous morphemes.

This web of indexical relations is not to be dismissed as a redundant, counter-functional encumbrance of the morphology. The fact that morphophonemic alternations are not uniformly curtailed and eliminated in the history of a language, but may be reformulated and retained as productive formal means, suggests that they may have some vital function beyond the obvious one of providing useful cues for the speakers in decoding messages. It is reasonable to see that function in their ability to diagram paradigmatic relations among signata.

Since innovations in alternations, by virtue of the indexical value of derived alternants, tend to be system motivated, the following sections will — with the exception of 5.5.2.1 — merely point to diagrammatic aspects of the types of innovations already reviewed in 5.3–5.4.

5.5.2.1 Retroduction: Indeterminacies in the locus of an alternation or in the indexical value of its derived alternants may lead to various types of innovation — including the extension of the alternation — as seen in 5.4. Retroduction might serve as the name of a type of innovation by which an alternation is extended through the creation of base forms that have no support in speech data.

South Russian dialects — which characteristically neutralize the opposition *o : a* in unstressed syllables, realizing both vowels as [a] — have a strong tendency to switch end-stressed 2nd conjugation verbs to a mobile stress pattern. By this change, stem vowels which have previously been unstressed come to be stressed, and the previously pretonic [a] commonly appears as a stressed *o* (e.g. in such verbs as Standard Russian *val,ít,, vop,ít,, dar,ít,, zvon,ít,, kat,ít,, sad,ít,, plat,ít,*; cf. Avanesov — Orlova 1965:157f.); see (22).

(22)

	North Russian dialects			South Russian dialects		
	Mobile	End-stressed				
Inf.	*nos,í-t,*	*zvon,í-t,*	*dar,í-t,*	*nas,í-t,*	*zvan,í-t,*	*dar,í-t,*
1 sg.	*noš-ú*	*zvon,-ú*	*dar,ú*	*naš-ú*	*zvan,-ú*	*dar,-ú*
2 sg.	*nós,-i-š*	*zvon,-í-š*	*dar,-í-š*	*nós,-i-š*	*zvón,-i-š*	*dór,-i-š*

There is no doubt that the neutralization rule produces unstressed [a] from underlying *o* and *a*, and the innovated verb forms can only be understood as hypothetical base forms which come to the surface thanks to the stress pattern innovation. It is significant that some verbs with original pretonic *o* through the innovation in stress pattern come to have a stressed stem vowel *a* (e.g. *lov,ít,, sol,ít,*; cf. loc.cit); see (23).

(23)

	North Russian dialects		South Russian dialects	
	Mobile	End-stressed		
Inf.	*gas,í-t,*	*sol,í-t,*	*γas,í-t,*	*sal,í-t,*
1 sg.	*gaš-ú*	*sol,-ú*	*γaš-ú*	*sal,-ú*
2 sg.	*gás,-i-š*	*sol,-í-š*	*γás,-i-š*	*sál,-i-š*

Retroductive innovations presuppose a learner's strategy to go behind surface forms to postulate underlying representations. The strategy applies an already acquired command of rules of the language, and the innovations to which it gives rise are thus system-motivated.

The preceding example illustrates retroduction involving a phonological rule. Russian nouns like *óčerk* 'sketch', *ótpusk* 'leave', retroduced

from derived imperfective verbs (earlier *očerčát*, 'outline', *otpuščát*, 'let
go') containing an ambiguous *č* — in spite of the existence of the perfective verbs *očert,ít, otpust,ít,*, the substantive *čertá* 'line', and the adjective
pustój 'empty, deserted', are examples of the same kind, only from
derivational morphology.

5.5.2.2   Alternations as diagrams: Morphophonemic alternations are
among the most complex semiotic phenomena of language. A derived
alternant represents, as a symbolic signatum, the basic alternant from
which it is derived. At the same time, it has an indexical signatum,
some element(s) of a contiguous morpheme. But in addition, it forms
together with its basic alternant a diagram, for the relation between the
two mirrors the relation between the elements of the context to which
each of them indexically refers.

Such diagrams arise by virtue of the fact that the derived (marked)
alternant — if the alternation is to be defined at all — must be assigned a
specific, indexical value. This may be achieved in two ways. Either a
narrowly defined part of the total range of environments in which the
alternants occur is specified as the privilege of occurrence of one of the
alternants, which thereby becomes marked. This possibility is illustrated,
for instance, by the *-s-* ~ *-x-* alternation in the Early Slavic aorist morpheme (5.3.1) and by the *-e-* ~ *-o-* alternation in the present tense of the
Russian type (C) dialects (5.3.2). Or — and this is the more interesting
possibility — one of the alternants is defined as an index of some specific,
intrinsically marked feature within the range of environments of the
alternation. In such cases, the markedness relation between the alternants diagrams the markedness values of terms of a phonological, grammatical, or lexical opposition, e.g. sharping (5.3.1), nasality (5.4.3.2),
number (5.3.2(B), 5.4.1, 5.4.3.2), animacy (5.3.2), quantifier (5.3.3).

The high frequency with which alternations are defined in such a way
that they diagram grammatical oppositions is reflected in the fact that,
when alternations are eliminated, it is as a rule the alternant proper to the
unmarked category (the singular, the third person, the present tense, the
indicative) that is generalized; cf. Mańczak's fourth law (1963) and
Vennemann 1972.

The principle according to which derived alternants are assigned to
marked contexts has been named markedness assimilation (Andersen
1968:75). The importance of this principle — which is undoubtedly
deeply rooted in man's faculties of mind — extends far beyond the limits
of morphophonemics (cf. Andersen 1972:44f.). But within morphophonemics it has the effect of projecting relations of equivalence in

markedness onto the syntagmatic axis, as relations of contiguity (cf. Jakobson 1964:358). In morphophonemic innovations, it has the effect of ensuring that alternations to the greatest possible extent are motivated by the system.

5.5.2.3 Diagrams with relative signantia: As a final example of diagrammatization through morphophonemic alternants I will mention the redistribution of desinence initial vowels in the endings of the locative, dative, and instrumental plural in Russian.

The Middle Russian desinences for these cases ((24) (A)) contained initial vowels which did not express case meaning and were distributed in a most complicated fashion, apparently by morphophonemic rules. In an abductive innovation, -*a*-, which had the inductive indexical signatum 'substantival stem' was made a deductive index of substantives and generalized. As a consequence, -*e*- became restricted to adjectival pronouns and -*o*- to the numerals 'three' and 'four', with the result that the desinence initial vowels all became indexes of parts of speech (cf. (24) (B)).

(24) (A) The Middle Russian locative, dative, and instrumental plural desinences.

	Substantives			Adjectives			
	I	II	III		'2'	'3, 4'	
loc.	*ex/ix ox*	*ax*	*ox*	*ix*	*(oj)u*	*om*	⎫
dat.	*om om*	*am*	*om*	*im*	*ema*	*om*	⎬ Nouns
instr.	*im,i*	*am,i*	*m,i*	*im,i*	*ema*	*m,i*	⎭

	Pers.	Anaph.			
loc.	*as*	*ix*	*ex/ix*	⎫
dat.	*am*	*im*	*em/im*	⎬ Pronouns
instr.	*am,i*	*im,i*	*em,i/im,i*	⎭

(B) The Modern Russian locative, dative, and instrumental plural desinences.

	Substantives	Pronom. adj.		Adjectives	'two'	'three, four'
loc.	*ax*	*ex*	*ix*	*ix*	*ux*	*ox*
dat.	*am*	*em*	*im*	*im*	*um*	*om*
instr.	*am,i*	*em,i*	*im,i*	*im,i*	*um,a*	*(o)m,a*

The resulting distribution of desinence initial vowels is not just a matter of a the five vowels functioning as absolute signantia with indexical value.

It is remarkable that the maximally unmarked vowel *a* corresponds to the least restricted nominal part of speech, the substantive. Among the unrounded vowels, the more marked *e* points to the closed class of adjectival pronouns, while the less marked *i* points to adjectives in general. The marked, rounded vowels index the most restricted nominal part of speech, the numerals, the more marked *o* corresponding to the less frequent 'three' and 'four', the less marked *u* to the more frequent 'two'.

Thus in these desinences, the relations among the nominal parts of speech are diagrammed by the markedness relations of the vowel system.

5.6 In closing this survey of abductive innovations it is appropriate to add some comments on the presentation of the examples.

I have tried to distinguish types of innovations which may arise out of indeterminacies in speech (5.2–5.4), types of innovations which are motivated by particular features of the system into which they are integrated (5.5), and types of innovations that are called forth by typological properties of the system (5.1). This division of the survey into major classes of innovations corresponds to a methodological requirement in the analysis and interpretation of innovations, that the different kinds of motivation be explicitly distinguished. It is not to be understood as a claim that in reality, innovations in inflectional morphology are of one or the other type.

In the presentation of the examples in 5.2–5.4, the main emphasis was on the indeterminacies in speech which allow of alternative resolutions in the abductive process. In the sections dealing with system-motivated innovations (5.5), we were able to return to several of these examples to show that the actual resolutions depend in part on the structure of the morphological system. Typological factors were considered explicitly only in 5.1, but it goes without saying that these abstract properties of the design of a language play a role in all kinds of innovations. This means that the examples that have been given here to illustrate individual kinds of innovation have been presented with considerable simplification, which is justified by their use here as examples, but which must be noted together with the other simplifications (mentioned in 4.0) imposed by the character of the presentation and the purpose it is intended to serve.

6.0 In the introduction I stated that the aim of a typology of change is to give a systematic account of our experience with different kinds of innovation, a categorization of the possible which can be used as a heuristic tool in investigating individual changes and as a framework for that sorting of our data which must precede any attempt to formulate laws of change.

The preceding attempt at a systematization possibly falls short of this goal in several ways. Important types of innovation in inflectional morphology may have been overlooked. Important aspects of some of the types that have been defined may have gone unnoticed. I may not have succeeded in defining all the types I have identified consistently and correctly. Such shortcomings are unavoidable in an account that is limited to one man's experience with languages of a particular type. But I would hope that the survey given here will stimulate discussion of types of innovation in the history of languages of other types, and that some of the distinctions that have been assumed as essential here will help focus interest on aspects of historical morphology which so far have received scant attention or none at all.

Despite its preliminary character, I hope to have demonstrated that the theoretical assumptions embodied in this typology of innovations make it applicable as a heuristic tool in the analysis of changes in morphology. It is clear that the more articulate one's model of change, and the more refined one's theory of morphology, the more relevant questions one can put to the data to be analysed, and the greater are the chances of getting pertinent answers. But whether the typology proposed here is adequate — and, if not, how it should be amended — these are questions that can only be answered if it is confronted with the experience of other linguists.

The ultimate aim of historical morphology, that of formulating laws of change, has not been particularly relevant to this survey. A few remarks about apparent learner's strategies have been made en passant, but on the whole it seems to be too early yet in the development of the discipline to speculate on laws of change. Before this can be done, considerable quantities of data from different types of languages will have to be analysed — in greater detail than has been customary — and categorized according to uniform criteria, perhaps along the lines suggested here.

The fact that I have made no use of the term analogy in this study, finally, requires a word of comment. The term and the notion have been so widely used to describe relations among surface forms at different stages of a language — that is, to describe diachronic correspondences — that they are best avoided altogether in a theory of change that consistently analyses diachronic correspondences into sequences of innovations. There are deductive innovations which can be described as analogical. But these are accounted for by referring to the synchronic rules that produce them, and not by citing similar surface forms. There are abductive innovations which can be described as analogical. But these, too, are more appropriately explained by reference to the features of the grammar that have motivated them. If one finds, for instance, at a certain stage, that one set of forms have been segmented in a similar way to another set of forms, the question must be asked whether this new segmentation was motivated by surface ambiguities in the forms in question, whether it conformed to existing rules of the language, whether it conformed to typological properties of the language, and whether it was dictated by some general principle of language structure manifested as a learner's strategy. If the discovery of a surface analogy prevents these questions from being asked — and this has too often been the case in the past — the term and the notion should be abandoned. If it does not prevent the investigator from asking and seeking to answer these questions, the term and the notion do no harm, but neither do they contribute anything. In the areas of historical morphology where the concept of analogy has had a legitimate function, in questions of explicating the mapping relations between content and expression, it seems better to avoid the term and redefine the notion as part of the semiotic conceptual framework that appears to be called for in the investigation of language.

References

Alexander, Ronelle
    1976   *Torlak accentuation (= Slavistische Beiträge 94)* (München: Otto Sagner).
Al'muxamedova, Z. M.
    1976   "O variantnosti osnov otymennyx prilagatel'nyx s suffiksom -*ušč*" [On the varia
            tion of denominal adjectives in -*ušč*] in: *Imennoe slovoobrazovanie russkogo
            jazyka*, edited by S. P. Lopušanskaja (Kazan': Izdatel'stvo Kazanskogo Univer
            siteta), 15–23.
Andersen, Henning
    1968   "IE *s after *i, u, r, k* in Baltic and Slavic", *Acta Linguistica Hafniensia*
            11:171–190.
    1969a "A study in diachronic morphophonemics: The Ukrainian prefixes", *Language*
            45:807–830.
    1969b "The peripheral plural desinences in East Slavic", *International Journal of Slavic
            Linguistics and Poetics* 12:19–32.
    1970   "Kashubian *dobëtk* 'dobytek' and its kind", *Welt der Slaven* 15:61–76.
    1972   "Diphthongization", *Language* 48:11–50.
    1973   "Abductive and deductive change", *Language* 49:567–595.
    1975   "Towards a typology of change: Bifurcating changes and binary relations", in:
            Historical Linguistics, edited by John M. Anderson and Charles Jones (Amst
            erdam: North-Holland), 2:18–62.
    1978   "Vocalic and consonantal languages", to appear in: *Studia linguistica A.V. Issa
            tschenko a collegis et amicis oblata* (Lisse: Peter de Ridder Press).
Anttila, Raimo
    1972   *An introduction to historical and comparative linguistics* (New York: Macmillan).
    1975   *The indexical element in morphology (= Innsbrucker Beiträge zur Sprach
            wissenschaft, Vorträge 12)* (Innsbruck: Institut für Sprachwissenschaft der
            Universität).

Avanesaw, R. I.
1964 *Narysy pa belaruskaj dyjalektalohii* [Outline of Byelorussian dialectology] (Minsk: Navuka i texnika).
Avanesov, R. I.—V. G. Orlova
1965 *Russkaja dialektologija* [Russian dialectology] (2nd edition) (Moskva: Nauka).
Borkovskij, V. I.—P. S. Kuznecov
1965 *Istoričeskaja grammatika russkogo jazyka* [A historical grammar of Russian] (2nd edition) (Moskva: Nauka).
Bromlej, S. V.—L. N. Bulatova
1972 *Očerki morfologii russkix govorov* [A morphological description of Russian dialects] (Moskva: Nauka).
Brugmann, Karl
1906 *Vergleichende Laut-, Stammbildungs- und Flexionslehre nebst Lehre vom Gebrauch der Wortformen*. 2.Bd.: *Lehre von den Wortformen und ihrem Gebrauch*, 1. Teil: *Allgemeines, Zusammensetzung (Komposita), Nominalstämme* (2nd edition) (Straßburg: Trübner).
Bulatova, L. N.
1973 "O redkom sposobe vyraženija form roda v russkix govorax" [On a rare means of expressing gender in Russian dialects] in: *Issledovanija po russkoj dialektologii*, edited by S. V. Bromlej (Moskva: Nauka), 214–216.
Bulaxovskij, L. A.
1958 *Istoričeskij kommentarij k russkomu literaturnomu jazyku* [Historical commentary on the Russian literary language] (5th edition) (Kiev: Radjans'ka škola).
Coseriu, Eugenio
1958 *Sincronía, diacronía e historia: el problema del cambio lingüístico* (Montevideo: Universidad de la República).
1962 "Sistema, norma y habla", in: *Teoría del lenguaje y lingüística general*, edited by Eugenio Coseriu (Madrid: Editorial Gredos), 11–113.
1968 "Sincronía, diacronía y tipología", in *Actos del XI Congreso Internacional de Lingüística i Filología Románicas* (Madrid), 1:269–283.
Dejna, Karol
1973 *Dialekty polskie* [Polish dialects] (Wrocław: Ossolineum).
Endzelīns, Jānis
1971 *Comparative phonology and morphology of the Baltic languages*, translated by William R. Schmalstieg and Benjamiņš Jēgers (The Hague: Mouton).
Gabelentz, Georg von der
1901 *Die Sprachwissenschaft. Ihre Aufgaben, Methoden und bisherige Ergebnisse* (2nd edition) (Leipzig: Tauchnitz).
Gołąb, Zbigniew
1959 "The influence of Turkish upon the Macedonian Slavonic dialects", *Folia Orientalia* 1:26–45.
Greenberg, Joseph H.
1963 "Some universals of grammar", in: *Universals of Language*, edited by Joseph H. Greenberg (Cambridge, Mass.: M.I.T. Press).
Gvozdev, A. N.
1949 *Formirovanie u rebënka grammatičeskogo stroja russkogo jazyka*, I–II [The formation of Russian grammatical structure in a child] (Moskva: Izdatel'stvo Akademii pedagogiceskix nauk).
Haas, William
1957 *Studies in linguistic analysis* (= *Special Publication of the Philological Society*).

[Reprinted in part as "Zero in linguistic description" in: *Linguistics in Great Britain* II, edited by Wolfgang Kühlwein (Tübingen: Niemeyer), 75–84.]

Halle, Morris
1959   *The sound pattern of Russian. A linguistic and acoustic investigation* (The Hague: Mouton).

Hjelmslev, Louis
1963   *Sproget. En introduktion* [Language. An introduction] (København: Berlingske Forlag).

Huntley, David G.
1968   "Two cases of analogical feature substitution in Slavic languages", *Language* 44:501–506.

Isačenko, Aleksander V.
1938–1939   "Versuch einer Typologie der slavischen Sprachen", *Linguistica Slovaca* 1–2:64–76.
1975   "Morphologische Motivierung phonologischer Merkmale", in: *Phonologica 1972*, edited by Wolfgang U. Dressler and František V. Mareš (München: Fink), 335–352.

Jakobson, Roman
1948   "Russian conjugation", *Word* 4:155–167. [Reprinted in Jakobson 1971:119–129.]
1957   *Shifters, verbal categories and the Russian verb* (Cambridge, Mass.: Harvard Slavic Department). [Reprinted In Jakobson 1971:130–147.]
1958   "Morfologičeskie nabljudenija nad slavjanskim skloneniem" [Morphological observations on declension in Slavic] in: *American Contributions to the Fourth International Congress of Slavicists* (The Hague: Mouton), 127–156. [Reprinted in Jakobson 1971:154–183.]
1964   "Linguistics and poetics", in: *Style in language*, edited by Thomas A. Sebeok (Cambridge, Mass.: M.I.T. Press), 350–377.
1965   "Quest for the essence of language", *Diogenes* 51:21–37. [Reprinted in Jakobson 1971:345–359.]
1966   "The relationship between Russian stem suffixes and verbal aspects", in: Jakobson 1971:198–202.
1971   *Selected writings, II. Word and language* (The Hague: Mouton).

Kernyc'kyj, I. M.
1967   *Systema slovozminy v ukrajinskij movi* [The system of inflection in Ukrainian] (Kyjiv: Naukova Dumka).

Kiparsky, Valentin
1967   *Russische historische Grammatik, II. Die Entwicklung des Formensystems* (Heidelberg: Carl Winter).

Klemensiewicz, Zenon — Tadeusz Lehr-Spławiński — Stanisław Urbańczyk
1965   *Gramatyka historyczna języka polskiego* [A historical grammar of the Polish language] (3rd edition) (Warszawa: PWN).

Kuryłowicz, Jerzy
1949   "La nature des procès dits 'analogiques'", *Acta Linguistica Hafniensia* 5:15–37.
1964   *The inflectional categories of Indoeuropean* (Heidelberg: Carl Winter).

Kuz'mina, I. B. — E. V. Nemčenko
1971   *Sintaksis pričastnyx form v russkix govorax* [The syntax of participial forms in Russian dialects] (Moskva: Nauka).

Leed, Richard L.
1970   "Distinctive features and analogy", *Lingua* 26:1–24.

Lounsbury, Floyd G.
  1953   *Oneida verb morphology* (New Haven: Yale University Press).
Malkiel, Yakov
  1968   "Studies in irreversible binomials", in: *Essays on linguistic themes*, Yakov Malkiel
          (Berkeley: University of California Press).
Mańczak, Witold
  1957–1958   "Tendances générales des changements analogiques", *Lingua* 7:298–325,
              387–420.
  1963   "Tendances générales du développement morphologique", *Lingua* 12:19–38.
Matthews, Peter H.
  1974   *Morphology. An introduction to the theory of word structure* (Cambridge: University Press).
Mirčev, Kiril
  1963   *Istoričeska gramatika na bălgarskija ezik* [A historical grammar of the Bulgarian
          language] (2nd edition) (Sofija: Nauka i izkustvo).
Obnorskij, S. P.
  1953   *Očerki po morfologii russkogo glagola* [Outline of the morphology of the Russian
          verb]; (Moskva: Izdatel'stvo Akademii Nauk).
Osthoff, Hermann
  1879   *Das physiologische und psychologische Moment in der sprachlichen Formenbildung* (Berlin: Habel).
Paul, Hermann
  1920   *Prinzipien der Sprachgeschichte* (5th edition) (Tübingen: Niemeyer).
Ringgård, Kristian
  1961   *Vestjysk stød* (Aarhus: Universitetsforlaget).
Samijlenko, S. P.
  1964   *Narysy z istoryčnoji morfolohiji ukrajins'koji movy* I [Outline of historical
          Ukrainian morphology] (Kyjiv: Radjans'ka škola).
  1970   *Narysy z istoryčnoji morfolohiji ukrajins'koji movy* II [Outline of historical
          Ukrainian morphology] (Kyjiv: Vyšča škola).
Samuels, M. L.
  1972   *Linguistic evolution with special reference to English* (Cambridge: University
          Press).
Sapir, Edward
  1921   *Language* (New York: Harcourt, Brace & World).
Senn, Alfred
  1966   *Handbuch der litauischen Sprache* I. *Grammatik* (Heidelberg: Carl Winter).
Shapiro, Michael
  1968   *Russian phonetic variants and phonostylistics* (= *University of California Publications in Linguistics* 49) (Berkeley and Los Angeles: University of California
          Press).
  1969   *Aspects of Russian morphology. A semiotic investigation* (Cambridge, Mass.:
          Slavica Publishers).
Stang, Christian S.
  1942   *Das slavische und baltische Verbum* (Oslo).
  1966   *Vergleichende Grammatik der baltischen Sprachen* (Oslo: Universitetsforlaget).
Stern, Gustav
  1931   *Meaning and change of meaning, with special reference to the English language.*
          Reprinted in the *Indiana University Studies in the History and Theory of Linguistics* (Bloomington, Ind.: University Press), 1964.

Schooneveld, Cornelius H. van
 1959   *A semantic analysis of the Old Russian finite preterite system* (The Hague: Mouton).
Vážný, Václav
 1963   *Historická mluvnice česká II. Tvarosloví. 1: Skloňování* [Historical Czech grammar II. Morphology. 1: Declension] (2nd edition) (Praha: Státní pedagogické nakladatelství)
Vennemann, Theo
 1972   "Rule inversion," *Lingua* 29:209–242.
Veyrenc, Jacques
 1962   *Les formes concurrentes du gérondif passé en russe (Publication des annales de la faculté des lettres)* (Aix-en-Provence: Editions Ophrys).
Wheeler, Benjamin Ide
 1887   *Analogy and the scope of its application in language.* Reprinted 1965 (New York: Johnson).
Žylko, F. T.
 1966   *Narysy z dialektolohiji ukrajins'koji movy* [Outline of Ukrainian dialectology] (2nd edition) (Kyjiv: Radjans'ka škola).

STEPHEN R. ANDERSON

On the development of morphology
from syntax

A recent upsurge of interest in historical syntax (as exemplified by the
papers in, e.g., Steever et al. 1976 and Li 1977) has focused a certain
amount of attention on the need for valid general procedures that would
be of use in the reconstruction of syntactic systems. Most writers have
recognized that, whatever their utility for phonological problems, the
basic principles of the comparative method have at best limited utility in
the domain of syntax. If historical syntax is to be a possible undertaking at
all, it is necessary to arrive at procedures for its investigation that can be
justified in terms of our knowledge of the nature of syntactic systems, and
of grammatical theory in general. The principles of historical change in
phonology are founded at least implicitly on assumptions about the
nature and regularity of phonological systems and processes, and their
relation to sound change; since there is no reason to believe that changes
in sentence patterns of a language are governed by anything like the
principles regulating sound changes, and indeed every reason to doubt
that syntax is interestingly similar to phonology in its underlying formal
properties, it is clear that new techniques (or at best radically new
foundations for old ones) are called for in historical syntax.

  One principle with a great deal of appeal was suggested by Givón
(1971): "Today's morphology is yesterday's syntax." In several cases
discussed by Givón (and others taken up in later literature), it appears
that morphological material has arisen through the "fossilization" of
earlier independent syntactic elements, and interestingly, the position of
this material is correlated with the syntactic structures of an earlier stage
of the language prior to the "fossilization". For example, in the Scandinavian languages most modifiers (adjectives, demonstratives, and except in
Icelandic, genitives) in the Noun Phrase precede the Noun. The inflected
definite article, however, follows the noun, as in Danish *bog*en "the
book", *land*et 'the country'. By itself, this is simply an isolated anomaly:
Scandinavian is just one among the comparatively few languages that
show postposed articles. When we look at the earliest attested stages of
Germanic, however (the runic inscriptions, as described for example by

Antonsen (1975)), we see that this anomaly is probably reflective of earlier word order: in this material, it appears that the order noun plus modifier predominates. In particular, demonstratives seem to have followed the noun, and the Scandinavian definite article represents a reduced and encliticized demonstrative. It is reasonable to suggest, then, that in the course of development of Scandinavian the word order shifted from noun-modifier to modifier-noun; but that in the circumstance where a demonstrative had reduced stress (by virtue of being used simply as a determiner, with considerably weakened demonstrative force) and thus formed part of a single phonological word with the preceding noun, it failed to change position. The morphological position of the post-posed article in Scandinavian thus represents a residual trace of the earlier syntatic system in which modifiers followed their heads.

It is clear that this sort of observation could be of great utility in reconstructing syntactic prehistory, if in fact it could be shown to be reliable. If morphological idiosyncrasies of this sort generally reflected earlier syntax, then they could of course be used to recover it, just as morphological idiosyncrasies of another sort (isolated or relic forms) can often give us important clues about earlier phonological processes. In order to assess the validity of this principle, however, we must ask whether it is generally the case that grammars are so organized that morphology and syntax will show the appropriate relationship. Is it the case, that is, that syntactic systems are subject to principles of formal organization so that morphological characteristics such as the position of inflectional material will in general reflect syntactic features of earlier stages of the language. If not, of course, then today's morphology will be unreliable as a guide to yesterday's syntax.

It is quite clear in some cases that independent principles interfere with this sort of reconstruction of syntax from morphology. A widely cited example of the validity of this principle, for example, concerns clitic pronouns such as the object pronouns in the Romance languages (e.g. French *Je* le *sais*). The fact that these elements precede the verb is invoked by Givón (1971) as a reflection of an earlier state of affairs in which corresponding independent elements preceded the verb — an "O–V" syntactic type. The explanatory force of this observation is quite limited, however. While the two features in question (preverbal clitic pronouns and earlier O-V syntax) may in fact co-occur in the history of Romance, they may actually have nothing to do with one another. Clitic elements in general have a tendency to relocate in one of a few preferred positions — most notable after the first independent sentence element — and as Steele (1977) has argued, this can result in the appearance of clitics in positions having no connection with the positions of independent elements in syntactic structure. For instance as shown by Chung (1976), Tongan and a few other Polynesian languages have subject clitics that precede the verb, though they (and most other languages of the family) otherwise display a general verb-first order. One might invoke the position of the clitics as evidence that Polynesian once had S–V–O order, but there is no other support for this notion. Those languages of the family (a few of the so-called "Outlier" languages) that have S–V–O order have manifestly changed from V–S–O to S–V–O in the recent past, and there is no reason to believe that Polynesian was ever other than V–S–O. Instead, the explanation for the preverbal position of the subject pronouns is simply the tendency of clitics to appear in second position: the verb is preceded by a tense element or other auxiliary word, and the clitics thus attach after this by a principle having nothing to do with the syntax of independently occurring NPs.

The other side of the coin is of course the fact that by no means all syntactic changes will be reflected in subsequent stages of the language by morphological elements. Many sorts of change are such that it is difficult to imagine any morphological consequences: if a language acquires a rule of topicalization to initial position, for instance, how could the morphology reflect the stage of the language prior to the appearance of the rule? Only a few sorts of syntactic rule are such that they can leave such residual effects in the morphology, and as we have seen, the effects themselves can also be caused by other principles.

Given these observations, we might well ask whether morphology is of any use in syntactic reconstruction. To determine this, we would have to ask whether there are any circumstances in which the relation between syntactic change and morphological structure is fairly determinate and well-defined. If there are changes of some characterizable sort from which morphological consequences could be expected to follow, then at least within this limited domain we might claim that syntax and morphology are related in such a way as to be of potential use in determining the course of linguistic history.

It is our purpose here to discuss some cases of this sort, in which syntactic changes can be expected to have morphological consequences. We will be concerned, in particular, with cases in which morphological material associated with some category of the grammar appears as the reflex of a syntactic state of affairs in which a particular sort of structural opacity motivates a reanalysis of a construction. Just in case derivational opacity (of a sort to be discussed and illustrated below) comes to be associated with a well-defined category of the grammar, we will argue that such reanalysis and associated morphological change occurs. If that is the case, we will have at least a kernel of cases in which the relation of syntax and morphology is fairly clear.

For an example of the sort of situation that will be of interest to us below, consider the most commonly used expression of the relation of possession in Chickasaw, a Muskogean language[1]:

(1) *Hattuk   at   ofi'   at   imaya'sha*
    (man   sbj   dog   sbj   him-it-be there, have)
    'The man has a dog'.

From the point of view of Chickasaw morphology, there are a number of unusual features to this construction:

1 In general, subjects of all sentence types, and only subjects, are followed by a "subject article" — usually *at*. In sentences like (1), however, both NPs are followed by *at*.

2 The verbal form consists of the stem *aya'sha*, meaning roughly 'be somewhere', preceded by an agreement marker *im* agreeing with *hattuk* 'man' in person, as well as an implicit marker Ø agreeing with *ofi'* 'dog'.[1] Subjects in Chickasaw are marked with agreement formatives from one or the other of two sets, depending on the class of the verb; but *im* is not a member of either of those sets. It is rather a member of the 'oblique' set of agreement markers, used otherwise to mark indirect objects, benefactives, and the oblique objects of a few verbs such as 'love'.

3 The verb form *aya'sha* is clearly from the paradigm of a verb meaning to be at some place, or to exist. This is one of a set of verbs in Chickasaw that show suppletion for number, however, and the form *aya'sha* is explicitly a plural form (as opposed to *ahanta*, singular, and *ahanshwa*, dual). Neither the NP *hattuk* nor *ofi'* is plural, however. If we vary the number of both, the verb form does not change.

The explanation of these anomalies is not difficult to find in view of the way possession is expressed in the languages of the world. As is well-known (cf. Benveniste 1960), many languages express a possessive relationship with a construction of the type *mihi est aliquid*, where the possessor is formally in an oblique relation (dative, locative, etc.), the possessed is formally subject of the construction, and the verb is a copula or existential. Such a construction is clearly at the base of example (1): we might gloss it as something like 'a dog exists for the man'. This would account for the agreement markers on the verb, as well as for the presence of *at* after *ofi'* 'dog'. If we further assume that the plural form has become specialized in the sense 'have', we would further have an account of the invariance of the form for number: only verbs of positional location in Chickasaw appear to show the three-way number suppletion of *ahan-*

ta/ahanshwa/aya'sha, and if *aya'sha* in this construction has taken on a non-positional sense, it would not be expected to show this pattern.

This account would still leave us with two problems, however:

1 If *ofi'* is subject of (1), why is it not sentence-initial? Word order in Chickasaw is quite strictly subject-initial (and verb-final, though adverbial elements can sometimes follow the verb);

2 Why does *hattuk* 'man' have a subject article? Oblique complements in Chickasaw are unmarked or followed by one of a set of non-subject articles.

We could account for these facts as well if we suggested that the syntactic structure of (1) was not that suggested by the morphology of the *mihi est aliquid* construction, but rather that of a straightforward transitive verb: *hattuk* is the subject, and *ofi'* the object. In that case, *hattuk* would appropriately appear in sentence initial position and be followed by a subject article. But this move would put us back in our original dilemma: how now to explain the article following *ofi'* and the verbal agreement pattern?

In order to resolve this apparent contradiction, it is necessary to have tive verb; *hattuk* is the subject, and *ofi'* the object. In that case, *hattuk* and *ofi'* in (1) which is independent of their morphological properties. The notion of subject is after all a syntactic one; and though it may be reflected in the morphology of a language, this reflection is often complex and non-unitary (cf. Anderson 1976 for some discussion of this connection between grammatical relations and morphology). It is only by looking to the syntactic rules of a language that we can assign genuine significance to the assertion that some NP is (or is not) a subject. We look, that is, to rules of the general class that are sensitive to grammatical relations (as opposed to rules of semantic interpretation and lexical rules, which appear to be sensitive to relations of a more semantic sort, called "thematic"; cf. Anderson 1976, 1977a, 1977b for some further discussion) in order to determine which NP in a clause has the syntactic properties of a subject. In Chickasaw there are several such rules: as in many other American Indian languages, for example, Chickasaw coordination is based on a device of "switch reference," which requires an indication whether coordinated clauses have the same subject or different subjects. Furthermore, the language displays principles which delete (or interpret, in a different syntactic framework) the subjects of certain embeddings, similar to English Equi-NP deletion. Only subjects can serve as the antecedents for reflexive forms. And so on: the range of syntactic processes typically found to be sensitive to the distinction between subjects and non-subjects in other languages can be found here too, and can be used as the basis of a genuinely syntactic test for subjecthood. In the case of sentences like (1), the result of this test is quite unambiguous: the first NP, *hattuk*, the possessor, displays all of the properties of a subject, and these properties are not associated with *ofi'*, the possessed. Only the morphology runs against this conclusion, and the morphology is not a reliable guide, as shown by a wide variety of languages in which grammatical categories are not consistently indicated in morphological categories.

We suggest, then, that the following has taken place. A construction for expressing 'have' was originally formed in Muskogean on the *mihi est aliquid* model. In the original form of this construction, the possessed NP was indeed the subject, and the possessor an oblique complement. the morphological marking of the verb and of the possessed NP with a subject article was thus appropriate. Subsequently however, the meaning of 'have' became specialized in the verb form *aya'sha*, and the relation between possessor and possessed was interpreted as a straightforward transitive one — perhaps on the model of other expressions for possession in Chickasaw, such as (2):

(2) *Hattuk   at   ishhola sochi'   i'shta*
     (man   sbj   pencil   (he-) (it-) holds)
     'The man has a pencil'.

The verb *i'shta*, a durative form of a verb meaning 'take hold of', can also be used to express (temporary) possession, and is constructed as any other transitive verb.

The reanalysis of the possessive construction in (1), then, involved reinterpreting the possessor as subject, the possessed as object, and the verb as transitive (rather than intransitive with an oblique complement). After the reinterpretation its most important consequence, the assignment of syntactic subject-hood to the possessor, was reflected in the sentence-initial position of this element and the assignment of a subject article to it. The conclusion that this was not the original state of affairs is supported, not only by the morphology, but by the fact that in related languages the possessed NP shows some subject properties: Heath (1976) reports that in Choctaw, a closely related language, either possessor or possessed can be treated as subject. Notice that the reinterpretation in Chickasaw is primarily a structural one, though, with minimal consequences for the surface form of sentences. The verb form continues to be marked as originally, and the possessed NP continues to be assigned a subject article (though no other subject properties).

This is apparently a case, then, in which today's morphology does reflect yesterday's syntax, and we would like to know what has motivated such a change. We suggest that the basis is as follows. As illustrated by the wide distribution of *mihi est aliquid* constructions to express possession, this structure is semantically appropriate to the notion; but as evidenced by the frequent replacement of such constructions with the model *habeo aliquid*, with ordinary transitive verb, it is syntactically inappropriate. When possession is thought of as expressed by a unitary verb, it seems that the most natural construction is a transitive one with possessor as subject and possessed as object.

As a result of this situation, the oblique construction for possession was only motivated as long as the status of the verb was clearly that of the locational/existential. As soon as the verb form *aya'sha* became specialized in the sense of possession, and hence in part dissociated from the locative/existential verb, the oblique construction was no longer syntactically motivated (though of course it was still indicated morphologically). The resulting reanalysis, then, can be seen as the reinterpretation of the morphology associated with the oblique construction not as significant of syntactic structure, but rather as the mark of the possessive sense of the verb *aya'sha*. When the original syntactic structure ceased to be motivated, that is, it became to that extent "opaque" (in a sense similar to that associated with this term in phonology). The structure was then reanalyzed as the syntactically most natural one, and the original morphology interpreted as if it were connected not with the syntax but with the category of possession. As noted above, this reinterpretation and reduction of syntactic opacity had minimal consequences for the surface shapes of sentences, but profound ones for the syntactic structures of those sentences.

We should now proceed to examine the nature of the "opacity" which results in such a reanalysis, in order to clarify as far as possible the circumstances in which we might expect such a reflection of earlier syntax in morphology. In this case, the opacity resulted from the fact that the syntactic structure associated with a particular verb ceased to be motivated as that verb became specialized in a different sense. In this example, the opacity and resulting reanalysis are associated with the semantics of a particular verb; but in fact essentially the same principle can be seen at work in other examples in which rather more of the structure of the language is affected.

A number of useful examples are furnished by the study of the development of ergativity in language. Consider, for instance, the syntactic history of a Polynesian language like Tongan (as established by Chung 1976, 1977). Chung shows that it is possible to establish a number of facts about the syntax of "Proto-Polynesian":

1   subjects, whether of transitive or of intransitive verbs, were originally unmarked;

2 objects of transitive verbs were marked with the particle *'i*, an accusative marker, and were in fact direct, rather than oblique objects;

3 a passive construction promoted objects to subject position, and marked the (demoted) underlying subjects with a particle *'e*, while adding a suffix (C)*ia* to the verb (where C is a consonant determined idiosyncratically by the given verb). This is essentially the situation of modern Maori, but the various aspects of it can be established by comparative procedures for the family as a whole, as Chung demonstrates.

In modern Tongan, the situation is quite different:

1 while intransitive subjects are unmarked (or marked with a Tongan innovation, the particle *'a*, in conservative speech), transitive subjects are marked with *'e*;

2 objects of transitive verbs, on the other hand, are unmarked (or marked with *'a* in conservative speech);

3 there is no longer an active/passive opposition, although a great many transitive verbs end in an element -(C)*ia*

Tongan morphology, that is, has replaced the nominative/accusative pattern of "Proto-Polynesian" with an ergative/absolutive one. It is also clear that this pattern has arisen by generalizing the original passive construction at the expense of the original active one. Such a generalization is entirely consistent with the facts of Polynesian: as Chung notes, even in Maori and other Polynesian languages which retain the active/passive opposition, the passive forms are used in a much wider range of environments than is characteristic for passives in a language like, for example, English. It would be perfectly reasonable to propose that Tongan and a few other languages simply carried this generalization of the use of passives to its logical conclusion, completely replacing actives.

In a passive construction, the (derived) subject is not the underlying subject, the agent, but rather the underlying object. If all that has happened in Tongan is the generalization of passive structures, then, we would expect to find that the NP corresponding to the object of a transitive verb should display subject properties. In a sentence like (3), that is, we would expect the NP *'a Sione* to display the syntactic characteristics of a subject:

(3) *na'e   taa'i   'e   Mele   'a   Sione*
     (past hit   prt Mary   prt John)
     'Mary hit John'.

As Chung shows, however, this is not the case: the NP which displays the characteristics of a subject is not *'a Sione*, but *'e Mele*. Tongan has several rules that distinguish between subjects and non-subjects, and these all treat the NP in the position of *'e Mele* as the syntactic subject. This is not a property of the passive construction in Polynesian: in languages like Maori, where passives are opposed to actives, it is the NP in the position of *'a Sione* in a passive sentence parallel to (3) that behaves like a syntactic subject. It also has nothing to do with the surface word order of the two NP's in (3): these can be freely permuted without affecting their syntactic behavior.

The conclusion to be drawn from this, then, is that Tongan has reanalyzed its (originally) passive structures as basic active ones, with the "agent" NP in syntactic subject position, while retaining the morphological marks of the earlier derived status of the construction. Again, there has been essentially no change in the surface shape of sentences in the language, but rather a major reinterpretation of their syntactic structure. Sentences which originally were derived structures, with their underlying grammatical relations changed by a rule of passive, are now treated as if those grammatical relations were left in their most basic, unchanged form. The morphology originally associated with the structural change of passive (Ø or *'a* marking for underlying object, *'e* marking for underlying subject, and -(C) *ia* added to the verb) has simply been reinterpreted as the mark of a transitive construction, rather than as the consequences of a syntactic rule altering clause structure. Again, the morphology of the resulting ergative construction reflects not the syntactic organization of a clause in modern Tongan, but rather the syntax of the historically antecedent passive construction.

Here there is of course no semantic specialization involved, and we might well ask whether the example is at all parallel to the Chickasaw possessive construction discussed above. It is our contention, however, that the two cases are in fact quite parallel: in both instances, the reinterpretation of a syntactic structure as a more "basic" one, and of the morphological marks of the original construction as simply formal baggage, is motivated in both cases by the development of opacity in the syntactic structure involved. In Chickasaw, this came about through the dissociation of the sense of possession from the original locative/existential sense of particular verb forms. In Tongan, on the other hand, it comes about through the thoroughgoing replacement of active structures by passive ones. As the basic active structures from which the passive ones were (originally) derived disappeared from the language, that is, the derived status of the passive lost its motivation. The absence of surface structures displaying the putative underlying structure removed the motivation for deriving the occurring forms from something else by a rule that changes grammatical relations; and these were thus reinterpreted as if they were in fact the most natural underlying structures, unaffected by any syntactic reorganization at all. The morphology originally associated with passive was then simply seen as part of the formal marking of transitive clauses, rather than as directly indicative of the syntactic structure of a derived passive.

There is a similarity between the Chickasaw and Tongan cases, then: in both, a reanalysis takes place, in which an originally non-basic syntactic structure for transitive constructions is reinterpreted as if it were the most basic, natural construction of that type; and furthermore, the original morphology (while it formerly indicated syntactic categories fairly accurately) is taken to be an unmotivated formal property of the construction. In both cases, we can perceive a type of syntactic opacity, which we would like to characterize. It seems reasonable to suggest that, where the surface structure of a transitive construction differs from that in which (roughly) the agent of a transitive verb is its subject and the theme or patient is object, such a structure must have a motivation in the syntax of the language. In both cases this was originally true: in Chickasaw, the motivation came originally from the syntax of locational verbs, one of which had been pressed into service for semantic reasons to indicate possession; and in Tongan, the motivation came originally from the productive relation between active and passive. Subsequent change obscures these motivations: in Chickasaw, the verb expressing possession becomes partially dissociated from the locative/existential, certainly in sense and to some extent in form; and in Tongan the original active structures disappear over time from the surface data available to the language learner as the use of the passive is generalized to more and more discourse environments. In each case, as the motivation disappears, the non-basic transitive structure becomes opaque; and the reanalyses we have seen are the result.

In the Tongan case, the opacity that provokes reanalysis results from a rule becoming (effectively) obligatory, and we would expect that this would be a frequent source of examples of the type we are interested in. Whenever all of the surface structures expressing a given meaning or range of meanings have a particular form (perhaps by virtue of their all having undergone the same obligatory rule), it is natural to suggest that the derivation of these structures from something else more basic will be unmotivated and opaque; and to that extent, they will be interpreted as if they were themselves basic. Furthermore, we might expect that whatever morphological peculiarities the surface construction exhibits will be associated with the meanings or range of meanings that it conveys, rather than with the (unmotivated) non-basic character of the structure. In the Chickasaw case, the morphology was thus associated with the sense of "have"; in the Tongan case, it was associated with transitive constructions in general. It is also possible to find examples in which such reanalyzed morphology is associated with categories intermediate between the specific semantics of a particular verb and the general notion of transitive structures.

When we examine other instances of ergative morphology, we find that in quite a few instances it is associated not with all transitive structures, but only with some. Typically, for instance, we find ergativity confined to sentences in which the verb is in a perfect tense (or in a tense deriving from an original perfect, generally simply a past). This is the case in many of the modern Indic and Iranian languages, for example, as well as in Classical Armenian (with some reservations), Georgian, and Burushaski. In some of these cases, we can see that the motivation for this is in the historical source of the perfect. As discussed by Anderson (1977a), as well as by Benveniste (1952), when a language creates a new perfect for transitive verbs, there are two common sources which are employed for this purpose in a variety of languages. In some languages, an original passive comes to be employed in the sense of a perfect (the relation between passive or middle and perfect being well established, as discussed by e.g. Kuryłowicz 1964). This was apparently the source of the perfect tense forms which are the antecedents of the past tense forms that display ergative morphology in modern Indic languages such as Hindi and Nepali. In others, an original possessive construction is employed in a similar sense: thus, "I have (the book (read))" comes to be employed to mean "I have read the book". Coupled with the use in some languages of an oblique construction of the *mihi est aliquid* type to express possession, this results in a decidedly non-basic structure: roughly "to-me is (the book (read))" to express the perfect tense corresponding to "I read the book". This development seems to be responsible for the creation of a perfect form in Iranian.

In a language like Hindi, though, we can see that while the perfect tense form may originally have been a syntactically derived passive (hence with underlying object functioning as subject, and underlying subject relegated to an oblique agent phrase of some sort), it is no longer so. In a sentence like (4) below, that is, it is not *kuttā* 'dog', but *larke* 'boy' that displays the properties of a syntactic subject:

(4) *larke-ne   kuttā   dekhā   hai*
    (boy-erg   dog   seen   has)
    'The boy saw a dog'.

Only *larke*, for example, can serve as the antecedent of a reflexive, the deleted NP under Equi–NP type rules, etc. in Hindi. Thus although the perfect forms are morphologically ergative, they are structurally not passive but straightforwardly active.

We can clearly see here another instance of the same sort of change that affected Tongan, though on a more interesting and limited scale. In the history of Indic, that is, after the disappearance of the original inflected perfect of Sanskrit, the surface forms expressing perfect aspect that were available to a language learner were obligatorily those with passive structure. As a result, we can hypothesize that their motivated derivation from more basic active structures became opaque; they were thus reanalyzed as basic actives, with subject properties assigned to the agent phrase, and the complex morphology of the passive construction reinterpreted as simply (part of) the formal marking of the category "perfect". Here again, the obligatory use of a derived construction leads to opacity and consequent reanalysis; but since the obligatoriness is confined to a particular morphological category ("perfect tense"), the reanalysis is similarly confined, and the reinterpretation of the morphology takes it to be a formal mark of just that category.

Another instance in which the obligatory application of a rule within a grammatically characterizable environment leads to reanalysis is probably to be found in the history of the Algonquian family. Studies of the independent indicative of the transitive animate verb in Algonquian (e.g., Goddard 1967) have traditionally distinguished among direct forms, inverse forms, and local (or "you-and-me") forms. The distinction among these is insightfully described by Hockett (1966) in terms of a hierarchy of proximity of "person": speaker and hearer are strictly local to the speech act, a third person is further away, and another person (the "obviative" or "fourth person") may be yet more distant, conceptually. The local forms of the transitive animate paradigm are used when both speaker and hearer are involved as agent and goal (or vice versa). Of the other sets, the direct forms are used when a nearer referent is agent and a further referent goal, and the inverse forms when the further referent acts on the nearer. Thus, when first or second person acts on third or obviative, or when third acts on obviative, a direct form of the verb is used; while if third or obviative acts on first or second person, or obviative on proximate third person, an inverse form is required.

Our interest here is in the shape of the inverse forms. A complete (or even partial) description of the morphology of an Algonquian language is well beyond the scope of this paper (but cf. Anderson 1977c for a formalization of the inflectional system of Potawatomi, and Rhodes 1976 for a treatment of Central Ojibwa). It can be noted, however, that rules involved elsewhere in the grammar for the description of the intransitive paradigms and of the transitive inanimate forms handle most of the work of describing the direct forms of the transitive animate paradigm. The inverse forms are the ones that raise special problems.

The individual languages of the family have their own minor indiosyncracies, but overall the inverse forms show the same two distinguishing features:

1   a special formative (in Potawatomi, /-uko-/, and in other languages generally a form close to this or directly cognate) is added to the verb in place of the usual transitive animate theme sign; and

2   the marking of the verb for its object is virtually the same as the method of subject marking in other paradigms, and vice versa.

The effect of this property of the inverse forms is that in any given sentence, the participant closest to the speech act (i.e., first or second person if the other is third or obviative, proximate if the other is obviative) is the one shown by the "subject" morphology, and the more distant participant is the one shown by the "non-subject" morphology. In the direct forms, this is of course because what distinguishes the direct paradigm is precisely the fact that the subject is the nearer participant; in the inverse forms, it is by virtue of the peculiar, "inverse", nature of the forms themselves.

The mechanism underlying the formation of the inverse paradigm is not far to seek. In fact, it is quite apparent from a comparison of the languages of the family that the other distinguishing feature of the inverse paradigm holds the key: the additional formative (e.g., Potawatomi /-uko-/) is also employed in several of the languages to form a (generally agentless) passive, We can plausibly suggest, then, that the inverse forms are passive in origin, and that the apparent interchange of subject and object marking is due to the interchange of subject and non-subject relations which is associated with passive rules. Apparently, then, at an early point in the history of Algonquian, passive became an obligatory rule whenever the situation described did not conform to the "preferred" direction of action: first or second person acting on non-local participant, proximate acting on obviative. Whenever this situation did not obtain, passive was applied obligatorily, with the result that the "nearer" participant came to occupy the position of (derived) subject.

This sort of situation with respect to passivization is in fact not at all unprecedented in American Indian languages. A particularly well-known case is the passive in Navajo. As described by Frishberg (1972) and Creamer (1974), Navajo has a principle by which all nouns can be arranged in a hierarchy corresponding roughly to the (perceived) capacity of their referents to act independently. Thus, all persons (except babies) outrank everything else; next come babies and large animals such as horses, bulls, etc.; then animals such as sheep and goats, chicks, etc.;

then small animals; then insects; then natural forces; then plants and inanimate objects, like rocks; and finally abstractions, like old age, disease, etc. The importance of this hierarchy is that when a sentence contains two third person participants, the one that ranks higher on the hierarchy must occupy the position of subject. This is accomplished through the operation of a syntactic rule of passive, interchanging subject and object in derived structure and substituting the agreement marker *bi* for basic *yi*. It should be pointed out that this rule is completely obligatory when the two participants differ in position on the "activity" hierarchy: it is quite ungrammatical to say 'the bee stung the boy', and the sentence must be converted into 'the boy was stung by the bee'. When both participants are at the same level on the hierarchy, however, passive is optional: one can thus say either 'the bull gored the horse' or 'the horse was gored by the bull'. The condition of obligatory passive to "enforce" a preferred way of organizing the participants is nonetheless similar to the state of affairs suggested for Algonquian.

An even closer parallel is found in another American Indian language: Nitinaht of the Wakashan family (as well as the related languages "Nootka" and Makah). As described by Klokeid (1977), participants in a clause in Nitinaht can be ranked in the "chain of being" with first and second persons highest, then other animates, and finally inanimates. Further investigation might reveal some further, finer gradation of these categories, but these at least seem well established. The function of this hierarchy is similar to that of the others we have examined. If one orders the grammatical positions in a clause with subject highest, then direct object, then indirect object, the Nitinaht hierarchy requires that where participants occupy different ranks on the "chain-of-being" hierarchy, the higher ranking participant must occupy a higher position on the grammatical hierarchy. This is accomplished through the interaction of rules of passive, indirect-object promotion (or dative shift), and demotion of objects to oblique status (where they no longer are relevant to the hierarchical constraints). As in Navajo, one thus cannot say 'the rock hit the man', but only 'the man was hit by the rock'; further, one cannot say 'I made a canoe for my brother', but only 'I made my brother a canoe', etc. The rules involved are optional as long as the hierarchical status of participants is equal, but when it is not, their operation is determined strictly obligatorily. Again, the situation is like that suggested for Algonquian.

In these cases, then, rules of passive (and other relation-changing rules as well in Nitinaht) are obligatory under certain circumstances, and we might expect, on the analogy of the cases considered at the beginning of this paper, that such a situation would create opacity that would be eliminated through reanalysis. When we look at the Algonquian languages, that is what we apparently find. The question to be asked here is, which of the NPs in a clause with an inverse verb form is the subject? To put it another way, are the inverse verb forms still derived as passives, or have they been reanalyzed as basic, active sentence types despite their inverse morphology?

It is difficult, given the structure of Algonquian to find unambiguous evidence bearing on this question. Since the forms we are concerned with are from the independent indicative set, and not from e.g. the conjunct paradigms (which have their own structure and problems); and since embeddings that undergo any rule that might tell us about grammatical relations, such as Equi–Np deletion or raising would be in the conjunct form rather than the independent indicative, these rules are not available to us as tests for subjecthood. Conjunction formation is relatively free in these languages, and does not seem to be sensitive to grammatical relations in any interesting way; reflexive has the effect of converting the verb from a transitive to an intransitive animate form, and thus of removing it from the area of concern, etc. There are two points that do seem significant, however. First of all, most of the languages retain, in addition to the direct and inverse forms, an independent (generally agent-less) passive form for the transitive animate verb. While it would probably not be completely impossible for a language to have two distinct passive rules, this would certainly be an unusual situation. The existence of a genuine passive, with the constraint (frequently encountered in natural languages) that passive forms involve deletion or omission of reference to an agent, argues against the construal of the inverse forms as synchronically derived by passive also.

Secondly, the inverse forms have the property that not only is their object indicated by the morphology of other subjects, but their agent is indicated as other objects would be. Now Algonquian verbs are quite rigidly divided into animate and inanimate forms, depending on the gender of the subject (if intransitive) or of the object (if transitive). These frequently, though not always, come in pairs, differentiated by stem-final suffixes. For transitive verbs, the animacy of a given verb is determined by the gender of its object; and if passive really operated to interchange subject and object in the inverse forms, as suggested by their morphology, we might expect it to give rise to a conflict. In a sentence like 'the rock killed the man' the verb will be a transitive animate one. If the rock is obviative and the man proximate, an inverse form is required. If inverse forms involve an interchange of subject and object, however, this would make "the rock" object; and hence might be taken to require a transitive *in*animate verb form instead. Now apparently this is not found in any of the languages, which suggests that the inverse forms do not really involve an inversion of grammatical relations.

Better evidence than the above arguments would certainly be useful, but even in its absence it is reasonable to suggest that the inverse forms are not in fact synchronically derived by passive. Passive of the sort that would be involved is not an optional rule anywhere in Algonquian: language learners would never see evidence for the putative "active" structures from which the inverse forms were to be derived. There is no reason whatsoever, then, for them not to eliminate the opacity of a derivation involving passive by reanalyzing the inverse forms as active, basic structures and taking the peculiar morphology (including the formative like Potawatomi /-uko-/ that marks this paradigm) as simply one part of the highly complex system of person/number marking of an Algonquian language. This development presumably took place early in the history of the family; already in Goddard's (1967) reconstructed Proto-Algonquian paradigms, for instance, the actual passive forms differ in several respects from the inverse forms, implying that the two are distinguishable from the point of view of the family as a whole. However this may be, it appears plausible to suggest that the inverse forms arose through the reanalysis of a passive rule that was obligatory under certain conditions of person/number of the participants in a clause. The reanalysis had the consequences that both direct and inverse forms subsequently were taken to have the same syntactic structure (that of an active sentence), and the originally passive morphology of the inverse forms was taken to be simply a part of the agreement system of the language.

Now let us compare this conclusion with the state of affairs in the other languages we cited above, Navajo and Nitinaht. In those languages we must apparently reach a different conclusion. In both cases, the structures in which passive is obligatory have not undergone reanalysis, and the derived passives are indeed still derived. The evidence for this is reasonably clear: briefly, both languages have at least some rules which refer to the distinction between subjects and non-subjects, and in both cases, the NPs that display subject properties in the passive constructions are the underlying objects, not the underlying subjects.

Both in Algonquian and in Navajo and Nitinaht, passive rules can be seen to be (or have been) obligatory under certain circumstances. What is it that motivates the different results in the different cases? We might say simply that the kind of reanalysis that we have been discussing is a possible course for linguistic change, but not a necessary one: and that Navajo and Nitinaht have simply not undergone it (yet). It is probable, though, that there is more to the situation than that.

When we look at the difference between the two sorts of case, we see that there are two distinguishing factors:
1   In Algonquian, where we hypothesize that reanalysis has taken place, there are no circumstances under which passive is optional: thus, there are no cases of contrasting active/passive pairs. In both Navajo and Nitinaht, however, if participants are of equal status passive is optional, and thus there are some such pairs. As such, there is some motivation in Navajo and in Nitinaht for positing a rule of passive, and its opacity is thereby reduced (even though it is obligatory in some circumstances).
2   In Algonquian, the circumstances under which passive was obligatory can be defined in terms of independently functioning features of the grammatical system of the language. First and second person, proximate and obviative have independent existence in the language, and serve to define the class of inverse forms. When reanalysis took place, then, the language provided a ready set of features that the original passive morphology could be taken as markers for. In both Navajo and Nitinaht, however, the hierarchy that is relevant to determining the circumstances of obligatory passivization involves features that do not play a role in the grammar of the language otherwise. If reanalysis were to occur in either language, there is no motivated grammatical category that the morphological material of passivization could be "rationalized" by.

These two features serve to constrain the operation of the reanalysis mechanism we have been discussing, we would suggest. Where there are some environments where a derived structure is motivated, this reduces the opacity that would otherwise be associated with it where it is obligatory. And where there is no basis in the grammar of a language for defining the class of environments in which some clustering of morphological material appears, it is apparently not possible to ignore it by reanalyzing it as syntactically irrelevant. Of course, one might suggest that where only one of these factors enters in, a change might be motivated to eliminate it: thus, if a derived structure were obligatory in some well-defined category, it might well also become obligatory elsewhere and thus facilitate reanalysis. Examples of this sort are not known to us, however, and this must remain pure speculation.

The cases we have been discussing present an interesting situation: they are precisely those in which a grammar-constructor has a free choice between a strictly morphological and a strictly syntactic account of the same data. The fact that reanalysis seems to favour the rationalization of the syntax at the expense of complicating the morphology should probably be taken to have some importance for the construction of an evaluation procedure for grammars.

In conclusion, we have been examining here a special case of the development of morphology out of earlier syntactic structure. If we have not found that today's morphology can be taken reliably to be yesterday's syntax, we have at least seen that there are some clear circumstances in which today's syntax can be expected to become tomorrow's morphology.

Note

1. Information on Chickasaw comes from my own research, conducted in collaboration with Pamela Munro. I would like to express my appreciation to Mrs. Catherine Willmond of Los Angeles for her patient help in teaching us some of her language.

References

Anderson, Stephen R.
   1976 "On the notion of subject in ergative languages", in Li (ed.) 1976:3–23.
   1977a "On mechanisms by which languages become ergative", in Li (ed.) 1977:317–363.
   1977b "Comments on Wasow: The role of the *theme* in lexical relations", in Culicover et al. (eds.) 1977:361–377.
   1977c "On the formal description of inflection", *Papers from the Regional Meeting of the Chicago Linguistic Society* 13:15–44.
Antonsen, Elmer H.
   1975 *A concise grammar of the older Runic inscriptions* (Tübingen: Niemeyer).
Benveniste, Emil
   1952 "La construction passive du parfait transitif", *BSL* 48:52–62.
   1960 " 'Etre' et 'avoir' dans leurs fonctions linguistiques", *BSL* 55:113–134.
Chung, Sandra
   1976 *Case marking and grammatical relations in Polynesian.* Unpublished Ph.D. dissertation (Harvard).
   1977 "On the gradual nature of syntactic change", in Li (ed.) 1977:3–55.
Creamer, Mary H.
   1974 "Ranking in Navajo nouns", *Dine Bizaad Nanil'iih/Navajo Language Review* 1:29–38.
Culicover, Peter et al. (eds.)
   1977 *Formal syntax* (New York: Academic Press).
Frishberg, Nancy
   1972 "Navajo object markers and the Great Chain of Being", *Syntax and Semantics* 1:259–66.
Givón, Talmy
   1971 "Historical syntax and synchronic morphology: An archeologist's fieldtrip", *Papers from the Regional Meeting of the Chicago Linguistic Society* 7:394–415.
Goddard, R. H. Ives
   1967 "The Algonquian independent indicative", National Museum of Canada, *Bulletin* 214:66–106.

Heath, Jeffrey
  1976   "Choctaw cases", *Papers from BLS* 3:204–213.
Hockett, Charles F.
  1966   "What Algonquian is really like", *IJAL* 32:59–73.
Klokeid, Terry J.
  1977   "Syntactic and conceptual relations in Nitinaht", *Papers from the 12th International Conference on Salish Languages*, 1–68.
Kuryłowicz, Jerzy
  1964   *The inflectional categories of Indo-European* (Heidelberg: Carl Winter).
Li, Charles (ed.)
  1976   *Subject and topic* (Austin: University of Texas Press).
  1977   *Mechanisms of syntactic change* (Austin: University of Texas Press).
Rhodes, R.
  1976   *The morphosyntax of the Central Ojibwa verb.* Unpublished Ph.D. dissertation (University of Michigan).
Steele, Susan
  1977   "Clisis in diachrony", in Li (ed.) 1977:539–582.
Steever, S. et al. (eds.)
  1976   *Diachronic syntax* (Chicago: Linguistic Society).

MARK ARONOFF

The relevance of productivity in a synchronic description of word formation[1]

1   The question of productivity has always been a difficult one for modern linguistic theories. In those areas where productivity is not a central concern, it has simply been swept under some convenient rug, or dealt with summarily, so that the field could go on to more important matters. In syntax, for example, rules are classified as either optional or obligatory, punkt. The question of the degree to which a rule is optional is not of interest, except perhaps to sociolinguists and stylisticians. In phonology, alternations were very early divided into automatic (phonemic) and nonautomatic (morphophonemic), with no in-betweens. Generative Phonology abolished this simple classification on various grounds, one of which was that it did not distinguish between completely suppletive alternations and partially predictable ones. The solution was to treat all alternations in the same fashion as the completely regular ones. Again the issue of productivity was successfully avoided.

There is one area, however, in which the question of productivity cannot be ignored if one is to do serious work. That is the area of word formation. For many years, the response of American linguistics to this problem was simply not to attempt to work on word formation. Recently, however, mainly because of new developments in syntactic and phonological theory, people have been forced to pay more attention to word formation, with the result that interest in the general nature of productivity has revived. Scholars are beginning to ask the question, what does it mean for one Word Formation Rule to be more productive than another? This paper provides one small part of the answer to this question. In fact, it answers one small preliminary to the general question, that is, whether productivity of word formation is a synchronic or a diachronic matter.

At first glance, it seems more plausible to think of productivity in purely diachronic terms. According to this view, one would say that Rule A is more productive than Rule B if more words formed according to Rule A enter the language in the time between two given points T_i and T_2.

Thus, since productivity is computed by comparing points in the history of a language, it is a diachronic matter. Yet this approach seems unsatisfactory. Surely one would like to say that Rule A is more productive than Rule B at one particular point, without reference to a seemingly arbitrarily chosen point in the past. A simple version of this synchronic view is the following. Rule A is more productive than Rule B at a given time T_i if there exists in the lexicon of the language at time T_i a greater number of words formed according to A than according to B. However, I have shown elsewhere (Aronoff 1976, Chapter 3) that this simple version must be wrong for several reasons. The most important of these is that a numerical measure such as this can only tell us about the actual words of the language, those which have been formed already, and tells us nothing about the possible but not actual words, those which might be formed. What we need is more dynamic framework, one which can deal with the potential of the system. Within such a dynamic framework, the productivity of a given rule at a given time would tell us how likely it is that a new word will be used which is formed according to that pattern rather than according to another. The more productive the rule, the more likely the word. Productivity would thus be incorporated into a synchronic grammar, but expressed in terms of probability.

This seems like a reasonable position, but how do we go about discovering whether it has any utility? Its novelty is the stressing of the notion "possible word" as opposed to "actual word". It is difficult to see, however, how we can deal with these elusive "possible but not actual" entities. By definition, they are not to be found in the dictionaries and word lists which are the familiar tools of the morphologist's trade. Let us therefore look for analogues in other areas of linguistics to the notion "possible word". The one which comes to mind most readily is the use of the term "grammatical sentence" in generative syntax. Can we therefore test the productivity of word formation rules in the same way that syntactic theories are tested?

The most common analytic tool of the modern syntactician is the grammaticality judgment. The investigator constructs sentences the grammaticality of which is predicted by a hypothesis. The value of the investigator's hypothesis is determined by the extent to which its predictions agree with the judgement of native speakers. Though this method is not perfect, it has greatly expanded our syntactic horizons. On the analogy of this syntactic method, we should be able to make up words in accordance with a certain morphological hypothesis and submit them to speakers for judgement. Such a simple test, however, is blocked by speakers' reluctance to deal with new words, even when they are well formed, and by the variation in productivity of the word formation rules.

Faced with this human problem, the linguist turns for help to the psychologist.

Psychologists have long been interested in words (much more so than in sentences, traditionally) and the ways in which people use and process them. Recently, workers in cognitive psychology have developed reliable techniques for investigating the semantic, phonological, and orthographic structures of words, as well as the ways in which people process these structures.

One of these techniques is known as the "lexical-decision task". In this task, people are required to judge whether various stimuli are instances of English words or not. Both the decision (yes or no) and the time taken to reach the decision provide data for testing hypotheses about linguistic structures and the psychological processes which represent and use these structures. Several recent experiments have used the lexical-decision task to investigate the role of linguistic structure in recognizing words and nonwords.

Rubenstein, Lewis, and Rubenstein (1971) found that unpronounceable nonwords (e.g., BRAKV) are judged faster and more accurately than pronounceable nonwords (e.g., BLEAN). The latter were judged faster than nonwords whose pronunciation is homophonic with an actual word (e.g., BRUME, homophonic with BROOM). These findings suggest that the time required to classify nonwords in the lexical-decision task provides a scale of "wordness" according to phonological structure. The more a nonword embodies the phonological structure of words, the longer the time required for people to judge that it is a nonword.

Other recent experiments have shown that phonological structure influences lexical-decision performance with actual words as well as with nonwords (Schvaneveldt et al. 1973; Schvaneveldt et al. 1976). These investigators found that judgements about words were influenced by the orthographic and phonological similarity of the preceding word. For example, the word DIME is judged faster following TIME compared to an unrelated word. In contrast, LEMON is more difficult to judge following DEMON than following a dissimilar word. Presumably the phonological structure is responsible for the differences in the two cases. The important point for our purposes is that linguistic structure on a phonological level can be investigated for both words and nonwords in the lexical-decision task.

More directly related to our own work, a few studies have investigated morphological structure using the lexical-decision task. MacKay (1974) presented subjects with verbs (e.g., DECIDE) and asked them to produce a related noun (DECISION) as fast as possible by adding either

ment, ence, ór *ion.* Reaction times and errors were related to morphological and morphophonological complexity.

Taft and Forster (1975) found evidence to support the hypothesis that,
in a lexical-decision task, prefixed words are analyzed into their constituent morphemes before lexical access occurs. They found that nonwords which are the stems of prefixed words (e.g., JUVENATE) take
longer to classify than nonwords which are not stems (e.g., PERTOIRE).
They also found that prefixed nonwords took longer to classify when they
contained a real stem (e.g., DEJUVENATE) compared with control
items which did not (e.g., DEPERTOIRE). Thus nonwords which are
morphologically closer to real words take longer to react to.

All these studies led me to believe that my hypothesis about the
synchronic reality of productivity could be tested experimentally. We
would use the techniques of cognitive psychology, but the experiment
which we would perform was to be a linguistic one. We were not concerned with the manner in which productivity affected people's linguistic
abilities, but simply with whether productivity was a factor in synchronic
word formation, or, as I prefer to think of it, morphological competence.

2   The productivity experiment

Our central concern is the possible but non-occurring word. Among such
words, we claim that there is a ranking of probability of occurrence, a
ranking which is associated with productivity. If a given Word Formation
rule is more productive than another such rule, then words formed by the
former are more likely to be used in the language than those formed by
the latter. The experiment which we designed was quite simple. We chose
two English suffixes which we know attach to words of the same class to
form words of another syntactically identical class, but which differ in
productivity and shape. We presented native speakers of English with
words which they had never seen before, which were formed by using
these two suffixes. Our hypothesis predicts that speakers will choose the
words formed by the more productive rule more often than words formed
by the less productive rule. We did not concern ourselves with explaining
why they did this or how they did it, but merely with ascertaining that they
behaved as expected. The experiment is described in detail below.

2.1   Material: *Xive#ness* and *Xiv+ity*
The English nominal suffixes *-ness* and *-ity* are "rivals" in that they
both often attach to the same morphological and semantic class of adjectives (CONGRUOUS / CONGRUOUSNESS / CONGRUITY;

POROUS / POROUSNESS / POROSITY; IMMENSE / IMMENSE-
NESS / IMMENSITY; SCARCE / SCARCENESS / SCARCITY).
The productivity of each of the suffixes varies with the morphology of
the base: *-ity* is more productive with bases ending in *-ic* (ELEC-
TRIC / ELECTRICITY) and *-ile* (SENILE / SENILITY), while *-ness* is
more productive with *-ous* (DEVIOUS / DEVIOUSNESS), and *-ive*
(DECISIVE / DECISIVENESS). Note that though one suffix is more
productive with a certain class of base, the other is not impossible;
SPECIFICNESS, JUVENILENESS, UNCTUOSITY and DECEP-
TIVITY are all attested.

Productivity and its analogues can thus be studied in a very narrow
range; the attachment of two rival affixes to bases of the same morphological class. The experiment deals with *-ness* and *-ity* attached to bases of the
form *Xive*, where we know that *-ness* is by far the more productive. This is
easily demonstrated by the analytic techniques of Aronoff (1976); most
obviously, there exist only 28 words of the form *Xivity* in Walker (1936),
versus 140 of the form *Xiveness*. Similar studies can be done with *-ness*
and *-ity* attached to other bases, as well as with other rival pairs of suffixes.

2.2 Design

In this experiment there are three different types of items, each consisting
of an equal number of letter strings of the form *Xiveness* and *Xivity*. The
three types are defined as follows: (a) words — actual words in the
language (listed in Webster's Collegiate Dictionary); (b) possible words
— these items do not occur in the language but the form *Xive* does; (c) nonwords — these items do not occur in the language, nor does the
form *Xive*, nor does the form *X*.

Each subject judges 40 words, 100 possible words, and 40 nonwords.
All subjects judge the same 40 words, but the possible words and the
nonwords come from two different lists such as that a particular *Xive* form
will appear as *Xivity* in one list and as *Xiveness* in the other. This
counter-balancing ensures that performance on the possible words and
nonwords can be attributed to the ending (*ness* and *ity*) and not to any
peculiar characteristics of the *Xive* items. Furthermore, each subject
judges a particular *Xive* stem only once, precluding any effects of repeat-
ing the stems.

An outline of the assignment of materials in the experiment is shown in
Table 1. Table 2 contains a complete list of the materials we used in the
experiment.

The choice of a 2:5:2 ratio for the three item types was motivated by
the hypotheses at issue. The subject should see some clear cases of words,
some clear cases of nonwords, and many instances which could be judged

Table 1

Type of stem	Suffix	Number per subject	Examples from List 1	List 2
word	*ness*	20	*perceptiveness*	*perceptiveness*
	ity	20	*captivity*	*captivity*
possible word	*ness*	50	*augmentiveness*	*propulsiveness*
	ity	50	*propulsivity*	*augmentivity*
nonword	*ness*	20	*depulsiveness*	*remortiveness*
	ity	20	*remortivity*	*depulsivity*

Table 2. Materials used

A. Words: 20 words of the form *Xivity* and 20 words of the form *Xiveness*.

proclivity	*productivity*	*creativity*	*retroactivity*
negativity	*sensitivity*	*perceptivity*	*reactivity*
relativity	*captivity*	*positivity*	*passivity*
activity	*nativity*	*conductivity*	*receptivity*
objectivity	*festivity*	*subjectivity*	*selectivity*
decisiveness	*explosiveness*	*permissiveness*	*effectiveness*
compulsiveness	*massiveness*	*exclusiveness*	*destructiveness*
expansiveness	*aggressiveness*	*elusiveness*	*primitiveness*
offensiveness	*expressiveness*	*obtrusiveness*	*deceptiveness*
responsiveness	*possessiveness*	*attractiveness*	*assertiveness*

B. Possible words: The list contains 100 words of the form *Xive*. From each of these is formed a pair of words of the forms *Xivity* and *Xiveness*.

effervescive	*vellicative*	*granulative*	*remonstrative*
abrasive	*supplicative*	*inflammative*	*eructative*
propulsive	*explicative*	*affirmative*	*cantative*
ascensive	*domesticative*	*reformative*	*mutative*
ostensive	*inculcative*	*rheumative*	*extenuative*
implosive	*reciprocative*	*emanative*	*enervative*
errosive	*evocative*	*combinative*	*relaxative*
aspersive	*gradative*	*subordinative*	*tractive*
contorsive	*oxidative*	*contaminative*	*reflective*
recursive	*fecundative*	*culminative*	*inflective*
accessive	*exudative*	*illuminative*	*maledictive*
assuasive	*permeative*	*agglutinative*	*deductive*

Table 2 *(continued)*

egressive	*derogative*	*inchoative*	*structive*
irrepressive	*arrogative*	*emancipative*	*inhibitive*
suppressive	*conjugative*	*extirpative*	*exploitive*
obsessive	*mediative*	*adumbrative*	*inceptive*
omissive	*retaliative*	*reverberative*	*redemptive*
concussive	*expiative*	*enumerative*	*presumptive*
tussive	*initiative*	*vituperative*	*invertive*
refusive	*ablative*	*asseverative*	*assortive*
extrusive	*dilative*	*elaborative*	*contrastive*
contusive	*extrapolative*	*invigorative*	*congestive*
siccative	*legislative*	*pejorative*	*insistive*
indicative	*emulative*	*impetrative*	*portative*
amplificative	*stimulative*	*administrative*	*deflective*

C. Nonwords: The list contains 40 nonwords of the form *Xive*. From each
of these is formed a pair of words of the forms *Xivity* and *Xiveness*.

remortive	*nebiative*	*marbicative*	*promutative*
ditestive	*tulsive*	*fulgurative*	*exputitive*
malipestive	*carmosive*	*ramitive*	*intusive*
transemptive	*valiative*	*lugative*	*redunsive*
affentive	*incrative*	*quentive*	*florsive*
mortentive	*pulmerative*	*pervictive*	*ancotive*
amnective	*argitive*	*allomutive*	*entractive*
condictive	*sebutive*	*rubicitive*	*hortentive*
rassive	*agrancive*	*laspative*	*plastive*
ollutive	*permulsive*	*prensive*	*axiative*

either way. The selected ratio should encourage subjects to discriminate
among the possible words, judging some to be words and some, nonwords. The hypothesis makes clear predictions about which possible
words are more likely to be judged words.

An additional variable in this experiment is the instructions given to the
subjects. One group is asked to judge whether the items are in their
vocabulary. Another group judges whether the items are English words.
A third group judges whether the items are meaningful words. This
instructional manipulation should provide some useful information about
the effect of altering the task criterion. We expect the proportions of
affirmative judgements for possible words to change with instructions,
but the predictions should still hold.

78   *Mark Aronoff*

2.3 Procedure

We asked 141 students at the State University of New York at Stony Brook to make judgements about the items listed in Table 2. The students were divided into three groups of 47 people each, and each group was given different instructions as described above. The suffixes *-ity* and *-ness* were counterbalanced with the stems for the possible words and the nonwords. The items were presented in six random orders on mimeographed sheets. Subjects made yes or no judgements by circling Y or N in adjacent columns. Obviously, we were not able to collect response time with this procedure. This makes our study different from most experiments involving the lexical-decision task, where response time is considered the central variable. Our decision was motivated by several considerations. For one, many people are suspicious of reaction time, which they feel to be too sensitive to extraneous factors to be reliable. If we can prove our case without the reaction time, we finesse these. Secondly, the items that we are testing are different from most of those used in previous experiments of this type: We are interested in possible words, rather than simple words or nonwords. Finally, by not measuring reaction time, we make the experiment much simpler to perform. It can be administered to large numbers of subjects in a very short time.

2.4 Anticipated results

If speakers can consistently distinguish productivity, we expect that non-existent words of the form *Xiveness* will be judged to be actual words more often than non-existent words of the form *Xivity*. We also expect results both within and across speakers, as well as within and across *Xive* stems. This may tell us something about the extent to which productivity of word formation rules is an individual or social phenomenon and the extent to which productivity holds for particular words.

2.5 Results

The results are shown in Tables 3, 4 and 5. As can be seen from Table 3, the expected results were obtained with the possible words. People responded affirmatively to the possible words with *-ness* suffixes more than they did with *-ity* suffixes, regardless of the instructions. This effect is statistically reliable.

The instructions were effective in varying the proportion of positive judgements people made, with .42, .50 and .54 of the total responses being affirmative with vocabulary, English word, and meaningful word instructions, respectively. The instructional effect shows that people can vary their criterion for what counts as a word, but more importantly for our purpose, such variations have little effect on the influence of mor-

Table 3. Proportion of "Yes" responses

Instruction (Question)	Suffix	Words	Possible Words	Nonwords
In your vocabulary?	+ity	.88	.28	.09
	#ness	.84	.34	.10
An English word?	+ity	.90	.39	.18
	#ness	.87	.46	.20
A meaningful word?	+ity	.92	.47	.20
	#ness	.93	.52	.19

Table 4. Number of items

| | Possible words | | |
	Vocabulary	Language	Meaning
More "Yes" answers to *-ity* form	33	27	38
Equal "Yes" answers to *-ity* and *-ness* forms	5	9	6
More "Yes" answers to *-ness* form	62	64	56
Sign test	p<.01 *	p<.01 *	p<.05 *

* Significantly different from chance ($x = .05$)

phological structure on their judgement. In other words, the possible words show a very similar influence of morphological structure for the different instructions. We take this to mean that the phenomenon is robust.

The actual words and the nonwords showed less influence of morphological structure. This may reflect the relatively leisurely judgements people were allowed to make in the experiment. With the words, different items are involved in the two suffix categories and since they were selected as foils, no effort was made to control for other factors. The addition of a reaction time measure may show effects where the judge-

Table 5. Individual subjects

Instruction	Words			Possible words			Non words		
	V	L	M	V	L	M	V	L	M
More "Yes" answers for *-ity* items	21	20	12	12	11	13	12	12	19
Equal "Yes" answers for *-ity* and *-ness* items	14	13	15	3	2	2	22	10	10
More "Yes" answers for *-ness* items	12	14	20	32	34	32	13	25	18
Sign test	p=.25	p<.25	p=.25	p<.01	p<.01	p=.01	p>.25	p=.05	p>.25
Sign test				*	*	*		*	

* significantly different from chance ($\alpha = .05$)

ment proportions do not. Particularly with the nonwords we used the final judgement may not be affected by the suffix but the process of arriving at the judgement could be different for the two suffixes.

In Tables 4 and 5 the data are broken down according to individual items and individual subjects. The results of these analyses give added support to our conclusions. Looking just at Table 4, which is in terms of individual possible words, we find that significantly more *-ness* forms than *-ity* forms receive a higher proportion of Yes responses, as we predict. Furthermore, the proportion stays more or less constant, regardless of instructions. This latter result is expected. Differences in instructions should affect the total proportion of positive responses, but should not affect the ratio of positive *-ness* to positive *-ity* responses.

In Table 5, the data are broken down for individual subjects. Here our findings are parallel. Out of 141 subjects, the number (98) giving more yes responses for *-ness* items is significantly greater than the number (36) giving more Yes responses to *-ity* items. Seven subjects give equal numbers of responses to both sets. Here the proportions are almost exactly constant across instructions, as we predict.

3 Conclusion

Native speakers of English, when asked to judge the acceptability of novel words, are found to be sensitive to the productivity of the word formation rules which are used to form these words. It follows from these findings that productivity must be represented in synchronic descriptions of linguistic competence, and that the productivity of a rule is not a purely historical artifact. One might now turn the tables and ask how this new notion of productivity figures in the theory of linguistic change. I have not done so in this paper.

Note

1. This paper is based on a study done jointly with Roger Schvaneveldt and published in *Annals of the New York Academy of Science* under the title "Testing morphological productivity".

References

Aronoff, M.
  1976 *Word formation in generative grammar (Linguistic Inquiry Monograph 1)* (Cambridge, Mass.: M.I.T. Press).

Aronoff, M. — R. W. Schvaneveldt
   1978   "Testing morphological hypotheses", *Annals of the New York Academy of Science*
          318: 106–114.
Chomsky, N. — M. Halle
   1968   *The sound pattern of English* (New York: Harper & Row).
Kornblum, S. (ed.)
   1973   *Attention and performance* 4 (New York: Academic Press).
MacKay, D.
   1974   "Derivational rules: Dead souls or living people in the perception, production and
          storage of words?", Paper presented at the Psycholinguistic Circle of New York.
Rubenstein, H. — S. S. Lewis — M. A. Rubenstein
   1971   "Evidence for phonemic recoding in visual word recognition", *Journal of Verbal
          Learning and Verbal Behavior* 10: 645–657.
Schvaneveldt, R. W. — D. E. Meyer
   1973   "Retrieval and comparison processes in semantic memory", in: S. Kornblum (ed.)
          1973: 395–409.
Schvaneveldt, R. W. — D. E. Meyer — C. A. Becker
   1976   "Lexical ambiguity, semantic context and visual word recognition", *Journal of
          Experimental Psychology. Human Perception and Performance:* 243–256.
Taft, M. — K. Forster
   1975   "Lexical storage and retrieval of prefixed words", *Journal of Verbal Learning and
          Verbal Behavior* 14: 638–647.
Walker, J.
   1936   *Walker's rhyming dictionary,* revised and enlarged by L. H. Dawson (New York:
          Dutton).

BERNARD COMRIE

Morphology and word order reconstruction:
problems and prospects*

In section 1 we examine the general proposition that the order of morphemes at a given stage of a language's history represents, to the extent
that those morphemes derive historically from separate words, the word
order at an earlier period, and following from this the possibility of using
current morpheme order in reconstructing word order at an earlier
period. A number of examples are cited, involving both affixal and
compound-word morphology, where good results are obtained in this
way, by comparison with attested earlier stages of the language concerned, though some problems are also encountered. In section 2, the
body of the paper, a particular problem is examined in detail, namely the
development of person-and-number suffixes in Mongolian languages, a
phenomenon which runs directly counter to the hypothesis that morpheme order directly reflects earlier basic word order. Some possible
reasons for this discrepancy are suggested, with an examination of their
repercussions on the general validity of this method of reconstructing
word order.

1   Word order and morpheme order

1.1   Affixal morphemes

Historical linguists are familiar with numerous instances where what now
appears as an affix derives historically from a separate word, through a
gradual process of loss of independent word status. For instance, com-
mitativity in standard Finnish can be expressed by means of the genitive
and the postposition *kanssa*, less commonly also the post-position *kera-
(lla)*. These postpositions function as separate words, for instance in
that native speakers of Finnish will cite them as separate citation forms,
and that they can bear stress where appropriate. There are also certain
criteria internal to the majority of Balto-Finnic languages according to
which these positions also appear to be separate words: First, adjectives
agree in case with their head noun, but there is no agreement in postposi-

tion between an adjective and its head, e.g. Finnish *hyvä-n poja-n kanssa* (good-Gen. boy-Gen. with), 'with (a) good boy', where the attributive *hyvä* agrees in case (genitive) with *poja-n,* but there is no repetition of the postposition after the attribute.[1] Secondly, case endings (e.g. Finnish inessive *-ssa/-ssä* 'in') are normally subject to vowel harmony if they contain the vowels *a, o, u* (front equivalents *ä, ö, ü,* the last written *y* in Finnish), whereas *kanssa and kera(lla)* are not thus affected: *talo-ssa* 'in the house', *käde-ssä* 'in the hand', but *tytö-n kanssa* 'with the girl'. In most of the other Balto-Finnic languages, and also in some Finnish dialects, however, these postpositions have given rise to bound affixes that in the extreme cases behave just like case suffixes. Thus Estonian has a comitative suffix *-ga,* although adjectives accompanying a noun in the comitative do not take this suffix (and Estonian lacks vowel harmony over all). In the Kukkosi dialect of Vepsian, the suffix *-kā* is subject to vowel harmony, e.g. *lāhsē-kā* 'with the child', but *lehmǟ-kā̄* 'with the cow'. In some dialects of Karelian, both vowel harmony and agreement are found: *kolme-n-kela lapše-n-kela* 'with three children', but *tütö-n-kelä* 'with the girl'.[2]

One characteristic of the development from postposition to suffix suggested by these Balto-Finnic forms is that the earlier order of the separate words (noun followed by postposition) is exactly mirrored by the subsequent order of morphemes (noun stem, or rather here noun in its genitive form, followed by a suffix). Other things being equal, this is what one might expect: phonetic attrition of a word following another word would lead to a suffix, phonetic attrition of a word preceding another word would lead to a prefix. In principle, then, one could suggest inverting this historical development as a tool in historical reconstruction, as follows:

Hypothesis 1: The order of morphemes in a word reflects, in so far as those morphemes derive etymologically from separate words, the order of those separate words at the time they started being fused together into a single word.

One might even generalize this hypothesis somewhat, to give:

Hypothesis 2: The order of morphemes in a word reflects, in so far as those morphemes derive etymologically from separate words, the basic word order of the language concerned at the time those separate words started being fused together into a single word.

Hypothesis 1 and 2 are distinct, since under Hypothesis 1 it would be possible for the current morpheme order X – Y to derive from an atypical word order X – Y, where the typical word order was Y – X; Hypothesis 2 excludes this possibility. Both hypotheses make use of an oft-noted difference between order of words and order of morphemes, the former tending to be much less rigid than the latter. This can be observed synchronically, in that many languages have partially free word order with preservation of cognitive synonymy (though not necessarily of topic-comment structure), while freedom of order of morphemes within a word is exceptional. Diachronically, there are numerous attested examples of change in basic word order (e.g. SOV to SVO in the development from Latin to the Romance languages), whereas change in the order of morphemes within a word is again quite exceptional.[3] Given this, Hypothesis 2, if valid, would provide an important tool in syntactic reconstruction, since it would provide us with a window onto word order at an earlier stage of the language in question: If, at the present moment, we find the morpheme order X – Y, and these morphemes can be shown to derive from separate words, then at an earlier stage the basic word order must have been X – Y; and this is so irrespective of the basic word order at present (X – Y, Y – X, or free). Hypothesis 1 would allow us to make only a much weaker claim: if, at the present moment, we find the morpheme order X – Y, and these morphemes can be shown to derive from separate words, then at an earlier stage the word order X – Y must have been possible (but may not have been the basic word order).

1.2   Compound words

Another area where one might expect the order of morphemes to represent, in a frozen state, the earlier order of words is with compounds, such as English *blackbird*, where the order Adjective-Noun reflects the earlier, and still current, order of words Adjective–Noun, as in *black bird*. Thus the order of elements in a pattern of compound formation, under Hypothesis 2, would reflect the basic word order of those elements when that pattern developed.[4]

Although the English Adjective–Noun compounds reflect equally the synchronic word order, this is not true of compounds with a verb or verbal derivative as head and an object noun phrase or adverbial as adjunct: such compounds have the verb in final position, whereas as separate words the verb would precede the noun: *nutcracker* (cp. *crack nuts*), *corn-grinding* (verbal noun or adjective; cp. *grind corn*); *everlasting* (cp. *last for ever*). Given the observation that English has developed from a language with basically verb-final word order (SOV) to a language with basic SVO word order, we can say that the current order in these compounds does indeed reflect the earlier verb-final word order.[5]

1.3   Clitics

The aim of this section is not to look in any detail at clitic phenomena, but rather just to point out the possible relevance of clitics to our general discussion, and to note some problems that arise once one considers clitics. Clitics stand in many ways between separate words and bound morphemes, and in many instances one may surmise that they are also, diachronically, a possible stage between separate words and a single word with one or more affixes. However, clitics present a number of ordering possibilities and restrictions of their own, which do not always seem to fit in with Hypotheses 1 and 2 above: The order of clitics is usually more restricted than that of separate words, but more free than that of morphemes, and a diachronic repercussion of this is that changes in element order can take place at the clitic stage that are not mirrored by changes in the order of separate words, so that the order of clitics, and any morpheme order based on the new order of clitics, does not necessarily reflect the earlier order of separate words.

One particularly clear instance of this is the widespread phenomenon of second position clitics, whereby clitics stand immediately after the first constituent (sometimes, but not invariably, after the first major constituent) of the sentence, irrespective of what function that first constituent may play in the sentence. Second position is extremely rare as a required position for separate words — the only example that comes readily to mind is the position of the verb in declarative main clauses in German and some related languages —, and in those languages with second position clitics for which we have detailed historical material, e.g. West and South Slavic languages, the second position of clitics does not seem to continue directly any feature of the order of the corresponding separate words, indeed the order of, say, clitic pronouns is markedly different from that of stressed pronouns.

One possible consequence that one could draw from second position clitics, in particular, is that clitics should simply be excluded from work on word order reconstruction. But ideally, one would want some principled basis for making this exclusion. One suggested basis for the origin of second person clitics is that such elements were originally attracted into the position between the topic (theme) and the comment (rheme) of the sentence, i.e. into the main intonation break within the sentence. This possibility is mentioned, but subsequently discounted, by Steele (1977: 551, 563–564) for Uto-Aztecan languages, the skeptical conclusion resting on the fact that the attested history of the Uto-Aztecan languages shows no sign of close correlation between topic-comment break and second position clitics, even at the earliest stages of the appearance of second position clitics. Recent work by Svedstedt (1976) on the position of unstressed pronouns in Russian, which are showing some of the initial stages of clitic-like behaviour, and have a tendency to be positioned in the main intonation break of the sentence, suggests that there may still be something to the suggested topic-comment basis for second position clitics. This would also provide a principled basis for excluding second position clitics from discussions of the reconstruction of the relative order of grammatical relations (e.g. of subject and object relative to the verb), given that the position of the clitics would be dependent rather on the relative order of topic to the rest of the sentence, and in principle any grammatical relation can fulfil the role of the topic.

2 Person-and-number suffixes in SOV languages

2.1 The dilemma

In recent work on word order typology, one of the main types that has been discussed is the SOV type, referring to a type with the following characteristics: (i) the basic word order in the sentence is Sub-ject–Object–Verb (SOV); (ii) the basic word order in the noun phrase is Attribute–Head noun (AN) (where the attribute may be either an adjective or a possessive); (iii) the language has postpositions rather than prepositions, i.e. Noun–Postposition; and (generally) (iv) the language has suffixes rather than prefixes, i.e. Stem–Suffix. For present purposes, it is sufficient that languages of this type should exist, irrespective of how important the constellation of these four features is considered for a general typology of language. This type is represented, for instance, by the Turkic and Mongolian languages. Since much of the ensuing discussion will involve primarily data from Buryat, a Mongolian language, we shall cite illustrative examples from this language.[6]

(1) *exe-ń xübǖ-gē daxin xilēmen-de el'gē-be.*
(mother-his son-Refl.-Acc. again bread-Dat. send-Past).
'The mother sent her son again for bread'.
(2) *eseg-īn ger*
(father-Gen. house)
'father's house'
(3) *sagān xuha-d-ai dunda*
(white birch-Pl.-Gen. among)
'among the white birch-trees'.

Sentence (1) illustrates the basic word order SOV; examples (2) and (3) illustrate the order AN (possessive attribute in (2), adjective in (3)), while (3) also illustrates postpositions; all three examples illustrate the use of suffixes (case, possession, tense). Some of the Uralic languages also come very close to this SOV type, especially the more easterly Uralic

languages (Samoyedic, Ob-Ugric); the more westerly languages have
departed from this type, primarily in permitting the SVO word order to
gain the ascendency, to a much lesser extent in permitting prepositions
and prefixes (though still with predominance of postpositions and suffixes). In the Turkic and Mongolian languages, the orders Stem–Suffix
and Noun–Postposition are quite rigid, and the order Attribute–Head
noun virtually so. The order SOV is subject to much greater variation,
expecially in the spoken varieties of these languages, where the verb does
not have to occur sentence-finally; it remains, however, true that SOV is
the basic (unmarked, most frequent, least context-bound) word order in
these languages.

The Turkic, Mongolian, and Uralic languages typically have person-
and-number suffixes, added either to verbs, where they code the person-
and-number of the subject, or to nouns, where they code the person-and-
number of the possessor. In the first and second persons, the similarity
of these suffixes to the full forms of pronouns is apparent, to varying
degrees in different languages. In Finnish, for instance, the first person
plural pronoun is *me* 'we'; the corresponding verbal ending is *-mme*, e.g.
laula-mme 'we sing', as is the corresponding possessive ending, e.g.
talo-mme 'our house'. Although phonetic changes and analogical
developments have obscured the relationship in some of the other
person-and-number combinations, the etymological derivation of
person-and-number suffixes from independent pronouns can be traced
with relatively little difficulty for Finnish and many other Uralic languages. In the case of Buryat, the similarity between pronouns and
suffixes is even more apparent, as can be seen from the forms in Table 1.

Table 1. Pronouns and person-and-number affixes in Buryat

	Pronoun (Nom.)	Verb ending	Pronoun (Gen.)	Noun ending
Sg1	*bi*	*-b*	*minī*	*-m(ni),-ni*
Sg2	*ši*	*-š*	*šinī*	*-š(ni)*
Pl1	*bide*	*-bdi*	*manai*	*-(m)nai*
Pl2	*ta*	*-t*	*tanai*	*-tnai*

These person-and-number suffixes are clearly phonetically reduced
forms of the corresponding nominative or genitive pronouns. However,
in Buryat, as in the Turkic, Mongolian, and to a large extent Uralic
languages, this means that the current morpheme order does not directly
reflect the current word order. Since the word order is SOV (or SVO in

some Uralic languages — in any event, S precedes V), subject pronouns precede their verb, yet these languages consistently present us with subject affixes after the verb. Since attributes precede their head noun, we find, with separate words, the order possessive pronoun before head noun, but possessive suffixes following the noun. The mirror-image relation between word and suffix can be seen in these Buryat examples: *bi jaba-na-b* (I go-Pres.-1sg.) 'I am going'; *miñī axa* (I-Gen. elder-brother) or *axa-m(ni)* (elder-brother-1sg.) 'my elder brother'.

If we apply Hypothesis 2 above, then we are forced to the conclusion that at an earlier stage, the basic word orders were not SOV and AN, but rather VS and NA.[7] Now, however far back we go in the history of the Mongolian, Turkic, and Uralic languages — and in the case of Turkic we can go back to around the eighth century, in the case of Mongolian to around the thirteenth century — we find no evidence that these languages were any less SOV in type than they are now; indeed, in the case of the western Uralic languages, the evidence is that they were if anything more SOV. One might try to save Hypothesis 2 by maintaining that the current order of morphemes represents a word order that held long before the appearance of written texts in any of these languages, and that at this stage the basic word orders were indeed VS and NA. There is no evidence for such a stage, but at least it would be consistent with what we have said so far and with Hypothesis 2. However, we shall show that Hypothesis 2 cannot be saved in this way, because evidence from the Mongolian languages shows that the development of person-and-number suffixes in these languages is very recent, certainly postdating the earliest written texts, so that these person-and-number suffixes must have arisen at a time when the basic word orders were SV and AN.

2.2   Evidence from the Mongolian languages

In the Mongolian languages, the person-and-number suffixes as illustrated in Table 1 for Buryat are of relatively recent origin.[8] In Classical Mongolian, they are absent. The possessive suffixes are found in probably all of the modern languages, though the degree of phonetic reduction from the genitive of the pronoun varies considerably: Buryat represents the greatest degree of reduction found. In Khalkha we find the least degree of reduction: 'my' is *minī*, suffix *-mini*; 'thy' is *činī*, suffix *-čini*; 'our' is *manai*, suffix *-mani/-māni*; 'your' is *tanai*, suffix *-tani/-tāni*, although the suffixes for plural possessors are of restricted occurrence. Khalkha orthography writes these suffixes as separate words, and as will be seen from the forms cited the only difference between the preposed genitive pronoun and the postposed possessive suffix is the reduction of the final vowel or dipthong to *-i* (which may be omitted in spoken

Khalkha).[9] The subject agreement suffixes on verbs are of even more recent origin, and are found only in Buryat, Oirat, Kalmyk, Dagur, and Moghol.[10] In other words, the development of person-and-number suffixes in the Mongolian languages took place during the period of their recorded history, during the whole of which period these languages were clearly SOV languages, both with regard to the order SOV and with regard to the order AN. On the basis of these data, Hypothesis 2 is untenable as a general statement.

However, although SOV and AN have been the basic word orders throughout the recorded history of the Mongolian languages, they have not been the only orders. Deviations from these basic orders are found even in Classical Mongolian. There are fewest deviations from the order AN, but one class of such deviations (in fact, the main one) is particularly interesting for the origin of possessive suffixes, since it concerns pronouns as attributes in the genitive case, i.e. *minü* 'my', *činü* 'thy', *manu* 'our', *tanu* 'your'. Although in general these precede their head noun in Classical Mongolian, they can also be postposed, in which case they are unemphatic, e.g. *minü morin* '*my* horse', but *morin minü* 'my *horse*' (Sanžeev 1953:179). In Classical Mongolian, apart from, presumably, lack of phonetic stress, there was no difference between preposed and postposed genitive pronouns, in particular no phonetic reduction of the latter: such phonetic reduction belongs to the later history of the individual Mongolian languages. There is thus no evidence for considering these Classical Mongolian postposed genitives as suffixes, so that we can say that Classical Mongolian allowed NA as a nonbasic word order, and that it is from this word order that the possessive suffixes developed. This is in keeping with Hypothesis 1. Note, incidentally, that Classical Mongolian does not permit both a preposed and a postposed genitive together, i.e. **minü morin minü*; nor does Buryat permit both a preposed genitive and a possessive suffix, i.e. not **minī axa-m(ni)*. Kalmyk, however, always requires presence of the possessive suffix, i.e. *möre-m* or *minī möre-m*, but not **minī mören* 'my horse'.

Similarly, although SV has always been the basic order of subject relative to verb during the recorded history of the Mongolian languages, numerous deviations are attested, one class of which comprises unstressed subject pronouns. Such examples are found both in Classical Mongolian (Sanžeev 1963:87) and in colloquial Khalkha. Thus the Khalkha for 'I know' is normally *bi med-ne* (I know-Pres.), but in the colloquial language, if the subject pronoun is unstressed, it can also be *med-ne bi*. It is this second possibility in older Mongolian that gave rise to the subject agreement suffixes in such modern Mongolian languages as Buryat, and this is consistent with Hypothesis 1. There is one important difference between the status of nominal and verbal suffixes of person-and-number in Buryat (and, probably, the other Mongolian languages that have person-and-number verbal suffixes): the nominal suffix is mutually exclusive with a preposed genitive pronoun; however, the verbal suffix is obligatory when the subject is first or second person — the subject pronoun may be present or omitted, but the suffix must always be there, i.e. either *bi jaba-na-b* 'I am going' or *jaba-na-b*, but never simply **bi jaba-na*. On the other hand, Khalkha, with the possibility of postposing the subject but no subject affixes, has *bi med-ne* and *med-ne bi*, but not **bi med-ne bi*.

If we had simply the data from modern Buryat, and were to apply our hypotheses to these data to try and reconstruct the word order at an earlier stage of the language, then Hypothesis 2 would clearly give us an incorrect result, since it would lead us to the conclusion that the Buryat suffixes developed at a time when the basic word orders were VS and NA. Hypothesis 1 would lead us to the conclusion that VS and NA were possible, though not necessarily the only or even the basic word orders at this time. The Mongolian material is certainly consistent with this weaker hypothesis — but Hypothesis 1 is very much weaker than Hypothesis 2. If we had only the modern Buryat data, then Hypothesis 1 would tell us that at an earlier stage the orders VS and NA were possible, but would give us no indication as to the role of these word orders within the language at the period to which the reconstruction applies. Since we do have data from the earlier period, we can see that Hypothesis 1 in fact allows us to reconstruct only very atypical word orders of the earlier period, but does not tell us that the reconstructed word orders are in fact atypical. In effect, the only set of circumstances where Hypothesis 1 would provide us with any specific new information would be if, synchronically, a given word order were absolutely excluded, but reconstructed by Hypothesis 1; this would tell us that the language at an earlier stage had a word order at least slightly less rigid than at present. The only possible counterexample to Hypothesis 1 would be if some word order were absolutely excluded at the time when affixes were formed, yet still those affixes reflect the excluded word order.

2.3   Possible explanations

The rejection of Hypothesis 2 does leave us with a problem in describing the history of person-and-number suffixes in SOV languages: If the basic word order in these languages is SOV and AN, then why is it that affixes develop very consistently on the basis of a nonbasic word order VS and NA? The discussion here will be fairly speculative, but at least certain plausible suggestions can be made. We may note first that there is no general principle placing affixes at the opposite side of their head from the position they occupied as separate words; in section 1.1 we noted that the current order Noun stem — Case suffix often follows the earlier order Noun — Postposition without any such inversion, moreover many basically SOV languages do have person-and-number prefixes, at least in addition to suffixes (e.g. many Caucasian languages). We shall assume that at the inception of the process of affixation, both SV and VS, both AN and NA are possible word orders, although SV and AN are by far the more usual. The problem then is to explain why affixes should arise on the basis of the S of VS and the A of NA, rather than on the basis of the S of SV and the A of AN. Since, as we have already noted, some SOV languages do develop prefixes in such instances (i.e. from SV and AN), we shall be asking primarily what pressures there may be setting up a tendency (not an absolute prohibition) against the development from the basic word order and in favour of the development from the nonbasic word order. Below, we give three possible reasons; they are not necessarily mutually exclusive, so that conceivably the major reason is the combination of these three factors pushing in the same direction.

(i) Since the languages in question are already exclusively or overwhelmingly suffixing, preference is given, in deriving affixes, to that word order which produces further suffixes rather than introducing prefixes, i.e. in accordance with the existing patterns of the language.

(ii) The languages in question in general do not have constructions where an adjunct completely lacking independent stress precedes its head constituent.[11] Here the observations on stress in the Mongolian languages come into play: postposing the independent pronoun correlates with lack of independent stress on that pronoun, thus avoiding the sequence of unstressed adjunct followed by head, and providing a form (head plus unstressed adjunct) on the basis of which suffixes can develop by phonetic attrition.

(iii) The general characteristic of the SOV type is that in each construction (except, possibly, Noun–Postposition) the head constituent occurs last. Thus the subject precedes its verb, and a possessive precedes its noun, but there is no requirement that they should immediately precede the head constituent. Indeed, except in sentences consisting just of a subject noun phrase and a verb, the subject will normally be separated from its verb by object noun phrases and adverbials. Similarly, a possessive attribute will often be separated from its head noun by other attributes (e.g. adjectives). A pronoun can only become an affix to its verb or head noun if it is adjacent to that verb or head noun. The orders SV and AN, or rather S ... V and A ... N, do not invariably satisfy this requirement of adjacency. On the other hand, since postposing constituents after the noun or verb is so rare, the orders VS and NA (hardly ever, if at all, V . . . S or N . . . A) do satisfy this requirement. The latter are thus more likely to lead to affixation on the verb or noun than are S . . . V or A . . . N.

It should be noted that if we can uncover an explanation for the discrepancy between basic word order and morpheme order in these instances, then there may still remain the possibility that Hypothesis 2 is applicable to ranges of data to which this explanation does not apply. For instance, if (i) above is correct, and given the observation that there are few if any languages that avoid suffixes in the way some languages avoid prefixes, then it might still be true that person-and-number prefixes always arise on the basis of SV or AN, never on the basis of VS or NA, as basic word orders. Although Hypothesis 2 in the forms stated in the Introduction is not applicable to affixal morphology, it is still possible that some more restricted version of Hypothesis 2 may be applicable.

3 Conclusions

In our discussion, we started from the assumption that, other things being equal, morpheme order will reflect earlier word order. However, in the course of the discussion we have noted several instances where other things are not equal, i.e. where there are pressures against morpheme order simply reflecting the earlier word order, especially if this is taken to mean the earlier basic word order. In section 2.3 we noted several possible reasons why morpheme order might continue a possible, but atypical, word order from an earlier period, and in section 1.3 we noted the possibility that clitic phenomena (especially second position clitics) may give rise to morpheme order possibilities that do not necessarily reflect any previous word order possibility.

The most obvious repercussion of this for syntactic reconstruction is that such reconstruction must proceed with extreme care, since one cannot accept as a general principle that morpheme order reflects earlier (basic, or even possible) word order. It is conceivable that further work may enable us to isolate those factors that lead morpheme order to diverge from earlier word order, thus leaving a residue of types where morpheme order can be used as a reliable guide to the (partial) reconstruction of earlier word order. But the first task is then to establish this inventory of factors leading to discrepancies between word order and morpheme order, and not to apply blindly a reconstructional technique which we know to give provably incorrect results in a number of cases.

Notes

* This work was supported by a grant from the Social Science Research Council, London, for investigation of the linguistic typology of the non-Slavic languages of the Soviet Union. Much of the general line of this paper has grown out of correspondence and discussion with Talmy Givón. While the paper crystallizes mutual disagreement rather than agreement, without these discussions it is doubtful whether the paper would have crystallized at all. I am grateful to Denis Creissels and Katalin Radics for drawing my attention to the Buryat data, and to Susan Steele for discussion of second-position clitics. The following abbreviations are used:

1sg. — first person singular; 3pl. — third person plural; A — attribute; Abs. — absolutive; Adv. —adverbial; Dat. —dative; Erg. —ergative; Gen. —genitive; Instr. —instrumental; Loc. —locative; N — head noun; Nom. —nominative; O —object; Pl. — plural; Pres. —present; Refl.-Acc. —reflexive-accusative; S —subject; Sg. —singular; Superess. — superessive; V — verb.

1. Contrast the situation in Hungarian where those few attributes that agree with their head (i.e. the demonstrative adjectives *ez* 'this', *az* 'that') require repetition of postpositions, e.g. *ez előtt a ház előtt* (this before the house before) 'in front of this house'. The Finnish postposition *kanssa* derives etymologically from the inessive of *kansa*, i.e. **kansa-ssa* 'in the company (of)'. Likewise *kera(lla)* from the adessive of *kerta*, i.e. **kerra-lla* 'at the time (of)'.

2. For further discussion and references, see Tauli (1966:113).

3. To avoid misunderstanding, we would emphasize that there is a strong tendency for word order and morpheme order to be distinguished in this way according to the criterion of rigidity, although there are of course individual counterexamples were this to be advanced as an absolute rule. One occasionally finds alternative possible morpheme orders, as with some combinations of case and possessive suffixes in the Uralic language Mari (Cheremis), e.g. *čodra-m-lan* 'forest-1sg.-Dat.' or *čodra-lan-em* 'to my forest'. In Hungarian, the older order Case–Possessive in the superessive (earlier: locative) (suffix *-n* 'on'), still retained in frozen form in *bennem* 'in me' (for **bele-ne-m* 'inside-Loc.-1sg.'), has been inverted to Possessive–Case, e.g. *háza-m-on* (house-1sg.-Superess.) 'on my house', under the influence of this order with other case suffixes.

   This last kind of example is potentially damaging to both Hypotheses 1 and 2, since clearly if the order of morpheme can change then the new order will no longer directly reflect anything about order of words at an even earlier stage. However, such examples seem to be extremely rare, and there appear to be good chances of successfully isolating such examples where they do occur, given the very special circumstances that seem to be required to bring about a change in morpheme order. In the Hungarian example quoted, all other cases have the order Possessive–Case, and this provides a model for the shift to Possessive–Case in the superessive too. Except in such individual circumstances, this particular objection to Hypothesis 1 (whence also to the stronger Hypothesis 2) can reasonably safely be disregarded. For further discussion, see Comrie (1976).

4. Note that it is the pattern, rather than the individual compound, that reflects the earlier word order, since new compounds can be formed on the basis of an existing pattern, e.g. *speech-synthesizer* on the pattern Noun–Verb-*er*.

5. Verb–Object compounds do occur, though very rarely, e.g. *spoilsport*. Since this order is found from the Old English period, though always as very much a minority pattern, it might be more accurate to say that the overwhelming predominance of OV and AdvV compounds over VO and VAdv compounds reflects the earlier predominance of verb-final word order.

6. These Buryat examples are taken from Sanžeev et al. (1962). For a statement of Buryat grammar in English, see Poppe (1960).

7. The order of morphemes provides no evidence as to the ordering of O relative to S and V. Hypothesis 1 would make the weaker claim that VS and NA were possible orders.

8. The linguistic term 'Mongolian' is ambiguous, in that it can refer either to a family of closely related languages (impressionistically, varying about as much as English does from German), or to one language within this family. The prestige dialect of this single language is Khalkha, which forms the basis of the current standard language, and to avoid confusion we have used the term "Khalkha" in citing forms from this language. Although there is not absolute agreement among different authorities as to how many distinct Mongolian languages should be recognized, the list given by Poppe (1970:2) may be taken as representative: Mongolian (prestige dialect: Khalkha), Buryat, Oirat, Kalmyk, Moghol, Dagur, Monguor, Santa, Bao-an (Paongan), Yellow Uighur. We shall also refer to Classical Mongolian, attested as a written language from the thirteenth century; it represents an older stage of the Mongolian language family, probably before the current language divisions were more than minor dialect divisions.

9. In addition, the modern Mongolian languages have a third person possessive suffix *-ni/-ń* 'his, her, its, their', deriving from the Classical Mongolian genitive *inü* 'his, her, its', also 'their', which could be preposed or postposed like the other genitive pronouns. Other than as a possessive suffix, reflexes of *inü* have not survived into the modern languages.

10. The forms are listed by Sanžeev (1963:85). The suffixes in Dagur and Moghol are for the most part the same as the nominative of the pronouns, i.e. without any phonetic reduction.

11. This restriction is very rigid in at least most of the Turkic and Mongolian languages. The only exceptions known to me in Turkish are the use of unstressed *bir* 'one' as the indefinite article, and the conjunction *ve* 'and' Even in many Uralic languages that have otherwise moved far from the SOV type, exceptions are rare: in Hungarian, for instance, probably restricted to the definite article *a(z)*, the indefinite article *egy*, and some conjunctions. In the Mordvin languages (Uralic family) the definite article, which developed from a demonstrative adjective (preposed), occurs postposed, e.g. Erźa Mordvin *se kudo* 'this house', but *kudo-ś* 'the house', i.e. exactly the same as we observe with person-and-number affixes.

References

Comrie, Bernard
    1976   "The ordering of case and possessive suffixes in the Uralic languages", Ms. (available from the author).
Li, Charles N. (ed.)
    1977   *Mechanisms of syntactic change* (Austin: University of Texas Press).
Poppe, Nicholas
    1960   *Buriat grammar* (= *Indiana University Publications, Uralic and Altaic Series* 2) (The Hague: Mouton).
    1970   *Mongolian language handbook* (Washington, D.C.: Center for Applied Linguistics).
Sanžeev, G. D.
    1953   *Sravnitel'naja grammatika mongol'skix jazykov* [Comparative grammar of the Mongolian languages], Vol. 1 (Moskva: Izdatel'stvo AN SSSR).

1963   *Sravnitel'naja grammatika mongol'skix jazykov: Glagol* [Comparative grammar of the Mongolian languages: The verb] (Moskva: Izdatel'stvo Vostočnoj Literatury).

Sanžeev, G. D. et al. (eds.)

1962   *Grammatika burjatskogo jazyka: Fonetika i morfologija* [Grammar of the Buryat language: Phonetics and morphology] (Moskva: Izdatel'stvo Vostočnoj Literatury).

Steele, Susan

1977   "Clisis and diachrony", in Li (ed.) 1977:539–579.

Svedstedt, Dag

1976   *Position of objective personal pronouns: A study of word order in Modern Russian* (= *Stockholm Slavic Studies* 9) (Stockholm: Almqvist and Wiksell).

Tauli, Valter

1966   *Structural tendencies in Uralic languages* (= *Indiana University Publications, Uralic and Altaic Series* 17) (The Hague: Mouton).

XAVIER DEKEYSER

The diachrony of the gender systems in English and Dutch

0 Scope of the paper

0.1   Gender can be regarded as a grammatical category on the basis of which all nominal heads can be classified as masculine, feminine and neuter. This classification, which is primarily related to pronominal reference and modifier concord (see Lyons 1971:283–284), is comparable to, but often far from identical with the natural or extra-linguistic sex distinctions in terms of male, female and asexual. Indeed, it is common knowledge that in the ancient and modern Indo-European languages gender assignment, though probably once metaphorically conditioned, often operates along seemingly arbitrary, even erratic lines. To the best of my knowledge, Modern English assumes a notable position on that score in that its gender system is, to all intents and purposes, an almost perfect replica of the natural sex system. Anglicists also know that this "logical" structure is the outcome of a sweeping evolution which set in as early as the Old English period (in the North earlier than in the South) and reached its virtual completion in the course of Early Middle English (Mustanoja 1960:43ff.). The classical Old English gender system, however, is governed by the same principles as those of Modern German and some varieties of Modern Dutch, which does not imply a one-for-one correspondence between all the nominal heads in (Old) English and their modern equivalents, if any, in German or Dutch.

0.2   In the present paper I want to give a brief survey of the existing data concerning the OE/ME shift from grammatical to natural gender; next I shall deal with the gender system in Dutch (including regional dialects), which is linguistically very interesting because the category of gender has undergone a thorough re-structuring in some varieties of that language.

1 Grammatical gender in English

1.1 Old English nominal and adnominal elements

1.1.1 Old English nominal inflections signal case, gender and number distinctions; see e.g. Campbell (1959: chapter xi). Although some of the morphemes are not outspokenly gender-distinctive, or not at all (e.g. the weak class throughout, or *-e* in the dative singular, *-a* and *-um* resp. in the genitive and dative plural), it is evident that, on the whole, the OE language-user needed an innate gender (and case) feeling in order to be able to select the appropriate items from the nominal paradigms; the genitive singular masculine and neuter *-es*, and the nominative and accusative plural masculine *-as* are outstanding examples in this respect.

1.1.2 The adnominal categories were considerably more gender-distinctive than the heads; see Campbell (1959: chapter xii (adjectives) and xv (pronouns)). On the basis of congruential criteria items from the adnominal sets were selected in agreement with the inherent nominal gender, even if this was not overtly marked. This can be clearly seen in the article and deictic determiners (Campbell 1959:290–291): e.g. nom. masc. *se stan* 'the or that stone', nom. fem. *seo talu* 'the or that tale', neuter *þaet scip*; etc. Old English strong adjectives, which borrowed morphemes both from the determiner and the nominal inflection, are highly gender-distinctive, while the weak paradigms are not very functional, if at all, as a marker mechanism, these paradigms being virtually identical with the nominal weak paradigms, so mostly *-an* (Campbell 1959:262ff., 272). But then it must be borne in mind that weak adjectives, as in German, only patterned in post-determiner position, so that congruential gender did not need to be signalled by means of adjectival paradigms.

1.1.3 The use of a nominal head in an OE NP generally involved an intricate selection of paradigmatic items, dictated by the inherent grammatical gender of the head, in addition to case and number:

Rule 1

$$\text{Preposed adnominals} \longrightarrow \begin{bmatrix} \alpha \text{ case} \\ \beta \text{ number} \\ \gamma \text{ gender} \end{bmatrix} \Bigg/ -(X) \begin{bmatrix} \text{Nom. head} \\ \alpha \text{ case} \\ \beta \text{ number} \\ \gamma \text{ gender} \end{bmatrix}$$

Note: (X) symbolizes an optional weakly inflected adjective; γ stands for masculine, feminine or neuter.

1.2   Middle English nominal and adnominal elements

1.2.1   From Late Old English on, earlier in the North than in the South, nominal heads underwent drastic morphological changes resulting from the obscuration and reduction of the vowels in the inflectional morphemes and the extension of particular forms to other cases and genders (Systemzwang); see Mossé (1968: chapter v). Even a casual glance at the ME nominal paradigms suffices to see that gender distinctions are totally absent.

1.2.2   The same holds for the adnominal constituents of the NP. The class of determiners was drastically simplified. The definite article *se/þe*, later only *the*, was a relic of the *se-seo-þaet* paradigm and came to be used without any distinction of gender, case or number from Late Old English on (Mossé 1968:60–61). *An*, later also *a*, was the invariable indefinite article. The deictic determiners were (only) number-distinctive: singular *this*, plural *thise, these*; singular *that*, plural *thos(e)* (Mossé 1968:61). Rule 1 must be re-written as follows:

Rule 2

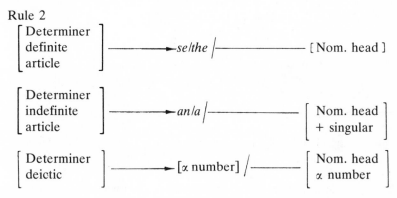

The highly distinctive OE adjective soon became a by and large unmarked class, with *-e* for the weak declension throughout, 0 for the strong declension singular, and *-e* for the plural (Mossé 1968:64–65).

1.2.3   The shift towards almost complete adnominal unmarkedness was not an overnight and smooth process; rather, there was an interim development, extending over a rather long period and characterized by seemingly erratic (probably idiolectal) usages.[1] In addition, there was also a great deal of dialectal variation, the dialects of the North being more advanced than those of the Midlands and the South.[2]

1.3 PRO forms in Old English/Middle English

1.3.1   It has been demonstrated in the preceding sections that grammatical gender was lost in the adnominal and nominal categories for sheer lack of gender-distinctive forms. Let us now turn to the pronominalized NPs. Strictly speaking, the historical gender system as it operated in Old English could be preserved here: the three-term contrast expressed by *he-heo-hit* was continued in the Middle English forms *he-she/sho-(h)it*; over and above these the possessive articles *his-hire-his* (with no distinction between masculine and neuter in Old English/Early Middle English) could be employed to mark a contrast in terms of masculine/neuter vs. feminine. As is commonly known, grammatical gender did not survive here either, giving way to a three-term contrast that was referentially determined: male–female–asexual; see Mustanoja (1960:43ff.). The stage of a consistent use of natural gender in PRO forms was already reached in the *Final Continuation* (1132–1154) of the *Peterborough Chronicle* (Clark 1957:111).

1.3.2   When reading Moore (1921), I was struck by one of his major findings: "The fact is that in Old English the use of the gender-distinctive forms of *he, heo, hit* was almost the same as our own use of them" (p. 89). Indeed, Moore provides numerical evidence from which it appears that "conflicts with natural gender" only amount to approximately 3% of the gender-distinctive PRO forms in Old English, and to about 4.3% in Middle English; particularly the low rate for Old English is highly surprising, if not suspect. It must be added that the same scholar arrives at an even lower percentage of "conflicts" with regard to Gothic, Old High German and Old Saxon. I am not in doubt about the fact that in a piece of discourse actual conflicts with natural gender are not rife. But does this prove anything as to the gender properties of PRO forms? I think not. If Moore were right here, we should have to accept two gender systems for Old English: a grammatical system governing the adnominal and nominal categories and marked by congruential rules, and a natural one, based on reference and pertaining to the PRO forms (with a few deviations due to the grammatical gender of the antecedent NP overriding natural gender).[3] I maintain that Moore's rates need adjusting and re-assessing. Impressionistically I would believe that persons are the most frequent "topical items" in a piece of Old English discourse; this implies that a great deal of PRO forms are related to animates, for which category conflicts with gender are virtually non-extant.[4] Neuter inanimates do not give rise to conflicts either. The crucial group are the historically masculine and feminine inanimates, such as *wisdom* (masc.) or *lar* (fem.), and then only in the singular, as plural PRO forms are not gender-distinctive.

Undoubtedly pronominalized NPs of this category constitute but a small proportion in Moore's total of gender-distinctive forms; and if we singled out (singular) masculine and feminine inanimates, the rates for "conflicts with natural gender" would be a great deal higher.

That Moore has grossly overrated the share of natural gender may also appear from the evidence of the *Peterborough Chronicle.* Clark (1957:110–111) states that gender-pronouns (note: i.e. PRO forms reflecting grammatical gender) are *commonly used* (my own emphasis) to refer to inanimate nouns; the use of neuter PRO forms for historical masculine or feminine inanimate nouns is sporadic; when animates are involved, sex-governed forms are the universal practice, even when gender conflicts with sex (e.g. *þaet wif*). In Clark's article there is no mention of masculine PRO forms referring to historical feminine or neuter heads, which I think bears out Jones' thesis (see note 2) that the increasing use of the masculine marker (*-ne*) should not be viewed as masculinization, but primarily as extension of a *case*-marker, which happens to signal masculine gender as well, to feminine and neuter nouns. "In the *Final Continuation,*" Clark goes on to write, "pronouns of reference are . . . governed solely by the sex, or lack of it, of the person or object in question" (1957:111).

1.3.3   The Old English situation can be aptly summed up as follows: with the vast majority of animates and with the neuter inanimates there is no scope for a gender/sex conflict; as far as masculine and feminine inanimates are concerned, there is an (incipient?) tendency in pronominalized NPs for natural gender (asexualness) to prevail over grammatical gender, though the historical system as a whole is still upheld. But, as Clark (1957:115) points out, it "carried the seeds of its own decay". This is particularly noticeable when there is a certain distance between the head and the pronominalized form, as in the following extract from the *Preface* to the *Cura Pastoralis*:

. . . *þaet þu þone wisdom þe þe God sealde, þaer þaer þu* hiene [masc.]
'that you that wisdom which to-you God gave, there where you *him*
befaestan maege, befaeste. Geþenc hwelc witu us þa becomon
[= it] implant may, implant. Think what punishments to-us then came
for þisse worulde, þa þa we hit *nohwaeþer ne selfe ne*
for this world, when we *it* neither ourselves
lufodon, ne eac oþrum monnum ne lefdon . . .
loved, nor other men allowed . . .'
[quoted from Rigg 1968:183; my own emphasis].

And when grammatical gender was no longer supported by adnominal and nominal flection, it was quite natural for the masculine and feminine PRO forms signalling inanimates to join the already existing system of natural gender (masculine and feminine animates and a fair number of neuter inanimates) and to become neuter (the asexual category). In this way the present-day "logical" system was by and large arrived at in Early Middle English. The Old English/Early Middle English evidence seems to suggest that the process of nominal and adnominal deflection (and consequently the loss of congruential gender) and the restructuring of the PRO forms were simultaneous rather than sequential, and that there is a causal relationship between the former and the latter.

Before trying to advance more fundamental conclusions regarding the relationship between the gender of NPs and that of their pronominalizations, I shall now highlight some features of the gender system in present-day Dutch.

2   Grammatical gender in Dutch: A dynamic synchrony

2.1   Socio-linguistically and dialectally speaking the situation is utterly complex, while at the same time highly interesting, as regards gender in Modern Dutch. I shall treat three varieties of Dutch, and what is offered must be looked upon as an unrefined approximation of the matter as far as details go; yet, since we only view general trends and principles, I believe this treatment to be sufficient and valid here. Variety 1 is Standard Dutch as spoken by educated speakers in the Netherlands; Standard Dutch as used by educated speakers in the northern part of Belgium (Flanders) differs to some extent from variety 1, and will be referred to as Variety 2.[5] The regional dialects spoken in Belgium will be called Variety 3.

2.2   Gender in Variety 1

2.2.1   Adnominal and nominal categories

On the basis of adnominal distinctions all nouns have to be assigned to two classes: the so-called *de*-words (historically both masculine and feminine nouns), and the *het*-words (historically neuter); e.g.

de-words	*het*-words
de man 'the man'	*het kind* 'the child'
de vrouw 'the woman'	*het boek* 'the book'
de straat 'the street'	*het water* 'the water'.

De and *het* are definite articles; only *de* can feature in the plural. The indefinite article is invariably *een: een man, een vrouw, een boek.* Neither the definite nor the indefinite article are case-distinctive. Possessive articles, such as *mijn man* 'my husband' or *mijn vrouw* 'my wife', etc. also constitute a totally unmarked class. Deictic determiners show the same binary contrast as the definite articles: *deze* 'this' goes with *de*-words, *dit* with *het*-words, similarly *die* and *dat* 'that', while only *deze* and *die* can occur with plural heads.

Rule 3

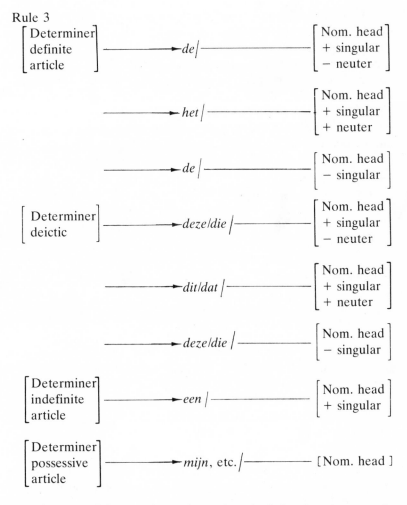

The marking of the non-determiner adnominal class is rather complex and cannot be rendered by means of a single rule. On the whole there is a contrast between *-e* and Ø, which sometimes matches the *de-het* contrast:

de-words	*het*-words
(a) *de goede man* 'the good man'	*het goede kind* 'the good child'
de goede vrouw 'the good woman'	
(b) *een goed(e) man* 'a good man'	*een goed kind* 'a good child'
een goede vrouw 'a good woman'	
(c) *goede wijn* 'good wine'	*goed fruit* 'good fruit'
goede trouw 'good faith'	

In the plural there is alternation between -*e* and Ø depending on the morphological complexity of the adjective.

It can be inferred from this scanty evidence that adnominal gender contrasts boil down to a binary opposition +neuter vs. −neuter in definite and deictic determiners, singular, and in a subsidiary way in adjectives.

Note: The nominal heads themselves are almost totally deflected, there being only a contrast between singular and plural: *man* and *mannen*, *boek* and *boeken*, etc.

2.2.2   PRO forms

2.2.2.1   Nouns [±human]

These are nearly always marked by a two-term contrast based on sex:

man:	*hij*	'he'	*vrouw* 'woman':	*hij*	'she'
	hem	'him'		*haar*	'her'
	zijn	'his'		*haar*	'her'

Diminutives, which are neuter, may select "natural" PRO forms by the side of grammatical gender: *het meisje* 'the girl': *het* 'it' or *zij* 'she'; the choice is often determined by the principle of distance: the further away the PRO form is from the antecedent, the greater the probability is that the natural gender forms are used.

2.2.2.2   Nouns [−human]

The situation is so complex here that it defies simplicity of description. The following could be tentatively advanced: most *de*-words (historically both masculine AND feminine nouns) have masculine PRO forms: *hij* 'he' — *hem* 'him' — *zijn* 'his', all the *het*-words (historically neuter nouns) have neuter PRO forms: *het* 'it' — *zijn* 'its'; a few nouns, which were historically feminine, have preserved feminine PRO forms, see 2.2.3.2.

A few examples: $\begin{cases}de\ weg \\ de\ straat\end{cases}$ 'the way' — *hij* ...
                                         'the street' — *hij*. ...
                          het pad   'the path' — *het* ...
                          (*de goedheid* 'the goodness' — *zij* ...)

The important point to note here is that, historically, the Dutch language had a grammatical gender system comparable to that of Old English and present-day German. *Weg* has always been a masculine noun, but *straat* is historically feminine; cf. OE *seo stræt*; and this holds for thousands of former feminine nouns. The restructuring of the adnominal classes, due to deflection,[6] resulted in a contrast reduced to *de/het*, very subsidiarily *-e*/Ø (see 2.2.1). The system of PRO forms was adapted accordingly, which involved a shift from a three-term set: *hij-zij-het* to a two-term contrast: *hij-het*.[7]

2.2.2.3   The distribution of the gender PRO forms with regard to nouns in present-day (northern) Standard Dutch can be mapped out as follows:

Rule 4

PRO forms

$\begin{bmatrix} \text{Noun} \\ + \text{human} \\ + \text{male} \end{bmatrix}$ (*de*-words) ⟶ *hij*, etc.   (hist. masc.)

$\begin{bmatrix} \text{Noun} \\ + \text{human} \\ - \text{male} \end{bmatrix}$ (*de*-words) ⟶ *zij*, etc.   (hist. fem.)

$\begin{bmatrix} \text{Noun} \\ - \text{human} \\ + \text{de} \end{bmatrix}$ (*de*-words) ⟶ *hij*, etc.   (hist. masc. and fem.)

$\begin{bmatrix} \text{Noun} \\ + \text{het} \end{bmatrix}$ (*het*-words) ⟶ *het*, etc.   (hist. neuter)

2.2.3   In summary

2.2.3.1   Adnominal contrasts have basically been reduced to *de* (historically both masc. and fem.) and *het* (neuter). When nouns [+human] are involved, PRO forms reflect sex distinctions; a few nouns have to be assigned to the neuter class, viz. diminutives, and *het kind* 'the child', *het wijf* (in Standard Dutch an abusive term for 'woman'), and may have either gender or sex PRO forms. In the aggregate nouns [−human] select either *hij* or *het*: the historically neuter nouns have preserved their gender; the *hij*-class covers both historically masculine and feminine nouns. The massive shift from *zij* to *hij* has to be regarded as a concomitant feature of the inflectional unmarkedness in the adnominal categories.

2.2.3.2 It should be added immediately that the above is a somewhat simplified account of the matter. First, the shift towards the *hij*-class is not yet fully completed: there are still a number of feminine words that defy the process of "masculinization", notably very often words referring to female animals, depending on the macro-context, and also quite a number of abstract nouns, where the suffix tends to support the historical gender: *diepte* 'depth' *grootheid* 'greatness', etc. In neither case can hard-and-fast rules be spelled out, though. Next, there seems to be a discrepancy between *some* normative grammars and the language-user's competence, and also perhaps between the older and the younger generations (see *Woordenlijst van de Nederlandse taal: ix–xxii*).

However, these restrictions do not invalidate the general principles which we have highlighted in the foregoing sections: the vast majority of Dutch nouns select either *hij* or *het* PRO forms, following the adnominal contrast between *de* and *het*; the *zij* PRO form is supported by the sex feature of the referent, and is only consistently used with nouns [+human], there being a tendency to assign nouns referring to female animals to the *hij*-class.

2.3   Gender in Variety 3

2.3.1   Adnominal categories

I shall take my own regional dialect (Brabant) as sample evidence.[8] First and foremost it must be pointed out that the historical three-term gender contrast has been preserved, as evinced by the following sample rules:

Rule 5

$$\text{Preposed adnominals}\longrightarrow[\alpha\ \text{gender}]/ \underline{\quad\quad} \begin{bmatrix} \text{Nom. head} \\ +\ \text{singular} \\ \alpha\ \text{gender} \end{bmatrix}$$

where α = masculine, feminine or neuter.

This general rule can be mapped out as follows:[9]

$$\begin{bmatrix} \text{Determiner} \\ \text{definite/deictic} \end{bmatrix} \longrightarrow \begin{bmatrix} \textit{diene (n)} \\ \textit{die} \\ \textit{da (t)} \end{bmatrix} \Bigg/ \underline{\hspace{1cm}} \begin{bmatrix} \text{Nom. head} \\ + \text{masculine} \\ + \text{feminine} \\ + \text{neuter} \end{bmatrix}$$

$$\begin{bmatrix} \text{Determiner} \\ \text{indefinite} \end{bmatrix} \longrightarrow \begin{bmatrix} \textit{ne(n)} \text{ /nə(n)/} \\ \textit{een} \text{ /ən/} \\ \textit{e} \text{ or } \textit{een} \text{ /ə(n)/} \end{bmatrix} \Bigg/ \underline{\hspace{0.5cm}} \begin{bmatrix} \text{Nom. head} \\ + \text{masculine} \\ + \text{feminine} \\ + \text{neuter} \end{bmatrix}$$

$$[\text{ Adjective }] \longrightarrow \begin{bmatrix} - e \\ - e/\emptyset \\ \emptyset \end{bmatrix} \Bigg/ \underline{\hspace{1cm}} \begin{bmatrix} \text{Nom. head} \\ + \text{masculine} \\ + \text{feminine} \\ + \text{neuter} \end{bmatrix}$$

Let it be repeated that the above is only meant as an outline of the adnominal marking system in my dialect. By the side of *diene(n)* and *die* also *de(n)* (masc.) and *de* (fem.) are used as definite article (not deictic). There is also variation between masculine determiners with and without /n/, depending on the first sound of the following noun or adjective; this also holds for /ə/ and /ən/ in the neuter class. The distribution of marked and unmarked adjectives patterning with feminine nouns again defies simplicity of description. Anyway, the limited evidence I have been able to offer suffices to prove that the singular nominal group is gender-distinctive along the traditional lines of a Germanic language, and that the use of a singular NP more often than not entails gender selection on the part of the language-user.

Cases are not specifically marked, and in the plural the definite article is invariably *die* or *de*.

2.3.2 PRO forms

These are selected in agreement with grammatical gender, which, as we have just seen, is signalled by means of the adnominal categories. (See Rule 6 on page 108.) This correlation holds for all nominal heads in Variety 3 and is almost faultlessly applied by speakers of that kind of Dutch. The only exceptions are, once more, neuter nouns [+human], with which sex reference may override gender. The crucial difference between this variety and 1 is the marking of feminine nouns (adnominally), which no doubt accounts for the preservation of the traditional tri-partite system.

Rule 6

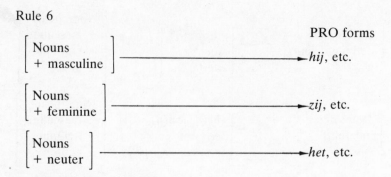

PRO forms

$\left[\begin{array}{l}\text{Nouns} \\ \text{+ masculine}\end{array}\right]$ ——————————————→ *hij*, etc.

$\left[\begin{array}{l}\text{Nouns} \\ \text{+ feminine}\end{array}\right]$ ——————————————→ *zij*, etc.

$\left[\begin{array}{l}\text{Nouns} \\ \text{+ neuter}\end{array}\right]$ ——————————————→ *het*, etc.

2.4   Gender in Variety 2

What has been said regarding the adnominal features of Variety 1 (see
2.2.1) also applies here: a binary contrast between *de/het* nouns, which no
longer reflects the traditional three-term contrast. However, and this is of
the utmost importance, PRO forms still pattern according to the long-
standing tri-partite division. Here are a few examples (to be compared
with the ones adduced in 2.2.2.2):

Masculine:	*de weg*	'the way'	— *hij* ...
	de stoel	'the chair'	— *hij* ...
Feminine:	*de straat*	'the street'	— *zij* ... (but *hij* in Var. I)
	de tafel	'the table'	. — *zij* ... (idem)
Neuter:	*het pad*	'the path'	— *het* ...
	het huis	'the house'	— *het* ...

We can account for this odd situation if we know a little of the sociolinguistic background as regards the Dutch language in Belgium. Most of
the speakers of Standard Dutch in Belgium (Variety 2) — and they
constitute a minority — also speak their regional dialect (Variety 3); and
their competence in the field of historical PRO forms is nurtured by their
dialect. Speakers of 2 do not generally encounter any difficulty in assigning *hij* to *stoel* or *weg*, but *zij* to *tafel* or *straat*, although these nouns are no
longer adnominally (or congruentially) marked for the category of gen-
der. In their regional dialect, however, these speakers very nicely distinguish between masc. *ne stoel* and fem. *een tafel*; see note 9. It stands to
reason that it is the adnominal markedness of the (underlying) regional
dialect that supports their competence in historical gender PRO forms.
Yet, as the regional dialects in Belgium tend to be losing ground among
some (educated) speakers these days, I have the impression that the
feeling for a tri-partite system is increasingly blurred in the speech of
these speakers: we sometimes find ourselves switching to Variety 1, at

least sporadically. In other words, a shift from the feminine gender to the masculine class in *de*-nouns seems to be *incipient* in Variety 2. This may be a long and slow process, but eventually Variety 2 may well have the same binary system of PRO forms as Variety 1; in the long run this will depend on how long and to what extent the regional dialects survive among speakers of Standard Dutch in Belgium.

3   Conclusions

The evidence provided by English and Dutch, both diachronic and synchronic, allows us to advance the following principles:

(a) The gender system of PRO forms operates basically along the same lines as that of the adnominal classes: tri-partite in Old English, in earlier strata of Dutch and still in many of its regional dialects (Flemish); bi-partite, at least to a very great extent, in present-day (northern) Dutch.

$$\begin{bmatrix} \text{NP} \\ \alpha \text{ gender} \end{bmatrix} \longrightarrow \begin{bmatrix} \text{PRO form} \\ \alpha \text{ gender} \end{bmatrix}$$

Standard Dutch, Variety 2, does not follow this rule for the reasons explained in 2.4.

(b) When the adnominal constituents lack gender distinction, as in Middle and Modern English, PRO forms are characterized by natural gender, i.e. they are selected on the basis of sex assignment (or the absence of it): [+male], [+female], or [−male] [−female].

$$\begin{bmatrix} \text{NP} \\ - \text{ gender} \end{bmatrix} \longrightarrow \begin{bmatrix} \text{PRO form} \\ + \text{ sex} \end{bmatrix}$$

(c) The gender of pronominalizations of neuter nouns with animate reference is determined by the (grammatical) gender of the pronominalized NP or by the sex of the referent.

$$\begin{bmatrix} \text{Noun} \\ + \text{ animate} \\ + \text{ neuter} \end{bmatrix} \longrightarrow \begin{bmatrix} \text{PRO form} \\ \left\{ \begin{matrix} + \text{ sex} \\ + \text{ neuter} \end{matrix} \right\} \end{bmatrix}$$

(d) A diachronic re-structuring of the adnominal classes in point of gender distinctiveness entails a re-structuring in the field of PRO forms, as well: Old and Middle English, and present-day Standard Dutch.

(e) Relevant evidence in German and the Romance languages seems to bear out these rules. A widening of the scope to other languages might eventually answer the question whether they tend to have universal validity or not.

Notes

1. Thus in the EME *Ancrene Wisse* the gender-distinctive determiners *þes* (masc.), *þis* (neuter), *þeos* (fem.) are still currently used; see Mossé 1968:61.
2. Recent research in the field of congruential gender (Jones 1967a, b) has shown that some Late Old English/Early Middle English texts exhibit a temporary re-structuring of their determiner system: on the one hand there is an ever-increasing tendency to use fully unmarked forms: *se* or *þe*, on the other hand there is a (temporary) re-deployment or extension of historically masculine morphemes in accusative and dative forms, presumably to mark the V–O relationship; e.g. *in þone cyrce* (hist. fem. head), or *to þone mynstre* (hist. neuter head), etc. Neuter determiners, e.g. *þ boc*, are sometimes found in congruence with historically masculine or feminine nouns, when anaphoric reference is involved; see Jones (1971:198–219).
3. Traugott (1972:87) asserts that Old English PRO forms conformed to a dual system: one based on grammatical gender (of the pronominalized NP) and another one supported by the natural gender of the referent; see also Baron (1971).
4. Old English nouns with animate reference with which gender clashes occurred are e.g. *se wifman* (masc.) 'the woman', *þaet cild* (neuter), *þaet wif* (neuter), *þaet bearn* (neuter) 'the child'.
5. Variety 2 is my Standard Dialect; the difference between 1 and 2 can be best explained in terms of the contrast between British and American English.
6. This process of deflection started in Late Middle Dutch; see de Vooys (1952:48) and Geerts (1966).
7. The question why *zij* was superseded by *hij*, and not vice versa, will be left untouched here.
8. Impressionistically I would say that most of the evidence provided by this dialect, if not all of it, holds for most of the other southern dialects as well.

9. Here are some examples in a more or less standardized spelling:

(a)	masculine:				
	diene (+ Def.)	*ne* (– Def.)	*rijke*	*man*	'the/a rich man'
	diene	*ne*	*slechte*	*stoel*	'the/a bad chair'
(b)	feminine:				
	die (+ Def.)	*een* (– Def.)	*rijke*	*vrouw*	'the/a rich woman'
	die	*een*	*slechte*	*tafel*	'the/a bad table'
(c)	neuter:				
	da (+ Def.)	*e* /ə/(– Def.)	*rijk*	*kind*	'the/a rich child'
	da	*e*	*groot*	*huis*	'the/a big house'

References

Baron, Naomi
  1971   "A reanalysis of English grammatical gender", *Lingua* 27:113–140.
Campbell, Alistair
  1959   *Old English grammar* (London: Oxford University Press).
Clark, C.
  1957   "Gender in *The Peterborough Chronicle* 1070–1154", *English Studies* 38:109–115 and 174.
De Vooys, C. G. N.
  1952³   *Nederlandse spraakkunst (met medewerking van M. Schönfeld)* (Antwerpen: De Sikkel).
Geerts, Guido
  1966   *Genus en geslacht in de Gouden Eeuw* (= *Bouwstoffen en Studiën voor de geschiedenis en de lexicografie van het Nederlands* 10) (Belgisch Interuniversitair Centrum voor Neerlandistiek).
Jones, Charles
  1967a   "The functional motivation of linguistic change", *English Studies* 48:97–111.
  1967b   "The grammatical category of gender in Early Middle English", *English Studies* 48:289–305.
  1971   "Some features of determiner usage in the Old English glosses to the *Lindisfarne gospels* and the *Durham ritual*", *Indogermanische Forschungen* 75:198–219.
  1972   *An introduction to Middle English* (New York: Holt, Rinehart and Winston).
Lyons, John
  1971   *Introduction to theoretical linguistics* (Cambridge: University Press).
Moore, Samuel
  1921   "Grammatical and natural gender in Middle English", *PMLA*:79–103.
Mossé, Fernand
  1968⁵   *A handbook of Middle English* (translated by James A. Walker) (Baltimore: Johns Hopkins University Press).
Mustanoja, Tauno F.
  1960   *A Middle English syntax, Part One: Parts of speech* (= *Mémoirs de la Société Néophilologique de Helsinki* 23) (Helsinki: Société Néophilologique).
Rigg, A. G. (ed.)
  1968   *The English language: A historical reader* (New York: Appleton-Century-Crofts).
Ross, A. S. C.
  1936   "Sex and gender in the Lindisfarne gospels", *JEGPh* 35: 321–30.
Schönfeld, M. – A. van Loey
  1964⁷   *Schönfelds historische grammatica van het Nederlands. Klankleer, vormleer, woordvorming* (Zutphen: W. J. Thieme and Cie).
Traugott, Elizabeth Closs
  1972   *A history of English syntax: A transformational approach to the history of English sentence structure* (New York: Holt, Rinehart and Winston).
Vachek, Josef
  1976   "Notes on gender in Modern English", in *Selected writings in English and general linguistics* (Prague: Academia), 386–392.
Woordenlijst . . .
  1954   *Woordenlijst van de Nederlandse taal. Samengesteld in opdracht van de Nederlandse en de Belgische Regering* ('s-Gravenhage: Staatsdrukkerij- en Uitgeversbedrijf).

JAMES DINGLEY

Some notes on Byelorussian historical morphology

1 The material for this article is based on a study of the noun morphology
of sixteenth-century Byelorussian texts contained in Koršunaŭ (1975).
The texts are the *Otpisy*[1] of Filon Kmita-Čarnabylski to the Lords-in-
Council of the Grand Duchy of Lithuania (1573–1574) and the Barkulabaŭ Chronicle[2], an anonymous work dating from some time after
1633. Both texts are of great importance for our knowledge of events
within the Grand Duchy at a crucial stage in its history. The *Otpisy* deal
almost exclusively with first-hand accounts, gathered from spies, of Ivan
the Terrible's doings, in particular his military preparations and reactions
to the election of Henry de Valois to the throne of the Polish-Lithuanian
Commonwealth and his sudden disappearance. The Chronicle is made up
of four separate elements — the life of the village of Barkulabaŭ and its
surroundings, comments on political events affecting the whole country,
official documents of the period, and legends of popular origin.

Both texts pose considerable historical and literary problems; at the
same time, because of their mostly nonofficial nature[3], they are of great
linguistic interest. Both were included among documents from which
information was taken for *Narysy* (1957), but neither has been subjected
to a linguistic analysis of the type carried out by Stang (1935) for official
state papers, by Nadson (1968) for the crucial memoirs of the
Navahrudak county judge Jeŭlašeŭski, and by Alt (1977) for the
sixteenth-century law codes of the Grand Duchy. The publication of
Wexler (1977), and the promise of publication of volume two of Jankoŭski (1974) and of a historical morphology of Byelorussian in 1978,
mean that the fundamental ground-work laid by Karskij and Stang is
being used to construct a systematic study of the history of the Byelorussian language[4], particularly of the time when it was used as the state
language of the Grand Duchy of Lithuania.

2 The nouns taken from the *Otpisy* (O) and the Barkulabaŭ Chronicle
(B) are here subdivided, for the sake of convenience, according to the
traditional stem-type pattern[5]:

2.1 *-a-*stem, mostly feminines (all masculines denote human beings, e.g. *sluga, starosta, ezuita, patriarxa*):

(a) nominative singular: the ending is always *-a* (including one example of *bura* for *burja* in B);

(b) accusative singular: *-u* for all feminines and for masculine animates (e.g., *na Oku reku; vspominaet mene, slugu*[6]);

(c) genitive singular: *-y* (e.g., *do kazny svoee, ryby, vody, pracy*) or, after velars, *-i* (e.g., *z laski božoj, do Pol'ski, Patriarxi*). After /š/ and /šč/, either ending is possible (*do Orši* but *Takovoe roskošy*); the two possibilities *do Vil'ny* and *do Vil'ni* are likely to reflect two distinct nominative singular forms *Vil'na* and *Vil'nja*, the latter being identical to the modern Byelorussian form;

(d) dative singular: *-e* causes morphophonemic velar-dental alternations in stem-final consonants (e.g., *panu L'vu Sapeze* [: *Sapega*], *dočce* [: *dočka*]); there is one example of an absence of alternation in O: *mne, sluge, vpn.*;

(e) instrumental singular: the ending is *-oju* (e.g., *z korolevoju, dočkoju, za obytnicoju*), except after /č/ (*pered strečeju, z dobyčeju; čeremisju* occurs once alongside *čeremisoju*); the ending *-om* is found once with an *a-*stem masculine, *patriarxom*;

(f) locative singular: the ending is *-e*, causing morphophonemic velardental alternations in stem-final consonants (e.g., *na slobode, u sprave, v doroze, v lasce božej, po patriarse*), *-i* with stems in /š/ and /šč/ (e.g., *na Orši, u pušči, v Polšči*), or *-y* with stems in original /c/ (e.g., *na stolicy, v Starycy, u Rečicy*; there is one example of *-y* after stem-final /dz/, *u nendzy* — cf. Polish *nędza*);

(g) nominative plural: the ending is *-y*, except after velars, when it is written as *-i* (e.g., *noviny, ordy, metelicy, slugi, utiski*);

(h) accusative plural: identical to the nominative plural for inanimates (there are no examples for animates);

(i) genitive plural: *-Ø* (e.g., *novin, ot granic, z otčizn, s obu storon*) or, after /č/, *-ej* (*šest' tisečej/tysečej*); once, *-ov* is found with an *-a-*stem masculine (*patriarxov*);

(j) dative plural: *-am* (e.g., *ku tym že službam, slugam, po vsim storonam*); there is one example of *-om* with an *-a-*stem masculine (*voevodom*);

(k) instrumental plural: *-ami* (e.g., *službami, obema rukami*); once, *-y* is found in O (*s takovymi noviny*);

(l) locative plural: *-ax* (e.g., *o novinax, vo vsix ukrainax, po dorogax*); once, *-ex* occurs (*v krivdex*).

2.2 *-ja-*stem, predominantly feminines (the stem final consonant is soft or /j/):

(a) nominative singular: *-a* (graphically *-ja*, e.g., *bestyja, unija, gosudarinja*); there are also two words ending in *-i* (*pani, gosudarini* — the latter also with *-ja*);

(b) accusative singular: *-u* (graphically *-ju*, e.g., *v nedelju, u viliju, na koronaceju, na svjatago Iliju*);

(c) genitive singular: *-i* (*z zemli neprijatel'skoe, z brat'i, okolo stacei, do Merei*);

(d) dative singular: *-i* (*k večeri, k zemli, ku voli, gosudarini moee*);

(e) instrumental singular: *-eju* (*zemleju, knjagineju, pred svjatym Il'eju, z' sem''eju*);

(f) locative singular: *-i* (*v zemli, na svjatoj nedeli, v revizii, na merei*);

(g) vocative singular: *-e* is attested in *gosudarine*;

(h) nominative plural: the ending is *-i* in *nedeli, oracyi*; there is one example of *-e* after /j/ (*novye ceremonie*);

(i) for inanimates, nominative and accusative plural are identical; no animate forms are attested;

(j) genitive plural: the ending is mostly *-∅* (*sto mil', zo vsix zemel'/zeml', dlja takovyx okazej* [from unattested *okazija* or *okazeja*?]); *ej* is found in *ot vsix zemlej, panej*;

(k) dative plural: *-am* (graphically *-jam*: *dekljaracijam*);

(l) instrumental and locative plural are not attested.

2.3 Masculine *-o*-stems:

(a) nominative singular: *-∅* (*list, čas, nočleg, pan gosudar, monastyr, služebnik, bojarin*);

(b) accusative singular: identical to the nominative singular for inanimates, to the genitive singular for animates;

(c) genitive singular: *-a* for nouns denoting persons (*špega, pana, cara, poslan'ca*), place-names (*Men'ska, Dorogobŭža, Šlova, Novgoroda* [but also *do Novagorodu*], *Kieva*), months (*mesjaca avgusta*); *-u* for inanimates and the collective animate *ljud* (*s togo sejmu, z dvoru, ot morozu, bez snegu, do novogo kalendaru, z rokošu, dlja plaču, togo ž času*);

(d) dative singular: the ending is predominantly *-u* (*panu, gospodu bogu, k tomu roku, narodu ruskomu*); *-ovi* is found in *senatorovi, getmanovi, časovi, responsovi* (all but the first one are from B);

(e) instrumental singular: *-om* (*vsim porjadkom, s panom Romanom Xodkevičom, pod onym časom*);

(f) locative singular: *-u* for stems in velar or /c/ (*v tom roku, na tom nočlegu, v mestečku Orši, o svoem poslancu, u Meščersku*); *-e* elsewhere (*na z'' ezde, o živote moem, v osoblivom liste*); one example of *na sejmu* is found in B, as well as expected *na sejme*;

(g) vocative singular: *-e* is found in *pane, biskupe, bože, -u* in *gosudar-ju/gosudaru*;

(h) nominative plural: *-e* is found where the nominative singular would be expected to end in *-in* (*seljane, smoljane, bojare*) and in *žolnere; -ove* in the human animates *tatarove, panove, senatorove, mazurove, francuzove; -y* or *-i* (mostly after velars) elsewhere (*gody, tovary, gorody, domy, nagajcy, tatary, ovoščy, doždy; tri čeloveki, zamki, žolneri*);

(i) accusative plural: identical to the nominative plural for inanimates, to the genitive plural for male human beings; note, however, the use of forms identical to the nominative plural after certain prepositions (*čerez špegi moi; čerez nekotorye kupčiki; čerez častye poslancy; movi dux božij na pogany*);[7]

(j) genitive plural: *-ov* (*tyx časov, protivko nemcov, poslov, ovoščov*); or *-∅* (*ot rimljan, tatar, sused*); or *-ej* (*grošej dvadcat', mesjacej šest'*);

(k) dative plural: *-om* (*kupcom, tatarom, špegom, vološčanom, kanclerom*); there is one case of *-am* in O (*po tym gorodam*);

(l) instrumental plural: *-y* or, after velar, *-i* (*s tatary nagajskimi, z nagajcy, s tymi meščany, z listy, s tovary svoimi; velikimi dostatki*); or *-ami* (*z detkami moimi, špegami moimi, z nagajcami*); or *-mi* (*z obema synmi svoimi, s poljacmi, z zemjanmi*);

(m) locative plural: three variants occur: *-ex* (*v svoix listex, po vsix gradex, po inšix gorodex, na lesex, o synex, na tyx časex, v otpisex, v naezdex, po roznyx panex*); *-ox* (*u goncox, u dolgox, pri panox*); *-ax* (*v tyx časax, po zamkax, pri poslancax, pri ix životax*).

2.4   Neuter *-o-* stems:

(a) Nominative singular: *-o* (*vojsko*; one example of *-e* in *mestce*, where /c/ is probably hard);

(b) accusative singular: identical to the nominative singular;

(c) genitive singular: *-a* (*togo vojska*);

(d) dative singular: not attested;

(e) instrumental singular: *-om* (*z vojskom*);

(f) locative singular: *-u* following velar or /c/ (*o vojsku, na mestcu*), *-e* elsewhere (*v skorom dele*); *mestu* is found beside expected *meste*[8];

(g) nominative plural: *-a* (*vojska, vsi rycerstva, starye sela*);

(h) accusative plural: identical in form to the nominative plural;

(i) genitive plural: *-∅* (*do tyx carstv, tyx panstv, mnogo sel*); there may be one case of *-ov* (*senov malo bylo statku*);

(j) dative plural: *-om* (*vojskom, nizkim mestom*);

(k) instrumental plural: the ending is *-y* or, after velar, *-i* (*tymi slovy, z dely, z gorly našimi, mežy panstvy; z vojski velikimi*); or *-ami* (*nad vojskami, z delami*), or *-mi* (*kolenmi*);

(l) locative plural: *-ax* (*po selax i mestax, pri obex tyx carstvax*) or *-ex* (*v inšyx delex, na derevex, v letex*).

2.5 Masculine *-jo-* stems (the stem-final consonant is soft or /j/):

(a) nominative singular: *-∅* (*korol', knjaz'*);

(b) accusative singular: identical to the nominative singular for inanimates, to the genitive singular for animates;

(c) genitive singular: *-a* (graphically *-ja*) for nouns denoting persons (*Ostafeja Volloviča, gospodarja, knjazja, do svjatogo Jur'ja*), months (*dnja aprelja*), places (*okolo Berestja*), *-u* (graphically *-ju*) elsewhere (*z sego kraju, z žalju*[9];

(d) dative singular: *-u*, graphically *-ju* (*dnju, knjazju, korolju*);

(e) instrumental singular: *-em* (*tym že obyčaem, s korolem*);

(f) locative singular: beside *-u*, graphically *-ju* (*o neprijatelju, v špitalju, o knjazju velikom, v pokoju, na privilju*), there are, in B, some examples of *-i* (*o poludni, u Beresti; u Berestju* is also found);

(g) vocative singular: *-e* (one case, *knjaže*);

(h) nominative plural: only *kroleve obadva* (B) and *obovatele* (O) belong here;

(i) accusative plural: no examples attested for inanimates; forms denoting male humans identical to genitive plurals;

(j) genitive plural: the endings incurred are *-ev* (*fortelev, rublev, vjaznev, kraev, obyvatelev*), *-ej* (*konej, vjaznej, gospodarej*[10], *losej*), *-∅* (*ot neprijatel' svoix*);

(k) dative plural: *-em* (*iereem, prezviterem*);

(l) instrumental plural: the sole example is *kon'mi* (B);

(m) locative plural: *-ex* (*pri oboix korolex*) and *-ax* (*u tyx krajax*).

2.6 Neuter *-jo-* stems (the stem-final consonant in soft or /j/[11]):

(a) nominative singular: *-e* (*knjažen'e, vesele*);

(b) accusative singular: identical in form with the nominative singular;

(c) genitive singular: *-a*, graphically *-ja* (*zdorovja, zvrocenja*);

(d) dative singular: *-u*, graphically *-ju* (*z'exanju, bačenju*);

(e) instrumental singular: *-em* (*za dozvolenem, so obrezaniem*);

(f) locative singular: *-i* (*na poli, po vzjati* [a misspelling?]) and *-u*, graphically *-ju* (*u vezenju, pri dobrom zdorovju, o zvrocenju borzom, po vzjatiju*);

(g) locative plural (the only plural ending attested): *-ax*, graphically *jax* (*na poljax, pri rosputijax*).

2.7 *-i-* stems, all inanimate feminines (stem-final consonant soft or hardened[12]):

(a) nominative singular: -∅ (*švyren', bran', cerkov, noč*);

(b) accusative singular: identical in form to the nominative singular (*krov xristianskuju, u vosen' straž velikuju, za Reč Pospolituju, moc*);

(c) genitive singular: -*i* (*z žičlivosti, do moee smerti*) or -*y* (*takovoe roskošy, see že nočy*); there is one example of -*e* (*krve našoj* O, B);

(d) dative singular: -*i* (*k Reči Pospolitoj*);

(e) instrumental singular: -*ju*, with variation in the spelling of preceding material (*pred milostyju, za vedomostju, pomoč'ju, za pečat'ju, moc"ju*);

(f) locative singular: -*i* (*o gotovnosti, pri bytnosti, v noči, v cerkvi, v Reči Pospolitoj*);

(g) nominative plural: -*i* (*reči*; also *rečy*);

(h) accusative plural: identical to nominative plural;

(i) genitive plural: -*ej* (*rečej*); one case of -*ij* in *žyvostij*;

(j) dative plural: -*am* in O (*vašym panskim milostjam*), -*em* in B (*vsim ix milostem*);

(k) instrumental plural: -*mi* (*za pečatmi, takimi rečmi*) and -*ami* (*pod pečatjami, rečami, živnostjami*);

(l) locative plural: -*ex* (*v trudnostex, vo vsex ščastlivostex, pri ix milostex*) and -*ax* (*v doleglostjax, na čestjax, vo cerkvax, v rečax*).

2.8   Variant patterns; pluralia tantum:

(a)   historic consonant-stem neuters (incomplete paradigms only):

singular	nominative	*knjaža*[13]
	genitive	*do knjažati, do sego ščenjati*
	instrumental	*z knjažati*
	locative	*na osljati*
plural	nominative	*panjata, xlopjata*
	genitive	*do knjažat, xlopjat*

(b)   *ljudi:*

plural	nominative	*ljudi* (B), *ljude* (O, B)
	genitive	*ljudej*
	dative	*ljudem*
	instrumental	*ljudmi*

(c)   *deti:*

[singular	nominative	*ditjatko*]
	[dative	*ditjatku*]
[plural	nominative	*detki*]
[	accusative	*detki* (B)]
	dative	*detem* (O)
[	instrumental	*detkami*]

(d)   relics of the dual:

from O: *do uši*; from B: *na dve godine, dve dole, po dve kope, dve mile* (an odd form, if the noun really does have a soft stem-final consonant, cf. *dve nedeli* which could either be a dual survival or the nominative plural).

3   Commentary

In this section, the data cited above will be compared with the noun paradigms given by Ivan Uževič in his manuscript grammars of 1643 (written in Paris, cited here as P) and 1645 (kept in the Arras Municipal Library, cited as A) see Bilodid—Kudryc'kyj (1970). I have elsewhere (Dingley 1972) attempted to place Uževič's grammars within the context of the history of Byelorussian rather than Ukrainian.

3.1   *-a-* stems

Uževič assigns nouns of this pattern to his 'declinatio prima', giving as an example *starosta* in both P and A. All of Uževič's endings of the singular are attested in O and B, with the exception of a vocative in *-o*. For the plural, a curious vocative ending *-ove* is given[14], but not repeated for the nominative or accusative. The genitive plural is either *-∅* or *-ov*, the latter reserved for masculine nouns only. The dative is said to end in either *-om* or *-am*. Morphophonemic alternation is dealt with in detail only in A (A 21 verso) and only for the dative case.[15] For some reason the change /h/ > /z/ produces a dative singular ending *-i* (e.g., *sluga: sluzi*), although elsewhere the ending is *-e* (*zvloka: zvloce*).

3.2   *-ja-* stems

Uževič combines *-ja-* and *-i*-stem nouns in both versions of his grammar as 'declinatio quarta', with some confusing results. His example of a *-ja-*stem is *laznja* with all the endings corresponding to the evidence of O and B. For information on *-i*-stem nouns see section 3.5 below.

3.3   Masculine and neuter *-o-* stems

Uževič's examples are *pan"* and (P) *bozstvo*, (A) *slovo*. Only *-a* is given in the paradigms as the ending of the genitive singular, although a number of nouns occur with the *-u* ending in sample sentences elsewhere in the grammars (e.g., *do domu, Rimu, golosu, roku, času, koštu*). The dative singular ending *-ovi* is not listed, although it does occur four times: *carevi* (three times in A 14 recto), *Bogovi* (A 19 recto, next to *Bogu*). Because Uževič finds it difficult to include a locative in a paradigm of Latin type, no separate ending is given for this case (only the instrumental *-om* is listed under the heading 'ablativus'); in the section 'De casibus nominum vagabundis' (P 17 verso, A 34 recto), the following examples of the locative singular are included: *na obedi, v železi* or *v železe*. The ending *-u* occurs in sample sentences with the nouns *Bog, mešok, Pariž,* i.e., with stems ending in a velar or a hush-sibilant. Stang (1935) gives a morphophonological explanation of the ending *-i*, seeing it as a reflex of the change *ě* > *e* in unstressed syllables rather than the result of Ukrainian influence. He finds the ending *-u* in nouns with velar stem-final consonants, and in certain other nouns when governed by the prepositions *v* or *na* (cf. *na mestu, na sejmu* in B). All this certainly agrees with the information gleaned from the two texts under examination, although special mention must be made of *v tom že Vendoroži* in B (cf. B *u Beresti / u Berestju*).

Uževič gives *-y* and *-ove* for the nominative plural of masculines, *-a* for that of neuters, and only *-ov* for the genitive plural. He makes no mention of *-y* for the instrumental plural, but lists only *-ami* (and *-ax* for the 'ablative'); no examples of an instrumental in *-y* occur in either version of the grammar. Stang, who divides his study of 1935 into two periods, 1496–1548 and 1548–1632, observes the more frequent occurrence of the *-ami* ending towards the end of the second period. The fact that *-y* is used in O and B in all manner of contructions makes it difficult to regard it as entirely archaic by the end of the sixteenth century, although it may well have become so during the first decades of the seventeenth. Stang also observed a predominance of *-ami* with masculine nouns whose stem ends in a velar. In O and B, we find *detkami, špegami, kozakami,* but the corpus is scarcely large enough for any statistical inference to be made. *-om* of the dative plural and *-ox* and *-ex* of the locative plural are not found in Uževic. Stang notes a predominance of *-ox* with stems in velar. The evidence of O and B is such that no precise pattern of distribution can be determined. Alt (1977) has made a significant contribution to the study of stress position as a decisive factor in the choice of locative plural ending.

3.4   Masculine and neuter *-jo-* stems; neuter consonant stems
The combination of two historically separate patterns leads to some confusion in Uževuč's paradigms; his examples on P 14 recto are *kamen', gultaj, zbavene, telja*. Disregarding for the moment the pattern of *telja*, we find in the singular endings that correspond to those in O and B (plus a vocative *kamenju, gultaju*). Two endings, *-i* and *-e*, are given for the nominative plural, two, *-ev* and *-e* (with *kamenev"* as an example!) for the accusative plural, one, *-ev*, for the genitive, and one, *-jami*, for the instrumental plural. However, a genitive plural in *-ij* is found once (P 62 verso) for a noun listed by Uževič as belonging to this pattern: *za tyx"*

dnij; -ej is attested in *vele u tebe est' gostej* (P 68 recto). The instrumental plural in *-mi* occurs in *keruju konmi* (P 59 verso); the example of *kolenmi* (cited above B 4 k [iii]) might be derived from a *-jo-* stem, but as in B only the accusative plural *kolena* occurs, there is insufficient evidence to assign just one form to a totally different pattern.

By linking *telja* (and *gusja, porosja, ščenja,* etc.) with original *-jo*-stem nouns, Uževič has to some extent preempted developments actually found in modern literary Byelorussian (cf. Hurski et al. 1968:218), where nouns like *imja* have been wholly absorbed into the declension pattern of nouns like *agon'*, and those like *cjalja, jagnja* partially so. The genitive singular given by Uževič is *teljata*, although on P 15 recto he makes a mistake which allows us to assume the possibility of an ending *-ti* (cf. Polish *cielę: cielęcia*, Byelorussian *cjalja: cjaljaci*). The 'ablative' is *teljate,* the nominative plural *teljata;* no further forms are given.

3.5 Feminine *-i-* stems

Uževič combines nouns of this pattern with *-ja-* stems (see 3.2 above). All singular and plural endings coincide with the evidence from O and B, except for the 'ablative' (i.e., instrumental) singular of his *-i*-stem example, *pesn',* which he lists as *pesneju,* in full agreement with *lazneju: laznja.* Since *pesneju* is found in both P and A, we cannot assume a spelling error.

The genitive plural ending is *-ej,* that of the instrumental plural, *-jami.* Note the comment: 'Ad hanc declinationem pertinent faeminina desinentia in '' ut *moc'', peč'', tvar''* ' (P 16 recto).

4 Conclusion

The number of noun forms actually extracted from O and B is probably too small to allow any categorial conclusions to be made on the problems that arise. One of the most obvious problems connected with noun morphology of the period is the multiplicity of endings possible for certain cases within the same text. In seeking to establish a precise delineation of, e.g., conditions for the occurrence of *-a* and *-u* in the genitive singular of masculine nouns, we may simply be wasting our time when attempting to do more than work out broad principles along the lines of Stang (1935), or of Unbegaun (1935) for sixteenth-century Russian. There will probably always be an area where either ending is used without fitting into our categories. Something may be gained by reference to the published volumes of *Słownik staropolski* and *Słownik polszczyzni XVI wieku,* but we are then faced with the task of deciding between cases of morphological influence and of chance agreement. Polish influence on verb forms and lexis is perfectly obvious (in the texts under discussion here as well as in many others dating from the second half of the sixteenth century), but it may well be that developments in noun morphology in the period under examination were the result of internal rather than of external influence. It may well be impossible to find a meaningful distribution for the ending variants of instrumental and locative plural, apart from one on a time scale on which some become archaic and others gain in importance.

It is worth adding that, despite widespread literacy and several normative grammars, there are still many variant case forms in modern literary Byelorussian. The language described by Taraškievič (1918) uses on occasion morphological devices completely different from those in Hurski et al. (1968); some of these different devices are still insisted upon in the written language by some Byelorussians in the diaspora (Pashkievich 1974: 150: *na beragox*). The spheres of usage of the masculine genitive singular endings -*a* and -*u* have frequently been the subject of heated debate (cf. Kramko et al. 1968: 155–338). Lapioškin (1977) finds a great deal of material on which to base a survey of various endings for the masculine and neuter instrumental plural in the modern literary language.

Uževič's description of the noun declensions of the language appears to be an attempt to produce a clear-cut system out of the wide range of possibilities before him, and to fit that system neatly into the Latin pattern. In so doing, he cites only a small number of possible endings in the paradigms but, perhaps as a result of carelessness, allows a greater variety to creep into his sample sentences elsewhere in the grammars. The fact that not every possible form is listed must not detract from the importance of Uževič's attempt to describe the literary language of the Grand Duchy of Lithuania in the first half of the seventeenth century.

The work of Karskij, Stang, and Alt, combined with the promised historical dictionaries of Ukrainian and Byelorussian, must surely make it possible for a comprehensive morphological survey to be produced on a level with Unbegaun (1935). Such a work will not only further our understanding of the process of Polonisation of the language in the sixteenth-century Grand Duchy, but also of the Polonisation process in general, leading to the 1696 decree banning Byelorussian (or Ruthenian, or whatever we call it) from use as a state language.

Notes

1. *The analysis of the Otpisy* and the Barkulabaŭ Chronicle has been carried out on the basis of the texts published in *Pomniki* (1975). I have been unable to trace the whereabouts of the original manuscripts of the *Otpisy*. The text in *Pomniki* (1975) is based on

previous publications—*Źródła* (1844: 243–305, in Polish spelling) and *Akty* (1848: 164–177, in Russified spelling).

2. The Barkulabaŭ Chronicle has received considerably more attention than the Otpisy having been published in full or in part many times; it appeared, in the same year as *Pomniki* (1975), in *PSRL* 32:174–192.

3. Obviously much of Filon's writing is concerned with official reports and thus is couched in official terminology. However, he frequently becomes so angry in his denunciations of inefficiency and treachery in high places that we gain a real insight into the kind of language he must have spoken.

4. I offer no excuses for being so forthright here. Alt (1977:403–411) makes a good case for the term 'Ruthenian'. The clear demarcation of Byelorussian and Ukrainian in the sixteenth century is fraught with difficulties, by no means all of a linguistic nature. See Shevelov (1974) for a survey of the criteria involved; the confusion of Aničenka (1969), particularly in the word list purporting to distinguish between the two languages, shows how problematical the task is. Obviously Polish linguistic features are easier to recognize, especially in verb forms.

5. Such a division by 'historical' categories, although obviously based on the procedures of comparative Slavonic philology, must inevitabley take into account the actual state of the language. Therefore *den'* is assigned to the pattern of masculine -*jo* -stem nouns; the hush-sibilants are classified as hard (as against Stang 1935, who places *groš* and *ratuš* in the -*jo*-stem pattern); the nominative plural ending -*e* of masculine nouns with the suffix *tel* is regarded as a variant ending, alongside -*i*.

6. There is a curious case of what looks like a nominative singular after an imperative: *postavi, gospodi, zakonodavca* (the masculine suffix -*ca* is well attested in the language of the period); this may be either a straightforward mistake or go back to an underlying nominative singular in -*ec*.

7. Alt (1977:215–227) discusses this point in detail.

8. *mestu* is the one form cited by Stang (1935) from the documents under investigation.

9. *žal'* is clearly masculine, as it still is in modern Polish and Byelorussian.

10. Nouns with a stem-final /r/ show considerable fluctuation because of the hardening process. The nominative singular *gospodar* contrasts with the genitive singular *gospodarja* (but note *car: cara*).

11. In practice we may assume that original stem-final *Cjo* had already yielded *C'C'e* by this time.

12. Hardened consonants in Byelorussian are /c/, /r/, and the hush-sibilants.

13. The gender of *knjaža* is clearly neuter in *knjaža semigradskoe,* but masculine at other times: *knjaža im otkazal; knjaža, žalem budučy porušonyj.*

14. Alt (1977) finds a nominative plural *zločincove* in the 1529 Statute.

15. Uževič has great difficulty with the locative, lumping it together with the instrumental as 'ablativus' and describing it as a 'casus vagabundus'.

Note added in print: Due to circumstances beyond the control of the author and the series editor, *g* in the transliterated words should be replaced by *h*.

References

Akty ...
 1848 *Akty, otnosjaščijesja k istorii Zapadnoj Rossii* III [Documents relating to the history of Western Russia] (St. Peterburg).

124   *James Dingley*

Alt, T.
1977   *The language of the Lithuanian Statute of 1529: Orthography, phonology, inflec-tions.* Unpublished Ph.D. dissertation (Columbia University).

Aničenka, U. V.
1969   *Bielaruska-úkrainskija piśmova-moúnyja suviazi* [Byelorussian-Ukrainian liter-ary and linguistic connections] (Minsk: Vyšejšaja Škola).

Bilodid, I. K. — E. M. Kudryc'kyj (eds.)
1970   *Hramatyka slov'jans'ka I. Uževiča* [The Slavonic grammar of I. Uževič] (Kiev: Naukova Dumka).

Dingley, James
1972   "The two versions of the Gramatyka Slovenskaja of Ivan Uževič", *Journal of Byelorussian Studies* 11: 369–384.

Hurski, M. I. et al.
1968   *Bielaruskaja mova I* [Byelorussian] (Minsk: Vyšejšaja Škola).

Jankoŭski, F. M.
1974   *Histaryčnaja hramatyka bielaruskaj movy I* [Historical Byelorussian grammar] (Minsk: Vyšejšaja Škola).

Koršunaŭ, A. F. (ed.)
1975   *Pomniki staražytnaj bielaruskaj piśmennaści* [Monuments of ancient Byelorus-sian literature] (Minsk: Navuka i texnika).

Kramko, I. I. et al (eds.)
1968   *Historyja bielaruskaj litaraturnaj movy II* [History of literary Byelorussian] (Minsk: Navuka i texnika).

Lapioškin, V.U.
1977   "Varyjantnyja formy nazoúnikaŭ bielaruskaj movy u tvornym sklonie množnaha liku" [Variants of Byelorussian nouns in the instrumental of the plural], *Bielarus-kaja linhvistyka* 11:21–28.

Nadson, A.
1968   "The memoirs of Theodore Jeŭłaseŭski, Assessor of *Navahrudak* (1546–1604)", *Journal of Byelorussian Studies* 1:269–348.

Narysy ...
1957   *Narysy pa historyi bielaruskaj movy* [Notes on the history of Byelorussian] (Minsk: Dziaržaŭnaje vučebna-piedahahičnaje vydaviectva Ministerstva Aśviety BSSR).

Pashkievich, V.
1974   *Fundamental Byelorussian I* (Toronto: Byelorussian-Canadian Coordinating Committee).

Pomniki ...
1975   *Pomniki staražytnaj bielaruskaj piśmennaści* [Monuments of ancient Byelorus-sian literature] (Minsk: Navuka i texnika).

PSRL
1975   *Polnoe sobranie russkix letopisej 32* [Complete collection of Russian chronicles] (Moskva: Nauka).

Shevelov, A.Y.
1974   "Belorussian versus Ukrainian: Delimitation of texts before A.D. 1564", *Journal of Byelorussian Studies* 11:145–156.

Stang, C.S.
1935   *Die westrussische Kanzleisprache des Großfürstentums Litauen* (Oslo: J. Dybwad).

Taraškievič, B.
1918   *Bielaruskaja hramatyka dla skol* [Byelorussian grammar for schools] (Vilnia).

Unbegaun, B.O.
1935   *La langue russe au XVIe siècle (1500–1550), I: La flexion des noms* (Paris: Champion).
Uževič, Ivan
1970   *Hramatyka slov"jans"ka I. Uževiča* [The Slavonic grammar of I. Vženvič] (edited by I.K. Bilodid and E.M. Kudryc'kyj (Kiev: Naukova Dumka).
Wexler, P.
1977   *A historical phonology of the Belorussian language* (Heidelberg: Winter).
Źródła . . .
1844   *Źródła do dziejów polskich II* [Sources of Polish history] (Wilno).

STIG ELIASSON

Case, word order and coding in a historical linguistic perspective

1   Theoretical background

One major innovation introduced into linguistic theory by Chomsky was to regard grammar as an enumerative device, i.e., as a mechanism for enumerating the set of grammatical sentences of a language. Thus he states, for instance (1964a: 240f.):

The central notion to be defined in linguistic theory is, I believe, the notion *grammar of L* for an arbitrary natural language *L*. A grammar of *L* is a device which enumerates the sentences of *L* in such a way that a structural description can be mechanically derived for each enumerated sentence.

And similarly (ibid. 218):

We can avoid many complex and rather artificial problems altogether by recon-struing the goal of linguistic analysis as the construction of a grammar of a fixed form . . . which enumerates all and only the sentences of the language.

But the idea that mere enumeration of this sort is sufficient as a goal for sentence generation will allow for a wide range of grammatical models which are strongly at variance with the main functions of linguistic per-formance, perception and production, as these are commonly under-stood. Especially psycholinguists, but also linguists, have therefore time and again been tempted to reinterpret such enumerative devices in per-formance terms (by and large, in terms of speech production, due to the set-up of most variants of transformational generative grammar).
   Among other things, these two views of generative grammar imply certain definite positions on the question of inter-level directionality, that is, whether there is any linguistically significant direction to the mappings between levels and, if so, what that direction is. In the first case, we have to do with a non-directional model where any apparent direction in the mappings is purely notational, and, in the second one, with a kind of unidirectional model where derivations proceed from one level to

another, but not the other way around. The non-directional interpretation is the one that is usually maintained in generative theory, when the
problem of directionality is being explicitly discussed. The undirectional
interpretation receives considerable support from generative practice. In
Zwicky's words (1972:107 [italics added]):

It is instructive to compare theory with practice in generative grammar. *Most of
the actual work on* the *syntax* of specific languages *has assumed* that there is a
directionality in description, and has been concerned with the form of rules, the
ordering of rules, and the content of remote representations. By and large,
directionality has been an issue only to the extent that analysts have needed to
determine WHICH direction was to be associated with a particular mapping.
These matters have been especially clear *in phonology,* where no one is inclined to
be suspicious of the fact that the mapping (s,P) of systematic phonological
representations to systematic phonetic representations is partitioned into a set of
mappings called rules, and where *the directionality of particular rules is uncon-
troversial.*

Either standpoint, however, appears to fit poorly with a host of facts and
considerations from many different areas of linguistics such as descriptive
phonology and syntax, language acquisition, linguistic performance, and
historical change. Relevant arguments include the following:

(a)   Many linguistic processes which convert one representation into
      another are bidirectional rather than unidirectional. Hence, these
      processes allow for a good deal of two-way transduction through the
      linguistic system, i.e., either in the direction from semantics to
      phonetics or vice versa.
(b)   A good many unidirectional processes (which uniquely permit only
      one-way transduction in the direction from semantics to phonetics)
      are amended by other structural mechanisms so as to enhance or
      ensure transduction in the other direction. Thus, bidirectional pro-
      cesses may interlock with unidirectional ones in such a way that the
      latter are disambiguated, or the neutralizing effects of unidirec-
      tional processes may be partially or fully offset by means of separate
      anti-ambiguity constraints.
(c)   Not infrequently languages contain special surface markers whose
      primary purpose must be to signal deeper structural relations, thus
      again enabling inferability in the direction from phonetics to semantics.
(d)   Numerous historical changes have apparently been at least partly
      motivated by a tendency to preserve or to introduce a substantial
      portion of one-to-one matchings between lower and higher levels.
(e)   The description of linguistic performance, especially perception,

will be considerably simplified if linguistic models are allowed to contain not only unidirectional, but also bidirectional rules. Insofar as the linguistic system can be assumed to be directly involved in linguistic processing, perceptual processing may often operate with local strategies employing bidirectional rules rather than exclusively by means of global strategies utilizing unidirectional rules in combination with mechanisms for provisional analysis and trial-and-error type matching.

Still other considerations may be extracted from the literature on biuniqueness, recoverability, and directionality (cf., e.g., Eliasson 1974, 1975, 1977, forthcoming a, b and references there).

Specifically, such data appear to suggest a model which is not just neutrally non-directional or basically unidirectional, but which involves instead a combination of bidirectional and unidirectional relationships. In other words, instead of assuming that the connections between two adjacent linguistic levels must be described as in (1a) or (1b), we seem justified to reckon with the inter-level relationships of (1c).

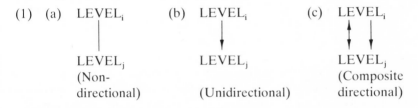

(1) (a) LEVEL$_i$ (b) LEVEL$_i$ (c) LEVEL$_i$

        LEVEL$_j$ LEVEL$_j$ LEVEL$_j$
        (Non-   (Composite
        directional)   (Unidirectional)   directional)

Consequently, we will also have to reconsider the notion of rule, dividing linguistic rules grossly into the two major classes indicated above, i.e., bidirectional and unidirectional ones. Bidirectional rules are two-way processes which can be equally well used for inferring a deeper representation from a more superficial one as for deriving the more superficial representation from the deeper one. Unidirectional rules, on the other hand, are one-way processes which yield unique outputs only in derivation; when used for 'backwards derivation' or inference without being amended by structural anti-ambiguity devices, they must therefore necessarily presuppose disambiguation by means of general cognitive operations. From what has now been said, it is clear that the derivational and the inferential modality of linguistic structure are not regarded as being entirely symmetric. The inferential modality is, in a sense, less elaborated, but the resulting structural indeterminacies of the linguistic code are remedied by the language user's general cognitive capacity. However, from the fact that the linguistic system does not afford completely unique transduction in the inferential mode, it does not follow that the inferential modality can be more or less neglected or even entirely excluded. In this paper, we would like to point to still another linguistic phenomenon which seems relevant to the issue of inter-level directionality.

2   The historical interplay between case marking and word order

The phenomenon we would like to refer to here emanates from the interface of historical morphology and syntax. Specifically, we will discuss an important theoretical implication emerging from the interdependence between case and word order which has been observed in many languages. It is, of course, a commonplace in the linguistic literature that, as overt case marking gradually breaks down, greater demands are put on the rigidity of syntactic frames. If we consider, for instance, works on the Central Scandinavian languages (Danish, Norwegian and Swedish), we find that this traditional view is hinted at or openly expressed in many historical handbooks such as Haugen (1976:79, 268), Knudsen (1976:9, 23, 24f., and passim), Skard (1967:103, 154, also 12f.), Skautrup (1968; vol. 1: 275), Wessén (1965:202) and so forth.[1] This interplay between relatively fixed word order and the gradual abolition of case marking is explored further in a paper by Teleman (1975), who asks how it might have been possible to predict the particular course of the case reductions that took place in the Central Scandinavian languages. On the whole, he opposes to each other two alternative principles of explanation: complexity and distinctiveness. Dealing first with the notion of grammatical complexity, he relates briefly how a generative grammar handles the category of case. At some point, he says, the grammar will produce the tree diagram in (2) (Teleman 1975:695):

(2)

Structures of this sort will then trigger case assignment rules such as those in (3) (ibid. 696). At a somewhat later stage in the derivation, other rules will provide abstract inflectional markers of declensional class, case,

(3) Let NP be NOM if immediately dominated by S   unless . . . .
    ,,   ,,   ,, ACC ,,   ,,   ,,   ,, VP   ,, ...
    ,,   ,,   ,, DAT ,,   ,,   ,,   ,, PrepP   ,, ...
    ,,   ,,   ,, GEN ,,   ,,   ,,   ,, NP   ,, ...

number, gender, etc., with phonological content (ibid.).[2] Teleman now asks how complexity in terms of this framework might be used to explain the case reductions in Central Scandinavian. Evidently, Old Scandinavian and the modern Central Scandinavian dialects do not differ much in regard to the basic syntactic structures as in (2), so a putative difference in complexity cannot reside there. In regard to the rules in (3), on the other hand, the question naturally arises whether there exists a hierarchy of complexity within the case system itself such that the loss of particular case distinctions would proceed in accordance with it. However, Teleman finds no really convincing evidence for this hypothesis and concludes that the notion of simplicity in the formal grammar is apparently not by itself enough to predict the course of the case reductions in Central Scandinavian. Therefore, he turns instead to the concept of distinctiveness which he finds much more promising. He points out that word order, selectional restrictions, and concord usually suffice to indicate subjects, direct objects, and indirect objects in Middle Scandinavian. Consequently, the case differences in these noun phrases, as opposed to the genitive in possessive constructions, could easily be allowed to disappear. Distinctiveness rather than complexity appears as a primary factor governing the specific course of how the case morphology of Central Scandinavian breaks down.[3]

3   The case/word-order drift as an instance of a coding shift

The basic principle underlying the gradual replacement of case by increased reliance on word order recurs in many other types of historical developments, one of which may be especially worth recalling here. In a suggestive paper, Sigurd (1961) discusses the important Old Norse (or Common Scandinavian) changes of syncope, umlaut and breaking from the point of view of two formal codes *A* and *B*. Code *A* contains only two elementary signals, *a* and *b*. To yield a large number of 'words', these two units must be permitted to combine in a number of ways such as *aa*, *aba*, *bb*, *bab*, *aabb*, *bbaa*, etc. It is obvious that, due to the scarcity of signals, a large vocabulary in this code will necessarily have to include many long words. Code *B*, on the other hand, involves ten elementary signals, *a* through *j* in the alphabet, and will clearly allow for a substantial vocabulary made up of much shorter words than in code *A*, such as *c*, *d*, *e*, *ca*, *ad*, and so on. Turning now to the actual Old Norse changes, we recall that mutation (umlaut), and, to some extent, breaking, produced a series of new segmental distinctions, while syncope decreased somewhat the average word length. For instance, by *i*-umlaut and syncope, older **fōtiR* 'feet' was converted into **fötR* with contracted syntagmatics and a new vowel phoneme *ö*. Hence, the later stage of the language displays a channelling of information from the unstressed syllables into the root syllables, which is reminiscent of a change from one formal code to another. In Sigurd's words (1961:18):

> The two stages of Old Norse can be compared to the two codes above, *A* and *B*. *A* is characterized by few signals and, as a consequence, long words; *B* is character- ized by a greater number of signals and shorter words. ... living languages are different from the codes *A* and *B* in that they have a certain amount of redun- dancy, since only a fraction of the theoretically possible words is used. But since this fraction is probably fairly constant and does not vary too much from one language to another, the comparison with the codes *A* and *B* is relevant. Living languages are of the type *A* or *B*, but for the fact that a certain percentage of the words is eliminated. From this point of view the development in Old Norse can be described as a development from a code of the type *A* to a code of the type *B*, a development towards a code with a higher number of signals and shorter words.

And, similarly (ibid. 21):

> Syncope, mutation and breaking in Old Norse should not be regarded as isolated events that only lead to dropping of unstressed syllables and changes of the stem vowels according to the quality of the following vowels respectively. Syncope, mutation and breaking together imply a change in the linguistic code, a change to a code with more signals and shorter groups ... The code shift is essentially brought about by introducing new vowel phonemes in the stem syllable and thus in transferring to this syllable the information of the syncopated phonemes.

It is clear that the historical change analyzed by Sigurd has a certain similarity to the developments discussed earlier which led to a greater dependence on word order as a means for grammatical distinctions and to a drastic reduction of case morphology. Schematically:[4]

(4) (a) GREATER WORD   (b) LESS FIXED WORD
          LENGTH —   ORDER — CASE
          SMALLER PHONEME   MARKING
          INVENTORY

                    >   >

DECREASED WORD LENGTH —
MORE PHONEMIC DISTINCTIONS

MORE FIXED WORD ORDER —
REDUCTION OF CASE MARKING

In both cases, we obviously have to do with a shift in coding, and it is most important to note that, in both cases, distinctiveness is preserved.

4   Coding shifts and models of grammar

Coding shifts have certain implications for the organization of grammatical models, specifically for those parts of the models which account for inter-level relationships (rather than mere distributional properties of a single level). An obvious example of a device which interrelates different levels is the transformational component of a standard generative grammar. As we know, in early generative grammar, transformations were thought of as performing such operations as deletion, simple replacement, expansion, reduction, addition, and permutation (Bach 1964:73–79; but cf. Chomsky 1965:144, 147). Schematically:

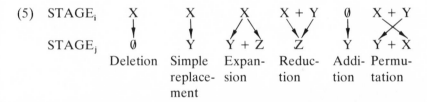

(5)   STAGE$_i$ X   X   X   X + Y   0   X + Y

STAGE$_j$ 0   Y   Y + Z   Z   Y   Y + X

Deletion   Simple replacement   Expansion   Reduction   Addition   Permutation

Clearly, these operations entail a relatively unconstrained description of the connections that hold between the two syntactic levels. In these general conditions, a wide variety of derivationally complex relations is hidden, which is not always taken care of by context specifications in the transformational rules. Bach (1964:79) indicates that the principles for deriving phrase markers by means of transformations must be made more precise in certain ways, but, as we know, Bach's formulation of the conditions is on the whole quite characteristic of the way in which transformations were viewed in early generative theory. Eventually, the requirement of unique recoverability for deletion and substitution transformations was added (Chomsky 1964b:71; Katz — Postal 1964:78-81; Chomsky 1965: 144f., 177–82), the role of ambiguity as a constraining force on stylistic transformations was recognized (Chomsky 1965:127), and so forth. All of these added conditions imply stricter restrictions on the relationships depicted in (5). Nevertheless, it does not appear too unjust to say that recoverability never became a key notion in generative theory. In particular, it seems fairly clear that generativists did not draw the full consequences of this notion for their models of grammar.

It is against this background that we have to view, for instance, the classic paper by Bever and Langendoen (1972) on how speech perception interacts with generative grammars in linguistic history, A generative or 'predictive' grammar, they say, is organized as in (6) (Bever—Langendoen 1972:34).

(6)
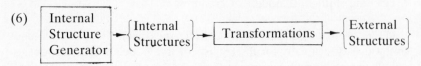

Their model for speech perception, on the other hand, includes the configuration in (7) (1972:41).

(7) | External structures | → | Perceptual Mechanisms | → | Internal structures |

The perceptual mechanisms comprise, in turn, "an ordered set of perceptual strategies which directly map external strings onto their internal structures" (1972:42). Examples of such non-grammatical perceptual strategies are (8a) and (8b)

(8) (a) X_1 Nominal $V_f X_2$ ⟶ $[_s X_1$ Nominal $V_f X_2]$
     (b) $[_s X V_f$ (Nominal) ⟶ $[_s X V_f$ (Nominal)$]_s$

which state that a noun phrase and a finite verb inflected in agreement with the noun phrase mark the beginning of an underlying sentence (8a) and that the verb phrase, which may optionally contain a noun phrase, is the end of such a sentence (8b) (1972:45). In Bever — Langendoen 1971 (436 fn. 1 [1976:118 fn. 1]), the authors "emphasize that such strategies . . . are *explicitly probabilistic*, and *should not be confused with syntactic rules*" [emphasis added] (cf. also Bever 1970 [1976:69]). As for the role of grammar and the perception model in language history, Bever and Langendoen (1972:40) note that the notion of simplification in the grammar is *"the only potentially explanatory device*" which the *structure* of a predictive grammar offers to the historical linguist in his quest for causes of historical developments" and state further that "[t]o find the causes of historical change we must therefore *look beyond the structures offered by predictive linguistic grammars*, to the structure of the interaction between the predictive and the behavioral system of language" [again, my italics]. The perceptual strategies constrain grammars and, especially, the constraint holds that the sentences generated by the grammar "must be *in general perceptually analyzable*" (1972:48). From this summary of Bever and Langendoen's conception it is clear that they adhere, on the whole, to a purely synthetic or unidirectional view of linguistic structure. Most notably, the potential role of intra-structurally recoverable processes remains almost totally unexplored and no consequences are drawn for the form of grammar.

But coding shifts as described in section 3 above indicate that the notion of intra-structural recoverability should move much more into the foreground of linguistic theory. The shift from case to word-order marking of sentential relations is, in vital respects, a structural matter. Just as deeper sentential relations can frequently be read off, or inferred, by the same rules as assign or derive case, so can these relations quite often be retrieved by the same rules as linearize sentence components. In other words, both case assignment rules and ordinary transformations are not seldom bidirectional, if not in customary formalizations, so at least in actual fact. We believe this to be an extremely important, indeed a fundamental, property of language which cannot be slighted. The import of the case/word-order exchange is that it provides yet another striking example of the crucial role of upwards signalling in linguistic structure. For what happens in a coding shift is not that bidirectionality is simply lost, but that a function previously handled by one set of partly bidirectional relations is gradually taken over by another set of partly bidirectional relations. Thus bidirectionality has been kept largely constant, only the means to effectuate it have changed. Furthermore, the change has, to a large extent, been a change within the grammatical system itself. The outside constraint is that the code has to distinguish different semantic contents. The grammar-internal effect is to secure a sufficient degree of two-way coding. Consequently, our model of grammar must reflect this situation by explicitly incorporating the corresponding bidirectional rules.

5 Conclusion

Inherent in our discussion are three diverging suggestions about the explanation of historical change and the form of grammars. One is the idea, characterized by Bever and Langendoen (1971:443 [1976:126]), that

a linguistic change represents an "improved" grammar in formal terms. The primary attempts have been to argue that structural changes produce formally "simpler" grammars, or grammars with more general application of particular rules.

Another suggestion is the counterproposal, advanced by these two authors, which was summarized above in section 4. Here, historical changes are explained in functional terms and mainly by causes outside the linguist's grammar. Still another alternative would emphasize both functional explanations and intra-structural causes. In Kiparsky's words, "[f]unctional conditions ... enter the linguistic system in a grammaticalized form" (Kiparsky 1972:224). With the understanding that this is a simplified scheme, the differences are summed up in the table in (9).

(9)	Functional explanation (as opposed to explanation in terms of simplicity)?	Development describable within the grammatical system itself (i.e., within competence as opposed to performance)?
'Standard' generative theory	No	Yes
Generative psycholinguistics (Bever-Langendoen)	Yes	Largely no
A third possibility	Yes, to a considerable extent	Yes, in certain important respects

Furthermore, we have suggested that the almost universally accepted view of case/word-order shifts is pertinent to model construction in linguistics. This traditional insight has a direct bearing upon standard generative grammars, both under the non-directional and the unidirectional interpretation. First, it entails that directionality is in fact a relevant consideration in grammar, thus ruling out the merely enumerative approach. Secondly, it indicates that a largely top-down unidirectionality (in the direction from deep structure — or the like — to sound) is insufficient and must be complemented with a partial inverse derivability, which may be utilized by the perceptual strategies in linguistic performance.[5] The overall picture which emerges is then the one in (10).

(10)

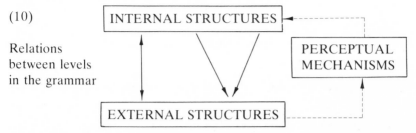

Relations
between levels
in the grammar

In particular, this means that both bidirectional and unidirectional relationships are recognized in the grammar and that non-grammatical perceptual operations are a natural complement to strictly linguistic structure.

Notes

1. For Germanic in general, cf. e.g. Meillet (1917:187f., 191f. [1923:113f., 116]). Note also Jespersen (1922; [1964:361f.]), Chomsky (1966:45, 101 fn. 82), and many others.
2. Cf. also, of course, Chomsky (1965:170–176), Bierwisch (1967), etc. Sigurd (1965:43f.) formulates some rules for case in Old Swedish in terms of the early generative model.
3. The role of distinctiveness in the historical development of case systems has recently been explored in greater detail by Plank (1978 and this volume).
4. The relation between a small phoneme inventory and word length is amply illustrated in the Polynesian languages, although the effect is, on one hand, further accentuated by fairly heavy restrictions on phonotactics and, on the other, diminished by the fact that a good deal of lexical homonymy is allowed. See, e.g., Krupa (1966) on Maori. Similarly, case and word order are not, of course, the only interactive factors in the coding of sentential relationships and it may even occur that both are absent at the same time. On the latter point, cf. Li and Thompson (1976:472–475).
5. Cf., e.g., Chomsky — Lasnik (1977:434): "It is reasonable to suppose that the design of language should facilitate the perceptual strategies that are used by the hearer". Note, incidentally, also that it might be possible to characterize trace theory (e.g., Chomsky 1975:82–118) as an implicit acknowledgement of the need for inverse derivability in grammar.

References

Bach, Emmon
   1964   *An introduction to transformational grammar* (New York: Holt, Rinehart and Winston).
Bever, Thomas G.
   1970   "The influence of speech performance on linguistic structure", in Flores d'Arcais —Levelt (eds.) 1970:21–50. [Reprinted in Bever—Katz—Langendoen (eds.) 1976:65–88.]

138   Stig Eliasson

Bever, Thomas G.—Jerrold J. Katz—D. Terence Langendoen (eds.)
   1976   An integrated theory of linguistic ability (New York: Thomas Y. Crowell).
Bever, Thomas G. — D. Terence Langendoen
   1971   "A dynamic model of the evolution of language", Linguistic Inquiry 2:433–
          463. [Reprinted in Bever—Katz—Langendoen (eds.) 1976:115–147.]
   1972   "The interaction of speech perception and grammatical structure in the evolution
          of language", in Stockwell — Macaulay (eds.) 1972:32–95.
Bierwisch, Manfred
   1966   "Syntactic features in morphology: General problems of so-called pronominal
          inflection in German", in To honor Roman Jakobson (The Hague: Mouton),
          239–270.
Chomsky, Noam
   1964a "A transformational approach to syntax", in Fodor — Katz (eds.) 1964:211–
          245.
   1964b "Current issues in linguistic theory", in Fodor — Katz (eds.) 1964:50–118.
   1965   Aspects of the theory of syntax (Cambridge, Mass.: MIT Press).
   1966   Cartesian linguistics (New York: Harper and Row).
   1975   Reflections on language (New York: Pantheon Books).
Chomsky, Noam – Howard Lasnik
   1977   "Filters and control", Linguistic Inquiry 8:425–504.
Dahl, Östen (ed.)
   1974   Papers from the First Scandinavian Conference of Linguistics (Göteborg: Depart-
          ment of Linguistics, University of Göteborg).
Dahlstedt, Karl-Hampus (ed.)
   1975   The Nordic languages and modern linguistics 2. Proceedings of the Second Interna-
          tional Conference of Nordic and General Linguistics, Umeå 1973. (Stockholm:
          Almqvist & Wiksell).
Dressler, Wolfgang U.—Wolfgang Meid (eds.)
   1978   Proceedings of the 12th International Congress of Linguists, Vienna, 1977
          (=Innsbrucker Beiträge zur Sprachwissenschaft) (Innsbruck: Institut für
          Sprachwissenschaft der Universität Innsbruck).
Eliasson, Stig
   1974   "Diakroni och direktionalitet", in Dahl (ed.) 1974:71–85.
   1975   "On the issue of directionality", in Dahlstedt (ed.) 1975:421–444.
   1977   "Cognitive processes and models of language", in de Mey et al. (eds.), 60–72.
   forthcoming a   "Analytic vs. synthetic aspects of phonological structure", in Goyvaerts
          (ed.)
   forthcoming b   "Historical change and phonological directionality".
Flores d'Arcais, G. B.—J. M. Levelt (eds.)
   1970   Advances in psycholinguistics (Amsterdam: North-Holland).
Fodor, Jerry A. — Jerrold J. Katz (eds.)
   1964   The structure of language. Readings in the philosophy of language (Englewood
          Cliffs, N.J.: Prentice-Hall).
Goyvaerts, Didier L. (ed.)
   forthcoming   Phonology in the 1970's.
Haugen, Einar
   1976   The Scandinavian languages. An introduction to their history (London: Faber and
          Faber).
Jespersen, Otto
   1922   Language. Its nature, development and origin (London: Allen & Unwin). [1964
          reprinted (New York: Norton).]

Katz, Jerrold J. — Paul M. Postal
  1964 *An integrated theory of linguistic descriptions* (Cambridge, Mass.: MIT).
Kiparsky, Paul
  1972 "Explanation in Phonology", in Peters (ed.) 1972:189–227.
Knudsen, Trygve
  1976 *Kasuslære, I: Innledning—nominativ—akkusativ* (2nd edition) (Oslo: Universitetsforlaget).
Krupa, Viktor
  1966 *Morpheme and word in Maori* (The Hague: Mouton).
Li, Charles (ed.)
  1976 *Subject and topic* (New York: Academic Press).
Li, Charles – Sandra A. Thompson
  1976 "Subject and topic: A new typology of language", in Li (ed.) 1976:457–489.
Meillet, Antoine
  1917 *Caractères généraux des langues germaniques* (Paris: Hachette). Norwegian translation of the 2nd edition 1922: Almindelig karakteristik av de germanske sprog (Kristiania: Aschehoug, 1923).]
de Mey, M. et al. (eds.)
  1977 *International Workshop on the Cognitive Viewpoint, University of Ghent, 24–26 III 77* (Gent: Werkgroep voor de Studie van Communicatieve en Cognitieve Processen, Rijkuniversiteit Gent).
Peters, Stanley (ed.)
  1972 *Goals of linguistic theory* (Englewood Cliffs, N. J.: Prentice-Hall).
Plank, Frans
  1978 "Case syncretism and coding syncretism", in Dressler — Meid (eds.) 1978: 405–407.
  this volume "Encoding grammatical relations: Acceptable and unacceptable nondistinctness".
Sigurd, Bengt
  1961 "The code shift in Old Norse", *Studia Linguistica* 15:10–21.
  1966 "Generative grammar and historical linguistics", *Acta Linguistica Hafniensia* 10:35–48.
Skard, Vemund
  1967 *Norsk språkhistorie I* (Oslo: Universitetsforlaget).
Skautrup, Peter
  1968 *Det danske sprogs historie*, vols. 1–4 (2nd edition) (København: Gyldendalske Boghandel Nordisk Forlag).
Stockwell, Robert P. – Ronald K. S. Macaulay (eds.)
  1972 *Linguistic change and generative theory* (Bloomington: Indiana University Press).
Teleman, Ulf
  1975 "Reductions of a morphological case system", in Dahlstedt (ed.) 1975:692–703.
Wessén, Elias
  1965 *Svensk språkhistoria, III: Grundlinjer till en historisk syntax* (2nd edition) (Stockholm: Almqvist & Wiksell).
Zwicky, Arnold M.
  1972 "Remarks on directionality", *Journal of Linguistics* 8:103–109.

MARTIN HARRIS

The marking of definiteness in Romance*

In recent years, it has come to be widely acknowledged that there are important areas of semantic overlap, amounting at times to near-identity of meaning, between the categories traditionally known as 'personal pronouns' and 'definite articles', with demonstrative adjectives and pronouns also having closely related functions on many occasions. Such a view is reinforced by the significant degree of morphological similarity, both synchronically and diachronically, between the exponents of these categories, a similarity which is perhaps nowhere more apparent than in Romance. Some linguists (e.g. Postal 1966) have gone so far as to claim that personal pronouns are in fact derived from definite articles, while others (e.g. Sommerstein 1972) have drawn the opposite conclusion from very similar data.

The present paper will attempt to establish at the outset, independently of any particular exponents, a range of semantic features that will serve as an adequate framework within which to analyse the situation at any given moment in Romance (and which, hopefully, will also have a wider applicability). This will be followed by an analysis of the uses made of one particular form, *ille*, and its derivatives, together with related forms, and the paper will conclude by re-examining the relationship between definite articles and (certain) personal pronouns, both in Romance and elsewhere.

From among the very many features which may be associated with any given NP in a (semantically defined) underlying level of structure, we shall be considering primarily three: grammatical person, definiteness and "demonstrativeness". As regards the first of these, we shall accept the time-honoured analysis of three persons in each of two numbers, passing over as irrelevant to the present discussion such obvious difficulties as "polite" usages where a plural form may have singular value or where a form which is morphologically third person may be semantically second person. We shall be concerned here only with the third person, singular and plural.

The feature [± definite], we shall claim, is associated in underlying structure with any NP, whether or not the positive selection of the feature is actually marked on the surface in a given language or in a given context. It is especially important to distinguish rigorously between such a seman- tic feature and the distribution of any one or more morphological ele- ments. Specifically, the feature may normally be not explicitly marked in surface structure (as was the case in Classical Latin), while conversely a form which can have as one of its functions the marking of definiteness is not necessarily playing this role whenever it appears (as is the case with the "definite article" in contemporary French — see the penultimate paragraph of this paper). Notice that the feature [+ definite], when selected, is associated initially with the NP as a whole; realization rules for the language and context in question determine whether and how the feature is marked in surface structure.

The feature [± demonstrative] is closely related to [± definite], in that it can only be selected if the latter feature is positively marked. In our view, moreover — and this is slightly more contentious — the selection of [+ demonstrative] automatically implies the marking of "proximity"[1], the choice being either binary (as in English or French) or ternary (as in Latin or Spanish). In other words, the concept of a demonstrative unmarked for proximity is not allowed for within the framework adopted here. We shall indeed argue strongly that many of the difficulties encountered by Romance linguists in this field are due, in part at least, to the establish- ment and retention of a category described as a "demonstrative unmarked for proximity", particularly within the pronominal system (e.g. *CL is*) but also — in French, at least — within the system of determiners (the so-called *démonstratif neutre* or *démonstratif simple*; cf. Brunot — Bruneau 1969: §§181, 194). To this one may add at times an extreme reluctance to accept that a form originally demonstrative in value (in our full sense) may eventually cease to be so.

The selection of the feature [+ demonstrative], then, necessarily implies the selection also of one of two or three degrees of proximity, depending on the language in question. The choice available in Romance may thus be represented as follows: [+ definite] → [± demonstrative]; [+ demonstrative] → [1,2] or [1,2,3 proximity] or, in a more abbreviated form for convenience, as: [+ definite] [−,1,2,] or [−,1,2,3 proximity]. The category [+ definite, − proximity] will be the centre of our concern throughout this paper.

One final point before we attempt to analyse the Romance data. So far, nothing has been said of a distinction between elements which necessarily colligate with a nominal ("articles" or "determiners", in the context of this discussion) and those which can themselves serve as sufficient expo- nents of an NP, namely "personal", "demonstrative" and "anaphoric" pronouns. This omission is deliberate and reflects our view that such distinctions are surface structure characteristics of particular languages at particular moments. Put in other words, when a given feature, for example [+ definite], occurs in conjunction solely with grammatical person, it may be realized in surface structure as what is traditionally labelled a pronoun, whereas exactly the same feature when it occurs in conjunction with other features such that a noun or noun equivalent is selected from the lexicon, may be realized as an "adjectival" form, i.e. as a determiner. In each case, whether this feature is overtly marked morphologically and if so how, and in particular whether "adjectival" and "pronominal" forms are distinguished, are purely surface phenomena of the language in question. It follows from this that the converse situation, in which various determiners and the semantically equivalent pronouns are morphologically identical, or where there is interaction between the members of two relevant sets, is far from surprising. We are after all dealing with one and the same semantic feature, leaving only the grammatical distinction between *pre-* (or *post-*) nominal form and *pro-*nominal form — a distinction generally self-evident in any case from the context — to be marked or not marked by the language or dialect in question.

Let us now begin an examination of the Romance data. In Classical Latin, we need to consider primarily four forms, all marked as [+ definite] and corresponding in our view to the four categories defined above; these are [1 proximity]: *hic*; [2 proximity]: *iste*; [3 proximity]: *ille*; [− proximity]: *is*. All of these forms could be used both adjectivally and pronominally, but in the latter case if the total feature specification was [+ definite, − proximity], the surface realization in subject position was generally[2] zero. Put in more familiar terms, the distribution of *is* was exactly the same as that of the other subject pronouns of Classical Latin, also marked for person and as [+ definite].[3] Quite simply, when such pronouns functioned as subjects, the information they conveyed in respect of person was already clearly marked by a set of post-verbal affixes, while definiteness was not marked overtly in Classical Latin; in non-subject position, however, the information about person was not otherwise marked and the pronoun was therefore generally necessary in surface structure. In other words, the very omission of an overt subject — with an active verb form at least[4] — would be interpreted as indicating that the subject was [+ definite], with the verb form marking person. If the subject was [− definite] — e.g. 'someone', 'something' etc. — or if some additional information was to be conveyed (e.g. proximity), then of course pronouns were generally required in subject position also.

In the case of determiners, here once again — as is well known — the

feature [+ definite] was generally not explicitly marked in surface structure in Classical Latin.

In essence, then, our claim is that there existed in Classical Latin a set of
three "demonstrative" forms, *hic, iste* and *ille*, differentiated in respect of
proximity and a fourth form, *is*, traditionally also called a demonstrative,
which served rather as the exponent of [+ definite, − proximity] in those
contexts, both "adjectival" and "pronominal" where such a feature was
overtly marked in that language.[5] In particular, we should note that this
form *is* was the normal "anaphoric" pronoun — for example, as the
antecedent of relative clauses, where no opposition of proximity is generally found — whereas it was (above all) *hic* and *ille* which were used when
an opposition of proximity was to be clearly marked.[6] We must bear in
mind finally, however, that, as all pedagogical grammars and commen-
tators agree, there was a certain fluidity in the use of all of these forms
which seems at times to belie the simplicity of the analysis which has just
been presented.

The main theme of this paper, we have said, is to trace the morphosyntactic development of one of the forms mentioned above, namely *ille* and
its derivatives, through Vulgar Latin to French and Spanish. Once again,
we shall be concentrating largely on a single set of changes, those which
eventually prevailed, whereas in reality the Vulgar Latin period in particular saw a whole set of competing developments in this field.

The most important change in Vulgar Latin, within a radical redistribution of the available forms, was a considerable expansion in the role of *ille*
at the expense of *is* and the consequential neutralization of one of the
distinctions outlined above. If we look first at the pronominal system, we
find that *ille*, while retaining its role as a marker of [3 proximity], came to
serve also in the [+ definite, − proximity] role discussed earlier. After a
fairly prolonged period of resistance, at least in the written language
(Trager 1932:15), *is* was lost from Romance[7], as was *hic* (but see also
below, note 8), the generally accepted reason in both cases being the
attrition of these very short forms during a period of rapid phonological
change. For reasons outside the scope of this paper, the functions of *iste*
and an originally identitive form, *ipse*, also changed, with the result that a
Vulgar Latin system emerged as follows: [+ definite, 1 proximity]: *iste*;
[+ definite, 2 proximity]: *ipse*; [+ definite, 3 proximity] and [+ definite,
− proximity]: *ille*. This naturally meant that *ille* was now the appropriate
form to serve as an "anaphoric" pronoun, and also as a "personal"
pronoun in those contexts where such was required in surface structure.

At first sight, it may seem strange for a single form to serve both as a
"true" demonstrative (i.e. marked for proximity) and as a "definite" (but
not demonstrative) pronoun. Examination of the Indo-European lan-

guages reveals, however, that this is by no means unusual. In fact, there are at least three patterns: (a) the [2 proximity] or [3 proximity] forms — depending on whether the language in question has a binary or ternary opposition of proximity — are distinct from the [– proximity] forms (e.g. Classical Latin, Modern Spanish); (b) they are the same (e.g. Vulgar Latin and modern spoken German); or (c) they are distinguished at times but not consistently (e.g. English).

If we look briefly for a moment at English, we find '*the ones* I bought yesterday' (a [+ definite, – proximity] form) and '*those* I bought yesterday' (a basically [+ definite, 3 proximity] form) used virtually interchangeably. (Such constraints as there are appear to be syntactic rather than semantic; note that in certain contexts, such as with a genitive noun, a zero form is used, thus *it is Peter's* (= 'that/the one of Peter').) The important thing to bear in mind at this stage is that where a "demonstrative" form is used, it is the remote form *that* which is pressed into service. Equally, in Vulgar Latin it is no accident that it is the "remote" demonstrative, *ille*, which serves to make good the deficiency caused by the loss of *is*. It seems clear, in fact, by virtue of considerable morphological and syntactic evidence, that a "non-proximate" demonstrative may very often serve in addition as the unmarked member of that particular paradigm, i.e. with a [+ definite, – proximity] value.

Some English evidence therefore exists for the overlap of *that* in its unmarked role and *the one*, which we have seen to be one pronominal marker of the category [+ definite, – proximity]. (We should observe, of course, that one can also say *thóse which Peter bought* (*not thése*), where the emphatic stress makes it clear we are now back within the realms of true demonstratives.) It is no accident that it is *that* (rather than *this*) which occurs in structures such as *that is* (cf. Latin *id est*) and the like and why, in those dialects of English where one finds overlap between "demonstrative" and "personal" pronouns — these latter not, of course, being marked for proximity — it is *that* and *those* which ring the changes with *it, they* and *them*. Equally in Italian, the normal anaphoric form is *quello*, which serves also as a remote demonstrative in that language (cf. also note 18). Further evidence on this point will be presented below in a discussion of the role of *ille* as a determiner. We should note at this stage, however, that overlap between "demonstrative" and "anaphoric" pronouns is apparently independent of overlap between either of these categories and third person "personal pronouns"; thus in Italian, as we have seen, anaphorics and remote demonstratives, functioning as unmarked forms, overlap, but not personal pronouns, whereas in Spanish anaphorics and personal pronouns overlap although — in the modern languages — remote demonstratives are morphologically distinct. (As we shall see shortly, it is in Spanish that one finds by far the neatest distribution of forms.)

The attribution of both "remote" and "unmarked" functions to one and the same member of the "demonstrative" paradigm would also explain very neatly the often noted significantly greater frequency of such forms in comparison with the exponents of the [1 proximity] category. For example, Gougenheim et al.'s recent survey of contemporary French (1964:216) observes "il faut noter que les formes en *-ci* sont rares" while Trager observes (1932:184–185) that the form *iste*, definitely a [1 proximity] form in Vulgar Latin, is "very uncommon". One may legitimately suppose that *this* and *that* and their equivalents in their full demonstrative sense occur with roughly equal frequency, but that the occurrences of the latter are considerably inflated by the unmarked functions which they also have.[8]

So there seems to be no reason in principle why the analysis of Vulgar Latin pronominal forms presented above should be unacceptable, and it certainly seems to account elegantly and economically for the observable data. We must now turn to the determiner system of Vulgar Latin, to see to what extent parallel changes can be observed there.

As one might expect on the basis of what has gone before, the determiner system of Vulgar Latin underwent a complex change, as the ultimate result of which *ille* ended up with a greatly expanded role. Briefly, as part of the well-known and general tendency for Vulgar Latin and Romance to mark explicitly and distinctly in surface structure elements of meaning marked either agglutinatively or not (overtly) at all in Classical Latin (the "development from synthesis to analysis"), the feature [+ definite, − proximity] came to be marked more and more often in Vulgar Latin. (In other words, a "definite article" became steadily more frequent.) The obvious candidate for such a role, however, namely *is*, was, as we have already seen, lost in Vulgar Latin, and once again *ille* extended its role to fill the vacant slot. (There is one important complication here, however, not found to anything like the same extent within the pronominal system, which is that *ille* as a (non-pronominal) marker of [+ definite, − proximity] was significantly rivalled by *ipse*; in the end, however, *ille* predominated almost everywhere.[9]) *Ille* therefore came as a determiner to have the same double function as we have already ascribed to it when acting pronominally.

In essence, then, *ille* maintained in Vulgar Latin its value as a marker of [+ definite, 3 proximity] and came to mark also [+ definite, − proximity]. As a result of this change, *ille*, while retaining at first at least its demonstrative functions, was also used both as a 'personal' and an 'anaphoric' pronoun (these both also being [+ definite, − proximity]), and additionally came to be used more and more pre-nominally (in Romanian, post-nominally) as the appropriate determiner to mark a particular nominal unspecified in respect of proximity. It is from this starting point that the systems of the modern Romance languages all derive.

Before looking at French and Spanish in some detail, we must just examine briefly one further change which was clearly already well under way in Vulgar Latin. While we have seen that it is possible, particularly within the pronominal system, for one form to serve both as a "non-near" demonstrative and as a marker of [+ definite, − proximity], there are clearly times when it is important to have available a form which is unambiguously [+ definite, 3 proximity]. Use of emphatic stress is one way to circumvent this difficulty, context — as with pairs of adversatives — another; but at times a distinct form may well be desirable, to put it no more highly. In Vulgar Latin, as a concomitant to the increasing use of *ille* and *ipse* as definite articles and as personal and anaphoric pronouns, new reinforced forms came into use when [2 proximity] or [3 proximity] was to be clearly marked; and, presumably by analogy, similar reinforced forms were introduced to mark [1 proximity] although *iste* was, for the reasons discussed earlier, rarely if ever used to mark [+ definite, − proximity]. The details of these reinforced forms need not concern us here (cf. Harris 1978a:70–71); suffice it to say that, ultimately, forms prefixed by the elements **accu-* or *ecce* came to be used in certain circumstances by all the Romance languages.

Let us now examine the functions which *ille* has retained and those which **accu-ille* or *ecce-ille* have taken over. Looking first at determiners, we find a clear distinction between reflexes of *ille*, used to mark [+ definite, − proximity] and reflexes of **accu-/ecce-ille*, which were pressed into service to mark [2 proximity] (within binary systems) or [3 proximity] (within ternary systems). If we look initially at Spanish, we find the position unchanged to this day: *el* etc. (<*ille*) is used (among other things) as the exponent of [+ definite, − proximity], while *aquel* etc. (< **accu-ille*) is used as the exponent of [+ definite, 3 proximity]. In other words, a Classical Latin system where these two values were marked by zero and *ille* respectively gave way to a Vulgar Latin system where the same form *ille* served with both values, while the categories came — within the determiner system under discussion here — to be redifferentiated in Spanish, *el* being opposed to *aquel*. (The situation within the pronominal system is discussed below.) Interestingly, the reinforcing participle **accu* — introduced, it will be recalled, to indicate clearly the demonstrative value of a particular form — has been lost in the case of the [1 proximity] and [2 proximity] forms, OSp *aqueste* and *aquese* losing out to their unreinforced rivals *este* and *ese*. This is clearly possible once a final choice of exponent for the category [+ definite, − proximity] (the "definite article") has been made, since while *aquel* remains opposed to *el* as we have seen, *(aqu)este* and *(aqu)ese* are invariably demonstrative in value.[10]

In Old French, the position was in essence similar, except that the ternary opposition of proximity of Vulgar Latin, maintained as we have seen in Spanish, had been reduced to a binary one in Old French. Thus we find *le* etc. (< *ille*) opposed to *cil* etc. (< *ecce ille*), the [1 proximity] demonstrative in this case being *cist* (< *ille iste*). Note that the unreinforced form *ist*, which one might have expected in view of the pattern we have just observed in Spanish, did not in fact survive the earliest texts.[11] The situation has subsequently changed considerably in French, as we shall see in due course.[12]

Having established the — fairly unsurprising — evolution of these elements within the determiner system, let us now look at the corresponding pronominal system, first of all in Spanish. Here, a very striking pattern emerges, which appears to validate the semantic analysis presented at the outset of this paper. The form *el*, which we have seen to be used to mark [+ definite, − proximity] within the determiner system, is also used as both an "anaphoric" and as a (third person) "personal" pronoun. (Purely orthographic accents are ignored in this discussion.) Of course there are allomorphic variants within the *el* paradigm and its equivalents elsewhere in Romance whose precise distribution in different syntactic contexts needs to be handled by detailed realization rules of the kind proposed by Raposo (1973:386). (This is particularly true in respect of conjunctive subject pronouns, for clear historical reasons.) This purely morphological variation, where the forms concerned are, with only trivial exceptions, in complementary distribution, should not obscure the fact that every one of the traditionally separate categories whose essential semantic value is [+ definite, − proximity] has in fact the same exponent in Spanish, whereas forms marking [1] [2] or [3 proximity] — whether "adjectivally" or "pronominally" — are morphologically distinguished in some way. It is interesting to note that all of the functions gained by *ille* etc. in Vulgar Latin are retained by *el* etc. in Spanish, whereas the original Classical Latin function of that form — to indicate remote proximity — is now marked by the reinforced form *aquel*, so that the situation which we suggested must have existed in Vulgar Latin — with one and the same form having both a marked and unmarked value in respect of proximity — has been significantly changed, each element of meaning now being consistently indicated and distinguished.

We should also note, before leaving Spanish, that formal near-identity between "adjectival" and "pronominal" markers of a given semantic category is a widespread feature of the language. Such a situation exists with the "true" demonstratives, with indefinites, with possessives and so on. Modern French, on the other hand, as we shall see, (though not Old French), systematically differentiates morphologically between syntactically — but not semantically — distinct functions. In the case of the category [+ definite, − proximity], the differences between the two languages are less than elsewhere, because the retention of case distinctions within the personal pronoun paradigm but not within those of the definite article or the anaphoric pronoun necessarily leads to more morphological variation in the former category. Note that even here, however, the distinction in Spanish is not between "pronoun" and "determiner" but between "personal pronoun" and "anaphoric pronoun" + "determiner", the last two categories having identical exponents.

We are now in a position to turn once again to the situation in French. We have already seen that Old French developed within its determiner system an opposition between *le* etc. [+ definite, − proximity] *cest* etc. [+ definite, 1 proximity] and *cel* etc. [+ definite, 2 proximity].[13] The two latter forms could serve in principle with both adjectival and pronominal functions, although in general rather fuller forms, capable of bearing stress, were selected from the two fairly complex paradigms[14] in contexts where a pronoun was required. When one makes allowance for the retention of case distinctions within the personal pronoun system (cf. note 13), then one can say exactly the same about the definite article/personal pronoun forms as about those of the demonstrative: one complex paradigm, derived in this instance from (unreinforced) *ille*, provides all the forms necessary for both these two traditionally distinct categories, each with the value [+ definite, − proximity].

The Old French system, therefore, was not at all unlike that of modern Spanish. There is, nonetheless, one important observation which needs to be made, and this concerns "anaphoric" pronouns. It is clear that Old French hesitated between *le* etc. and *cel* etc., in this role[15] (cf. Väänänen 1967:§275; Foulet 1968:§70); had the choice been in favour of the former, then the system of oppositions within Old French would have been almost identical with that of Spanish. In fact, the *cel* set early prevailed. One obvious reason why French may have eliminated *le, la, les* in this role is the ongoing development in that language of an increasingly rigid distinction between items capable of bearing stress and those not so capable, itself part of the move towards the adoption of phrasal stress as the norm in modern French; by this token, *le, la, les*, perfectly acceptable as "definite articles" or "conjunctive object pronouns", would no longer be suitable as (disjunctive) anaphoric pronouns. In such a situation, the remote demonstrative in its unmarked capacity, already discussed, could clearly be expected to make good the deficiency; hence the use of *cel*. The position only remained thus briefly, however, by virtue of a development which we are about to discuss.

It is evident that the opposition between [1 proximity] and [2 proximity] demonstratives is no longer made in French by the selection of forms derived from the *ecce iste* or the *ecce ille* paradigms respectively. For reasons discussed in detail by Price (1969), this morphological distinction gave way, within both the determiner and the pronominal system, to one based on the selection of one or other of two postposed elements, *-ci* and *-là*. (In other words, Old French *cest livre* is replaced by *ce livre-ci*, while *cel livre* is replaced by *ce livre-là*.) This change gave rise, apparently by chance, to the possibility of a structure *ce livre*, potentially differentiated both from *le livre* on the one hand and *ce livre-ci/-là* on the other, and to a corresponding additional possibility within the pronoun system (*celui* as opposed to *celui-ci/-là*). The use made of these additional possibilities is discussed shortly.

Let us now remind ourselves of a point made earlier: that French — unlike Spanish — systematically differentiates morphologically between determiners and the corresponding pronouns. A very clear example, not forming part of the topic under examination here, is the almost total divergence in French between the forms of the possessive adjectives and those of the possessive pronouns, whereas in Spanish, with the exception of the reduced pronominal forms *mi, tu* and *su*, one set of forms can be used with either adjectival function (i.e. as determiners) or as pronouns. This fairly systematic differentiation between determiners and the equivalent pronouns is however a relatively recent development in French, the reasons for which have been noted briefly above in connection with the discussion of anaphoric pronouns. As part of this process, demonstrative adjectives and pronouns, still virtually identical in Spanish, are now wholly separate in the modern language, *ce, cette* and *ces* (with *-ci/-là*) being opposed to *celui, celle, ceux* and *celles* (also with *-ci/-là*). That these forms remain semantically related, however, no one doubts; and yet, with one minor exception,[16] the formal relationship between the demonstrative adjective (a conjunctive form) and the demonstrative pronoun (a disjunctive form) is strikingly similar to that between the "definite article" and the corresponding[17] forms of the "personal pronoun", i.e. the disjunctive forms, as the tabulation opposite shows; once again we find strong morphological support for regarding definite articles, personal pronouns and anaphoric pronouns as differing surface realizations of but one underlying semantic category.

Once allowance has been made for the differentiation or non-differentiation of determiners and pronouns in French and Spanish, one

	demonstratives (with -ci/là)	definite articles: third person pronouns
conjunctive (determiner)	ce cette ces	le la les
disjunctive (pronoun)	celui celle ceux celles	lui elle eux elles

observes the striking parallels in the basic structure of these languages in the area under discussion. One distinguishing feature remains to be highlighted, however: the use of *celui* (without -*ci* or -*là*) as an anaphoric pronoun in French.

I have argued elsewhere (Harris 1977) that *celui* without -*ci* or -*là* should not, despite its etymology, be analyzed in synchronic terms as a demonstrative, in that it does not — cannot — serve to mark proximity. In our terms, then, the *celui* paradigm is, like the personal pronouns, a marker of the category [+ definite, − proximity]. It seems clear, as was noted earlier, that this set of forms came to serve as the normal anaphoric pronoun in French while it was still functioning also as the remote demonstrative (i.e. *cel* as opposed to *cest*), a dual marked:unmarked role which we have seen to be widespread in the case of non-near demonstratives. In this case, however, the marked role was gradually taken over by *celui-là*, leaving *celui* as a syntactically conditioned variant of the personal pronoun (*not* of the demonstrative pronoun) occurring as the marker of [+ definite, − proximity] in certain specifiable environments, e.g. as the antecedent of a restrictive relative clause or a prepositional phrase. (For a similar conclusion in respect of Portuguese, where however the current anaphoric pronoun, unlike *celui*, has never had demonstrative value, see Raposo 1973:385–386.)

The occurrence of forms not marked in respect of proximity as anaphoric pronouns (in the sense in which that term is used throughout this paper) is semantically to be expected, in that the item under discussion is generally precisely specified by the linguistic context ('the ones I bought yesterday', 'the one on the table'). Equally, it is not surprising to find a non-near demonstrative used with its unmarked value (as in Italian[18], Old French and, at times, in English). When the marking of proximity is semantically motivated, however, then a demonstrative is perfectly acceptable, in English as in all the Romance languages. (For representative French examples, see Grevisse 1975:§532.)

So here too the difference between French and Spanish is more apparent than real, the former language merely having a higher degree of syntactically conditioned allomorphy in respect of the category [+ definite, − proximity].

We may thus conclude the main body of this paper by reiterating the view that, within the Romance family at least and very probably in many other languages also, important insights may be gained if one recalls that the traditionally distinct categories of "definite article" "(third person) personal pronoun" and "anaphoric pronoun" all have in common the marking of the element of meaning [+ definite, − proximity]. In languages which typically do not distinguish between determiners and the corresponding pronouns, one set of forms may accordingly be expected to fill all these functions; and indeed, in Spanish, only the greater range of case distinctions retained within the personal pronoun paradigm obscures this pattern. The Spanish exponents of the categories listed above have a common etymon, *ille*, which itself had these same functions in Vulgar Latin, with the added complication that it served also as a "non-proximate" demonstrative; we have argued that it is not unusual for one form both to serve as a non-proximate demonstrative and to be used with at least some of the [− proximity] values under discussion here.[19] In Old French, the position was much the same as in Modern Spanish, except that *le* etc. was early rivalled by *cel* as the appropriate anaphoric pronoun form. One must add to this the progressive divorce during the evolution of Old to Modern French between adjectival and pronominal forms, which tends to obscure the fact that *le, il/lui* and *celui* (without *-ci* or *-là*) are, to this day, purely formal variants which all derive ultimately from that one Vulgar Latin form, *ille*, which has come to mark the [+ definite, − proximity] category so widely in Romance.

A short postscript appears to be in order to conclude this paper. Linguistic change is a never-ending process and appears once again to be affecting this particular area of French — and, to a lesser extent, the other Romance languages — in a way discussed at some length in Harris 1977 and 1978a. Briefly, *le/la/les* have acquired a number of functions over and above that of marking [+ definite, − proximity], discussed here. Certain additional occurrences of *le/la/les*, such as their use with nouns generic in value, may conceivably be accountable for by the addition of another semantic feature to the range which we have been considering hitherto; certain others seem to be explicable only in syntactic terms, *le* now serving as the appropriate "unmarked" determiner in surface structure when no determiner is semantically motivated, in the same way that *il*, in addition to being opposed to *je, tu, elle* etc., is used also as the "unmarked" subject pronoun — for example, with impersonal verbs — when there would otherwise be an unacceptable void in subject position in surface structure.

(Note how, once again, derivatives of *ille* come to play a certain role regardless of whether the appropriate surface realization is as a determiner or as a pronoun). *Le/la/les*, therefore, while certainly still serving often as the marker of [+ definite, − proximity], are to some extent at least compromised in this role by the multiplicity of their other uses. In French[20], however, an alternative paradigm is available which can increasingly serve as a "definite article" whenever required, namely *ce/cette/ces* (without, of course, postposed *-ci* or *-là*). This is not the place to expand an argument recently developed elsewhere; but it is interesting to note that, just as the *il/le/lui* paradigm alternates with that of *celui* to mark the "definite pronouns", so *le* and *ce* now alternate as "definite determiners" (with *celui . . . -ci/-là* and *ce . . . -ci/-là* available for truly demonstrative uses). Whereas the choice between *il/le/lui* and *celui* is largely syntactically regulated, as we have seen, that between *le* and *ce* is less clearly determined, *ce* being most likely where *le* is in some way inadequate, by virtue of its other functions, as a marker of [+ definite, − proximity] (e.g. with abstract nouns) but found also in other contexts from time to time. It seems clear, therefore, that the existence of the *ce/cette/ces* paradigm, which arose largely by accident, would enable French to maintain its present system of marking definiteness and demonstrativeness even if the 'definite articles' *le/la/les* come at some future date to be, for instance, nothing but the formal markers of the presence of a noun, and to lose entirely their value as markers of [+ definite, − proximity].

In Classical Latin, then, an element of meaning [+ definite, − proximity] was not normally marked, whether as a determiner or as a personal pronoun, in surface structure, though a form, *is*, was available when required. In Vulgar Latin, the remote demonstrative *ille*, doubling up as an unmarked form, served with this value when required, which was increasingly often, as part of the increasing tendency in Vulgar Latin to mark elements of meaning analytically and explicitly. In modern Romance, [+ definite, − proximity] must be marked, normally by derivatives of *ille*, when colligated with a nominal, as it must also with a verb in French, in which contexts it may still be omitted from surface structure in Spanish when functioning as surface subject. Finally, inasmuch as an "unmarked" determiner or personal pronoun has developed — particularly in French — this too shares the same exponent, once again derived from *ille*. The study of the history of one particular morphological item, *ille*, its predecessor *is*, and its derivatives in contemporary Romance provides striking confirmation of the initial hypothesis that definite articles, (third person) personal pronouns and anaphoric pronouns are best regarded as one single class of elements with a common semantic value and with

surface formal variation to be explained in terms of syntactically conditioned allomorphy.

Comments made by a number of colleagues at the conference point
quite clearly to the view that an analysis such as that presented here is in
no way limited in its application to the field of Romance. I have gratefully
followed up these suggestions and the results of this further investigation
appear in Harris 1980.

Notes

* As the final version of this paper was being prepared, I was able to consult C. G. Lyons'
  Ph.D. thesis *Constituents of the determiner and their evolution in Romance.* I am happy to
  acknowledge the extent to which reading and discussing this work helped to clarify my
  attitude towards several of the points discussed in this paper.
1. Recall, with Price (1971:p.121, n.1), that "the distinction between ... "nearness"
   and ... "distance" is a subjective, not an objective one: it is fundamentally one of
   nearness or remoteness of interest". We should note also that this set of oppositions is at
   times pressed into service with a secondary function, e.g. to add a pejorative overtone,
   but this is beyond the scope of the present paper.
2. As with other subject pronouns, *is* could be used when emphatic or adversative.
3. For a discussion of this point in the context of a more general examination of deixis, cf.
   Lyons (1968:276).
4. For the position with passive or reflexive verbs, cf. Harris 1978b.
5. Trager summarizes a similar view when he writes (1932:13–14): "The "that" character
   of *is* is not very marked in the adjective uses, and is almost wholly absent in the
   pronominal ones". Trager was describing the situation in (written) Vulgar Latin, in this
   respect at least little different from the Classical Latin position under discussion here.
6. *Hic* and *ille* were accordingly used to mark such contrasts as 'the former': 'the latter'. See,
   for example, Gildersleeve and Lodge (1895:§307).
7. Except in a very few cases such as Italian *desso* (< ID IPSU(M)); cf. Väänänen,
   1967:§270.
8. We may now elaborate somewhat on the demise of *hic*, noted earlier. *Hic* was first ousted
   from its [1 proximity] role, where it was replaced, as we have seen, by *iste*, a process
   already underway in Classical Latin. (Väänänen, for instance, cites (1967:§271) a form
   iste *dies* 'this very day' in Juvenal.) *Hic* was not immediately lost, however, but seems to
   have been used for several centuries as an alternative to *is* as an exponent of the [+
   definite, – proximity] category, a use in which, as we have seen, *ille* eventually predominated. Thus Trager observes (1932:5), of *is* and *hic*, that "when either of them occurs in a
   context which implies no contrast, the meaning approaches that of the undifferentiated
   demonstrative, French *ce*". (Of this "undifferentiated demonstrative", we shall have
   more to say below.) This usage of *hic* accounts not only for such forms as OFr *ço* (>*ce*), It
   ciò (< *ecce hoc*), which have no connotations of proximity, but also for the fact that *hic*
   was much more frequent in Vulgar Latin (Trager, *loc. cit.*) than could easily be recon-
   ciled, as we have just seen, with a [1 proximity] value.
9. The principal exceptions are certain dialects of Catalan, and in Sardinian; Aebischer
   (1948) gives a full and fascinating survey of the conflict between *ille* and *ipse* as

"definite articles" in Romance. Note that we can now refine our earlier claim that "remote" demonstratives may also function as unmarked forms by observing that in languages with three-fold oppositions of proximity within their demonstrative systems, either [2 proximity] or [3 proximity] forms may apparently be used in an unmarked capacity at times; it is "near" demonstratives which seem to be wholly excluded from this role. The fact that when a three-term demonstrative system is reduced to two terms it is generally (as in French) the second and third degrees of proximity which merge lends further support to the view that the fundamental opposition is between "near" — [1] — and "far" — [2] and [3] — with the differentiation between [2] and [3] being secondary. (But cf. the final part of note 10.)

10. By the same token, one would expect dialects choosing derivatives of *ipse* as a definite article not to use unreinforced forms derived from the same etymon as a demonstrative. Catalan provides an interesting example of this, in that Eastern Catalan, retaining derivatives of *ipse* as a definite article to this day in certain areas, particularly the Balearic Islands, normally shows reinforced *aqueix* etc. as the "middle distance" demonstrative, whereas in Western Catalan, where derivates of *ille* are now almost universally found as definite articles, unreinforced demonstratives such as *eix* occur widely. (See, for example, Badía Margarit 1951:279–289, esp. p. 282.) (It seems appropriate to note also in this connection that, in spoken Catalan at least, the three-term demonstrative system has largely given way to the two-term one, with derivatives of *(accu-) iste* in certain dialects and *(accu-) ipse* in other dialects being used to mark both [1 proximity] and [2 proximity] (cf. Moll 1952:§470); this development therefore diverges from that suggested in note 9 to be the more widespread pattern.)

11. In the Strasbourg Oaths one finds, for instance, *d'ist di in avant.* The same text also includes the form *cist* with the same value.

12. In many dialects of Italian — i.e. those with a binary opposition of proximity — the position today is identical with that of Old French, *il* etc. (< *ille*) being opposed to *quello* etc. [<*accu ille*), the [1 demonstrative] form being *questo* etc. (<*accu iste*).

13. Here and henceforth the masculine oblique singular forms are cited. This is because virtually all modern French noun and adjective forms derive from the Vulgar Latin/Old French oblique case and not from the nominative. The allomorphic variation within the paradigm of the third person pronoun, both in Spanish (as discussed above) and in modern French, derives very largely from the exceptional survival of derivatives of the Latin nominative, dative and genitive cases.

14. For a readily accessible survey, cf. Foulet (1968:§236).

15. Foulet cites, for instance, (1968:§70), *ia de Dieu* (= *celle de Dieu*), *les sa mère* (= *ceux de sa mère*) etc.

16. The "minor exception" is the occurrence of *cette* rather than **ça* as the feminine singular demonstrative adjective.

17. Recall the retention of forms distinguished for case within this paradigm.

18. In Italian, *quello* functions both as a "remote" demonstrative and as an anaphoric pronoun. Here we find once again the situation alluded to earlier in which a "non-proximate" demonstrative may also have an unmarked value in non-contrastive structures. Note that, unlike *ille* in Vulgar Latin, *quello* can not also be found as a "definite article" or as a "personal pronoun".

19. Vulgar Latin appears to be exceptional in that all the [− proximity] uses could be marked at times by *ille*. As we saw earlier, however, reinforced forms such as *accu-ille* were already available when required in Vulgar Latin.

20. But not Spanish or Italian.

References

Aebisher, P.
   1948   "Contribution à la protohistoire des articles ILLE et IPSE dans les langues romanes", *Cultura Neolatina* 8:181–203.
Badía Margarit, A.
   1951   *Gramática histórica catalana* (Barcelona: Noguer).
Brunot, F. — C. Bruneau
   1969   *Précis de grammaire historique de la langue française* (Paris: Masson).
Dineen, F. P. (ed.)
   1966   *Georgetown Monograph Series on Languages and Linguistics* 19 (Washington, D.C.: Georgetown University Press).
Foulet, L.
   1968   *Petite syntaxe de l'ancien français* (Paris: Champion).
Gildersleeve, B. L. — G. Lodge
   1895   *Gildersleeve's Latin grammar* (New York/London: Macmillan).
Gougenheim, G. — P. Rivenc — R. Michea — A. Sauvageot
   1964   *L'élaboration du français fondamental* (1er degré) (New York: Chilton Books).
Grevisse, M.
   1975   *Le bon usage* (Gembloux: Duculut).
Harris, M. B.
   1977   " 'Demonstratives', 'articles' and 'third person pronouns' in French", *ZRPh* 93:249–261.
   1978a   *The evolution of French syntax: a comparative approach* (London: Longman).
   1978b   "Alternatives to the morphological passive in Romance", *Semasia* 5:65–87.
   1980   "The marking of definiteness: a diachronic perspective", in *Papers from the Fourth International Conference on Historical Linguistics*, edited by E. C. Traugott, R. Labrum and S. Shepherd (Amsterdam: Benjamins).
Lyons, C. G.
   1977   *Constituents of the determiner and their evolution in Romance* (unpublished Ph.D. dissertation, London).
Moll, F. de B.
   1952   *Gramática histórica catalana* (Madrid: Gredos).
Postal, P. M.
   1966   "On so-called 'pronouns' in English", in Dineen (ed.) 1966:177–206.
Price, G.
   1969   "La transformation du système français des démonstratifs", *ZRPh* 85:489–505.
   1971   *The French language: present and past* (London: Arnold).
Raposo, E. P.
   1973   "Sobre a forma *o* em português", *Boletim de Filologia* 22:361–415.
Sommerstein, A.
   1971   "On the so-called definite article in English", *Linguistic Inquiry* 3:197–209.
Trager, G. L.
   1932   *The use of the Latin demonstratives (especially ILLE and IPSE) up to 600 A.D., as the source of the Romance article* (New York: Publications of the Institute of French Studies).
Väänänen, V.
   1967   *Introduction au latin vulgaire* (Paris: Klincksieck).

JOAN BYBEE HOOPER

Child morphology and morphophonemic change

A controversy has raged for nearly a century over the influence of the child on linguistic development (see for example, Jespersen 1922).* In recent research there has been some attention given to the child's role in phonological change (Stampe 1973, Dressler 1974, Drachman 1976), and some comparisons drawn between child syntax and syntactic change (Baron 1977, Slobin 1975) but reports on the child's role in mor-phophonemic change have either been very general, or largely anecdotal. The present paper is an initial attempt to explore the relation of mor-phophonemic change and the acquisition of morphology in a more sys-tematic and detailed way.[1] It is based on progress made recently in the understanding of the acquisition of morphological systems. Several authors have formulated general principles which seem to govern the acquisition process (Slobin 1973, Simões — Stoel-Gammon 1977). These principles will be compared to the principles proposed to describe the general properties of morphophonemic change, such as the hypotheses of Kuryłowicz (1949), Mańczak (1958, 1963), and Ven-nemann (1972a). It is recognized that none of the principles applying to acquisition and change is absolute, for morphology seems always to admit exceptions. Furthermore, the entire framework is still rather general, as there is no well-articulated theory that explains the intricate interaction of formal and semantic properties in morphology. However, a close look at child morphology suggests a more elaborate framework that will be useful in the study of both the acquisition process and the process of change.

Given certain principles governing acquisition and change, the purpose of this paper is to ask whether the two sets of principles do in fact coincide in enough cases to make child language a plausible source for mor-phophonemic change. It is not enough, however, to show that the two processes exhibit similar characteristics, because this does not necessarily establish a causal relation between them. It will be necessary in addition to explicate the mechanism for implementation of a morphophonemic change originating in the language acquisition process. While I will make some suggestions concerning the latter point, I cannot treat this problem in any detail. I will concentrate instead on making a systematic comparison of the output of child morphology and morphophonemic change and I will give a detailed analysis of one aspect of the acquisition process which has interesting implications for both synchronic and diachronic morphophonemics.

1   There are two types of principles that have been formulated in an attempt to describe the dominant tendencies in child language and in morphophonemic change: principles based on semantic criteria and principles based on formal criteria. We begin with the semantic principles.

In language acquisition it is often observed that the forms of one inflectional category will predominate in the child's speech, largely replacing other related inflectional forms. For example, a widespread (if not universal) tendency is for children to use only the singular forms of nouns for a long period of time (Rūķe-Draviņa [1959] 1973). The singular form tends to be used in all situations before the singular/plural distinction is made semantically, and it continues to be used even when the concept of plurality is evident, as in the phrase "two shoe" (Rūķe-Draviņa [1959] 1973). The semantic concept is present before the formal marking of it appears. Until the proper formal marking is acquired, then, one inflectional form tends to replace all others, in this case the singular form of the noun replaces the plural form. This situation can be summed up by the generalization:

A.   Singular noun forms are acquired before plural noun forms.

Similar generalizations concerning the acquisition of inflectional morphology are as follows:

B.   Present tense is acquired before past tense (Rūķe-Draviņa 1959; Bates 1976; Simões — Stoel-Gammon 1978).
C.   Indicative mood is acquired before the subjunctive (Rūķe-Draviņa 1959; Simões — Stoel-Gammon 1978).
D.   The third singular verb form is acquired before other persons (Rūķe-Draviņa 1959; Bates 1976; Simões — Stoel-Gammon 1978).

It should be borne in mind that there are always exceptions to such generalizations in the speech of individual children. For instance, some verbs may be acquired initially in their first singular present indicative forms, while the majority appear first in the third singular.

These generalizations from the study of child morphology are paralleled by generalizations based on the study of analogical change. Particularly striking are four hypotheses by Mańczak (1958, 1963).

> *Hypothèse VI*: Les formes de l'indicatif provoquent plus souvent la réfection des formes des autres modes que vice versa (1958:387).
>
> *Hypothèse VII*: Les formes du présent provoquent plus souvent la réfection des formes des autres temps que vice versa (1958:388).
>
> *Hypothèse XIII*: Les radicaux et les désinences du singulier subissent moins de changement analogiques que ceux et celles des autres nombres (1963:30).
>
> *Hypothèse XIV*: Les radicaux et les désinences de la troisième personne subissent moins de changements analogiques que ceux et celles des autres personnes (1963:34).

These four hypotheses of Mańczak are the only ones that are based on semantic categories with the exception of three that deal with the very specific cases of geographic names and proper names. It is striking that the four dominant morphological categories he isolates are the same four that were isolated quite independently in the language acquisition literature.

Kuryłowicz (1949) also formulates some general principles of analogical change, although his approach is quite different from Mańczak's. Kuryłwoicz's formulas refer to relation among forms in a grammar, and are stated in terms of the base form of a paradigm:

> Formule II: Les actions dites "analogiques" suivent la direction: formes de fondation → formes fondées, dont le rapport découle de leurs sphères d'emploi (1949:23).

The comparability of the content of this formula to the language acquisition data rests heavily on the meaning of "sphères d'emploi". The accompanying illustrations and the discussion in Kuryłowicz 1968 indicate that the base form is chosen largely on semantic criteria, such that the stem of the semantically unmarked form of the paradigm usually serves as the base form.[2] Examples given are: nominative singular vs. other case forms, present vs. other tenses, indicative vs. other moods, and third person singular vs. other persons (Kuryłowicz 1968:75).

The parallelism between the semantic principles governing analogical change and the acquisition of morphology, then, are quite striking. It must be remembered, however, that in both realms the choice of an unmarked category may be determined by language-specific factors. For instance, in the Russian aspect system the imperfective is unmarked with respect to the perfective aspect (Jakobson 1932), while in Spanish and Portuguese the preterite is unmarked with respect to the imperfect (Comrie 1976).

Simões and Stoel-Gammon suggest a few other generalizations concerning the order of acquisition of different semantic oppositions. They observe that tense, aspect and mood differentiations appear before the differentiation of person, and that person markers are distinguished before number markers in verbs. The parallel for morphological change would be the generalization that certain semantic oppositions (those that are acquired later) are subject to loss before others (those that are acquired earlier). Thus we might predict that person markers on verbs would be lost before tense, aspect and mood markers, and this we know to be generally true (e.g. as in English and Irish).

Kuryłowicz's Formula V may perhaps apply here:

Formule V: Pour rétablir une différence d'ordre central la langue abondonne une différence d'ordre plus marginal (1949:31).

Again Kuryłowicz refers to the relations among forms in a grammar, without providing details concerning the criteria used in establishing the relation.[3] Still the formula suggests an interesting hypothesis: that certain morphological distinctions are more central or basic than others, and that these central distinctions are more stable over time. We will see below that the language acquisition data gives valuable information concerning the status of morphological oppositions in a language, and that this information provides accurate predictions concerning morphophonemic change.

2   On the basis of data concerning the acquisition of forty different languages, Slobin (1973) formulates a series of "Operating Principles" that describe some of the analytic strategies evident in child language. Several of the principles have to do with the acquisition of morphology. They are all based on criteria relating to the formal expression of morphological categories. We will compare Slobin's principles to formal principles formulated to describe morphophonemic change.

Slobin's first principle dealing strictly with morphological form is:

Operating Principle E: Underlying semantic relations should be marked overtly and clearly.

This is a very general principle and corresponds to the very general principle of linguistic change that Vennemann (1972) calls Humboldt's Universal:

> Humboldt's Universal: Suppletion is undesireable, uniformity of linguistic symbolization is desireable: Both roots and grammatical markers should be unique and constant (1972:184).

Vennemann explicitly relates this principle to the acquisition process, saying that it is an "innate principle of linguistic change" (1972:184). How well this principle describes the strategies of children can be seen by comparing Slobin's descriptions of the more specific manifestations of Operating Principle E with other generalizations concerning morphophonemic change.

The first specific instance of Operating Principle E is:

> Universal E 1: A child will begin to mark a semantic notion earlier if its morphological realization is more salient perceptually (ceteris paribus) (Slobin 1973:202).

Slobin adds: "The notions of 'more salient perceptually' and 'ceteris paribus', of course, are in need of more precise definition" (p. 202). One of the instances of perceptual saliency that Slobin mentions is the position of the grammatical marker with respect to the rest of the word. He proposes that suffixes and postpositions are acquired earlier than prefixes and prepositions. No comparable principle of change has been suggested, although the well-known preponderance of suffixing and postpositional languages over prefixing and prepositional languages (Greenberg 1957) is probably relevant here.

One of Mańczak's hypotheses concerning analogical change seems to point to some significance for perceptual saliency.

> Hypothèse V: Les désinences monosyllabiques sont plus souvent remplacées par des désinences polysyllabiques que vice versa (1958:323).

It is not unreasonable to assume that polysyllabic desinences have greater perceptual saliency than monosyllabic desinences, provided that the segmental and suprasegmental composition of the desinences are also comparable. Beyond this, however, it is difficult to draw conclusions from Slobin's Universal E 1, without a well-defined notion of perceptual saliency.

Slobin's Universal E 2 is much clearer:

Universal E 2: There is a preference not to mark a semantic category by Ø ("zero morpheme"). If a category is sometimes marked by Ø and sometimes by some other overt phonological form, the latter will, at some stage, also replace the Ø (p. 202).

A footnote restricts this principle to semantically marked categories, since children do seem content to leave inflections off nominative singulars, third singular present forms, etc. Universal E 2 has a clear parallel among the principles governing analogical change, Mańczak's Hypothesis IV.

Hypothèse IV: Les désinences zéro sont plus souvent remplacées par les désinences pleines que vice versa (1958:321).

Slobin's Universal E 3 does not have such a clear parallel in morphological change:

Universal E 3: If there are homonymous forms in an inflectional system, those forms will tend not to be the earliest inflections acquired by the child; i.e. the child tends to select phonologically unique forms, when available, as the first realization of inflections (p. 203).

Slobin provides only one example to substantiate this hypothesis, the example of the choice of the masculine and neuter *-om* by Russian children as the expression of the instrumental case, rather than the more frequent feminine *-oy*. The latter suffix has five different homonyms in the adjective declensions, while the suffix *-om* has only one homonym, also in an adjective form.

Andersen (1974) mentions morphological changes motivated by the avoidance of homonymy, in which a synonymous inflectional marker with few or no homonyms replaces a marker with many homonyms. To my knowledge, however, no one has proposed a general principle of the form of Kuryłowicz's and Mańczak's, which predicts that morphophonemic changes will result in reduced homonymy more often than in increased homonymy. There is a need then to examine a number of cases of this nature. Let us consider here one example.

In many Spanish dialects of the Americas, the distinction between second and third conjugation is being lost. Except for the infinitive and forms related to this infinitive, i.e. the future and conditional, in the standard language these conjugations are distinct only in the first person plural of the present, e.g. 2nd conjugation *comemos* vs. 3rd conjugation *vivímos.* In the 2nd conjugation, the 1st plural present form is distinct from the 1st plural preterite form, but in the 3rd conjugation there is no distinction:

(1)		2nd conjugation	3rd conjugation
	present	*comémos*	*vivímos*
	preterite	*comímos*	*vivímos*

Some dialects have merged the two conjugations by extending the non-homonymous theme vowel *e* of the 2nd conjugation into the 3rd conjugation, giving a unique marker for 1st plural present (Rosenblat 1946):

(2)		2nd conjugation	3rd conjugation
	present	*comémos*	*vivémos*
	preterite	*comímos*	*vivímos*

While this is the sort of example predicted by Slobin's principle, it does not support a significant tendency in diachrony for the avoidance of homonymy, since in related dialects, the opposite change has occurred, creating greater homonymy: the vowel *í* has replaced *é* in the present tense of the 2nd conjugation, giving -*ímos* for both present and preterite.

Without more data it is rather difficult to assess the validity of Slobin's Universal E 3, and its relation to morphophonemic change. It should be observed here, however, that some language acquisition strategies may disappear too early in the language acquisition process to be of much significance to linguistic change. The diachronic changes we are discussing here take place on the edges of the system, or at the difficult, unstable points in the system. In relation to child language, the changes take place among items that would be acquired late, and the changes occur because such items are not acquired, or are only partially acquired. Therefore, the very first strategies of the child, which (s)he abandons early in the process may not relate at all to morphophonemic change. This should be borne in mind when considering Slobin's Operating Principle F and Universal F 1.

Operating Principle F: Avoid exceptions.

Universal F 1: The following stages of linguistic marking of a semantic notion are typically observed:
(1) no marking,
(2) appropriate marking in limited cases,
(3) overgeneralization of marking (often accompanied by redundant marking),

(4) full adult system (p. 205).

Operating Principle F is not too different from Operating Principle E. Its parallel in historical linguistics is well-known. It is the second half of Sturtevant's paradox, that analogical change creates regularity.

In Universal F 1 we see the various stages of acquisition of an inflection system. Stage (1) is extremely early; here all inflection is simply ignored. In stage (2) some marking occurs, and individual inflected words may be used appropriately, but they have been learned by rote, and no general rules have been formulated. In stage (3) there is abundant evidence of rules, since they are overapplied, and even forms that were correctly used in stage (2) are subject to the over-application of the rules. To attain stage (4), the full adult system, the rules must be properly restricted and exceptions appropriately marked. For changes in a full complex morphological system, stages (1) and (2) are transitted too early to be of importance. The changes we describe as analogical occur because of the overgeneralizations characteristic of stage (3), and the failure to acquire the restrictions and exceptions necessary to match the adult system.

In stage (3) are found both analogical extensions of markers and analogical leveling of alternations. Kuryłowicz's first formula describes extensions:

> Formula I: Un morphème bipartite tend à s'assimiler à un morphème isofonctionnel consistant uniquement en un des deux éléments, c.-à-d. le morphème composé remplace le morphème simple (1949:20).

As examples of this phenomenon, Kuryłowicz gives the extension of German umlaut, *Baum* > **Baum-chen* > *Bäumchen* in diminuitive formation, and in plural formation, *Wald* > *Wälder, Huhn* > *Hühner*.[4] The other sort of overgeneralization characteristic of stage (3) is comparable to analogical leveling, i.e. the failure to produce a morphophonemic alternation. An example in child language is the failure to produce the stem vowel alternation in a Portuguese verb such as [komu] *como* (1st singular present) [kɔmi] *come* (3rd singular present), where the child's forms are [kɔmu], [kɔmi]. Mańczak's Hypothesis II describes levelling:

> Hypothèse II: L'alternance du radical est plus souvent abolie qu'introduite.[5]

In the next section analogical levelling in children's speech is examined in further detail.

Slobin's final Operating Principle dealing with morphological form may be the most important.

> Operating Principle G: The use of grammatical markers should make semantic sense.

> Universal G 1: When selection of an appropriate inflection among a group of inflections performing the same semantic function is determined by arbitrary formal criteria (e.g. phonological shape of stem, number of syllables in stem, arbitrary gender of stem), the child initially tends to use a single form in all environments, ignoring formal selectional restrictions (p. 206).

This means that a one-to-one relation between sound and meaning is preferred (Humboldt's Universal again), and that semantic criteria for formal expression are easier to learn than phonological or other arbitrary criteria. There are numerous examples in recent theoretical discussions which show that reanalysis and changes in non-automatic alternations (extensions or levelling) are motivated by semantic criteria rather than phonological criteria. Among the examples are the case of Maori suffixes discussed by Hale (1971), and the parallel example of French liaison consonants discussed by Klausenberger (1976) and Baxter (1975), the cases of rule inversion in Vennemann (1972b), and the cases of reanalysis in Skousen (1975) and Hooper (1976a). Most of these cases can be explained by the Semantic Transparency Principle of Vennemann (1972b):

> "Usually in natural language, a semantic derivation of secondary conceptual categories from primitive ones, tertiary from secondary ones, etc., is reflected in a parallel syntactic or morphophonological derivation" (p. 240).

Thus the formal manifestation of a secondary category should be made up of the form of the primitive category, plus some modification, e.g. an affix, a stem change. This principle is proposed as a mechanism of change through reanalysis in the language acquisition process. It should be noted that Vennemann's principle subsumes a number of the other principles we have discussed, in particular the semantically-based principles of section 1, and some of the principles based on formal criteria, i.e. the avoidance of zero markers, and the principles behind extension and levelling. Slobin's observation suggests what I have argued (in Hooper 1978), that this semantic principle overrides all others, that the choice of the basic category is a purely semantic choice, and that for non-automatic alternations, the semantic criteria are primary, and formal criteria such as phonological predictability are secondary.

To conclude this section, then, closer examination of the language acquisition process and of morphophonemic change confirms our suspicions of a striking correspondence, such that categories and formal properties that are acquired late tend to change under the influence of categories and formal expressions that are acquired early. The child language data reveals that semantic and cognitive development precede the formal expression of a distinction. Semantic characteristics are primary, basic and acquired first, while the formal properties are added later. It follows that the formal complexities would be eliminated in favour of a more transparent sound-meaning relation. Thus levelling, extension and reanalysis of various types should be common morphophonemic changes, since they represent a move toward more direct expression of semantic categories. Furthermore, the order of acquisition of the semantic categories predicts that the unmarked categories will exert an influence over the marked categories rather than vice versa.

3   We turn now to an examination of the details of the acquisition of alternating, inflected forms, to see if the details support a relation between child language and morphophonemic change to the same extent that the general principles do. We are relying primarily here on the descriptions by Stoel-Gammon (1976) and Simões — Stoel-Gammon (1977) of four children acquiring the Brazilian Portuguese inflectional system. We will examine the way the acquisition process gives internal structure to a paradigm, influencing both the inflectional desinences and the stem alternations. We will discuss the implications for morphophonemic change as they arise.

In the Brazilian Portuguese verbal system, there are only two person distinctions indicated by inflection, the first person vs. the second/third person. (We will refer to the latter simply as the third person.) There are three conjugation classes, but distinctions between these classes are not made for every inflectional category. The forms for the singular in the present indicative are as follows:

	1st conjugation	2nd conjugation	3rd conjugation
infinitive	*falar* 'speak'	*bater* 'hit'	*abrir* 'open
first sg.	*falo*	*bato*	*abro*
second/third	*fala*	*bate*	*abre*

Simões and Stoel-Gammon report that the first forms used by children are the third singular forms, and they are substituted for all other forms. For instance, the third singular form is used in contexts where first person is clearly intended semantically. It is used with the first singular pronoun *eu* 'I' when this form appears. The appearance of the pronoun means of course that the semantic category has been acquired. Finally, the first person inflection *-o* appears on the verb. This distinction between first and third person singular is among the first distinctions to be marked by inflections.

A subclass of second and third conjugation verbs have a vowel alternation in the verb stem, such that if the third singular form contains the low vowels [ɛ] or [ɔ], the first singular form will contain the vowels [e] or [o] in second conjugation and [i] or [u] in third conjugation.

(3)	2nd conjugation		3rd conjugation	
infinitive	*comer* 'eat'	*beber* 'drink'	*dormir* 'sleep'	*conseguir* 'get'
first sg.	c[o]mo	b[e]bo	d[u]rmo	cons[i]go
third sg.	c[ɔ]me	b[ɛ]be	d[ɔ]rme	cons[ɛ]ge

Initially children produce first singular forms for these verbs with the proper inflection *-o*, but with the stem vowel as it is found in the third singular form (Stoel-Gammon 1976; Simões and Stoel-Gammon 1977). The first singular form, then, is built directly on the third singular stem:

(4)	c[ɔ]mo	b[ɛ]bo	d[ɔ]rmo	cons[ɛ]go

This sequence of events bears a clear relation to historical change. Note first that the inflectional suffix is acquired before the stem vowel alternation. This implies that the alternations are more susceptible to loss through levelling than the inflectional suffixes are, a generalization that is clearly supported by the historical facts (Mańczak 1958; 1963). Note secondly that the mechanisms by which root alternations are levelled, if the levelling has its source in child language, is by substitution of the neutral, third singular stem, for the stem in the other category. That is, a stem vowel is not changed to a vowel that is like that of the third singular stem, but rather, a new first singular form is constructed, using the third singular as the base.

Thus the acquisition of the stem forms shows the influence of the third singular on the first singular form within a single tense. The acquisition of the inflections in the other tenses, however, shows the influences, not of the other persons within the tense, but rather of the inflection for the same person in the other tenses. This is especially clear in the imperfect tense. (The imperfect is acquired after the preterite, but I treat the imperfect here to illustrate the influence of the inflections on one another.) By the time the imperfect is used, first and third singular forms are already distinct in the present and preterite tenses. In Portuguese, the first person singular forms of the imperfect are identical to the third person singular forms: e.g. *ele queria* 'he wanted', *eu queria* 'I wanted'. One of the children studied by Simões and Stoel-Gammon (1978), however, differentiated these forms, using the first singular marker *-o* from the present tense on the imperfect verbs. The child used the form *sabio* for *sabia* 'I knew', and *querilo* for *queria* 'I wanted'. The form *querilo* is particularly interesting. For the third singular form *queria*, the child used the form *querila*. Her first singular form was built on the third singular base *queril* plus the first singular inflection of the present tense (Simões — Stoel-Gammon 1978:16). The third singular stem affects the form of the stem in the other persons of the same tense, but the first person inflection affects first person forms across tenses. This generalization helps us understand the stages in the acquisition of the preterite person markers.

In the adult language the preterite forms are as follows:

(5)	1st conjugation	2nd conjugation	3rd conjugation
infinitive	*falar* 'speak'	*bater* 'hit'	*abrir* 'open'
first sg.	*falei*	*bati*	*abri*
third sg.	*falou*	*bateu*	*abriu*

The third singular forms for each conjugation class have a different inflection, *-ou*, *-eu* and *-iu*, and the first singular forms have two inflections, *-ei* for first conjugation, and *-i* for second and third. As with the present tense the children initially used the third person singular form with all subjects. Interestingly enough there is no evidence of confusion of conjugation classes for the third singular forms. Simões and Stoel-Gammon indicate that even from the earliest usage of preterite forms, the third singular forms are inflected correctly according to conjugation class.

This correct assignment of conjugation class is not, however, carried over to the first singular forms when they are acquired. Instead, the first conjugation inflection *-ei* is used for all first singular forms, giving, e.g. *comei* for *comi*, and *bebei* for *bebi*. This overgeneralization is somewhat perplexing in view of the fact that the children were already making correct conjugation class assignments for the third singular inflection. It can be explained, however, if we bear in mind that the third singular form affects the form of the *stem* of the first singular, but not the inflection. The influence on the inflection comes from the other existing first singular inflection, i.e. the present tense inflection. The present first singular inflection is the same for all conjugation classes, -*o*, and thus offers no model for differentiating conjugation classes.

Projecting now from this data, the direction of influence for stems is as follows:

(6)   STEM

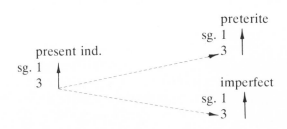

While the direction of influence for person markers is:

(7)   PERSON MARKERS

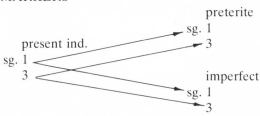

4   If child language is the source of morphophonemic change, then the direction of influence schematized in (6) and (7) will apply to diachronic change. Thus (7) predicts that a person marker in the preterite or imperfect can be replaced by the marker of the same person in the present tense. This diachronic hypothesis in turn implies a hypothesis about synchronic systems: that verbal inflections for person are very likely to be the same across tenses. Many examples of such systems are known, e.g. Latin person inflections, -*o* or -*m*, -*s*, -*t*, -*mus*, -*tis* and -*nt*, occur in every tense and aspect category. Unfortunately, the existence of such a system does not imply prior analogy of the form illustrated in (7), since situations of the predicted type can arise in another way as well. If person markers on verbs develop diachronically from subject pronouns, the identity of person markers across tenses is built into the system from its origin. Thus only attested morphophonemic changes can provide support or falsification for (7) as the direction of diachronic change. This is in contrast with (6) which provides a testable synchronic hypothesis.

The diachronic hypothesis derived from (6) is that a third singular stem form may replace the stems for other person categories of the same tense, but a non-third person stem in one tense will not replace the stem for the same person in another tense. For example, a first singular present stem form will not exert influence over a first singular form in some other tense. Thus the high vowel in Portuguese 1st singular present *sigo* (from *sequir*) will not show up at any point in first singular preterite *sequi*. [6] This hypothesis is testable, but it would be difficult to construct an appropriate corpus on which to test it.

The synchronic hypothesis that corresponds to (6) is more easily testable. The synchronic hypothesis is that alterations in verb stems will be restricted by tense, or aspect, but not by person. [7] That is, there may be a special stem or stem change that occurs in all persons of a particular tense or aspect, but there will not be any such stem or stem change that occurs in a particular person across tenses. Thus we find quite often in Indo-European language a special stem form for different tenses: the Germanic strong verbs had different stems for present, preterite and participle forms, [8] Old Irish strong verbs had present, subjunctive, future, preterite stems, Latin shows stem changes of several types in the perfect aspect, just to name a few. What we do not find is a special stem for, e.g. the first person singular throughout several tenses.

This hypothesis concerning synchronic states may be tested by examining stem alternations in a number of languages in order to determine whether these alternations ever correspond to person categories across tense or aspect categories. The hypothesis was applied to forty-four languages out of a fifty-language stratified probability sample constructed by Revere Perkins (Perkins 1978). The sample consists of one language from each phylum according to the Voegelin and Voegelin (1966) classification, as long as no two languages belong to the same geographical-cultural grouping according to Kenny (1974). This sampling method ensures the widest possible distribution, and controls for genetic similarity and areal influence. Only forty-four of the fifty languages were used in the present study since adequate information about morphology on the remaining six was not yet available.

Languages which do not have person inflections on verbs are not relevant for the study, and were thus excluded. [9] This amounted to twenty-six languages, and left eighteen on which the hypothesis could be tested. Of these eighteen, there were two (Santa Cruz, a Papuan language, and Pawnee, a Macro-Siouan language) for which no stem alternations were reported. In two other languages (Kutenai, of undetermined genetic affiliation, and Ojibwa, Macro-Algonquin) stem alternations occur, conditioned by a number of affixes, but no clear semantic correlation emerged. The remaining fourteen languages have stem alternations that correspond to tense, aspect, finiteness, number, animacy of direct object, but never to person. This generalization covers all verb stem alternations reported in the individual grammars, even alternations in highly irregular verbs.[10]

(8) Languages with verb stem alternations

Language (family)	Stem alternation corresponds to:	Stem alternation corresponds to person:
Acoma (Keres)	number	no
Basque (Undetermined)	tense	no
Burushaski (Undetermined)	tense/animacy of DO	no
Classical Nahuatl (Aztec-Tanoan)	tense	no
Diegueño (Hokan)	aspect/number	no
Georgian (Caucasian)	tense	no
Ket (Undetermined)	aspect/tense	no
Miwok (Penutian)	tense/aspect	no
West Greenlandic (American-Arctic- Paleo-Siberian)	tense	no
Quileute (Chimakua)	aspect	no
Serbo-Croatian (Indo-European)	tense/finiteness	no
Temiar (Malaya)	aspect	no
Touareg Berber (Afro-Asiatic)	aspect	no
Western Apache (Na-Dene)	tense/number	no

These findings overwhelmingly support the synchronic hypothesis and by implication the diachronic hypothesis. If morphophonemic stem changes by person across tenses occurred, then we would find some cases in which alternations correspond to person. Since no cases of this sort were found, we can conclude that changes of this type are extremely rare, if they exist at all.[11]

It should be noted that not all verb stem alternations are the result of morphophonemic change. Their original source is, of course, phonetic change. If the phonetic change is conditioned by the phonological properties of the tense marker, then the alternation will, from its beginning, correspond to a tense category, and morphologically-conditioned change need not be involved. Thus some stem alternations found may have a purely phonetic source and are therefore irrelevant to the study of morphophonemic change.

By the same token, it is possible for stem alternations to be conditioned by the phonetic properties of a particular person marker, giving rise to a stem alternation that corresponds to person across tenses. Since such a development is clearly possible, the synchronic hypothesis is stated too strongly, and is stronger than it needs to be to test the diachronic hypothesis.

Given the possibility of a stem alternation corresponding to person developing from a phonetic source, the findings of the cross-linguistic survey are all the more striking. The data suggest that stem alternations corresponding to tense and aspect categories are relatively stable, whether produced under phonetic or morphological conditioning, while similar alternations corresponding to person are less stable.

It cannot be over-emphasized that a rather modest amount of language acquisition data has suggested a strong hypothesis concerning diachronic morphophonemics and the synchronic organization of verbal paradigms, and that this hypothesis has withstood an extensive cross-linguistic survey. This is shining proof of the relevance of child morphology to the study of morphophonemic change. In the remaining sections, we discuss the implications of these findings.

5   The direction of influence for stems in the language acquisition data follows quite mechanically from the fact that tense distinctions are made earlier than person distinctions. This is true of Latvian (Rūķe-Draviņa [1959] 1973), and Italian (Bates 1976) as well as Portuguese (Simões — Stoel-Gammon 1978:27). There is a stage (A) in which the third singular present forms substitute for all others. This is followed by a stage (B) in which the present form is restricted to the present and the third singular preterite form substitutes for all preterite forms. Then person is differentiated in the two tenses (C and D). This is shown schematically in (9).

(9)

		present	preterite
A.	sg. 1	3rd sg. present	
	3	form	

	present	preterite
B. sg. 1 3	3rd sg. present	3rd sg. preterite

	present	preterite
C. sg. 1	1st sg. pres.	3rd sg.
3	3rd sg. pres.	preterite

	present	preterite
D. sg. 1	1st sg. pres.	1st sg. preterite
3	3rd sg. pres.	3rd sg. preterite

Note that there is never a point at which the first singular present form is substituted for the first singular preterite form, thus providing no opportunity for the stem of the former to influence the latter.

If person distinctions were acquired before tense distinctions, the following hypothetical stages would result:

(10)

	present	preterite
A'. sg. 1 3	3rd sg. present form	

	present	preterite
B'. sg. 1	1st sg. present	
3	3rd sg. present	

	present	preterite
C'. sg. 1	1st sg. present	
3	3rd sg. present	3rd sg. preterite

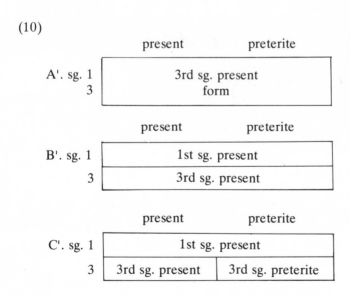

	present	preterite
D'. sg. 1	1st sg. present	1st sg. preterite
3	3rd sg. present	3rd sg. preterite

In this case the first singular present stem would substitute for the first singular preterite, allowing for the possibility of influence by person across tenses. Since this is not the order of acquisition of person and tense, however, we do not expect to find such substitutions historically.

It might be argued that the child's method of organizing and attacking the verb morphology is determined by the organization inherent in the system itself, and not by the child's cognitive development. That is, the existence in Portuguese of a class of verbs with a different stem for the present and the preterite (e.g. *fazer* 'do, make', *ter* 'have', *por* 'put, place') leads the child to organize the system the way (s)he does. This argument cannot hold, however, since there is no evidence that the child grasps this organization from the beginning. Rather the child tends to treat these verbs as having the same stem in the present and preterite. Simões and Stoel-Gammon (1978:15) report the following stages in the acquisition of the preterite forms for *fazer:* (Adult forms: *fiz, fez, fizemos, fizeram*)

Stage 1: *fez* repetition of third singular irregular form
       2: *fazeu* regularization of third singular form
       3: *fazei* first singular form with first conjugation inflection
       4: *fazi* first singular with second/third conjugation inflection
       5: *fiz* memorization of the irregular form

The tendency to make tense distinctions before person distinctions is not provoked by the formal properties of the conjugation system, but appears to depend upon the inherent nature of time versus person categories, and the cognitive development of the child. I cannot speculate further on why tense distinctions are made before person distinctions, nor what it is about the grammatical categories of tense and person that influence their hierarchical relation. Rather I will restrict myself to some general remarks concerning the relevance of such hierarchical relations to morphophonemic change.

5   The child's pattern of substitutions, the order of acquisition, and the distribution of stem alternations cross-linguistically provide evidence about the internal organization of verbal paradigms. In particular, we find that the persons within a tense are more closely related to one another

than they are to persons across tenses.[12] Or, to state the organization in another way the tenses are more autonomous (Zager 1978) than the persons within a tense.

Two predictions concerning morphophonemic change follow from this distinction. On the one hand, as Bolozky (1978) has suggested, forms that are more closely related (or less autonomous) are more likely to influence one another in morphophonemic change. The result is that the closer semantic relation is reflected in a closer phonological relation. Thus the data we have examined here predicts that morphophonemic stem changes are more likely within the persons of a tense, with the third singular influencing other forms, than they are among different tenses, with e.g. the third singular present affecting the third singular, and ultimately all persons of a past or future tense. Forms that are less closely related (or more autonomous) are less likely to influence one another, and are more likely to move apart both phonologically and semantically. Common examples of this sort involve words related by so-called derivational morphology, but the phenomenon is also found in inflectional morphology in the form of split paradigms. Here again we find evidence for the hierarchical organization of paradigms, since verbal paradigms tend to split along tense lines, never along person lines across tenses. Thus English *go* takes its past tense from *wend,* and English *be* has non-finite forms from OE *bēon,* present tense forms deriving ultimately from IE **esmi,* and past tense forms from OE *wesan.*

The relative autonomy of the tenses is represented in schema (6) above by the dotted line between the third singular present form and the other third singular forms. It is especially evident in the acquisition of the third singular preterite forms. As we mentioned above, the three conjugation class distinctions are made in the third singular preterite, and the children acquiring these forms rarely confused the conjugation classes, even though third singular present forms make only two conjugation class distinctions. This would suggest that third singular preterite forms are initially learned as unanalyzed wholes, and entered in the child's lexicon as separate words. The children are not so successful with the conjugation class membership of first singular preterite forms, suggesting that these forms are not learned as separate items, but are generated from the third singular stem form, by adding *-ei,* the first conjugation marker of first singular preterite. This process reflects the lesser autonomy of the persons within the tense.

7   It should be apparent, then, that child language data contains precisely the clues needed for the understanding of evolutive morphophonemic innovations, and the organization of synchronic systems.

Using child language data we have been able to refine considerably certain predictions concerning the direction of morphophonemic or analogical change. Mańczak predicts that the third singular will affect other persons and the present other tenses, but his hypotheses do not rule out the possibility of some other person in the present affecting the stem of the same person in another tense. We have, however, only scratched the surface since we have only examined the relation of two categories, person and tense. Presumably, similar relations can be established among all morphological categories, given appropriate information concerning the child's order of acquisition and patterns of substitution. For instance, it would be interesting to study the relation of person to number, and of tense to mood, just to name a few.

The productivity of such a line of research may be illustrated by examining another case from the Brazilian Portuguese data, the acquisition of gender and number in adjectives.

In both Latvian and Portuguese (Stoel-Gammon 1976), gender distinctions develop before number distinctions. In Portuguese, before gender distinctions emerge, the masculine singular form of the adjective is usually (but not always) used in all contexts (stage A) (Stoel-Gammon 1976). Then the two genders are distinguished (B) and lastly number (C):

(11)

	masculine	feminine
A. singular plural	masculine singular	

	masculine	feminine
B. singular plural	masculine singular	feminine singular

	masculine	feminine
C. singular	masculine singular	feminine singular
plural	masculine plural	feminine plural

For the purposes of levelling in the stem, the direction of influence would be as in (12). This organization allows the possibility of the singular forms affecting the plurals or of the masculine singular affecting the feminine,

(12)

but disallows the possibility of the masculine plural form affecting the feminine plural, even though this would be a case of a relatively unmarked category affecting a more marked category.

Certain Portuguese adjectives have stem vowel alternations similar to those found in verbs. A typical adjective paradigm with the alternation is:

(13)
	masculine	feminine
singular	n[o]vo	n[ɔ]va
plural	n[ɔ]vos	n[ɔ]vas

The acquisition of the alternation supports our hypothesis. When the gender distinction first emerges, the stem vowels are used correctly. Thus, for stage B the general masculine form is n[o]vo and the feminine is n[ɔ]va. The plural forms are then based directly on these two, giving the following forms for stage C:

(14)
	masculine	feminine
singular	n[o]vo	n[ɔ]va
plural	n[o]vos	n[ɔ]vas

The lower vowel in the masculine plural is acquired very late (after the child has been in school several years) (Stoel-Gammon 1976).

There are several interesting points to observe in this process. The masculine and the feminine forms are relatively autonomous, appearing with a difference in vowels established right from the beginning. The plural forms, however, are based quite directly on the singulars in each gender, and share a common stem vowel. This seems to indicate that the relation between singulars and plurals is much closer than the relation between masculines and feminines (at least in Portuguese). Finally, we can observe that the vowels of the feminine forms seem to be no help at all in acquiring the masculine plural form, a definite indication of the hierarchial organization of the inflectional system.

8   To this point, then, we have seen that the very general principles of morphological change parallel nicely the general principles of the acquisition of morphology. We have also seen that the details of the acquisition process suggest a mechanism, substitution, for analogical levelling. The

acquisition data also provide evidence concerning the way the child organizes paradigms, and a hypothesis that can be checked against morphophonemic changes. We turn now to one more fact that points to a relation between language acquisition and morphophonemic change.

The treatment of highly frequent irregular forms also forms a nice parallel between morphophonemic change and child language. In early stages children produce frequent irregular forms correctly, apparently having learned them by rote, without imposing any analysis on them. In some cases, once the child has formulated some rules, the irregular forms are remade on the basis of regular forms, as shown for *fazer* above, with the irregular forms re-learned later. In other cases, however, irregular forms are treated as irregular throughout the learning period. Thus high-frequency monosyllabic verbs in Portuguese do not undergo the same regularization process as other verbs, but are learned more or less by rote (Simões — Stoel-Gammon 1978). Because of their high frequency the forms of these verbs are available to be learned by memorization, and this type of learning is desirable because the highly irregular monosyllabic verbs are difficult to analyze on any regular pattern. These facts correspond well to the facts of morphophonemic change, where it is observed that the highly frequent forms are the most resistant to analogical levelling (Schuchardt [1885] 1972; Paul [1890] 1970; and see also Vincent, this volume). In fact, the general pattern of lexical diffusion of analogical changes supports the hypothesis that such changes come about by imperfect learning (Hooper 1976b). The less frequent forms tend to be regularized early because their forms are not reinforced to the extent that the forms of frequent items are.

9   It is time now to bring adult speakers into the picture. Jespersen (1922) points out that adults also produce analogical formations. He argues that "The important distinction is not really one of age, which is evidently one of degree only, but that between the first learners of the sound or word in question and those who use it after having once learned it" (1922:178). Jespersen also notes that the conditions under which analogical formations come about are the same for both adults and children: "Some one feels an impulse to express something, and at the moment has not got the traditional form at command, and so is driven to evolve a form of his own from the rest of the linguistic material" (p. 163). But while the conditions under which analogical formations are produced may be the same for adults and children, it is not clear that the resulting forms will be the same. Differences will surely result from the fact that adults know more of the system than children do. This is unavoidable, and probably trivial. The important question is whether or not the adult's

analogical formations are governed by the same principles as the child's. Unfortunately, adults' analogical formations have not been studied as systematically as children's speech and analogical change. However, from what we know about the latter two areas, we can infer that the adult's morphological system, and thus his analogical formation must be based on the same principles as are evident in child language, and that the adults must to some extent participate in the implementation of morphophonemic change.

The parties responsible for morphophonemic change are either (1) adults, (2) children or (3) both. (I discard "neither" as a possible answer on the assumption that it is the speakers of the language who produce these changes.) We have seen that the principles governing morphophonemic change are quite similar to the principles governing the acquisition of morphology. If it is the adults, rather than the children, who are responsible for morphophonemic change, then these same principles must govern adult morphological systems, and cause them to produce the requisite sorts of analogical forms.

If, on the other hand, the major blame is to be laid on children, we cannot help but implicate the adults, for it is they who let the little ones get away with it. For a child's analogical innovation to effect a change in the language at large, it must be acceptable to the speech community. As Andersen (1974) points out, analogical innovations, which are deductive innovations, can be accepted by the speech community, despite their deviations from the norm, because "they manifest the underlying structural relations of grammars" (p. 24). In other words, the child's innovations will succeed in producing a change if the speech community (including the adults) can view the innovation as compatible with the system as internalized in their own grammars. An example would be the widespread acceptance of *brung* as the past tense and past participle of *bring*. This form follows the dominant pattern of verbs in *ing,* which practically all form the past participle in *ung,* and furthermore tend to replace the past tense with the past participle form. My own experience is that I cannot correct my son every time he says *brung.* However, when he produced the form [fowt] as a past tense of *fight* (possibly on the basis of the forms *write, wrote*), all communications ceased, and he learned very quickly that he had to use *fought* (or *fighted*) if he wanted to be understood. The form [fowt] never appeared again. Thus even if children are the primary innovators, successful morphophonemic changes depend to a large extent on the speech community, which inevitably includes adults. Again, we are lead to the conclusion that the principles that govern morphophonemic change and acquisition also govern the adults' morphological system.

Thus under any of these views of morphological change, it is necessary to assume that the adults participate, and that the adult system is constructed on the same principles as the child's system. We cannot, then, expect to find the party responsible for morphophonemic change by comparing children's analogical formations to those of adults, since they will in all likelihood manifest the same properties (except, of course, that the adult has a more complete system on which to base his creation).

Children are, however, the more likely candidates. They are much more often in a situation where innovation is required, since they have not mastered all the forms of the adult system. The facts at hand, then, suggest a scenario such as that described above, in which children create the innovations, and their interlocutors (of all ages) either reject them totally, as in the case of [fowt], or tolerate them, overlook them in the interest of getting the message. The tolerated innovations eventually become accepted changes.

One final remark concerning general linguistic theory seems in order. We have seen in this preliminary attempt at a systematic comparison of child morphology and morphophonemic change that there seems to be a single set of principles at work determining the structure of these two processes. Further, I have just argued that these same principles must govern adults' morphological systems as well. It follows, then, that even the study of synchronic morphology, and particularly the development of a theory of morphophonemics, must proceed from the study of language acquisition and diachronic morphophonemics.

Notes

* A number of clarifications of the ideas presented here have come from discussions with Henning Andersen, Deborah Keller-Cohen, and David Zager. I would like to thank Caroline Stoel-Gammon for making her paper available to me in prepublication form, and for commenting on my interpretation of the data. I am especially grateful to Revere Perkins for allowing me to use the sample of grammars he so painstakingly has collected.

1. In this paper, the terms morphological change and morphophonemic change will be used as defined in Andersen (1969 and this volume). Morphological change refers to "changes in the relations among linguistic signs", while morphophonemic change refers to "change in the relations among variants (allomorphs) of signantia". The changes we will be concerned with are changes in the variants of morphemes, thus they are morphophonemic. It will be shown, however, that these changes are determined quite directly by the relations among linguistic signs and their order of acquisition. We are studying, then, child morphology, but morphophonemic change.

2. However, Kuryłowicz (1968) indicates that the form from which all other forms are phonologically predictable may be chosen as basic even if it does not occur in the unmarked category. In Hooper 1978 I have argued that for morphologically-

conditioned alternations morphological criteria take precedence over phonological criteria. The language acquisition data and the diachronic data support this view.

3. The example he gives here concerns the loss of case marking and the retention of number marking in Romance. It is not clear that this is a morphological change pure and simple, since it is accompanied by a complete change in the syntactic structure of the language. Nor is case as a morphological category necessarily lost, since word order restrictions and prepositions develop to mark grammatical relations.

4. As with Kuryłowicz's other formulae the basic terms remain undefined. When a stem change accompanies the addition of a desinence, one doesn't know if the stem change is an alternation, i.e. suppletion scheduled for levelling, or a meaningful element, i.e. a bipartite morpheme scheduled for extension.

5. Mańczak 1958 seems to think that Kuryłowicz's Formula I is in direct contradiction to his own Hypothesis II. However, Kuryłowicz's formula clearly deals with stem changes that are considered morphemes, i.e. associated with meaning, while Mańczak's hypothesis refers to arbitrary alternations. If this distinction is made, as Kruszewski advocated, the two principles are both valid. The problem (see note 4) is how to make this distinction.

6. The case of Italian *-iamo* discussed by Vincent (this volume) would appear to be a counter-example to several of the claims made here, since for some verbs stem changes occurred with the first plural (and no other persons) of the present indicative. Such a change goes against the hypothesis that the indicative affects other moods, and that a person category in one tense, aspect or mood cannot affect a person in another. The explanation for this case, however, fits in well with the rest of the child language data. The first plural subjunctive in Italian has the same form as the first plural imperative. Given a fairly early acquisition of imperatives, well before subjunctives (Rūķe-Dravina 1959; Bates 1976) and probably before first plural of the indicative, it is quite plausible that this substitution took place in just the way the child language data examined here would predict, that when the time came to use a first plural indicative form, the imperative, which was already acquired with first person markings, was substituted. This example raises the question of the order of acquisition of imperatives and indicatives. In Portuguese the third singular present indicative has the same form as the singular familiar imperative, so that it is not clear whether the basic form the child uses is an indicative or an imperative. However, in Latvian and Italian where such a formal difference exists, the third singular indicative precedes the imperative (Rūķe-Dravina 1959; Bates 1976).

7. For the purposes of the present study, I have lumped tense and aspect together in order to avoid the difficulty of distinguishing them. The important distinction I make here is between person categories on the one hand and categories such as tense, aspect and mood on the other.

8. Stem changes in Germanic strong verbs sometimes coincide with singular/plural distinctions within a single tense, or with a single person category within a tense (e.g. Old English preterite: *band, bunde, bundon*), but never with a single person in more than one tense.

9. To qualify as person inflections, the morphemes in question must:
   (1) agree with the subject (or mark subject if no overt nominal is present)
   (2) occur contiguous to the verb and its affixes
   (3) occur in a fixed position
   (4) be obligatory in any finite clause (except for third person which may be $\emptyset$)
   (5) be distinct from, and occur with, subject pronouns
   (6) signal at least 3rd and non-third person (as opposed, e.g. to markers that signal only inclusion or exclusion).

10. The second column of the chart list some of the categories that major stem alternations correspond to. It is not intended as an exhaustive list, it is only illustrative of the types of alternations reported.

11. During the conference at Boszkowo, Jonathan Kaye (Université de Québec à Montréal) reported an analogical formation in the speech of pre-adolescent Quebecois speakers. According to Kaye the third person plural imperfect of *être* occurs in the speech of these children as *sontait* [sɔ̃te], presumably formed from the third plural present *sont* [sɔ̃] by the addition of [te]. If only morphological conditioning is involved in this change, it provides a counter-example to the hypothesis defended in the text. I have not had access to further data on this formation.

12. It is perhaps no accident that our traditional method of presenting paradigms on paper reflects nicely their internal organization, since verb forms are always presented in groups according to tense, aspect and mood. Does the other possibility illustrated below with a Spanish verb, seem strange because we are unaccustomed to it, or because it is at odds with our internal grammars?

	1st sg.	2nd sg.	3rd sg.
pres. ind.	*amo*	*amas*	*ama*
pres. subj.	*ame*	*ames*	*ame*
preterite	*amé*	*amaste*	*amó*
imp. ind.	*amaba*	*amabas*	*amaba*
imp. subj.	*amara*	*amaras*	*amara*
future	*amaré*	*amarás*	*amará*
conditional	*amaría*	*amarías*	*amaría*

References

Andersen, Henning
   1974   "Towards a typology of change: Bifurcating changes and binary relations", in Anderson and Jones (eds.) 1974: 17–60.
   this volume "Morphological change: Towards a typology".
Anderson, J. — C. Jones (eds.)
   1974   *Historical linguistics: Proceedings of the First International Conference on Historical Linguistics* (Amsterdam: North-Holland).
Baron, Naomi
   1977   *Language acquisition and historical change* (Amsterdam: North Holland).
Bates, Elisabeth
   1976   *Language and context: The acquisition of pragmatics* (New York: Academic Press).
Baxter, A. R. W.
   1975   *Some aspects of naturalness in phonological theory* (unpublished B.Lit. thesis, Oxford University).
Bolozky, Shmuel
   1977   "Paradigm coherence: Evidence from Modern Hebrew", *Afro-Asiatic Linguistics*.
Christie, William (ed.)
   1976   *Current progress in historical linguistics* (Amsterdam: North-Holland).
Comrie, Bernard
   1976   *Aspect* (Cambridge: University Press).

Dinnsen, Daniel (ed.)
  1978   *Current phonological theories* (Bloomington: University of Indiana Press).
Drachman, Gaberell
  1978   "Child language and language change: A conjecture and some refutations", in
          Fisiak (ed.) 1978: 123–144.
Dressler, Wolfgang
  1974   "Diachronic puzzles for natural phonology", in *Natural Phonology Parasession*
          (Chicago: Linguistic Society), 95–102.
Ferguson, C. A. — D. I. Slobin (eds.)
  1973   *Studies in child language development* (New York: Holt, Rinehart and Winston).
Fisiak, Jacek (ed.)
  1978   *Recent developments in historical phonology* (The Hague: Mouton).
Greenberg, Joseph H.
  1957   "Order of affixing: A study in general linguistics", in J. H. Greenberg, *Essays in
          Australian example"*, in Sebeok et al. (eds.).
Hale, Kenneth
  1971   "Deep-surface canonical disparities in relation to analysis and change: An
          Australian example", in Sebeok et al. (eds).
Hooper, Joan Bybee
  1976a *Introduction to natural generative phonology* (New York: Academic Press).
  1976b "Word frequency in lexical diffusion and the source of morpho-phonological
          change", in Christie (ed.), 95–105.
  1978   "Substantive principles in natural generative phonology", in Dinnsen (ed.) 1978.
Jakobson, Roman
  1932   "Zur Struktur des russischen Verbums", reprinted in Roman Jakobson, *Selected
          Writings* II (The Hague: Mouton), 3–15.
Jespersen, Otto
  1922   *Language: Its nature, development and origin* (London: Allen & Unwin).
Kenny, J.
  1974   *A numerical taxonomy of ethnic units using Murdock's 1967 world sample* (unpub-
          lished Ph.D. dissertation, University of Indiana).
Klausenburger, Jürgen
  1976   "(De) morphologization in Latin", *Lingua* 40: 305–320.
  1977   "The relevance of Kruszewski's theory of morphophonology today", Ms.
Kuryłowicz, Jerzy
  1949   "La nature des proces dits 'analogiques'", *Acta Linguistica* 5:15–37.
  1968   "The notion of morpho(pho)neme", in Lehmann — Malkiel (eds.) 1968:66–
          81.
Lehmann, Winfred P. — Yakov Malkiel (eds.)
  1968   *Directions for historical linguistics* (Austin: University of Texas Press).
Mańczak, Witold
  1958   "Tendances générales des changements analogiques", *Lingua* 7:298–325 and
          387–420.
  1963   "Tendances générales du développement morphologique", *Lingua* 12:19–38.
Paul, Hermann
  1970   *Principles of the history of language,* [1890] translated by H. A. Strong (College
          Park, MD.: McGrath Publishing Company).
Perkins, Revere
  1978   "A stratified probability sample of fifty languages with bibliography", *Behavioral
          Science Research.*

Rosenblat, A.
  1946   *Biblioteca de dialectología hispanoamerica*, II (Buenos Aires: Facultad de Filosofía y Letras de la Universidad de Buenos Aires, Instituto de Filología).
Rūķe-Draviņa, Velta
  1959   "On the emergence of inflection in child language: A contribution based on Latvian speech data", in Ferguson — Slobin (eds.), 252–267.
Schuchardt, Hugo
  1885   "On sound laws: Against the Neogrammarians", in Vennemann — Wilbur
  [1972]   (eds.) 1972: 39–72.
Sebeok, Thomas et al. (eds.)
  1971   *Current trends in linguistics* 2 (The Hague: Mouton).
Simões, Maria C. P. — Carol Stoel-Gammon
  1978   "The acquisition of inflections in Portuguese: A study of the development of person markers on verbs", *Journal of Child Language* 6:53–67.
Skousen, Royal
  1975   *Substantive evidence in phonology* (The Hague: Mouton).
Slobin, D. I.
  1973   "Cognitive prerequisites for the development of grammar", in Ferguson — Slobin (eds.) 1973:175–208.
  1977   "Language change in childhood and in history", in *Language learning and thought*, edited by John Macnamara (New York: Academic), 185–214.
Stampe, David
  1973   *A dissertation on natural phonology* (unpublished Ph.D. Dissertation, University of Chicago).
Stoel-Gammon, Carol
  1976   "Metaphony in Portuguese: Analysis and acquisition", Paper presented at the Colloquium on Hispanic and Luso-Brasilian Linguistics, Oswego, NY; Ms.
Vennemann, Theo
  1972a   "Phonetic analogy and conceptual analogy", in Vennemann — Wilbur (eds.) 1972:181–*204.*
  1972b   "Rule inversion", Lingua 29:209–242.
Vennemann, Theo — Terence H. Wilbur (eds.)
  1972   *Schuchardt, the Neogrammarians, and the transformational theory of phonological change* (Frankfurt/M. Athenäum).
Vincent, Nigel
  this volume "Words versus morphemes in morphological change: The case of Italian *-iamo*".
Voegelin, Charles F. — Florence M. Voegelin
  1966   *Anthropological linguistics: Index to languages of the world*, Vol 6 and 7 (Bloomington: Indiana University).
Zager, David
  1978   "A grey area of morphology", Ms.

Grammars consulted

1 Languages with subject marking inflection on the verb

ACOMA (Keres)
    Miller, Wick R.
    1965   *Acoma grammar and tests* (Berkeley: California UP).
BASQUE (undetermined)
    N'Diaye, Geneviève
    1970   *Structure du dialecte Basque de Maya* (The Hague: Mouton).
BURUSHASKI (undetermined)
    Lorimer, D.L.R.
    1935   *The Burushaski* language (Oslo).
CLASSICAL NAHUATL (Aztec-Tanoan)
    Andrews, Richard
    1975   *Introduction to Classical Nahuatl* (Austin: Texas UP).
DIEGUEÑO (Hokan)
    Langdon, Margaret
    1970   *A grammar of Diegueño* (Berkeley: California UP).
GEORGIAN (Caucasian)
    Marr, N. — M. Brière
    1931   *La langue géorgienne* (Firmin-Didot).
KET (undetermined)
KUTENAI (undetermined)
    Garvin, Paul
    1948   "Kutenai II: Morpheme variations", *IJAL* 14.
MIWOK (Penutian)
    Broadbent, Sylvia M.
    1964   *The Southern Sierra Miwok language* (Berkeley: California UP).
OJIBWA (Macro-Algonquin)
    Bloomfield, Leonard
    1957   *Eastern Ojibwa* (Ann Arbor: Michigan UP).
PAWNEE (Macro-Sionan)
    Parks, Douglas
    n.d.   *A grammar of Pawnee* (dissertation, Berkeley).
POLAR ESKIMO (West Greenlandic-American-Arctic-Paleo-Siberian)
    Schultz-Lorentzen
    1945   *A grammar of the West Greenland language* (København: C. A. Reitzels
        Forlag).
QUILEUTE (Chimakua)
    Andrade, Manuel J.
    1933   *Quileute* (Columbia, N.Y.). [Reprint from *Handbook of North American Indian
        languages 3.*]
SANTA CRUZ (Papuan)
    Wurm, Stephen A.
    1969   *The linguistic situation in the Reef and Santa Cruz Islands* (= *Papers in linguistics
        of Melanesia* 2) (Australian National University, Canberra).
SERBO-CROATIAN (Indo-European)
    Partridge, Monica

1964   *Serbo-Croatian. Practical grammar and reader*
(Beograd: Publishers Jugoslavia).
TEMIAR (Malaya)
Cary, Iskandar
1961   *Tengleq Kui Serok* (Kuala Lumpur: Dewan Bahasa dan Pustaka).
TOUAREG BERBER (Afro-Asiatic)
Cortade, Jean-Marie
1969   *Grammaire touareg* (Université D'Alger).
WESTERN APACHE (Na-Dene)
Durbin, Marshall Elza
1964   *A componential analysis of the San Carlos dialect of Western Apache* (dissertation, SUNY, Buffalo).

2   Languages without subject marking inflection

AINU
Batchelor, John Obe
1938   *An Ainu-English-Japanese dictionary* (4th edition) (Tokyo: Iwanami Shoten).
ANDAMANESE
Portman, M. V.
1887   *A manual of the Andamane language* (London: W. H. Allen).
APINAYE
Callow, John Campbell
1962   *The Apinayé language: phonology and grammar* (dissertation, London).
CAMBODIAN
Jacob, Judith M.
1968   *Introduction to Cambodian* (London: Oxford UP).
GARO
Burling, Robbins
1961   *A Garo grammar* (Poona: Linguistic Society of India).
GOAJIRO
Holmer, N. M.
1949   "Goajiro", *IJAL* 15.
HAITIAN
Breton, P. R.
n.d. *Grammaire caribe* Paris: Adam-Leclerc).
HOTTENTOT (NAMA)
Schills, G.H.
1891   *Grammaire complète de la langue des Namas* (Louvain: Leferer).
IATMUL
Laycock, D. C.
1965   *The Ndu language family* (Canberra: The Australian National Univeristy).
KARANKAWA
Swanton, John R.
1970   *Linguistic materials from the tribes of Southern Texas and Northeastern Mexico* (Washington, D.C.: United States Government Printing).
KHASI
Rabel. Lili
1961   *Khasi, a language of Assam* (Louisiana State UP).

KHMER
  Gorgoniyev, Y. A.
  1966   *The Khmer language* (Moskva: Nauka).
KIWAI
  Baxter, E. Riley
  n.d.   *A grammar of the Kiwai language* (Fly Delta, Papua).
KOREAN
  Martin, Samuel E.
  1960   *Korean reference grammar* (Cleveland: American Council of Learned Societies).
MALAYALAM
  Frohnmeyer, L. J.
  1913   *A progressive grammar of the Malayalam language for Europeans* (2nd, revised
         edition) (Mangalore: Basel Mission Book and Tract Depository).
NICOBARESE
  Braine, Jean Critchfield
  1970   *Nicobarese grammar (Car dialect)* (dissertation, Berkeley).
PALAUNG
  Milne, Leslie
  1921   *An elementary Palaung grammar* (Oxford: Clarendon).
SONAY
  Prost, R. P. A.
  1956   *La langue sonay et ses dialectes* (Aakar, Senegal: Institut Fondamental d'Afrique
         Noire).
SUSU
  Lacan, R. P. P.
  1942   *Grammaire et dictionnaire français-soussou et soussou-français* (Bordeaux:
         Conakry).
TARASCAN
  Foster, M. L.
  1969   *The Tarascan language* (Berkeley: California UP).
TASMANIAN
  Roth, H. Ling
  1899   *The aborigines of Tasmania* (Halifax: F. King & Sons).
TIMUCUA
  Gatschet, Albert S.
  1880   "The Timucua language", *Proceedings of the American Philosophical Society*
         28:105.
TONGAN
  Churchward, C. M.
  1953   *Tongan grammar* (London: Oxford UP).
VIETNAMESE
  Thompson, Laurence C.
  1965   *A Vietnamese grammar* (Seattle: Washington UP).
YANOMAMA
  Migliazza, Ernest Cesar
  1972   *Yanomama grammar and intelligibility* (dissertation, Indiana University,
         Bloomington).
ZAPOTEC
  Briggs, Elinor
  1961   *Mitla Zapotec grammar* (México: Instituto lingüístico de Verano y centrales
         investigaciones antropológicas de México).

DAVID HUNTLEY

The evolution of genitive-accusative animate and personal nouns in Slavic dialects

The main purpose of the present discussion is to show how grammatical oppositions vary over time, and how, as a result, such oppositions vary at a particular time within an area in which related dialects are spoken. The oppositions of animate versus inanimate, or of male personal versus others that have evolved in various Slavic dialects have been selected for discussion here, because they give a good illustration of the principles involved, and because we have enough information to give a fairly good picture of the contemporary distribution of these forms in various dialects, and of the ways in which they have evolved.

Hjelmslev (1956), and Stieber (1971:15–17) give good outlines of the material, but so far a general survey for all Slavic dialects of all the historical developments of these oppositions has not yet been offered in the literature. In the present paper, these developments will be surveyed from the standpoint that there are two major types of grammatical opposition, clearly differentiated one from another as explained by Fasske (1975:6–18). One type is the equipollent, or symmetric opposition in which one grammatical unit always signals a certain content, while another grammatical unit signals the opposite content, there being no purely grammatical overlap in the content of either unit. I shall call this type of opposition an unmarked opposition. The other type is the privative, or asymmetric opposition in which one grammatical unit (the marked form) always signals a certain content, while another grammatical unit (the unmarked form) may implicitly signal this content, but also will explicitly signal its opposite. I shall call this type of opposition a marked opposition.

In a marked opposition, the unmarked form can be used to replace the marked to a different degree from one period to another in the history of a particular dialect, or from one related dialect to another at any particular time. When the unmarked member relatively frequently replaces the marked member, I shall call this a weak opposition, and when the unmarked member relatively infrequently replaces the marked member, I shall call this a strong opposition, saying that in the first instance the marked member is weakly correlated, and in the second instance that the marked member is strongly correlated. While marked oppositions are diametrically opposed to unmarked oppositions, weak and strong oppositions are simply gradual variations within a marked opposition and would appear to have no systemic status.

However, it is well known that new items arising in a language typically do not replace the old item, but for a time the old and the new exist side by side. Consider a system, say a case system, in which Case A always expresses Content(s) I, but in which Case B always expresses Content(s) II. The opposition is clearly an unmarked one. If, for some reason, certain instances of Case A regardless of syntactic or stylistic factors begin to signal at least part of Content(s) II, this part of II becomes involved in a marked opposition where what should now be called Case A–B is at first weakly marked with respect to B in signalling this part of II. Over time, A–B may become more strongly correlated with respect to B, but if ever only A–B always comes to signal this part of II, and always replaces B, which is now never used to signal this part of II, the correlation will be broken and a new unmarked opposition will have arisen. Conversely, if within a marked opposition the unmarked member gradually replaces the marked member over a period of time, the opposition itself disappears. In the latter type of development, either the formerly marked form disappears, or else remains as a lexically or stylistically marked exception. I shall now illustrate these general postulates by examining the genitive-accusative of nouns in the various dialects of Slavic for which I have information, both synchronically and diachronically.

Animate and male personal forms have arisen in various dialects of Slavic at different times, not only in the noun but also in adjectives, pronouns, demonstratives, numerals, and participles, including a participle that has been used to form finite past tense(s). An adequate survey of the material would have to consider all these forms. After examining their history, and contemporary geographical distribution, I have come to the conclusion that the central stream of evolution runs in the noun, so that my discussion will largely, but not entirely, ignore the other forms.

In this paper, I shall examine first the singular forms of nouns, and then the plural in all contemporary Slavic dialects for which I have information, making reference to the literary languages only en passant. Then I shall examine the historical evolution, first of the singular, and then of the plural. Finally, I shall make some remarks concerning the nature of the factors that have influenced the evolution, and concerning the nature of the evolution itself.

In all contemporary Slavic dialects, except for Bulgarian and Macedonian, genitive-accusative singular is obligatory for all masculine animates, that is for both animals and male persons. In Russian, for instance, animate singular masculine has nominative *pop* 'priest' with zero inflection, whereas accusative *popa* has -*a* inflection homonymous with the genitive, as are all its modifiers. Inanimate singular masculine has the zero inflection in both nominative and accusative, e.g., *stol* 'table', and all its modifiers have homonymous nominative and accusative. In various of these dialects, certain inanimate masculine nouns may also have genitive-accusative, at least in certain constructions. However, these inanimate genitive-accusatives are all either lexically, syntactically, or stylistically marked, and a detailed discussion would be mainly of an empirical nature. Lexically, syntactically, and stylistically unmarked nouns in these dialects all have obligatory genitive-accusative for animates, and nominative-accusative for inanimates, so that the opposition is an unmarked one.

Nouns have lost their case inflections in Bulgarian and Macedonian, but some dialects do have the -*a* inflection for the accusative singular of masculine proper names and kinship terms (Stojkov 1962:138). The opposition involves a restricted set of male personal nouns, and is marked in some dialects, and unmarked in others (Stojkov and Bernštejn 1964, maps 158, 159).

In the plural, and in the dual in Sorbian, the structures are in many dialects more complex than in the singular, and they vary considerably from one dialect to another. Bulgarian and Macedonian do not distinguish nominative from accusative at all in the plural. The structures in the other dialects will be outlined below going from the North-East (Russian) to the South-West (Serbo-Croatian).

Russian dialects do not have gender distinctions in the plural for any parts of speech. Instead, they distinguish animates which have accusative plural homonymous with genitive plural, from inanimates which have accusative plural homonymous with nominative plural, e.g., animates:nominative plural *popy* 'priests', *koni* 'steeds', *materi* 'mothers', *suki* 'bitches' (where -*y*, -*i* are allophonic variants), accusative plural *popov*, *konej*, *materej*, *suk* (where -*ov*, -*ej*, -*∅* are allomorphs of both accusative plural and genitive plural), inanimates: nominative-accusative plural *stoly* 'tables', *nogi* 'legs'. In certain syntactically and lexically marked bound phrases, some animates use the nominative-accusative form, e.g., *on postupil v officianty* 'he became a waiter'. However, in Russian the basic grammatical opposition of animate ~ inanimate is an unmarked one in the plural, just as it is within the masculine singular. A few examples of nominative-accusative plural for certain animals have been observed by Seliščev (1921:129), Orlova (1949:60), and Kuznecov (1949:90), but these seem to be lexically and stylistically marked examples, for as Avanesov and Orlova (1965:97) point out, the category animate ~ inanimate is uniform throughout all Russian dialects.

In North-Eastern Ukranian dialects, the structure is identical with that of Russian. In many South-Eastern dialects, accusative plural for animals is optionally identical either with the genitive or with the nominative, and in some of these dialects all animates have such optional forms (Żylko 1966:83). Where all animates have such forms, the opposition is privative, with genitive-accusative marked for Animate. Where only animals have such forms, there are three binary oppositions, two marked oppositions, animals ~ persons, and animals ~ inanimates, and one unmarked opposition persons ~ inanimates. Nominative-accusative is the marked form in the animals ~ persons opposition since it specifies the feature Non-human. In the animals ~ inanimate opposition, the genitive-accusitive is the marked form, specifying the feature Animate. In some South-Western dialects, genitive-accusative is used only for male persons (Samijlenko 1964:181), so that here there is is an unmarked opposition, male persons ~ others.

North-Eastern Belorussian dialects have the unmarked animate ~ inanimate opposition, as in Russian and North-Eastern Ukrainian. Immediately to the South-West of this area, some Belorussian dialects have obligatory genitive-accusative plural for persons, and animals that have masculine forms in the singular, but optional nominative-accusative for animals that have feminine forms in the singular. Since the two groups of animal nouns may have genitive plural *-ow* for masculines, and *-ø* for feminines, there is a gender distinction within the accusative plural of animal nouns. These dialects have three oppositions, feminine animals ~ persons and masculine animals, where nominative-accusative is marked, feminine animals ~ inanimates where genitive-accusative is marked, and an unmarked opposition of persons and masculine animals ~ inanimates. Further South and West, masculine animals also have the optional forms until in some dialects genitive-accusative is used only for persons in the plural (for the distribution of the forms for animals, see Avanesov — Krapiva — Mackevič 1963: maps 209, 210). Oppositions where animals have the optional forms are the same as those described above for Ukrainian. In these dialects of Belorussian, nominative-accusative is more strongly marked for feminine animals than for masculine animals in the animals ~ persons opposition and becomes stronger as one goes South-West, whereas in the animals ~ inanimates opposition genitive-accusative is more weakly marked for feminines than for masculines, and becomes weaker as one goes South-West, until there are some dialects which have an unmarked opposition persons ~ non-persons in the plural.

Zieniukowa (1974) quite rightly emphasizes that the oppositions of male personal, and of animate in the plural have not yet been adequately described for Polish dialects (for a survey of the distribution of the forms other than genitive-accusative plural, see Dejna 1973:232–4, and map 70). In literary Polish the grammatical distinction in the plural is male persons ~ others, an unmarked opposition characterized by special nominative plural forms for male personal nouns and forms congruent with them, as well as by genitive-acusative. In highly stylistically marked, particularly pejorative utterances male personal referents may, however, have the non-personal forms. Thus, in stylistically unmarked discourse one uses for male persons, e.g., *Ci dobrzy chłopi już przyszli* 'These good fellows have come already', (where *-y* and *-i* are phonologically predictable variants for male personal nominative plural forms), *Znam tych dobrych chłopów* 'I know these good fellows', (where *-ych*, *-ów* are male personal accusative plural forms homonymous with genitive plural). In discourse with marked pejorative reference, one may use, on the other hand, *Te pijane chłopy już przyszły* 'These drunk guys have come already', *Znam te pijane chłopy* 'I know these drunk guys'. Here the grammatical opposition in neutral style is reutilized for stylistical purposes, and within the male personal category the grammatically male personal forms are stylistically unmarked.

In Eastern Polish dialects, the special male personal forms are not used at all for nouns, but genitive-accusative plural is used in many of these dialects much more widely than it is used in the literary language. In a description of one of these dialects, Moszyński (1958:39, 49) shows that genitive-accusative plural is obligatory for male persons, but optional for other nouns, including even inanimates. It will be interesting to see whether, in the light of further investigations which Zieniukowa advocates, nominative-accusative, the marked form for such Eastern dialects, becomes more strongly marked as one goes westwards until it eventually ousts genitive-accusative for nouns other than the male personal.

While genitive-accusative plural is used for male persons only in many Western dialects, the special nominative plural forms do not occur in many North-Western Polish dialects, but are used in Kashubian and in South-Western Polish. In other Western dialects, the special nominative plural forms are optional for male persons (Zagórski 1967:24–7, map 8), but here the optional nominatives of the *chłopy* type do not appear to have pejorative meaning ("nie ma tu znaczenia pogardliwego", Nitsch 1915:299–300, 1923:427, "nie ma tu znaczenia pejoratywnego," Nitsch 1957:69).

An excellent summary of studies of the forms that occur in Slovak dialects is given in Kondrašov 1954. Some Eastern Slovak dialects have an unmarked opposition within the masculine plural of animates ~

inanimates, where the animates have special nominative forms and the genitive-accusative. As one goes westwards, these forms are used less frequently for animals, so that within the masculine there is a marked opposition non-human ~ human. In many Central and Western Slovak dialects only three animal nouns have such forms, and then only optionally. Only two of these have special nominative plural forms. The phonemic forms are either nominative /vtáci/ 'birds', /vlci/ 'wolves', /psi/ 'dogs', genitive-accusative /vtákow/, /vlkow/, /psow/, or nominative-accusative /vtáki/, /vlki/, /psi/. In such dialects, these animal nouns are not a part of the grammatical opposition, but are lexically marked, and the grammatical opposition is an unmarked one, male persons ~ others, as in Western Polish.

The best description of the forms for many Slavic dialects is the exhaustive and detailed account for Sorbian in Fasske (1975:39-93). Sorbian dialectologists distinguish three groups of dialects: Lower Sorbian in the North, Upper Sorbian in the South, and between them, the transitional dialects. Whereas in East Slavic, and in most West Slavic dialects the animate, or male personal plural forms vary along an East-West axis, in Sorbian there is one wave that extends from the North (Lower Sorbian), and another that extends from the South (Upper Sorbian). These waves meet one another in the transitional dialects.

Within the masculine, Lower Sorbian distinguishes animate nouns from inanimate nouns by means of genitive-accusative in the dual, and when nouns are conbined with the numerals 3 and 4 (the paucal). In the dual, the opposition is unmarked, as in the singular. In most North-Eastern dialects, the opposition is strongly marked, or even unmarked in the paucal, but is elsewhere less strongly marked. The North-Eastern Horno dialect distinguishes animates from inanimates only in the masculine singular. Lower Sorbian dialects do not have nominative plural forms for male animates that are grammatically distinct from those for inanimates or female animates, and genitive-accusative does not occur in the plural (except in the paucal constructions).

Most Upper Sorbian dialects distinguish male personal nouns from others only in the plural, by means of special nominative plural forms, and by genitive-accusative. These forms are used especially frequently only in the South-East, where the forms are in general strongly correlated, and are even obligatory in at least two dialects, where the opposition is thus an unmarked one. The male personal plural forms are used especially infrequently in the North-East, where the forms are weakly correlated, and in two of these dialects the forms are not used at all, so that in these dialects the opposition does not exist.

In some Southern dialects, the dual has been lost altogether, and in the

North-West, accusative dual is homonymous with the nominative for all nouns. A few other dialects do have genitive-accusative dual for male persons, while a few Northern dialects have the form for male persons and animals. The genitive accusative dual is, in general, weakly correlated.

Thus outside of the singular, Lower Sorbian has animate ~ inanimate in dual and paucal, while Upper Sorbian has male persons ~ others in the plural. The transitional dialects have a combination of these two, with animate ~ inanimate in dual and paucal, and male persons ~ others in the plural. Some dialects have an unmarked opposition in dual and paucal, with a marked opposition in the plural. Dialects with a marked opposition in the paucal have male persons more strongly marked than animals. While nearly all the transitional dialects have an unmarked opposition in the dual, only one dialect, Weisskeissel, has unmarked oppositions recorded in dual, paucal and plural. As in Lower Sorbian, the transitional dialects do not have special nominative plural forms for male persons, but a few examples are recorded in extreme Southern transitional dialects.

The systems occurring in Czech dialects are described by Bělić (1972: passim). Genitive-accusative plural, and special nominative plural forms are found only in Silesian dialects bordering on Polish, and in some Moravian dialects bordering on Slovak. Most Moravian, and some Bohemian dialects distinguish masculine animates from others by special nominative plural forms of demonstratives and possessive adjectives, but do not have genitive-accusative. Masculine animate nouns and adjectives with stem-final velars, or -t-, -d-, -n-, -r-, have a stem-final alternation of the consonant in nominative plural, e.g., animate nominative plural /tī naší staří haďi/ 'these old snakes of ours', accusative /ti naše stari hadi/; inanimate nominative-accusative /ti naše stari hradi/ 'these old castles of ours'.

In a number of Southern Bohemian dialects, the distinction is also expressed by vowel length in the nominative plural animate masculines, e.g., nominative /haďī/, accusative /haďi/; nominative-accusative /hradi/. In these dialects, the stem-final alternations occur in both nominative and accusative plural of the stem-types listed above.

In most Bohemian dialects, the grammatical category of inanimate has disappeared in the plural, and nominative and accusative forms are identical for all nouns and modifiers in the plural. However, masculine animates with the stem-finals referred to above have the consonant alternations in both nominative and accusative plural, while certain masculine animate nouns are lexically marked for taking nominative-accusative plural inflection /-ovē/. I have not had access to any reliable information concerning the degree to which any of the above-mentioned oppositions in Czech dialects are marked; it is clear, though, that in many dialects these are unmarked oppositions.

In Slovenian, and in most Serbo-Croatian dialects, there are no distinctions between animate and inanimate outside of the singular. Some Western (Čakavian) Serbo-Croatian dialects do have such distinctions in the plural, expressed by the genitive plural. In some dialects, e.g., Cres (Tentor 1909:169), and Novi (Steinhauer 1973:183), there is an unmarked opposition, male persons ~ others. In the Susak dialect (Hamm — Hraste — Guberina 1956:101), genitive-accusative plural is obligatory for animate masculines, and optional for inanimate masculines. In this dialect there are three oppositions:— an unmarked opposition, masculine animates ~ non-masculine, and two marked oppositions, inanimate masculine ~ animate masculine, with marked nominative-accusative, and inanimate masculine ~ non-masculine, with marked genitive-accusative.

In examining the diachronic developments, one must note that Old Slavonic texts, the oldest extant Slavic texts, are basically Bulgaro-Macedonian, and that at first, Bulgaro-Macedonian seems to have been more innovating with respect to the use of genitive-accusative than were other Slavic dialects. These texts are considerably altered copies, probably from the late tenth to eleventh centuries, of lost ninth to tenth-century originals, nearly all of which are translations from the Greek. Meillet (1897) points out that in the oldest reconstructable layer of these texts, genitive-accusative singular is used only for certain nouns, adjectives and participles denoting male persons. Within the masculine singular, all substantivized definite adjectives and participles, all proper nouns and most common nouns denoting mature male persons other than spirits had obligatory genitive-accusative. The interrogative pronoun also had obligatory genitive-accusative, *kogo* 'whom'. A few common male personal nouns are attested with genitive-accusative when definite, e.g., *raba* 'the slave', but with nominative-accusative, e.g., *rabŭ* 'a slave', when indefinite. The original opposition appears to have been, within the major masculine declension, definite mature human ~ others.

The pattern of attestation appears to be such that genitive-accusative singular then became obligatory for all male persons, so that there was an opposition within the singular of the major masculine declension, male persons ~ others. However, the Old Slavonic texts also contain some younger examples of genitive-accusative singular for masculine animals. Thus for late Old Slavonic (eleventh century), there is some evidence for three oppositions within the masculine singular:- male persons ~ inanimate with unmarked members; animals ~ inanimates with weakly marked genitive-accusative; animals ~ male persons with strongly marked nominative-accusative. In the fourteenth-century Bulgarian material analysed in Boissin (1946), both male personal and animal nouns are always attested with genitive-accusative singular in the masculine, showing that at least in some dialects there was now within the masculine singular a single unmarked opposition, animate ∼ inanimate.

From the eleventh to the fourteenth centuries, genitive-accusative was extended in Bulgaro-Macedonian to nouns of a minor feminine declension with genitive singular in -*e*. Meillet (71) states that in this declension genitive-accusative *matere* 'mother', and *dŭštere* 'daughter' arose by analogy with the genitive-accusatives *ot'ca* 'father', and *syna* 'son'. However, both Old Slavonic and later Bulgaro-Macedonian texts have genitive-accusative also for inanimates of this declension, so that here the form became a feature of this declension and did not participate in the animate ∼ inanimate opposition.

Subsequently, along with the general loss of case inflections in Bulgaro-Macedonian, most animate nouns lost the -*a* inflection, which has now become restricted to a small group of male personal nouns in some Eastern Bulgarian dialects.

Apart from the genitive-accusative -*e* inflection, which was a specifically Bulgaro-Macedonian innovation, most Slavic dialects appear to have followed the same chronological sequence, namely genitive-accusative singular first became optional for male persons, but gradually became obligatory for male persons, and subsequently for all masculine animates. It seems likely that genitive-accusative became marginally optional for animals, before the form became obligatory for male persons. This would give rise to male persons ∼ inanimates with strongly marked genitive-accusative, and animals ∼ inanimates with weakly marked genitive-accusative. At such a stage, genitive-accusative singular would be relatively frequent for male persons, while nominative-accusative would be relatively infrequent, and the opposite situation would hold for animals. One may call such an opposition a relatively unmarked opposition.

While all Slavic dialects appear to have shared a common relative chronology in the evolution in the singular, there is no common absolute chronology. In Serbo-Croatian, the evolution appears to be somewhat slower than in Bulgaro-Macedonian. Belić (1962:9) points out that in twelfth-century Serbian texts, genitive-accusative singular is still optional for male persons, while masculine animal nouns normally have nominative-accusative singular. However, Svane (1958:26) finds that in an extensive corpus of fifteenth-century Serbian material, all masculine animates have genitive-accusative singular.

Slovenian seems to show a similar chronology, for the few examples in the eleventh-century *Freising Folia* have nominative-accusative for masculine nouns denoting spirits, and genitive-accusative for other male persons, while nouns denoting animals are not attested. In all the fifteenth and sixteenth century Slovenian texts examined by Oblak (1888:528), all masculine animates have genitive accusative singular.

In the North, in West and East Slavic, with the possible exception of Sorbian, the form evolved much more slowly. It is clear from Unbegaun (1935:266–7), Kuznecov (1959:99), Kedajtene (1961:185–6), and Cocron (1962:98–9), that in the singular the form became obligatory for male persons in East Slavic only by the fifteenth century, and for animals in Russian only in the seventeenth century. A similar pattern in seventeenth-century Ukrainian is observed by Samijlenko (1964:178), and Kedajtene (1961:188), who along with Karskij (1956:115–16, 126–7) make similar remarks for seventeenth-century Byelorussian. Before the fifteenth century, genitive-accusative is attested quite frequently for male persons in the singular in Old East Slavic texts, but only very rarely for animals.

The chronology in Polish (Grappin 1956:26–32), Slovak (Stanislav 1967:51–2), and Czech (Gebauer 1960:26–7) is very close to that of East Slavic, with the form becoming normal in the singular for male persons in the fifteenth century, but for animals not until the seventeenth century. In Sorbian, the developments are earlier than in the rest of Northern Slavic, for sixteenth-century texts have genitive-accusative singular for all animate masculines (Lötzsch 1964:494). Polabian is extant only in late seventeenth to early eighteenth-century texts, but here the developments may have been slowest of all, since nominative-accusatives *büg* 'God', and *vål* 'ox' are attested, alongside the more usual genitive-accusative singular animate masculine (Schleicher 1871:199).

While none of the oldest texts except Sorbian has genitive-accusative in the plural, with respect to the present discussion it is necessary to examine the oldest attested forms for nominative and accusative plural of the major masculine and feminine declensions. Here there were predictable alternations in masculine accusative, and feminine nominative and accusative depending on whether the stem ended in a 'hard' consonant, or in a 'soft' consonant. In the major masculine declension, nominative plural -*i* for hard and soft stems was distinct from accusative -*y* (high central unrounded vowel) for hard stems, and -*ę* (front nasal vowel) in South Slavic, -*ě* (front diphthong) in North Slavic for hard stems. The major feminine declension had for both nominative and accusative plural inflections that were homonymous with the masculine accusative plural. Thus nominative plural masculine hard stems: *rabi* 'slaves, servants', *gadi* 'serpents', *stoli* 'tables, thrones', soft stems: *ot'ci* 'fathers', *koni* 'horses', *noži* 'knives'; accusative plural: *raby, gady, stoly, ot'cę* (-*ě*), *konę* (-*ě*), *nožę* (-*ě*); nominative and accusative plural feminine: *ženy* 'women, wives', *ov'cę* (-*ě*) 'sheep'.

Kuryłowicz (1947) points out that in Russian and Polish *i* and *y* became allophones of the same phoneme by at least the twelfth century, so that nominative and accusative plural of the masculine hard stems became distinct, not by the vowel inflections, but by consonant alternations of the stem-final consonant which was palatalized before -*i*, but not before -*y*. There was a tendency for nominative and accusative plural of the hard stems to become homonymous, by the loss of the feature of palatalization in the stem-final consonant of the nominative plural. It must be pointed out that the same situation arose in Belorussian, Slovak, Czech, and Sorbian. In Ukrainian, *i* and *y* conflated phonetically into a mid-high front-central vowel, which I shall indicate also by *y*, and the feature of palatalization was lost by consonants before the new *y* by the thirteenth century (Bezpal'ko et al. 1962:160–62). Thus, in Ukrainian, nominative and accusative plural of the masculine hard stems conflated as the result of purely phonetical developments.

In South Slavic, there arose a development similar to that in Ukrainian, for here *y* > *i* in Slovenian by the eleventh century (*Freising Folia*), and in Serbo-Croatian and Bulgaro-Macedonian in the twelfth to thirteenth centuries (Belić 1960:74, Mirčev 1963:116). In Bulgaro-Macedonian, this development had no further consequences in noun morphology, since case inflections were lost from the fourteenth century onwards. Up to that time, Bulgaro-Macedonian was as innovating with respect to other dialects in the plural as it was in the singular, for younger Old Slavonic forms have genitive-accusative plural of definite adjectives and participles referring to male persons, a feature that becomes the norm for fourteenth-century Bulgarian texts. In Slovenian and Serbo-Croatian, however, the phonetical conflation of nominative and accusative plural of the hard-stem masculines was blocked as the result of the analogical conflation of hard stems with soft stems. Here *ę* > *e*, so that both hard-stem and soft-stem masculines emerged with nominative plural -*i*, accusative plural -*e* after the hard-stem masculines had acquired soft-stem endings. One cannot be sure of the relative chronology of this analogical development and of *y* > *i*, since the results of both processes are reflected in the *Freising Folia*, while in Serbo-Croatian the analogical change is attested for some nouns in the earliest twelfth-century texts (Belić 1962:15), and may have preceded the onset of the phonetical change. The inflection -*e* for accusative plural of hard stems is shown by Oblak (1890:372) to be normal for fifteenth- to sixteenth-century Slovenian, and for fifteenth-century Serbo-Croatian by Svane (1958:47). In most Serbo-Croatian dialects, the *-i/-e* distinction has been maintained in the masculine plural. In the Cres, Novi, and Susak types, accusative plural masculine subsequently fell together with nominative, giving *-i* for both cases, with a subsequent development of genitive-accusative plural for male persons, and then in the Susak type for animals and even for some inanimates.

In North Slavic, nominative and accusative plural masculine conflated earliest and most consistently in Russian and in North-East Byelorussian. Here, the most general development was that soft stems acquired hard-stem endings. While Karskij (1956:149) cites instances from Byelorussian from the fourteenth century onwards, Kuznecov (1959:59) states that no such analogical influence of hard stems on soft stems is attested in the Russian *Laurentian Chronicle* of 1377 in the accusative plural of masculine soft stems. In fact, this manuscript contains a number of younger forms where soft-stem masculine and feminine nouns have acquired hard-stem endings in a number of noun inflections including for older masculine accusative plural *mužě* a younger *muži* 'men' which is now homonymous with the nominative plural.

In Russian, from the fourteenth century nominative plural of hard-stem masculines lost the consonant alternation, first for inanimates, then for animals, and finally for male persons, until in the early sixteenth century only a few male personal nouns are lexically marked for the alternation in the nominative plural (Unbegaun 1935: 154–7). In the meanwhile, genitive-accusative was replacing the old accusative plural for male personal nouns, and by the early sixteenth century had become obligatory when male personal nouns were the verbal object, and optional when they were governed by prepositions in the accusative plural (Unbegaun 1935:229–34). At this stage, attribute adjectives had lost the distinctions of gender in the nominative plural, so that animate masculines and feminines were distinct in the accusative plural, *staryx popov* 'old priests', *staryjě baby* 'old women', but not in the nominative plural, *staryjě popy, staryjě baby*. By the late seventeenth century (Cocron 1962:101), feminine nouns and their qualifiers had strongly marked genitive-accusative in the plural, while nouns denoting animals are attested with genitive-accusative plural somewhat less frequently. By the eighteenth century, the contemporary unmarked animate ~ inanimate opposition had been firmly established in Russian. In North-Eastern Byelorussian dialects, the developments are similar to those of Russian; in South-Western dialects nouns denoting animals may still have nominative-accusative to the present day.

After the conflation of nominative and accusative plural hard-stem masculines in Ukrainian, *ě* > *i*, giving rise to a new *i*, before which consonants did not dispalatalize (Bezpal'ko et al. 1962:151). By the sixteenth century, nominative plural of soft-stem masculines analogically acquired the accusative inflection (now -*i*) (Kernyc'kyj 1967:53). Thus both nominative and accusative masculine had the same inflection as the feminine hard stems *stoly, baby*, soft stems *koni, zemli*. Male personal nouns had only optional genitive-accusative plural in sixteenth-century Ukrainian texts, while the structure of adjectives was as in Russian, but with optional genitive-accusative for male persons (Kernyc'kyj 1967:61, 117–19). Male personal genitive-accusative is not the norm in Ukrainian texts until the end of the seventeenth century (Samijlenko 1964:180–81; Kedajtene 1961:189–91), and the unmarked animate ~ inanimate opposition occurs only in some contemporary Ukrainian dialects.

In fifteenth-century Polish texts inanimate masculine nouns have lost the consonant alternation in nominative plural, and nouns denoting animals are attested without the alternation from that time onwards, but the old forms are still attested for animals up to the nineteenth century (Grappin 1956:64). Since male persons had acquired the genitive-accusative inflection -*a* in the fifteenth century, and since nominative-accusative masculine also had this inflection in the dual, accusative dual and accusative singular had become homonymous for male persons. Grappin (1956:107–112) shows that in fifteenth-century Polish texts, some male personal nouns have genitive-accusative dual -*u* in the place of the old accusative -*a*, and claims that in the sixteenth century, with the loss of the dual, genitive-accusative was extended into the plural to male persons modified by numerals, and then to male persons unmodified by numerals. Kuraszkiewicz 1961, analyzing an extensive corpus of fifteenth- to sixteenth-century texts, agrees that genitive-accusative arose in nouns in the dual in Polish, and was then extended to the plural, but points out that in the sixteenth century genitive-accusative plural was normal only for pronouns, and substantivized adjectives denoting male persons, and did not become normal for nouns until the seventeenth century.

Grappin (1956:112–14), observing that nouns denoting animals are also attested with genitive-accusative in sixteenth- and seventeenth-century Polish texts, concludes that genitive-accusative plural developed in Polish for both male persons and animals, but that nouns denoting animals ceased to have genitive-accusative plural during the course of the eighteenth and early nineteenth centuries. One cannot be sure whether such forms in the texts are of Western or Eastern Polish provenance, without a more detailed study of the texts and of contemporary Polish dialects.

Turska (1953) and Grappin (1956:83–8) point out that in eighteenth-

and nineteenth-century Polish texts male personal nouns are attested without consonant alternation in the nominative plural, that is, with the same structure as masculine animals, inanimates and feminines. According to Turska (1953:154–5), the old and new nominative plural forms had become optional for male persons in spoken Polish in general; this is borne out by what we know of contemporary Polish dialects. Turska adds that from the end of the eighteenth century, new nominative plurals, such as *chłopy*, were being utilized in literature with optional pejorative meaning, and by the fourth quarter of the nineteenth century nominative-accusatives of the *chłopy* type had acquired obligatory pejorative meaning in literary Polish.

Although the corpus of older Slovak texts is much smaller than that which is extant for Polish, it is clear from Stanislav (1967:83) that nouns denoting animals and inanimates occur without the consonant alternations in the nominative plural masculine in fifteenth-century Slovak texts, that masculine personal nouns are attested with genitive-accusative plural in the sixteenth century, and that masculine nouns denoting animals are attested with genitive-accusative plural from the late seventeenth century.

In Upper Sorbian, by the sixteenth century, masculine nouns denoting animals and inanimates had conflated nominative plural with accusative plural, so that there was an unmarked opposition of male persons ~ others in the plural, expressed by the genitive-accusative and special nominative plural forms (Fasske 1972:18–20, 30). Apart from Slovenian, which developed genitive-accusative only in the singular, only Sorbian dialects have retained the dual till modern times. In Sorbian, as previously in Polish, the masculine genitive-accusative singular -*a* was homonymous with masculine accusative dual, and in Sorbian genitive-accusative dual developed for all masculine animates (Lötzsch 1964; Fasske 1972:43–5). In Upper Sorbian genitive-accusative dual is attested for all masculine animates up to the middle of the nineteenth century. However, the genitive dual inflection -*ow* in Upper Sorbian was homonymous with genitive plural. In the meantime, in seventeenth-century Upper Sorbian, the old nominative dual -*a* inflection was replaced by a new inflection -*aj*, distinct from both genitive-accusative masculine singular and from genitive plural. From the middle of the nineteenth century onwards, this new nominative dual ending replaced the genitive-accusative dual inflection for all animals in Southern Upper Sorbian dialects, and in many of them for male persons as well. Genitive-accusative dual is retained (and then only optionally) for male persons and animals in Upper Sorbian only in some Northern dialects. Fasske (1972:45–6) accounts for this regional differentiation on the grounds that special nominative plural forms were strongly retained for male persons only in Southern dialects for nouns and all parts of speech congruent with them. In other dialects special forms had been lost for parts of speech congruent with male personal nouns, and genitive-accusative plural had developed less strongly for the male personal forms. According to Fasske, the decline of genitive-accusative animate dual in Upper Sorbian arose as a result of asymmetry between the male personal category in the plural, and the animate category in the dual. The stronger the male personal category was in the plural, the weaker did the animate category become in the dual during the last hundred years.

In Lower Sorbian, the developments were quite different (Lötzsch 1964, 1970; Fasske 1972:20–26). By the seventeenth century, the old masculine nominative plural forms were almost entirely lost, even for nouns denoting male persons, genitive-accusative plural never became wholly obligatory for male persons, and is occasionally attested for masculine animals, and even for female persons (Lötzsch 1970:118–123, especially 123 fn. 36). In the dual, however, the development was quite consistent. The nominative dual masculine retained the old -*a* inflection, and the genitive dual -*owu* is not homonymous with genitive plural -*ow* in Lower Sorbian, and nearly all the dialects have obligatory genitive-accusative animate dual today. In the plural, however, from the mid-nineteenth century, genitive-accusative has been lost, first for masculine animals, and then for persons, except when the nouns are combined with the numerals 3 and 4. Lötzsch (1970) states that genitive-accusative animate was retained with the numerals 3 and 4 as a result of the influence of the dual. Fasske (1972:35–42) sees the development as being the result of the development of the system of numerals. When numerals from 5 upwards are in the accusative, they have governed the genitive plural of all nouns in Slavic from the time of the earliest texts. The numerals 3 and 4 had special forms for masculine nouns in the nominative, and the reflexes of these numerals retained the old nominative forms for animates in Lower Sorbian, after the animate nouns themselves had lost the old nominative forms. The numerals 3 and 4 then developed special forms in the oblique cases for animates, including genitive-accusative, in Lower Sorbian. These special animate masculine forms were then transferred to the numerals 5 and upwards. When genitive-accusative animate masculine was lost in Lower Sorbian during the last hundred years, the numerals were not affected, and neither were the nouns that they governed, so that in contemporary Lower Sorbian dialects genitive-accusative animate is retained in the paucal as well as in the dual. The complex structures of the contemporary transitional dialects that have been sketched above clearly arose as the result of the

impingement upon one another of the male personal category developing
in the plural in the South, and of the animate category developing in dual
and paucal in the North.

In Czech, masculine inanimate nouns, and parts of speech congruent
with them, had conflated nominative plural with accusative plural by the
beginning of the seventeenth century (Gebauer 1960:46–7, 103–4).
There was now an unmarked opposition of animate ~ inanimate in the
masculine, expressed only by the retention of the old nominative forms by
animates, since genitive-accusative plural developed only in a few Eastern Czech dialects. This opposition was expressed throughout parts of
speech congruent with animate masculine nouns in all dialects, but in
most dialects, as the result of some earlier phonological changes, not all
hard-stem masculine animate nouns distinguished nominative plural
from accusative plural. Up to the fourteenth century, Czech labials and
dentals were palatalized before -*i*, but not before -*y*. During the fourteenth century, labials and dentals other than -*t*-, -*d*-, -*n*-, -*r*- lost the
feature of palatalization in most dialects, and then, in many dialects, *y* > *i*
(Komárek 1962:123–4, 167–8). Thus by the seventeenth century,
nominative and accusative plural of masculine animate nouns were distinct only for soft stems, for certain dental stems, for velar stems (which
preserved an ancient alternation), and for nouns with nominative plural
in -*ové*. For other stems, the distinction was signalled only by the modifiers, e.g., nominative plural /ťi slabī xlapi/ 'these weak fellows', accusative /ti slabē xlapi/. Most Bohemian dialects subsequently conflated
nominative and accusative plural of these nouns and their modifiers in
such a way that today they have lost the animate ~ inanimate opposition,
and in its stead there are the rules that certain animate masculine nouns
are lexically marked for the nominative-accusative plural -*ové* inflection,
and that animate masculines with velar stems, and certain dental stems
have consonant alternations of the stem in nominative and accusative
plural (and in some dialects throughout the plural).

In some Southern Bohemian dialects, the distinction has been preserved by vowel length in the nominative plural of masculine animates,
probably the result of analogy with a minor declension, as suggested by
Belić (1972:155). Most Moravian dialects preserve the distinction, in the
modifiers, and in nouns of the stem-types referred to above. The male
personal category, with genitive-accusative plural in Silesian, and in some
Eastern Moravian dialects, occurs in areas which are contiguous with
Polish and Slovak, respectively.

In Northern Slavic, genitive-accusative was restricted to the masculine
singular, not only in Czech, but also in Polabian, which, in the plural,
expressed the animate ~ inanimate distinction by retaining the old

nominative plural forms for masculine animates (Schleicher 1871:202–203).

In discussing the rise of genitive-accusative in Slavic, I shall cite as Common Slavic certain Old Slavonic forms which happen to correspond with the forms we can reconstruct for late Common Slavic. In my view, the major factor influencing the original development of genitive-accusative in Common Slavic was the asymmetry between nominative and accusative of the personal interrogative, and of the nouns to which that interrogative referred. The interrogative had distinct forms for nominative *kŭto* 'who', and accusative *kogo* 'whom', and the latter was homonymous with the genitive. All nouns of the major feminine declension, and therefore all the feminine personal nouns of this declension, also had distinct forms for nominative singular, e.g., *žena*, and accusative singular *ženǫ* (genitive singular *ženy*), whereas nouns of the major masculine declension had conflated nominative and accusative singular, e.g. *prorokŭ* 'prophet'. Similarly, the definite adjective had nominative singular feminine *novaja* 'the new one', accusative *novǫjǫ*, but nominative-accusative singular masculine *novŭj*. The genitive singular masculine, *novajego*, had the terminal suffix *-ego*, the soft-stem equivalent of the *-ogo* suffix of the personal interrogative. The asymmetry between the personal interrogative and personal feminine definite adjectives on the one hand, and between personal masculine definite adjectives on the other, was removed by utilizing the *-ego/-ogo* suffix for the accusative of the personal masculine definite adjective as well as for the personal interrogative. From here, genitive-accusative singular was extended to definite participles referring to male persons, and then to masculine nouns referring to definite male persons. The account given here is a modification of that given in Meillet (1897); both accounts proceed from the necessity of explaining why the distinction in the oldest extractable layer in Old Slavonic intimately involves the distinction definite ~ indefinite.

Tomson (1908) takes issue with Meillet on this point, and states that the distinction arose in order to distinguish Agent from Patient. In Old Slavonic, however, genitive-accusative singular is used just as regularly in prepositional phrases as it is when the noun is the object of the verb. In Old East Slavic, Old Czech, and Old Polish, the form is used most frequently as the object of the verb, and less frequently in prepositional phrases. The reason for this is that Bulgaro-Macedonian was highly innovating with respect to the extension of genitive-accusative singular. Genitive-accusative singular, then, first arose by distinguishing nominative and accusative of masculine singular nominals referring to definite persons, but was extended to distinguish these cases for all masculine singular nominals referring to persons, and particularly to distinguish Patient from Agent. At various times, in all Slavic dialects, the male personal category in the singular was transformed into an animate category within the masculine singular. While these dialects shared a common point of departure, the subsequent evolution in the singular represents, at least in Northern Slavic, a set of parallel innovations within related dialects, rather than a single innovatory wave which spread across the whole area. It is possible, in view of the time lag between Bulgaro-Macedonian and Serbo-Croatian, that in South Slavic there was a single innovatory wave spreading from the South to the North. In East Slavic, Polish, Slovak, and Czech the developments seem to be contemporaneous one with another, so that the absence of a time lag points here to parallel innovations, rather than to a single innovatory wave.

In the Old East Slavic *Primary Chronicle*, there is a passage which, in my opinion, provides strong confirmation of Meillet's statement that genitive-accusative in Slavic arose first of all to distinguish definite from indefinite masculine personal nouns. From the five oldest witnesses, it is clear that this passage contains one example of the old nominative-accusative *bykŭ* 'bull', and three examples of the younger genitive-accusative *byka*. This passage occurs in some texts under the year 992, and in others under the year 993, but was almost certainly composed not later than the early twelfth century. In the *Hypatian Chronicle* the forms have been changed to *volŭ, vola* 'ox', respectively, but the original hand clearly has *bykŭ, byka*. The passage may be normalized:- *I nalězoša bykŭ velikŭ i sil'nŭ. I povelě razdražiti byka, i vŭzložiša na n' želěza goräča. I pustiša byka, i poběže bykŭ mimo i. I poxvati byka rukoju za bokŭ.* 'And they found a large and strong bull. And he ordered them to annoy the bull, and they put hot irons on it. And they let the bull go and it started to run away past him. And he grabbed the bull by the side with his hand.' In the first sentence, the reference is indefinite 'a bull', and the Old East Slavic uses the nominative-accusative. When 'bull' is mentioned again, the reference is to the same previously-mentioned bull, so that the reference becomes definite, and the verbs *razdražiti* 'to irritate', *pustiša* 'they let go', and *poxvati* 'he took hold of', which all govern the accusative case, now have a definite object which appears in the form of the genitive-accusative *byka*. In the Old East Slavic Primary Chronicle the only masculine nouns that have obligatory genitive-accusative singular are all proper nouns. Since proper nouns are a subclass of the class of definite nouns, in Old East Slavic of this period the feature Definite was still a relevant factor in triggering the genitive-accusative singular for male personal nouns. Since genitive-accusative for nouns denoting animals is wholly exceptional for twelfth-century Old East Slavic, the unusual occurrence of three such genitive-accusatives in the passage cited above can be explained on the grounds that the feature Definite played a role in Old East Slavic in triggering genitive-accusative for masculine nouns denoting animals, as well as for those denoting persons. Thus Old East Slavic, as well as Old Slavonic, provides data supporting Meillet's contention that genitive-accusative singular first arose in Slavic as a means of distinguishing definite objects from indefinite objects.

In the plural, there is a division between North Slavic, where genitive-accusative plural evolved at one time or another in nearly all dialects, and between South Slavic, where, in the plural, the form occurs in very few dialects. In South Slavic, case inflections were lost in Bulgaro-Macedonian, but in Slovenian and Serbo-Croatian, nominative plural masculine -*i* was kept distinct from accusative -*e* as a result of the analogical influence of the soft stems on the hard stems. After accusative plural masculine conflated with the nominative in certain *Čakavian* dialects, genitive-accusative plural arose as a means of distinguishing Object from Subject for male persons, since only masculine nouns had the form in the singular, and the subject of a transitive verb is more frequently personal than impersonal. From male personal nouns, the form was extended in the plural in some of these dialects, to other masculine nouns. Here, the evolution was clearly independent from, and therefore clearly parallel with, the rise of genitive-accusative plural in most of the Northern Slavic dialects.

In East Slavic, by the sixteenth century, nominative and accusative plural masculine had almost entirely conflated. The paths leading to that conflation were quite different in Ukrainian on the one hand, and in Russian and North-Eastern Byelorussian on the other. While the Russian and Byelorussian developments were part of a single innovatory wave, Ukrainian arrived at a similar result through quite a different path, so that the similar outcome in these two regions was coincidental, and not a parallel innovation. Genitive-accusative was extended to male personal nouns during the fifteenth to seventeenth centuries in East Slavic, partly as a means of keeping Object distinct from Subject, as in Čakavian, but also for the reason that genitive-accusative was now becoming obligatory for male persons in the singular. In addition, forms of the masculine plural declension were now assimilated to those of the feminine, and along with this general trend, genitive-accusative was being extended to feminine personal nouns in the plural, and then later to plural nouns referring to animals. The extension of genitive-accusative plural beyond the sphere of the male personal is, in East Slavic, an innovatory wave that spread from

Russian westwards, and gradually petered out in Western Byelorussian and Western and Southern Ukrainian.

In Polish and Slovak, the rise of genitive-accusative plural is in no way linked in the first instance with the distinction between Subject and Object, for in Eastern Slovak, and possibly in Eastern Polish, genitive-accusative plural was extended to male persons and animals, which, particularly in Eastern Slovak, also retained the old distinction between nominative and accusative more strongly than did inanimate masculine nouns. Here the development was strongly influenced by the development of obligatory genitive-accusative in the singular. The rise of the male personal plural genitive-accusative in Central and Western Slovak and in Western Polish was under a similar influence. Thus in Čakavian, the rise of genitive-accusative plural was primarily influenced by relationships within the plural, in Polish and Slovak mainly by the influence of the singular on the plural, and in East Slavic both factors ought to be given equal weight. Certainly, there has been an East-West innovatory wave from Slovak to Czech, running today from animate genitive-accusative in the East to the absence of the animate category in the plural in the West. In Polish one may speak of a single innovatory wave, with genitive-accusative plural strongest in the East, and the male personal nominative plural forms being stronger in the West. It might be tempting to look for a single innovatory wave spreading from East Slavic right across these two West Slavic regions. More detailed information on the dialects across the whole area might give one a better basis on which to discuss this issue. In Polish, it seems very likely that the dual had an influence on the plural; such was probably also the case in Sorbian. Ought one to look, then for a single innovatory wave that spreads right over to Sorbian?

The detailed localized information for Sorbian given in Fasske (1975) leads one to look for more detailed information on local developments; innovations may have spread out from all sorts of centres, and one may well have had a whole series of innovations, partly parallel and partly diverging one from the other.

It is clear, though, that the development of genitive-accusative in Slavic does give a good model of the ways in which privative oppositions may arise in languages, of how they may be transformed into equipollent oppositions, or how an opposition may disappear altogether.

The particular semantic and morphological relations involved, and the various phonological and analogical developments that have brought about those relations are, of course, peculiar to the categories of animate and male personal in Slavic. However, the kind of diachronic and synchronic relations between oppositions revealed by this material seems to be quite general in nature. For example, there is an ancient opposition in

Slavic within the imperfective aspect between verbs of motion which characterize the motion as being carried out in one direction, e.g., *nes-* 'carry', and verbs which do not characterize the motion in this way, e.g., *nos-* 'carry'. In Old Slavonic, the unmarked *nos-* could be used to refer to a motion carried out in one direction on one occasion, e.g., *pridǫ na grobǔ nosęštę ježe ugotovašę aromaty* 'they came to the tomb carrying the spices they had prepared'. In two out of the three attested readings in Old Slavonic, the indetermined *nos-* occurs in this passage, as above, in the *Zographensis* and the *Marianus*, whereas the *Assemanianus* has *nesǫštę* from determined *nes-*. Similarly, in the Old East Slavic *Laurentian Chronicle*, and *Hypatian Chronicle: pride nosǎ Igorǎ dět'ska* 'he came carrying the young Igor', *nos-* is used where modern East Slavic would have to use *nes-*. The reason for this is that the determined verbs were less strongly marked in Old East Slavic than they are today. A similar evolution has occurred in West Slavic. In South Slavic, however, the unmarked indetermined forms gradually replaced the marked forms in most dialects, so that today, for example, in Bulgaro-Macedonian only *nos-* has the meaning 'carry', in one direction, or several directions. Where *nes-* is used, it normally has the meaning 'lay an egg'.

There are, of course, other types of change that must be investigated. For example, definite adjectives in Old East Slavic (and probably in Common Slavic) were the explicitly marked form, but particularly in nominalizations had the implication of a generic quality, 'the one who . . .'. In Contemporary Standard Russian, the reflexes of the indefinite adjectives are used with lexical and syntactical restrictions, but some of them do have relations involving the reflexes of the definite adjectives in features Specific ~ Generic. However, with the verbs of motion, and with the adjectives, the semantic features involved are more controversial, and more abstract than the features Animate and Personal. Still, if we attempt to investigate the history of oppositions involving fairly simple features, we will surely throw some light on the history of oppositions involving more complex features, and in my view, the animate and personal oppositions in Slavic provide an excellent pilot study for this type of investigation.

References

Avanesov, R. I. — K. K. Krapiva — J. F. Mackevič
    1963 *Dyalektalagičny atlas belaruskaj movy* [Dialectological atlas of Byelorussian]
          (Minsk: Akademija navuk BSSR).
Avanesov, R. I. — V. G. Orlova
    1965 *Russkaja dialektologija* [Russian dialectology] (Moskva: Nauka).

Belić, A.
1960 *Osnova istorije srpskohrvatskog jezika, Fonetika* [Foundations of the history of Serbo-Croatian, Phonetics] (Beograd: Nolit).
1962 *Istorija srpskohrvatskog jezika, knj. 2, sv. 1, Reči sa deklinacijom* [History of Serbo-Croatian 2.1: Declined words] (2nd edition) (Beograd: Naučna knjiga).
Bělić, J.
1972 *Nástin české dialektologie* [An outline of Czech dialectology] (Praha: Státní pedagogické nakladatelství).
Bezpal'ko, O. P. — M. K. Bojčuk — M. A. Žovtobrjuk — S. P. Samijlenko – I. J. Taranenko
1962 *Istoryčna hramatyka ukrajin'skoji movy* [Ukrainian historical grammar](Kiev: Radjan'ska škola).
Boisson, H.
1946 *Le Manassès moyen-bulgare, étude linguistique* (Paris: Droz).
Cocron, F.
1962 *La langue russe dans la seconde moitié du XVIIe siècle* (Paris: Institut d'études slaves).
Dejna, K.
1973 *Dialekty polskie* [Polish dialects] (Wrocław: Zakład Narodowy im. Ossolińskich).
Fasske, H.
1972 "Wuwiće ak./gen. jako wuraz kategorije žiwosće resp. kategorije racionalosće w serbščinje" [The development of the accusative/genitive as an expression of the category 'animate' or 'rational', respectively, in Sorbian], *Lětopis Instituta za serbski ludispyt w Budyšinje, Rjad A*, 19:18–51.
1975 *Sorbischer Sprachatlas, Band II* (Budyšin: Domowina).
Gebauer, J.
1896 [1960] *Historická mluvnice jazyka českého, 3: Tvarosloví, 1: Skloňování* [Historical grammar of the Czech language, 3: The verb, 1: Inflection] (Praha: Československá Akademie věd).
Grappin, H.
1956 *Histoire de la flexion du nom en polonais* (Wrocław: Zakład Narodowy im. Ossolińskich).
Hamm, J. — M. Hraste — P. Guberina
1956 "Govor otoka Suska" [The dialect of the island of Susak], *Hrvatski dijalektološki zbornik* 1:7–213 (Zagreb: Jugoslavenska Akademija znanosti i umjetnosti).
Hjelmslev, L.
1956 "Animé et inanimé, personnel et non-personnel", *Travaux de l'Institut de linguistique* 1:155–199.
Karskij, E. F.
1911 [1956] *Belorusy. Jazyk belorusskogo naroda. Istoričeskij očerk slovoobrazovanija i slovoizmenenija v belorusskom jazyke* [The Byelorussians. Byelorussian — a historical outline of word formation and word change] (Moskva: Akademija nauk SSSR).
Kedajtene, E. I.
1961 "K voprusu o razvitii form roditel'nogo-vinitel'nogo padeža (na materiale vostočnoslavjanskix jazykov)" [On the problem of the development of the forms of the genitive-accusative (based on East Slavonic data)], *Issledovanija po leksikologii i grammatike russkogo jazyka* (Moskva: Akademija nauk SSSR), 185–193.
Kernyc'kyj, I. M.
1967 *Sistema slovozminy v ukrajin'skij movi na materialax pam'jatok XVI st.* [The

system of word change in Ukrainian based on data from the 16th century] (Kiev: Naukova Dumka).

Komárek, M.
1962 *Historická mluvnice česká, I: Hláskosloví* [Historical Czech grammar, I: Phonology] (Praha: Státní pedagogické nakladatelství).

Kondrašov, N. A.
1954 "Kategorija ličnosti imen suščestvitel'nyx v slovackom jazyke" [The category of person in Slovak nouns], *Slavjanskaja filologija* 2:38–67.

Kuraszkiewicz, W.
1961 "Uwagi o gen.-acc. pl. męskich form osobowych w XVI wieku" [Notes on the genitive-accusative plurals of masculine personal forms in the 16th century], *Język Polski* 41:288–295.

Kuryłowicz, J.
1947 "Męski acc.-gen. i nom.-acc. w języku polskim" [The Masculine accusative-genitive and nominative- accusative in Polish], *Sprawozdania Polskiej Akademii Umiejętności w Krakowie* 48:12–16.

Kuznecov, P. S.
1949 "Očerk morfologičeskoj sistemy pil'masozerskogo govora" [An outline of the morphological system of the dialect of Pil'masozero], *Materialy i issledovanija po russkoj dialektologii* 2:72–127. ·
1959 *Očerki istoričeskoj morfologii russkogo jazyka* [Notes on the historical morphology of Russian], (Moskva: Akademija nauk SSSR).

Lötzsch, R.
1964 "Die Verbreitung des Gen.-Akk. Du. in den sorbischen Dialekten und das Problem seiner Genese", *Zeitschrift für Slawistik* 9:485–499.
1970 "Osobennosti razvitija roditel'nogo-vinitel'nogo padeža množestvennogo čisla v sobstvenno nižnelužickix govorax i v nižnelužicko-verxnelužickix perexodnyx dialektax" [Peculiarities of the development of the genitive-accusative of the plural in genuine Lower Sorbian and in transitional Lower-Upper Sorbian dialects], *Issledovanija po serbolužickim jazykam*, 111–125.

Meillet, A.
1897 *Recherches sur l'emploi du génitif-accusatif en vieux-slave* (= *Bulletin de l'Ecole des hautes études 115*) (Paris: Bouillon).

Mirčev, K.
1963 *Istoričeska gramatika na bŭlgarskija ezik* [Historical grammar of Bulgarian] (2nd edition) (Sofia: Nauka i izkustvo).

Moszyński, L.
1958 "Szkic monograficzny gwary wsi Rudy pow. Pulawy" [A monographical sketch of the dialect of the village of Ruda, region of Pulawa], *Studia z filologii polskiej i słowiańskiej* 3:7–60.

Nitsch, K.
1915 "Dialekty języka polskiego" [Polish dialects], *Encyklopedia Polska* 3/2:238–343. [2nd edition in: *Gramatyka języka polskiego*, edited by T. Benni et al. (Kraków: Polska Akademia Umiejętności, 1923), 3rd edition (Wrocław: Zakład Narodowy im. Ossolińskich, 1957).]

Oblak, V.
1888–1890 "Zur Geschichte der nominalen Declination im Slovenischen", *Archiv für slavische Philologie* 11:523–561, 12:358–450.

Orlova, V. G.
1949 "O govore sela Permas Nikol'skogo rajona Vologodskoj oblasti" [On the dialect

of the village Permas (county of Nikol'sk, region of Vologda)], *Materialy i issledovanija po russkoj dialektologii* 1:45–70.

Samijlenko, S. P.
1964 *Narysy z istoryčnoji morfologiji ukrajin'skoji movy 1* [Notes on the historical morphology of Ukrainian] (Kiev: Radjan'ska škola).

Schleicher, A.
1871 *Laut- und Formenlehre der polabischen Sprache* (Wiesbaden: Sändig).

Seliščev, A. M.
1921 *Dialektologičeskij očerk Sibiri* [A dialectological sketch of Siberia] (Irkutsk: Irkutskij universitet).

Stanislav, J.
1967 *Dejiny slovenskéeho jazyka 2* [History of Slovak] (3rd edition) (Bratislava: Slovenská Akadémia vied).

Steinhauer, H.
1973 *Čakavian studies* (The Hague: Mouton).

Stieber, Z.
1971 *Zarys gramatyki porównawczej języków słowiańskich 2/1* [An outline of the comparative grammar of Slavic languages] (Warszawa: Państwowe Wydawnictwo Naukowe).

Stojkov, S.
1962 *Bŭlgarska dialektologija* [Bulgarian dialectology] (Sofia: Nauka i izkustvo).

Stojkov, S. — S. B. Bernštejn
1964 *Bŭlgarski dialekten atlas 1* [Bulgarian dialect atlas] (Sofia: Bŭlgarska Akademija na naukite).

Svane, G.
1958 *Die Flexionen in štokavischen Texten aus dem Zeitraum 1350—1400* (Aarhus: Universitetsforlaget).

Tentor, M.
1909 "Der čakavische Dialekt der Stadt Cres", *Archiv für slavische Philologie* 30:146–204.

Tomson, A. I.
1908 "Roditel'nyj-vinitel'nyj padež pri nazvanijax živyx sušcestv v slavjanskix jazykax" [Genitive-accusative of animate nouns in Slavic languages], *Izvestija otdelenija russkogo jazyka i slovesnosti* 13.2:232–264.

Turska, H.
1953 "Mianownik 1. mn. typu *chłopy, draby* w języku ogólnopolskim" [The nominative plural of the type *chłopy, draby* in Common Polish], *Język Polski* 33:129–155.

Unbegaun, B.
1935 *La langue russe au XVIe siècle* (Paris: Champion).

Zagórski, Z.
1967 *Wewnętrzne tendencje rozwojowe gwar północnowielkopolskich* [Internal developmental tendencies of North Great Polish dialects] (Poznań: Uniwersytet im. Adama Mickiewicza).

Zieniukowa, J.
1974 "Rodzaj męskoosobowy w dialektach polskich (w świetle opracowań dialektologicznych)" [Masculine personal gender in Polish dialects (in the light of dialectological investigations)], *Studia z filologii polskiej i słowianskiej* 13:55–63.

Žylko, F. T.
1966 *Narysy z dialektologiji ukrajin'skoji movy* [Notes on Ukrainian dialectology] (2nd edition) (Kiev: Radjan'ska škola).

DIETER KASTOVSKY

Zero in morphology: a means of making up for phonological losses?[1]

1.1.1   If one compares generative-transformational grammar to the grammatical model it has more or less superseded, viz. taxonomic linguistics, one notices a remarkable difference in the role of morphology in these two linguistic models. In the heydays of classical structuralism, syntax was considered a subsection of morphology taken in a broad sense, which in turn was opposed to phonology; and grammar itself was defined as consisting of "(1) *the morphemes used in the language*, and (2) *the arrangements in which these morphemes occur relative to each other in utterances*" (Hockett 1958:129; italics by Hockett). In early generative grammar, especially before the development of generative phonology, this view remained essentially unchanged, as is evident from the following statement found in Buckalew's *Generative grammar of Gothic morphology* (1964:2): "The grammar has two divisions: phonology and morphology in the broad sense . . . The inventory of morphemes and the rules which specify the permitted combinations and alterations of morphemes constitute the morphology in the broad sense. This division in turn contains the two sub-divisions of morphology in the narrow sense [inflection and word-formation, D. K.] and syntax."

    Hockett's definition of a grammar as quoted above is typical of the Item and Arrangement model of classical structuralism, where the grammatical levels of morphology and phonology were kept strictly apart. But the rivalling Item and Process model (cf. Hockett 1954) already at that time drew attention to the close interrelation between morphology and phonology in that it replaced the morpheme alternants of IA by corresponding morphophonemic processes. The development of generative phonology as a system of rules relating underlying morphophonemic (i.e. systematic phonemic) representations to systematic phonetic (i.e. surface) representations in conjunction with the abandoning of the phoneme as a relevant linguistic unit[2] finally led to a complete reassessment of the role of morphology in the grammar. Many generative linguists now no longer recognize a separate morphological component, but distribute its functions between the phonological component and the readjustment rules, which adapt the output of the syntactic component to the requirements of the phonological component (cf., e.g., Chomsky — Halle 1968:9ff.). As a consequence, the various surface realizations of a morpheme, i.e. its allomorphs, will be derived in different components of the grammar. Thus the purely phonologically conditioned allomorphs will automatically be derived in the phonological component from underlying systematic phonemic (morphophonemic) base forms by phonological rules needed elsewhere. The base forms in turn are probably introduced by the readjustment rules, although this is not quite clear. Morphologically conditioned allomorphs are either also derived in the phonological component by phonological rules governed by morphological exception features on lexical items, or they are introduced directly by some of the readjustment rules. And for some realizations, e.g. the zero allomorphs postulated in taxonomic linguistics as representations of the morphemes {PRET (ERITE)} and {PART (ICIPLE) II} with verbs such as *bet, bid, cut*, etc., it is questionable whether they can be accounted for at all in the present framework. It is this problem which forms the background of this paper, which will investigate the description of these verbs both from a synchronic and a diachronic point of view.

1.1.2   One of the major problems with this model is the status of the readjustment rules, which was never really made clear, as Barnes (1971:7 ff.) correctly pointed out. On the one hand, readjustment rules seem to contain those morphological rules which replace morphosyntactic features by the appropriate morphemes, and the latter by the corresponding morphophonemic base forms of the phonologically conditioned allomorphs, or by the morphologically conditioned allomorphs. But on the other hand, they are also said to contain rules which reduce or "flatten" syntactic surface structure; and Chomsky — Halle (1968:371) state "that it is very difficult to separate the study of these processes from the study of the theory of performance in any principled way." If these latter rules indeed account for factors of performance — and this seems to be the case —, the set of readjustment rules postulated by Chomsky — Halle would no longer form a homogeneous component, since the morphological rules mentioned above definitely refer to the speaker's competence, and not to his performance.

Furthermore, the distribution of the derivations of the various surface representations of one linguistic item (morpheme) among several components of the grammar may have the effect of destroying the functional unity of this item, which is due to its paradigmatic surface status, as was pointed out by Dik (1967). Several generative linguists, e.g. Barnes (1971:7ff.), Bierwisch (1967), Leitner (1972; 1974:18), Wurzel

(1970:18ff.), and myself (Kastovsky 1971:7ff.) have therefore suggested retaining a separate morphological component. There, inflectional (and probably also derivational) morphemes will be inserted for the respective morphosyntactic features or feature combinations. These morphemes are then replaced by their respective morphophonemic base forms (i.e. those underlying the various phonologically conditioned allomorphs) or by those morphologically conditioned allomorphs which cannot be derived by phonological rules, even in conjunction with a morphological exception feature as, e.g., the zero allomorph of the morpheme {PLURAL} in *sheep, trout, grouse*, etc., or the allomorph /t/ of {PRET}, {PART II} in *dealt, bought, built, sent*, etc. Allomorphs which are derivable by general or morphologically conditioned phonological rules of the phonological component will be derived from their common morphophonemic base form. This functions as a uniting factor for the various surface representations, since these can be traced back to this underlying representation, which in turn is linked to the morphologically conditioned allomorphs and ultimately to the respective abstract morpheme by the rules of the morphological component. In this manner, the functional unity of linguistic items having several surface representations can be preserved in spite of the fact that some of them are derived in the phonological component.

1.2.1 The setting up of zero elements as surface representations of morphological categories is based mainly on functional considerations. In structuralist morphology, such elements were used to mark a significant absence of an element in a paradigm, as, e.g., with the preterite/second participle of the verbs *cut, hit, bid*, etc., or the plural of the nouns *sheep, trout, grouse*, etc.; there, zero was justified by the comparison of these forms with the preterites/second participles *sliced, payed, wanted* and the plurals *cats, dogs, horses*, etc., respectively. This use of zero has an old tradition reaching as far back as Pāṇini (cf. Allen 1955; Saussure 1973:380; Schifko 1973:1, fn. 4); but, as Schifko (1973:1) quite rightly points out, it was only after the publication of Ferdinand de Saussure's *Cours de linguistique générale* (1916) that it was employed on a larger scale.

Some remarks as to the conditions on setting up zero elements seem to be required at this stage, although a detailed discussion of this problem is not possible here.[3] Saussure based his zero signs ultimately on the claim that the functioning of language as a system of signs rests on the paradigmatic oppositions and syntagmatic contrasts of these signs. Signs therefore are not characterized positively by what they are, but negatively by their differences from other signs: "dans la langue, il n'y a que des différences" (Saussure 1916:166). But the signs taking part in these oppositions need not all be explicit, because "la langue peut se contenter de l'opposition de quelque chose avec rien" (Saussure 1916:124). This then has to be interpreted as the meaningful absence of an element in a paradigm in a syntagmatic position where one would normally expect an overt marker of the respective category. Saussure exemplified this with the Czech example *žen* (gen. pl.) of *žena* (nom. sg.) 'woman', *ženu* (acc. sg.), *ženy* (nom. pl.), where *žen* is said to contain a "signe zéro". Historically speaking, this zero sign replaces a phonologically overt formative, because the Old Church Slavonic form of the gen. pl. is *ženĭ*, where *ĭ* is the continuation of the corresponding IE inflectional ending. Saussure thus postulates a zero sign for structural reasons in order to account for the fact that a certain morphological category in a paradigm has no corresponding formal exponent. Zero is thus used to regularize a paradigm, i.e. to make it symmetrical. Furthermore, it is interesting to note that zero takes the place of a formative which at an earlier stage of the language was realized overtly, but was subsequently lost due to certain regular sound changes.

1.2.2   Saussure's definition of a zero sign has to be modified, however, since it suggests that zero may be based on any privative opposition, a situation which would invariably lead to an uncontrollable proliferation of zero elements. This conclusion was in fact drawn by Frei (1950), who set up zeros wherever the possibility of privative oppositions existed. He therefore postulated a complex structure *Ø-père-Ø* on the basis of an opposition between *père, beau-père* and *père-adoptif*, or a zero element in *je Ø chante* because of its opposition to *je ne chante pas*. But these zero elements obviously have no functional content. Godel (1953) therefore argued that the basic criterion for zero should be the non-equivalence of *a* and *a-Ø* (or *Ø-a*), both of which are not identical with the bare stem. Consequently zero can only be established on the basis of a proportional opposition of the type $a : a\text{-}Ø = b : bc$, where $Ø$ is functionally (or semantically) equivalent to *c*. This restriction was taken over by Bally, whose definition of zero will be adopted for the present purpose: "Un signe zéro est donc un signe qui, sans signifiant positif, figure avec une valeur déterminée à une place déterminée d'un syntagme échangeable avec un ou plusieurs syntagmes de même espèce ou ce suffixe[4] a une forme explicite" (Bally 1944:160).

2.1   In structuralist descriptions of English morphology, it was customary to postulate zero allomorphs as representations of the morphemes {PRET}, {PART II}, and {PLURAL} in cases such as *cut, hit, bid*, or *sheep, trout*, etc.[5] A zero allomorph of {GEN (ITIVE)} was furthermore assumed to occur in *James's* in the pronunciation [ǰeymz], as well as in the plural form *boys', girls'*, etc.

The justification of these zero allomorphs from a surface structural point of view is relatively easy, since there are always overt realizations of the same morphological category in other environments. The justification of zero morphemes is somewhat more difficult, however. Zero morphemes are usually postulated in derivational morphology for the process termed conversion by some linguists, but more appropriately called zero derivation (cf. Jespersen 1942:85; Kastovsky 1968:31ff.; Marchand 1969:359ff.). Such zero morphemes characterize verbs such as *clean* (< *clean* adj.), *cash* (< *cash* sb.), or nouns such as *cheat* (< *cheat* vb.), *stop* (< *stop* vb.), etc. These cases will not be discussed in this paper, however.

In early generative-transformational grammar, zero morphemes were also set up for the singular of nouns and the plural of verbs (Chomsky 1957:29, fn. 3; 39; 64). However, this was done solely in order to simplify the formulation of certain transformations, e.g. DO-Insertion, and not on the basis of a structural analysis of the relevant morphological oppositions. The status of these zero morphemes is highly suspect, therefore, because they do not satisfy the definition of zero quoted above, but remind one of the zero elements postulated on the basis of a simple privative opposition by Frei. It seems preferable, therefore, to treat singular nouns and present tense verbs in English as unmarked forms, from which the few inflected forms are derived by adding the respective morphemes.[6] The only exceptions to this are the copula *be* and the personal pronouns, which have preserved some of the former inflectional categories. These will best be treated as separate lexical categories, which do not characterize the overall morphological pattern of the language.

2.2   It was mentioned above that Saussure exemplified the use of zero signs with the Czech form *žen*, where the zero sign replaces an explicit inflectional ending present at an earlier stage in the language but subsequently lost by some phonological change. Zero in this case could thus be regarded as a descriptive device which for the purposes of a synchronic description is set up to fill a gap in the paradigm, differentiating the respective form from the bare stem and marking its inflectional function. From a diachronic point of view, it could also be interpreted as a descriptive device which is set up to compensate for the loss of phonological material having morphological relevance, thus again preserving the functional oppositions within the paradigm. In the following I will try to show that the same is true of the zero allomorphs postulated in English as surface representations of the morphemes {PRET}, {PART II} with the verbs *beat, bet, bid, burst, cast, cost, cut, hit, hurt, let, put, quit, rid, set, shed, shit(ted), shut, slit(ted), spit, split, spread, sweat(ted), thrust, wed(ded), wet.* Here, too, the postulation of a zero allomorph is made necessary by the loss of phonological material having morphological relevance. Furthermore, it can be shown that this loss is synchronically recoverable, i.e. the historical process is still reflected by the morphophonemic rules of the language.[7]

The description of these forms presented in this paper should also be seen as an attempt to reconcile the surface-structural analysis of taxonomic linguistics with the process-oriented approach of generative grammar, which relates underlying representations to surface representations by a system of syntactic, morphological, and phonological rules. So far, no one has disputed that surface structure has to be regarded as a relevant linguistic level exhibiting its own type of structure, and one task of the rules deriving the surface representations of sentences is in fact to account for their internal structures. This applies not only to syntactic, but also to morphological structures. We will therefore have to ask how the rules of generative-transformational grammar account for morphological surface structures established independently on the basis of the functional morphological oppositions characterizing a language. As will be shown in the following, the preterites/second participles of verbs such as *bet, bid, cut,* etc. prove to be of particular interest in this respect, since with these verbs, the respective morphemes are not realized overtly. This creates certain problems for the generative description of the respective forms.

2.3.1   Generative morphology so far has not been concerned specifically with the derivation of these forms[8], but has mainly dealt with the derivation of the explicit allomorphs of the respective morphemes, especially /id/, /d/, and /t/, and the corresponding surface realizations of the so-called sibilant morphemes {PLURAL}, {GENITIVE}, and {3. PERS. SG.}, viz. /iz/, /z/, and /s/. The specific problem posed by these allomorphs is the choice of their underlying representation, from which the various surface representations can be derived by general phonological rules.

Two major alternatives are discussed in the literature[9]: (1) one of the vowelless forms, usually /d/, is assumed as basic, and /id/ is derived by a rule which inserts a vowel between a stem-final dental stop and this base form; (2) the form containing a vowel, i.e. /id/, is assumed as basic, and the vowelless forms are derived by a rule deleting the vowel. In both cases, the form /t/ is derived by a rule assimilating /d/ to a preceding stem-final voiceless consonant[10], since English does not tolerate the immediate succession of two stops or fricatives contrasting in the feature [voice] in word-final position. The same options exist for the sibilant morphemes.

Vowel Insertion is usually justified by referring to general phonotactic restrictions of English, which exclude clusters consisting of two identical consonants in certain positions. According to this analysis, a vowel /i/ would automatically be inserted into the underlying representation /nɔd#d/ of *nodded* in order to break up this consonant cluster yielding /nɔd#id/. The alternation /id~ d~ t/ could then be treated as completely automatic.[11]

However, the status of phonotactic surface constraints with regard to phonological rules is less than clear (Zwicky 1974:210). Moreover, Vowel Deletion has the additional advantage of also accounting for the reduced forms of *is* in *he's here, it's here, John's here*, as against *Charles is here*. And finally Vowel Deletion is parallel to the historical process of Vowel Syncopation, which has brought about the present distribution of the respective allomorphs (Kastovsky 1971:65–123; Miner 1975:350f.). In fact, Vowel Insertion would have to assume restructuring, since the original underlying representations of these morphemes, viz. /iz/, /id/, would have to be replaced by the new base forms /z/, /d/. But according to Miner (1975:351), there is no evidence that restructuring has taken place, and medieval spelling practice generalizing the spelling *-ed* unambiguously points to /id/ as the underlying representation at this stage. Thus the Vowel Deletion hypothesis on the whole seems to be more plausible than the Vowel Insertion hypothesis and will therefore be adopted here.

2.3.2.1   The verbs *bet, bid, burst*, etc., are exceptional in both analyses with regard to the formation of their preterites and second participles in that these do not show an overt inflectional ending. They will therefore have to be provided with a suitable exception feature in the lexicon.

It could be argued that the simplest solution would be to specify these verbs as selecting a zero allomorph of the respective morphological categories, and to derive their surface forms by an appropriate rule in the morphological component, i.e. to treat this zero allomorph as completely morphologically conditioned. It would thus be handled in the same way as the surface representation /t/ occurring in *dealt, built, bent*, etc. But this solution is inadequate, since it does not relate the occurrence of zero to the fact that only verbs ending in a dental stop have this zero allomorph. On its own, this would not provide a cogent argument for the proposed phonological rules. Rather, we would be confronted with the same situation as with Hoard and Sloat's rule of devoicing (cf. note 10), which was rejected as ad hoc, because, although it was statable in phonological terms, it was morphologically governed, and was not needed elsewhere. I therefore argued for treating /t/ as a purely morphologically conditioned allomorph, which should be introduced directly in the morphological component. The same arguments would be valid here, if it were not for an additional factor which suggests that the presence of a zero allomorph is indeed related to the type of consonant occurring in final position. This additional factor is the behaviour of the allomorphs representing {GEN}. This morpheme is realized as zero if it is preceded by one of the regular plural allomorphs /iz ~ z ~ s/, i.e. by an allomorph containing a sibilant, cf. *mothers', sisters', aunts', nieces'*, etc., as against *men's, children's, addenda's*, etc., where the plural is formed by one of the irregular non-sibilant allomorphs.[12] Furthermore, there is free variation between /iz/ and zero with singular proper names ending in a sibilant, cf. *Charles's, Dickens's*, etc. There is thus an obvious correlation between the occurrence of zero allomorphs, the stem-final consonant and the consonant of the inflectional base form in that zero is more or less restricted to cases where the stem-final consonant and the consonant of the inflectional ending belong to the same class, i.e. are both dental stops or sibilants.[13]

2.3.2.2   This relationship should somehow be captured by the morphophonemic rules deriving the surface representations of the repsective morphemes. The simplest way to do this is to use the independently motivated rule of Cluster Simplification,[14] which specifies that one of two identical consonants is deleted (Chomsky — Halle 1968:46, 221). In this form, the rule is an overgeneralization, and I will return to its more exact formulation below. The clusters required as input to this rule arise in connection with the rule of Vowel Deletion (or Vowel Insertion). As a preliminary hypothesis, it could be argued that in the framework using Vowel Deletion, the respective verbs *bet, bid, burst*, etc. are characterized by an exception feature in the lexicon marking them as obligatorily undergoing this rule, although they contradict its structural description, which states that this rule is inapplicable if the verb ends in a dental stop. Similarly, {GEN} would be marked as obligatorily deleting the vowel of its base form if preceded by {PLURAL}, which in turn (just as the genitive singular) does not delete its vowel if the stem-final consonant is a sibilant. Vowel Deletion itself could best be formulated in terms of a negative environment statement, expressed by the condition which in the following formulation (1) is introduced by "except" (cf. Zwicky 1974:214 and fn. 7).

In the framework using Vowel Insertion, the respective verbs (and {GEN}) would have to be marked as not permitting Vowel Insertion, although its structural description is met. Here the relevant environment

(1)

$$i \to \emptyset \; / \; \# \underline{\hspace{1.5cm}} \begin{bmatrix} - \text{son} \\ + \text{cor} \\ - \text{dist} \\ \chi \;\; \text{stri} \end{bmatrix} \# \;\; \text{except} \; / \begin{bmatrix} + \text{cor} \\ - \text{dist} \\ \chi \;\; \text{stri} \end{bmatrix} \# \underline{\hspace{1.5cm}} \begin{bmatrix} + \text{cor} \\ - \text{dist} \\ \chi \;\; \text{stri} \end{bmatrix}^{15} \#$$

could be specified positively. We thus have the two alternatives of negative environment and positive exception feature or positive environment and negative exception feature; in 2.3.4 below, however, a different solution in terms of boundary features will be proposed. Vowel Deletion applied to the items marked as exceptions produces unacceptable consonant clusters, cf.

(2) a. /bet#id/ → */bet#d/
    b. /bid#id/ → */bid#d/
    c. /bɔs#iz#iz/ → */bɔs#iz#z/

The same is true in case Vowel Insertion is omitted under the same circumstances. Only what in (2) appears as output will be the underlying representation in this alternative analysis.

For example (2a), we need Voice Assimilation as an additional rule in order to produce a cluster of identical consonants, which would then provide the input to the Cluster Simplification rule. Voice Assimilation is also needed to derive the surface representations *kissed* [kist], *lacked* [lækt], *cats* [kæts], *puffs* [pʌfs] from the intermediate representations /kis#d/, /læk#d/, /kæt#z/, /pʌf#z/. Since Voice Assimilation is needed anyway, its application to cases such as (2a) seems rather more plausible than the addition of a specification to Cluster Simplification, which states that it is insensitive to voice differences between the adjacent consonants, as is proposed by Hoard and Sloat (1971:51).

Now Cluster Simplification applies and deletes one of the identical consonants, thus producing the surface representations [bet], [bid], *bosses'* [bɔsiz].

2.3.3.1 Let us now turn to a closer examination of Cluster Simplification. This rule, which in phonetic terms could be described as complete assimilation, is in fact the phonological process (both synchronically and diachronically) for which the zero allomorphs postulated in *bet, hit*, etc. can be considered as the morphological surface compensation in the sense discussed in 1.2.1 and 2.2 above.

This rule is introduced by Chomsky and Halle (1968:46) in order to simplify the final consonant cluster in the underlying representations of

caréss, haráss, viz. *kVress, hVræss*, which is required for the explanation
of the stress pattern of these words. Phonetically, these words contain a
weak final syllable, to which the Main Stress Rule could not have assigned
the stress; but the assumption of two underlying final consonants makes
the final cluster strong, and the Main Stress Rule will then correctly assign
the stress to this syllable. The correct surface representation is derived by
the rule of Cluster Simplification, which in informal terms states that "the
first of two identical consonants is deleted", i.e. it can be represented
as

(3)   C → Ø before an identical consonant
        (Chomsky – Halle 1968:148, rule 156).

This rule also simplifies the identical consonant clusters present in
/æs=sist/, /æs=sembl/, etc. (intermediate representations of *assist,
assemble*, etc.), which protect these words from undergoing voicing of
intervocalic /s/, cf. *resist, resemble, design, presume* with [z] as against
consist, semblance, consign, consume with [s], where [z] is derived from
underlying /s/ by this voicing rule.[16] /æs=sist/, etc. in turn are derived from
/æd=sist/, etc. by a rule that assimilates /æd=/ to the following consonant
under certain conditions, thus producing the identical consonant clusters.
This Assimilation Rule, together with Cluster Simplification, is also
involved in the derivation of *attest* [ætest] < /æt=test/ < /æd=test/,
appear [æpīyr] < /æp=pēr/ < /æb=pēr/, etc. (Chomsky — Halle
1968:222).

Chomsky and Halle's formulation of Cluster Simplification is, however, unduly simplified. Not all sequences of identical consonants are
affected, nor does the rule always delete the first consonant of a given
cluster.

2.3.3.2   Cluster Simplification does not normally function across word
boundaries, cf. *went to, met Tom*, where the two consonants are usually
preserved. Only when the word boundary (#) is weakened, i.e. replaced
by the weaker formative boundary (+) (cf. Chomsky — Halle 1968:66f.;
369f.), does Cluster Simplification apply, as in the derivation of *gotta* <
got to, wanna < *want to*. The same applies to compounds and derivatives,
both prefixed, and suffixed. Thus *hop-picker, gas-stove, blood-disease,
blood-donor* contain an internal # boundary, since they consist of words
bounded by # . The same is true of prefixed derivatives such as *unnerve,
unnatural, unnavigable, misspell* (i.e. *un#nerve*, etc.), or suffixed derivatives like *oneness, openness, evenness* (i.e. *one#ness*), where the presence
of two identical consonants at the level of phonetic representation points

to # as the internal boundary. Cluster Simplification thus seems to be blocked by #.

This is corroborated by the behaviour of the prefixes *dis-* and *in-*. With *dis-*, we have to distinguish two cases, viz. *dis-* as an etymological element having no constant semantic value as in *dissemble, dissect, dissent, dissident*, etc., and *dis-* as a productive word-formative prefix with negative, ablative, or reversative meaning, which is attached to adjectives, nouns, and verbs also occurring independently in English, as in *dissimilar, dissatisfy, dissever*, etc. The former is invariably subject to Cluster Simplification and may undergo Intervocalic Voicing, cf. *disaster, dissolve* with internal [z], which points to the presence of the boundary = (as in *re=solve* [ri'zɔlv] as against *re#solve* [ˌriy'sɔlv]; Chomsky — Halle 1968–95) rather than + or #.[17] Contrary to Chomsky and Halle (1968:94), who assume morphological analysability in these cases, *dis-* here is a purely phonological, not a morphological unit. With productive *dis-*, on the other hand, pronunciation varies, i.e. some speakers preserve the identical consonant cluster, while some have Cluster Simplification; and some even have both forms. Thus Windsor Lewis (1972) only lists forms with simple [s], whereas Jones (1958) in many cases gives alternative pronunciations with or without Cluster Simplification, and even quotes [di'zɑːm], [di'zeibl] with internal voicing as possible alternatives. This can be explained by assuming that all words containing etymological *dis-* will be listed in the lexicon as words containing the = boundary, while the productive prefix *dis-* will be added to the respective adjectives, nouns, and verbs by the morphological component as a lexicalization of the semantic features underlying this prefix. This will produce a structure [$_A$ # *dis*[$_A$ # *similar* #]$_A$#]$_A$, where # will block Cluster Simplification. We could now assume that speakers having Cluster Simplification in these cases have generalized the = boundary occurring with *dis-* in *dissemble* to all occurrences of *dis-*. A better solution, however, would be to assume that productive *dis-* (as against phonological-etymological *dis-*) is invariably entered as /dis#/, but that speakers having Cluster Simplification weaken the boundary between this prefix and the stem to =, after which Cluster Simplification is regularly applicable. Speakers using [di'zɑːm] rather than [dis'ɑːm] will have an additional rule feature triggering Intervocalic Voicing. This rule of Boundary Weakening, which is needed elsewhere (see below), is triggered by a positive rule feature in lexical items (including prefixes and suffixes) undergoing it, while items not affected by this rule are not specified with regard to it. In the case of *dis-*, its presence is obviously due to the analogy with etymological *dis-* as in *dissemble*, etc. In this manner, the two functionally different elements *dis-* can be formally distinguished, and the relationship between Cluster Simplification and boundary types can be preserved.

The prefix *in-*[18], on the other hand, always involves Cluster Simplification, regardless of whether it is present as a purely etymological-phonological unit in lexical representations, as in *immaculate, innocent, illicit*, etc., or is introduced by the morphological component as a word-formative prefix representing NEG, as in *illogical, irregular, impossible, innumerable*. Assimilation and Cluster Simplification thus require the absence of #; and while *innocent, illicit*, etc. are represented with = already in the lexical representation, word-formative *in-* may be specified as obligatorily undergoing Boundary Weakening to =. There is one exceptional case, however, viz. *innavigable*, which is listed in Jones (1958) with the alternative pronunciation ['in'nævigəbl]. Here, Boundary Weakening does not take place, probably in direct analogy to the rivalling form *unnavigable*, where # is present as in all *un-* formations.

Thus Cluster Simplification seems to be blocked if # intervenes between two consonants, but may occur across a weaker boundary (= as in the above examples, or +, see below).

2.3.3.3 There is one additional factor, however, which complicates the situation. Chomsky and Halle have argued that Cluster Simplification deletes the first of two identical consonants. The examples quoted so far corroborate this, i.e. it is intuitively more plausible to interpret *illogical, innumerable, dissimilar* as having lost the consonant of the prefix rather than the stem-initial consonant. For *harass* and *caress*, no such intuitive judgement seems possible, so here the choice seems to be free. But Chomsky and Halle are not consistent in applying Cluster Simplification only to the first of two identical consonants. Thus they state that *singly* [siŋgly] is derived from "phonological /siNgl#ly/, with the /l/ of /#ly/ dropping after /Cl/" (1968:85). It is thus parallel to *normally, casually, really, civilly, fully*, etc., where the identical consonant cluster is also simplified, whereas it is preserved in *frailly, palely, genteelly, servilely, futilely, hostilely, vilely, wholly, solely, drolly, foully, coolly*, etc. Chomsky and Halle restrict their discussion to *singly*, however. Now this dropping of /l/ after /Cl/ (and in the other environments) bears a remarkable resemblance to Cluster Simplification, except for three points: (1) it affects the second of two identical consonants; (2) it requires the specification of some phonological environment beyond the identical consonant (i.e. this must be preceded by another consonant as in *singly*, or a vowel, as in *normally, civilly, fully*, etc., but it may not be preceded by a glide, i.e. by [w] or [y][19] (these additional conditions are not mentioned by Chomsky and Halle); and (3) it operates across #. Chomsky and Halle do not subsume this process under Cluster Simplification, probably because this rule in their formulation does not apply to clusters where the identical consonants are separated by #. But they do not say this explicitly.

It is logical to assume that it would be preferable if all processes resulting in the loss of one of two identical consonants could be treated by one rule. In order to do this, however, we will have to account for the three factors distinguishing the simplification of /l#ly/ from the instances of Cluster Simplification discussed above.

2.3.3.4   The first point mentioned above concerned the fact that according to Chomsky and Halle it is the second consonant which is deleted in *singly*. And indeed it cannot be denied that intuitively it is the second of the two consonants which is lost in this case, just as it seems intuitively more justified to speak of the deletion of the second consonant in *bet+t* (*<bet+d*),[20] *bid+d, burst+t* (*<burst+d*), the forms underlying the pre-terites/second participles *bet, bid, burst*, etc. rather than assuming deletion of the first, stem-final consonant. In view of these latter cases, Hoard and Sloat (1971:51) opt for the deletion of the second consonant in all instances of Cluster Simplification. But this decision is obviously just as questionable as Chomsky and Halle's proposal to always delete the first consonant, because, as has already been mentioned, it seems intuitively more plausible to interpret *dissimilar*, etc. as instances where the first of the two identical consonants is deleted.

There is one feature, however, which these cases have in common, and which permits us to treat Cluster Simplification, despite the seeming differences, as a unified process. In all the examples cited, i.e. in *dissimilar, illogical* (deletion of the first consonant), as well as in *singly, bet* (deletion of the second consonant), it is the consonant forming part of the affix which is deleted, while the consonant belonging to the word-stem is preserved. Now there is a widespread tendency, according to which stems are much more resistant to phonological change than affixes, and the phenomenon under discussion seems to be a reflex of this tendency. It thus is likely that Cluster Simplification itself is a homogeneous process, but that the result of its application is determined by the morphological status of the formatives to which it is applied. It will therefore have to be constrained so as to delete the consonant of the affix rather than that of the stem if the two identical consonants are separated by a boundary, i.e. by + or =, since, as will be remembered, Cluster Simplification is blocked by #.

2.3.3.5   This still leaves us with the problem that Cluster Simplification in *singly* occurs across a # boundary and requires an additional environment specification. These two facts are obviously related. In order to save our hypothesis that Cluster Simplification is nevertheless involved in *singly*, we have to find an explanation for these exceptions. One possibility would be to assume that Cluster Simplification is directly related to some environment specification of the type

$$
/ \left\{ \begin{matrix} \begin{bmatrix} + \text{ son} \\ - \text{ cons} \\ + \text{ voc} \end{bmatrix} \\ \begin{bmatrix} - \text{ son} \\ + \text{ cons} \\ - \text{ voc} \end{bmatrix} \end{matrix} \right\} \quad 1 \; \# \text{\_\_\_\_}
$$

Such a solution does not work, however. The contrast between *singly* ['siŋgli] vs. *wrinkleless* ['rıŋklles] shows that Cluster Simplification cannot be made dependent on a purely phonological environment, since despite the practically identical phonological structure the two words behave differently with regard to this rule. Thus it seems that some morphological feature is involved, relating Cluster Simplification directly to the suffix *-ly*, but not to *-less*. Now above we were confronted with a similar situation in connection with the discussion of the prefixes *dis-* and *in-*, where Cluster Simplification also occurs in cases where one would expect a # boundary to intervene between identical consonants, as, e.g., in *dis#similar, in#numerable*. There the problem was solved by postulating the application of Boundary Weakening, which depended on a morphological feature present in the affixes. It is obvious that a similar solution is required here in order to explain the different behaviour of the suffixes *-ly* and *-less* with regard to Cluster Simplification. Thus, rather than specifying Cluster Simplification for additional environments, the affixes themselves will be provided with an appropriate rule feature. But *-ly* will not be specified by a feature making direct reference to Cluster Simplification, because this would miss the obvious generalization that Cluster Simplification depends on the boundary separating the two identical consonants. Therefore, Boundary Weakening must be involved again, as with *dis-* and *in-*, and consequently the suffix *-ly* will be marked as undergoing Boundary Weakening at least in the environments specified above with reference to Cluster Simplification. A simpler formulation, however, would make *-ly* subject to Boundary Weakening everywhere except if it is preceded by /l/, and this in turn is preceded by a glide. Cluster Simplification in *singly, civilly, normally, fully*, etc. is thus accounted for by the previous application of Boundary Weakening and does not require any additional environmental specification.

Cluster Simplification can thus be treated as a unified phonological process, which is blocked if # intervenes between two identical consonants, and in which affixal consonants have deletion priority over consonants belonging to stems. It presupposes a rule of Boundary Weakening, which, however, is well-motivated.

2.3.4.1 We will now have to reconsider the derivation of the preterites and second participles *bet, bid, burst*, etc. in the light of the restriction placed on Cluster Simplification. Regardless of our decision whether Vowel Insertion or Vowel Deletion accounts for the surface forms of the respective morphemes, the representations immediately preceeding the application of Cluster Simplification so far are /bet#t/, /bid#d/, etc., because inflectional endings in English are always preceded by # at the level of underlying representation.[21] But Cluster Simplification is not applicable to these representations because of the intervening # boundary. It would of course be possible to add a condition to this rule making it obligatory in word-final position irrespective of an intervening # boundary. But the exceptional status of the verbs involved does not justify this solution, since it would only be on their account that such an additional specification of the rule would be required. The obvious solution is therefore to use the already well-motivated rule of Boundary Weakening. That this solution is correct is corroborated by the behaviour of some other types of irregular verbs.

In one class of irregular verbs instanced by *keep — kept, sleep — slept, weep — wept*, etc., the stem-vowel alternates between /iy/ and /e/. Originally, these verbs had the vowel /ē/ in all forms, cf. OE *cēpan — cēpte*, etc., but this vowel was shortened in the preterite/second participle forms in Middle English by a fairly regular process affecting long vowels before certain mainly non-dental consonant clusters. This development in conjunction with the changes caused by the Great Vowel Shift led to the Modern English alternation. Now Chomsky and Halle, in order to account for these alternations, assume the existence of a Laxing rule in Modern English, which in fact is a synchronic reflex of this historical development:

(4)
$$V \rightarrow [- \text{ tense}] / - [+ \text{ cons}] \begin{bmatrix} + \text{ cons} \\ - \text{voc} \end{bmatrix}$$

(Chomsky — Halle 1968: 241, Rule 20. III; cf. also 175).

This rule does not apply, however, if the consonant cluster mentioned in the environment contains a # boundary, cf. *wiped* [waypt] < /wīp#t/ < /wīp#d/ vs. *produce* [prɔ'djuws] — *product* ['prɔdʌkt]. The vowel alternation in the above-mentioned verbs can be explained by assuming that the underlying representation of, e.g., *kept*, viz. $[_v[_v\#kēp\#]_vd\#]_v$,[22] must be replaced by $[_v\#[kēp+d]\#]_v$, where the + boundary now no longer blocks the application of the Laxing rule (4). Chomsky and Halle consider two alternatives to account for this replacement, i.e. elimination of # by a language-specific rule "the applicability of which defines the subcategory of irregular verbs that contains *keep, lose, weep*, etc." (1968:369), or elimination of the internal structure of these verbs, i.e. the internal brackets, before the insertion of #. They assume furthermore that this boundary symbol "is automatically inserted at the beginning and end of every string dominated by a major category" (Chomsky — Halle 1968:366). The latter alternative replaces $[_v[_vkēp]_v\ d]_v$ by $[_v\ kēp+d]_v$, where the lack of internal structure and the presence of + blocks the insertion of a boundary between *kēp* and *d*. For morphological reasons it seems preferable, however, to retain the internal structure, thus preserving the structural parallelism with the other verbs and also the morphological status of the affix. These verbs will therefore, according to the first alternative, be marked in the lexicon as undergoing Boundary Weakening if followed by {PRET}, {PART II}. After the replacement of # by +, the Laxing rule applies, quite regularly deriving the correct surface forms.

There is another group of verbs, exhibiting the same type of alternation as *keep* — *kept*, but distinct insofar as they select the purely morphologically conditioned allomorph /t/ (cf. 2.3.2.1) viz. *deal, kneel, feel, lose, lean*, etc. These verbs are also marked for Boundary Weakening in order to provide the environment for the application of Laxing, but in addition they will have to be positively specified for this latter rule, since most of them end in dental clusters, and Laxing usually does not take place before dental clusters, cf. *bind, wind, kind, mild, gold, field*, etc.

It seems reasonable to assume that the verbs *bet, bid, burst*, etc. in fact belong to the same subclass of verbs, all of which are characterized by Boundary Weakening before the morphemes {PRET}, {PART II}.[23] Whereas this process makes the first two subsets eligible for the application of the Laxing rule, the latter subgroup can now be subjected to Cluster Simplification. *Beat* is exceptional in that it does not undergo Laxing and must therefore be marked accordingly in the lexicon (cf. Hoard – Sloat 1971:51); otherwise, it would pattern like *bleed* — *bled*. This is corroborated by a fourth group of verbs, viz. *bleed* — *bled, lead* — *led, read* — *read, feed* — *fed, hide* — *hid, slide* — *slid, shoot* — *shot*, etc., which might be described as undergoing all three rules, viz. Boundary Weakening, Laxing and Cluster Simplification.[24] Cluster Simplification thus need not be complicated by any additional specification, since the assumption of Boundary Weakening creates the necessary input to this rule and at the same time accounts for the similar behaviour of a substantial subset of irregular verbs, which have the morphological rule feature [+ Boundary Weakening] in common.[25]

2.3.4.2   We must now once again return to the rule of.Vowel Deletion (the same would apply to Vowel Insertion, if this alternative is chosen), which will have to be modified so as to take the above analysis based on Boundary Weakening into account. It is now no longer necessary to provide *bet, bid, burst*, etc. with an exception feature referring to Vowel Deletion. Instead, this rule itself will make reference to the type of boundary by allowing it to operate after # as well as +:

(5)

$$i \rightarrow \emptyset \ \bigg/ \ \left\{ {\# \atop +} \right\} \text{---} \begin{bmatrix} - \text{son} \\ + \text{cor} \\ - \text{dist} \\ \alpha \ \text{stri} \end{bmatrix} \# \ \text{except} \ \begin{bmatrix} + \text{cor} \\ - \text{dist} \\ \alpha \ \text{stri} \end{bmatrix} \# \text{---} \begin{bmatrix} + \text{cor} \\ - \text{dist} \\ \alpha \ \text{stri} \end{bmatrix} \#$$

This addition of + in the environmental specification guarantees that the rule will delete /i/ between a dental or a sibilant, if it is preceded by +, while the exception feature of the rule blocks it from applying after # in this environment. Thus it correctly derives /bet+d/ from /bet+id/ (after Boundary Weakening), but does not affect /flit#id/ (without Boundary Weakening).

2.3.4.3   Vowel Deletion, Voice Assimilation, and Cluster Simplification are phonological rules having morphological consequences in that they derive surface variants of certain inflectional morphemes. Of these, Vowel Deletion and Voice Assimilation are unproblematic, since they still leave a phonological trace of the underlying representation: the remaining consonants (i.e. /z/, /s/ or /d/, /t/) are easily identifiable as the representations of the respective morphemes. The same is true of Cluster Simplification, as long as it deletes only part of the phonological representation of a morpheme, as in *dissimilar, illogical, singly*, where it creates a surface alternant, i.e. /di/ besides /dis/, /i/ besides /in/, or /i/ besides /li/. But in *bet, bid*, etc., Cluster Simplification eliminates the last phonological trace of the underlying representations /id/, /iz/ of the respective morphemes, so that these morphemes now no longer have any surface representations with these verbs. This is the effect if Cluster Simplification is formulated as a purely phonological rule, e.g. in the following tentative formalization:

(6) $C_i \rightarrow \emptyset \% \; [C_i(=)]_{stem} \text{———}^{26}.$

$\emptyset$ in this formulation only denotes that the item to the left of the arrow is deleted under certain conditions, not that it is replaced by zero. The resulting surface forms would thus be *bet, bid, burst, bosses'* ['bɔsiz], etc. This is obvious from the general function of phonological rules, which are set up to derive phonetic surface representations. As was pointed out above (2.1, 2.2), however, the morphological surface analysis on the basis of the functional oppositions of the language results in postulating zero allomorphs of the respective morphemes, i.e. the meaningful absence of an element in a morphologically relevant position. Morphologically, we therefore have the surface representations *bet-$\emptyset$, bid-$\emptyset$ bosses-$\emptyset$*, etc. If it is assumed that morphological surface structure is a relevant linguistic level — and the widespread phenomenon of analogical levelling within and between inflectional paradigms strongly argues in favour of this assumption —, then we are faced with a problem, because our rules so far do not account for the respective morphological surface structure in the case of *bet, bid, bosses'*, etc. We can solve this problem, and at the same time reconcile taxonomic surface morphology and generative morphology in this respect, by postulating the following general convention:

(7)   Zero Convention

> If a phonological rule deletes a segment which exhaustively represents a formative, then $\emptyset$ resulting from the deletion operation has morphological surface status.

This convention thus states that the respective segment is not simply deleted, but in fact is replaced by $\emptyset$, which can be regarded as a descriptive device signalling the absence of a phonological surface representation of a formative (morpheme). It is not unlikely that this convention belongs to the formal universals characterizing phonological theory, and the interaction between phonology and morphology.[27]

With this convention added to the general theory, the output of rule (6) in the case of [dis='similə] would still be [di='similə], since /s/, the deleted segment, does not exhaustively represent a formative, but is only part of the representation of a formative. But with /bet+t/, the output would now be [bet+Ø], because [t] in [bet+t] represents {PRET}, {PART II} (< /d/ by Voice Assimilation < /id/ by Vowel Deletion). This now also explains, why zero in certain cases may in fact be regarded as a surface-structural descriptive device compensating for phonological losses: this is exactly what rule (6) in conjunction with (7) does in the case of *bet*, etc.; a phonological rule replaces a phonological representation of a morpheme by zero, i.e. its meaningful absence.

2.3.4.4   Above it was suggested that verbs such as *bleed — bled, feed — fed, hide — hid*, etc. may be analysed parallel to *bet — bet* and *deal — dealt*. The same applies to *bend — bent, send — sent*, etc. But such an analysis again results in a contradiction. According to the analysis presented above, *bled* and *lent* would be derived as follows:

(8)   a.   [blēd#id]   : Boundary Weakening →
           [blēd+id]   : Vowel Deletion →
           [blēd+d]   : Laxing →
           [bled+d]   : Cluster Simplification →
           [bled+Ø]

      b.   [lend#t]   : Boundary Weakening →
           [lend+t]   : Voice Assimilation →
           [lent+t]   : Cluster Simplification →
           [lent+Ø]

Surface-structurally, we would thus get the forms *bled-Ø* and *lent-Ø*, where *bled* and *lent* would have to be regarded as morphologically conditioned allomorphs of {BLEED}, {LEND}, occurring before Ø (the conditioning factor), whereas elsewhere the forms /bliyd/ and /lend/ are found. This in fact is the analysis already proposed by Bloch (1947:407). But as was already pointed out by Nida (1948:415, 427; cf. also Hockett 1947:340), it would be counterintuitive to locate the functional difference between present and preterite/second participle in an invisible zero, and treat the fomal, i.e. phonological, difference /iy/: /e/, /d/: /t/ as nonfunctional.[28] Consequently, these forms were reanalysed as containing the replacives /e ←iy/, /t←d/ as representations of the respective inflectional morphemes. Is there any possibility of reconciling the structural (surface) analysis of these forms with the generative description presented above in the same way as the structural and the generative descriptions of *bet, bid*, etc. could be matched? For the type *bleed — bled*, etc, there seems to be an attractive solution in terms of restructuring. English has a number of verbs forming their preterites and second participles by vowel change, e.g. *sing — sang — sung, hang — hung — hung*, etc., a reflex of the Indo-European ablaut pattern. It is therefore reasonable to assume that the verbs *bleed —bled*, etc. — despite their historical origin as weak verbs and the applicability of the rules discussed above — in Modern English have changed their inflectional class and joined the verbs having ablaut pattern, thus introducing a new alternation into this group. Restructuring here thus concerns the morphological features of the verbs.[29] I am not sure, however, whether the type *bend —bent* should be treated in the same way, since the alternation type is so far restricted to vocalic alternations. There would thus be no parallel pattern which could have caused this restructuring by analogy. On the other hand, the similarity to the type *leave —left, mean —meant*, etc., rather argues in favour of classing *bend —bent*, etc. with the non-vocalic preterite formations. I will therefore assume that *bend, lend*, etc., have not undergone restructuring, and derive their preterites/past participles as illustrated in (8b).

2.3.4.5   As a conclusion to this discussion of the synchronic relationship between morphological zero and phonological rules it should be added that the zero allomorphs in *sheep, trout, fish*, etc. cannot be explained in the same way in Modern English, since there is no phonological basis for their derivation. They will therefore have to be introduced directly by a morphological rule as purely morphologically conditioned variants of the plural morpheme. The same is obviously true for the zero morphemes set up in word-formation to characterize *cheat* sb., *clean* vb., *cash* vb. as against *cheat* vb., *clean* adj., *cash* sb. It is likely, however, that at an earlier stage of the language these zero allomorphs had a status similar to those discussed above.

3.1   Synchronic morphophonemic or phonological rules such as those discussed above in most cases have a historical rationale. This was in fact one of the arguments presented in favour of Vowel Deletion. The same is true of Cluster Simplification, and, moreover, just as Vowel Deletion and Cluster Simplification interact synchronically in that the former feeds the latter, so Vowel Syncopation and Shortening of long consonants, their diachronic counterparts, are both responsible for the historical origin of the inflectional pattern *bet — bet — bet*.

The relevant phonological changes took place mainly in pre-Old English, but are reflected in the Old English phonological system. Thus the best starting-point for the historical investigation of this pattern is Old English, although only one half of the verbs exhibiting it in Modern English are in fact Old English. Of these *beat, bid, burst, let, shed, shit* originally belonged to the inflectional class of vocalic (strong) verbs and first adopted this pattern in Middle English, so that only *hit* (late Old English < ON *hitta*), *set, shut, spit, spread, sweat, wet, knit*, and probably *slit* (not attested in Old English, but cf. G *schlitzen*), *cut* and *put* (both not attested in Old English, but probably of Old English origin) are direct continuations of the Old English forms. *Bet, cast, cost, hurt, quit, split*, and *thrust* are later loans mainly from Old Norse and Old French (*split* is MDu).

3.2   The pattern originated with Class 1 weak (consonantal) verbs, which on account of various phonological processes exhibited several subclasses characterized by certain morphophonemic alternations, while Class 2 verbs were completely regular.[30] Both verb classes exhibit the following morphological structure:

(9)   a.   root + stem formative[31] (+ preterite) + person/number
      b.   root + stem formative + 2nd part. (+ stem formative)
           (+ case/number)

which is evident in the preterites *frem*+*e*+*d*+*e* 'supported', *luf*+*o*+*d*+*e* 'loved'.

The stem formatives here are -*e*- and -*o*-, respectively, which act as markers of the inflectional class to which the verb belongs. They thus form part of the stem[32], and the base form of the preterite/second participle morphemes at this stage is /d/. In the following, I will only be concerned with Class I verbs, which are characterized by *i*-mutation, cf. the pairs *dōm* — *dēman, full* — *fyllan, fōd* — *fēdan, gram* — *gremman*, etc. This can be accounted for by assuming that the stem formative originally was a palatal, viz. /j/, and in a synchronic description of Old English morphophonemics it is also postulated that /j/ underlies the surface representation [e] of this formative (cf. Wagner 1969:220; Erdmann 1972).

This stem-formative element probably was originally a derivational affix, which, however, already in Old English had lost its function and served as an inflectional class marker. Due to this functional shift, we will have to assume that in the denominal and deadjectival verbs *dēman* < **dōm-j-an* : *dōm, trymman* < **trum-j-an* : *trum*, etc., the derivational marker in Old English is zero, as it is in Modern English *clean* adj. < *clean*/Ø vb., etc. on account of the parallel with *legal* : *legalize*. In this case we thus have a substitution of zero for an explicit element for functional, not phonological reasons.

This underlying representation /j/ appears as /ij/ after a heavy or unstressed syllable (Erdmann 1972:410f.), as /i/ (surface-structurally [e]) before a consonant such as the base form /d/ of the preterite and second participle morphemes, and as /j/ elsewhere. In all environments it produces *i*-mutation, and /j/ additionally lengthens a preceding stem-final consonant (except /r/) in a short stressed syllable, cf. *trum* : *trymman* vs. *andswaru* : *andswerian*;/j/ is then lost except after /r/, cf. *dēman* vs. *nerian*.

Weak verbs are thus generally characterized by stem formatives (thematic vowels, verbal extensions). There are certain exceptions, however. A small class of verbs including *bringan — brōhte* and the preterite-presents *āgan — āhte, magan — meahte*, etc. never had a stem formative and will therefore have to be analysed as a class of its own. Another group of verbs, traditionally regarded as a subclass of Class 1 verbs, i.e. those characterized by the so-called "Rückumlaut", and instanced by *sēcan — sōhte, bycgan — bohte, þencan — þōhte, þyncan — þūhte, wyrcan — worhte*, had the stem formative /j/ only in the present stem but not in the stem underlying the preterite/second participle. This is evident from the lack of *i*-mutation in the latter forms. For these we will assume a separate stem formative (Wagner's verbal extension [2 Ext$_v$], cf. Wagner 1969:220), which has the two morphologically conditioned variants ∅ and /j/. Their distribution will not be handled by a phonological rule, but by the following morphological rule:

(10)

$$[2\ \text{Ext}_v] \longrightarrow \left\{ \begin{array}{l} \emptyset\ /\underline{\hspace{2cm}} + \left\{ \begin{array}{l} \{\text{PRET}\} \\ \{\text{PART II}\} \end{array} \right\} \\ \\ /j/ \end{array} \right\}$$

3.3 In the transition from Common Germanic to Old English, the representation /i/ of the stem formative /j/ (= Wagner's [1 Ext$_v$] characterizing the bulk of Class 1 verbs) was either reduced to [e], or it was syncopated in certain environments. We have to distinguish two stages in this development, according to whether syncopation took place before or after *i*-mutation became effective and resulted in the phonemicization of the mutated vowels. With a number of verbs ending in /k/ or /l/, *i*-syncopation occurred before *i*-mutation vowels had become phonemicized, thus removing the factor conditioning *i*-mutation in the preterites and second participles of these verbs. This produced the Old English alternations *cweccan — cweahte* 'shake', *dreccan — dreahte* 'afflict', *leccan — leahte* 'moisten', *reccan — reahte* 'narrate', *streccan — streahte* 'stretch', *þeccan — þeahte* 'cover', *weccan — weahte* 'wake' *rǣcan — rāhte* 'reach', *tǣcan — tāhte* 'teach', *cwellan — cwealde* 'kill', *dwellan — dwealde* 'hinder', *sellan — sealde* 'sell', *stellan — stealde* 'place', *tellan —*

tealde 'count'. After the loss of /i/, these verbs closely resembled those of the type *sēcan — sōhte*, and it is reasonable to assume that they changed their class marker (verbal extension) from [1 Ext$_V$] to [2 Ext$_V$]. Thus at this stage no rule of Vowel Deletion need yet be added to the phonological rules; the respective alternations can still be handled on the purely morphological level in terms of a verbal stem extension with the alternants /j/ and Ø.

The second stage of *i*-syncopation, however, occurs after *i*-mutation immediately before the beginning of the Old English period, and causes the addition of a new phonological rule to the existing rule system, viz. Vowel Deletion. This rule captures the historical development according to which /i/ representing the stem formative before a consonant, e.g. before /d/ as the base form of {PRET}, {PART II}, is lost after having caused *i*-mutation. Syncopation is restricted to certain environments, however; /i/ is generally syncopated only after long syllables (i.e. those containing a long vowel or ending in a consonant cluster), if /d/ is followed in turn by a vowel, and after short syllables ending in a dental stop, again if /d/ is followed by a vowel; it is optionally syncopated after dental stops (both in long and short syllables), when /d/ is followed by #, i.e. in uninflected participles, and when /d/ is followed by a consonant, i.e. in inflected participles where the inflectional ending begins with a consonant. Elsewhere, /i/ is retained and changed to [e]. These developments result in the following Old English surface patterns:

(11) a. *ner+i+an − ner+e+d+e − ge+ner+e+d − ge+ner+e+d+ne*
        (short stem, no Vowel Deletion)
      b. *dēm+an − dēm+d+e − ge+dēm+e+d −*
        ge+dēm+e+d+ne (long stem, Vowel Deletion in the preterite)
      c. *send+an − send+e − ge+send+e+d/ge+send −*
        ge+send+e +d+ne/ge+send+ne
        (long stem ending in a dental stop; Vowel Deletion in the preterite obligatory, in the participle optional)
      d. *sett+an − set+t+e − ge+set+e+d/ge+set −*
        ge+set+e+d +ne/ge+set+ne
        (short stem ending in a dental stop; Vowel Deletion in the preterite obligatory, in the participle optional)

This loss of the stem-forming vowel in certain positions, which is captured in Old English by a purely phonologically conditioned rule at least in the earlier period, is the origin of the Modern English rule of Vowel Deletion. It was only in late Old English, when Vowel Deletion was extended to other environments as well, and especially in Middle

English, where the conditioning factors were obscured by various phonological changes, that Vowel Deletion came to be a morphologically conditioned rule for some time (Kastovsky 1971:99ff.). In conjunction with this change, the stem formatives lost their function, since they no longer distinguished the two classes of weak verbs, and became part of the underlying representation of {PRET}, {PART II}, which from then on had a vocalic segment. Only when Vowel Deletion was generalized did the rule become phonologically conditioned again.

3.4   For our present purposes, this sketch of the development of Vowel Deletion will suffice. What is really relevant are the results of the various historical changes as mirrored by the Old English phonological rules, especially in those cases where a stem ended in a dental stop. Thus the stems underlying the verbs *sendan, settan* are /sand+/, /sat+/, respectively. Correspondingly, the underlying representations of the preterite and the uninflected second participle are /sand+j+d+a/, /sand+j+d#/ and /sat+j+d+a/, /sat+j+d#/,[33] which are converted to /sand+i+d+a/, /sand+i+d#/ and /sat+i+d+a/, /sat+i+d#/ by the rule changing /j/ to /i/ before a following consonant. Then the rule corresponding to the historical process of *i*-mutation raises the stem vowel to /e/, after which Vowel Deletion applies. Taking into account, furthermore, the changes affecting unstressed vowels, i.e. /i/, /a/ > /e/, the resulting representations are /send+d+e/ and /send+e+d#/ ~ /send+d#/, /set+d+e/ and /set+e-+d#/ ~ /set+d#/. The same alternative forms occur in inflected participles. The sequence /t+d/ is automatically assimilated to /t+t/ by the same rule which still operates in Modern English. Vowel Deletion thus produces clusters of identical consonants, i.e. geminates (long consonants).

So far, the morphemes {PRET} and {PART II} would still be overtly represented everywhere by a dental stop, which, however, together with the preceding stem-final consonant, forms a long consonant in those instances where Vowel Deletion has applied. Old English, in contrast to Modern English, permitted long consonants in intervocalic position, cf. the contrast between *cwelan* 'die' and *cwellan* 'kill'. It originally apparently also had long consonants in word-final position, but these were simplified rather early; in preconsonantal position, long stops and fricatives occurred only before sonorants, cf. *æpplas, bettra*, etc., but apparently in free variation with simple consonants, cf. the spellings *æplas, betra*, etc.; in post-consonantal position, long consonants were not permitted (cf. Kurath 1956:435f.). We thus have to assume the existence of a rule of Cluster Simplification for Old English as well, for which Wagner (1969:232) proposes the following formulation:

(12) $C^2 \to C$ if: $<C>$ ___ $<C>$.

But this formulation is incomplete, since it does not include a restriction referring to word-final position. A possible restatement, using angled brackets to indicate that the rule operates whenever one of the environmental elements or a combination of them is present, would be

(13)

$$C_i \to \emptyset \: / \: <C> \: C_i \: (=) \quad \underline{} < \left\{ \begin{array}{c} [- \text{ voc}] \\ \# \end{array} \right\} >$$

$[-\text{voc}]$ excludes liquids and vowels from this position, since before these, long consonants were permitted. Alternatively, and much simpler, the rule could be stated in terms of a negative environment as

(14) $C_i \to \emptyset \: / \: C_i \: (=)$ ___ except $/ \: VC_i$ ___$[+ \text{ voc}]$.

In this form, the rules are probably incomplete, because they only deal with clusters in stem-internal position or between a stem and a suffix. In order to cover prefixes as well, the rule will have to be reformulated along the lines of (6), using the mirror image convention and an index referring to "stem". A complete formulation is not necessary for the present purpose, however. As in (6), only = is explicitly mentioned, so that (13) or (14) also apply across + (cf. note 26), but not across #. The development from Old English to Modern English, characterized by the loss of long consonants, would thus merely consist in the concomitant loss of the exception feature placed on the environment.

If we applied this rule to the intermediate representations quoted above without using at the same time the convention stated in (7), we would get /send+e#/, /send#/, and /set#/, where the representations of the preterite and second participle morphemes have been completely deleted. We are thus faced with the same problem of accounting for the morphological surface structure as in our discussion of the Modern English equivalents. Morphologically speaking, these forms are analysed as *send+Ø+e, ge+send+Ø,* and *ge+set+Ø,* and similarly the inflected participles *ge+send+Ø+ne, ge+set+Ø+ne.* This is all the more obvious, since we have allomorphic variation between *Ø* and explicit realization of the same morphosyntactic category within one verb. Thus in *ge+send+Ø* and *ge+send+e+d, ge+send+Ø+ne* and *ge+send+e+d+ne,* /d/ and *Ø* seem to alternate freely; and the same is true in the respective forms of *settan.* Furthermore, in *set+t+e* the preterite is realized by /t/, in *send+Ø+e* again by *Ø.* In order to allow for this morphological surface analysis, we will therefore have to use convention (7) when applying (13) or (14).

Rules (13) or (14) are thus the origin of the Modern English pattern *set* – *set* – *set*, but in Old English there existed a phonologically conditioned alternation between /d/ or /t/ and Ø with one and the same verb, while in Modern English Ø has been generalized with these verbs, except for those cases where Ø and /id/ are in free variation, as in *bet/betted, wed/wedded*, etc.

3.5   Cluster Simplification as formulated above for Old English only makes reference to optional = as internal boundary, but not to #. Correspondingly, the input to this rule must not contain #; in the examples discussed above, the inflectional endings were therefore preceded by +. In Modern English, however, the boundary separating the inflectional affixes from the stem is #, which requires an additional rule of Boundary Weakening. We must now ask ourselves whether for Old English we should indeed assume + as the internal boundary, or whether the boundary between stem and inflectional ending in fact was not #, with Boundary Weakening applying throughout. There are, however, strong reasons to adopt the first solution. In Modern English, word and stem are often identical, i.e. even an uninflected word has a rather autonomous status, and at least one inflectional ending, viz. the genitive, may not only be added to words, but also to whole syntactic groups, i.e. sequences of words, e.g. in *the Queen of England's grandson*. This was not possible in Old English.[34] There, the major word classes, viz. nouns, adjectives, and verbs, exhibited a full set of inflectional endings, often preceded by a stem formative, and in fact could not occur without these elements in sentences, except as stems in word-formation, where they are linked to other stems or derivative suffixes. Thus the stem without inflectional endings had no independent status, and it is therefore highly plausible to assume that a word-boundary only occurred after, but never before inflectional endings. One of the major phonological changes in the history of English, probably in conjunction with the almost total loss of inflectional endings and the resulting identity of stem and word, was therefore the replacement of + by # before the remaining inflectional endings. This development must have occurred in the course of the general restructuring of the inflectional system during the Middle English period, as will be shown below.

3.6   Two sound changes, the shortening of long vowels in certain environments in the transition from Old to Middle English, and the loss of long consonants during the Middle English period, are of importance for the further development of the verbs under consideration. The first sound change affected verbs having a long stem vowel, e.g. *blēdan — blēdde, fēdan —fedde, mētan —mette, lǣdan —lǣdde,* etc., which was shortened before the long consonant, resulting in an alternation between long and short stem vowels. The long stem vowel was later affected by the Great Vowel Shift, which added a qualitative alternation to the quantitative one. These alternations are captured by the Modern English laxing and vowel shift rules. The loss of the final vowels in *mette, fedde,* etc., and the general loss of long consonants in Middle English produced the Modern English alternation pattern *bleed — bled, meet — met,* etc. As was suggested above, this should no longer be handled on the basis of an underlying representation /id/ of {PRET}, {PART II}, but in the same way as the vowel alternations in *fling —flung, drink —drank —drunk, bind — bound,* etc. It has become questionable, however, whether these can really be handled by phonological rules in Modern English.

The loss of long consonants and final unstressed vowels in Middle English is also responsible for the regularization of the Old English alternations *set+t+e* vs. *ge+set+Ø ~ ge+set+e+d,* etc. by reducing *set+t+e* to *set+Ø* and generalizing the forms without inflectional endings in the participle. This pattern involving zero was much more common in Middle English than it is today, since it was extended to a number of originally strong verbs, e.g. *bid, burst, let, shed, shit,* and was adopted by various loans, e.g. *bet, cast, cost, hurt, quit, split.* Moreover, many verbs which today are inflected regularly, had preterites and second participles without explicit inflectional endings in Middle English and Early Modern English, e.g. *light, start, bolt, lift,* etc., and were thus recategorized later on. (For details, cf. Brunner 1962:261ff., and Jespersen 1942:34ff.)

Another interesting phenomenon is also linked to this pattern and illustrates its productivity in Middle English. English in this period borrowed numerous French and Latin participles (or verbs in participial form) ending in -*t,* e.g. *anoint, discomfit, corrupt, separate, approbate,* etc. When these came to be used as verbs, the participles often, although not always, kept their original form, which partly was also extended to the preterite, so that these fitted into the pattern *set — set — set.* Partly, however, -*ed* was regularly added in the preterite and participle on analogy with verbs not affected by Vowel Deletion after a dental stop. Now Reuter (1934) assumes that the pattern *cut — cut — cut* played a major part in this borrowing process, and that it was mainly on analogy with this pattern that the original participles extended their function to the other verbal categories, e.g. the infinitive, present, and preterite, while only at a much later stage -*ed* was added to the preterites and second participles. Although this is undoubtedly true in a number of cases, the analogy to the *burst, cut, set* pattern apparently was not the only factor determining the borrowing process. As Marchand (1969: 256ff.) points out, the correlation between *-ate* and *-ation* (*create* ~ *creation*) also played an important role, leading to the back-formation of verbs in *-ate* from nouns ending in *-ation*. Nevertheless, and this is also admitted by Marchand, surface analogy to *cut, burst, put, cast*, etc., certainly was involved, too, at least in the earlier stages of the borrowing process. But it is strange that the analogy only worked for a limited period, viz. from about 1225 to about 1475, and from then on the regular pattern automatically adding *-ed* to a loan ending in *-t* became the norm. This is actually the major criticism raised by Marchand (1969:257) against Reuter's hypothesis, who did not explain this change in the behaviour of the loans.

3.7.1   It appears that the solution of this problem involves the rules discussed in connection with the derivation of the preterites/second participles of verbs like *bet, cut, burst*, etc., in Modern English, viz, Boundary Weakening, Vowel Deletion, and Cluster Simplification. We are now faced with the following phenomena, which require an explanation: 1) replacement of + by # before inflectional endings; 2) greater productivity of the pattern *cut — cut — cut* in Middle English and later recategorization of many verbs originally following this pattern; 3) prevalence of the pattern 'borrowed French or Latin participle in *-t* → homophonous infinitive/present/preterite' from about 1225 to 1475 (Marchand 1969:257, following Reuter), then complete replacement of this pattern by the rivalling pattern adding *-ed* to the participle and preterite. Since the pattern *cut — cut — cut* continued to exist with a number of verbs, why was it dropped with the borrowed participles?

I think that there is a definite connection between these latter two phenomena, the change of the boundary before inflectional endings from + to #, and the introduction of /əd/ (or /id/) as the underlying representation of the inflectional morphemes involved, which thus replaced the original base form /d/.

3.7.2   The loss of unstressed vowels in word-final position led to a considerable reduction in the number of inflectional endings, i.e. only those ending in a dental stop or a sibilant were ultimately preserved, except for participial *-ing* and a few cases ending in *-en*, as in the strong participles *written, broken*, etc., or the irregular plurals *oxen, children*. At the same time, this loss automatically resulted in the replacement of original + separating the stem from the inflectional ending by #, while in those cases where the inflectional endings were preserved, + still remained as boundary. But the loss of the inflectional endings, especially in such syntactically neutral forms as the infinitive or the nominative singular, in conjunction with the replacement of + by #, automatically changed the status of these forms. They were no longer considered as inflected forms among others, but, due to their formally independent status, which was especially obvious on account of the boundary #, became the base forms of the respective inflectional paradigms. More precisely, their status changed from stem plus zero ending to word without inflectional ending, i.e., to an unmarked base form. As a consequence, inflection now no longer operated on the basis of stems followed by +, but on the basis of words bounded by #. This led to the introduction of # also before the remaining inflectional endings, i.e. to the generalization of #. It is obvious that this whole process was gradual and much more involved than this sketch indicates, especially if we take the dialectal variation of Middle English into account. Nevertheless, it seems clear that the loss of final vowels, eliminating many inflectional categories, caused the stem as basic inflectional category to be replaced by the word, which is an autonomous syntactic unit.

3.7.3   At the same time, Vowel Deletion, which in Old English was predictable on the basis of the shape of the stem and thus was a purely phonologically conditioned rule, came to be a purely morphologically conditioned operation, i.e. each verb had to be specified in the lexicon as to whether it permitted Vowel Deletion or not.[35] Thus ME *enden — endede — ended* (OE *endian — endode — geendod*) preserves its vowel, while the phonologically parallel ME *blenden — blende — (y)blend/(y)blent* (OE *blendan — blende — geblend(ed)*) was subject to Vowel Deletion. This situation resulted from the merger of the two classes of old English weak verbs, which was brought about by the coalescence of their different stem formatives in /ə/. As a consequence, the stem formatives lost their function and ultimately became part of the underlying representations of the inflectional morphemes. Again this process was gradual, and it led to two rivalling patterns for verbs ending in a dental stop, which now no longer were kept apart by different stem formatives, i.e. by phonological criteria, but solely by the morphological feature governing Vowel Deletion. It is reasonable to assume that in such a situation phonological surface analogy will have played an important role in determining the categorization of verbs, and that class shifts due to phonological analogy will have been frequent. It is at this stage that French and Latin participles in *-t* probably were categorized mainly in terms of phonetic similarity to English verbs, and there the pattern *cut — cut — cut* may have facilitated the borrowing, since no explicit native inflectional ending had to be added to a foreign stem in the preterite and the second participle. This would explain why in this period the pattern of borrowing involving no addition of *-ed* to the participle was relatively strong, since the presence or absence of this ending depended solely on the incorporation into one or another almost equally productive class.

Vowel Deletion, being determined by a morphological feature, was independent of the type of boundary separating stem and affix. Moreover, Cluster Simplification gradually was generalized to all positions except those where the two consonants were separated by #, thus reaching the stage formulated in (6). But inflectional endings were not yet generally preceded by #, but, at least in the earlier period, by +, so that Cluster Simplification would operate freely without any additional rule such as Boundary Weakening. Therefore, the pattern *cut —cut —cut* was completely regular at this stage. It only presupposed a morphological feature [+ Vowel Deletion] present in the lexical entry of the verb, and this feature it shared with many other verbs not ending in a dental stop and thus having explicit realizations of the preterite/second participle morphemes. The deletion of the surface realizations of these morphemes was therefore still completely regular and solely due to the automatic application of Cluster Simplification.

3.7.4   This roughly describes the situation prevailing at the beginning of the 14th century. In the 14th century, however, spreading from the North to the South, Vowel Deletion became more and more general, first leading to free variation between deleted and undeleted forms, until finally the deleted forms won out, except after dental stops and sibilants. The morphological conditioning of Vowel Deletion became phonological again. This stage was reached, according to Strang (1970:178–180), in the late 16th century. But why did this development reduce rather than increase the number of verbs patterning like *cut,* i.e., why was the vowel preserved after a dental stop (or a sibilant with the sibilant morphemes)? And why did the pattern '*separate* (participle) → *separate* (verb)' suddenly cease to be productive?

The answer to these questions is obviously tied up with the introduction of # before inflectional endings, and the reinterpretation of the stem formatives as part of the underlying representations /əd/, /əz/ (or already /id/, /iz/) of the respective inflectional morphemes. Both developments must have happened either shortly before the generalization of Vowel Deletion or at least parallel to it. As has been stated above, the loss of unstressed final vowels not protected by a consonant was probably the first development[36] and established # as the boundary after what in the remaining inflected forms appeared as a stem followed by +. The reinterpretation of the uninflected forms as unmarked base forms must have led to a gradual replacement of + by # also before the remaining inflectional endings. It is not improbable that this boundary change was in fact the ultimate cause of the loss of the vowel in the inflectional endings, i.e. caused the generalization of Vowel Deletion. But two factors now prevented the spread of Vowel Deletion to verbs ending in a dental stop or nouns ending in a sibilant.

In the earlier stages of Middle English, the status of the vowel representing the original stem formatives probably was indeterminate between forming part of the stem and forming part of the inflectional ending, with an increasing tendency towards the latter alternative. Correspondingly, the underlying representations of the inflectional endings gradually changed from/d/, /s/ to /əd/, /əs/ (later /id/, /iz/). During this transition period, there was considerable vacillation from dialect to dialect, and probably even within one and the same idiolect. But eventually /id/ and /iz/ came to be established as base forms everywhere, which is corroborated by the extension of the spelling *-ed* to cases where Vowel Deletion must have occurred regularly ever since Old English, as in *deemed* (OE *dēmde*), *kissed* (OE *cyste*).[37] So /id/, /iz/ as underlying representations must have had a certain psychological reality, which strengthened their position and made their retention after dental stops and sibilants more likely than the complete deletion of the formative, which would have resulted if Vowel Deletion had applied in this environment. Moreover, Vowel Deletion after the introduction of # before inflectional endings would produce clusters of the type /t#t/, /d#d/, etc., which could not form the input to Cluster Simplification, except if this rule contained a corresponding specification at this stage. But since apparently Cluster Simplification did not operate across # in Old English, and does not in Modern English either, this assumption is very unlikely. Thus the boundary must have been weakened to + again in order to make Cluster Simplification applicable, or, more precisely, it was never changed to # at all in those cases which permitted Vowel Deletion after a dental stop or sibilant. For a synchronic description, however, this requires the introduction of a new rule, viz. Boundary Weakening, which may have already existed at the time in other morphological patterns, and had only to be made applicable to a new environment. As is obvious from the description of Modern English, this is basically a morphologically conditioned rule. Thus it involves the introduction of a morphological feature governing this rule into the lexical entries of those verbs which were subject to it, while the others neither had this feature nor underwent this rule, a rule, furthermore, which was contrary to the general tendency of separating the inflectional endings from the stem by #. Consequently, the pattern *cut — cut — cut* for the first time became totally exceptional, which is why the regular forms in /id/ prevailed. This also explains the death of the pattern 'participle (without *-ed*) → verb', which was replaced by the regular pattern adding *-ed* to mark the functions of the participle and preterite overtly. Since this pattern was given up at the end of the 15th century, we may assume that by then the above developments were largely complete. It also explains why many verbs originally inflected like *cut*, etc., subsequently joined the regular class and added *-ed*, while only a few monosyllabics retained their Middle English inflectional pattern.

4   The above considerations have shown that the zero allomorphs postulated for verbs like *cut, bet, burst*, etc., are indeed structural compensations for a (synchronic and diachronic) phonological loss. However, the analysis of the forms in question has also shed some light on certain other aspects of historical English morphology. If the above sketch of the Middle English developments is correct, then the change of inflectional boundaries from + to # played a major role in the generalization of Vowel Deletion, which, contrary to Miner's assumption (Miner 1975:350) was not added to English phonology in the transition from Middle English to Early Modern English, but is much older. What happened at this stage was that the rule became phonologically conditioned again, at the same time marking the verbs preserving Vowel Deletion after dental stops as irregular, whereas before they had been completely regular. Their irregularity in Modern English is best accounted for by making them subject to a rule of Boundary Weakening, thus indicating that they have preserved an earlier morphological pattern which involved + instead of # as the boundary preceding inflectional affixes. The rule of Cluster Simplification, immediately responsible for the zero realizations of the inflectional affixes in *cut*, etc., reached its present formulation already in Middle English, but in fact also dates back to Old English, where, however, it was less general. If surface structure also plays a role in morphology and not only in syntax, then Cluster Simplification will be subject to a general convention which specifies that Ø resulting from the deletion of a phonological segment has morphological status, if the deleted segment exhaustively represents a formative. The various analogical changes in the history of the English language, which are mainly due to surface analogy, strongly argue in favour of this assumption.

Notes

1. I should like to thank Martin D. Pam for many helpful comments on this paper. I am also very grateful for a number of valuable suggestions made by various participants at

the conference, notably Mark Aronoff, Broder Carstensen, James Fidelholtz, Joan Hooper, P. Neubauer, Jerzy Rubach and Werner Winter, who helped me to clarify a number of points.

2. But cf. Schane (1971) for a defense of the phoneme concept in order to state relevant surface contrasts.

3. For an extensive discussion of this problem, cf. Meier (1961), Frei (1950), Godel (1953), Haas (1962), Kastovsky (1968:31–53), Schifko (1973).

4. Godel (1953) amends this to "signe".

5. Cf., e.g., Gleason (1961:98, 102).

6. The origin of this principle will be discussed below in 3.7.2.

7. For a more detailed discussion of this development, cf. Kastovsky (1971:65–123).

8. An exception is Hoard — Sloat (1971:49 ff.). I did not know their article, however, when I wrote this paper, and I am very grateful to James Fidelholtz for bringing it to my attention.

9. For a comprehensive survey, cf. Zwicky (1974).

10. This applies to the forms *kicked* /kikt/, *laughed* /lɑːft/, etc., but not, of course, to cases such as *dealt* /delt/, *sent* /sent/, etc., where /t/ as the surface realization of the respective morphemes has to be introduced directly as a morphologically conditioned allomorph in the morphological component. This seems to be a more appropriate and much simpler solution than postulating an additional, but otherwise quite unmotivated rule of devoicing, as is suggested by Hoard and Sloat (1973:113–114, fn. 9), viz. $d \rightarrow t$ / [+consonantal, −syllabic] + — #, which has to be morphologically governed in any case in order to differentiate *healed*, *billed* from *spoilt*, *dwelt*.

11. Cf. already Hockett (1958:280), and the arguments in Shibatani (1973). Hoard and Sloat (1971:47 f.) insert this vowel as part of the stem, thus obtaining /nodi#d/ as the result of Vowel Insertion, which seems to be rather counterintuitive. There does not seem to be any principled way of choosing between these two alternatives, which adds further weight to the arguments usually adduced against Vowel Insertion.

12. Zwicky (1974:216) lists the nouns *feet*, *teeth*, *mice*, *geese*, *lice* "ending in obstruents" as exceptions to this tendency. The latter three could be accounted for by including them in the general derivational framework, if Vowel Deletion is made obligatory for {GEN} preceded by {PLURAL} (cf. also note 25). In this case, Cluster Simplification (see below) would eliminate the overt realization of {GEN} in the same way as in the other genitive plurals. *Teeth* and *feet*, however, would have to be regarded as truly exceptional, but then inanimate nouns usually reject the "Saxon genitive" anyway.

13. This does not mean, of course, that zero allomorphs are not found elsewhere, cf. *sheep*, *trout*, *grouse*, *giraffe*, etc. Allan (1976) has pointed out, however, that these nouns apparently form a natural semantic class in that they all denote animals which are either regularly used as food, or are hunted as game, and that nouns like *giraffe*, *elephant*, etc. select the zero plural in fact only if they are considered as objects of hunting, but require the sibilant allomorphs in all other contexts. In this case, the zero allomorph representing {PLURAL} will have to be introduced directly in the morphological component on the basis of a morphological exception feature. But this feature could be made dependent on a morphological redundancy rule in the lexicon introducing it into the respective lexical items on the basis of their semantic specification, if Allan's generalization proves to be correct.

14. Hoard and Sloat (1971:50 f.) also use Cluster Simplification to account for these forms, but since their base form is /t/ rather than /id/ or /d/, their treatment of these forms is rather different. In their 1973 article (1973:114, fn. 9), they opt for the base form /d/,

without, however, considering the consequences this choice has for their overall analysis, and especially for the formulation of Cluster Simplification.

15. This is basically Zwicky's rule (9) (1974:214), which is derived from Miner's rule (15) (Miner 1975:356), except for the replacement of /ə/ by /i/ to conform to the phonology of British English. The internal boundaries prevent this rule from applying to words such as *morbid*, *acid*, or *premise*, *promise*, *treatise*, etc., where /id/, /iz/ are not preceded by a boundary, since they are not formatives. This also applies to Vennemann's arguments mentioned in Miner (1975:356, fn. 13), according to which /əd/, /əz/ and a syncopation rule could no longer be motivated for English on account of words such as *insipid*, *rabid*, *focus*, which should undergo vowel deletion but in fact don't. Miner mainly counters this by reference to phonological aspects, but I think that the morphological aspect, i.e. the fact that /iz/, /id/ (or /əz/, /əd/) represent morphemes in one case but not in the other is decisive. Consequently, /id/ in *rabid*, *insipid*, etc. will not be preceded by a # boundary and thus does not satisfy the structural description of rule (1). Moreover, *focus* would be pertinent as a problem only in dialects which have /əz/ as inflectional endings, i.e. not in British English, where *focus* ends in /əs/ (note the voiceless sibilant!), and the inflectional ending is /iz/. But here the same argument involving the lack of an internal boundary applies. Actually, as will be shown below, some restructuring took place in Middle English, but this concerned the removal of the morpheme boundary between the stem-forming (thematic) vowel and the inflectional ending. It was this process which made the vowel part of the underlying representation of these morphemes.

16. Other pairs exhibiting this alternation are *gymnasium* vs. *potassium*, *music* vs. *russet* (cf. *musket*).

17. This = boundary is neither a word- nor a formative boundary and is used by Chomsky and Halle (1968:66 f., 94, 371) to characterize verbs and nouns of the type *permit*, *concur*, *compel*, etc., which etymologically are derived from Latin prefixal verbs, but where neither "prefix" nor "stem" have independent status in the lexicon. This boundary is introduced for purely phonological reasons, e.g. correct stress placement on the final syllable even if this is a weak cluster, as in *permit*, etc.

18. The following only applies to the negative prefix *in-*; the situation with the locative particle *in-* occurring in *income, immigrate*, etc. is more complicated and seems to involve reference to the distinction between native and foreign formations.

19. I have to thank several participants of the conference, notably Jerzy Rubach and Werner Winter, for pointing out the inadequacies of my original analysis, which, due to insufficient data, included stressed vowels in this environment. As *fully* shows, this is incorrect. On the other hand, the great number of examples, of which the above instances are only a selection, warrants the analysis in terms of Boundary Weakening suggested below, and thus counters the objection that only very few exceptional cases are subject to this rule.

20. The presence of + instead of # in these instances will be explained in 2.3.4 below.

21. Cf. Chomsky — Halle 1968: 369; for an historical explanation of this fact, cf. 3.5, 3.7.2 below.

22. Chomsky and Halle apparently opt for Vowel Insertion.

23. Cf. also Hoard and Sloat (1971:48 f.), who treat these classes as cases of internal sandhi (with a + boundary), as against the completely regular verbs, which exhibit external sandhi, due to the presence of # before the affix.

24. Although this analysis correctly accounts for the surface forms of these verbs, and moreover, reflects their historical development, thus corroborating the above rules, it nevertheless presents serious problems, cf. below 2.3.4.4.

25. The morpheme {GEN} probably contains a similar exception feature specifying that its boundary is weakened to + after the plural morpheme; cf. also Hoard and Sloat (1971:55, fn. 33), who consider a similar solution, but restrict it to the sibilant allomorphs of {PLURAL}, since they do not consider forms such as *mice', lice', geese',* mentioned in note 12 above.

26. This attempt at formalizing Cluster Simplification uses the mirror image convention as suggested in Anderson (1974:114 ff. It thus is an abbreviation of the following more explicit formulation.

(6')

$$
C_i \rightarrow \emptyset \quad \Big/ \left\{ \begin{array}{c} [C_i \ (=)]\text{stem} \ \underline{\quad\quad} \\ \underline{\quad\quad} [\ (=) \ C_i]\text{stem} \end{array} \right\}
$$

The index *stem* indicates that the environmental consonant, i.e. the one not deleted, always must form part of the stem. The boundary = is optional in order to accommodate both *dissimilar, illicit, assist,* etc. with = and *harass, caress,* etc. without intervening boundary between the identical consonants; since in the latter examples both consonants belong to a stem, the rule is applicable. The + boundary need not be mentioned explicitly, if it is assumed that any rule applying "to a string of the form XYZ also applies to strings of the form X + Y + Z, XY + Z, X + YZ, where X, Y, Z stand for sequences of zero or more units and + represents formative boundary" (Chomsky — Halle 1968:364). Since # must be mentioned explicitly in a rule, (6) is excluded from applying to the sequence C_i # C_i.

27. As Werner Winter pointed out in the discussion of this paper, this convention is in fact a more formalized version of a principle postulated by him in order to restrict the use of morphological zero, cf.: "... in the special case that the total phonic substance of a morpheme consists of one phoneme subject to phonologically conditioned partial loss, a zero-allomorph of this one-phoneme morpheme can be admitted" (Winter 1964:16). As the above examples have shown, however, this is only the last step in the progressive reduction of the representation of a morpheme; i.e. Winter's restriction is too strong if it is applied to the underlying representation (base form) of a morpheme directly, which may consist of more than one phoneme, since this may nevertheless ultimately yield a zero allomorph in the course of the application of several different deletion rules.

28. For an extensive discussion of these problems, cf. also Haas (1962).

29. This would then be an instance of the morphologization of a phonological rule, which is described in Wolfgang Wurzel's paper also presented at the Historical Morphology Conference in Poznań (Wurzel, this volume), i.e. an originally purely phonological alternation becomes itself the marker of a morphological opposition.

30. There are a few relics of a third class, e.g. *libban, habban, hycgan,* which, however, joined the other two classes during Old English, so that for our purposes we need not recognize a separate class to accommodate them.

31. Buckalew (1964) uses the term "stem formative", Barnes (1971) calls this element "thematic vowel", and Wagner (1969) speaks of "verbal extension".

32. As Erdmann (1974:19) has shown, this analysis can no longer be maintained for the nominal inflection which was originally also based on the pattern 'root + stem formative + case/number'. Due to various phonological changes, the stem formative was fused with the case/number endings, a process which spread to the verbal paradigm in the transition to Middle English (cf. Kastovsky 1971:98 ff., and 3.3, 3.7.3 below).

33. The prefix *ge-* /ji/ characterizing the second participle is omitted here. The presence of + rather than # before the inflectional endings will be explained in 3.5, 3.7.2 below.
34. Neither was it possible in Middle English, cf. Chaucer's *The wife's tale of Bath.*
35. For details, cf. Kastovsky (1971:98 ff.).
36. Cf. Jespersen (1909:187 ff.).
37. Cf. Jespersen (1942:26) and Miner (1975:351).

References

Allan, K.
  1976 "Collectivizing", *Archivum Linguisticum* 7:99–117.
Allen, W.S.
  1955 "Zero and Pānini", *Indian Linguistics* 16:106–113.
Anderson, S.R.
  1974 *The organization of phonology* (New York: Academic Press).
Bally, Ch.
  1944 *Linguistique générale et linguistique française* (Berne:Franke).
Barnes, M.R.
  1971 *Phonological and morphological rules in Old Saxon* (Unpublished Ph.D. Dissertation, U.C.L.A.).
Bierwisch, M.
  1968 "Syntactic features in morphology: General problems of so-called pronominal inflection in German", in *To honor Roman Jakobson* (The Hague:Mouton), 239–270.
Bloch, B.
  1947 "English verb inflection", *Language* 23:399–418.
Brunner, K.
  1962 *Die englische Sprache.Ihre geschichtliche Entwicklung, II* (Tübingen:Niemeyer).
Chomsky, N.
  1957 *Syntactic structures* (The Hague:Mouton).
Chomsky, N. — M. Halle
  1968 *The sound pattern of English* (New York: Harper & Row).
Dik, S.C.
  1967 "Some critical remarks on the treatment of morphological structure in generative grammar", *Lingua* 18:352–383.
Erdmann, P.
  1972 "Suffixal *j* in Germanic", *Language* 48:407–415.
  1974 "Die Ableitung der altenglischen Substantivparadigmen", *Linguistics* 130:5–53.
Frei, H.
  1950 "Zéro, vide et intermittent", *Zeitschrift für Phonetik und allgemeine Sprachwissenschaft* 4:161–191.
Gleason, H.A.
  1961 *An introduction to descriptive linguistics* (New York: Holt, Rinehart and Winston).
Haas, W.
  1962 "Zero in linguistic description", in *Studies in linguistic analysis* (Special volume of the Philological Society) (Oxford: Blackwell), 33–53.

Hoard, J.E. — C. Sloat
1971 "The inflectional morphology of English", *Glossa* 5:47–56.
1973 "English irregular verbs", *Language* 49:107–120.
Hockett, C.F.
1947 "Problems of morphemic analysis", *Language* 23:321–343.
1954 "Two models of grammatical description", *Word* 10:210–231.
1958 *A course in modern linguistics* (New York: Harcourt & Brace).
Hyldgaard-Jensen, K. (ed.)
1972 *Linguistic 1971. Referate des 6. Linguistichen Kolloquiums, 11–14 August 1971 in Kopenhagen* (Frankfurt/M: Athenäum).
Jespersen, O.
1909 *A Modern English grammar on historical principles. Part I: Sounds and spelling* (København/London: Munksgaard/Allen & Unwin).
1942 *A Modern English grammar on historical principles. Part VI: Morphology* (København/London: Munksgaard/Allen & Unwin).
Jones, D.
1958 *English pronouncing dictionary (11th edition)* (London:Dent).
Kastovsky, D.
1968 *Old English deverbal substantives derived by means of a zero morpheme* (Unpublished Ph.D. dissertation, University of Tübingen).
1971 *Studies in morphology. Aspects of English and German verb inflection* (Tübingen: Narr).
Kurath, H.
1956 "The loss of long consonants and the rise of voiced fricatives in Middle English", *Language* 32:435–445.
Leitner, G.
1972 "Argumente für eine morphologische Ebene in einem TG-Modell", in Hyldgaard-Jensen (ed.) 1972:236–251.
1974 *Denominale Verbalisierung im Englischen. Eine Analyse der Derivation im Rahmen der generativen Grammatik* (= *Linguistische Arbeiten* 21) (Tübingen:Niemeyer).
Marchand, H.
1969² *The categories and types of present-day English word-formation* (München: C.H. Beck'sche Verlagsbuchhandlung).
Meier, G.F.
1961 *Das Zero-Problem in der Linguistik* (Berlin: Akademie).
Miner, K.L.
1975 "English inflectional endings and unordered rules", *Foundations of Language* 12:339–365.
Nida, E.
1948 "The identification of morphemes", *Language* 24:414–441.
Reuter, O.
1934 *On the development of English verbs from Latin and French participles* (Helsinki: Societas Scientiarum Fennica).
Saussure, F. de
1916 *Cours de linguistique générale* (Paris: Payot).
1973 *Cours de linguistique générale* (Edition critique préparé par Tullio de Mauro) (Paris: Payot).
Schifko, P.
1973 "Zero in der allgemeinen und romanischen Sprachwissenschaft", *Zeitschrift für Romanische Philologie* 89:1-51.

250 *Dieter Kastovsky*

Shibatani, M.
  1973 "The role of surface phonetic constraints in generative phonology", *Language* 49:87–106.
Strang, B.H.M.
  1970 *A history of English* (London: Methuen).
Wagner, K.H.
  1969 *Generative grammatical studies in the Old English language* (Heidelberg: Julius Gross Verlag).
Windsor Lewis, J.
  1972 *A concise pronouncing dictionary of British and American English* (London: Oxford University Press).
Winter, W.
  1964 "Form and meaning in morphological analysis", *Linguistics* 3:5–18.
Wurzel, W.U.
  1970 *Studien zur deutschen Lautstruktur* (=*Studia Grammatica* 8) (Berlin: Akademie Verlag).
This volume "Ways of morphologizing phonological rules".
Zwicky, A.
  1974 "Bibliography V: The English inflectional endings", *Ohio State University Working Papers in Linguistics* 17:206–221.

ROGER LASS

Paradigm coherence and the conditioning of sound change: Yiddish 'schwa-deletion' again*

1. Introduction

It sometimes happens that what is supposed to be a case of something interesting turns out not to be; but with luck it turns out to be something even more interesting. It also happens that what is supposed to be a clear-cut instance of one thing turns out to be a rather fuzzier instance of whatever it is. Both of these points relate to the methodological importance of not getting one's information on language history out of footnotes or small exemplary samples (as we all do from time to time).

My starting point is a discussion by King (1969:123ff.)[1], which attempts to make a theoretical point about sound change. The point itself — that 'sound change' can be responsive to non-phonetic properties — is not particularly controversial now (though see Hock 1976); but the basic issues are worth summing up as a frame for the discussion to follow, since the data I will be examining focusses directly on this problem.

In what is generally (and loosely) called the 'Neogrammarian Model', sound change (unless interfered with by analogy, etc.) is automatic; it proceeds classically 'mit blinder Notwendigkeit', and no non-phonetic factors are available for its conditioning. The standard (putative) 'Ausnahmslosigkeit' of sound change is a consequence of this: a given segment in a given environment changes uniformly in all lexemes where the appropriate configuration occurs (cf. Bloomfield 1933: ch. 20).

This notion of change was of course originally proposed within an unformalized theory: but it gives rise to assumptions that can be — and have been — incorporated into more formalized ones ('structural' of various kinds, 'generative' and 'natural generative' — the latter at least as far as exceptionlessness in the usual sense is concerned).

The question King addresses in his discussion is this: can information from one grammatical level be made available to another for the conditioning of change? Can information (say) from morphology be available to (higher or lower level) phonology? The 'structuralist' answer, Neogrammarian in spirit, is no. (Neo)Bloomfieldian methodologies — at least those that espouse any form of separation of levels — presuppose a rigidly stratified or hierarchized grammar, with no possibility of feedback or interlevel communication (in the name of 'text signalling its own structure', or whatever). A formalization of this kind of theory gives us a set of one-way mappings (exponencies) from level to level, with in fact no 'grammar' as a whole to serve as information focus. In principle a phonological process cannot have recourse to morphosyntactic information.

The generative answer (while with respect to 'exceptions' it is still in general Neogrammarian: cf. Anttila 1975) is yes. In a generative grammar information coded in underlying structures can be carried through a derivation (since in characteristic TG derivations, levels may be 'theoretically significant' without being strictly 'separate'). Information — in standard theory, at least categorial information — from virtually anywhere can be available virtually anywhere else, if needed. King's discussion is essentially concerned with justifying a particular representation of change within this kind of model.

But the widening of grammatical horizons to allow morphosyntactic information transfer, as it is usually conceived, is not enough. The particular change that King invokes as a crucial example of morphosyntactic *categorial* information is in fact an example of something else. And this something else requires the admission not merely of categories, but of such classically 'epiphenomenal' material as overall paradigm shapes as primitives.[2] The total picture of the change King is concerned with, when looked at in detail, leads to a more complex and interesting (and in some ways puzzling) view of the relations between components of a grammar than King's rather simple exposition would suggest. In particular, the morphological and lexical conditioning are more far-reaching than King shows, and some interesting issues arise concerning the nature of a speaker's access to certain aspects of lexical and morphological structure.

2   The schwa-deletion rule and its minor exceptions

King is concerned with a putative rule of final schwa-deletion in Yiddish, which is supposed to be a paradigm case of 'morphologically conditioned sound change' (where 'morphological' = 'invoking simple category labels'). He writes (1969:123):

In the development of standard Yiddish from something similar to Middle High German we find that final unstressed *e*, phonetically [ə][3], has been lost: *tage > teg* 'days', *erde > erd* 'earth' *gibe >gib* 'I give' ... In some cases, however, final [ə] is not lost, principally when the *e* is an adjective inflectional ending: *di groyse shtot* 'the big city', *dos alte land* 'the old country', *a sheyne froy* 'a pretty woman'. A few other final unaccented *e*'s are retained, erratically, but these too are confined to specific morphological environments, e.g. *gesele* 'little street', where (*e*)*le* is the diminutive ending.

King states the deletion rule as follows (1969:123):

$$
(1) \quad
\begin{bmatrix} V \\ -\text{ stress} \end{bmatrix}
\longrightarrow
\left\{
\begin{array}{l}
[- \text{ next rule}] \: / + \underline{\hspace{2cm}}) \\
\qquad\qquad\qquad\qquad \text{Adjective} \\
\emptyset \: / \underline{\hspace{2cm}} \#
\end{array}
\right\}
$$

Or, in Joan Hooper's revision (1976: 103, n. 6), properly eliminating '[− next rule]':

$$
(2) \quad
\begin{bmatrix} V \\ -\text{ stress} \\ -\text{ adjective} \end{bmatrix}
\longrightarrow
\emptyset \: / \underline{\hspace{2cm}} \#
$$

To put it in context, let us look at a typical modern Yiddish adjective paradigm (cf. Weinreich 1965b: 39–40; Birnbaum 1966: 39–40). Standard Yiddish has three genders (masculine, feminine, neuter), and two adjective declensions, paralleling the usual Germanic weak (definite) and strong (indefinite).[4] Here are paradigms for three nouns, one of each gender (*man* 'man' m., *štot* 'city' f., and *land* 'country' n.), illustrated by the nom. sg./pl. and the adjective *grojs* 'big'[5]:

(3)

DEF	sg.	*der grojser man*	*di grojsė štot*	*dos grojsė land*
	pl.	*di grojsė men*	*di grojsė štet*	*di grojsė lender*
IND	sg.	*a grojser man*	*a grojsė štot*	*a grojs land*[6]
	pl.	*grojsė men*	*grojsė štet*	*grojsė lender*

Now on the face of it there is something odd about calling this retention of -*ė* in adjectives an 'exception to a phonological rule'; since the base (i.e. predicative or citation) forms of the adjective have no ending anyhow (*di štot iz grojs* 'the city is big', etc.). This looks more like a (nonphonological) fact about Yiddish morphology. At least it would unless it could be convincingly shown that there was in fact a truly general and clearly phonological 'elsewhere' rule of *ė*-deletion, to which this is a genuine morphological exception. I will claim that although this is in fact such an exception, it is so only in a rather marginal sense: the bulk of exceptions to rule (1) — which King does not mention (see below and section 3) — are of a rather different type. And none of the environments for the deletion rule, in fact, are really 'phonological'.

The deletion that King discusses covers three basic classes of original final -*ė*:

(i) In noun plurals: *štot/štet, tog/teg* 'day', *hant/hent* 'hand', *fus/fis* 'foot', etc.

(ii) Pres. 1 sg. of verbs: *ix gib, ix gej* 'I go', *ix hob* 'I have'.

(iii) Non-inflectional *-ė* in monomorphemic words: *erd* 'earth', *harc* 'heart', *kac* 'cat'.

Category (iii) is of course the 'real' (apparently non-morphological) deletion, to which the adjectival retentions are supposed to be 'exceptions'. And it is in fact this category — properly expanded — that provides much better evidence for non-phonological control of an apparently phonological rule than King suggests. The situation here is exceedingly complex, and comes out looking nothing like what King (or Hooper) would claim.[7]

The trouble is this. The facts about part of the deletion process have been easily available to the non-specialist at least since they were pointed out by Sapir over sixty years ago (1915). In a very useful study of a Lithuanian Yiddish dialect, Sapir remarks that virtually all Middle High German *-ė* were lost in final position[8]; the only exception he mentions is the diminutive suffix, also mentioned by King. (Note, by the way, that King fails to include the diminutives in his rule, which if correctly formulated on the basis of the data he cites would require a disjunction in the environment).

The purely lexical dimension, however, also has a part to play among the minor exceptions. We can begin by citing a few other exceptions of Middle High German origin: *béjdė* 'both', *étlexė* 'several', *ánderė* 'some, others', *dos íberigė* 'the rest'[9]; old adverbial datives like *sérštė* 'firstly', *cvéjtė* 'secondly', *sbéstė* 'at best', *dervájlė* 'meanwhile'; and nouns like *líbė* 'love affair', *frágė* 'question', *gešíxtė* 'history', *cíbelė* 'onion' (not < Pol. *cybula* but MHG *zibolle* ~ *zibülle*: Mieses 1924: 226), *brúnė* 'well', *zónė* 'sun(rise)'.[10]

There are also what appear to be morphological exceptions in some verbs: e.g. *kvíčn* 'complain', pres. 1 sg. *ix kvičė, líben zix* 'make love', pres. 1 sg. *ix libė mix*, where we would expect **kvič, *lib*. These *ė*'s however are not to be taken as 'really' affixal, but as stem-final or thematic — which is of course still a problem with respect to the deletion rule. Thus compare *er kvičėt* 'he complains' with *-ėt*, past participle *gekvičėt* with *er kract* 'he scratches' < *krácn*, past participle *gekráct*, with *-t*. I will return to these verbs and some related problematic forms in 7 below.

3 The major exceptions

Even given his (venial) understatement with respect to exceptions, King's formulation of the deletion rule is still misleading, because he fails to consider the really massive classes of exceptions. It is in fact rather easy to be misled by Sapir's 1915 paper, or even an account like that in the classic history of Yiddish (Mieses 1924). Thus Mieses says (28) that "Das Schluß -e wird im Jd. in allen deutschen Worten apocopiert . . . Ausgenommen sind bloß einige Worte auf -n . . . die Feminin- und Plural-endungen von Adjektiven . . . und Eigennamen . . ." (he doesn't mention diminutives here, nor some of the lexical exceptions I cited above; though he cites most of them elsewhere).

The problem is the lack of emphasis in 'allen deutschen Worten' — this also arises in Sapir's treatment, which is confined to the history of Middle High German sounds in Yiddish. Note that King also speaks of the development of Yiddish from "something similar to Middle High German".[11] "Similar", yes; but with some crucial differences. It is a mistake to equate "the history" (or "structure") of Yiddish with the history or structure of the Middle High German element alone. Or even, more broadly, with the German or Germanic element alone. This is tantamount to talking about English stress, morphophonemics and lexis without reference to the Romance element.

That is: there are two very extensive, ancient, and important subsets of the Yiddish lexicon that are entirely unaffected by *è*-deletion: words of Hebrew (or Aramaic) origin, and words of Slavic origin — regardless of their category-membership or phonological structure. And both these major components contain a good deal of 'core' vocabulary (as well as much else) — even to the extent of Hebrew or Slavic kinship and body-part terms having replaced Germanic ones. The size and nature of these components can be illustrated by the following highly selective lists, which contain only forms with retained final *-è* (i.e. excluding the large amount of everyday lexis irrelevant to our concerns here).

A. HEBREW

almónè 'window'; *avéjrè* 'sin'; *balególè* 'coachman'; *balkójrè* 'Torah reader'; *behéjmè* 'cow'; *bérjè* 'energetic woman'; *bróxè* 'blessing'; *cevúè* 'testament'; *cúrè* 'trouble'; *éjcè* 'advice'; *gábè* 'committee member'; *gedílè* 'joy'; *gehénè* 'hell'; *gvúrè* 'strength'; *haclóxè* 'luck'; *haláxè* 'Jewish

Law'; *haskálė* 'enlightenment'; *jedíjė* 'knowledge'; *ješívė* 'Yeshiva';
jéjcer-hórė 'evil inclination'; *kálė* 'bride'; *kálfė* 'ballot-box'; *kapójrė*
'scapegoat'; *kášė* 'question'; *kehílė* 'community'; *kínė* 'jealousy'; *kvíjrė*
'burial'; *levájė* 'funeral'; *levónė* 'moon'; *lóšn-hórė* 'vilification'; *mácė*
'unleavened bread'; *májsė* 'story, Märchen'; *mákė* 'plague'; *málkė*
'queen'; *másė* 'burden'; *matbájė* 'coin'; *matónė* 'gift'; *maxšúve* 'idea';
mecíjė 'bargain'; *medínė* 'country'; *megílė* 'scroll, elaborate discourse';
mekánė 'envious'; *melóxė* 'craft, trade'; *menójrė* 'candelabrum'; *mešúgė*
'crazy'; *mešúnė* 'fate'; *mexájė* 'pleasure; *mexílė* 'forgiveness'; *mezúzė*
'Mezuzza, talisman hung on doorpost'; *mícvė* 'good deed, covenant';
míkvė 'ritual bath'; *milxómė* 'war'; *mistómė* 'perhaps'; *mišpóxė* 'family';
mníxė 'peace'; *náfkė* 'prostitute'; *náxlė* 'inheritance'; *nedóvė* 'alms';
nešómė 'soul'; *nevúė* 'prophecy'; *nexómė* 'comfort'; *néxpė* 'epilepsy';
ójlem-házė 'this world'; *parnúsė* 'earnings'; *rébė* 'rabbi'; *rfíjė* 'medica-
ment'; *rójfė* 'army surgeon'; *róšė* 'enemy of the Jews'; *roš-hašónė* 'Rosh
Hashona, Jewish New Year'; *símxė* 'joy'; *skúnė* 'danger'; *sójnė* 'enemy';
sréjfė 'burning'; *súkė* 'Succah, booth for Feast of Tabernacles'; *svúrė*
'sight'; *šexínė* 'Spiritus Dei'; *šexítė* 'ritual slaughter'; *šíksė* 'gentile girl';
šívė 'mourning' [12]; *šójtė* 'fool'; *tfísė* 'prison'; *tójrė* 'Torah, Pentateuch';
tójvė 'good' (n)[13]; *xájė* 'animal'[14]; *xálė* 'Sabbath loaf'; *xásenė* 'Wedding';
xévrė 'comradeship, association; *xníjfė* 'hypocrisy'; *xólė* 'malediction';
xolílė 'God forbid'; *xórvė* 'destruction'; *xóxmė* 'wisdom'; *xúcpė* 'nerve,
arrogance'; *xúpė* 'wedding canopy'.

B.   SLAVIC

amíšnė 'intentionally'; *bábskė* 'female'; *bájkė* 'tale'; *bánkė* 'cup (for med-
ical cupping)'; *békesė* 'caftan'; *bíškė* 'stork'; *berjózė* 'birch'; *blíncė* 'pan-
cake'; *blótė* 'mud'; *bóbė* 'grandmother'[15]; *bóbkė* 'bean, goat turd'; *búbė*
'midwife'; *búlbė* 'potato'; *búlkė* '(bread) roll'; *ǰábė* 'frog'; *Fráncevatė*
'having syphilis'[16]; *fútė* 'fur coat'; *gžíbė* 'cowlick'; *jágedė* 'strawberry';
jármulkė 'skullcap'; *jáščerkė* 'lizard; *káljekė* 'cripple'; *káčkė* 'duck';
kapótė 'coat'; *kášė* 'buckwheat groats'; *kázė* 'nannygoat'; *kiškė* 'intes-
tine'; *kósė* 'goat'; *krétšmė* 'public house'; *kúrvė* 'whore'; *kúpė* 'group';
lánkė 'meadow'; *lápė* 'paw'; *lípė* 'lime tree'; *ljálkė* 'doll'; *ljúlkė*
'(tobacco) pipe'; *lópetė* 'spade'; *lúžė* 'puddle'; *málinė* 'raspberry'; *máplė*
'monkey'; *máslinė* 'olive'; *márdė* 'snout'; *múraškė* 'ant'; *njánjė* 'nurse';
nóvenė 'change'; *padkóvė* 'horseshoe'; *padlógė* 'floor'; *paskúdnė* 'disgusting'; *pétuškė* 'parsley'; *pjátė* 'heel'; *pjávkė* 'leech'; *pléjcė* 'shoulder';
pljátkė 'gossip'; *pólė* 'lappet'; *povečénjė* 'cobwebs'; *prásė* 'millet'; *próstė*
'simple, crude'; *púškė* 'kitty (money-box)'; *róžinkė* 'raisin'; *sámė*
'same'[17]; *sásnė* 'spruce'; *sémenčkė* 'sunflower'; *slínė* 'saliva'; *smarkátė*
'snotty'; *srákė* 'magpie'; *stádė* 'herd'; *stéjkė* 'path'; *šmátė* 'rag'; *tákė*

'indeed'; *tátė* 'father'; *táčkė* 'wheelbarrow'; *témnė* 'dark';[18] *térpkė* 'sour (of fruit)'; *tšaprínė* 'mane'; *tšátškė* 'toy';[19] *tšéredė* 'herd'; *vánė* 'bathtub'; *vésnė* 'springtime'; *vérvė* 'willow'; *vóncė* 'moustache'; *vránė* 'raven'; *xátė* 'hut'; *xmáljė* 'blow, clout'; *xoljérjė* 'cholera';[20] *zéjdė* 'grandfather'.[21]

Some exemplary loans from other languages follow:
(a) from Romance, either direct or via Slavic: *ádjė* 'adieu'; *asimilácjė* 'assimilation'; *blúzė* 'blouse'; *ekzekúcjė* 'execution'; *epidémjė* 'epidemic', *filosófjė* 'philosophy'; *histórjė* 'history'; *kártė* 'map'; *legéndė* 'legend'; *lékcjė* 'lesson'; *profésjė* 'profession'; *rásė* 'race'; *rólė* 'rôle'; *rózė* 'rose'; *spázmė* 'cramp'; *tradícjė* 'tradition', and perhaps *cóbitė* 'old shoe' (It. *ciobota*: cf. Mieses 1924:239);
(b) from Hungarian (Mieses 1924:236): *áfinė* 'bilberry' (H. *afonya); císmė* 'boot' (H. *czisma); píčė* 'small' (H. *pici*).

4 The Hebrew and Slavic components: Origin and integration

The forms exemplified in the lists in the last section would pose no problem for King's rule if one of the following points could be established:
(a)   That they are in some way not fully integrated into the language;
(b)   that they postdate *ė*-deletion;
(c)   that the various (historical) qualities of unstressed Hebrew vowels now collapsed in *-ė* were not levelled with Middle High German *-ė* at the time of the deletion.
None of these conditions appears to hold. I will deal with (a) and the relevant external history in this section, and take up the dating and levelling problems in 5.

It seems clear that the Hebrew component (in all dialects) and the Slavic (mainly in East Yiddish)[22] are as integrated as, e.g. the French element in English. In the following examples, Hebrew forms are in normal print:

(i) c. 1400–1425 (Birnbaum 1965:3):
ix hōn gybroxyn di haskòmys, *di di* rabōnym *hon gymaxt⟨*
'I have broken the commandments that the rabbis have established'
(ii) c. 1514 (Birnbaum 1965:6):
as fil as di koxōvym balaily
'as numerous as the stars at night'
(*ba* 'in', *laily* < H. *laila* 'night').

The transliterations here are Birnbaum's; for the use of *y* see note 30 below. It is worth noting here, however (and I will take this up again below), the different Hebrew vowels that have collapsed in what is spelled *y: -os* in *haskōmys*, *-im* in *rabōnym, koxōvym, -a* in *laily*.

  (iii) 20th c. (Guggenheim-Grünberg 1954:53):
        bə'hɛjmaz *hods 'mɛi vi* sus·ɪm
        (cows has it more than horses)
        'there will be more cows than horses'
  (iv) 20th c. (Guggenheim-Grunberg 1954:55)
        mər hot saị 'gsɛ:rəs *mit di* ɛ'rufəs
        'one has one's troubles with the guarantees'.

And so on. The Hebrew forms here retain their morphological integrity, though they are often phonologically modified (i.e. 'Yiddishized', restressed, with vowel changes, etc.) But in no sense can utterances like these be taken as uncharacteristic or odd (in the sense of 'macaronic', or full of 'foreign' terms): the Yiddish word for 'cow' simply is *behéjmè*, and so on. (Though nowadays one would use *štéren* rather than *koxóvim*, and *sus* and *ferd* are doublets.) In fact the use of Hebrew forms in these sentences is no odder than the French *troubles* and *guarantees* in the gloss to (iv).[23]

Points (b) and (c) are of course considerably more important than (a), and I will preface the treatment of them in the next section with an excursus on the external history of Yiddish, which will explain the integration phenomenon — as well as providing background.

Yiddish — even though its structural groundwork is 'German' in a very clear sense — is nonetheless what might be called a 'fusion language' (M. Weinreich 1954:75). That is, a language in which at least four strata of material have to be reckoned with (I am not here considering English, which would add a fifth component to the discussion of British and American Yiddish). These four are: (a) Hebrew/Aramaic; (b) Western/Southern Loez (Romance: see below); (c) German; and (d) Slavic. The integration of these components can be explained on the grounds of two important and perennial properties of post-Diaspora Jewry: separation from their non-Jewish surrounds (endogamy, etc.), and mobility (voluntary or forced).

From earliest post-Biblical times there has been a strong tendency for Jews in any case to keep themselves separate from the gentile communities they lived in: this in itself largely accounts for the survival of Judaism as a religion-cum-culture through the Egyptian and Babylonian captivities, and through the Diaspora. And even though it was the case that Jews historically spoke the vernaculars of the communities they lived in, the fact of their separateness led to their speaking specifically Jewish — and recognizably Jewish — versions.[24]

To lead up to the relevant period: the destruction of the Third Temple in Jerusalem by Titus in A.D. 70 led to the dispersal of the Palestinian Jewish community in two main directions: into other parts of the Middle East, and into Europe, especially the Mediterranean Littoral. The dispersed Jews were already a linguistically complex community: largely Aramaic speaking, but with Hebrew, in one form or another, as their liturgical and scholarly language. The Hebrew element is fully integrated into all the Jewish vernaculars: not only Yiddish but Judeo-Spanish (Ladino), Judeo-Aramaic ('Targumic'), Judeo-Arabic (Yahudic), Judeo-Slavic (Knaanic), etc.

In the 9th century (M. Weinreich 1954:78), Jews from Southern Europe began entering the region they called *Loter*:[25] i.e. the Moselle basin and the left bank of the Rhine between Cologne and Speyer. This was apparently where the nucleus of what was later to be the Yiddish-speaking community (*Ashkenazim*) was formed.

These Jews came from France and Italy with two Judeo-Romance vernaculars: Western Loez (Jewish Old French) and Southern Loez (Jewish Old Italian). But they also had Hebrew (or Hebrew/Aramaic), and with this heritage they came in contact for the first time with German dialects. This contact can be said to mark the beginning of Yiddish proper.

Before the 13th century, however, there was little settlement in Germany outside the "Grenzstreifen" (Mieses 1924:274) Cologne/Trier/Metz; some typical first dates are 1255 Heidelberg, 1230 Baden, 1341 Württemberg, 1342 Tübingen, 1350 Stuttgart. The earliest mention of settlements in Austria is earlier (Salzburg as early as c. 800: though these are probably Jews from the East).

During this period there were extensive migrations into eastern Europe: there were settlements from the west in Poland around 1100, with further migrations in the 13th and 14th centuries. As various European countries expelled their Jews in the 14th–16th centuries, successive waves of migration passed through Poland, and what is now Rumania in the south, Lithuania in the north, and points further east, with Ashkenazic settlements in Russia by the 16th century.

There is thus no doubt about either the antiquity or the provenance of the Hebrew component; but the problem with Slavic, from the external point of view, is much more complex. The difficulty is that just because we may have documentary records of Jews in a Slavic-speaking area, this doesn't mean that they are Yiddish-speaking: indeed, in the case of the earliest records it is quite clear that they can't be (e.g. in Kiev in the 8th

century). Much of the evidence that we do have involves Hebrew inscriptions (e.g. 11th-century bracteates from Poland: Mieses 1924:288), and
this tells us nothing of the origin of these Jews.

In fact, what we can find out about contact between German Jews and
Slavic-speakers in the relevant period is confused and problematical. The
only real certainty, in fact, seems to be that during the bulk of the
medieval period there was considerable commerce in both directions:
Jews moving into Germany from Slavic areas, and Jews moving out. The
situation may be summed up by Mieses' observation (309) that there
were certainly Slavic speakers in Austria as late as the 14th century, and
German-speaking Jews as early as the 9th.[26] Thus at least some of the
Slavic lexis may in principle date from the earliest formative stages of
Yiddish. As far as the east is concerned, it is at least clear that German-
speaking Jews were moving into Poland in considerable numbers from
the 13th century on — though it was not until the 16th that Poland
became "ein Judenland par excellence" (Mieses 314).

Thus there is no reason to doubt the antiquity of the Slavic component
— though of course it does postdate the Hebrew. The origin of specific
forms (e.g. those that are unequivocally from Russian) may be late, but
the majority are clearly early. What remains to be seen, of course, is how
all this squares with the dating for *ė*-deletion. In a sense, of course, the
Slavic element doesn't really matter: even if *ė*-deletion could be shown to
postdate the bulk of the Slavic borrowings (say we could fix it in the 11th
or 12th century), we would still have the Hebrew to explain. The only
difference would be a reduction in the number of items involved, not a
change in principle.

5   The date of *ė*-deletion

The earliest extensive literary document in Yiddish is a manuscript now in
Cambridge, written c. 1382 (Fuks 1957). An examination of this material
shows final *-ė* intact in umlaut plurals, verb endings, and (generally) in
monomorphemic forms. To take a few characteristic examples, we find
the following (Fuks 1957, II; identified by MS facsimile page and line
number; the forms are given in transliteration):

(4)		Item	Modern Yiddish	New High German
	20.178	*hrzė*[27]	*harc*	'Herz'
	30.411	*vnė*	*on*	'ohne'
	37.7	*vxsė*	*oxs*	'Ochse'
	60.469	*tgė*	*teg*[28]	'Tage'
	18.132	*ridė ix*	*red ix*	'rede ich'

There are very few instances of missing MHG -*ė*: among them are *zit* (= NHG *Sitte*) 16.82, 28.349, *erd* (= NHG *Erde*) 10.78, and *brk* (= NHG *Barke*) 48.158. (The latter is of course a Romance loan.) These could be examples of deletion beginning to diffuse, or scribal errors; there are too few instances to allow firm conclusions. But it is clear that as late as the end of the 14th century -*ė* was largely intact in all the major categories where it was later lost in forms of Middle High German origin.

The wide chronological and regional sample of short texts in Birnbaum (1965) gives some indication of a possible dating not only for deletion, but for the other important event mentioned above (section 4): the levelling of unstressed Hebrew vowels with Middle High German ones. The picture given by Birnbaum's selection can be sketched out as follows (and cf. the examples above in 4):

    (i) The earliest texts (15th century) showing large numbers of Hebrew loans show all final unstressed vowels, regardless of source, spelled the same way, whether they were originally unstressed or unstressed by the Ashkenazic stress-shift[29]; these are levelled with MHG -*ė*. Thus in the 15th-century Apology of Zimlin of Ulm (ex. (i) in 4 above) we find in addition to the cited forms *mišpoxy* < H. *mišpoxá* (and cf. the MHG *gyvëzyn, gybroxyn, gymaxt, ubyl*).[30] Another 15th-c. text (no. 2) shows *šabys* 'Sabbath' < H. *sabáṭ*[31] and *mošy* 'Moses' < H. *mošé*.

    (ii) All the 15th-century texts in Birnbaum's selection show evidence of retained -*ė*: e.g. in text 4 (15th c., copied c. 1574) we find *gründy* (= NHG *Gründe*), *erdy* (= *Erde*) and *verdy* 'worthy' (presumably = *würdig*, with -*ė* < reduced -*ig*).

But there is a problem. As Mieses points out (1924:29),

Dem ältesten Jd. war die Apocope des auslautenden -e nicht eigen. Im Gegenteil, das Endungs-e wurde übermäßig von Juden angebracht. In den jd. Glossen aus dem XII., XIII. Jahrh. heißt es: Reitwege, Kochre, Aale, Stachle.

And further (ibid.):

Im xv. Jahrh. tritt Isserlein für die schreibweise Taubre, Egre, Basle ein, er erklärt, daß man in vielen Ländern "Haus" sagt, dennoch sprechen solche, die scharf (explosiv) reden, nur Hause. Joseph Kolon . . . schrieb im 15. Jahrh. '*avlm'a*[32] (Ulm). Levita schrieb zu Beginn des XVI Jahrh. "grope" (*grvp'a*) fur grob. Noch im XVII. Jahrh. schrieb Gluckel von Hameln "dere" statt "der", "ich weise", "mage" fur "weiß", "mag".

The question that arises here of course is whether these final vowel letters are in fact phonetic, or represent inverse spellings due to a change in progress. Mieses suggests (ibid.) that this "auslautende, übermäßige e ist altes Deutsch", and cites numerous Middle High German doublets with final unstressed vowels in places where we would not expect to find them. He also cites Old High German forms like *unde, vrouwe*: and there is surely no question of *ė*-deletion and inverse spelling at this stage.

After detailed argument and consideration of the evidence, Mieses concludes (1924:30) that genuine inverse spellings don't appear in quantity until considerably later; with the gradual extension of apocope,

Das Schluß-Alef dünkte manchem als überflüssige Zierde und wurde nach einer jd. orthographischen Regel aus dem XVI. Jahrh. bereits damals nach Vokalen, wie "zwei, drei" als "Zier" verwendet . . . Das stumme Alef als "Zier" erscheint bei den Juden in Polen im 16. 17. Jh. . . .

He cites forms like (again in my transliteration) *pvzn'a* (Posen), *vjn'a* (Wien), *premjsl'a* (Przemysl), *k'ap'a* (*Kopf*) and *l'advnk'a* (*Ladung*). This suggests a date for substantial loss around the middle-to-late 16th century, if this "Zierde" is in fact an inverse spelling.[33]

The history of *ė*-deletion is, to say the least, rather murky; but it is pretty clearly a post-medieval development, which makes it clear that we need to explain the immunity of both Hebrew and Slavic forms to its operation. There seems no doubt that all of the Hebrew and probably the bulk of the Slavic lexis coexisted for a considerable time with deletion-free Middle High German forms.

6 A sketch for an explanation

It now seems that if we leave out the minor morphological categories (diminutives, proper names) and the purely lexical Middle High German exceptions, the deletion-rule must be formulated something like this:

$$(5) \quad \begin{bmatrix} V \\ -\text{ stress} \\ +\text{ MHG} \\ -\text{ Adj} \end{bmatrix} \longrightarrow \emptyset \ / \underline{\qquad} \#$$

But what kind of rule is this? Why should two well-integrated subsets of the lexicon be immune to the effects of what looks on the face of it to be a rather simple rule? Or better, how can speakers be aware of the relevant distinctions? Are they really sensitive to etymology? (This might be plausible to some extent if (a) all speakers of Yiddish were literate in both Yiddish and Hebrew (but not all were: and certainly not women, which poses a problem in acquisition, in a matriarchal society); and if (b) they actually paid attention to which words they met first in Hebrew; and (c) that only adults were involved in the change. I don't think these conditions can be shown to be met.) Surely we need some other kind of explanation.

We can eliminate at the outset the possibility that there is some systematic phonological discrepancy or idiosyncracy that characterizes the Hebrew-Slavic (and Romance) strata as a whole. The only distinctive segmental properties are sporadic: e.g. the presence of non-Germanic clusters (*gvúrė, tfísė, mníxė, gžíbe*) or segments (*ž, ĵ*), or 'normal' segments in odd places (e.g. initial *x-*). But otherwise, even if we take stress-placement into account, the majority of the foreign forms could perfectly well be Germanic. Thus a stress pattern V̆.V́.V̆ as in *behéjmė* can be duplicated in any prefixed disyllabic German infinitive or participle (*bacéjlen* 'pay', *farfálen* 'lost'); a pattern V́.V̆.V̆ as in *káljeke* can be found in derivatives like *géselė*; and of course V́.V̆ as in *símxė, káčke* is the most typical Germanic pattern for disyllables. So any explanation of this general type is a non-starter.

But the non-Middle High German element does have one significantly idiosyncratic property, and this I suspect is at least part of the answer — though there are some problems, as we will see. This is a matter of inflexional morphology. If we look at the characteristic noun-plural formatives of Middle High German, we find the following (Helm 1966: §§ 57 ff.; von Kienle 1969:169):[34]

(6) a. *-e*
     b. *-(e)n*
     c. umlaut + *-e*
     d. Ø

Of these only-*(e)n*, zero, and umlaut (without following-*e*) now remain in Yiddish; the *-e* (with or without umlaut) is of course one of the casualties of the deletion rule.

But if we look at the Hebrew and Slavic vocabulary, we find a striking difference: all Slavic plurals are formed with *-(e)s*, and all Hebrew plurals either with *-(e)s* or a complex pattern involving (frequent) vowel-change,

plus stress-shift and a suffix *-im* (for details cf. Birnbaum 1922:36 ff.).[35]
The *-im* plurals are largely restricted to original Hebrew masculines
(normally consonant-final), e.g. *xázer* 'pig', pl. *xazéjrim, kabcen* 'pauper',
pl. *kabcónim*.[36] But the typical paradigm for the forms of the type shown
in section 3 is with *-s: behéjmè/behéjmes, mícvè/mícves* for Hebrew, and
búlbè/búlbes, šmátè/šmátes for Slavic.

The origin of this *-s* plural is clear: it is the Hebrew feminine *-(x)t̪*, later
(o) θ > Ashkenazic *-(o)s*, with vowel reduction in Yiddish.[37] What is
curious, however, is its occurrence in Slavic forms: these are as far as I
know given this plural without exception (and cf. Mieses 116). We can at
the outset get rid of any possibility of a Slavic source: the only consonantal elements to be found in the relevant Slavic plurals, as far as I know, are
m, v, x (cf. Entwistle – Morison 1964: §§ 114, 164). For some problems
connected with this ending see 7 below.

So far one thing is clear: at least as far as nouns (which constitute by far
the bulk of the borrowed material) are concerned, the Hebrew/Slavic
stratum is a morphologically coherent subset of the lexicon. Nouns of this
stratum have a distinct 'paradigmatic identity' — possession of 'deviant'
plural morphology. I suggest that this may have been sufficient to keep
them apart from the Middle High German element, whose plurals were
'regular'.

If this is the case, it suggests that not only categorial information, but
information like 'paradigm-type' can (a) be available to speakers, and (b)
serve to trigger 'exceptionality' with respect to phonological rules (or
whatever kind of rule the *è*-deletion is). This can be sketched out in a
(non-explanatory) formalization as follows:

(7)
a. $\begin{bmatrix} + \text{ Noun} \\ + s\text{-Plural} \end{bmatrix} \longrightarrow [- \dot{e}\text{-deletion}]$

b. $\begin{bmatrix} V \\ - \text{ stress} \\ - \text{ Adjective} \end{bmatrix} \longrightarrow \emptyset \: / \text{_____} \#$

i.e. the actual deletion rule is in fact the same as King's; only we have
managed, in the 'readjustment rule' or whatever it is (7a) to mark the
Hebrew/Slavic component as an exception, without having to identify it
etymologically.

There is of course another version, which would incorporate the adjectival exception in (7a). This is in the present state of our knowledge
merely a notational equivalent of (7a, b), or at least (7a) plus the

[-adjective] specification of (7b). I do not think the question 'which is correct' is intelligible.

Let us note finally that the rules in (7), or the possible alternative formulations, do not 'explain' why the exceptions fall out as they do; they merely suggest a model for how they can. This kind of 'plausibilistic' claim is probably the best we can do in any historical investigation of this kind. Whether it is enough is of course another question, and perhaps the central one in historical linguistics; but that is the subject for a monograph (for suggestions, see Lass 1980).

7   Residual problems

I want to discuss two things in this final section: (a) the problem of how Slavic loans get *s*-plurals, and (b) the status of some forms that cannot be explained under the assumptions behind the argument in 6.

The first difficulty is accounting for the fact that all Slavic forms get (Hebrew) *s*-plurals: none of them seem to get either *-im* plurals or any of the various Germanic ones (even though their own plurals would in many cases quite naturally become Middle High German *-ė* by normal Germanic reduction) — unlike the case with Hebrew forms, some of which get German plurals.

Now the *s*-plural is the type that is in fact extended to virtually all loans, of whatever origin; the best solution would seem to be that at the time of borrowing from Slavic (and later English — see below) all plurals except *-s* had become nonproductive, so that this was 'the only one left'. This seems reasonable at first: we observe that for instance in this century, in American Yiddish, *-s* is extended to nearly all English loans — even these that have /ɪz/ or /z/ plurals in English (both of which could be canonical Yiddish finals: cf. *iz* 'is', *hojz* 'house' and all forms of this type with 'lost' Auslautverhärtung). Thus we get *der víndė, di víndes* 'window' (replacing *dos fénster*), *évenjė, -s* 'avenue', *pjánė, -s* 'piano', *pijámė, -s* 'pyjama', etc.

But other plural types are not totally unproductive: the *-er* plural is as we have seen borrowed from standard German (some time after the 17th century), and we even get umlaut in English borrowings, like the semi-calque *švic-šop, -šeper* 'sweatshop'.

The answer would seem to be something like decreasing productivity of other plurals, reaching nearly vanishing point by the late 19th–early 20th century, when most of the English loans come in: but this still leaves us with the Slavic problem: if German loans can come in with totally new types of plurals (*-er*) much later than the bulk of the Slavic loans, why weren't some of the latter taken in with their own plural endings, which could so easily be remodeled on a German pattern?

The more serious problem is the applicability of the morphological explanation I proposed above to a class (admittedly fairly small, but still not worthy of being swept under the rug) of non-nominal forms without *ė*-deletion. Some of these appear in the lists in section 3: mainly adjectives and adverbs; but there is also another class, which I mentioned briefly in 2 — verbs which keep their *-ė* in the 1 sg. present. I give some more extensive exemplification of these forms below, unsorted as to etymology:

A. ADJECTIVES

bábskė 'female'; *bírnė* 'sad'; *bíšlojmė* 'granted'; *číkavė* 'curious'; *mádnė* 'odd'; *mekánė* 'envious'; *mešúpė* 'steep'; *mútnė* 'muddy'; *parsívė* 'cheap'; *párvė* 'neither flesh nor dairy'; *paskúdnė* 'disgusting'; *pavóljė* 'slow'; *píčė* 'small'; *próstė* 'simple'; *témnė* 'dark'; *térpkė* 'sour'.

B. ADVERBS AND MISCELLANEOUS

afílė 'even'; *bejsmájsė* 'meanwhile'; *bórex-hábė* 'welcome'; *dávkė* 'necessarily'; *sámė* 'very'; *tákė* 'indeed'.

C. VERBS

búrčn 'grumble'; *gríjn* 'gnaw, complain'; *hánfn* 'flatter'; *klípn* 'sob'; *kójln* 'slaughter'; *kvíčn* 'complain'; *líbn zix* 'make love'; *mékn* 'bleat'; *múčn* 'torment'; *nújn* 'bother'; *právn* 'celebrate'; *rátevn* 'save'; *sójščn* 'chirp'; *strašn* 'threaten'; *šepšn* 'whisper'; *tájnen* 'claim'; *tópn* 'stamp'.

The forms in A and B are few enough in number so that it seems reasonable to invoke lexical diffusion (even though in a methodological sense it's a last resort, the empirical evidence for it seems beyond dispute: Chen 1972, etc.). One way of getting at some kind of answer here would be a really large-scale survey of the Yiddish lexicon, to determine just how many forms of the A and B types there are, and what percentage of all non-nominals borrowed from Hebrew and Slavic show retained *-ė*. If nearly all of them do, then we need a systematic explanation, not a contingent one, like aborted diffusion. But this work remains to be done.[38]

The verbs, however, are more of a problem. These all belong to Mieses' class V (1929:163), and the group consists of:

... einige deutsche Verben mit vokalischem Wurzelauslaut: sajyn (= säen), krajyn (= krähen), wie auch alle jene hebräischen Zeitwörter, die einen Kehl-.

oder Lippenlaut zum Endkonsonant haben . . . einige hebräische verben auf -sch gehören auch hierher . . .

This takes care of a few forms in a systematic (i.e. phonological) way: but not e.g. *líbn zix* or *kvíčn* (= G. *quietschen*). But, as Mieses adds in the same passage, unfortunately all Slavic verbs (even those borrowed in early Middle High German times) show this class V pattern (essentially a thematic vowel throughout the conjugation, and an *-ė* in the 1 sg. present: thus *ix búrčė, du búrčest, er búrčet, mir búrčen, ijr búrčet, zej búrčen*). Some of the odd German forms might be left simply as 'exceptions' (failed diffusion, or whatever); but the total systematicity of the Slavic forms cries out for an explanation. The only obvious one — that they were all borrowed after *ė*-deletion had ceased to be productive — is (a) false on the historical evidence, and (b) in principle outlandish, since it suggests that all early borrowing from Slavic was categorially selective in a bizarre way (everything but verbs could be borrowed). I have no solution to offer here.

It seems in retrospect that the morphological analysis in terms of 'paradigm-coherence' will do nicely for the nominal material, which of course constitutes the great bulk of the exceptions. But for the verbs there seems to be no explanation, and for the remaining forms we will have to invoke sporadic and contingent factors, like late borrowing where possible (as seems to be the case with *frágė, gešíxtė*), or failed lexical diffusion. This is in the end somewhat sloppy, but maybe language history is too.

Notes

* I am grateful to Maurice Chayen for advice on Hebraistic matters, and to Ken Albrow and Bernard Comrie for assistance with Slavic. They are needless to say not to be blamed for any mess I have made out of areas outside my competence. I am also grateful for comments on earlier oral presentations of some of this material to Jim Hurford, Nigel Vincent, and Paul Werth. My special gratitude to my father, for checking many of the forms, and furnishing me with lexical and grammatical information; and to both my father and my mother for teaching me (often inadvertently) what Yiddish I know.

1. Basically following Postal (1968: Part II).
2. Paradigmatic information is allowed in some more recent generative theories, e.g. in Kiparsky (1971), but not, to my knowledge, quite in the sense I will propose here. For further discussion of the basic issues involved cf. Vincent (1977:227–8).
3. There is no particular reason, by the way, judging either from modern German or most Yiddish dialects, to assume anything as 'neutral' as [ə] for unstressed final *-ė*. Except in certain environments, e.g. before [ł] or [x], it is in most dialects of Yiddish that I have

heard a distinctly front vowel, in the general range [ι ~ ë ~ ë], occasionally nearly fully central, but if so in the higher ranges, i.e. around [ɨ - ɘ].

4. On the development of standard Yiddish see Birnbaum (1954) and Schaechter (1969). In the nonstandard dialects the gender systems are often quite different: for a summary see Wolf (1969). There are other endings involved as well (e.g. masc. acc. sg. -*n*), but these are not relevant here.

5. Yiddish is (and always has been) written, like the other Jewish vernaculars, in Hebrew characters. In citing Yiddish forms here I will use a quasi-orthographic (generally = phonemic) transcription, following pretty much the practice of most of the contributors to Herzog et al. (1969). Yiddish forms cited without reference are from my own speaking knowledge of the language, checked where possible against informants, the glossaries in Weinreich (1965b), Birnbaum (1966), and citations in Mieses (1924), Birnbaum (1922).

   I will follow the practice of Birnbaum (1966) and mark unstressed final -*e* with a superscript point (*ė*), e.g. *grojsė*. In Modern Yiddish it is normally spelled *áyin*, which is the spelling also for stressed *e* ([ɛ]). The transcriptions, unless otherwise indicated, represent the standard ('*literariš*') Yiddish taught e.g. in Weinreich (1965b). The symbols have roughly the following values: *i* [ɪ], *e* [ɛ], *a* [ɐ], *u* [ʊ], *o* [ɔ]; in diphthongs *j* =[i̯]; *t, d, n* are dental; *l*=[ɫ]; *c* [ts], *č* [tʃ], *š* [ʃ], *ž* [ʒ], *j* [dʒ], *x* [x, χ], *r* [ʀ]. Stress is marked with an acute.

6. The zero ending in the neuter indefinite singular may go back to a Middle High German alternative form: cf. Birnbaum (1954:65), who considers it a typical 'Old Central German' characteristic.

7. The end result is even less like what Hooper's 'strong regularity hypothesis (1976:102) would predict than what King's analysis produces. Hooper would predict erosion of morphological or lexical control in the direction of phonological ('natural') control; but there is no evidence whatever for this in this case, only evidence for a continuing morpholexical control. Cf. the discussion below in 3ff.

8. Middle High German -*ė* is lost in many other German dialects as well, but generally without the special complications arising in Yiddish. According to the information in Keller (1961), this occurred to a greater or lesser degree in Alemannic (e.g. Züritüütsch, 33), Alsatian (121), Rhenish Franconian (164), Upper Austrian (204), Luxemburgish (252) and North Saxon (341). Middle High German -*ė* is generally preserved in Westphalian (302), and of course in various forms of modern standard German. For detailed discussion of the loss of -*ė* in German cf. von Kienle (1969: § 65.4) and Mieses (1924:29ff.).

9. *Étlexė*, etc. are of course ultimately adjectival, and might be expected to escape the deletion; except that they maintain their -*ė* when according to the paradigm in (3) they might be expected to lose it, e.g. in nominalizations (*di ánderė zint gekómen* 'the others came') where syntactically at least *ánderė* is not '+adjective'.

10. Some of these forms (*frágė, gešíxtė*) may be late borrowings from standard German: cf. the discussion of this problem in the lexis of an 18th-century Yiddish text in Herzog (1965a: §§ 3.1–2). Certainly *frágė* is 'literary' or 'German'; the usual word for 'question' is the Hebrew *káše*, as in *fregn a káše* 'to ask a question', *klóc káses* 'easy questions, questions for simpletons'. *Gešíxtė* is also rather literary: the more usual term is *histórje*. The word *kánė* 'enema' may also belong here, if it is related to G. *Kanne* (?).

11. Exactly what Yiddish developed from is a problem; literary Middle High German as we know it (which is really kind of a *koiné*) is no more the ancestor of Yiddish than the Old English 'poetic dialect' is of any form of Modern English. On the problems here see Mieses (1924), M. Weinreich (1954) and Birnbaum (1954).

12. Literally 'seven', referring to the seven days of obligatory mourning (H. *ševá*): thus *zícn šívè*, English 'to sit Shivah'.
13. In the toasting formula *lexájim tójvè vešólem* 'to health, good(ness) and peace'. Note that this is all Hebrew, including the preposition *le* 'to' and the conjunction *ve* 'and': but the Hebrew forms are restressed, and H. *ō* in *tójvè < tōvā* has undergone Yiddish diphthongization.
14. Most commonly in the collocation *vildè xájè* 'wild beast', but elsewhere as well. I am not aware of any cognate to G. *Tier*.
15. Perhaps doubtful. Mieses (224) cites Middle High German *baba* 'altes Weib' which by lengthening in open syllables would give *bāba*, and by normal Yiddish rounding of *ā* and loss of length would give (after unstressed vowel reduction) the attested *bóbè*; he also cites Bavarian use of *Baba* in the sense of 'grandmother', which in any case would not be surprising.
16. Pol. *francovaty*. The *franc-* refers to '*Morbus gallicus*'. The suffix *-vatè* is reasonably productive: I have heard *kílevatè* 'having a hernia' (I don't know the source of *kílè*, but it is another form without *è*-deletion), and the semi-calque *káltevatè* 'having a cold'.
17. Perhaps doubtful. See Mieses (1924:220).
18. Cf. Pol. *ciemny*. Many Yiddish loans show *t-* for Pol. *ci-*. For discussion cf. Mieses (230ff.).
19. Cf. Slovak *čača*; also Mieses (233).
20. Most often not literal, but as a curse: *a xoljérjè ojf dir* 'a plague on you', or *xap a xoljérjè* 'catch a plague'.
21. Possibly originally a Germanic loan into Slavic (Mieses 1924:232).
22. Yiddish dialects are grouped roughly as follows (cf. Joffe 1954): West Yiddish (Germany, Holland, Alsace, Switzerland, Czechoslovakia, Hungary); East Yiddish (NE: Lithuania, White Russia; SE: Poland, the Ukraine, the rest of Russia to the Black Sea, Bessarabia, Rumania).
23. And in colloquial Yiddish as well, of course. Cf. set phrases like *a gedílè ojf dajn púpik* 'be happy, congratulations', lit. 'a joy (Heb.) on your navel (Sl.)' *freg mir nit kejn kášes* Don't ask me questions (H)', *di góldenè medínè* 'America', lit. 'land of gold', *bóbèmájsè* 'tall tale', lit. 'grandmother (Sl) story (H)', *šejn vi di levónè* 'lovely as the moon', etc. In many cases there is simply no Germanic word for certain basic vocabulary items: e.g. no cognate to *Mond* but only *levónè*, only *pónim* (H) for 'face', *béjcim* (H) for 'testicles', but doublets *tóxes* (H) and *hintn* for 'arse', and so on.
24. For some socio-cultural commentary cf. Polack – Lawrence (1976: ch. 1); for specifically linguistic discussion M. Weinreich (1954), Birnbaum (1954). On the complexities of Jewish migrations see the detailed discussion in Mieses (1924:273ff.).
25. Not that there weren't already some Jews in the area before: as early as the 2nd c. A.D. according to Dimont (1962:242). But these were mainly leftovers from Roman-Jewish legionaries. The Jews begin to attract documentary attention only later: Aachen 820, Metz 888, Mainz 906, later in Trier, Speyer, Worms (Mieses 1924:273).
26. In other Slavic-speaking areas, the earliest dates seem to be: Bohemia 903, Moravia 1063, Prague 965 (Mieses 288). Aside from the epigraphic evidence mentioned above, Jews appear in Polish documents beginning in 1085; and we know of migrations from Bohemia to Poland (and Hungary) in 1098 (ibid.). The earliest Jewish records in Russia are much earlier, beginning in the 8th century: but these are surely not Ashkenazim (who didn't exist), but Jews from the east.
27. In this MS *'aleph* is written for final unstressed *è*, unlike modern practice, which is to use *áyin* (cf. note 5 above). Yiddish was written then as now in an essentially alphabetic way, using the Hebrew characters that stood for non-Germanic sounds as vowel letters

270   *Roger Lass*

(e.g. *'aleph* [ʔ], *áyin* probably [ʕ]). The omission of the stressed vowel symbols in *hrzè*, *tgè* is an old Yiddish tradition, which persisted until the 19th century, allowing short *a* not to be written (cf. Sand 1965:33–34).

28. This later form is of course not strictly the 'descendant' of Middle High German *tage*, but an analogical reformation (cf. NHG *Hände*).
29. On the development of Ashkenazic stress see Leibel (1965).
30. The *y*-spellings are a German Yiddishist convention for representing [ɪ] or [ɨ] type vowels; raising (with some centralization) seems to have been the general fate of *-è* in Yiddish, whatever its origin. The earliest texts sometimes write *yud* (normally = [i, j]) for this sound (Mieses 1924:27f.).
31. Yiddish-*s* here is from earlier *θ*, which is the development of velarized or pharyngalized ('emphatic') *t*. On this see Birnbaum (1922:20–21).
32. Here and in the next citations I transliterate the Hebrew forms given by Mieses: the two forms here are spelled respectively *'aleph-vov-lamed-mem-'aleph* and *gimel-reš-vov-pe-'aleph*.
33. But (Mieses 1924:30): 'Dennoch ist est möglich, daß das Alef gar nicht in diesen angeführten Worten im Auslaut damals stumm war. Zitiertes Beispiel *premjsl'a* lautet noch heute im Jd. Premysły . . .' (is this a spelling-pronunciation?).
34. NHG *-er* is missing here. Its development in many umlauting nouns began in late Middle High German times, but it became widespread only in the 17th–18th centuries: for a sketch of its history see von Kienle (1969: § 170). Many Yiddish umlauting nouns now have *-er* plurals (e.g. *búx/bíxer* 'book'); but this is probably due to late borrowing from German, a process which has persisted to some extent throughout the whole history of the language (cf. Herzog 1965a §§ 7.12–13).
35. There are sporadic exceptions, where Germanic plurals have gotten attached to Hebrew nouns: thus *tóxes/téxeser* 'arse', *pónim/pénemer* face', *kól/kéler* 'voice'; *maxlójkis*, *-isn* 'quarrel', *hisxávis*, *-isn* 'duty', as well as the names of some of the letters of the alphabet, e.g. *xes*, *-n* 'Cheth' (cf. Birnbaum 1922:39).
36. The inverse of the situation described in note 35 also occurs: e.g. *-im* plurals, often with a stem-'extension' in German words: *nár/narúním* 'fool', *ójg/ojgánim* 'eye'; also *-s* plurals, e.g. *šúster*, *-s* 'shoemaker', *lígner*, *-s* 'liar' (Birnbaum 1922:37).
37. This has been contested: for some discussion of other suggested origins see Birnbaum (1922:37) and Mieses (1924:124ff.).
38. A few items in A and B just might be explained phonotactically: thus if we had *è*-deletion in *paskúdnè, mútnè, pavóljè* we would get uncanonical final clusters, i.e. **-dn, *-tn, *-lj*. But this will only cover some of the examples: *afílè* > **afíl*, *sámè* > **sam*, *bírnè* > **bírn* would give perfectly legal (though as it happens nonexistent) outputs. This explanation would not work, as far as I know, for any of the verbs.

References

Anttila, R.
  1972 *An introduction to historical and comparative linguistics* (New York: Macmillan).
  1975 "Exceptions as regularity in phonology", in: Dressler and Mareš (eds.) 1975:91–100.
Birnbaum, S.
  1922 *Das hebräische und aramäische Element in der jiddischen Sprache* (Leipzig: Gustav Engel).

1954 "Two problems of Yiddish linguistics", in: Weinreich (ed.) 1954:63–72.
1965 "Specimens of Yiddish from eight centuries", in: Weinreich (ed.) 1965a:1–23.
1966 *Grammatik der jiddischen Sprache* (2nd edition) (Hamburg: Buske Verlag).
Bloomfield, L.
1933 *Language* (New York: Holt).
Chen, M.
1972 "The time dimension: Contribution toward a theory of sound change", *Foundations of Language* 8:457–498,
Dimont, M. I.
1962 *Jews, God and history* (New York: Simon and Schuster).
Dingwall, W. O. (ed.)
1971 *A survey of linguistic science* (College Park: University of Maryland, Linguistics Program).
Dressler, W. U. — F. V. Mareš (eds.)
1972 *Phonologica 1972. Akten der zweiten internationalen Phonologie-Tagung, Wien 5–8 September 1972* (München/Salzburg: Wihelm Fink Verlag).
Entwistle, W. J. — W. A. Morrison
1964 *Russian and the Slavonic languages* (2nd edition) (London: Faber).
Guggenheim-Grünberg, F.
1954 "The horse dealer's language of the Swiss Jews in Endingen and Lengnau", in: Weinreich (ed.) 1954:48–62.
Herzog, M. I.
1965a "Grammatical features of Markuze's *Seyfer Refues* (1790)", in: Weinreich (ed.) 1965a:49–62.
1965b *The Yiddish language in Northern Poland: Its geography and history* (IJAL 31,2, Part III) (= *Indiana University Research Center in Anthropology, Folklore and Linguistics*, 37).
Herzog, M. I. — W. Ravid — U. Weinreich (eds.)
1969 *The field of Yiddish. Studies in language, folklore and literature. Third collection* (The Hague: Mouton).
Helm, K.
1966 *Abriß der mittelhochdeutschen Grammatik*, revised by E. Ebbinghaus (3rd edition) (Tübingen: Niemeyer).
Hock, H. H.
1976 Review of Anttila 1972, *Language* 52:202–220.
Hooper, J. B.
1976 *An introduction to natural generative phonology* (New York: Academic Press).
Joffe, J. A.
1954 "Dating the origin of Yiddish dialects", in: Weinreich (ed.) 1954: 102–121.
Keller, R. E.
1961 *German dialects. Phonology and morphology* (Manchester: Manchester University Press).
King, R. D.
1969 *Historical linguistics and generative grammar* (Englewood Cliffs, N.J.: Prentice-Hall).
Kiparsky, P.
1971 "Historical linguistics", in: Dingwall (ed.) 1971:576–649.
Lass, R.
1980 *On explaining language change* (Cambridge: U.P.).

Leibel, D.
  1965   "On Ashkenazic stress", in: Weinreich (ed.) 1965b:63–71.
Mieses, M.
  1924   *Die jiddische Sprache. Eine historische Grammatik des Idioms der integralen Juden Ost- und Mitteleuropas* (Berlin/Wien: Benjamin Harz).
Polack, A. I. – J. Lawrence
  1976   *Cup of life: A short history of post-biblical judaism* (London: SPCK).
Postal, P. M.
  1968   *Aspects of phonological theory* (New York: Harper & Row).
Sand, I. Z.
  1965   "A linguistic comparison of five versions of the *Mayse-Bukh* (16th–18th Centuries)", in: Weinreich (ed.) 1965b:24–48.
Sapir, E.
  1915   "Notes on Judeo-German phonology", *The Jewish Quarterly Review, n.s.* 6:231–266.
Schaechter, M.
  1969   "The 'hidden standard': A study of competing influences in standardization", in: Herzog et al. (eds.) 1969:284–304.
Vincent, N.
  1977   Review of S. R. Anderson, *The organization of phonology, York Papers in Linguistics* 7:225–234.
Weinreich, M.
  1954   "Prehistory and early history of Yiddish in facts and conceptual framework", in: Weinreich (ed.) 1954:73–101.
Weinreich, U. (ed.)
  1954   *The field of Yiddish*, 1 (= *Publications of the Linguistic Circle of New York* 3) (New York: LSNY).
  1965a *The field of Yiddish*, 2 (The Hague: Mouton).
  1965b *College Yiddish* (4th edition) (New York: Yivo Institute for Jewish Research).
Wolf, M.
  1969   "The geography of Yiddish case and gender variation", in: Herzog et al. (eds.) 1969:102–215.

HELMUT LÜDTKE

The place of morphology in a universal cybernetic theory of language change

1 Morphology: An idiosyncratic device of language

Language is a natural (i.e. biologically given) procedure of communication by means of phono-acoustic symbolising, peculiar to mankind. The outstanding specific properties of language can perhaps best be understood by comparing language with sign-systems. The fundamental differences between the two may be stated as follows:

(a) Sign-systems are devised, created, and set in operation within a given frame of reference or cultural setting that includes as a prerequisite, or antecedent condition, the functioning of a particular *langue* (henceforth "L_i"), i.e. a socially established variety of the biologically given *langage* (henceforth "L"). Language, on the other hand, is its own prerequisite, in the sense that though L_i presupposes L plus interaction between individuals in society, no external communication system is required to institute L_i; hence we may say that language is autogenetic or self-instituted. A momentous consequence of this difference between sign-systems and language is that the former consist of items plus rules prior to operation, while the latter shows circularity, which means that the L_i potential in the brain is continually built up (i.e. reinforced, modified etc.) through speech acts which in turn presuppose the existence of some L_i potential.

(b) Sign-systems are characterised by the principle of immediate representation: aliquid stat pro aliquo. Language, on the contrary, is two-staged (or "doubly patterned"), i.e. has an intervening variable between signal (speech-wave) and meaning; in other terms: the signal does not "stand for" its meaning, but has to be interpreted as containing cues for it. This entails complex strategies on the part of both speaker and hearer, in order to assure the fulfillment of communicative needs with optimal effort.

(c) The economy principle that governs communication as well as production of goods and services is implemented differently in sign-systems and in language. Economy in communication systems is linked with the notion of size (of a sign or signal), which is susceptible of various definitions such as "space required in exhibition", "degree of complexity or sophistication", or "effort displayed in production"; for a semantactic or meaning unit in L_i, size can be defined as the amount of physical exertion required to produce the signal that carries the cues necessary for the identification of the unit in question. Economy may be either present or absent; if present it may work on an absolute or on a relative scale: the latter means that size co-varies with some other quantity, most usually frequency of occurrence. It is a well-known fact that in language as well as in some sign-systems the products (or some measures related to, but more complex than, the linear products) of size and frequency of different units differ little. Only language goes a decisive step further by using relative location beside frequency as a factor that rules the variation of size: this is what lies behind the device called morphology.

The principle works as follows. The unilinear flow of the sound-wave continuum is fraught with a multilinear succession of cues for semantactic units. The set of the semantactic units thus represented, i.e. mediately present, in the speech event is divided into two paradigmatic subsets or classes, viz. lexemes and grammatical morphemes, the former being characterized by freedom of occurrence in different parts of an utterance (initial, medial, and final), the latter by formal restrictions of location. Along with this difference in locational properties goes a difference in size: while lexemes are relatively large-sized so that they can be identified by the hearer on account of their size × frequency product, grammatical morphemes — small-sized as they are — in order to be correctly identified need to be scheduled, which means that their occurrence must be more or less foreseeable in given environments. This requires some sort of forced choice among a small number of alternative possibilities at those places. Therefore, high locational constraint occurs in conjunction both with small size (which in turn is connected with high frequency) and with paucity of alternatives. What may be called the "identification potential" (IP) of a semantactic unit (I) — regardless of whether this be a lexeme or a grammatical morpheme — is illustrated by the formula

$$IP = \frac{(S + 1) \cdot L \cdot F}{A}$$

whose constituant quantities, L(ocation constraint), A(lternatives), S(ize), F(requency), have the following limitations:

$$S_\emptyset^n / \ L_\emptyset^1 \ / \ F_\emptyset^1 / A_1^n .$$

Morphology is a language-specific device that makes use of locational constraints and its corollaries, and in so doing provides the possibility of processing a maximal number of semantic units with minimal effort, while maintaining a workable identification potential.

2 Universal laws of language change

As an autogenetic system, language (L) is both self-instituted and self-regulating: regulation is brought about — as a natural corollary — by a great number of speech acts. Speech activity is governed by two fundamental principles, viz. variability and optimisation. The parameters for which optimisation is relevant include:

— the overall effort displayed both in producing and in perceiving speech signals (goal: minimum)
— the endeavour of learning one's L_i (goal: minimum)
— the range of communication, i.e. the number of people that can be reached with a given learning and production effort (goal: maximum).

Whereas variability is a prerequisite for change, optimisation is a cause of it.

Language (= any L_i) is homeorhetic, i.e. keeps changing, by necessity, in order to keep functioning as a system of communication. Optimisation — as a never-ending activity, a Sisyphean task — is required to prevent language (L and L_i) from degeneration.

Language change is governed by principles of compensation concerning the following parameters:

(a) alteration of a given state of communication possibilities: centripetal vs. centrifugal
(b) negentropy of the signal (in relation to given items of what may be communicated through speech): decrease vs. increase
(c) semantactic unit ratio, i.e. number of semantactic units in relation to a given amount of signal negentropy: increase vs. decrease.

Centrifugal alteration of a given state of communication possibilities (implying diminution of the range of communication) is a natural outcome of a bundle of long-term processes which any L_i is liable to undergo. While these processes themselves can hardly be detained by any measures, their detrimental effect on the range of communication is usually

counterbalanced by consciously undertaken short-term changes that tend
to diminish linguistic heterogeneity.

While the above-mentioned principle of compensation (a) opposes two
categorically different types of language change stemming from different
sources (centripetal change being contingent upon social factors, centrifugal change resulting from universal, innate tendencies in speech
activity), quantitative compensation as stated under (b) and (c) is confined to the sphere of centrifugal long-term change.

Long-term change in language (L_i) is characterized by irreversibility of
processes and balance of relations. On the phonetological level, the size
of a given semantactic item at a time t_o will tend to diminish (like Latin
aqua developing into French /o/):

$$S_i(t_o) \geqslant S_i(t_1) \geqslant S_i(t_2) \ldots \ldots \geqslant S_i(t_n)$$

On the semantactic level, the opposite applies: the number of semantactic
units employed to convey a given idea will tend to increase (like Latin
aqua developing into what may be written *de-illa-aqua*, the etymological
ancestor of French *de l'eau*):

$$\Sigma U(t_o) \leqslant \Sigma U(t_1) \leqslant \Sigma U(t_2) \ldots \ldots \leqslant \Sigma U(t_n)$$

If semantactic increase keeps pace with phonetological decrease, the
amount of signalling negentropy produced in order to convey a given idea
will remain the same (like French *de l'eau* differing from Latin *aqua* in
quality, but not in quantity: two syllables each).

Without the third principle of compensation stated under (c), at a time
t_∞ there would be an infinitely great number of infinitely small-sized
semantactic units — which is in flagrant contradiction with the limited
storage capacity of the human brain. The solution is: merger of syntag-
matically adjacent units. Thus an ordinary French speaker analysing
aujourd'hui will not be able to split this complex into as many significant
parts as would his linguistic ancestor in analysing the corresponding
ancestral form *ad-ill-um-di-urn-um-de-ho-di-e*.

This is the way language change works: homeorhetically. In spite of
incessant irreversible processes, quantitative relations only oscillate.
Language changes in order to remain unaltered.

3   Panchronic morphology

3.1   General laws

(1)   There is no absolute necessity for morphology to exist in a given L_i.

Indeed, we observe its absence in early child language, in pidgins and incipient creoles. These are marginal cases, to be sure, and we also find that extant morphology begins to be acquired by children around age 2 and that new morphologies develop once a creole becomes stabilized. All this is easily explained by the principle of optimisation: while pidgins and incipient creoles require a (near) minimum of learning endeavour, but lavish effort of production and perception, "normal" languages have a more balanced economy which is more appropriate to non-extreme cultural settings.

(2) All grammatical morphemes derive from former lexemes. Any lexeme is — in the long run (however long that may be) — doomed to lose its identity: it may either get cancelled from the list (= frequency drop to zero), or merge with another unit adjacent in the syntagmatic string, or become morphologized (i.e. develop into a grammatical morpheme).

(3) Morphological systems owe both their origin and their inexorable decay to irreversible processes due to optimisation.

3.2 Formalised implications

If "$X \rightarrow Y$" means "if X becomes Y" and "$\Rightarrow$" is understood as "then it follows that . . .", starting from the "identification potential" formula

$$IP = \frac{(S + 1) \cdot L \cdot F}{A}$$

we may state the following implications:

(a)	(F	$\rightarrow$	$\emptyset$)	$\Rightarrow$	(I	$\rightarrow$	$\emptyset$)
(b)	(L	$\rightarrow$	$\emptyset$)	$\Rightarrow$	(I	$\rightarrow$	$\emptyset$)
(c)	(A	$\rightarrow$	∞	$\Rightarrow$	(I	$\rightarrow$	$\emptyset$)

where (a) means that any semantactic unit may be lost through a drop in frequency; (b) that there must always be some sort of locational constraint (albeit only semantic) and (c) that the number of alternatives must not be too high, if semantactic units are to be identified:

(d) $(S \rightarrow \emptyset)$ (if $(F > \emptyset) \wedge (L > \emptyset) \wedge (A < \infty)$) $\Rightarrow (I \rightarrow n)$.

hence the size of a given semantactic unit may become zero without the unit in question ceasing to be identifiable: e.g. the phonetological representation of what is usually called "present tense" in French /ilʃãt∅/ (il chante) by zero is sufficient because of high locational constraint (L = 1) of the unit and of paucity of alternatives (/ɛ/ and /r/ for imperfect and future/conditional respectively).

3.3   Formalised dynamics

Dynamism in morphology is determined by the following three principles: irreversibility, compensation, repercussion. Two irreversible processes inherent in human speech activity, viz. phonetological reduction
and semantactic augmentation, have been shown to be the fundamental
cause of language change (cf. Lüdtke 1970, 1971, 1977); their opposite
effects compensate each other insofar as signal negentropy is concerned,
while together they tend to diminish the mean size of semantactic units; this
latter effect is in turn compensated by merger, which tends to increase
size.

There would be no morphology if the impact on size did not instigate a
chain reaction upon the other factors that determine the identification
potential of semantactic units (viz. frequency, locational constraint,
number of alternatives). Such a chain reaction or multiple repercussion is
a more subtle means of compensating the gradual diminution of size
through continuous phonetological reduction (which works more or less
alike upon all, or nearly all, the units of an L_i) than the merger of lexemes
(e.g. Engl. *cupboard, forehead, blackboard*; French *jeune fille, pomme de
terre, loup-garou*; It. *pomodoro*; dialectal Arabic *bnædem*, from *'ibn
'Adam* 'Adam's son'), which — though universal — is not very frequent in
any L_i. The first step in the reaction to decrease of IP (identification
potential) through diminution of S is usually an increase of F (frequency).
If this happens, the unit in question may for some time escape elimination
by compensating decrease of S with increase of F, thus keeping the S × F
product stable and, in so doing, preserving the identification potential

$$IP = \frac{(S + 1) \cdot L \cdot F}{A}.$$

The origin of morphology lies in a split of the set of lexemes (of a given
L_i) into three subsets, viz. those that are not (or rather: not yet!) in
jeopardy because their IP is far above the threshold; those that go
downhill towards elimination and finally, a subset of units that become
more and more small-sized and at the same time more and more frequent,
thus developing into grammatical morphemes.

This latter subset then splits further into two sub-subsets: derivational
and inflexional morphemes. The difference between the two lies in the
degree of capability of entering into syntagmatic combinations with particular lexemes, or classes of lexemes: while derivational morphemes
undergo semantic or haphazard restrictions as to such combinations,
inflexional morphemes tend to be grouped into classes that form Cartesian products with other classes (of both lexemes and other inflexional

morphemes). In the long run, derivational morphemes will merge with adjacent lexemes, and in so doing increase the mean size of the latter. Inflexional morphemes, on the other hand, will tend to form complex systems of classes and subclasses among themselves, thus constituting "grammar", in the narrower sense of the word, i.e. as opposed to the stock of lexemes (plus derivational morphology).

The further development of established inflexional systems is conditioned by another repercussion-type reaction ultimately due to the corroding effect of phonetological reduction (decrease of size). When compensation through rise in frequency reaches a threshold of tolerance, the L and A factors come into play. An IP increase can be achieved by raising locational constraint (clustering and coalescence of "–fixes"), or by reducing the number of alternatives, or by both. In Latin, combinations of *scribere +habere* were both locationally free (*scribere habeo/habeo scribere/habeo illud scribere/illud scribere habeo*/etc.) and susceptible of full conjugation (*scribere habeo/scribere habeam/scribere habebam/scribere haberem/scribere habebo/scribere habui*/etc.). On the way to French, out of ten alternatives eight got lost, two were retained: *scribere habeo* > *écrirai/scribere habebam* > *écrirais*; at the same time, *écrir-* and *-ai/-ais* became inseparable. Supplanting *scribam* and *scriberem*, *écrirai* and *écrirais* have greatly augmented their frequency of occurrence, while suffering a reduction in size from six to three syllables.

3.4   Origin, development, and decay of morphological systems

The advantage of morphology lies in the fact that grammatically (not lexically) processed information (i.e. cognition items) is communicated with comparatively little physical exertion (small size of units; easy articulation) and little expense of time. On the other hand, grammatical morphemes need lexemes, i.e. semantactic units with a high S × F product, as location markers. It is certainly not due to chance that the most complex morphological systems develop in post-lexeme, not in pre-lexeme position, but rather to the linear processing of the speech-signal, which entails that units with a low S × F product and a high $\frac{L}{A}$ quotient are better perceived if the place where they are to be expected is indicated beforehand. These facts put a limit to the growth of morphology.

To give an example for the rise of a new morphological system I shall adduce the verb-aspect system that originated about the end of the 17th century on Réunion Island (formerly called Ile Bourbon) in the then incipient French-based creole language which was afterwards (in the 18th century) carried to other island groups, viz. Mauritius and the Seychelles. The material — taken from A. Bollée (1977:141–2) — is apt to show at least part of the process of development that led from the strongly

French-influenced creole of Réunion to the more independent and fully-fledged creoles of the other islands.

	réun.	maur.	seych.
1 passé récent	sort vyĕd, vyen	fek	fek
2 plus-que- parfait	te fin(i) te i fin	ti'n (ti fin)	ti'n (ti fin)
3 passé	(le)te i	ti	ti
4 aspect accompli	la, fin(i) la fin(i)	fin, in, n	fin, in, n
5 présent	i	Ø	Ø
6 aspect progressif	(le) apre (le) ãtrĕ(d) po	(a)pe	(a)pe
7 imparfait (passé + progressif)	(le)te apre (le)te ãtrĕ(d)	ti pe	ti ape
8 futur	a, (a)va sa(a), sava (le) pur	a, ava, (va) pu	a(va) pu
9 futur antérieur	lora (fini) nora (fini)	a fin, a'n pu fin	a(va)'n pu'n
10 conditionnel (futur du passé)	te i sa (le) te pur	ti a ti pu	ti a(va) ti pu
11 conditionnel passé	lore (te fini) nore (te fini) te fini	ti a fin ti a'n ti pu fin	ti a(va)'n ti pu'n
12 impératif	Ø alõ, anu	Ø anõ, anu	Ø anu

Established morphologies are usually characterized by a fair equilibrium of gain and loss. In medieval and modern French, e.g., the tense-and-aspect system has continually acquired new periphrastic formations while at the same time being stripped of some of the inherited morphological categories through phonetological attrition. How this latter process impairs morphology at the very peak of its efficiency may be illustrated by the following argument:

Suppose two semantactic units are in binary contrast $(A = 1)$, and let there be maximum locational constraint $(L = 1)$; the ideal distribution of size would be $S_1 = \emptyset$ for the more frequent, $S_2 = n$ for the less frequent unit. Once this paramount stage is reached, further phonological attrition — which goes on inexorably — will bring the size of the less frequent unit down from n to $\emptyset$; this, however, entails loss of the distinction between S_1 and S_2: *sic transit efficientia morphologiae.*

References

Bollée, Annegret
1977   "Remarques sur la genèse des parlers créoles de l'Océan Indien", in: *Langues en contact*, edited by Jürgen M. Meisel (Tübingen: Narr), 137–149.
Lüdtke, Helmut
1970   "Sprache als kybernetisches Phänomen", *Bibliotheca Phonetica* 9:34–50.
1971   "Zur Theoriebildung in der Phonetik", *Folia Linguistica* 5:331–354.
1977   "Epistemological remarks on language change and language universals", *Journal of Maltese Studies* 11:3–18.
1980   "Auf dem Weg zu einer Theorie des Sprachwandels", in *Kommunikations theoretische Grundlagen des Sprachwandels*, edited by Helmut Lüdtke (Berlin: De Gruyter), 182–252.

WITOLD MAŃCZAK

Laws of analogy

The difference between Kuryłowicz's works on comparative grammar and those written by other comparatists lies in the fact that Kuryłowicz tries to base them on laws of analogy, a development which is particularly striking in his works published after 1949, where he gave a final form to his conception of analogy by formulating the following six laws:

"I. Un morphème bipartite tend à s'assimiler un morphème isofonctionnel consistant uniquement en un des deux éléments, c'est-à-dire le morphème composé remplace le morphème simple ["morphème simple" = affix or ending, "morphème composé" = affix or ending + alternation of the stem].

II. Les actions dites "analogiques" suivent la direction de formes de fondation → formes fondées, dont le rapport découle de leurs sphères d'emploi.

III. Une structure consistant en membre constitutif plus membre subordonné forme le fondement du membre constitutif isolé, mais isofonctionnel.

IV. Quand à la suite d'une transformation morphologique une forme subit la différenciation, la forme nouvelle correspond à sa fonction primaire (de fondation), la forme ancienne est réservée pour la fonction secondaire (fondée).

V. Pour rétablir une différence d'ordre central la langue abandonne une différence d'ordre plus marginal.

VI. Le premier et le second terme d'une proportion appartiennent à l'origine à des systèmes différents: l'un appartient au parler imité, l'autre au parler imitant."

In order to give an example of the application of these laws to the solving of problems of comparative grammar, it is enough to mention that Kuryłowicz's view of the origin of the Indo-European apophony *e/o* is nothing but a consequence of his first law of analogical development, according to which analogy consists in introducing alternations. Formerly, it was thought that the apophony *e/o* was caused by phonetic factors, whereas Kuryłowicz (1956), convinced of the validity of his first

law, maintains that the ablaut in question is almost exclusively of analogical origin, cf. also Mańczak (1960a).

In 1958, I published an article on analogy, which was followed by a
controversy between Kuryłowicz (1958 and 1960) and me (1960). The
difference between Kuryłowicz's laws and mine is fundamental: whereas
his laws are a priori and are only illustrated by a minimal number of
examples, I attempted to give an inductive character to my hypotheses by
testing them against thousands of facts registered in historical grammars
and etymological dictionaries of different languages.

To my mind, the following four cases can be distinguished in the
analogical development:

(1) A remains, while B disappears;
(2) A keeps an archaic character, whereas B undergoes analogical
change;
(3) A causes a re-formation of B;
(4) A replaces B.

Taking account of these four possibilities, I finally formulated the
following five laws of analogical evolution:

I. The number of morphemes having the same meaning more often
diminishes than increases.

II. In the case of
(a) shorter morphemes — longer morphemes,
(b) shorter words — longer words,
(c) words — word-groups,
the latter more often replace the former than vice versa.

III. In the case of
(a) shorter morphemes — longer morphemes,
(b) shorter words — longer words,
(c) words — word-groups,
the former more often remain than the latter,
the former keep an archaic character for a longer time than the latter,
the former cause a re-formation of the latter more often than vice
versa.

IV. In the case of more frequent forms and less frequent ones, e.g.
(a) those of the singular — those of the other numbers,
(b) those of the indicative — those of the other moods,
(c) those of the present — those of the other tenses,
(d) those of the third person — those of the other persons,
(e) inferior numerals — superior numerals,
(f) cardinal numerals — ordinal numerals,

the former remain more often than the latter,
the former keep an archaic character more often than the latter,
the former cause a re-formation of the latter more often than vice versa,
the former replace the latter more often than vice versa.

V. In the case of
    (a) the local cases of the geographical names — the same cases of the common nouns,
    (b) the non-local cases of the common nouns — the same cases of the geographical names,
    (c) the common nouns — the personal names,
the former keep an archaic character more often than the latter.

For a long time, the controversy between Kuryłowicz and me aroused no interest. It was only in 1973 that Best's doctoral thesis appeared, one half of which dealt with this matter. Best's book was reviewed by Mayerthaler (1974), Anttila (1975), and Faust (1977). In addition, Vincent's lecture on the controversy was published in 1974, and Anttila devoted several pages to the topic in his book on analogy (1974:112–118).

Best (1973:78) thinks that "Kuryłowicz' Theorie in weiten Bereichen nicht nachvollziehbar ist und deshalb auch weder verifiziert noch falsifiziert werden kann". As to my laws of analogy, Best applied some statistical tests in order to verify them and came to the conclusion that these tests confirm my first, second, and third law, and refute the fourth one, whereas the verification of my fifth law is impossible because of the lack of statistical data.

As to my fifth law, it seemed to me of no use to collect statistical data because the validity of this law is obvious. Here are some examples. In Classical Latin, the locative remained only in a couple of common nouns (e.g. *domi*), whereas there are hundreds or even thousands of geographical names which show a locative, e.g. *Romae, Arimini*, etc. In German, ıne dative is a local case, cf. *in Berlin, nach Berlin, aus Berlin*, and, in the German-speaking countries, there are thousands of geographical names of the type *Eberswalde, Kahlenberg, Bayern* (which show the generalization of the local case which the dative is), while with common nouns, this phenomenon is very infrequent. In French, the plural is normally expressed by -*s*, which continues the endings of the acc. plur. in such forms as *tabulas, populos*, etc. With common nouns, there are few which are invariable, that is to say which show no -*s* in the plural: it is a question only of some compounds and recent loan-words such as *les abat-jour* or *les veto*. In the case of family names, the situation is reversed: with the exception of a few surnames like *les Bourbons* or *les Plantagenêts*, practically all French family names, numbering approximately 80,000 (cf. Dauzat 1951:VII), are invariable, cf. *les Cheval, les Chevalier*, etc. In Polish, there is not a single surname whose declension does not show innovations in relation to that of a common noun. The situation is to a certain extent similar in German, cf. *die Müller, die Könige, die Körner* but *die Müllers, die Königs, die Korns.*

Best (1973:92–93) writes: "Mańczak beruft sich bei der Aufstellung seiner Statistiken immer auf Grammatiken und Wörterbücher. Solche Werke behandeln naturgemäss nur eine subjektive Auswahl aus dem gesamten Sprachmaterial, das eine Sprache bietet". Although one does not know exactly what he means by "das gesamte Sprachmaterial, das eine Sprache bietet", Best raises a fundamental linguistic question. According to Saussure, grammar + vocabulary = "langue", whereas texts = "parole". To my mind, language is everything which is spoken or written; in other words, the texts (spoken or written) constitute the language, while grammars and dictionaries are only abstractions isolated from the texts by linguists. Identifying the grammar and the vocabulary of a language with the language in question is as erroneous as identifying Mendeleyev's system of chemical elements with nature. Being convinced that the texts constitute the language, I have suggested a new method of classifying languages: while all language classifications are based on an arbitrary choice of grammatical or lexical traits, a rational classification of languages should rest upon the comparison of parallel texts and not of some linguistic traits chosen at random (1958a).

Therefore, I must explain why I checked the laws of analogy by using historical grammars and etymological dictionaries:

(1)   Some tests convinced me that, in the case of analogical evolution, there are no great difficulties between the results obtained by scrutinizing grammars and dictionaries and those obtained by scrutinizing texts.

(2)   In some cases, there are different ways of interpreting an analogical form, e.g. Fr. *chante* for Lat. *cantet* may be considered as analogical with *chante* < *cantat*, with *entre* < *intret*, or with *vende* < *vendat*. The linguist scrutinizing a text might be tempted to choose the interpretation which suits his thesis. This temptation does not exist if one decides to scrutinize an historical grammar and to accept all the interpretations of its author.

(3)   In order to scrutinize a text, an excellent knowledge of the historical grammar of the language in question is necessary. Since I wanted to confront my hypotheses with the data offered by the most diverse languages (even non-Indo-European), I was obliged to resort to grammars and dictionaries.

Here is, however, an example showing that the scrutinizing of texts confirms my fourth law, according to which there is a connection between analogy and frequency. I scrutinized the first and the second act of Molière's *L'école des femmes*, where, altogether, I found 824 verbal forms, which, from the point of view of number, tense, mood, and person, are as follows:

	Regular forms	Analogical forms	χ^2 test
Singular	396	250	41,2 > 3,84
Plural	60	118	
Present	421	295	26,5 > 3,84
Other tenses	35	73	
Indicative	423	248	78,2 > 3,84
Other moods	33	120	
Third person	371	100	244,2 > 3,84
Other persons	85	268	

My chief criticism of Best's argument is that, while he applied the χ^2 and other statistical texts to my materials, he did not confront Kuryłowicz's laws and mine with the linguistic reality (for more details, see Mańczak 1978). Therefore, I repeat once more: if somebody wishes to know whether Kuryłowicz's laws or mine are true, theoretical speculations are of no use. The only way to solve this problem is to examine at least one historical grammar, etymological dictionary, or text and to count how many analogical changes confirm or refute each of Kuryłowicz's and my laws. Strangely enough, nobody had checked these laws in this way, although such a test could be done in a few days.

References

Anderson, John — Charles Jones (eds.)
  1974   *Proceedings of the First International Conference on Historical Linguistics* (Amsterdam: North-Holland).
Anttila, Raimo
  1974   *Analogy* (Helsinki: University). [Revised edition 1977, The Hague: Mouton.]
  1975   Review of *Probleme der Analogieforschung* by Best, *Historiographia Linguistica* 2:91–95.
Best, Karl-Heinz
  1973   *Probleme der Analogieforschung* (München: Hueber).
Dauzat, Albert
  1951   *Dictionnaire étymologique des noms de famille et prénoms de France* (Paris: Larousse).

Faust, Manfred
  1977   Review of *Probleme der Analogieforschung* by Best, *Zeitschrift für Dialektologie und Linguistik* 14:183–187.
Kuryłowicz, Jerzy
  1949   "La nature des procès dits 'analogiques'", *Acta Linguistica* 5:15–37.
  1956   *L'apophonie en indo-européen* (Wrocław: Ossolineum).
  1958   "Ogólne tendencje zmian analogicznych" [General tendencies of analogical changes], *Biul. Pol. Tow. Jęz* 17:207–219.
  1960   "Odpowiedź językoznawstwa" [A linguistic answer], *Biul. Pol. Tow. Jęz.* 19:203–210.
Mańczak, Witold
  1958   "Tendances générales des changements analogiques", *Lingua* 7:298–325, 387–420.
  1958a "Problem klasyfikacji genealogicznej języków słowiańskich" [Problems of the genetic classification of Slavic languages], *Z polskich studiów slawistycznych. Prace językoznawcze i etnogenetyczne na IV Międzynarodowy Kongres Slawistów w Moskwie 1958* (Warszawa: PWN), 35–51.
  1960   "Odpowiedź Prof. J. Kuryłowiczowi" [An answer to Professor J. Kuryłowicz] *Biul. Pol. Tow. Jęz.* 19:191–201.
  1960a "Origine de l'apophonie *e*/*o* en indo-européen", *Lingua* 9:277–287.
  1978   "Les lois du développement analogique", *Linguistics* 205:53–60.
Meyerthaler, Willi
  1974   Review of *Probleme der Analogieforschung* by Best, *Papiere zur Linguistik* (München: Fink), 124–130.
Vincent, Nigel
  1974   "Analogy reconsidered", in: Anderson and Jones (eds.) 1974:427–445.

FRANS PLANK

Encoding grammatical relations: acceptable and unacceptable non-distinctness*

With the renewed interest in grammatical relations, more attention has again been paid recently to those overt morphological and syntactic devices that are used in natural languages to encode these relations. These had for quite a while been neglected in favour of less superficial, underlying principles of grammatical organization which were believed to provide an appropriate basis for generalizations with a universal import. That this belief was, partly, mistaken and that the regularities pertaining to relational coding do have typological, historical and universal significance was clearly demonstrated by recent, and not so recent, theories about constituent order or case systems. In this respect, case and linear order theories represent, at least potentially, a considerable advance in our knowledge about what is accidental and language-particular and what is predictable on more general grounds. In another respect, though, they too are bound to fall short of explanatory adequacy, on account of their failure to address themselves to a range of empirical phenomena that forms a natural domain. The only natural domain for a theory concerned with relational encoding, I contend, is the ensemble of formal means available to natural languages for the purpose of encoding grammatical relations in its entirety. Although separate theories about individual coding devices, such as nominal case inflection (occasionally accompanied by patterns of segmental or suprasegmental modification), agreement or cross-reference[1], adpositions, and linear constituent order, may be able to arrive at partially explanatory generalizations, they cannot meaningfully ask, much less answer, important questions like the following. Which particular coding devices can, and which cannot, be utilized in individual languages at the same time? (Why, for instance, should there exist affinities between agreement and case inflection, or incompatibilities of case and order?) Which influences can be exerted upon syntactic processes by different coding devices? In which manner and for which reasons do languages change in time with regard to coding properties of their grammatical relations? If such problems are at issue, an integral theory about the interdependencies of alternative and/or complementary coding devices, rather than a neat compartmentalization of case, agreement, word order and other coding systems, is called for. To demonstrate that such problems indeed have to be at issue, is what I am presently concerned with.

It is obvious, for example, that case and serialization theories individually cannot explain a diachronic exchange of coding systems as happened in the history of the Germanic, Romance, Slavic and many other languages. But "drifts" towards analyticity are only the most conspicuous example of the non-random nature of the way one ensemble of coding devices gains predominance over another. The common accounts of such developments — the phonetically induced decay of inflectional morphology had to be compensated for by new syntactic means of relational encoding — essentially are post hoc attempts at stating what has happened rather than genuine explanations. And even as such they are anything but adequate, in so far as they are at odds with the empirical evidence that quite generally suggests that analytic encoding increases prior to morphological decay (Plank 1977a; 1980).

The present paper takes up a fairly traditional issue, which is usually situated entirely within the confines of one particular coding system, viz. that of case morphology. I am referring to the notion of syncretism, which is often understood as involving formal coincidence of entries of a declensional paradigm, although in another, more traditional usage of the term, case syncretism implies more than mere formal identity.[2] For the present purpose, the question of complete neutralization of paradigmatic categories, on the form as well as the content side, can be disregarded; what is of interest here is formal identity since the relevant categories are such that their distinctness on the functional level can safely be taken for granted. I submit that it is only within a general coding theory that a certain pattern of syncretism, or rather: avoidance of syncretism, emerges. Although the amount of cross-linguistic evidence adduced in support of this claim is necessarily limited, the proposed pattern of coding, rather than case, syncretism appears to be universally significant. The generalization that different grammatical relations are affected differently by syncretism would have to be missed if declensional paradigms alone were taken into account (cf. also Plank 1978a). There no doubt are a number of previous studies that quite convincingly show the non-random patterning of case syncretism to be a consequence of syntactico-semantic determinants of morphology[3]; they still do not sufficiently emphasize the principled manner of the interaction of alternative and simultaneous coding devices in serving their ultimately common purpose.

But what exactly is the purpose of relational coding devices? According to functional explanations, as advocated by Comrie (1975) or Martinet (1979) among others (cf. also Boeder 1971), their essential raison d'être is simply to distinguish the various grammatical relations co-occurring in actual sentences, especially if other clues to the relational identity of terms are lacking. Thus, coding by means of case marking, which is commonly regarded as an independent domain of such functional principles, has to guarantee that in transitive clauses subjects (S) are overtly distinguishable from direct objects (dO), whereas in intransitive clauses and clause types with only a single term being governed by the predicate (e.g. subjectless transitive imperatives) there is no need to distinguish anything, the particular case used to encode single terms, consequently, being largely arbitrary.[4] As far as I am aware, the absolute distinctness requirement on multi-term configurations at the heart of the functional principle has been assumed to apply with equal force to all grammatical relations potentially co-present in a single sentence, although occasionally particular prominence has been accorded to an allegedly central relational distinction: "those [ambiguities] resulting from the neutralization of substantive S.O distinctions are of a particularly damaging nature" (Vennemann 1975:295; similarly Wurzel 1977:136). In my opinion, these evaluations are both counterfactual. There as a matter of fact do exist priorities with respect to distinctive coding, but rather than pertaining to the S-dO configuration, they single out the non-clausal grammatical relation holding between an attributive term (A) and its head. After substantiating this claim by showing that, synchronically, there is a universal constraint against non-distinctive encoding of A, which is instrumental diachronically in bringing about or preventing pertinent changes of coding systems, I shall suggest an explanation of the differential toleration of relational non-distinctness that simultaneously entails certain modifications of the functional principle.

A few familiar examples suffice to demonstrate that the Modern English predominantly order-based coding system does not entirely successfully prevent S-dO relational ambiguity:

(1) *Mary is too young to marry.*
(2) *Joe likes Sue more than Bill.*
(3) *The chickens are ready to eat.*

The overt main clause subjects are of course clearly distinguishable; what cannot be determined, at least not on account of their encoding, is the relation they are holding with regard to the non-finite or unexpressed verbs.[5] Or consider coordinate clauses in Chukchee, and otherwise highly ergative language with case- and agreement-based coding:

(4) *ətləg-e talaywə-nen ekək ənkʔam ekwet-gʔi*
    (father-instr. beat-3sg3sg son(absol.) and leave-3sg)
    'The father beat his son and /father or son/ left'
(5) *keyŋ-ən na-nmə-gʔan ənkʔam yara-k qača wa-rkən*
    (bear-absol. 3pl-kill-3sg and house-loc. near be-pres. 3sg)
    'They killed a bear and /it/ is near the house'.

Apparently, control in Chukchee identity deletions does not obligatorily conform to an ergative pattern, and verb agreement sometimes (as in(5)) but not always (cf. (4)) helps to avoid relational ambiguities resulting from ambiguous S and dO behaviour and control (cf. Nedjalkov 1979). It could, thus, at first sight look as if S-dO ambiguities are likely to turn up only in non-basic constructions such as nominalizations or complex elliptical sentences, but even a superficial cross-linguistic survey quickly proves this assumption wrong. No matter which particular coding devices are predominant, many (probably most) languages tolerate non-distinctive coding of S and dO to a certain extent. It seems that of all coding systems, relationally determined linear order would be the one best suited to avoid S-dO ambiguities in the long-run, at least in (non-elliptical) basic sentences, because ordering rules are inherently simpler than rules of inflectional morphology, and thus presumably more resistant to diachronic change; nevertheless, most predominantly order-based languages tend to admit variable order even in basic sentences for purposes other than relational encoding (e.g. topicalization), and thus increase the risk of relational ambiguity.

Here are a few instances of languages tolerating non-distinctive S-dO encoding.

— The rather frequent ergative-absolutive case syncretisms in various Basque dialects often cannot be compensated for by verb agreement (Jacobsen 1972).

— Case marking in Tongan formerly failed to distinguish agents and patients, at least with conceptually transitive verbs (such as 'eat') accompanied by a single term, and in the absence of a voice distinction or distinctive S- or dO-orientation in the predicate, this single term could be taken for a (passive or active) S as well as for a dO (Tchekhoff 1979).

— With 3rd person plural S and dO, Huichol cannot avoid relational ambiguity, both orders OSV and SOV being in principle available (Grimes 1964:69).

— In Dakota, 3rd person singular S and dO in main clauses likewise lead to relational ambiguity (Schwartz 1976).

— Lisu (a Lolo-Burmese language) apparently allows S-dO ambiguity in all transitive main clauses, ordering restrictions being largely of a non-relational nature (Hope 1973).

— Wolof has relationally ambiguous relative clauses if the verb of the relative clause is transitive and either the S or the dO has been relativized (Schwartz 1976).

— In Southern Paiute, the different 3rd person enclitics have no distinctive case forms, and their relative ordering is determined by class (inanimate precedes animate) rather than by grammatical relations; hence S-dO ambiguity is often unavoidable (Sapir — Swadesh 1946).

— In Mandarin Chinese, grammatical relations are encoded by linear order and/or prepositions (cf. *chī jī le* '(someone) eat chicken PAST' with distinctive VdO order, *bǎ jī chī le* 'OBJ chicken eat PAST' with distinctive object preposition, *gěi jī chī le* 'AGENT chicken eat PAST' with distinctive agentive preposition), not quite reliably, though, since sentences like *jī chī le* 'chicken eat PAST' are also acceptable, inspite of their having two readings, 'the chicken has eaten' and 'someone has eaten the chicken' (='the chicken was eaten') (Li 1971).

— Most Indo-European languages often do not overtly distinguish the nominative (S) and the accusative (dO), especially in neuter and in all plural paradigms; complementary coding devices often do not suffice to clear up these relational ambiguities.

— In Hiri Motu, which uses postpositions and cross-reference for coding purposes, 3rd person singular dO's usually are not expressed overtly, and then the transitive S postposition may also be dropped; thus *boroma ese ia ia itaia* (pig S_t-marker him (dO) it (S) saw) 'the pig saw him' becomes *boroma ia itaia* (pig it/he (S) saw), which, however, is ambiguous between 'the pig saw him' and 'he saw the pig' (Dutton — Voorhoeve 1974).

— Certain German dialects give up S-dO case distinctions in paradigms other than neuter, by overgeneralizing either the nominative (cf. Rhenish *Otto hat der Mann gesehen* 'the man has seen Otto' or 'Otto has seen the man', instead of the distinctive Standard German *den Mann),* or the accusative (cf. Low German *Wen is dat gewesen?* 'Who was that?', instead of Standard German *Wer).*

— The Israeli Sign Language lacks a reliable S-dO distinction as the temporal order of signs is not, or at least not consistently, relationally determined; often, the result is failure of communication if there are no appropriate situational or semantic cues (Schlesinger 1971).

Such examples of textually[6] tolerated S-dO ambiguity could be multiplied almost ad libitum, as, on the other hand, no doubt could examples of languages that, obligatorily or optionally, employ coding strategies to prevent this same kind of relational ambiguity.[7] One such strategy, which appears to be fairly common, is to distinctively mark dO's only if the risk of actual ambiguity is relatively high, i.e. if they have some of the semantic or pragmatic properties (such as animateness, topicality, definiteness) normally characteristic of subjects. A rather language-particular strategy with the same effect is encountered in Jacaltec (cf. Craig 1977:211–30); here, S and dO are identified essentially by their position (VSO) and also by verb agreement[8], and relational ambiguity potentially ensuing from movement or deletion of the S or dO term is obviated by the obligatory introduction of a verbal suffix that merely indicates any deviation from the standard VSO pattern on the part of the S term, and additionally by deleting the S-agreement marker of the verb. The reliance upon an otherwise relationally non-distinctive coding device has been said to be another such strategy, for instance in Russian, where constituent order is claimed to be restricted to SVO if accusative and nominative are not distinctively marked:

(6) *mat' l'ubit doč*
    (mother (nom./acc.) loves daughter (nom./acc.))
    'the mother loves the daughter'

But certainly, this is no general law, and perhaps not even a tendency; it seems to be much more common to rely on contextual rather than compensatory textual disambiguation of S-dO ambiguity, as does German, despite occasional claims to the contrary.[9] Sanžeev (1969) mentions the disambiguating function of parallelism, as in (7):

(7) *Den Vater liebt der Sohn und die Mutter die Tochter*
    (the father (acc.) loves the son (nom.) and the mother (nom./acc.)
    the daughter (nom./acc.))
    'the son loves the father and the daughter the mother'

but this is a contextual rather than textual way of reducing the risk of relational ambiguity.

It was only recently that serious attempts were made to come to terms with the important distinction between acceptable (tolerable) and unacceptable (intolerable) ambiguity.[10] The notion of unacceptable ambiguity has so far been resorted to in situations of the following kind. Certain grammatically well-formed sentences, which on account of the general rules utilized in their derivation (or, more neutrally, in their generation) ought to be derivable from two or more different underlying representations (or, more neutrally, ought to be analysable in two or more different ways), in fact are not ambiguous, all but one of their potential readings being suppressed, independently of their context of use. Gapped coordinate constructions like (8a) and (9a), and extraposed relatives like (10a) illustrate this:

(8) a. *Max gave Sally a nickel, and Harvey a dime.*
   b. *Max gave Sally a nickel, and* (Max gave) *Harvey a dime.*
   c. *Max gave Sally a nickel, and Harvey* (gave Sally) *a dime.*
(9) a. *The press characterized Agnew as colourless, and Nixon as low-keyed.*
   b. *. . ., and* (the press characterized) *Nixon as low-keyed.*
   c. *. . ., and Nixon* (characterized Agnew) *as low-keyed.*
(10) a. *A man looked for his brother, who was blind.*
   b. *A man, who was blind, looked for his brother.*

(8a) and (9a) cannot result from a deletion of VO (as indicated in (8c) and (9c)), although the identity requirement of Gapping is met by VO as well as by SV in the second conjuncts. (10a) likewise cannot result from an extraposition of the relative clause in (10b), although an appropriate structural constraint on the application of the extraposition rule would be difficult to motivate. To complicate these matters even further, it often happens that one of the potential readings is not suppressed completely. Whereas (9) is a hard and fast case of unacceptable ambiguity, (8) and (10) apparently are such instances where one of the potential readings (8b, 10a) is clearly preferred over its a priori just as likely alternative (8c, 10b), without these latter interpretations being excluded as a matter of grammatical principle.[11]

In the absence of a truly explanatory theory of ambiguity it is not surprising that hardly any attention has so far been paid to another, more drastic way of getting rid of undesirable ambiguity, which simply is not to accept any of the potential readings of an ambiguously coded construction, i.e. to stigmatize potentially ambiguous constructions as ungrammatical, irrespective of any potentially disambiguating context of use.[12] An adequate theory of ambiguity would have to be able to predict under what circumstances ambiguities are likely to arise, are likely to be suppressed by obligatory non-contextual disambiguation, or are likely to result in plain ungrammaticality. With this ultimate aim in mind, I think it is significant first to observe that non-distinctive and eventually ambiguous coding of the non-clausal relation of an A to its head as a rule entails ungrammaticality of the attributive construction, whereas there is a tendency for S-dO ambiguity to be universally acceptable. To pave the way for a somewhat more precise formulation of this generalization, here is a sample of the evidence that is highly suggestive of an entirely different reaction to non-distinctive coding of S-dO and of A-head.

Indefinite plural nouns in German do not cooccur with a determiner, and their own genitival suffix formally coincides with nominative and accusative plural suffixes. Moreover, the relative order of the genitive and its head is not exactly free but neither is it strictly relationally determined. Hence there is no way of encoding a synthetic genitival A in an absolutely distinctive manner under these circumstances. Ungrammaticality is the result, if the analytic prepositional alternative (11b) is not resorted to:

(11) a. *Benachteiligungen Frauen/Männer/Schotten*
        'discriminations (against) women/men/Scots'
     b. *Benachteiligungen von Frauen/Männern/Schotten.*

Adjectives, on the other hand, do have distinctively genitival suffixes, and, thus, can render constructions like (11a) perfectly grammatical:

(12) a. *Benachteiligungen andersgläubiger Frauen/Männer/Schotten*
        '... against heterodox women/men/Scots'
     b. *Benachteiligungen Andersgläubiger*
        '... against heterdox (ones)'.

That the suffix *-er* is distinctively genitival is slightly inaccurate; nominative singular masculine adjectives also take *-er* if not preceded by a definite determiner. This syncretism, however, may be considered irrelevant since singular adjectives would hardly ever occur without distinctive determiner. Feminine nouns likewise lack a distinctive genitive suffix in the singular; if unaccompanied by a determiner or adjective, such nouns (typically mass nouns) also lead to ungrammaticality when used as synthetic A's:[13]

(13) a. *Ich bin kein Freund Milch/Schokolade.*
        'I'm no friend (of) milk/chocolate'
     b. *Ich bin kein Freund von Milch/Schokolade.*

In German certain proper names ending in a dental and alveolar fricative (s, z, sch) also have no distinctive genitive, which bars their use as synthetic A's:

(14) a. *Bewohner Moskaus/Londons/*Paris/*Graz*
        'inhabitants (of) Moscow/London/Paris/Graz'
     b. *Bewohner von Moskau/London/Paris/Graz.*

Another, less common alternative is to use two inflectional affixes simultaneously: *Graz +en +s*; *-en*, from the paradigm of the weak nouns, not only prevents the genitive *-s* from being phonetically amalgamated with the stem-final consonants, it also helps to create a maximally distinctive genitive form (cf. also innovations like *Herz +en +s* 'heart (gen.sg.)' instead of *Herzen* or *Herzes*).

In present-day German, certain masculine and neuter adjectives and adjectival pronouns fluctuate between the weak and strong declensional paradigms in the genitive singular without separate determiner:

(15) a. *der Konkurs welches/erwähntes Mann*es
     'the bankruptcy (of) which /said man'
   b. *der Konkurs welchen/erwähnten Mann*es.

Here the noun itself bears the distinctive marker *-es*. If, however, the substantival declension does not distinguish the genitive from other cases, the weak and strong adjectival forms are no longer in free variation, the distinctive *-es* of the adjective now being obligatory:

(16) *der Konkurs welch*es*/erwähnt*es*/*welchen/*erwähnter*
     Konkurrenten
     (*Konkurrenten* 'rival' could be gen./dat./acc.sg. and nom./gen./dat./acc.pl.).

The weak adjectival forms of the genitive are innovations already found in the 17th century. It is remarkable, though, that this morphological change, commonly said to be due to euphonic reasons, did not succeed entirely; the old strong forms linger on, and have to be resorted to only in cases of emergency, viz. in order to mark A's that lack other morphological indications of A-hood.

A quite restricted class of German cardinal numerals[14] has an inflectional suffix in the genitive; this inflected form must be used if the numeral is part of an otherwise morphologically non-distinctive genitive:

(17) a. *der Konkurs zwei/zwei*er *alt*er *Konkurrenten*
     'the bankruptcy of two old rivals'
   b. *der Konkurs zwei*er*/*zwei Konkurrenten*
   c. **der Konkurs siebener/sieben Konkurrenten*.

Numerals like *sieben* '7', which have no inflected form, require the analytic prepositional construction.

These were four different instances where strong pressure is brought to bear upon the absolute avoidance of non-distinctive encoding of attributive genitives in Modern German, if necessary by inhibiting certain morphological changes. Notably, the analytic coding device most commonly resorted to in order to avoid ungrammaticality ensuing from nondistinctive morphological coding was an increase in the use of prepositional A's rather than a restriction on the linear order of genitival A's.

That this last observation concerning preferred ambiguity avoidance strategies cannot necessarily be generalized is demonstrated by the following example from the history of English. Throughout the development of English towards analyticity there occasionally occurred what looks like a syncretism of the genitive singular, otherwise one of the last nominal relics of syntheticity, with the suffixless non-attributive noun form:

(18) Early Middle English (Orrmulum, data from Lehnert 1953):
      hiss a₃henn broþer wif, inn hiss Faderr bosemm, þe kyng sonne, þe leffdi₃ lac, off twellf winnterr elde, inn hiss moderr wambe, inn ani₃ kinne sinne.

(19) Early Modern English and later dialects (cf. Ekwall 1913):
      the emperoure moder, the Frenche Kyng dowthur, Patrik house, The Abbot of Redyng place, Master Wyllde bequest, the oulde goose fether, Thomas Gillman wiff.

These case syncretisms, however, do by no means amount to coding syncretisms. The formerly free genitive order had already been stabilized considerably as early as late Old English (cf. Fries 1940), so that even an uninflected noun preceding another noun could be identified with reasonable certainty as the attributive element.[15] As so often, word order change, from relationally free to relationally determined, antedated morphological change, and made possible the abandonment of one of the most crucial relational distinctions of inflectional morphology. What is also noteworthy is that the lexical elements in those attributive constructions encoded by order rather than inflection fall into semantically natural classes; the heads preferably are typical relational nouns, and the A's preferably denote persons or at least animates and are definite and in the singular. This configuration seems to indicate almost automatically which element is the A and which the head, and hence does not require much relational encoding at all to obviate misunderstanding (cf. Plank 1979). But such functional considerations did not play a prominent role in the further development of English. If adnominal A's were to be postposed, from around 1250 onwards the analytic prepositional construction with *of* was obligatory. It seems that already in early Middle English postposed synthetic genitives such as (20) hardly ever occurred;

(20) *an bite bræd*ess, *shippennd all*re *shaffte* (Orrmulum)

and if they did, they displayed a distinctive genitive suffix. As far as I was able to ascertain, the few Old English nouns with a syncretistic genitive singular (e.g. *bropor*) had to be accompanied by a distinctive determiner or adjective when used attributively. Finally, even if genitive nouns keep their *-s* there still is some case and number syncretism in standard Modern English, with the genitive singular being identical with all plural cases including the genitive. Due to the distinctive analytic coding devices (e.g. *the old sailors'/sailor's ships*), phonological and morphological changes of the earlier declensional system did not need to pay any attention to the requirement of keeping A's distinct morphologically.

The drift towards analyticity in the Romance languages in several respects resembled the Germanic developments; certainly analytic relational coding by means of linear order and prepositions had already gained predominance prior to the decay of crucial morphological distinctions. With respect to the encoding of A, one stage in the development of Old French from Vulgar Latin is particularly reminiscent of the English pattern sketched above (cf. Westholm 1899; Plank 1979). As the Latin system of six cases had been reduced to a two-case system (nominative vs. oblique), with the A being encoded by means of prepositions (*de*, *ad*), Old French had a pattern of attributive constructions without distinctive cases or prepositions:[16]

(21) *la roi fille, fil maistre Henri, le chienet sa niece, li serf sum pedre, la fille le roi*

The A's in this construction denote exclusively persons and most often are definite and specific (cf. *por l'amor mon pere* vs. *por l'amor d'un pere*) and in the singular; they are, thus, typical possessors (Plank 1979), which generally can often afford abandoning distinctive encoding. Such functional considerations notwithstanding, is this an instance of non-distinctive A encoding? Obviously not. Constituent order had already become largely relationally determined so that the second of two adjacent nouns could safely be taken to be the A. The pattern with the A preceding the head (cf. first example under (21)) played a less prominent role and disappeared in the 11th or 12th century; even here, the A could clearly be told from the head since preceding A's as a rule lacked a determiner. Thus, of two adjacent nouns preceded by a determiner, the first could only be an A.

These examples from German, English, and French evince a pattern that recurs in so large a number of languages of diverse genetic and typological affiliation that the following generalizations seem well motivated: Diachronically speaking, developments affecting synthetic coding devices cannot interfere with the distinctive encoding of A unless analytic coding devices are already available. Synchronically speaking, whenever one coding device is unable to encode the A relation distinctively, another coding device steps in to prevent the intolerable non-distinctness of A's. So far, I have only surveyed languages that are undergoing, or have undergone, one particular type of coding change, viz. a drift towards analyticity, for which reason other regularities concerning supplementary and complementary A encodings and their interactions may have gone unnoticed. If there is a target of optimal A encoding that analytic developments in general aim at in the long run, it would seem to be the use of adpositions. One probable reservation is that developments may be slightly different with A's that semantically are typical possessors.

Consider now a few further examples of requirements on the encoding of A's. First Old Irish, which has a fairly well developed system of nominal case inflection. Syncretisms of either nominative singular and genitive singular, or nominative singular and genitive plural, or genitive singular and nominative plural, or nominative and genitive plural are surprisingly widespread among the 13 declensional paradigms given by Thurneysen (1946) — in fact, only four of them are not syncretistic at all in these respects. However, at least in prose style it is precisely the attributive construction that is characterized by a complete lack of positional variability; the A relation is absolutely distinctively encoded by postnominal position of the nominal A.

Similarly in Modern Georgian, which to a large degree depends on morphological coding: "Si l'orde des termes dans les groupes nominaux est très rigide [adnominal genitives precede their heads], cèlui des termes de la proposition (verbe, sujet et régime) est absolument libre" (Vogt 1974:48).

The non-distinctive S-dO encoding in the Israeli Sign Language was already mentioned above; the A-head relation, on the other hand, is distinctively encoded: the attributive modifier consistently follows its head (Schlesinger 1971).

In Ostyak, there is only one "case" (in fact, the nominal stem) that encodes S, dO and A. To clear up textual S-dO ambiguities, it may be necessary to appeal to semantic or contextual factors. A-head ambiguities, on the other hand, are obviated textually, since A's consistently precede their heads (Sasse 1977:94–5).

Basque has distinctive case suffixes to encode A's: *etchear-en nausia* 'the house (gen. sg.) the master', *nausiar-en etchea* 'the master (gen.sg.) the house'. Apart from a few idiosyncratic exceptions (e.g. *aita-*

familiakoa 'the father of the family', *San Antonio Padukoa* 'St. Anthony of Padua'; cf. Lafitte 1962:420), A's precede their heads. Thus the possibility of suppressing the genitival suffix as in *ama oitura* 'the mother's costume' (Campion 1884:199–200) does not conflict with the distinctness requirement on A's, as position alone suffices for purposes of relational distinction. It is another question why Basque throughout its entire history has never made a serious attempt to abandon that part of its inflectional morphology that is strictly speaking redundant for the purpose of A encoding.

There is a similar interplay of synthetic and analytic A encoding in Hungarian (Lotz 1968:631). If possessive A's are in the dative case, which is distinctive vis-a-vis other cases, their order relative to their heads is not fixed. If, however, A's are in the nominative, which case also encodes S's, their order is strictly relationally determined; then they always precede their head.[17] Word order also becomes relationally distinctive in another situation in a few Ural-Altaic languages that I have looked at cursorily (e.g. Finnish and Uzbek). Normally, unique identification of A's is guaranteed by case inflection, probably in conjunction with cross-reference on the head; possessive nominal forms, however, often are syncretistic (Finnish *taloni* 'my house-nom./gen. etc. sg.', Uzbek *otiŋni* 'your horse-acc./gen. sg.'), and then linear order takes over the task of encoding A's. Notice, furthermore, that it is no mere accident that it is possessive nouns which are particularly prone to lose or not to develop distinctive A morphology. The reason is again of a functional nature; they are inherently predestined to A-hood, and totally unsuited to be employed as heads in attributive constructions, which apparently makes it superflous to specifically encode them as A's when this is their characteristic function anyway (but cf. Plank 1979).

The Scandinavian languages could have been mentioned above since their case systems are reduced as in the other Germanic languages; in most of them the genitive is one of the last relics of synthetic relational encoding (cf. Teleman 1975). In Swedish, for example, genitives continue to be encoded by case suffixes, and, this is an analytic innovation, by linear order, with A's preceding their heads. Thus, the distinctness requirement on the encoding of A's is met even if case suffixes are absent, which as a matter of fact happens in a few well-defined circumstances (cf. Wessén 1968:25), essentially with place names holding the A relation and heads that are not further modified by adjectives:

(22) *Uppsala domkyrka* vs. *Uppsalas nya domkyrka*
'Uppsala's (new) cathedral'

These "fasta förbindelser" (Wessén) are genuine A's and, again, typical possessors rather than first elements of compound nouns. This is not the place to enter into a general cross-linguistic discussion of the relationship between A's and modifier-modified structures of compounds; I only note in passing that compound modifiers usually are encoded fairly distinctively, and in so far resemble genuine A's. Their particular coding devices, however, may differ considerably, since stress, which plays a prominent role as compound indicator, apparently is only marginally, if at all, used to encode A's, and also S's and dO's.

Russian too has some syncretism of the genitive. According to Jakobson (1939), reliance upon "l'ordre zéro" head+genitive in such circumstances (cf. (23)) is a safe way of ensuring an unambiguous identification of A's and heads.

(23) a. *dočeri prijatel'nicy*
       (daughter-nom.pl./gen.sg. friend-gen.sg./nom.pl.)
       'the daughters of the friend'
   b. *prijatel'nicy dočeri*
       'the friends of the daughter'.

Another morphological innovation in the Slavic languages endangered the morphological distinctiveness of A's, viz. the accusative case form for animate or personal nominals, which is homophonous with the genitive (for recent surveys cf. Thomason 1976 and Huntley, this volume). Again, an A in construction with a personal/animate dO could be distinguished from this type of head by its position (following the head). In addition to supplementary analytic coding, throughout historical changes of the Russian nominal declensions high priority has always been given to avoiding case syncretism between the genitive and the nominative/accusative, if necessary by supplementing homophonous substantival desinences by an alternating stress pattern:[18]

(24)   gen.sg.   nom./acc.pl.
            svečí   *svéči*   'candle'
            xóloda   *xolodá*   'cold'
            slóva   *slová*   'word'
            mésta   *mestá*   'place'

This pattern may not have become a productive paradigm, and the need of number distinction may have been another force instrumental in its creation; it still fits in very well with the overall tendency to maintain and develop distinctive A rather than distinctive S and dO encoding.[19] In other Slavic languages the genitive occasionally is syncretistic (cf. Polish *rzeczy, pieśni* (gen./nom.pl.), Czech *duše* (gen./nom.sg.), *pole, paní, znamení* with syncretism of all singular cases), but significantly this happens more often the more a language has already progressed towards analyticity.

Although Arabic has, or rather had, available a coding device of inflectional morphology (case, verb agreement) to distinguish between independent (theme, agent), dependent (adnominal A), and subordinate (dO) status, "the system itself neutralizes the distinction in a considerable number of cases (nouns ending in -*ā*, substantives with the pronoun -*ī* attached, singular and plural demonstratives, etc.)" (Beeston 1970:54). But whereas with S-dO case syncretism an appeal has to be made to contextual clues to resolve ambiguities due to non-distinctive coding because constituent order on the clause level is relationally fairly free[20], linear order is relationally significant in the attributive "annexion" structure: the head obligatorily precedes the nominal A. In addition, the head is distinguished from its A by being unable to co-occur with a determiner of its own.

It seems appropriate to mention in the present context phenomena such as the "status constructus" and the "izāfat" construction characteristic of Semitic and Iranian languages respectively, and especially the alleged analogue in Eskimo, the "super-ordinative" case.[21] In these cases, the head itself, instead of (Semitic, Iranian), or in addition to (Eskimo), the A, is overtly marked as being the superordinate member of an attributive construction. Especially with double morphological marking of the head and the A, the probability of an A being mistaken for a head or vice versa, on account of accidental coding deficiencies is systematically reduced to a minimum.

Although agreement/cross-reference is a coding device that is perhaps more familiar in connection with the S and dO relations, it is in many languages also used to encode the A relation. With respect to S-dO, agreement/cross reference, without complementary analytic or synthetic coding, appears to be of rather limited utility because this indirect method of S-dO identification has to rely on a restricted set of (pronominal) identifying categories (such as person, number, gender/class; cf. Moravcsik 1971) that often do not suffice to absolutely distinguish the particular terms they are supposed to cross-reference or agree with. The Russian example (6), quoted above, illustrates this inherent deficiency. The 3rd person singular verb suffix cannot uniquely identify the S, since both terms, the S and the dO, are 3rd person singular. Although there is no strict distinctness requirement on S and dO, it is probably for this reason that languages with agreement/cross-reference as their sole relational coding device appear to be the exception rather than the rule. But notice that things are quite different if agreement/cross-reference is used to encode attributive constructions as is illustrated in (25) and (26).[22]

(25) a. Bantu (Meinhof 1936:88–90)
           vi-ti vi̱-a mzungu (chairs they-gen. marker European)
           'the chairs of the European'
      b. Ful (Meinhof 1936:90)
           putj-u ṅgu lami'do (horse it chief) 'the horse of the chief'

(26) a. Hixkaryana (Carib; Derbyshire 1977)
           toto yowanà (man his-chest) 'the man's chest'
      b. Turkish
           tren-in hareket-i (train-gen. departure-3rd.pers.possessive)
           'the trains's departure'
           sehir plan-ı (city map-3rd.pers.poss.) 'the map of the city'[23].

Irrespective of whether the A agrees with/cross-references the head (as in (25)), or the head the A (as in (26)), there never can be any danger of failure to distinguish the head from its A, since in both cases only one of them bears the distinguishing marker. And obviously, no matter how low the degree of differentiation of agreement/cross-reference categories might be, this does not at all interfere adversely with the functional task of relational distinction. Considering the hypothesis that non-distinctive coding of A is intolerable, it thus should not come as a surprise if languages were not particularly reluctant to base their coding of the A relation entirely upon agreement/cross-reference. There are no doubt additional reasons for the rise of pertinent attributive constructions in languages such as English and German (cf. (27)),

(27) *for Jesus Christ his sake, the king his havens;*
       dem König seine Häfen (with A in the possessive dative),

but it appears, nevertheless, significant that the coding device of agreement/cross-reference simultaneously gains prominence in the attributive construction and loses ground as far as the S and dO relations are concerned.

As a last example, let us consider in somewhat more detail some synchronic and diachronic phenomena in Latin, which heavily relies upon morphological coding, apparently without much support by analytic coding systems. Whereas in most Classical Latin declensional paradigms, genitives do have a distinctive desinence, there also is occasional syncretism:

(28) a. gen.sg. = nom.sg.
3rd declension substantives: *collis, civis, turris, finis, panis, canis, Neapolis* ...; and corresponding adjectival paradigms: *facilis, natalis, Aprilis, memorabilis* ...
b. gen.sg. = nom.pl.
1st and 2nd declensions: *mensae, pueri, horti* ...
4th declension: *fructūs, senatūs* ...

In early Latin, 5th declension substantives could also have been listed under (28a), but the syncretistic genitive was subsequently replaced by a new distinctive form (cf. *dies, diei*). Masculine substantives like *poeta* also occasionally had similar nom./gen.sg. forms in early Latin (*poetās, poetas*), but this syncretism was likewise eliminated later on (*poeta, poetae*). 4th declension substantives distinguish the genitive and the nominative singular only by vowel length (*fructus, fructūs; senatus, senatūs*); but in this class there continually occurred analogical restructurings, one obvious tendency being to maintain the nom.-gen.sg. distinction (originally *senatus, senatuos;* later analogical genitives like *senati, domuis*). Also, in early and still in Classical Latin many 3rd declension adjectives have parallel *-us/-a/-um* forms (*hilaris/hilarus, inermis/inermus, auxiliaris/auxiliarius*), the abandonment of which in late Latin eliminated this possibility of obviating nominative-genitive case syncretism. (For some of these and other developments see Coleman 1976.)

Anyway, there certainly was some nominative-genitive case syncretism in Latin, and the ways in which the language reacts to it provide an opportunity to attempt a more precise formulation of the distinctness requirement on A, since up to now it was intentionally left open whether the ungrammaticality of attributive constructions was a matter of actual textual ambiguity or — and this would constitute an even stronger requirement — a matter of syncretistic, non-distinctive coding of the A alone. To take the stronger interpretation first: Does this requirement state that irrespective of any context of use of an A, including the encoding of the head, paradigmatic non-distinctness of its encoding by itself suffices to rule out the attributive construction? "Paradigmatic" is to be understood here, of course, as referring to the entire ensemble of devices a language may utilize to encode the A relation. Accordingly, the above Latin substantives and adjectives, if not accompanied by another, distinctive element, should be unable to occur as attributive genitives regardless of the contextually determined case marking of their heads. The hypothesis would thus predict that not only the attributive constructions in (29a) but also those in (29b) are ungrammatical, although in the latter case the head constituents could not be mistaken for A's, on account of their distinctive accusative desinences.

(29)   a.   *canis civis* 'the dog of the citizen/citizen of the dog'
            turris canis 'tower of the dog/dog of the tower'
            senatūs Neapolis 'senates of Naples/the Naples of the senate'
       b.   *canem civis, turrem canis, pueros Neapolis* 'the boys-acc. of Naples'.

The second interpretation is that it is only actual textual ambiguities that are prohibited by this constraint; i.e. that attributive constructions are ungrammatical if on account of their coding both the head could be mistaken for the A, and the A for the head. The examples in (29b) would then not violate this constraint against unacceptable ambiguity since here non-distinctness of A's does not amount to actual relational ambiguity. Notice, furthermore, that such constructions as those in (29a) might still be able to escape both the strong and the weak version of the constraint. One of the synthetic coding devices for the S relation (and also the dO relation, with certain periphrastic verb constructions) is verb agreement, and if a complex phrase such as *senatūs Neapolis,* with different number specifications of the A and the head, is used as S (or dO), singular or plural verb agreement helps to uniquely identify the head of the attributive construction, and thus prevents not only textual ambiguity but also non-distinctness of A's.[24] Which alternative of the constraint is empirically preferable is, at the moment, difficult to decide, especially on the basis of a dead language like Latin. Nevertheless, a general tendency is clearly noticeable to avoid, irrespective of actual contexts of use, any coding syncretisms of A's, in particular vis-a-vis the unmarked paradigmatic term form, i.e. the form used for the purpose of citation.[25] Thus, in both cases, (29a) and (b), attributive adjectives (*civilis, caninus, Neapolitanus*) would seem to be equally welcome alternatives to non-distinctive or ambiguous nominal A's. The more restrictive interpretation is probably also suggested by the ungrammatical German examples (11a, 13a, 14a, 16, 17b–c) above, which remain ungrammatical even if the linguistic context requires another, distinctively encoded case of the head term.

Examples like the following could incline one to believe that the restrictive interpretation is basically correct even for Latin. The alternative constructions (30a/b) are possible with neuter adjectives of the 2nd declension, which if used as partitive genitives (30b) could be regarded as nominalizations (cf. Hofmann 1965:57–8).

(30) a. *aliquid bonum* 'something-nom./acc. good-nom./acc.'
 b. *aliquid boni* 'something-nom./acc. good-gen.sg.'

The genitive desinence of 3rd declension adjectives (see (28a) above), on the other hand, is not absolutely distinctive. The neuter genitive *-is* could as well be a masculine or feminine nominative singular; and although this paradigmatic identification would conflict with the neuter *aliquid*, the analogue of (30b), viz. (3lb), is almost never found and is probably ungrammatical.

(31) a. *aliquid memorabile* 'something remarkable'
 b. **aliquid memorabilis.*

If partitive genitives as in (31b) can be used at all, then as conjuncts of a distinctively genitival *o*-stem adjective (*quicquam . . . non dico civilis, sed humani*), but even in this kind of context the alternative (31a) is the rule (*nil novi nihilque difficile*).

In Classical Latin there are a few substantives with defective declensional paradigms; *vis* 'force', for example, only has a nominative singular and an accusative (*vim*) and ablative (*vi*) singular. The absence of a genitive has been explained as an attempt to avoid nominative-genitive syncretism (e.g. by Wackernagel 1926:296). Such substantives, then, appear to be among the first which are encoded analytically (*de vi*) when used as A's.

And finally, there in fact are actual textual ambiguities in Latin concerning the A status of genitives (examples from Jespersen 1922:343):

(32) a. *Menenii patris munus* 'the gift of the father of Menenius/of father Menenius'
 b. *expers illius periculi* 'free from that person's danger/free from that danger'.

Here the genitives *Menenii* and *illius* can either be genuine A's, or appositive elements (32a) or determiners (32b) agreeing with a genitive (*patris, periculi*), without any ungrammaticality resulting from this structural ambiguity. Since all genitives here, nevertheless, are distinctively encoded, this type of acceptable ambiguity does not conflict with a constraint against paradigmatic non-distinctness of A's; it rather seems to favour this, in another sense more restrictive, interpretation of the coding requirement on A's over the anti-ambiguity version. It is noteworthy, though, that precisely this particular ambiguity potential tended to be eliminated rather early by analytic coding; Väänänen (1956:13) mentions that of two recursive A's one is usually encoded by means of a preposition (*in presentia de domino servi,* rather than *in presentia servi domini*)[26].

So far we looked at the Latin case system basically from a synchronic perspective; the few analogical developments considered above essentially tended to eliminate nominative-genitive syncretisms. The most prominent, if not the only, trespassers against the distinctness constraint for A's were certain paradigms (vowel stems) of the 3rd declension; and since the distinctness of A's is, according to the hypothesis advocated here, the most crucial relational distinction, one would not expect, from a diachronic perspective, that other paradigms with distinctive A case joined this particular 3rd declension pattern. But such a development in fact occurred, quite sporadically in Classical Latin, with substantives like *mens, mensis* analogically replacing their nominative form by the genitive form (*mensis, mensis*; also *canis, navis*), but on a large scale in postclassical and especially in Vulgar Latin (cf. Plank 1979). As a rule, imparisyllabic substantives of the 3rd declension (consonant stems) became parisyllabic; if there was stress alternation as in *aéstas, aestátis* (as opposed to *nómen, nóminis*), it automatically disappeared in this process. This pattern of intraparadigmatic[27] levelling is illustrated in (33):

(33)   Classical Latin   Vulgar Latin
      a. *mors, mortis*   *mortis, mortis*
         mons, montis   *montis, montis*
         flos, floris   *floris, floris*
         aéstas, aestátis   *aestátis, aestátis*
         léo, leónis   *leónis, leónis*
         vírtus, virtútis   *virtútis, virtútis*
      b. *sánguis, sánguinis*   *sanguis, sanguis*
         héres, herédis   *heres, heris*

The diachronic target of parisyllabicity was, thus, attained in two different ways; the paradigmatic nominative-genitive opposition was neutralized either by giving up the erstwhile distinctive nominative form (33a), or, less commonly, the erstwhile distinctive genitive form (33b). In the present context, the crucial problem is not how to predict these two opposite directions of levelling, but how to reconcile this pattern of case syncretism with the hypothesis that A's have to be encoded distinctively. In other words, does this case syncretism amount to coding syncretism? To answer this question it is important to determine when these morphological changes took place, relative to other coding changes in Latin or Romance. According to Gildersleeve and Lodge (1895:430–1), even in early Latin word order in attributive constructions was not entirely free; rather, the genitival attribute, as opposed to the adjectival attribute, tended to follow its head. But this view is highly controversial (cf. Hofmann 1965:408–9); linear order is certainly no absolutely reliable indicator of A-hood in Classical Latin, nor, presumably, at the later period when the morphological changes at issue were initiated. However, the other analytic coding device for A's, viz. prepositions (*de, ex, ad*), was already competing with the synthetic genitive in Classical Latin, and it was at any rate rapidly gaining ground from the 1st century A.D. onwards (Hofmann 1965:51; Väänänen 1956), certainly prior to the onset of the large-scale nominative-genitive levelling in the 3rd declension. The Latin and Romance developments, thus, turn out to be another instance of the familiar picture: distinctive synthetic A encoding can only be dispensed with if alternative or supplementary analytic coding devices have already rendered it redundant.

Prepositional encoding of A did, however, not replace morphological A's (i.e. genitives, and later also datives: *magister convivio*, cf. Dardel 1964) in a wholesale manner; possessive A's continued to be encoded synthetically long after the other functions of the genitive, such as the partitive one, had already been taken over by prepositions (Väänänen 1956; cf. also the Old French pattern above). Significantly, the few exceptions to the paradigmatic levelling illustrated in (33) have a common lexical-semantic denominator; they are extremely likely to be members of possessive relations. Here is a representative list of the substantives that remain imparisyllabic in Vulgar Latin:

(34) a. *hómo, hóminis* 'man'; *cómes, cómitis* 'companion'; *imperátor, imperatóris* 'ruler'; *pástor, pastóris* 'shepherd'; *cántor, cantóris* 'singer'; *népos, nepótis* 'nephew'; *ínfans, infántis* 'child'
   b. *témpus, témporis* 'time'; *péctus, péctoris* 'breast'; *nómen, nóminis* 'name'; *cor, cordis* 'heart'; *fel, fellis* 'gall'.

The first group of exceptions to levelling are masculines denoting persons (34a); it is particularly useful for them to retain the morphological nominative-genitive distinction since they are either typically relational nouns predestined to function as heads (e.g. *comes, nepos*), or, as [+human], typical possessors predestined to function as A's. The second group of exceptions are neuters (34b), and most of them denote entities, such as body parts, that are inalienably possessed; i.e. they are also substantives predestined to function as heads in attributive constructions. The standard handbooks (cf. Rheinfelder 1967:13–4) account for this pattern of levelling vs. non-levelling differently; the [+human] substantives in (34a) are also likely to be used in the vocative, and the vocative form is identical to, and thus supports the retention of, the nominative form, and the nominative of the neuters in (34b) is supposedly supported by the formally identical accusative. It may be true that these paradigmatic identities were a peripheral factor in preventing this paradigmatic change, but this does not lessen the explanatory value of functional semantic and syntactic considerations, whose relevance for morphological change would seem to be much more general. From a cross-linguistic perspective it is, at any rate, no accident that in Latin and Romance the synthetic encoding of possessive A's was more resistant to the analytic drift than that of other A's (probably because the necessity of absolute relational distinction, the force behind analytic drifts, is more urgent in the case of non-possessive than of typically possessive A's), and that the need to distinguish A's from their heads, be it synthetically or analytically, was instrumental in preventing and inducing changes in the relational coding system, more so than the need to distinguish S's and dO's.

This concludes my survey of pertinent diachronic and synchronic phenomena, and on this empirical basis I would now like to suggest the following observational generalization:[28]

(35) a. Textually ambiguous, or paradigmatically non-distinctive, encoding of the grammatical relations S and dO is, in principle, tolerable.

b. Paradigmatically non-distinctive, but at any rate textually ambiguous, encoding of the grammatical relation A (vis-a-vis its head) is intolerable; rather than necessitating textual disambiguation, this kind of intolerable ambiguity or non-distinctness leads to ungrammaticality.

Although the present evidence seems highly suggestive, an even more extensive analysis of the coding systems of a wide variety of natural languages along such lines would be required before this generalization can be established as a universally valid part of a general relational coding theory. For the rest of the present paper I presuppose that its universal significance can eventually be ascertained, and turn to matters of explanation instead. For this purpose I first propose a yet more general formulation of (35), and this reformulation appeals to the different syntactico-semantic constitution of the relations S, dO, and A.

(36) a. Textually ambiguous, or paradigmatically non-distinctive, encoding of *lexically* governed grammatical relations is, in principle, tolerable.

b. Paradigmatically non-distinctive, or textually ambiguous, encoding of *constructionally* governed grammatical relations is intolerable.

With the notions of lexical and constructional government it is not intended to distinguish between such coding rules that have to, and ones that do not have to, refer to particular lexical items or classes of lexical items. This distinction is, rather, based on whether the relational term to be encoded itself is demanded or selected by a lexical item or class of lexical items, or whether it is selected by, or rather compatible with, a syntactic configuration whose optional constituent part it is, without any even indirect reference to individual co-constituent lexical items or classes of lexical items. Or, to put it differently, terms holding lexically governed relations are demanded by the inherent valence of the governing lexical items, whereas the co-constituents of terms in constructional governed relations do not possess any actual syntactic valence.[29] Although in some respects the notion of valence poses more problems than it helps solve, it clearly motivates the classification of dO's, and also of indirects objects[30], as lexically governed relations, even if all dO's were encoded by the same case and/or the same position, which obviously could be accomplished without reference to particular verb classes. It also identifies the S relation as lexically rather than constructionally governed, although the actual encoding of S's (e.g. the assignment of the nominative or the ergative[31] or the absolutive case or of preverbal position) is not directly contingent upon inherent characteristics of particular predicates. Moreover, in so far as the choice of one particular term as (basic or derived) grammatical subject is ultimately dependent upon the predicate, there is additional justification for the assumption that S's are lexically governed.[32]

A potentially controversial issue concerns raising (A.c.I./N.c.I.) constructions. It is indeed doubtful whether in sentences such as (37) (from Latin) the raised term, *te*, can be regarded as governed by the main clause predicate, as far as its (syntactic or semantic) valence is concerned.

(37)   *Aio te, Æacida, Romanos vincere posse.*
       (I-tell you (acc.), Æacida, the-Romans (acc.) defeat can)
       'you can defeat the Romans/the Romans can defeat you'.

At least conceptually, the raised term is required by the embedded predicate(s) (*vincere, posse*), though. It, in a sense, is simultaneously governed by the matrix predicate as well, since the rule of raising surely is governed and cannot apply in the constructional context of any arbitrary matrix verb. That (37) in fact is notoriously relationally ambiguous, nicely attests to the correctness of the classification of raised terms as holding lexically rather than constructionally governed relations. Additional evidence that in this type of construction relational ambiguity is, to a certain extent, tolerable, comes from pertinent coding changes in late Middle High/early New High German (cf. Bondzio 1958 for relevant data). In contradistinction to constructionally governed relations, where any risk of non-distinctive encoding is always avoided well in advance, there at first are no comparable measures of precaution here, although the only coding device available at the time, viz. case marking[33], often proved to be unreliable. Ambiguities as in (38) were, thus, tolerated (and probably still are),

(38)   *Lass den Mörder mich finden!/Lass mich den Mörder finden!*
        'Let me find the murderer/let the murderer find me!'

before gradually, in the 15th and 16th centuries, analytic devices such as linear order (raised term precedes embedded dO) and prepositions (marking the agent) became available and could help avoid these ambiguities textually. In a recent study of ambiguity-avoidance strategies, Sweetser (1977) assumes that raising constructions such as (38) can never be textually ambiguous in Modern German on account of a fixed word-order constraint: the first of two adjacent accusative terms supposedly is the raised term (underlying S), and the second the dO of the embedded clause. This assumption is no doubt counterfactual, but what is more interesting is that Sweetser postulates another supposedly universal constraint on extraction rules removing one of these adjacent accusative terms: extraction rules whose targets are definite terms can only apply to (underlying) S's in such raising constructions, while extraction rules with indefinite targets can only apply to (underlying) dO's. This constraint is supposed to disambiguate sentences like (39a) and to prevent dO preposing as in (39b):

(39) a. *Der Freund, den ich meinen Bruder anrufen liess, . . .*
         (the friend that (acc.) I my brother (acc.) call let . . .)
         'the friend that I had call my brother'
     b. **Den Wein habe ich meinen Freund holen lassen.*
         'I let the wine (acc.) be brought by my friend (acc.)'.

What makes this constraint interesting in the present context is its claim that the textual ambiguity of certain lexically governed relations is intolerable, which is not exactly incompatible with my generalization (36a).

Given that (36a) and (36b) are valid, one would, however, expect such constraints with respect to constructionally rather than lexically governed relations. And as a matter of fact, the German evidence does not support Sweetser's hypothesis at all; sentences like (39a) indeed are textually ambiguous (the reading 'the friend that I had my brother call' is certainly not suppressed textually, *pace* Sweetser's "six volunteer native informants"), and sentences like (39b) are perfectly grammatical. I cannot evaluate Sweetser's supplementary evidence from Icelandic, Tzotzil, and Navajo, but clearly her constraint against textual ambiguity of certain lexically governed relations is not universally valid.

Occasionally, there are situations where the assumption that all A's indiscriminately are instances of constructional government could seem controversial. In Basque, for example, A's can be in (at least) two different cases, the "génitif possessif" (40a) or the "génitif locatif" (40b):

(40) a. *etchearen nausia* 'of-the-house the master' (proprietor)
  b. *etcheko nausia* 'in-the-house the master'.

From the way Lafitte (1962:419–20) describes the criteria for choosing one or the other alternative for encoding A's:

"Quand le complément exprime l'*appartenance* ou détermine des noms pris dans un sens *abstrait*, on le met au génitif possessif . . . . Quand le complément exprime *le lieu* ou détermine des noms *concrets*, on le met au génitif locatif . . .",

one could probably infer that the case assignment rules for A's are directly contingent upon the lexical item that forms the head of the attributive construction. There still can be no question of there being a bond of valence between A's and their heads, which was our criterion for distinguishing between lexical and constructional government. Moreover, I suspect that it is not the meaning (abstract or concrete) of particular lexical items that ultimately determines the choice of the A case, but rather the constructional meaning of attribution as such ('possession', 'location', 'material' etc.).[34]

How does the distinction of lexical and constructional government of grammatical relations tie in with the functional principle that was mentioned earlier in this paper, according to which the essential task of case marking and other coding devices merely is to overtly distinguish those terms that are co-present in actual sentences? This question presupposes that another, more fundamental question concerning the adequacy of the functional principle is answered first: Do coding systems that conform to the functional principle already prevent relational ambiguities? They in fact do not, since formally distinctive coding by itself does not suffice yet to link the thus encoded co-occurring terms unambiguously with a specific grammatical relation and, most importantly, a specific semantic role (such as agent, patient, experiencer, and the like). What is important in addition to overt distinguishability of terms is that from their coding it is recoverable which grammatical relation and semantic role each term is to be associated with. The grammaticalization of unified designations for all relations, i.e. the systematic existence of equivalences between relations and their distinctive encoding, could seem to ideally guarantee recoverability, were it not for the obvious import of an economy principle seriously limiting the number of differently encoded grammatical relations vis-a-vis the much greater number of semantic roles. But notice that with respect to recoverability, coding systems are already adequate if there exist no more than implications between the relations and specific coding features, and these can be established, as far as the relations S and dO are concerned, by appropriately linking the coding of one-term clauses with that of two-term clauses.[35]

One could now conceive of the manner of interaction of these two functional tasks of distinction and identification (recoverability) fairly straightforwardly as follows: Identification necessarily presupposes distinction. But why is it, then, that overt distinguishability, as was demonstrated above, is much more crucial if the relation to be encoded is that of A rather than S or dO? It seems to me, and this would explain the generalization (36), that in situations of constructional government, in the absence of any bond based on valence, identification really does presuppose distinction of the members of the attributive construction, whereas with lexical government identification to a certain degree is possible even if absolutely distinctive coding is lacking. In particular, the semantics of the governing lexical item, in conjunction with coding-independent pragmatic and semantic S and dO properties (S's typically are highly referential, topical, high in the hierarchy of potential agency, whereas dO's typically are indefinite, commentative, lower in the agency hierarchy, etc.), provides fairly reliable safeguards against misidentification of non-distinctively encoded lexically governed terms. It is true that on account of their inherently relational nature some terms are more predestined than others to assume the status of heads, so that in attributive constructions consisting of members like those listed in (41) particular identifications of heads (41a) and A's (41b) would seem to suggest themselves, even in the absence of any distinctive encoding.

(41)   a. *brother*   b. *John*
           voice   *speaker*
           wheel   *car*
           shooting   *hunters*
           top   *hill*

Other semantic features serving the same purpose are definiteness, animateness, and possessivity (cf. Plank 1979). The linguistic context of attributive constructions of course can also help identify heads and A's; entire attributive constructions may function as S or dO, and as such enter agreement relations determined by the head and incompatible with the A, with the result that external coding accomplishes textual avoidance of internal relational ambiguity or non-distinctness. Although there are obvious parallels between the A-head and the S/dO-predicate relationships, I, nevertheless, think that these similarities are vastly exaggerated if it is claimed that heads of attributive constructions and predicates of clausal constructions determine the selection of the terms governed by them in an exactly analogous manner.[36] Despite the inherently relational nature of some terms, and despite typical attribute and head properties, there surely are no systematic constraints against attributive constructions with two equally relational or non-relational, typically attributive or non-attributive, members. In common patterns like (42), one can hardly succeed in identifying heads and A's without clues provided by their encoding.

(42)   a. *the uncle*   b. *the neighbour*
           the father   *the brother*
           the king   *the enemy*

It seems that in principle almost any term an co-occur with almost any other in an attributive construction; and since semantic role distinctions, thus, appear to be neutralized in attributive constructions to a much greater extent than in clausal constructions[37], the greater systematic emphasis upon insuring distinctive encoding of A's becomes understandable, paradigmatic identification otherwise being almost impossible, or more or less random.

In conclusion, what bearing have the specific results of this paper on questions of a general coding theory? The hypothesis that there are differently severe distinctness, or anti-ambiguity, requirements on S/dO and on A suggests that an interplay of different coding devices is more crucial in attributive than in clausal constructions, in particular if the predominant coding devices prove unreliable as to their distinctive function. The tentative generalization might not be too implausible that a greater variety of coding devices is utilized to encode A's than is used to encode S's and dO's, if one of the traditional coding devices is potentially unreliable. If there are any incompatibilities between individual coding devices that are in principle available, case and order is probably the only good candidate; case marking, agreement/cross-reference, adpositions, and fixed order are all found alone as well as in varying combinations, and not necessarily in accordance with the analytic or synthetic coding devices for the S and dO relations. There are also significant diachronic implications, which are beyond the scope of particularistic coding theories, especially some current constituent order theories. Although analogy-based serialization rules ought to link clausal (SVdO) with noun phrase-internal (e.g. A-head) patterns — ideally, all instances of modifier-modified patterns ought to be in 'harmony' with each other—, they often fail to do so.[38] Counteranalogical serialization of adnominal A's vis-a-vis the allegedly crucial model of the V-dO order is often observable, as are different manners and rates in the diachronic development of these two patterns. Rather than subscribing to the view that there merely is a unidirectional analogy from innovative verb phrase (i.e. V-dO) ordering to noun phrase-internal ordering, which, accordingly, often displays survival patterns of earlier harmonious serialization, I submit that it is rather the different, i.e. differently severe, distinctness requirements on the encoding of S/dO and A that are essentially responsible for non-analogical serialization. Constituent order is only one of the coding devices potentially available, and it seems to interact differently with the entire ensemble of coding devices in different types of construction. If a general coding theory can suggest a generalization linking lexically (S, dO) and constructionally (A) governed relations, then it might be like this: if a predominantly synthetic language drifts towards analyticity, analytic coding by means of linear order and/or adpositions tends to first occupy a prominent position with A's, before it assumes distinctive function for lexically governed grammatical relations. And if in this process of constituent order fixation analogy plays any role at all, it ought to be the A relation that provides the model for clausal relations, rather than vice versa.[39]

Notes

*   I am indebted to Steve Anderson, Lyle Campbell, Bernard Comrie, Stig Eliasson, Jim
     Fidelholtz, Dieter Kastovsky, Helmut Lüdtke, Josef Vachek, and especially Winfried
     Boeder for helpful comments and suggestions on earlier versions of this paper.

1. In the present paper not much attention is being paid to the distinction between cross-reference (based on genuine pronominal forms) and agreement (based on bound forms unable to independently fulfill grammatical functions); cf. Hutchinson (1977) for some discussion.

2. Cf. Delbrück's (1907) classic treatment of case syncretism in Germanic and Indo-European, and also the discussions of syncretism, neutralization, homonymy by Hjelmslev, Trnka, Martinet and others.

3. E.g., Jakobson (1936; 1958), Georgiev (1973), Boeder (1976).

4. Evidence for this view comes from languages such as Finnish or (Old) North Russian, where dO's of transitive imperatives are in the nominative, which case also encodes transitive and intransitive S's.

5. In a way, examples like *Miller sells well on college campuses* or *the shooting of the hunters* are similar; the surface relations S and A are encoded distinctively, but it cannot be determined uniquely what 'underlying' relations S or dO, they correspond to.

6. Obviously, textual ambiguity need not amount to actual ambiguity within a particular context.

7. Cf. Schwartz (1976), who tries to formulate generalizations about the manner of textual relational disambiguation on the basis of markedness considerations. Givón (1975) also investigates strategies that allow relational identification of terms; from his discussion it looks as if avoidance of S-dO relational ambiguity were indeed of particular importance in derived rather than basic constructions.

8. Craig (1977) actually analyzes these verbal markers as nominal case affixes that are associated with the verb by movement rules!

9. Thus Chomsky (1965:126–7) erroneously claims that sentences like *Die Mutter sieht die Tochter* 'the mother (nom./acc.) sees the daughter (nom./acc.)' are textually not ambiguous, the pre-verbal term invariably being interpreted as S (unless it has contrastive stress), and concludes — also erroneously — that "in any language, stylistic inversion of 'major constituents' . . . is tolerated up to ambiguity". The reading that is the only one possible according to Chomsky may very well be the preferred one, but the interpretation of the pre-verbal term as dO is certainly not textually excluded, irrespective of any reference to contrastive stress, which does not seem to play a major role in relational disambiguation anyway. In contradistinction to Chomsky, Müller (1977:25) claims that syntactic rules (in the above example: dO Fronting) cannot be sensitive to accidents of inflectional morphology, and he consequently looks for other ways to account for the different degrees of acceptability of the two readings of the above mother-daughter example. But Müller thus simply neglects the substantial body of evidence suggesting that syntactic rules can be sensitive to morphological and even phonological factors. Elsewhere (Plank 1977a) I argue that constraints on the generality of syntactic rules due to inflectional morphology can even be a factor contributing to the exchange of morphological coding devices in favour of analytic ones.

10. This discussion was largely stimulated by Hankamer (1973). Also relevant is the notion of transderivational constraints (cf. Lakoff 1973), which have been used in derivational theories to exclude unacceptable ambiguities.

11. That (un-)acceptable ambiguity often is a matter of degree, and not of principle (as Hankamer 1973 suggests), was pointed out by Channon (1974); cf. also Müller (1977).

12. Cf. Plank (1976) for probably another instance of this kind of unacceptable ambiguity, viz. complement subject deletion in English. — Cf. Eliasson (1975) for an account of analogous anti-ambiguity restrictions in phonology; in Swedish, for instance, adjectives ending in *dd* lack an indefinite singular neuter form (*en rädd pojke* 'a scared boy' vs. **ett rätt barn* 'a scared child'), and the reason for this paradigmatic gap apparently is that the

adjective stem is not uniquely recoverable from surface phonetic forms like *rätt*.
13. A more detailed analysis of this set of data can be found in Plank (1978b:§3). Notice
    that in possessive dative constructions the A may lack a distinctive case indicator (*dem
    Mann sein Hut* 'the man (dat.) his hat' vs. *Zille sein Berlin* 'Zille his Berlin'), but rather
    than case, cross-reference and order are the distinctive coding devices in this type of
    attributive construction. — In German, and in other languages (cf. Old English *he lætte
    ænne drope blod*), certain 'genitives' can be construed differently, and these variants
    look as if they did not require a distinctive case suffix: *ein Glas Milch, ein Glas kalte*
    (nom.)/*kalter* (gen.) *Milch* 'a glass of (cold) milk'. However, it is not clear that this kind
    of numeral classifier construction involves the A relation in the first place;
    moreover, constituent order still is an absolutely distinctive coding device here, and the
    inherent lexical characteristics of the nouns involved can also be relied on for the
    purpose of relational identification.
14. The inflected form of numerals such as *hundert* '100' and *tausend* '1000' has a different
    meaning, viz. 'several hundred/thousand'. — There are slight complications if the
    numerals themselves are heads of partitive constructions, the entire partitive construc-
    tion being an A. Apparently, the distinctness requirement is already met if one element
    of the partitive construction, and not necessarily its head (viz. the numeral), has a
    distinctive genitive suffix: *der Konkurs sieben meiner Konkurrenten* 'the bankruptcy of
    seven of my rivals'. — The alternation between inflection and non-inflection with
    quantifiers like *all(e)* 'all' is regulated by entirely different principles.
15. Or, more generally, as the modifying element, if compounds are also taken into
    account. The above examples clearly are no compounds, though.
16. Cf. Modern French relics like *fête-Dieu, l'hôtel-Dieu, la place Mercier*.
17. For similar phenomena in other Finno-Ugric languages cf. Kont (1973). The eastern
    Finno-Ugric languages additionally have a cross-reference marker on the head.
18. Cf. especially Jakobson (1957), and also Shapiro (1971a, b), who mentions that there
    are only two exceptions to pattern (24) (*rukavá* 'sleeves', *obšlagá* 'cuffs'), and these are
    remnants or replicas of old dual forms.
19. Diachronically, such patterns of purely suprasegmental case differentiation are prob-
    ably not very stable; for phonetic reasons, they ought to be likely to develop into
    patterns of segmental differentiation (preservation of stressed, and reduction of
    unstressed, desinential vowel).
20. Essentially, it is regulated by thematic (topic-comment) principles. Cf. Beeston
    (1970:45–8, 51–5).
21. Cf. Hammerich (1951) and Boeder (1972), according to whom the superordinative
    really is a case rather than a possessive suffix on the head cross-referencing the A.
22. It is unclear to me whether the manner of encoding A's that is used, for instance, in
    Shilha (cf. Meinhof 1936:88–90), where the A is accompanied by a pronominal copy of
    itself (*tigimi u-gellíd* (house he-king) 'house of the king'), ought to be considered a
    variety of agreement. At any rate, it is absolutely distinctive. For overviews of these and
    other varieties of A encoding see Royen (1929:899–909) and Knobloch (1950).
23. Without the genitive marker, the two members of the construction form a closer,
    inseparable unit, which is a prerequisite for compounding.
24. Not uncommonly, nominative singular-genitive plural and nominative plural-genitive
    singular syncretism is tolerated in languages with number agreement/cross-reference
    between the S and the predicate; at least if the A accompanies the S, the A and the head
    can be identified from attribute-external coding.
25. Notice that in ergative languages with inflectional coding, the ergative case; unlike the
    nominative in nominative-accusative languages, is morphologically marked, and the

unmarked absolutive typically serves as citation form. It is probably significant that the ergative in fact is often homophonous with the genitive (cf. Eskimo, Burushaski, Chukchee, Caucasian and Mayan languages). For some discussion of such systematic rather than accidental syncretism cf. Plank ((ed.) 1979)

26. Even with a preposition such constructions are still ambiguous ('in the presence of the master of the servant/of the servant of the master'), unless linear order is to some extent relationally distinctive. Cf. Hofmann (1965:65–6) for more examples of multiple A's, which seem to indicate that order was not absolutely distinctive with recursive A's; it may have been with simultaneous occurrences of subjective and objective genitives ('John's shooting of the hunters').

27. Probably also interparadigmatic, if the 3rd declension is analyzed as consisting of two different paradigms (vowel vs. consonant stems).

28. Probably Jacobi (1897) was hinting at a similar generalization when he claimed that the genitive differed from both the nominative and accusative in always requiring a formal marker. His statement is, nevertheless, inaccurate in so far as A's may very well be encoded by fixed linear order instead of segmental markers (such as adpositions or case inflections). Teleman (1975:698–9) also notices that genitives are in greater need of distinctive encoding than nominatives and accusatives. His attempt at an explanation draws on perceptual strategies that supposedly determine the way sentences are processed from left to right by the decoder, and from these strategies he infers that a segmental marker (suffix or preposition) is absolutely essential. In my opinion, this attempt fails because it does not take into account the wide variety of coding devices for A, S, and dO found in natural languages, which often do not conform to the predictions of perceptual strategies like those mentioned by Teleman.

29. Nominalizations, perhaps the most obvious candidates for lexical government in attributive constructions, are, nevertheless, characterized by a loss of syntactic valence vis-a-vis the corresponding verbs (*shooting* Ø-valent, *shoot* bivalent, monovalent if passive).

30. In languages where this relation can be defined.

31. Ergative terms need not necessarily be transitive S's in all ergative-type languages; in some of these languages they can presumably be analyzed as oblique terms which are not required by the inherent valence of the verb. Under such circumstances, ergative terms could be constructionally rather than lexically governed, demanding absolutely distinctive encoding just like A's, which might contribute to the affinity of genitives and ergatives mentioned in note 25.

32. Here are a few examples to illustrate this kind of lexical government of S's: Take a verb like *lican/like* in Old and Modern English, and it becomes obvious that it is due to the verb that different terms are allowed to assume (primary) S status. Or, in Modern German, it is also the verb that determines which objects can (viz. accusative ones) and which cannot (non-accusative ones) be promoted to S status through passivization.

33. Term order was not relationally distinctive; it was, rather, determined by rhythmical principles.

34. The material relation in German, for example, cannot be encoded with an inflectional but only with a prepositional A or with a compound or an attributive adjective (**ein Kessel Kupfers* 'a kettle (made) of copper', but *ein Kessel aus Kupfer, Kupferkessel, kupferner Kessel*). It is again the constructional meaning that determines the encoding of A, and not a particular lexical item functioning as head.

35. I am drawing here on Bechert's (1977) critique of the functional principle in the version of Comrie (1975); Bechert emphasizes in some detail the role of the recoverability requirement in different relational systems. Cf. also Plank (1979).

36. This seems to be the claim made by Boeder (1972:190–1).
37. I.e., the S and dO relations in general are semantically more transparent than the highly opaque A relation. On relational transparency/opacity cf. Plank (1977b).
38. Hsieh (1977) has recently shown that the noun-modifier order cannot be regarded as a simple consequence of the verb-dO order. Canale (1976) has demonstrated, with particular reference to the history of English, that the diachronic development of nounphrase-internal ordering is independent of word order changes on the clausal level.
39. Schmidt (1926), unlike later serialization theorists in the Greenberg tradition, in fact considered the encoding of genitives as basic for the prediction of other structural, especially word order, phenomena.

Note added in proof: Concerning pp. 292ff. (non-distinctive S/dO encoding), cf. now also E. A. Moravcsik (1978), "On the limits of subject-object ambiguity tolerance", *Papers in Linguistics* 11:255–259. Concerning pp. 306ff. (Latin *aliquid bonum/boni*), cf. now also P. Baldi (1978), "The influence of speech perception on inflectional morphology in Latin", *General Linguistics* 18:61–89.

References

Bechert, J.
    1977   "Zur funktionalen Erklärung des Ergativsystems", *Papiere zur Linguistik* 12:57–86.
Beeston, A. F. L.
    1970   *The Arabic language today* (London: Hutchinson).
Boeder, W.
    1971   "Neue Forschungen zur Kasustheorie", *Biuletyn Fonograficzny* 12:3–27.
    1972   "Transitivität und Possessivität", in: Haarmann — Studemund (eds.) 1972:179–209.
    1976   "Morphologische Kategorien", in: Braunmüller — Kürschner (eds.) 1976:117–126.
Bondzio, W.
    1958   *Zum Widerstreit der Objektverbindungen in deutschen Infinitivkonstruktionen* (Ph.D. dissertation, Humboldt-Universität Berlin).
Braunmüller, K. — W. Kürschner (eds.)
    1976   *Grammatik. Akten des 10. Linguistischen Kolloquiums, Tübingen 1975. Band 2* (Tübingen: Niemeyer).
Campion, A.
    1884   *Gramática de los cuatro dialectos literarios de la lengua euskara* (Tolosa: Lopez).
Canale, M.
    1976   "Implicational hierarchies of word order relationships", in: Christie (ed.) 1976:39–69.
Channon, R.
    1974   "The NAC and how not to get it", *North Eastern Linguistic Society* 5:276–298.
Chomsky, N.
    1965   *Aspects of the theory of syntax* (Cambridge, Mass.: MIT Press).
Christie, W. M., Jr. (ed.)
    1976   *Current progress in historical linguistics* (Amsterdam: North-Holland).
Coleman, R.
    1976   "Patterns of syncretism in Latin", in: Morpurgo Davies — Meid (eds.) 1976:47–56.

Comrie, B.
  1975 "The antiergative: Finland's answer to Basque", in: Grossman — San — Vance
        (eds.) 1975:112–121.
Craig, C. G.
  1977 *The structure of Jacaltec* (Austin: University of Texas Press).
Dahlstedt, K.-H. (ed.)
  1975 *The Nordic languages and modern linguistics 2* (Stockholm: Almqvist & Wikseli).
Dardel, R. de
  1964 "Considérations sur la déclinaison romane à trois cas", *Cahiers Ferdinand de
        Saussure* 21:7–23.
Delbrück, B.
  1907 *Synkretismus. Ein Beitrag zur germanischen Kasuslehre* (Strassburg: Trübner).
Derbyshire, D. C.
  1977 "First report on an OVS language", hand-out of a paper read to LAGB Spring
        Meeting, Walsall.
Drachman, G. (ed.)
  1977 *Akten der 2. Salzburger Frühlingstagung für Linguistik, Salzburg 1975* (Tübingen:
        Narr).
Dressler, W. U. — W. Meid (eds.)
  1978 *Proceedings of the 12th International Congress of Linguists* (Innsbruck:
        Innsbrucker Beiträge zur Sprachwissenschaft).
Dutton, T. E. — C. L. Voorhoeve
  1974 *Beginning Hiri Motu* (= *Pacific Linguistics* D-24) (Canberra: ANU).
Ekwall, E.
  1913 "The *s*-less genitive in Early Modern English", in: *Minneskrift till Axel Erdmann*
        (Uppsala/Stockholm), 53–67.
Eliasson, S.
  1975 "On the issue of directionality", in: Dahlstedt (ed.) 1975:421–445.
Fries, C. C.
  1940 "On the development of the structural use of word-order in Modern English",
        Language 16:199–208.
Georgiev, V. I.
  1973 "Interdependenz von Syntax und Morphologie", in: Redard (ed.) 1973:59–65.
Gildersleeve, B. L. — G. Lodge
  1895 *Gildersleeve's Latin grammar* (3rd edition) (London: Macmillan).
Givón, T.
  1975 "Promotion, accessibility and case marking: toward understanding grammars",
        Working Papers on Language Universals 19:55–125.
Grimes, J. E.
  1964 *Huichol syntax* (The Hague: Mouton).
Grossman, R. E. — L. J. San — T. J. Vance (eds.)
  1975 *Papers from the Eleventh Regional Meeting, Chicago Linguistic Society* (Chicago:
        Linguistic Society).
Haarmann, H. — M. Studemund (eds.)
  1972 *Beiträge zur Romanistik und Allgemeinen Sprachwissenschaft. Festschrift Wilhelm
        Giese* (Hamburg: Buske).
Hammerich, L. J.
  1951 "The cases of Eskimo", *International Journal of American Linguistics* 17:18–22.
Hankamer, J.
  1973 "Unacceptable ambiguity", *Linguistic Inquiry* 4:17–68.

Hofmann, J. B.
    1965   *Lateinische Syntax und Stilistik* (neubearbeitet von A. Szantyr) (München: Beck).
Hope, E.
    1973   "Non-syntactic constraints on Lisu noun phrase order", *Foundations of Language*
            10:79–109.
Hsieh, H.-I
    1977   "Noun-modifier order as a consequence of VSO order", *Lingua* 42:91–109.
Huntley, D.
    this volume   "The evolution of genitive-accusative animate and personal nouns in Slavic
            dialects".
Hutchinson, L. G.
    1977   "Cross-reference", in: Drachman (ed.) 1977:127–140.
Jacobi, H.
    1897   *Compositum und Nebensatz* (Bonn: Cohen).
Jacobsen, W. H., Jr.
    1972   "Nominative-ergative syncretism in Basque", *Anuario del Seminario de Filología
            Vasca 'Julio de Urquijo'* 6:67–109.
Jakobson, R.
    1936   "Beitrag zur allgemeinen Kasuslehre. Gesamtbedeutungen der russischen
            Kasus", *Travaux du Cercle Linguistique de Prague* 6:240–288.
    1939   "Signe zéro", in: *Mélanges de linguistique, offerts à Charles Bally* (Geneva:
            Georg), 143–152.
    1957   "The relationship between genitive and plural in the declension of Russian
            nouns", *Scando-Slavica* 3:181–6.
    1958   "Morfologičeskie nabljudenija nad slavjanskim skloneniem" [Morphological
            observations on declension in Slavic], in: *American contributions to the Fourth
            International Congress of Slavicists* (The Hague: Mouton), 127–156.
Jespersen, O.
    1922   *Language. Its nature, development and origin* (London: Allen & Unwin).
Kachru, B. B. et al. (eds.)
    1973   *Issues in linguistics. Papers in honor of Henry and Renée Kahane* (Urbana:
            University of Illinois Press).
Knobloch, J.
    1950   "Zur Vorgeschichte des indogermanischen Genitivs der *o*-Stämme auf *-sjo*", *Die
            Sprache* 2:131–149.
Kont, K.
    1973   "Nominatiivis ja genitiivis esinevast substantiivsest atribuudist soome-ugri
            keeltes" [Nominative and genitive substantive attributes in Finno-Ugric lan-
            guages], in *Commentationes fenno-ugricae in honorem Erkki Itkonen sexagenarii
            die XXVI mensis aprilis anno 1973* (Helsinki: Suomalais-ugrilainen seura), 165–
            173.
Lafitte, P.
    1962   *Grammaire basque (Navarro-labourdin littéraire)* (Bayonne: Éditions des 'Amis
            du Musée Basque' et 'Ikas').
Lakoff, G.
    1973   "Some thoughts on transderivational constraints", in: Kachru et al. (eds.)
            1973:442–453.
Lehnert, M.
    1953   *Sprachform und Sprachfunktion im 'Orrmulum' (um 1200). Die Deklination*
            (Berlin: Deutscher Verlag der Wissenschaften).

Li, C. N. (ed.)
1975 *Word order and word order change* (Austin: University of Texas Press).
Li, Ying-che
1971 "Interactions of semantics and syntax in Chinese", *Journal of Chinese Language Teachers Association* 6.2:58–78.
Lotz, J.
1968 "Grammatical derivability. The pronominal suffix {-É} 'that of ...' in Hungarian", *Lingua* 21:627–637.
Martinet, A.
1979 "Shunting on to accusative or ergative", in Plank (ed.) 1979:39–43.
Meinhof, C.
1936 *Die Entstehung flektierender Sprachen* (Berlin: Reimer).
Moravcsik, E. A.
1971 "Agreement", *Working Papers on Language Universals* 5:A1-A69.
Morpurgo Davies, A. — W. Meid (eds.)
1976 *Studies in Greek, Italic, and Indo-European linguistics offered to L. R. Palmer* (Innsbruck: Innsbrucker Beiträge zur Sprachwissenschaft).
Morton, J. (ed.)
1971 *Biological and social factors in psycholinguistics* (London: Logos).
Müller, F.
1977 "Inner- und aussergrammatische Erklärungen von Akzeptabilitätsurteilen. Probleme der Datenbasis generativer Grammatiken", *Linguistische Berichte* 50:11–30.
Nedjalkov, V. P.
1979 "Degrees of ergativity in Chukchee", in Plank (ed.) 1979:241–262.
Plank, F.
1976 "Misunderstanding understood subjects: the Minimal Distance Principle in Montague grammar", *Amsterdam Papers in Formal Grammar* 1:194–216.
1977a "Can case marking and serialization theories that rely on the principle of ambiguity avoidance explain syntactic and morphological change in Old and Middle English?", paper read at 3rd International Conference on Historical Linguistics, Hamburg.
1977b "Agent, experiencer, and locative in diachronic relational grammar: antagonisms between transparency and functionality in the history of English", paper read at 12th International Congress of Linguists, Vienna, working group on case and valency grammar.
1978a "Case syncretism and coding syncretism", in Dressler — Meid (eds.) 1978: 405–407.
1978b "Die Determinationsrichtung in der Adjektiv-Substantiv-Attribution", unpublished MS.
1979 "The functional basis of case systems and declension classes: From Latin to Old French", *Linguistics* 17:611–640.
1980 "Subjectivity and object-differentiation in the history of English", unpublished MS.
Plank, F. (ed.)
1979 *Ergativity: Towards a theory of grammatical relations* (London: Academic Press).
Redard, G. (ed.)
1973 *Indogermanische und Allgemeine Sprachwissenschaft. Akten der IV. Fachtagung der Indogermanischen Gesellschaft, Bern 1969* (Wiesbaden: Reichert).
Rheinfelder, H.
1967 *Altfranzösische Grammatik. Zweiter Teil: Formenlehre* (München: Hueber).

Royen, G.
1929   *Die nominalen Klassifikations-Systeme in den Sprachen der Erde. Historisch-kritische Studie, mit besonderer Berücksichtigung des Indogermanischen* (Wien: Anthropos).
Sanžeev, G. D.
1969   "Projavlenie logiki veščej v jazyke" [The emergence of general logic in language], in: Vardul' (ed.) 1969:99–103.
Sapir, E. — M. Swadesh
1946   "American Indian grammatical categories", *Word* 2:103–112.
Sasse, H.-J.
1977   "Gedanken über Wortstellungsveränderung", *Papiere zur Linguistik* 13/14:82–142.
Schlesinger, I. M.
1971   "The grammar of sign language and the problem of language universals", in: Morton (ed.) 1971:98–121.
Schmidt, P. W.
1926   *Die Sprachfamilien und Sprachenkreise der Erde* (Heidelberg: Winter).
Schwartz, L. J.
1976   "Ambiguity avoidance and syntactic markedness", in: *Proceedings of the 1976 Mid-America Linguistics Conference* (to appear).
Shapiro, M.
1971a   "Observations on the Russian case system", *Linguistics* 69:81–86.
1971b   "Markedness and Russian stress", *Linguistics* 72:61–77.
Sweetser, E. E.
1977   "Ambiguity-avoidance: A universal constraint on extraction from NP sequences", in: Whistler et al. (eds.) 1977:400–453.
Tchekhoff, C.
1979   "From ergative to accusative in Tongan: An example of synchronic dynamics", in: Plank (ed.) 1979:407–418.
Teleman, U.
1975   "Reductions of a morphological case system", in: Dahlstedt (ed.) 1975:692–703.
Thomason, S. G.
1976   "Analogical change as grammar complication", in: Christie (ed.) 1976:401–409.
Thurneysen, R.
1946   *A grammar of Old Irish* (Dublin: Dublin Institute for Advanced Studies, revised and enlarged ed.).
Väänänen, V.
1956   "La préposition latine *de* et le génitif. Une mise au point", *Revue de linguistique romane* 20:1–20.
Vardul', I. F. (ed.)
1969   *Jazykovye universalii i lingvističeskaja tipologija* [Universals of language and linguistic typology] (Moskva: Nauka).
Vennemann, T.
1975   "An explanation of drift", in: Li (ed.) 1975:269–305.
Vogt, H.
1974   "L'ordre des mots en géorgien moderne", *Bedi Kartlisa* 32:48–56.
Wackernagel, J.
1926   *Vorlesungen über Syntax mit besonderer Berücksichtigung von Griechisch, Lateinisch und Deutsch. Erste Reihe* (Basel: Birkhäuser).

Wessén, E.
1968   *Vårt svenska språk* (Stockholm: Almqvist & Wiksell).
Westholm, A.
1899   *Etude historique sur la construction du type 'li filz le rei' en français* (Ph.D. dissertation, Uppsala).
Whistler, K. et al. (eds.)
1977   *Proceedings of the 3rd Annual Meeting of the Berkeley Linguistics Society* (Berkeley: Linguistics Society).
Wurzel, W. U.
1977   "Zur Stellung der Morphologie im Sprachsystem", *Linguistische Studien, Reihe A, Arbeitsberichte* 35:130–165.

BLAIR A. RUDES

The functional development of the verbal suffix +*esc*+ in Romance

A more appropriate title to this work might be, "Waste not — want not: a recipe for linguistic left-overs", since this would perhaps be more to the point of the discussion. The vicissitudes of syntactic, semantic, and morphological change occassionally strip morphemes of their semantic content or morpho-syntactic function in the wake of developing other aspects of the linguistic system, leaving them as meaningless, functionless residues. What then becomes of these casualties, for linguistic systems are notoriously intolerant of useless elements? They may of course be lost from the system as, for example, was the case with many inherited case markers in English (those which were not erroded away entirely by phonetic changes) when case functions came to be clearly marked by syntatic position and prepositions. But what happens to such semantically empty, functionless morphemes if they are not lost from the linguistic system? The purpose of the present work is not to answer this question in its entirety, but rather to show what happened in one language family when such a situation arose in the parent language. The focus of our attention will be the history of the verbal suffix +*sc*+ in the Romance languages with particular attention to its outcome in more easterly languages, Rhaeto-Romance, Dalmatian and, in particular, Romanian.

1 The suffix +*sc*+ in Latin and Proto-Romance

In Latin, the suffix +*sc*+ was added to sequences of verb stem + theme vowel to form the inchoative aspect. For example, there were pairs such as: *amo* 'I love', *amasco* 'I begin to love'; *florere* 'to flower', *florescĕre* 'to begin to flower'; *dormīo* 'I sleep', *obdormĭsco* 'I begin to sleep, fall asleep'. The fact that we still find a few such paris of verbs in the modern Romance languages attests to the fact that +*sc*+ was also used to derive inchoative verbs in Proto-Romance.[2] In the modern Romance languages, however, +*sc*+ is no longer used to productively derive inchoative verbs, there being a number of other morphological and syntactic constructions used instead.[3] Yet, the suffix +*sc*+ itself lives on as a productive suffix in most of the Romance languages, though its use today has nothing to do wtih its earlier inchoative meaning.

According to Manoliu Manea (1971:173), the decline in the use of +*sc*+ to derive inchoative verbs may be viewed as but one more facet of the general devolution of aspect in favor of tense in Proto-Romance.[4] The loss in productivity of the derivational process forming inchoative verbs with +*sc*+ had, as one result, the reinterpretation of the suffix+*sc*+ as no longer being *the* marker of the inchoative aspect, but rather as being a simple stem-extender on some verbs. This shifts in meaning-function was aided by the loss of some of the non-inchoative partners of certain verbs in +*sc*+ and by shifts in meaning in some verbs taking the suffix +*sc*+ such that their "inchoative" relationship to their unsuffixed partners became opaque.

One additional change which occurred in verbs containing the suffix +*sc*+ was a resegmentation. Originally, such verbs had the morphologi cal structure stem+theme vowel+*sc*. At some point in Proto-Romance, these verbs were reanalyzed as consisting of stem+*Vsc;* that is, the theme vowel came to be viewed as part of the suffix +*sc*+. The evidence for this fact comes from the modern Romance languages where we find that, for example in Romanian and Rhaeto-Romance, the suffix +*sc*+ was transformed into +*esc*+ by the fusion of +*sc*+ with the theme vowel +*e*+ of 3rd conjugation verbs (see Graur 1968:223). In Romanian, +*esc*+ was then generalized from 3rd conjugation to 4th conjugation (*i*-stem) verbs, while in Rhaeto-Romance, for example Old Engadian, it was generalized to both 4th conjugation and 1st conjugation (*a*-stem) verbs (see Mourin 1971). Elsewhere in the Romance languages, for example in Calabrian, French, Portuguese, Sicilian, and Spanish, the suffix +*sc*+ was reshaped to +*isc*+ by fusion with the theme vowel of 4th conjugation verbs.

2 The development of the suffix +*Vsc*+

The suffix +*Vsc*+ (where *V* stands for either of the theme vowels which became associated with this suffix) continued as a simple stem-extender into Western Romance and parts of Italo-Romance. In Spanish, Portuguese, Sicilian, and Calabrian, the suffix spread to all forms of the verb paradigms in which it occurred giving rise to separate series of verbs in +*ecer* in Spanish and Portuguese, in +*iširi* in Calabrian, and in +*išire* in Sicilian (Meyer-Lübke 1895, II:269). In French, +*Vsc*+ (> +*iss*+) spread to all forms of 4th conjugation verbs except the infinitive, preterite, future, conditional, and past participle thus giving rise to suppletive stems such as {fin+} in *finir* 'to finish', *je finirai* 'I will finish', *fini* 'finished', and {finiss+} in *nous finissions* 'we — finished', *que je finisse* 'that I finish', *finissant* 'finishing'. In certain areas of the Romance speaking world, e.g. Sardinia, Veglia, Abruzzes, and the Lorraine (Meyer-Lübke 1895, II: 269), as well as in parts of the Romanian speaking areas (Meglenoromanian and Istroromanian), the suffix +*Vsc*+ lost its function as a stem-extender and disappeared from the morphological system. In Itallo-Romance and Eastern Romance, with the exceptions noted above, the Rhaeto-Romance, something else happened to +*Vsc*+, and it is this which shall interest us here.

3 The link between +*Vsc*+ and stress

The history of the suffix +*Vsc*+ in Italo-Romance, Eastern Romance, and Rhaeto-Romance is closely linked to the history of stress placement in the verbs systems of these languages. Briefly stated, the verbal suffix +*Vsc*+, along with certain other suffices (see the Appendix), came to serve as a vehicle for facilitating the spread of a specific productive stress pattern from non-finite and past finite verb forms to non-past finite verb forms, namely, the suffix-initial stress pattern which serves the demarcative function of distinguishing stems from verbal suffixes in Romance verbs. In order to illustrate what is meant here more closely, we must first examine the history of stress placement in verbs. The major trends in the development of stress patterns in Romance verbs are well illustrated by Romanian, and we shall therefore focus on this language.

The stress patterns encountered in the verb system of modern Romanian can be described by a single rule having three subparts (see Rudes 1977b for a more detailed presentation of this rule). The first subpart assigns stress to the highly "irregular" (read 'self-contained' class of verbs descended from Proto-Romance 3rd conjugation verbs in +*ĕre*. In Romanian, such verbs fall into one of two subclasses, the first consisting of those which form sigmatic preterites and pluperfects (i.e. *se*-perfects) and the second consisting of verbs which form asigmatic preterites and pluperfects (i.e. *u*-perfects). All 3rd conjugation verbs in Romanian receive stress on the last vowel of their stem in non-past finite and non-past non-finite verb forms. That is:

(1)   V → [+ stress] / _____ X] $\begin{bmatrix} \text{verb} \\ \text{stem} \\ \text{3rd} \\ -\text{ past} \\ -\text{ participle} \end{bmatrix}$ +

(X contains no [+ syllabic] elements.)

For example, the verbs *a merge* 'to go' (3rd conjugation, *se*-prefect) and *a începe* 'to begin' (3rd conjugation, *u*-perfect) are stressed as follows:[5]

Stem		merg +		încep +
Infinitive		(a) *mérge*	(a)	*încépe*
Present indicative	1sg	*mérg*		*încép*
	2sg	*mérgi̦*		*încépi̦*
	3sg	*mérge*		*încépe*
	1pl	*mérgem*		*încépem*
	2pl	*mérgeṭi̦*		*încépeṭi̦*
	3pl	*mérg*		*încép*
Present subjunctive	1sg	*mérg*		*încép*
	2sg	*mérgi̦*		*încépi̦*
	3sg	*me̦árgă*		*înce̦ápa*
	1pl	*mérgem*		*încépem*
	2pl	*mérgeṭi̦*		*încépeṭi̦*
	3pl	*me̦árgă*		*înce̦ápă*
Imperative	sg	*mérge*		*încépe*
	pl	*mérgeṭi̦*		*încépeṭi̦*

In addition, the *se*-perfect subclass of 3rd conjugation verbs also take stem-final stress in the third person forms of the preterite. That is:

$$(1') \quad V \rightarrow [+ \text{stress}] \, i \underline{\qquad} X] \begin{bmatrix} \text{verb} \\ \text{stem} \\ \text{3rd} \\ se\text{-perfect} \\ + \text{past} \\ + \text{perfect} \\ - \text{anterior} \\ + \text{3rd person} \end{bmatrix} +$$

We may illustrate this with the verbs *a merge* and *a rupe*, both of which belong to the *se*-perfect subclass.[6]

Perfect stem		mer +	rup +
Preterite	1sg	(*merséi̦*)	(*rupséi̦*)
	2sg	(*merséși*)	(*rupséși*)
	3sg	*mérse*	*rúpse*
	1pl	(*mersérăm*)	(*rupsérăm*)
	2pl	(*mersérăṭi̦*)	(*rupsérăṭi̦*)
	3pl	*mérseră*	*rúpseră*

Rules (1) and (1') may be collapsed into the following rule:

(1'') $V \rightarrow [+ \text{stress}] /\underline{\quad} X]$

$$
\begin{bmatrix}
\text{verb} \\
\text{stem} \\
\text{3rd} \\
\left\{
\begin{array}{l}
\left[\begin{array}{l} - \text{ past} \\ - \text{ participle} \end{array}\right] \\[1em]
\begin{array}{l}
se\text{-perfect} \\
+ \text{ past} \\
+ \text{ perfect} \\
- \text{ anterior} \\
+ \text{ 3rd person}
\end{array}
\end{array}
\right\}
\end{bmatrix} +
$$

The other forms of 3rd conjugation verbs in Romanian, i.e. the gerund, imperfect, pluperfect, the preterite of *u*-perfect verbs, and the non-third person forms of *se*-perfects are stressed like their equivalent forms in other conjugations which we will discuss in a moment.

The second subpart of the Romanian stress rule assigns stress to the non-past finite forms of non-3rd conjugation verbs. It is clearly a remnant of the Proto-Romance rule of phonologically predictable stress placement (from Hooper 1976:58),

$$
S \rightarrow [+\text{stress}] /\underline{\quad} \left(\begin{bmatrix} S \\ \text{weak} \end{bmatrix} \right) S \#] \text{ (where } S \text{ stands for a syllable).}
$$

The Romanian remnant of this rule in the verb system is:

(2) $V \rightarrow [+ \text{stress}] / \underline{\quad} C_1 (V) \#]$ $\begin{bmatrix} \text{verb} \\ - \text{ past} \\ + \text{ finite} \\ - \text{ 3rd} \end{bmatrix}$

That is, the last vowel before the last consonant (or consonant cluster) of non-past finite verb forms not belonging to the third conjugation is stressed. We may illustrate this with forms of the verbs *a afla* 'to find out' (1st conjugation), *a vedea* 'to see' (2nd conjugation), and *a oferi* 'to offer' (4th conjugation).

Present indicative				
	1sg	*áflu*	*văd*	*ofér*
	2sg	*áfli*	*vézi̯*	*oféri̯*
	3sg	*áflă*	*véde*	*oféră*
	1pl	*aflắm*	*vedém*	*oferím*
	2pl	*aflắți̯*	*vedéți̯*	*oferíți̯*
	3pl	*áflă*	*văd*	*oféră*

Present subjunctive	1sg	*áflu*	*văd*	*ofér*
	2sg	*aflị*	*vézị*	*oférị*
	3sg	*áfle*	*vádă*	*ofére*
	1pl	*aflắm*	*vedém*	*oferím*
	2pl	*afláțị*	*vedețị*	*oferíțị*
	3pl	*áfle*	*vádă*	*ofére*
Imperative	sg	*áfle*	*vézị*	*ofére*
	pl	*afláțị*	*vedéțị*	*oferíțị*

We should also note here the so-called class of "stress-retracting" verbs in Romanian which receive stress on the second to the last, rather than the last, vowel before the last consonant or consonant cluster of a verb form in the first, second, and third persons singular, and third person plural. We mark such verbs with the diacritic $\langle D \rangle$ and reformulate stress rule 2 as follows:[7]

$$(2')\quad V \to [+\text{stress}] / \underline{\quad} \text{ S C}_1 \text{ (V) }\#]\quad \begin{bmatrix} \text{verb} \\ -\text{ past} \\ +\text{ finite} \\ -\text{ 3rd} \end{bmatrix} \left\langle \begin{matrix} D \\ -\text{ 1st person} \\ -\text{ 2nd person} \\ +\text{ plural} \end{matrix} \right\rangle$$

An example of such a verb is *a cumpăra* 'to buy'.

Present indicative	1sg	*cúmpăr*
	2sg	*cúmperị*
	3sg	*cúmpără*
	1pl	*cumpărắm*
	2pl	*cumpăráțị*
	3pl	*cúmpără*

The last, and for our purposes, most important subpart of the Romanian stress rule assigns stress to the first vowel of the verbal suffixes, i.e. the first vowel after the stem, of the imperfect, pluperfect, and gerund of all verbs, the preterite, past participle, and infinitive of all except 3rd conjugation and certain "irregular" verbs. I call this the most important subpart of the Romanian stress rule not only because it affects more verb forms in the system than either of the other two subparts of the stress rule, but also because it is the most productive stress pattern in Romanian as may be demonstrated both from historical stress-shifts and from on-going changes in spoken Romanian. As we shall see, this subpart of the stress rule is crucially related to the history of the suffix $+Vsc+$ in Romanian. The rule may be formulated as follows:

(3)   V → [+ stress] /] $\begin{bmatrix} \text{verb} \\ \text{stem} \end{bmatrix}$ +X ___

       (*X* contains no [+ syllabic] elements)

We may illustrate this pattern of stress placement with forms of the verbs *a afla* 'to find out' (1st conjugation), *a vedea* 'to see' (2nd conjugation), *a merge* 'to go' (3rd conjugation, *se*-perfect), *a începe* 'to begin' (3rd conjugation, *u*-perfect), and *a oferi* 'to offer' (4th conjugation). (See table following page.)

The three subparts of the Romanian stress rule discussed above, rules 1″, 2', and 3, account for the stress patterns of all Romanian verbs including the "irregular" verbs *a avea* 'to have', *a bea* 'to drink', *a fi* 'to be', *a lua* 'to take', *a mînca* 'to eat', *a relua* 'to retake', *a sta* 'to stand', *a şti* 'to know', *a usca* 'to dry', *a voi* 'to want' and *a vrea* 'to want'. For a closer look at these verbs see Rudes 1977b:411-413.

We are now in a position to examine the behaviour of the Romanian reflex of the verbal suffix $+Vsc+$, i.e. $+esc+$. This suffix, as a productive aspect of Romanian morphology, has a rather peculiar distribution in that it occurs only on the first, second, and third persons singular and third person plural of the present indicative, present subjunctive, and imperative of 4th conjugation verbs. We may illustrate the distribution of $+esc+$ in Romanian with forms of the verbs *a citi* 'to read' and *a hotărî* 'to decide'.

Stem		*cit+*	*hotăr+*
Present indicative	1sg	*citésc*	*hotărắsc*
	2sg	*citéşti*	*hotărắşti*
	3sg	*citéşte*	*hotărắşte*
	1pl	*citím*	*hotărím*
	2pl	*citíţi*	*hotăríţi*
	3pl	*citésc*	*hotărắsc*
Present subjunctive	1sg	*citésc*	*hotărắsc*
	2sg	*citéşti*	*hotărắşti*
	3sg	*citęáscă*	*hotăráscă*
	1pl	*citím*	*hotărím*
	2pl	*citíţi*	*hotăríţi*
	3pl	*citęáscă*	*hotăráscă*
Imperative	sg	*citéşte*	*hotărắşte*
	pl	*citíţi*	*hotăríţi*

Stem	afl +	ved + /văz +	merg + /mer +	încep +	ofer +
Infinitive	(a) aflá	(a) vedéa	((a) mérge)	((a) încépe)	(a) oferí
Past participle	aflát	văzút	(mérs)	începút	oferít
Gerund	aflînd	văzînd	mergînd	începînd	oferínd
Imperfect 1sg	aflám	vedéam	mergéam	începéam	oferéam
2sg	aflái	vedéai	mergéai	începéai	oferéai
3sg	aflá	vedeá	mergeá	incepeá	oferéa
1pl	aflám	vedéam	mergéam	începéam	oferéam
2pl	afláţi	vedeáţi	mergeáţi	începeáţi	oferéaţi
3pl	afláu	vedeáu	mergeáu	începeáu	oferéau
Preterite 1sg	aflái	văzúi	merséi	începúi	oferíi
2sg	afláşi	văzúşi	merséşi	începúşi	oferíşi
3sg	aflá	văzú	(mérse)	începú	oferí
1pl	aflárăm	văzúrăm	mersérăm	începúrăm	oferírăm
2pl	afláráţi	văzúrăţi	mersérăţi	începurăţi	oferírăţi
3pl	afláră	văzúră	(merséră)	începúră	oferíră
Pluperfect 1sg	aflásem	văzúsem	mersésem	începúsem	oferísem
2sg	afláseşi	văzúseşi	merséseşi	începúseşi	oferíseşi
3sg	aflásе	văzúse	mersése	începúse	oferíse
1pl	afláserăm	văzúserăm	merséserăm	începúserăm	oferíserăm
2pl	afláserăţi	văzúserăţi	merséserăţi	incepuserăţi	oferíserăţi
3pl	afláseră	văzúseră	merséseră	începúseră	oferíseră

The absence of the suffix +*esc*+ in the past finite forms of these verbs may be illustrated with the forms of the preterite.

Preterite			
	1sg	*citíi̯*	*hotăríi̯*
	2sg	*citíși̯*	*hotăríși̯*
	3sg	*cití*	*hotărî́*
	1p	*citírăm*	*hotărî́răm*
	2p	*citírăți̯*	*hotărî́răți̯*
	3p	*citíră*	*hotărî́ră*

As in all of the other modern Romance languages, +*esc*+ as a verbal suffix is singularly meaningless as evidenced by the fact that first and second plural forms of non-past finite verbs, as well as all non-finite and past finite verb forms, which lack the suffix +*esc*+ have the same basic meaning as first, second, and third person singular and third person plural forms containing the suffix (see also comments in Graur 1968:222–224). Yet the suffix is today, and has been for some centuries, quite productive in that many neologisms and borrowings find themselves becoming 4th conjugation verbs and taking this suffix.[8] In discussing Old Romanian, the language of sixteenth and seventeenth century manuscripts, Densusianu (1932:204) notes that there were at least four verbs which lacked the suffix +*esc*+ but which always show it today: *a despărți* 'to separate from', *a împărți* 'to divide', *a omorî* 'to kill', and *a păți* 'to endure'. Further, he notes three verbs which in Old Romanian could be conjugated with or without the suffix +*esc*+ but which are always conjugated with this suffix in modern Romanian: *a luci* 'to shine', *a răpi* 'to kidnap', and *a slobozi* 'to liberate'. Rosetti (1968:544) gives a somewhat different, and slightly longer, list of such verbs in Old Romanian. Lacking familiarity with the manuscript material itself, I am not prepared to comment on the differences between Rosetti's and Densusianu's lists. The contrast between the Old Romanian verbs lacking +*esc*+ and the modern Romanian equivalents where the +*esc*+ is present is important for two reasons. First it shows that +*esc*+ has been a productive suffix in that its range of occurrence has expanded since the sixteenth century to include new verbs. Second, it reinforces our claim that the suffix +*esc*+ is meaningless since the verbs lacking the suffix in the sixteenth century meant the same as their modern counterparts exhibiting +*esc*+.

Given the meaninglessness of +*esc*+ in Romanian, we are forced to ask the question, why is it productive? This is not the first time this question has been raised. Graur (1968:222) gives the following reply to this question:[9]

Conjugarea fără -*ez* şi -*esc*, de tip arhaic, produce perturbări în economia flex-
iunilor: diferenţa de accent între persoanele 1 şi 2-a plural şi celelalte, ceea ce
cauzează diferenţe de vocalism şi chiar de consonatism . . . anarhia în conjugare
este în bună parte îndepărttată în momentul cînd se introduc -*ez* şi -*esc*.

Thus Graur notes that the addition of +*ez*+ and +esc+ in Romanian
verbs serves to preserve the identity of the stem by levelling allomorphy
produced by vowel and consonant alternations between stressed and
unstressed syllables. But he fails to note that the presence of these suffixes
results in the stress placement in the non-past forms. Thus he misses the
generalization, which we shall return to in a moment, that stress is
performing a demarcative function in Romanian, that of separating stem
from suffixes, and that this demarcative stress pattern is spreading from
the past verb forms to the non-past verb forms with the help of the suffixes
+*ez*+ and +*esc*+. A view similar to that of Graur has also been expressed
by Bourciez (1946) and Mourin (1974:27). Lombard (1954) infers that
the presence of +*esc*+ and +*ez*+ in Romanian verbs is due to the
tendency to distinctly mark the difference between persons in the verb.
Rosetti (1968) basically accepts Lombard's view. This explanation might
hold were it that these suffixes occurred only in the singular since they
would then serve the purpose of distinguishing the first or third person
singular form from the otherwise homophonous third person plural form.
However, these suffixes also occur on third person plural forms thus
causing them to remain homophonous with the first or third person
singular of the same verb, e.g. *citésc* 'I read', 'they read', *citeáscă* 'that
he/she/it reads', 'that they read'. While Graur's and Lombard's answers
to the question of "why is +*esc*+ productive in Romanian?" are not
entirely wrong, they are only part of the solution.

Returning to our discussion of the Romanian stress system for a
moment, we may remember that the most productive stress pattern in
verbs is that of suffix-initial stress. Romanian is not alone in showing a
preference for this pattern, for we may note that it is the most wide-spread
stress pattern in the non-finite and past finite verb forms of all the
Romance languages (excluding French which lacks a mobile stress). We
may warrantedly assume that stress placement in early Proto-Romance
was phonologically predictable, as it was in Classical Latin. That is, stress
would have fallen on the penultimate syllable of polysyllabic words if that
syllable was strong (i.e. contained a long vowel or a short vowel followed
by a consonant) and on the antepenultimate syllable if the penultimate
syllable was weak (i.e. ended in a short vowel). The change from a musical
accent to a dynamic accent, and the subsequent shifts in vowel quantity
and location of the accent in some words, resulted in the collapse of the

phonologically predictable rule of accent placement through the accumu-
lation of numerous exceptions. This situation was further aggravated by
the retention of accent patterns on loan words even when these patterns
did not conform to the norms of proto-Romance accent placement (see
Manoliu Manea 1971:77-80). During this period in the development of
Proto-Romance, stress placement became morphologized; that is, the
location of stress came to be determined by morphological rather than
phonological factors (for a detailed discussion of rule morphologization
see Hooper 1974). Two major trends in the morphologization of stress in
Proto-Romance may be singled out. The first affected only 3rd conjugation verbs where the location of stress came to be more and more
regularly fixed on the last vowel of the stem. This trend continues even
today in Romanian.

The second trend, which affected all non-3rd conjugation verbs, was to
locate stress on the first vowel after the stem, i.e. the first vowel of the
verbal suffixes. While both trends in stress placement served the same
function, that of delimiting stems from suffixes by denoting the end of one
or the beginning of the other, the trend toward suffix-initial stress placement became the most productive pattern, perhaps because of its less
restricted domain of applicability. In this regard we may note that the
Ibero-Romance languages have levelled out the stem-final stress pattern
on 3rd conjugation verbs completely while maintaining suffix-initial
stress as a productive process. In Romanian, we find plenty of evidence
for the favored status of suffix-inital stress in the verb system.

A number of stress shifts in the Romanian verb system can be
documented between Old Romanian, that found in sixteenth- and
seventeenth-century manuscripts, and modern Romanian. The most
important of these for our purposes concerns the accent pattern on
preterites. The dominant stress pattern in Old Romanian preterites was
to stress the last vowel of the stem except in the second person singular
where the first vowel of the verbal suffixes was stressed.[10] For example
(taken from Mourin 1968):

féciu 'I made'	*véniu* 'I came'	*dédiu* 'I gave'	*zíșu* 'I said'
fecéși	*vinéși*	*dedéși*	*ziséși*
féce	*víne*	*déde*	*zíse*
fécemu	*vínemu*	*dédemu*	*zísemu*
fécetu	*vínetu*	*dédetu*	*zísetu*
féceră	*víneră*	*déderă*	*zíseră*

In modern Romanian, the stress on preterites falls consistently on the first
vowel of the verbal suffixes, except in the case of 3rd conjugation,

se-perfect preterites as discussed previously. That is, except in the second person singular, stress has shifted on preterites from the last vowel of the stem to the first vowel of the verbal suffixes. The above verb forms in Old Romanian have as their modern Romanian equivalents:

făcúi̯	*veníi̯*	*dădúi̯*	*ziséi̯*
făcúși	*veníși*	*dădúși*	*ziséși*
făcú	*vení*	*dădú*	*zisé* ~ (*zíse*)
făcúrăm	*venírăm*	*dădúrăm*	*zisérăm*
făcúrăți̯	*veníráți̯*	*dădúrăți̯*	*ziséráți̯*
făcúră	*veníră*	*dădúră*	*ziséră* ~ (*zíseră*)

Of course, in addition to stress shift, or perhaps in order to effect stress shift, these verb forms have undergone major analogical remodelling. We refer here to verbs such as Old Romanian *féciu* and *dédiu* which were remodeled on the basis of verbs like Old Romanian *trecúiu* 'I crossed' which already had suffix-initial stress in Old Romanian. Compare the endings of the modern Romanian forms of *făcúi̯* and *dădúi̯* with those of Old Romanian *trecúiu*.

> *trecúiu*
> *trecúși*
> *trecú*
> *trecúmu*
> *trecútu*
> *trecúră*

Other than remodeling on the basis of verbs such as *trecúiu,* the only other analogical change in the form of these preterites (and also pluperfects) was the spread of the ending +*ră*+ from third person plural forms to all plural forms, perhaps to reinforce the distinctness of the plural endings. We may also note that a remnant of the Old Romanian stem stress on preterites still remains, optionally, on the third person singular and plural forms of verbs such as *ziséi̯.* However, such stem-stressed forms are generally considered literary or archaic and are rapidly disappearing from the spoken language.

We may also note the behaviour of stress on the synthetic conditional forms retained in some varieties of Romanian. There are four major varieties of Romanian: Dacoromanian (The Romanian spoken in the Socialist Republic of Romania and the variety from which Standard Literary Romanian is derived), Aromanian (spoken in southern Albania, southern Yugoslavia, Bulgaria, and northern Greece), Meglenoromanian (spoken in a small area on the border of Yugoslavia and Greece), and Istroromanian (spoken by a small number of people in the northern part of the Istrian peninsula).[11] In Dacoromanian, the variety of Romanian which we have been looking at so far in this work, and in Meglenoromanian, the old conditional formed from the perfect stem plust the suffix +re+ plus person and number markers was lost, although it was still present in Old Romanian.[12] However, in Aromanian and Istroromanian, the conditional survives.[13] In other Romance languages with mobile stress, the conditional occurs with stress on the first vowel after the subsequent marker (< +re+ historically).[14] We may illustrate this with examples from Italian, Portuguese, and Spanish.

Italian		Portuguese	Spanish
parleréi	'I would speak'	*falaría*	*hablaría*
parlerésti		*falarías*	*hablarías*
parlerébbe		*falaría*	*hablaría*
parlerémmo		*falaríamos*	*hablaríamos*
parleréste		*falaríeis*	*hablaríais*
parlerébbo		*falaríam*	*hablarían*

In each of these languages, the conditionals have the morphemic structure: stem + tense/aspect/mode vowel + subsequent marker + conditional person/number markers (e.g. Italian *parl*+*e*+*r*+*éi* 'I would speak', Portuguese *fal*+*a*+*r*+*ía,* Spanish *habl*+*a*+*r*+*ía*). Although the morphemic structure of the conditional forms in Aromanian and Istroromanian is exactly the same as in Italian, Portuguese, and Spanish, stress falls not on the vowel after the subsequent marker (+*r*+), but on the vowel preceding the subsequent marker.[15]

Aromanian		Istroromanian	
s-cîntárimu	'I would sing'	*aflǎr*	'I would find'
s-cîntári(și)		*aflǎri*	
s-cîntári		*aflǎre*	
s-cîntárimu		*aflǎrno*	
s-cîntáritu		*aflǎritu*	
s-cîntári		*aflǎru*	

Although it is clear that the conditional forms of Romanian, despite their superficial similarity, developed independently of the formation of the conditionals in the other Romance languages, it is still at first somewhat perplexing why the stress patterns should differ among the languages.[16] That is, since the morphemic structure of the conditional in all of these

languages is the same even to the point of including reflexes of the
subsequent marker +r+, and since all of these languages inherited essentially the same rule of stress placement from Proto-Romance, though
subject to later modifications, why should we find the stress falling on the
vowel before the subsequent marker in Romanian, but after it elsewhere
in the Romance languages? The only likely answer that I see to this
question at the moment involves the notion of demarcative, suffix-initial
stress placement which we have been discussing. As was discussed previously, all of the Romance languages show some degree of stress placement on the first vowel of the verbal sufixes, particularly in past finitive
and non-finitive verb forms; however, no other Romance language, with
the possible exceptions of Rhaeto-Romance and Dalmatian, shows as
strong a movement to spread suffix-initial stress placement throughout
the verb system. Remember that the vowel after the subsequent marker
of the conditional is not the first vowel of the verbal suffixes in any of the
Romance languages; rather, it is the tense/aspect/mode vowel which
precedes the subsequent marker. We may illustrate this using second
person plural forms of the conditional.

Italian		parl	+e	+r	+ *éste*
Portuguese		*fal*	+a	+r	+ *íeis*
Spanish		*habl*	+a	+r	+ *íais*
Aromanian	s+	*cînt*	+á	+r	+ *itu*
Istroromanian		*afl*	+ắ	+r	+ *itu*

Thus, only in Aromanian and Istroromanian does the stress fall on the
first vowel of the verbal suffixes, thereby aligning the stress pattern on
the conditionals in these varieties of Romanian with that of nonfinite and
past finite verb forms. From these facts it appears likely that the trend
towards demarcative, suffix-initial stress placement in Romanian had
become so strong, even during Common Romanian times when the
conditionals were formed, that it became part of the word formation rules
for verbs. Thus, when the conditionals were formed, stress was automatically assigned to the vowel before the subsequent marker; whereas in the
more westerly Romance languages, where the drive towards suffix-initial
stress was not so strong, the stress fell on the vowel after the subsequent
marker.

In all of the Romance languages except Dalmatian, Dolomite,
Rhaeto-Romance, and Romanian, the suffix-initial stress pattern is
restricted to non-finite and past finite verb forms. Only in the latter-
mentioned languages has this stress pattern penetrated into the non-past
finite verb forms. Non-past finite verb forms, i.e. present indicatives,

present subjunctives, and imperatives, in the Romance languages with mobile stress are characterized for the most part by an alternating stress pattern which is derived historically from the original Proto-Romance rule of phonologically predictable stress placement. We already noted that in Romanian this consists of stressing the last vowel before the last consonant of the word. If we examine the stress pattern on the present indicative, subjunctive, and imperative of a typical Romanian verb containing the suffix +*esc* +, we find that it can be said to fall on the last vowel before the last consonant of the word.

Present indicative	1sg	*citésc*	I read'
	2sg	*citéşțị*	
	3sg	*citéşte*	
	1pl	*citím*	
	2pl	*citíțị*	
	3pl	*citésc*	
Subjunctive	1sg	*citésc*	
	2sg	*citéşțị*	
	3sg	*citeáscă*	
	1pl	*citím*	
	2pl	*citíțị*	
	3pl	*citeáscă*	
Imperative	sg	*citéşte*	
	pl	*citíțị*	

But, unlike any other non-past finite verb forms (except those of +*ez* + verbs, see Appendix), Romanian verbs taking the suffix +*esc* + also may be said to receive stress on the first vowel of the verbal suffixes.

Stem		*cit* +	'read'
Present indicative	1sg	*cit* +*ésc*	
	2sg	*cit* +*éşt* +*ị*	
	3sg	*cit* +*éşt* +*e*	
	1pl	*cit* +*í* +*m*	
	2pl	*cit* +*í* +*țị*	
	3pl	*cit* +*ésc*	
Subjunctive	1sg	*cit* +*ésc*	
	2sg	*cit* +*éşt* +*ị*	
	3sg	*cit* +*eásc* +*ă*	
	1pl	*cit* +*í* +*m*	
	2pl	*cit* +*í* +*țị*	
	3pl	*cit* +*eásc* +*ă*	

Imperative   sg   *cit+éṣt+e*
                                    pl   *cit+í+ţi*

Here, in my opinion, lies the answer to the question as to why the
meaningless suffix *+esc+* has enjoyed such productivity in Romanian,
and why it has such a peculiar distribution, occurring as it does only on the
first, second, and third persons singular and third persons plural of
non-past finite verbs. If we were to remove the suffix *+esc+* from the
verb forms where it occurs, stress would have no choice but to fall on the
stem. We would be left with an alternation of stress between the stem on
singular and third person plural forms and on the verbal suffixes in first
and second plural forms. This is in fact the stress pattern we find on
non-past finite verb forms which do not take the suffix *+esc+* (or *+ez+*).
The extension of the verbal suffix *+esc+* in non-past finite verb forms in
Romanian provides a very convenient solution to the problem of reg-
ularizing stress in non-past verb forms. On those forms where it occurs,
stress remains regular for non-past finite verbs in that it falls on the last
vowel before the last consonant of the word, while, at the same time, the
presence of this suffix allows stress to fall on the first vowel of the verbal
suffixes by providing an extra, stressable syllable on the suffixes. Thus,
the productive demarcative, suffix-initial stress pattern can spread to
-non-past finite verb forms without entailing any major disturbance of
prior stress patterns in these forms or any major analogical remodeling
(note the remodeling that went on in the preterite of Romanian in order
to get suffix-initial stress as discussed previously). I conclude that the
productivity of *+esc+* in Romanian results from its performing the
function of serving as a vehicle for the smooth transmission of demarcative, stem-initial stress from non-finite and past finite verb forms to the
non-past verb forms.

The same analysis as that given above for the productivity of *+esc+* in
Romanian also holds true for this suffix in Dolomite, Rhaeto-Romance,
and the Ragusan dialect of Dalmatian (Tagliavini 1977:302). In these
languages, as in Romanian, the suffix *+esc+* has been spreading to new
verbs, but only to the first, second, and third persons singular, and third
persons plural of non-past finite verb forms. We may illustrate this with
examples from Dolomite, Old Engadian, and Old Surselvan (taken from
Mourin 1974).

Dolomite	Old Engadian	Old Surselvan	
	*bened*esch	*surv*esch	1st conj.
	*bened*esches	*surv*eschas	

	*benede*scha	*surve*scha	
	*bene*din	*surv*in	
	*bene*dis	*surv*its	
	*benede*schen	*surve*schan	

	*possid*esch		3rd conj.
	*possid*esch*es*		
	*possid*escha		
	*possid*ain		
	possidæs		
	*possid*eschen		

desflurësce	*glorifichi*esch	*persequit*esch	4th conj.
desflurësces	*glorifichi*esch*es*	*persequit*esch*as*	
desflurësc	*glorifichi*escha	*persequit*escha	
desflurion	*glorifichi*ain	*persequit*ein	
desfluriëis	*glorifichiæs*	*persequit*eits	
desflurësc	*glorifichi*eschen	*persequit*eschan	

The suffix +*esc*+ (the non-italicized portions above) behaves in these languages exactly as in Romanian, with Old Engadian having extended it the furthest to 1st and 3rd as well as 4th conjugation verbs. Also, in these languages, it is only those non-past finite conjugations where +*esc*+ appears that receive stress on the first vowel of the verbal suffix (with the exception of verbs taking the suffix +*ei*+ in Dolomite and +*ay*+ in the Vegliote dialect of Dalmation, for which see Appendix).

In summary, we have seen a morphological element, the suffix +*esc*+, originally serving a lexico-semantic function, that of deriving inchoative verbs, lose this function and appear as a semantically empty element, a stem-extender. Subsequently, in the more easterly areas of the Romance speaking territory, this suffix acquired a new function in the verb system, that of providing a vehicle for the spread of the productive, suffix-initial stress pattern into non-past finite verbs. The history of the suffix +*esc*+ in the Romance languages clearly illustrates how linguistic systems, intolerant as they are of meaningless, functionless elements, can put such an element back to work by providing it with a new function.

Appendix

We have already noted in the text that there exists another verbal suffix in Romanian which behaves identically with +*esc*+, namely +*ez*+. While the suffix +*esc*+ is restricted in Romanian to 4th conjugation (both *i*-stem and *î*-stem) verbs, +*ez*+ occurs only with 1st conjugation (*a*-stem) verbs. Like +*esc*+, +*ez*+ occurs only on the first, second, and third persons singular and third persons plural of non-past finite verb forms, and serves the purpose of allowing stress to fall on the first vowel of the verbal suffixes in these forms.

Stem		*vizit*+	'visit'
Present indicative	1sg	*vizitéz*	
	2sg	*vizitézi̧*	
	3sg	*vizitȩ́áză*	
	1pl	*vizităm*	
	2pl	*vizitáți̧*	
	3pl	*vizitȩ́áză*	
Subjunctive	1sg	*vizitéz*	
	2sg	*vizitézi̧*	
	3sg	*vizitéze*	
	1pl	*vizităm*	
	2pl	*vizitáți̧*	
	3pl	*vizitéze*	
Imperative	sg	*vizitézi̧*	
	pl	*vizitáți̧*	

Also, as with +*esc*+, +*ez*+ does not occur in past finite or non-finite verb forms.

Infinitive	(*a*) *vizitá*	
Gerund	*vizitînd*	
Past participle	*vizitát*	
Preterite	1sg	*vizitái̧*
	2sg	*vizitáși̧*
	3sg	*vizită*
	1pl	*vizitárăm*
	2pl	*vizitárăți̧*
	3pl	*vizitáră*

The development of +*ez*+ is more obscure than that of +*esc*+. It is known that it originated from verbs borrowed from Greek containing ιζω, e.g. *baptizare*. Such borrowings were particularly numerous in late Latin and Proto-Romance. However, the strategies by which ιζ in such verbs came to be segmented out as a suffix are unknown. What is clear is that, once this segmentation was accomplished, the resultant suffix underwent a development parallel to that of +*esc*+ in Romanian. As with +*esc*+, the evidence from sixteenth- and seventeenth-century Romanian shows that the suffix +*ez*+ was spreading to new verbs at this time as it is still doing today in spoken Romanian (see discussion in Rudes 1977c:206).

We also find in Dolomite another suffix functioning like +*esc*+, namely +*ei*+, which is restricted to 1st conjugation verbs (from Mourin 1974).

persequiteie   'I persecute'
persequiteies
persequitea
persequiton
persequitëis
persequitea

Further, in the Vegliote dialect of Dalmatian, there is a similar suffix, +*ay*+, which occurs only on the first, second, and third persons singular and third person plural forms of non-past finite verb forms (Tagliavini 1977:302; Bec 1971, II:408). According to Meyer-Lübke (1895, II:268), Vegliote +*ay*+ like Romanian +*ez*+ originated from the *ιξ* of Greek loan verbs. Since Dolomite +*ei*+ is restricted to 1st conjugation verbs as is Romanian +*ez*+ and, for the most part, Vegliote +*ay*+, and since the phonological relationship between Dolomite +*ei*+ and Vegliote +*ay*+ is clear (Vegliote +*ay*+ is generally reconstructed as *+*ei*+), we may assume a similar source for Dolomite +*ei*+.

Notes

1. I would like to express my gratitude to Editura Academiei R.S. România for allowing me to use portions of Rudes 1977b and 1977c in the preparation of this work. I would also like to thank Andrei Avram, Maria Manoliu Manea, Alexandru Nicolescu, and Elena Vasiliu for their most helpful assistance in researching this work, and their comments on the results. Of course, all responsibility for the final form of this work is my own.
2. For example, we may note Italian *parto* 'I leave', *partisco* 'I disassociate (myself) from it'; Romanian *împart* 'I disassociate (myself) from it'. *împărțesc* 'I give it freely' (in Moldavia).
3. See, for examples of such constructions, Manoliu Manea 1976.
4. "Incoativele indicau faptul că acțiunea se află în punctul inițial al săvîrșirii ei. Ele se derivau de la verbe, adjective și substantive cu ajutorul sufixului -*sc*- (-*asco*, -*esco*, *isco*) . . . În limbile romanice, sufixul a continuat să trăiască, dar ca simplă variantă combinatorie a formantului de prezent, dirijată de temele verbale. Formele de prezent incoativ au înlocuit, mai ales la conjugarea a IV-a, unele formele de prezent neincoativ,

fapt care dovedeşte că opoziţia aspectuală s-a degradat şi în acest cazsîn favoarea valorii temporale." (Manoliu Manea 1971:173).

5. All words in this paper are cited in standard orthography with the exception that, for Romanian, non-syllabic vowels are indicated with an inverted subscript breve accent, e.g. *i̯* represents a non-syllabic *i*. In Romanian, orthographic *ţ, ş, j, ă, î* have the values [ts], [š], [ž], [ə], [ɨ]. The letters *c* and *g* represent palatal affricates [tš] and [dž], respectively, before *i, i̯, e* and *g*, and velar stops [k] and [g] elsewhere. Stress is marked with an acute accent over the stressed vowel (for further details see Rudes 1977a).

6. They follow this stress pattern only in the preterite. In the pluperfect, stress regularly falls on the first vowel of the verbal suffixes as in other pluperfects (see rule 3).

7. For a discussion and justification of the use of a diacritic on these verbs in order to account for their stress pattern see Rudes 1977b:405–406.

8. In connection with our discussion of the productivity of +*esc*+ we might note the comment of Brâncuş (1976):14–15):

Verbele în *-ăi, -îi, -ui*, foarte multe dintre ele au origine onomatopeică, circulă în limba populară cu flexiune dublă, adică fie cu sufixul *-esc*, fie fără acest sufix.

The older forms of such verbs are among the group which take stress on the second, rather than the last, vowel before the last consonant of the word and thus must be marked with the diacritic ⟨D⟩ in order to be properly stressed by stress rule 1". The remodeled forms of these verbs, on the other hand, behave like other +*esc*+ verbs in taking stress on the first vowel of the verbal suffixes. Examples of such verbs are:

bîjbîi:	*bîjbîi̯e*	~	*bîjbîi̯éşte*	'he gropes'
scîrţîi:	*scîrţîi̯e*	~	*scîrţîi̯éşte*	'it squeaks'
bubui:	*búbui̯e*	~	*bubui̯éşte*	'it thunders'
dudui:	*dúdui̯e*	~	*dudui̯éşte*	'it shakes'
behăi:	*béhăi̯e*	~	*behăi̯éşte*	'it bleats'
moţăi:	*móţăi̯e*	~	*moţăi̯éşte*	'he dozes off'

Thus, the spread of +*esc*+ to these verbs in spoken Romanian assists the language to rid itself of the highly irregular stress pattern [V́ S C₁ (V)#] exemplified by the unsuffixed forms of these verbs.

9. We may translate this statement as follows:
'The archaic type of conjugation lacking the suffix *-ez* and *-esc* produced disturbances in the economy of inflexion: the difference in accent between first and second persons plural and the other persons created differences in the vowels and even the consonants (of the stem) . . . the anarchy in the conjugations is for the most part alleviated as soon as *-ez* and *-esc* are introduced.'

10. As we shall see in a moment, some preterites in Old Romanian already showed consistant suffix-initial stress placement in all persons.

11. For more detailed information on the geographical location, as well as the number of speakers, cultural history, relation to Dacoromanian, etc. see Caragiu-Marioţeanu 1975:189–191 for Istroromanian, 216–221 for Aromanian, and 266–267 for Meglenoromanian.

12. For comments on the conditional in sixteenth century Romanian see Caragiu-Marioţeanu 1975:115–117; Densusianu 1932:228–230; Rosetti 1968:549.

13. A detailed presentation of the conditionals in Aromanian may be found in Caragiu-Marioţeanu 1968 and 1975, and in Istroromanian in Caragiu-Marioţeanu 1975 and Puşcariu 1926.

14. See Caragiu-Marioțeanu 1975:116.
15. For a discussion of the somewhat aberrant personal endings on the Istroromanian conditional see Pușcariu 1926:185 f.
16. Stress placement on other verb forms in Aromanian and Istroromanian is essentially the same as in Dacoromanian except for the preterite which in Aromanian retains the stem-final stress, except on the second person singular, which has been leveled out in Dacoromanian (see discussion in text).

References

Bec, Pierre
1971 *Manuel pratique de philologie romane*, II (Paris: Picard).
Bourciez, E.
1946 *Eléments de linguistique romane* (4th edition) (Paris: Klincksieck).
Brâncuș, Grigoire
1976 *Limba Română contemporană: Morfologia verbului* [Contemporary Romanian: Verb morphology] (București: Universitatea din București).
Caragiu-Marioțeanu, Matilda
1968 *Fono-morfologie aromână* [Aromanian phonomorphology] (București: Editura Academiei R.S. România).
1975 *Compendiu de dialectologie română* [Compendium of Romanian dialectology] (București: Editura științifică și enciclopedică).
Densusianu, Ovide
1932 *Histoire de la langue roumaine*, II.2 (Paris: Leroux).
Graur, Al
1968 *Tendințele actuale ale limbii române* [Current tendencies in Romanian] (București: Editura științifică).
Hooper, Joan
1974 "Rule morphologization in natural generative phonology", *Papers from the parasession on natural phonology* (Chicago Linguistic Society), 160–170.
Lombard, Alf
1954 *Le verbe roumaine* 1 (Lund).
Manoliu Manea, Maria
1971 *Gramatica comparată a limbilor romanice* [A comparative grammar of the Romance languages] (București: Editura didactică și pedagogică).
1976 "Un modèle localiste de l'inchoatif roman", *Etudes romanes: Bulletin de la Société roumaine de linguistique romane* 9:47–62.
Meyer-Lübke, Wilhelm
1895 *Grammaire des langues romanes* (translated by A. Doutrepont and G. Doutrepont) (Paris: Welter).
Mourin, L.
1968 *Countribution à la description comparée des langues romanes*, III.3: *Les parfaits irreguliers* (Bruxelles: Presses universitaires de Bruxelles).
1971 *Contribution à la description comparée des langues romanes*, IV.6: *L'indicatif présent* (Buxelles: Presses universitaires de Bruxelles).
Pușcariu, Sextil
1926 *Studii istroromâne* II [Istro-Romanian studies] (București: Kultura).
Rosetti, Alexandru
1968 *Istoria limbii române de la origini pînă în secolul a XVII-lea* [History of Romanian

from the beginnings until the 17th century] (Bucureşti: Editura pentru literatură).

Rudes, Blair

    1977a   "A note on Romanian fast speech", *Revue roumaine de linguistique — Cahiers de linguistique théorique et appliquée* 14.1:87–97.

    1977b   "The history and function of stress in the Romanian verb system 1", *Revue roumaine de linguistique* 22.4:403–415.

    1977c   "The history and function of stress in the Romanian verb system 2", *Revue roumaine de linguistique — Cahiers de linguistique théorique et appliquée* 14.2:205–218.

Tagliavini, Carlo

    1977   *Originile limbilor neolatine* [The origins of the neo-Latin languages] (translated by A. Giurescu and M. Cârstea-Romaşcanu) (Bucureşti: Editura ştiinţifică şi enciclopedică).

RUSSEL G. SCHUH

Paradigmatic displacement

1 Introduction

1.1 The concept of paradigmatic displacement

When a paradigm shows irregularity at one or more points, the system is unstable. The typical linguistic reaction is either for analogical leveling to bring the offending point(s) in the paradigm into line with the more pervasive pattern or for the form felt to be the most "basic" to drive out other alternants.

The "pervasive pattern" model for leveling can be illustrated by a familiar example from Latin. In pre-Latin the root of the word 'honor' must be reconstructed as ending in *s (cf. *honestus*); later, through rhotacism, *s changed to r between vowels; and finally, in Classical Latin, since the majority of declensional forms had r, the final s of the nominative was replaced by r to make it conform to the overall paradigmatic pattern.

	Pre-Latin	Early Latin	Classical Latin
Nom.	*honōs	honōs	honor
Gen.	*honōsis	honōris	honōris
Dat.	*honōsī	honōrī	honōrī
Acc.	*honōsem	honōrem	honōrem
Abl.	*honōse	honōre	honōre

The "basic form" model for leveling can be illustrated from the history of English. Here, there has been a shift of large numbers of strong verbs, where the root has several morphologically conditioned alternants, to the class of weak verbs, where the form of the root does not alternate. The model for the analogically levelled root shape is the root as used in the infinitive and/or first person singular present:

	Old English	Modern English
1st sing. present	*help-e*	*help*
Infinitive	*help-an*	*to help*
1st sing. preterite	*healp*	*help-ed*
Plural preterite	*hulp-on*	*help-ed*
Past participle	*holp-en*	*help-ed*

Another possible reaction to irregularities in a paradigm is to shift the deviation from the original point to another point, either inside or outside the paradigm per se. The result is regularization at the original point(s) but creation of a new irregularity elsewhere. Several examples of such shifting have been identified in languages belonging to the Chadic family of West and Central Africa.

1.2 Identification of languages

The Chadic family is one of five branches of the Afroasiatic (= Hamito-Semitic) phylum. The most recent classification of Chadic languages (Newman 1977) divides the Chadic family into four major branches: West Chadic, spoken almost entirely in northern Nigeria and including Hausa, perhaps the largest indigenous language south of the Sahara; Biu-Mandara, spoken mainly in northern Cameroon and adjacent areas of Nigeria and Chad; East Chadic, spoken in western and central Chad; and Masa, spoken in Cameroon and Chad south of N'Djamena. The languages being considered here belong to the Bole-Tangale group of West Chadic. The languages of the Bole-Tangale group have perhaps the same closeness of relationship as the Romance languages. With the exception of Bolanci (Lukas 1971, 1970–1972) and Kanakuru (Newman 1974), there is very little published material on any of these languages. I have taken most of the data here from my own field work (especially Schuh 1978, n.d.).[1] Below is a family tree showing the relationship of the languages mentioned in this paper.

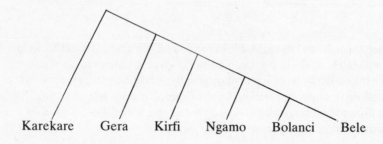

Karekare   Gera   Kirfi   Ngamo   Bolanci   Bele

2 Ngamo subject pronoun tone

2.1 Comparative background

Person, number, and gender of subjects in all these languages is marked by preverbal subject pronouns. These subject pronouns are generally analyzed as proclitics rather than inflectional prefixes. All these languages are tone languages with two contrastive tones.[2]

Of interest here is the tonal relation between the subject pronouns and the first syllable of the verb. In the reconstructed system and in most of the modern languages, tone of the verb can be predicted from the form of the verbal root (Schuh 1977). Only disyllabic verbs in the perfect aspect will be considered here. The only reconstructed disyllabic root shapes are *CVCu*, *CVCa*, *CVVCu* and *CVCCu*. All these languages have the tone pattern low-high for the latter three types. Karekare has this pattern for reconstructed *CVCu* verbs as well, but all the other languages have high-high for this type of verb. Following are examples of verbs of each root structure from Karekare and Bolanci. The verbs have a perfect suffix > *-ko* and the Bolanci citations have a suffix *-yí* used with transitive verbs when no object is expressed.

	CVCu	*CVCa*	*CVVCu*	*CVCCu*
	'hit'	'shoot'	'forgive'	'sew'
Karekare	dùk-kâu	bàsáa-kàu	yàafú-kàu	dànɗú-kàu
Bolanci	dúw-wòo-yí	bàsáa-wòo-yí	yàapú-wòo-yí	dònɗú-wòo-yí

Whereas the verb root is tonally uniform throughout the paradigm[3], the tones on the subject pronouns must be reconstructed as high in some persons, low in others: the first person singular pronoun must be reconstructed as low; the second persons singular (masculine and feminine) and the first and second persons plural must be reconstructed as high. In the reconstructed system, no subject pronouns are required in third person, but many modern languages now do require special third person pronouns. It appears that in the reconstructed system, there were optional third person pronouns which were reduced forms of the independent pronouns. Used as subject proclitics these third person pronouns had low tone.

The following Karekare paradigm will serve to illustrate what must be a system very close to the reconstructed system. We would expect the third person plural *sú* to have low tone. It has probably shifted to high on analogy with the high tone first and second persons. All the third person pronouns are optional in modern Karekare. For the *-an-* suffix with plural subjects, see note 3.

Karekare

'I shot'	*nà bàsáa-kàu*	'we shot'	*mú bàs-án-kàu*
'you (m.s.) shot'	*ká bàsáa-kàu*	'you (p.) shot'	*kú bàs-án-kàu*
'you (f.s.) shot'	*čí bàsáa-kàu*		
'he shot'	*(sà) bàsáa-kàu*	'they shot'	*(sú) bàs-án-kàu*
'she shot'	*(tà) bàsáa-kàu*		

As might be expected, a number of the modern languages have levelled out the tones on the subject pronouns. All the languages I know of where this has taken place have shifted all pronouns to low tone, apparently on analogy with the first person singular. A paradigm from Kirfi will illustrate this. In Kirfi, third person subject pronouns are obligatory when a noun subject is not present.

Kirfi

'I stepped'	*nà làɓɓú-wò*	'we stepped'	*mù làɓɓ-ín-kò*
'you (m.s.) stepped'	*kà làɓɓú-wò*	'you (p.) stepped'	*kù làɓɓ-ín-kò*
'you (f.s.) stepped'	*šì làɓɓú-wò*		
'he stepped'	*šì làɓɓú-wò*	'they stepped'	*sù làɓɓ-ín-kò*
'she stepped'	*tà làɓɓú-wò*		

There is little doubt that the system illustrated by Karekare represents the more archaic system. The principle upon which this conclusion rests has been called by Hetzron (1976) the "principle of archaic heterogeneity." Hetzron states this principle as follows:

"If a number of cognate languages each have a similar system to its homologues in the other languages in some respects, but different in other respects — unless one can find a clear conditioning factor for differentiation — the relatively most heterogeneous system might be considered the most archaic, the closest to the ancestor, and the more homogeneous ones might be assumed to have arisen as a result of simplification." (p. 93).

The Karekare system (and that of several other languages) is tonally the more heterogeneous, and there are no factors which could possibly account for the tonal differentiation of pronouns. Hence, it must be the more archaic.

2.2   Paradigmatic displacement in Ngamo

Ngamo, like Karekare, shows differing tones from one person to another.

Unlike Karekare this differentiation is not realized on the subject pronouns, but on the verb root. The subject pronouns are much more like
those in Kirfi in that they have low tone in all first and second persons.
Use of third person subject pronouns is optional. The third person
pronouns resemble the independent pronouns, having high tone in the
singular masculine and feminine and a termination -*ní* in the plural.[4] In
the following paradigm the reconstructed perfect suffix *-ko* does not
appear in the persons with singular subjects. This is regular for certain
classes of Ngamo verbs and is unrelated to the tone of the first syllable.

Ngamo

'I shot'	*nè bàsâ*	'we shot'	*mù bás-àn-kô*
'you (m.s.) shot'	*kò básâ*	'you (p.) shot'	*ŋgù bás-àn-kô*
'you (f.s.) shot'	*šì básâ*		
'he shot'	*(sí) bàsâ*	'they shot'	*(zùní) bàs-àn-kô*
'she shot'	*(té) bàsâ*		

Note that the tones of the first syllables of the verbs correspond
perfectly to the paradigmatic tonal system of the reconstructed subject
pronouns, illustrated above by Karekare. Thus, while Ngamo has regularized the tones in its subject pronoun paradigm, the original heterogeneous tone pattern is retained, having been shifted to the verb roots.

3 Bele object pronoun vowels

3.1 Comparative background

In the perfect aspect, pronoun direct objects are inserted between the
verb root and the reconstructed perfect marker, *-ko*. The following
Bolanci paradigm will illustrate this:

Bolanci

'he shot me'	*bàsáa-náa-wó*	'he shot us'	*bàsáa-mú-wó*
'he shot you (m.s.)'	*bàsá-káa-wó*	'he shot you (p.)'	*bàsáa-kú-wó*
'he shot you (f.s.)'	*bàsáa-ší-wó*		
'he shot him'	*bàsáa-nì-wò*	'he shot them'	*bàsáa-sú-wó*
'he shot her'	*bàsáa-táa-wó*		

The vowels of the object pronouns should probably be reconstructed as
short in all persons[5], but other than this the Bolanci object pronouns
illustrate not only the position of the object pronouns but also the vowel
quality and tones of the reconstructed object pronoun paradigm. Note

especially the low tone on the third masculine singular pronoun as opposed to high tone in all other persons.

Although pronoun vowels differ from person to person, almost all the object pronouns could be distinguished from each other by the consonants alone. Within singular persons the only pair which would not remain distinct if the vowel distinctions were neutralized are first singular and third masculine singular.[6] In a number of languages the vowel distinctions have been lost. One such language is Gera. Here, only the singular persons have been levelled. The plural persons retain the original -*u*. The reconstructed *-*ko* perfect marker has been replaced by -*mí*, a morpheme of unknown origin.

Gera

'he caught me'	*sì táw-nì-mí*	'he caught us'	*sì táw-mbù-mí*
'he caught you (m.s.)'	*sì táw-kì-mí*	'he caught you (p.)'	*sì táw-kùn-mí*[8]
'he caught you (f.s.)'	*sì táw-ši-mí*		
'he caught him'	*sì táw-sì-mí*	'he caught them'	*sì táw-sùn-mí*[8]
'he caught her'	*sì táw-ɗì-mí*[7]		

Gera has resolved the problem of the potential homophony of first and third persons singular by replacing third person masculine -*n*- with -*s*- on analogy with the third singular masculine subject and independent pronouns. The vowel -*i*- and low tone would appear to be on the model of the reconstructed third masculine singular *ni*, but this is the very pronoun which has been replaced in the new paradigm. The exact model for the levelling remains open to question, but Gera (and some other languages) show a preference for the vowel -*i* with low tone on bound pronouns elsewhere, viz. the singular subject pronouns have been levelled to become almost identical to the object pronouns. Compare the following subject paradigm with subject paradigms of the languages in section 1.

Gera

'I slaughtered'	*nì ɓâɗ-mí*	'we slaughtered'	*mù ɓâɗ-ìi-mí*
'you (m.s.) slaughtered'	*kì ɓâɗ-mí*	'you (p.) slaughtered'	*kù ɓâɗ-ìi-mí*
'you (f.s.) slaughtered'	*ši ɓâɗ-mí*		
'he slaughtered'	*sì ɓâɗ-mí*	'they slaughtered'	*sù ɓâɗ-ìi-mí*
'she slaughtered'	*tì ɓâɗ-mí*		

3.2   Paradigmatic displacement in Bele

Bele retains the reconstructed vowel and tone distinctions of the object pronouns, but as in the case of Ngamo subject tones, they do not appear in the reconstructed position in the paradigm. Consider the following paradigm:[9]

Bele

'he shot me'	*hì bàahí-ná-ŋó*	'he shot us'	*hì bàahí-má-ŋú*
'he shot you (m.s.)'	*hì bàahí-ká-ŋó*	'he shot you (p.)'	*hì bàahí-ká-ŋú*
'he shot you (f.s.)'	*hì bàahí-šá-ŋí*		
'he shot him'	*hí bàahí-nà-ŋì*	'he shot them'	*hì bàahí-há-ŋú*
'he shot her'	*hì bàahí-tá-ŋó*		

Here, the pronouns all have the vowel *-a-*, probably on analogy with the original first person singular pronoun. The original vowels of the pronouns now appear as the vowel on the **-ko* perfect marker, realized in Bele as *-ŋV*.[10] The final *-o* in three of the singular persons is not the *-o* of the perfect **ko*, but rather original **-a*, which has been widely shifted to *-o* in word final position in this group of languages. Even the aberrant low tone of the third masculine singular pronoun has been shifted to the perfect suffix though it is also retained on the pronoun.

4   Conditions for paradigmatic displacement

Two means of reducing relatively non-functional variations in paradigms have been illustrated here. By far the most common, both among West Chadic Languages as well as elsewhere in the world, is analogical levelling of original distinctions on the model of one or more members of the paradigm. The second, far less frequent, type of resolution of paradigmatic variation is to level the variation at its original position while shifting it to some other point. Two illustrations were given: Ngamo subject pronoun tone and Bele object pronoun vowels.

   Clearly, levelling with displacement and simple levelling without displacement are not mutually exclusive types of historical alteration which may affect paradigms since we have seen both operate to alter one and the same reconstructable point in a paradigm. Since displacement is by far the less common, it stands to reason that among all types of paradigmatic variation subject to levelling, only a subset of these types would be subject to displacement, and even there only as a less favored alternative to simple levelling.

   To date, only a few cases of displacement have been identified[11] so it is not likely that we can state all the factors that would be requisite to its taking place. At least two factors seem necessary, however: (1) there must be a site for the displaced distinction to be moved to, and (2) the displaced distinction cannot disrupt original distinctions to the point of impairing communicative efficiency.

The first point is obvious enough. Thus, if tonal distinctions are to be shifted there must be adjacent tone bearing segments and the tones on these segments must be distinct in at least some cases from the tones to be shifted. Were they identical, no shift could be detected. If a vowel distinction is to be displaced, there should be adjacent syllables containing vowels which are distinct from the displaced vowels. Another possibility would be for new vowels to be inserted to form a new syllable, e.g. one could envision a case such as the following:

*CaC > CaCa
*CiC > CaCi
*CuC > CaCu

This would require that the word structure be such that a new vowel could be added. For example, if the adjacent syllable already contained a vowel and the language had a restriction against sequences of vowels, no new vowel could be added.

The second point is the more important. Consider a case such as the Ngamo tonal displacement. Many African languages mark tense/aspect distinctions by tonal changes. A displacment of the tones which mark tense/aspect by tones from another syllable could obliterate important distinctions. In the case of the Bole-Tangale group, however, verb tone plays no such role. In fact, for the most part it has no functional role at all. Why Ngamo should choose to shift tonal variation from the subject pronoun to the verb is not clear, but it certainly has had no effect on communicative efficiency.

Similarly, in the case of Bele object pronouns, the following morpheme is the perfect marker *-ko. The vowel on this morpheme was originally *-o throughout. No other similar morpheme could appear in this position, so replacement of the original *-o by the pronoun vowels created no confusion. By contrast, consider the Bele subject pronouns. Like Gera (see end of section 3.1), Bele has levelled vowel distinctions in the singular subject pronouns. They are *nì* 'I', *kì* 'you (m.s.)', *šì* 'you (f.s.)', *hì* 'he', *tì* 'she'. Here, the original vowel distinctions have simply been lost. Had they been displaced to the following syllable as the vowels of the object pronouns were, they would have replaced the initial vowel of the verb root, making homophones of all those verbs distinguished only by the vowel of the first syllable. In addition, every verb in the language would have at least two alternants (three if the plural pronouns were involved), a high price to pay for achieving uniformity in the vowels of the subject pronouns.

Notes

1. I collected data on these languages intermittently from 1973–1975 while I was a Research Fellow at Ahmadu Bello University working in the Centre for the Study of Nigerian Languages at Abdullahi Bayero College (now Bayero University College). My thanks to Paul Newman and some of my colleagues at UCLA for comments on an earlier draft of this paper.

2. The tones are high, marked by acute accent (´), and low, marked by grave accent(`). There are also falling tones, marked by circumflex accent (^), which are analyzed as high-low on a single syllable. Double vowels indicate long vowels.

3. The tones of all verbs other than *CVCu* verbs do remain uniform as stated here. When the subject of a verb is plural, the verb replaces the final vowel of the root by a suffix reconstructable as *-an-*. When this suffix is added, even *CVCu* verbs take low-high tones, e.g. Bolanci *màté dùw-án-gòo-yí* 'they beat'.

4. When cited in isolation the singular third person pronouns have falling tone: *sî* 'him', *tê* 'her'. This may simply be a phrase final intonational phenomenon. The third person plural pronoun is *nzùní* 'them', differing from the form used as a subject by the presence of prenasalization of the initial *z*.

5. The vowel lengths I recorded for pronouns in my field notes, from which the paradigm here was taken, disagree with those given in Lukas (1970–1972:125). Lukas gives long vowels on all pronouns except third masculine singular *-nì-*. Lukas and I have recorded the same vowel qualities and tones throughout.

6. Even here the tonal difference could keep these persons distinct. I do not know of any language where this tonal distinction has been exploited in this way, however. As one might expect, the tonally aberrant third singular masculine pronoun has frequently been brought into line with the high tone of the other persons.

7. The expected feminine pronoun would be *-ti-*. The shift of medial *t* >*ɗ* is quite regular in Gera, e.g. *bòɗá* 'ashes', cf. Kirfi *bùtó*.

8. The plural Gera object pronouns are historically the same as the plural possessive pronouns, which are *-mbí, -kùní, -sùní*. These plural pronouns can be reconstructed as *-mùní, *-kùní, *-sùní* respectively. The first person plural pronoun has undergone the following historical development: *-mùní* > *-mní* > *-mmí* > *-mbí* (> *-mbú* before labial). These pronouns have the *-nV* plural termination already mentioned in connection with Ngamo in section 2.2.

9. There has been a regular sound shift *s* > *h* in Bele. The paradigm here illustrates this in the third singular masculine subject pronoun, the third plural object pronoun, and the verb root (cf. the Karekare, Ngamo, and Bolanci paradigms above where the verb 'shoot' is used).

10. The nasal *-ŋ-* instead of *-k-* suggests a nasal originally preceded the *-k-*. Cf. *hì bàahí-kò* 'he shot' but *màahá bàaháŋò* < *bàas-án-kò* 'they shot'. There are two or three candidates for what this nasal may have been. Perhaps the simplest explanation, suggested by Paul Newman, is an extension of the plural perfect marker *-ŋV* < *-n-kV* throughout the paradigm.

11. A few other cases similar to those illustrated here exist in the Bole-Tangale group. I do not know of any cases outside this group where the two features of these examples are found: both regularization of the original point of irregularity and retention of the irregularity by shifting it to some other point. Akin to this is umlaut in second and third person singular in Germanic verbs under the influence of high vowels previously appearing in the inflectional suffixes, e.g. *du trägst* but *ich trage*, and labialization and palatalization of root consonants in Ethiopian Semitic Gurage languages under the

influence of original *-u:* and *-i:* suffixes, e.g. *säpäru:* > *säpʷär* 'one broke' (my thanks to Robert Hetzron for providing this example). The difference between these examples and the Chadic examples is that the original conditioning factor for the displaced distinction is not present any longer, let alone having been regularized in some way.

References

Hetzron, Robert
  1976 "Two principles of genetic reconstruction", *Lingua* 38:89–108.
Lukas, Johannes
  1971 "Über das erweiterte Verb im Bolanci (Nordnigerien)", *Journal of African Languages* 10.1:1–14.
  1970–1972 "Die Personalia und das primäre Verb im Bolanci (Nordnigerien)", *Afrika und Übersee* 54:237–286; 55:114–139.
Newman, Paul
  1974 *The Kanakuru language* (= *West African Language Monographs* 9) (Leeds: Institute of Modern English Language Studies, University of Leeds).
  1977 "Chadic classification and reconstructions", *Afroasiatic Linguistics* 5.1:1–42.
Newman, Paul — Roxana Ma Newman (eds.)
  1977 *Papers in Chadic linguistics* (Leiden: Afrika-Studiecentrum).
Schuh, Russell G.
  1977 "West Chadic verb classes", in Newman — Newman (eds.) 1977:143–166.
  1978 *Bole-Tangale languages of the Bauchi area* (=*Marburger Studien zur Afrika- und Asienkunde* A 13) (Berlin:Reimer).
  n.d. "Ngamo perfect aspect", Ms.

SARAH GREY THOMASON

Morphological instability, with and without language contact*

Introduction

The claim has often been made that a language's morphology tends to be especially stable, by contrast to its syntax and phonology and, in particular, to its lexicon.[1] This claim has two aspects: on the one hand, the morphology is supposed to be resistant to internally-motivated changes, except for analogic changes that do not attack the basic structural organization of the morphological subsystems; and, on the other hand, the morphology is supposed to be immune to contact-induced language change, except for the intrusion of derivational affixes which make their way into the lexicon as attachments on loanwords. The hypothesized resistance to internally-motivated change is embodied, I think, in the view that the morphology, as the most highly structured part of the grammar, has internal cohesion that protects it from erosion. If this is true, then the morphology should change more slowly than other parts of the grammar, and the traditional wisdom holds that it does indeed do so. Internal systematic cohesion should also account for a lack of foreign interference in morphological structures. Again, the belief that there is such a lack is firmly entrenched in both the theory and the methodology of historical linguistics. Boas once commented, "I do not know . . . of any observations which would point to a radical modification of the morphological traits of a language through the influence of another language" (1911 [1966]:45)[2]; probably most historical linguists today would echo that sentiment.

The stable-morphology hypothesis has interesting implications for the study of genetic relationship in languages. If the morphology does change much more slowly than the rest of the language, and if it is not liable to be drastically restructured under the influence of other languages, then we should expect to find distantly related languages that share much morphology and little of anything else, in particular vocabulary. This in turn would mean that we should consider the use of shared morphological structure alone — not necessarily shared actual morphemes, but shared patterns even without cognate morphemes — as primary evidence for the establishment of a genetic relationship. In fact, this possibility for expanding the range of admissible evidence for genetic relationship has been explored only once in a careful enough way to impress many linguists favorably: in two articles (1955, 1956) Hymes proposed using morphological congruence as a primary tool for demonstrating genetic relationship in the Na-Déné group of languages (Athapaskan, Eyak, Tlingit, and Haida).[3]

This paper examines the basic premise, namely, that the morphology tends to resist both internally- and externally-motivated change. The results of this study indicate, as I will argue below, that morphological congruence without cognate morphemes cannot constitute presumptive evidence of genetic relationship. The argument rests on two conclusions. First, the morphology is by no means so stable as to justify the assumption that lexical cognates may vanish almost entirely while the morphology holds firm; and second, though much less vulnerable to contact-induced change than the lexicon, and somewhat less vulnerable than (at least) superficial aspects of the phonology and syntax, the morphology may be restructured to a considerable degree through the influence of another language.

1   Internally-motivated morphological change

I will not argue that the morphology changes as fast as other parts of the grammar, partly because I do not know of any way in which one could compare explicitly the rates of change in different parts of the grammar. Moreover, it still seems plausible that the more structured parts of the grammar will resist internally-motivated change to some extent; the Praguian notion of internal cohesion in a reasonably symmetrical phonological inventory should carry over into the morphology, and in an elaborate morphology the various well-integrated inflectional categories are likely to have a high functional load and to be, as a consequence, relatively stable.[4] However, even allowing for this tendency, one will hardly find a language which undergoes drastic changes in other parts of its grammar without undergoing considerable change in the morphology as well. Any reasonably diversified language family shows roughly comparable degrees of variation in all its grammatical subsystems.

The Indoeuropean language family is an obvious case in point. It is quite possible, by comparing the modern Indoeuropean languages, to identify a number of common typological traits. Among the most typical ones, in the areas of phonology and morphology, are the nearly universal existence of a voiced : voiceless opposition in stops; the presence of several fricatives, usually with some voiced : voiceless pairs; predominance of apical consonants, and a fairly equal distribution of labials and velars; lack of affricates other than apical stop plus sibilant; lack of vowel harmony, glottalized sounds, and post-velar consonants; lack of tones; numerous suffixes, a few derivational prefixes, but no infixes or reduplicative affixes; noun classes based on biological gender; a universal singular: plural opposition; lack of exclusive vs. inclusive 'we' and of grammatical gender in verb inflection; and isolating or flexional — but not agglutinative — morphology. Inspection of these common features, however, shows that they largely belong to typologically unmarked categories. This is not surprising in a family with the antiquity and the vast geographical range of Indoeuropean: the marked features that now occur in Indoeuropean languages are restricted to particular subgroups, both areal and genetic.

This is not to say that common trends cannot be identified in the history of Indoeuropean languages. In the morphology, the general pattern of development from flexional to isolating morphology is well known. But this progression is much more advanced in some branches of the family than others, and the least elaborate inflectional systems in modern Indoeuropean languages — those of the western European languages, say — bear little resemblance to the most elaborate systems, such as noun declension in most Balto-Slavic languages. It is not just a matter of a reduction in the number of cases or gender distinctions; often, the categories themselves have changed. In English, gender is gone as a morphological category (though not a syntactic one) in substantives; in Russian, to take an extreme example on the other side, the inherited Indoeuropean noun classification systems based on stem-final phoneme and biological gender have been supplemented by a new one based on animacy; and a phonological distinction between hard and soft stems has also acquired morphological significance in the declensional system. So although we can make some generally valid statements about inflectional changes in Indoeuropean — none of the languages have undergone systematic changes resulting in significant agglutination, except where intensive foreign interference can be established — the amount of current specific agreement in morphological structure among geographically separated subgroups of the family is quite small.

This degree of divergence is matched, but not obviously exceeded, by lexical developments. For instance, a 218-word diagnostic vocabulary list turns up forty English-Russian cognate pairs. Some of the words have undergone such drastic phonological modifications that they might not be spotted as cognates without prior knowledge of their etymologies, but at least thirty pairs are quite obvious, and they reveal numerous recurring sound correspondences.

A warning is in order here. Any assertion that the changes producing the divergent Indoeuropean grammatical systems were internally motivated would be risky, since investigators of virtually all Indoeuropean subgroups have claimed foreign interference in some developments. Traditional historical methodology in linguistics is so heavily biased in favor of internal causation that the absence of proof of interference might be thought to be sufficient evidence for internal causation. This position is probably untenable, but in the present case we at least have no compelling reason to claim significant foreign interference in the morphological history of Indoeuropean as a family, given the overall pattern of flexional-to-isolating development. The possibility, or probability, remains that the particular outcomes of this development in different Indoeuropean subgroups were determined partly by the influence of neighboring non-Indoeuropean languages. And, although Indoeuropean languages may have undergone more, and more different, types of interference as their speakers spread out than most language families are exposed to, there is no indication that Indoeuropean subgroups show an unusual amount of diversification by comparison to other families.

As another example of morphological diversification, consider Uralic, a relatively compact family whose members have a much closer lexical correspondence than modern Indoeuropean languages have. Common Uralic, according to Collinder (1965:54), had about six cases in its noun declension. Of the modern languages, some have developed much more extensive case systems: Finnish has fifteen or sixteen, and Hungarian is said to have twenty-three, though some of these are not productive. Other languages in the family have lost ground in this sub-system, e.g. Northern Ostyak (a Ugric language), which now has only two inflected cases. Most Uralic languages also add possessive suffixes to nouns, which form agglutinative constructions with the case suffixes. But the order of affixation varies in the different languages: in Finnish and Mordvin, for instance, case suffix precedes possessive suffix; in Ugric languages, case suffix follows possessive; and in the Permian languages some case suffixes precede the possessive, and some follow it:

Mordvin:	inessive sg./1st sg.:	*kudo+so+n*	'in my house'
	inessive sg./2nd sg.:	*kudo+so+t*	'in your house'
	ablative sg./1st sg.:	*kudo+do+n*	'from my house'
	ablative sg./2nd sg.:	*kudo+do+t*	'from your house'

Vogul
(Ob-Ugric): 1st sg./loc. sg.:   *haap +um +t*   'in my boat'
            2nd sg./loc. sg.:   *haap +yn +t*   'in your boat'
            1st sg./dat. sg.:   *haap +um +n*   'to my boat'
            2nd sg./dat. sg.:   *haap +yn +n*   'to your boat'

Votyak
(Permian):   dat. sg.:   *murt +ly*   'to the man'
            inst. sg.:   *murt +en*   'with the man'
            2nd sg.:   *murt +ed*   'your man'
            2nd sg./dat. sg.:   *murt +ed +ly*   'to your man'
            inst. sg./2nd sg.:   *murt +en +yd*   'with your man' (*+yd*
                                          and *+ed* are
                                          allomorphs of the 2nd
                                          sg. possessive
                                          morpheme)

Now, this sort of variation immediately suggests that the affixation of cases and possessives is a relatively recent event in the history of the family, and the Permian system calls the "degree of boundness" (cf. Weinreich 1968:29) of at least some of the suffixes into question. But even if some case markers and/or possessives should turn out to be enclitics rather than suffixes, the pattern of historical development in Uralic is clear: the family as a whole shows a progression toward an agglutinative morphology, but within that general movement considerable variation can be found.[5]

To take a final example, the Salishan languages of the Pacific Northwest in North America diverge in the order in which they affix person markers to verbs. Most or all of them affix both subject and object markers, but in at least three different relative orders: both suffixed, object preceding subject (Lillooet, Tillamook, Shuswap); both prefixed, object preceding subject (Kalispel); subject prefixed and object suffixed (Cowlitz, Okanagan).[6] As with Uralic case and possessive affixes, these varying orders may indicate a recent development of the systems of personal affixes, but again the general picture is one of divergent specific changes within a common pattern of development.

Some of these developments in Uralic and Salishan may well have been influenced by foreign contact; both North Asia and the Pacific Northwest are well-known Sprachbund areas. So, in considering the implications of the changes for genetic theory, we need to keep in mind both the fact that the divergences are variations on a single pattern within each family, and the strong probability that foreign interference is itself a virtually universal factor in linguistic diversification.

2   Externally-motivated morphological change

In examining contact-induced language change, it is important to recognize, first of all, that there are two fundamentally different types of foreign interference. One type occurs in a target language as the result of imperfect shift to the target language by speakers of some other language(s); this type of interference is most often (though too narrowly) known as substratum influence, though of course not all shifting groups can be classified as substrata. The other type of interference is borrowing — the incorporation of foreign elements into the speakers' native language. The results of these two types of interference are quite different in nature. In shifting to a target language, speakers typically acquire vocabulary first; phonology, morphology, syntax, and even lexical semantic structure come later. Accordingly, interference in a target language resulting from shift may not include much vocabulary, but it will include superficial phonological and syntactic features and, if extensive enough, morphological features as well. In borrowing situations, however, cultural pressure invariably leads first to lexical borrowing and only later, if at all, to borrowing in the more highly structured parts of the grammar.[7]

Unfortunately, but not surprisingly, situations of intensive cultural contact between speakers of two or more languages are not always so simple as to permit an easy determination of the source of an interference feature. Target language speakers, especially if they are newcomers to an area, are likely to be borrowing words from an indigenous language even while that language's speakers are shifting to the target language and incorporating some of their own native features into their version of the target language. If the shift is a slow process, and if a large number of target language native speakers are bilingual in the indigenous language, then the target language may borrow structural features as well as words. In addition, if the shifting group is large and/or prestigious (i.e. a superstratum rather than a substratum), target language speakers will be more inclined to imitate their version of the target language, and in that way structural features from the indigenous language may become fixed in the target language as a whole. Except in cases of very rapid shift, such complications are probably the rule rather than the exception. Nevertheless, even if the two types of interference often occur simultaneously, they represent two quite different historical processes.

In both types, morphological interference, particularly in inflectional systems, is less likely to occur than lexical, phonological, and syntactic interference. However, contact-induced changes do appear even in elaborate inflectional systems, and sometimes these changes are extensive enough to bring about considerable restructuring of the morphology.

A case showing moderate interference in the morphology as a result of language shift is that of the Ethiopic group of Semitic languages, described by Leslau in two articles (1945, 1952). When Semitic speakers conquered Ethiopia, the territory was occupied primarily by speakers of Cushitic languages. After the conquest, these Cushitic languages formed a substratum in the development of the Ethiopic languages, as Cushitic speakers gradually shifted to Semitic. The result, as Leslau observes, is that "the student of the Ethiopic languages, even though he knows that these languages belong to the Semitic group, cannot help being struck by their non-Semitic character" (1945:59).

Some of the morphological interference features mentioned by Leslau involve new means of expressing functional categories that already existed in Ethiopic: plural formation by reduplication of the second root-consonant; abstract and other derivational categories formed by suffixation; a negative perfect formation with a prefix-plus-suffix combination; a causative formation with a double prefix; and a frequentative stem formation by reduplication of the second root-consonant. These Ethiopic innovations match Cushitic and differ markedly from corresponding formations in other Semitic languages, though they hardly constitute drastic restructuring of the morphological system. They do, however, show that a target language's morphology can be adjusted to agree more closely with the morphology of the learners' native tongue, where there is already a high degree of functional correspondence between the two systems.[8]

But what happens when the two morphological systems do not correspond? Leslau's case study provides a clue to the answer. Where Cushitic interference leads to a change in the inventory of Ethiopic morphological categories, the result is almost always a reduction in their number. In contrast to other Semitic languages, Ethiopic has lost the dual number almost entirely; South Ethiopic has no consistent gender distinctions; and South Ethiopic dialects of the Gurage region have no plural markers on nouns. Leslau cites only one innovation resulting from Cushitic influence that clearly establishes a new morphological distinction in Ethiopic: this is the emergence, in some of the languages, of a special future tense in opposition to the present, in contrast to the typical Semitic "imperfect", which is used to refer to events in both present and future time.

Investigation of other case studies, including several discussed by Weinreich (1968:§2.3) and more recent examples like the one described by Gumperz and Wilson (1971), indicate that the Cushitic-Ethiopic situation reflects a general pattern, both for changes resulting from language shift and for changes resulting from direct borrowing: where the source language and the recipient language do not show functional congruence in their morphologies, the recipient language's morphological categories are likely to undergo reduction under the pressure of source-language interference, but they are not so likely to undergo corresponding expansion to match the source language's categories.

Exceptions to this pattern can be found. The most striking cases of morphological expansion under the influence of another language seem to be those in which a borrowing language is under intensive long-term pressure from the source language, with very widespread bilingualism among the borrowing language's speakers. Frequently, in such cases, the recipient language's speakers are gradually shifting to the source language, and a typical feature of these situations is the lack of a readily available standard language that might provide a model to inhibit recipient-language restructuring.

One instance of such restructuring, as described by Dawkins (1916), is that of the Modern Greek dialects spoken in Asia Minor.[9] These dialects are surrounded by Turkish and have been losing ground to Turkish, both linguistically and in terms of speaker figures, since at least the fifteenth century. The Greek speakers Dawkins interviewed were mostly bilingual in Turkish, and the historical record shows a steady, though slow, process of shift from Greek to Turkish through the centuries. In those Greek villages without a Greek school where standard Greek might be taught, Dawkins found some startling evidence of turkicization of the Greek dialects' grammar. For instance, Turkish derivational suffixes and even Turkish personal suffixes are frequently added to Greek verbs in these dialects.

Some of the interference, predictably, involved the loss of Greek morphological categories which were lacking in Turkish. Examples are the loss of case and gender inflection in adjectives used attributively (Turkish has no adjective-noun agreement) and the loss of grammatical gender even in nouns in the most-affected dialects (Turkish has no gender).

More unusual is the appearance of agglutinative structures in noun and verb inflection in several villages of Cappadocia. Noun formations consisting of noun stem + number suffix + case suffix, e.g. *nék +ez +yu* 'of the wives', correspond exactly to Turkish formations, e.g. *qïz +lar +ïn* 'of the girls', and contrast sharply with typical Indoeuropean — including other Greek dialects' — flexional patterns. This development, which surely constitutes "a radical modification of the morphological traits of a language through the influence of another language"[10], is accompanied by extensive interference in phonology and syntax, including such typical Turkish features as the development of vowel harmony and of SOV and relative clause + head noun word order patterns. In addition, the Asia Minor Greek dialects have vast numbers of loanwords from Turkish.

It may be that extensive interference leading to morphological expansion is actually confined to such long-term borrowing situations, and that it never occurs in a target language through the process of language shift. The most plausible candidates for cases of drastic morphological restructuring through shift might be pidgins and creoles; for instance, the English-based creole (ex-pidgin) Neomelanesian has a personal pronoun system built up with English morphemes and containing categories like singular : dual : trial : plural number and exclusive : inclusive 'we'. But it is questionable whether English, in contributing its lexicon to the pidgin, constituted a real target language in the usual sense of the word, since social factors militated against the acquisition of English itself, as a whole language. The same objection can be raised with other pidgins and creoles.

The Asia Minor Greek case, however, shows that contact-induced morphological restructuring involving expansion does occur, and the Ethiopic case, together with many similar studies, suggests that restructuring involving reduction in the morphology is a rather common occurrence.

3   Conclusion: Can morphological structure alone be used as a criterion for genetic relationship?

The morphological evidence adduced by Hymes (1955, 1956) in support of the hypothesized Na-Déné genetic grouping consists of a careful positional analysis of categories in complex verb forms. These verb forms comprise a maximum of thirteen prefixes and one suffix, though most of the languages lack one or more of the prefixes. The categories expressed include, among others, personal (subject, direct object, and indirect object); tense, aspect, mode; number (plural); and adverbials. The ordering of all these elements matches exactly in all the languages, but the shapes of the actual morphemes do not correspond in the posited Na-Déné subgroups. We are not concerned with evaluating the lexical evidence that has been offered, both before and since Hymes' articles appeared, in support of the Na-Déné hypothesis. The question here is this: can the precise morphological congruence in the elaborate Na-Déné verb complex constitute, all by itself, sufficient evidence of the genetic relationship of Athapaskan–Eyak and Tlingit? (Not Haida; see note 3.) The answer, I think, is no. As we saw above, language families that, like Indoeuropean, have undergone enough lexical diversification to reduce their cognate count to forty in a 218-word diagnostic list have also undergone a comparable amount of morphological diversification; and Indoeuropean languages which retain sufficient morphological structure still share cognate inflectional morphemes. All the evidence available from well-documented language families indicates that morphological diversification goes along with diversification elsewhere in the grammar, and historical linguistics will be in a sorry state if we must assume a radically different situation in language families that have no recorded history.[11] In other words, the Na-Déné positional correspondences are too exact, in the absence of a comparable number of lexical correspondences, to be the only relic of a distant genetic relationship. There is no language, as far as I know, that can be shown to have retained an elaborate set of morphological structures while replacing, or altering phonetically beyond recognition, all the actual morphemes.[12]

But if the order of affixes in Na-Déné verb forms is not due to direct genetic inheritance, how can we account for the spectacular agreement in the various languages? Chance is out of the question; what remains is convergence through contact-induced language change. To see whether convergence is a plausible hypothesis in this instance, we need to consider both the general likelihood of such a process, based on evidence from other cases, and the specific likelihood here, based on areal linguistic features.

Cases of clear one-way interference, as in Ethiopic (from Cushitic) and Asia Minor Greek (from Turkish), suggest that significant overall morphological expansion is likely to occur only in borrowing situations — and, therefore, that it should be accompanied by massive lexical borrowing, since words will be borrowed before morphological patterns. This framework does not fit the Na-Déné situation well, because here the problem is lack of lexical correspondences. However, as we have seen, the rearrangement and replacement of morphological means of expressing already existing categories is likely to occur either in a target language through shift or in borrowing situations, given intensive enough contact between two or more groups of speakers. It is reasonable to suppose, then, that two unrelated or distantly related languages that share a number of relevant morphological categories[13] could arrive at a very close agreement in affix ordering through contact-induced language change. I do not believe that the Na-Déné languages could plausibly have achieved their matching affix orders without a close prior agreement in the categories expressed by the affixes, but there is some evidence to support an assumption that they did already have the relevant categories.

As was mentioned above, the languages of the Pacific Northwest form a well-known Sprachbund. Most of the Na-Déné languages are located somewhat to the north of the densest cluster of languages in this Sprachbund, but they share many of the same typological features. Some of the most striking features are phonological — for instance, full series of glottalized stops, many velars and post-velars but few labial consonants, and lateral affricates. Others are morphological, and they include many of the morphological categories found in the Na-Déné verb complex: person-markers for subject, object, and often for indirect object as well; tense-aspect markers; and various adverbial affixes. Moreover, strings of prefixes are very common. Now, the actual ordering of affixes in the various languages is by no means uniform. Salishan, for instance, as we saw in paragraph 1, shows considerable variety in the ordering of personal affixes. But the presence of so many of the characteristic Na-Déné categories, together with the very widespread areal habit of putting affixes together in long strings, including many prefixes, makes it reasonable to assume that the Na-Déné languages had typologically similar structures to begin with; and that, in some former long-term situation of intensive contact, with either one-way interference or a Sprachbund-like convergence through mutual bilingualism, the Na-Déné languages evolved to a state of exact correspondence in categories and in their order within the verb complex.[14]

The question as to their ultimate genetic affiliation remains open. They may be genetically related. One or the other of the languages (treating Athapaskan-Eyak as a single language, i.e. Proto-Athapaskan-Eyak) may be related to one of the other Pacific Northwest groups — Salishan, Penutian, Wakashan, or Chemakuan. For that matter, of course, some or all of these — or none — may be related to each other. Whatever the answer to the genetic question might be, the extensive current morphological similarities in the Na-Déné languages are most likely to be due to contact-induced changes in systems that started out with a high level of agreement in morphological categories, and least likely to be due to direct genetic inheritance of the morphological categories in their present ordering relations.

Notes

* The idea for this paper arose out of an exchange of letters with Dell Hymes, and I owe whatever clarity my thinking on the subject has achieved to his acute comments. This does not, however, mean that he would agree with my conclusions.

1. See, for instance, the comment in Hymes (1956:634–635) to the effect that this view was held by Meillet, Sapir, Hoijer, Swadesh, et al.
2. Compare, in Weinreich (1968:29), similar quotations from Meillet and Sapir.
3. Research on Na-Déné since 1956 has resulted in a changed general view of Na-Déné relationships, though the genetic question is still a controversial one, at least with respect to Athapaskan-Eyak and Tlingit. The structural parallelisms that were previously assumed to link Haida with Athapaskan, Eyak, and Tlingit have largely evaporated in the light of new analyses of Haida (Michael E. Krauss, personal communication). Athapaskan and Eyak are now known to be genetically related, and the proof comes from traditional comparative-method sources (see Krauss 1976 for discussion). Hymes' analysis of Athapaskan, Eyak, and Tlingit positional categories is outdated in some details, but the basic outlines remain; so the question Hymes originally addressed is still a relevant one, even though the groups under consideration have in effect been reduced to two — Athapaskan-Eyak and Tlingit.
4. Even this cautious statement requires a caveat, since the inflectional morphology, while enjoying internal stability, is still liable to be radically restructured as a result of changes elsewhere in the grammar — notably in the phonology, as in the loss of case endings through a regular phonetic change that eliminates final syllables.
5. This account is somewhat oversimplified. Comrie (1976) shows that, although some Uralic case suffixes are certainly of recent origin, an original morpheme order CASE-+POSSESSIVE can be established for Uralic nouns. This original order has undergone changes in many of the languages, sometimes as a result of the later addition of new case suffixes, but sometimes — notably in Ob-Ugric — through reordering of old case and possessive suffixes.
6. Noonan (1976) points out that most Salish languages have V-o-s morpheme order within the verb, and he claims that the analysis of Kalispel as o-s-V is in error — that the forms in question are possessed nouns, not finite verbs (363–4). I am not a specialist in these difficult languages and so cannot judge the matter independently, but if Noonan . is right, the amount of variation in Salish affix ordering may be less than it appears here.
7. The framework for the analysis of contact-induced language change that I am using here is presented in detail in Thomason and Kaufman (1975 and forthcoming).
8. The importance of functional congruence in facilitating morphological interference is emphasized by Weinreich (1968:§2.3). Much of the pre-existing congruence in Semitic and Cushitic is explained, of course, by their relationship as two separate branches of the Afroasiatic language family.
9. This case is discussed in some detail in Thomason and Kaufman (1975 and forthcoming); see also Thomason and Kaufman 1976 for a description of Turkish phonological interference in these dialects.
10. Weinreich (1968:42) cites a study that parallels this Greek-Turkish case in a striking way: the morphology of Tadzhik (Persian), an Indoeuropean language of the Iranian subgroup, has been evolving from an isolating to an agglutinative type under the influence of the Turkic language Uzbek.
11. I do not mean to suggest, of course, that there will be no differences at all between the histories of well-documented language families and of largely undocumented ones, but only that it is still safe to project general inferences from the one group to the other.
12. Hymes (1955:21) quotes Lounsbury's comment on the great stability of affix order in Iroquoian morphology, and the relatively large amount of variability in the morphemes chosen to express the various affixal functions. This is of course a relevant point; but Iroquoian languages, unlike Na-Déné, show considerable lexical correspondence too,

and some affixes in verb complexes do correspond closely, even though many don't match.

13. I am using the phrase 'morphological category' loosely here, because I think the development is equally likely if some of the categories comprise only loosely bound, or even free, morphemes.

14. The suggestion that contact-induced changes are responsible for at least some Na-Déné morphological similarities is not new (see Krauss 1976:341 and the references cited there). Krauss concentrates, however, on the Na-Déné lexical dissimilarities and does not follow the line of argument presented here.

References

Boas, F.
1911 "Introduction", *Handbook of American Indian languages* (Washington: Government Printing Office). [Page reference in text to Preston Holder (ed.), *Franz Boas' Introduction and J. W. Powell's Indian linguistic families of America north of Mexico* (Lincoln: Nebraska UP).]
Christie, W. (ed.)
1976 *Current progress in historical linguistics: Proceedings of the 2nd International conference on Historical Linguistics* (Amsterdam: North-Holland).
Collinder, B.
1965 *An introduction to the Uralic languages* (Berkeley: California UP).
Comrie, B.
1976 "The ordering of case and possessive suffixes in the Uralic languages", Ms.
Dawkins, R. M.
1916 *Modern Greek in Asia Minor: A study of the dialects of Sílli, Cappadocia, and Phárasa with grammar, texts, translations and glossary* (Cambridge: Cambridge UP).
Gumperz, J. J. — R. W. Wilson
1971 "Convergence and creolization: A case from the Indo-Aryan/Dravidian border", in Hymes (ed.) 1971:151–167.
Hymes, D. H.
1955 "Positional analysis of categories: A frame for reconstruction", *Word* 11:10–23.
1956 "Na-Dene and positional analysis of categories", *AA* 58:624–638.
1971 (ed.) *Pidginization and creolization of languages* (Cambridge: Cambridge U.P.).
Krauss, M. E.
1976 "Na-Dene", in Sebeok (ed.) 1976:283–358.
Leslau, W.
1945 "The influence of Cushitic on the Semitic languages of Ethiopia: A problem of substratum", *Word* 1:59–82.
1952 "The influence of Sidamo on the Ethiopic languages of Gurage", *Language* 28:63–81.
Noonan, M.
1976 "On Proto-Salish word order: A reply to Ingram", *IJAL* 42:363–366.
Sebeok, T. A. (ed.)
1976 *Native languages of the Americas*, 1 (New York: Plenum).
Thomason, S. G. — T. Kaufman
1976 "Contact-induced language change: Loanwords and the borrowing language's pre-borrowing phonology", in Christie (ed.) 1976:167–179.

forthcoming   "Toward an adequate definition of creolization", Paper presented at the
            1975 International Conference on Pidgins and Creoles, Honolulu. [Currently
            under revision and expansion as a monograph entitled *Language contact, creoliza-
            tion and genetic linguistics.*]
Weinreich, U.
1968   *Languages in contact* (The Hague: Mouton).

JOSEF VACHEK

Problems of morphology seen from the structuralist and functionalist point of view

First of all, some delimitation of the subject to be treated here appears necessary.

In the present paper we exclude from our discussion of the morphological level of language all that is concerned with the word-formative analysis of words. In other words, morphology as delimited here deals with those modifications of words which do not change their lexico-semantic basis but are conditioned solely by the differences of the grammatical function performed by such words. To put the matter still differently, the centre of our attention in morphology will be paradigms, whether they use means commonly denoted as synthetic, inflexional (case endings of nouns, conjugational endings of verbs) or as analytical (prepositional phrases, grammaticalized positions of words within the sentence patterns, etc.). — It will be seen that this formulation is able to cover all the three "strategies" of linguistic research in morphology, as distinguished almost a quarter of a century ago by Hockett (1954), i.e. the WP-type, the IA-type, and the IP-type.

Admittedly, in any of the three strategies morphology is usually regarded as least problematic of all language levels. This is due to closer connection of words with facts of the extra-lingual reality than can be found in phonology (which, as is well known, does not deal with signs of this reality as wholes but — as was very aptly pointed out by Bühler (1931) — with diacritica of such signs). On the other hand, patterns of morphology appear to be less complex than those of syntax which reflect all complexity of facts and their relations observed in the said extra-lingual reality. This central position of morphology between phonology and syntax can perhaps account for the well-known fact that in practical language teaching greater stress is usually placed on morphology than on other language levels — one very often comes across simplistic classifications of paradigms into regular and irregular ones, with hardly any attention paid to the dynamism existing within the morphological system, particularly to the tension that may be observed between the two just-mentioned types of paradigms.

In our opinion, one of the permanent assets of the Prague structuralist and functionalist conception of language has been exactly this emphasis placed on the dynamic, non-static character of the system of language, in which one can ascertain a relatively firmly fixed centre, dominated by strict regularities, and a much vaguer peripheral area in which such regularities assert themselves much less consistently and sometimes even tend to become virtually disconnected with the centre to which they, after all, still belong. It should be stressed that this differentiation into the centre and the periphery is valid on all language levels, not only in the phonological subsystem where its existence has been demonstrated with a great deal of persuasiveness for many present-day languages. Perhaps the most obvious instance of a peripheral phonemic element is the phoneme /h/ in present day Standard English, which is isolated in its system both qualitatively and quantitatively and appears to be doomed to disappearance from it. It has already done so in the large majority of British English dialects: in them the sound [h] no longer has a phonemic status but rather constitutes what Trubetzkoy (1939) called a phonostylistic feature. Analogous instances of such peripheral phonic phenomena might of course be adduced from many other languages — see, e.g., the Modern Czech vocalic phoneme /ɔ:/, Modern French /œ/, etc.

On the lexical level a parallel differentiation might be spotted between the native word-stock which regularly represents the central part of the lexical subsystem, while the loan words constitute, as a rule, the periphery of the said subsystem (in Modern English this peripheral status is most clearly observed in the Graeco-Latin expressions implementing items of more or less specialized terminology). Since, however, our main concern here is the situation in morphology, we intend to concentrate on it in a couple of remarks.

On the morphological level the distinction between the centre and the periphery is implemented with especial clearness by what are commonly termed, respectively, productive and non-productive paradigms. See, e.g., the masculine *a*-stems in the declension of Old English nouns, as opposed to the *i*- and *u*-stems of masculine nouns in the same language; in the Old English verbal conjugation, again, the so-called weak conjugation ranks as central, as opposed to the strong one which is distinctly less central, and especially to the athematic verb group which is found in the extreme periphery of the verbal system, being absolutely non-productive (and upheld in the morphological system only by the high frequency of occurrence of its few items). Naturally, also among the central, productive types one can find various degrees of this central status: thus, e.g., of all the classes of the weak verbs, that of the type *sealfian* or *bodian* is certainly the "most central" (which is also underlined by its very high productivity, enriching the Old English vocabulary by a large number of nominative verbs), while the conjugational types *fremman, dēman*, and especially *þencean*, are decidedly "less central", but of course are still situated within the central, non-peripheral area of the morphological level of Old English.

It should be noted that the replacements of the less regular forms by the more regular ones, commonly ascribed to a mechanically operating morphological analogy (such as, e.g., of Npl. *₃ieste* by *₃iestas*, of Npl. *frīend* by *frēondas*, of Pret.sg. *slēp* by *slǣpte*, etc.) can be more appropriately qualified as shifts of such forms, standing farther from the centre, towards the innermost centre of the morphological subsystem. Such shifts, indeed, constitute another example of the integration of the peripheral elements of the language system into its centre, some specimens of which we discussed in an earlier paper (Vachek 1966). Since no semantic differentiation has been involved by such "analogical" changes, we can speak here of cases of simple integration (in the sense of our distinction formulated in the paper just referred to). But one can find in the development of English also instances of the other category of integrating changes, the so-called differentiative integration, in which a notable semantic change has been involved. This other category is represented by some cases of the development of English adjectives. As is well known, Modern English forms like *last, next*, going back to OE *lætesta, nīehsta*, are no longer synchronically evaluated as "irregular" superlative degrees of the Modern English positives *late, near*, but have become independent adjectives and thus integrated into a different, lexical subsystem of the English language — the superlative function, originally proper to them, has been taken over by new, regularly created forms *latest, nearest*, occupying the most central positions in their section of the morphological subsystem. (The same kind of change, naturally, has taken place in the Modern English adjective *latter*, which also has become lexicalized and so semantically independent of its original positive, and whose original comparative function is now performed by the regularly created form *later*.)

It is hardly necessary to stress the fact that the structural shifts instanced here testify to the dynamic, non-static character of the morphological system of English in both its old and middle periods. This dynamism has clearly been motivated by an effort — even though mostly unconscious — to adapt the structure of the given language level so as to make it capable to perform more efficiently its principal task, i.e. to serve as a dependable instrument of mutual communication among the members of the given language community.

Instances taken from the morphological level and from the processes of its development are particularly suited to demonstrate the functional motivation of the tendency to integrate peripheral elements into the more central area of the language system: since language, admittedly, constitutes a most intimate union of form and meaning, the existence in a language system of a greater number of formal means for one and the same grammatical function must necessarily be found redundant, and therefore functionally inadequate, especially if only very few instances reflect some of the said deviant formal means. The replacement of such minority cases by the majority ones (e.g., the replacement of the OE NPl. *3ieste* by *3iestas* or of the pret. *slēp* by *slæpte*) can thus be evaluated as a step towards higher functional efficiency of the morphological sub-system of the English language. Perhaps an even more eloquent proof of the functional motivation of the discussed processes is provided by the semantic differentiation taking place in those cases in which the original, more or less irregular form was kept in the language by the side of the newly installed analogously created regular form. This was the case of the above-mentioned lexicalization of the originally superlative forms like *last*, *next*, aside of the newly formed, more systematic superlatives *latest*, *nearest*. Needless to say, this semantic differentiation also clearly increases the functional efficiency of the language means. Moreover, it also provides additional support for the old maxim formulated by the Geneva school to the effect that no real synonyms exist in language, since some kind of semantic differentiation regularly intervenes in those instances in which an apparently genuine pair of synonymous forms might emerge.

The instances just quoted have revealed that processes taking place on the morphological level of language may have repercussions also on its lexical level. Undoubtedly the lexicalized forms of the type *last*, *next*, *latter* were to add to the English word-stock some hardly unimportant items. We have thus ascertained a case of interesting interrelation of two language levels; cases of this kind supply a very significant piece of evidence for another Prague thesis urging the existence of mutual relationships of all language levels within one and the same system of language. It should be pointed out, too, that morphology, constituting — as already noted briefly above — a central level of the given language system, simply cannot fail to be closely interrelated with all other levels of it. Its relations to syntax have, of course, been well known for many decades. It has been repeatedly admitted that the fixation of the word-order in Middle English and Early Modern English sentences was closely connected with the reshapement of the originally synthetic declension of nouns into the analytical one. But there are also other mutual inter-level relations which are usually overlooked.

In another paper (Vachek 1961) we hope to have shown that the phonological re-evaluation of the original Middle English opposition of voice in the paired consonant phonemes (voiced vs. voiceless) into the Late Middle English opposition of tension (lax vs. tense) was again closely linked with the above-discussed process of the morphological reshapement of the synthetic grammatical pattern into the analytical one. Particularly illuminating is the comparison of the Middle English structural situation with a similar situation found in Slavonic languages, such as Russian or Czech. In the latter two languages, paired voiced consonant phonemes came to stand in word-final position after the loss of the final "weak" semi-vowels (the yers). Thus, e.g., *plodi* 'fruit' > *plod;* in this word-final position, before a pause, the voiced /d/ lost its voice and so changed into its voiceless counterpart /t/, the pronunciation of the ana-lysed word-form being then [plot]. This loss of voice in word-final posi-tions testifies to the preservation of the phonological opposition of voice in paired consonant phonemes of the said Slavonic languages. The price paid for this preservation was, of course, the emergence of a number of new homonyms, because after the discussed changes of the type /d/ > /t/ the phonetic sequence [plot] came to implement not only the original word-form *plodi* 'fruit' but also the original word-form *ploti* 'fence'. So much, then, for the situation in the two Slavonic languages. What was the situation in Middle English?

As is well known, also in Late Middle English, thanks to the wholesale loss of the original inflexional endings like *-e*, *-en*, a large number of voiced paired consonant phonemes was to emerge in word-final posi-tions. As a result of this, one might also have expected a notable increase of homonymous word-pairs (such as *rib – rip*, *bag – back*, and also *plod – plot*). However, the surprising thing was that the phonic merger of members of such pairs has not taken place and that each of the members has still been clearly distinguished from its counterpart in the given pair. This fact can only be accounted for by a phonological re-evaluation of the phonic opposition of the type /t/: /d/, which was no longer interpreted in terms of voice but in terms of tension, /t/ being, further on, evaluated as tense, and /d/ as lax, or — in binary terms — as non-tense. This re-evaluation (discussed in some detail in the above-mentioned paper, Vachek 1961) was to make possible the keeping apart of members of the above-instanced word-pairs and, what should particularly be noted, to prevent a notable increase of homonyms in the Middle English vocabul-ary.

The question naturally emerges of why the development of English was here so diametrically opposed to that of the above-mentioned Slavonic languages. Why did the Slavonic languages not find objectionable the increase of homonymous word-pairs, while the English language was obviously so opposed to it that a specific phonological process was resorted to in order to prevent such increase? It appears that the solution of this problem should be sought in the differences of the morphological types represented by the compared languages: the Slavonic languages, preserving their synthetic, inflexional morphologies, have not grammaticalized the order of words in their sentences to such a high degree as English, whose morphological type has become analytical, with strong isolationist features. As a result of this difference, the English word-order in the sentence had already been so heavily functionally burdened that it could not take on itself the additional function of the contextual differentiation of newly arisen homonymous word-pairs. On the other hand, the Slavonic languages, having grammaticalized their word-orders to a much lower degree, could charge their word-orders and sentence contexts in general with the additional function of the contextual differentiation of a certain number of new homonymous word-pairs.

The conclusion that can be drawn from the differences of the morphological situation in the two language types is that any examination of the morphological level of language should be undertaken with constant regard to the situation on the other levels (or, subsystems) of the examined language — it is only this regard to the interdependence of all language levels that can do full justice to the dynamism characterizing the morphological level of language.

Another area of research in morphology which has greatly benefited from the work of the structuralist and functionalist linguistics of the Prague brand is also closely connected with the contact of the morphological and phonological levels. The specialized discipline dealing with these contacts is of course morpho-phonology (or, for short, morphonology) which, in Trubetzkoy's conception, examines the ways in which phonological materials are utilized for morphological purposes, whether one has to do with segmental or suprasegmental facts. Especially the very concept of the morphoneme, by which we understand — deviating here slightly from the Trubtzkoyan tradition — the repertoire of phonemes functioning in one and the same place of a morpheme within the various word-forms including it, proves to be a most useful tool of contrastive morphology (and morphological typology). In analysing various languages from the morphonological point of view, as Trubetzkoy himself did in his detailed morphonology of Modern Russian (Trubetzkoy 1934), one can certainly arrive at highly interesting typological results. But no less interesting conclusions can be arrived at in examining two various stages of the development of one and the same language. This is most graphically shown by a comparison of Old and Modern English: in its oldest period, when the morphological pattern was still prevailingly synthetic, the Old English paradigms exhibited quite a number of morphonemes — see, e.g., Nsg. *dæʒ* — Npl. *daʒas*, Nsg. *fōt* — Dsg. *fēt*, Nsg. *broþor* — Dsg. *brēþer*; Adj. posit. *grēat* — comp. *grīetra*, sup. *grīetsta*; 1. sg. Ind. pres. *ic sprece* — 3. sg. WSax. *hē spricþ*, 1.3 sg. Ind. pret. *wrāt* — pl. *writon*, and many other oppositions of the kind.

If one confronts the just-instanced Old English oppositions with the Modern English oppositions corresponding to them, one finds that virtually all morphonemes have been cancelled (see word-pairs like *day* — pl. *days; foot, brother* — Dsg. *to the foot, to the brother; great — greater — greatest; I speak — he speaks; I wrote — we wrote*, etc.). The only surviving morphoneme in the verbal conjugation of Modern English preterites is found, as is commonly known, in the word-pair *was — were* (which again, however, is discarded in many dialects). In the declension of nouns one only finds a very limited number of morphonemes in cases of archaic but very frequently occurring plural forms of the type *feet, geese, men*, and finally, in the adjectival area one comes across isolated instances of semantically specialized word-forms of comparative and superlative degrees *elder, eldest* (as opposed to the positive *old*) by the side of the regular *older, oldest*. It can hardly be overlooked that the decrease in the number of morphonemes in the development of English obviously went hand in hand with the typological reshapement of the English morphological system from synthesis to analysis. The decrease in the number of morphonemes in the development of English has naturally been so conspicuous that it could not escape the penetrating analysis of scholars surveying this development — see, e.g., Jespersen's remarks (1905), though formulated in a different terminology and in a different theoretical framework, as early as three quarters of a century ago.

The last set of problems which deserves to be mentioned here, at least in passing, is concerned with the question of how morphology of a language can be influenced in its development by the morphology of some other language which for political, social or economic reasons is known to have influenced the examined language in some periods of its development. Concretely, it was often argued that the analyticization of morphology in the Middle English period may have been motivated by the situation in French (both Norman and Central), whose morphological system had been analytical since the beginnings of the intensive contact of the two languages. However, although some limited influence of French on English morphology cannot be reasonably doubted, most scholars are now of the opinion that it only acted as a catalyser, furthering the operation of the analytical tendencies which had already been operating in Old English, when no strong impact of French upon English morphology can be thought of (cf. Baugh 1959:122). It appears indeed that the first impulses to the said analyticization may have been given by the sociolinguistic fact of the Scandinavian colonization of large areas of England as early as in the 8th and 9th centuries. This pet theory, formulated by Jespersen a long series of decades ago, finds some support in recent research done in the field of languages in contact. This research, inaugurated long before Weinreich's well-known monograph by some theses of the Prague linguist Havránek (1939), stresses the important part played in the development of the affected language by bilingual speakers who concentrate on the common features of the contacting languages and omit those features in which the two systems are found to differ. In the concrete case of English and Scandinavian such differences were mainly found in the inflexional endings which, in addition to this, were often added to word bases virtually identical in the two languages.

The limits set to the present paper have made it impossible to discuss other aspects of the involved problems, and forced us to concentrate on those features of morphological research which in our opinion have particularly benefited from the functionalist and structuralist approach of language facts. Even so, it may be safely asserted that any scholar ignoring the points commented upon here above would seriously misrepresent both the synchronic and the diachronic situation of the morphological subsystem of the language examined by him. It can only be added that research in all the fields enumerated here above should be positively encouraged in future functionalist treatment of the given issues. If our lines are regarded as a blueprint of such future research they will have achieved the purpose the present writer had in mind putting them down.

References

Baugh, A.C.
　1959　*A history of the English language* (London).
Bühler, K.
　1931　"Phonetik und Phonologie", *Travaux du Cercle Linguistique de Prague* 4: 22–53.
Havránek, B.
　1939　Answers to questionnaire", in: *IIIéme Congrés Internationale des Slavistes. Publication No. 3: Supplément* (Beograd), 41–43, 48–49.
Hockett, C.F.
　1954　"Two models of grammatical description", *Word* 10:210–231.
Jespersen, O.
　1905　*Growth and structure of the English language* (Leipzig: Tauchnitz).
Trubetzkoy, N.S.
　1934　*Das morphonologische System der russischen Sprache* (= *Travaux du Cercle Linguistique de Prague* 5.2) (Praha).
　1939　*Grundzüge der Phonologie* (= *Travaux du Cercle Linguistique de Prague* 7) (Praha).

Vachek, J.
  1961 "Some less familiar aspects of the analytical trend of English," *Brno Studies in English* 3:9–78.
  1966 "On the integration of the peripheral elements into the system of language", *Travaux Linguistiques de Prague* 2:23–37.

NIGEL VINCENT

Words versus morphemes in morphological change: the case of Italian *-iamo*

1   In historical grammars of a traditional cast, both morphologically simple and morphologically complex forms are adduced more or less indiscriminately as evidence for individual sound changes. Thus, both Lat. *octō*>It. *otto* and Lat. *factum* > It. *fatto* are cited as examples of the assimilation of stop clusters in the development of Latin into Italian, despite the fact that at the morphological level there is a boundary between the two consonants in *factum* (/fak + tum/, cf. fac*ere, amā*tum) but not in *octō*. A similar situation recurs in the case of Lat. *aqua* > It. *acqua* and Lat. *placuī* > It. *piacque*, where the gemination of [k] is attributed to the following semi-vowel regardless of the fact that in *aqua* the [w] is part of a monophonematic labiovelar /k^w/, whereas in *placuī* it is the segmental realization of the morpheme PERFECTIVE. It is the phonetic identity that counts and not the morphological discrepancy. The theoretical justification for this practice is, of course, the Neogrammarian legacy of the blind operation of sound laws. My task in the present paper will not be to contradict this metaprinciple of historical linguistic research, which I take to be still essentially correct, but rather to use the consequences of its application in the area of polymorphemic forms to point up some interesting questions in the theory of diachronic morphology.

One important aspect of linguistic theory which was not always made explicit in traditional accounts of linguistic change is what has come to be known as "the double articulation of language" (Martinet 1965: Ch.1) or "duality of patterning" (Hockett 1960), whereby utterances are structured at two levels, first as combinations of sounds organized into words or morphemes, and then as words or morphemes organized into higher order syntactic constructs. As both Martinet and Hockett observe, this principle is an indispensable characteristic of natural languages. As long as examples for sound shifts are drawn from the stock of monomorphemic forms, however, no gross theoretical damage will result from any failure to take the double articulation into account. Since the link between a lexical stem and its associated signifié is arbitrary, it is safe to assume that the group of sounds which make up the signifiant will be transmitted from one generation to the next as a whole. There is no evidence that speakers put sounds together to make words as they manifestly put words together to make sentences. It is this situation which Lightfoot (1977:191) is referring to when he writes:

One can reasonably claim that *chapter, captain* are in a way the same word as their historical antecedents, *chapiter, capitain* . . . An analogous view of syntax, however, is incoherent: it makes no sense to say that a certain sentence of Old English 'corresponds' to some sentence of Middle English.

Within these limitations an essentially Neogrammarian approach to the process, if not the result, of sound change may thus be adhered to without necessarily involving a rejection of structuralist and post-structuralist insights into the nature and working of language. This state of affairs is not disturbed by the discovery that a form which one generation takes to be unanlyzable may have been internally complex for a preceding generation. Klausenburger (1976) notes the case of verb stems like *rumpō* and *frangō* in Latin where the nasal consonant can be shown diachronically to be an infix, but is nevertheless best regarded as just another consonant in the stem from the synchronic point of view. We have here a classic instance of the Saussurean distinction between synchronic and diachronic explanation.

At the level of the second articulation, however, the situation is rather different. The central syntactic construct, the sentence, is clearly not transmitted whole across generations and, accordingly, it is not possible to say that Italian *Paolo disse che l'uomo era venuto* 'Paul said that the man had come' directly continues Latin *Paulus dixit hominem venisse* in the same way that we customarily state that the Italian stem *uom-* continues Lat. *hom-*.[1] Traditionally, though, It. *disse* is indeed said to be the reflex of Lat. *dixit* resulting from the cumulative effect of three sound changes: *-ks-* > *-ss-*; C> 0 word-finally; unstressed *ĭ* to *e*. Yet the form *disse* is synchronically segmentable in Italian and is (morpho)syntactically complex, so the question arises: at what point do we stop talking of direct reflexes and start to talk in terms of a rather vaguer notion of correspondences, as when we say that the analytic *era venuto* 'he had come' in Italian corresponds to the synthetic *venerat* in Latin? Of course, what we are here faced with is another variant of the age-old problem of how to separate morphology and syntax in inflecting languages. Mańczak (1976: § 92) invites reflection upon an interesting borderline case when he argues that the cluster [-km-] in Latin yields Italian [-mm-] as a result of assimilation, citing as his only example the equivalence of Latin *dīc mē* and Italian *dimmi*.[2] In this case we are not forced to accept the view that the syntagm of imperative verb plus object pronoun is transmitted as a whole, since we could equally well argue that Lat. *dīc* would give It. *di* by the normal loss of Latin final consonants, and that the doubling of /m/ in the syntactic nexus *dimmi* is due to an independently motivated rule of external sandhi which lengthens single consonants following stressed short vowels (cf. Modern Italian *parlò bene* [parlɔbbe:ne] 'he spoke well' and the discussion in Vogel 1977). There is thus no compelling evidence for treating the verb + clitic sequences as anything other than a syntactically generated construct from the synchronic viewpoint in both Latin and Italian. Whether *disse* is to be considered on a par with the clitic case, or as parallel to unanalyzable stems such as that contained in It. *sasso* 'stone' (< Lat. *saxum*) is a more difficult question, and one which it is part of the task of this paper to address.

2   Let us turn now from these ponderings on a traditional, though not always clearly recognized, problem to a similar issue which arises in connection with the treatment of regular and irregular allomorphy in the context of modern generative theory. In orthodox generative phonology as codified in Chomsky — Halle (1968), all the allomorphs of a given morpheme, apart from suppletive alternants, are generated by rule from a single underlying base form. Indeed, the achievement of such a state of affairs is the real raison d'être of much of the theoretical apparatus of that model. As Anderson (1974:51) puts it:

... the primary reason for incorporating phonological rules in a linguistic description (is) the need to describe alternations in shape which a morpheme undergoes in various environments.

In the derivation of the forms of a language some rules will always apply whenever their structural descriptions are met. The rule of homorganic nasal assimilation in Italian is a case in point. Thus:

(1)   /in + pɔssibile/   [impɔssibile]   'impossible'
         /in + formale/   [iɱformale]   'informal'
         /in + dɔtʃile/   [indɔtʃile]   'unmanageable'
         /in + koerɛnte/   [iŋkoerɛnte]   'incoherent'

Other rules may be controlled by a system of exception features and the use of the distinction between major and minor rules (Lightner 1968). In Italian, for example, we may posit a minor rule of diphthongization relevant only to the derivation of a handful of irregular verbs (e.g. *muovo* 'I move' vs. *moviamo* 'we move'; *vieni* 'you (sg) come' vs. *venite* 'you (pl) come') and some derivational alternations (e.g. *buono* 'good' vs. *bontà* 'goodness').[3]

In an influential paper Vennemann (1974) has criticized generative phonology for this approach to allomorphic patterning, arguing instead that "there is a gradation between suppletion and unrestricted productivity" (1974:349) and he proposes a new system according to which:

All paradigms are treated as lists in the lexicon. Differences in the regularities of paradigms are entirely captured by degrees of regularity of the rules, which function entirely as redundancy rules for forms already registered in the lexicon, and as generative rules only when unknown words are adapted to the lexicon or new words are created by a speaker.

I do not propose in the present context to attempt to refute all of Vennemann's model (which has parallels in more recent generative literature — see Halle 1973 and Jackendoff 1975), but I will rather concentrate on his counter-intuitive (to the traditional grammarian, at least) claim that all the forms of the paradigms in a language are represented in the mental lexicon as separate entries tied together by a network of lexical rules. I shall espouse instead a view closely akin to that adopted in traditional grammatical and pedagogical practice wherein a distinction is made between regular verbs, for which it suffices to provide a set of general rules for the composition of morphologically complex forms, and irregular verbs, where individual forms do indeed have to be learnt, and presumably therefore stored, as wholes which may or may not be partially decomposable by comparison with the forms of the regular paradigms.

It is notoriously difficult to find crucial evidence to decide the case one way or the other. Notice that the finite nature of paradigms makes it difficult if not impossible to exclude the lexicalist view a priori. Two areas where deciding evidence may be sought are a) psycholinguistic research and b) language history. Such psycholinguistic evidence as there is (Berko 1958; MacWhinney 1975) does indeed suggest that morphology is learnt by the construction of rule-based hypotheses compatible with the available data at a given stage of language acquisition and successively modified as more data presents itself. However, psychological testing of the kind pioneered by Berko always attempts to reveal the nature of the existing knowledge by inducing the subject to extend it to nonsense forms supplied by the investigator. Since it is part of Vennemann's claim that the existing patterns, though being consonant with the strategies used in 'new' situations, are not necessarily stored in terms of these strategies, the presently available psycholinguistic tests will not categorically refute his position. Following a line of reasoning which originates with Kiparsky (1968:174ff), we will therefore turn our attention to the area of linguistic change on the principle that distinctions made in change may be taken to reflect psychologically real distinctions for the speakers who participated in the change. In particular, what we need to find is a case where a linguistic change appears to distinguish between regular and irregular paradigms. I will now try to show that the generalization of the first person plural desinence *-iamo* from the present subjunctive to the present indicative in Italian is just such a case.

3   The essential facts are fairly simple to state. The verbal paradigms in Italian reflect quite closely the Latin system of conjugations, with different characteristic or thematic vowels intervening between the stem and the ending. Thus, the three verb forms *cantate* 'you (pl) sing', *temete* 'you (pl) fear', *dormite* 'you (pl) sleep' can all be reduced to a single canonical formula, viz.

(2)   STEM + TV + ENDING[4]

One place where the conjugational distinctions are not preserved involves the 1st pers. pl. of present tense verb forms, where we find, for the three verbs already cited: *cantiamo* 'we sing', *temiamo* 'we fear', *dormiamo* 'we sleep'. Furthermore, the corresponding forms of the subjunctive are identical: *cantiamo, temiamo, dormiamo*. The first problem to be solved regards the correct morphological segmentation of the ending *-iamo*. The portion /-mo/ presents no difficulty as it recurs without exception in every 1st pers. pl. verb form of the language. The /-ja-/ thus seems to occupy the TV slot, standing as it does between stem and ending. Further evidence that such is indeed the case is provided by a comparison of 2nd pers. pl. forms of the present indicative and subjunctive.

(3) | Indicative | Subjunctive |
       |------------|-------------|
       | *cantate* | *cantiate* |
       | *temete* | *temiate* |
       | *dormite* | *dormiate* |

Here *-ia* contrasts directly with the thematic vowel of the indicative. The forms with *-ia-* are thus seen to differ importantly from cases such as *canto* 'I sing', *temo* 'I fear', *dormo* 'I sleep' where there is simply no TV present on the surface.

Now these paradigmatic neutralizations involving the *-ia-* morph are a particular characteristic of the Florentine dialect underlying the modern standard language. Elsewhere the etymologically expected forms *cantamo*, *tememo*, *dormimo* survive (see Rohlfs 1968: § 530). Three questions therefore arise:

(i) what is the etymological source of the *-ia-* sequence?
(ii) how did it come to take over just these particular verb forms?
(iii) why did it take place when and where it did?

This last question will not concern us here. Our exposition of the main stages of development follows Wanner's (1975) excellently clear account, and the reader is referred there for an attempt at explanation.

It is generally agreed that the source of *-iamo* is Lat. *-eāmus* or *-iāmus*, that is to say the present subjunctive ending of verbs like *timēre*, *facere* and *dormīre*. Latin *e, i* in hiatus gave yod in Vulgar Latin by a well attested change, and this yod in turn exercised a phonetic effect on the preceding stem-final consonant, causing it to lengthen, and in the case of velars and dentals, to palatise as well. Thus:

(4)	Lat.	*fakiāmu(s)*	*(h)abeāmu(s)*
		fakjamu	*abjamu*
		fakkjamu	*abbjamu*
		fattʃamo	
	It.	*facciamo*	*abbiamo*

These changes took place both inside and outside the verbal paradigms. Compare:

(5)	Lat.	*fakiam*	'I do (subj.)'	*fakiam*	'face'
	It.	*faccia*		*faccia*	

By the time we come to the Old Florentine stage (approx. 12th — 13th C) we find *-iamo* has generalized to become part of the first conjugation as well as of the second and third in which it can be etymologically justified. Forms such as *portiamo* for etymological *portemo* (<Lat. *portēmus*) are the norm according to Castellani (1952).

Having become the general marker across all conjugations for the 1st pers. pl. subj., the next stage in the historical expansion of *-iamo* is its spread to the corresponding positions in the indicative paradigm.[5] The results of Alinei's multi-volume *spoglio* (1968) of early Italian texts attest the following pairs in 13th century Italian:

(6)   Indicative   Subjunctive
         dicemo   *diciamo*
         difendemo   *difendiamo*
         attendemo   *intendiamo.*

On the basis of forms such as these we might be tempted to think that the change which eliminates the forms of the indicative in (6) involves the transfer of the subjunctive ending to the indicative, an account on which the manuals generally agree. Rohlfs (1968: § 530) talks of "la sostituzione di *-amo, -emo, -imo* colla desinenza congiuntiva *-iamo* < eamus", while Tekavčić (1972: § 939) says "anche l'italiano letterario ha generalizzato la desinenza /jamo/ per tutte le classi". However, the following forms demonstrate that, for some verbs at least, the account cannot be as simple as this.

(7)   Indicative   Subjunctive
         facemo   *facciamo*
         avemo   *abbiamo*
         dovemo   *dobbiamo*
         volemo   *vogliamo*
         sapemo   *sappiamo*

In these cases the hypothesis of a simple change of ending would predict the following forms: **faciamo *aviamo, *doviamo, *voliamo, *sapiamo*, none of which occur to my knowledge. Here, rather, we are faced with two different allomorphs of the stem, both explicable on historical grounds. If we take *avemo/abbiamo* for the purposes of exemplification, we find:

(8)   *habēmus* > *avemo*   (*b* > *v* intervocalically,
                                                 cf. *caballum* > *cavallo, ripam* > *riva*)
         habeāmus > *abbiamo*   (cf. (4) above)

It seems then that what has happened historically is that, for the verbs in (7), the subjunctive forms have replaced those of the indicative in their entirety. In particular, it is to be noted that a form such as *abbiamo* in its indicative sense cannot be due to the synchronic effects of the initial /j/ in the *-iamo* ending for two reasons. In the first place, other evidence suggests that the gemination process had come to an end by this time, and secondly gemination, even if it had been in operation, would have produced **avviamo* and not *abbiamo*.[6]
A hypothesis of replacement at the level of the word rather than at the

level of the individual morpheme would also be compatible with the data in (6), so that it might appear that, in the interests of economy and a unified solution to the problem, we should treat both (6) and (7) as cases of word substitution, thereby confirming Vennemann's proposal rather than our own. Compare, however, the third set of forms listed in (9).

(9)   Indicative   Subjunctive
       vedemo   *veggiamo*
       ponemo   *pognamo* $(gn = [ɲɲ] < nj)$
       potemo   *possiamo*

In this instance the modern forms of the indicative/subjunctive are *poniamo* and *vediamo* for the first two words, while the form *potiamo* is also attested, though no longer current, the modern form being *possiamo*. The only appropriate account here is to regard the ending as having detached itself from the subjunctive stem and having reattached itself, with no sandhi effects, to the indicative stem. The present indicative of *vedere* 'to see' is thus:

(10)   *vedo*   *vediamo*
        vedi   *vedete*
        vede   *vedono*

In other words, it is an entirely regular verb with a single stem allomorph and clearly segmentable endings which are duplicated in the other regular verbs of the language.

4   The facts of the present case would seem to suggest a model of synchronic grammar in which a distinction is drawn or drawable between what, for want of a better term, we have been calling 'regular' and 'irregular' verbs. In particular, we need to be able to treat the irregular formations such as *abbiamo*, *facciamo* etc. as in the first instance words which are secondarily, and then not necessarily completely, decomposable into constituent morphs, while on the other hand giving logico-theoretical primacy to the individual morphs out of which the regular forms are then built up by means of a set of morphological composition rules. To put it in a nutshell, we need a word-and-paradigm (WP) model of morphology for the irregular formations and an Item-and-Arrangement/Item-and-Process (IA/IP) model for the regular ones. We now proceed to outline briefly the properties of a grammar which will satisfy this dual requirement (for further details, see Vincent (in preparation)).

As far as regular verbs are concerned the model does not diverge greatly from those proposals which follow the SPE tradition fairly closely, though with the inclusion of a specific morphological component to handle the insertion of inflectional affixes (see Wurzel 1970 and Wagner 1969). The stages in the synchronic derivation of a regular form such as *cantate* 'you sing' are as set out in (11).

(11)   a) a lexical verb-base (*canta-*) is selected and inserted into an appropriate deep-structure configuration;
       b) transformations gradually develop a complex of morphosyntactic features;
       c) the morphosyntactic features are given phonological realization (+ *te*) in a second lexical pass;
       d) the phonetic representation is derived through the application of the rules of the phonological component ([kan'ta:te]).

An irregular verb such as Italian *potere* 'to be able', on the other hand, will be represented as having a separate lexical entry for each form of the verb.[7] Thus, for the present singular forms, we have entries which can be set out as follows:

(12)   a) /pɔsso/   b) /puɔi/   c) /puɔ/
           ABLE   ABLE   ABLE
           Verb   Verb   Verb
           1st p.   2nd p.   3rd p.
           sing.   sing.   sing.
           pres.   pres.   pres.
           indic.   indic.   indic.

The principal reason which motivates storing these forms as separate words is that segmentation leaves stem variants that are not derivable from each other by means of rules having any phonetic plausibility or independent support in the phonology of Italian. However, the appropriate grammatical endings can be segmented off with no difficulty, viz. *-o,-i*, *-Ø* (cf. for a regular verb *canto, canti, canta*). A rule-based treatment of these forms would face a 'cranberry-morph' situation. If we segment off the recognizable bit, what do we do with the (synchronically) unrecognizable remainder? A lexical solution forestalls the dilemma by permitting bracketing of the following type, where only the known elements are labelled:

(13)   a) $_v[$pɔss $[o]_{Af}]_v$
         b) $_v[$puɔ$[i]_{Af}]_v$
         c) $_v[$puɔ$[Ø]_{Af}]_v$

With this much internal structure, lexical entries for verbs may be related
to the matrices which store inflectional endings in the second lexicon (cf.
Wagner 1969:73ff. and Vincent (in preparation)). Relatedness between
members of the same irregular paradigm can be handled on a pairwise
basis by means of non-directional lexical conditions along the lines of
Jackendoff (1975).

Of course, the question arises within such a framework as to how to
decide whether the forms of a given verb are to be represented lexically or
via the morphological rules. Regular and irregular represent two ends of a
continuum rather than a strictly binary opposition, as Vennemann has
recently re-emphasised. This state of affairs does not mean however that
the endpoints are not clearly distinguishable. Rather it implies an indeterminate area in the middle, and this seems to be in accord with what is
known of language acquisition (cf. in particular the interesting results of
Haber (1975)). Hence for any pair of speakers there may be slight
differences in the status of certain verbs. What, however, concerns us is
that for any general model of language, both possibilities will have to be
recognized, and our grammar is designed accordingly.

5   With the preceding proviso, and in the context of the theoretical
machinery outlined in the last section, let us turn to a reconsideration of
the historical source of the *-iamo* ending. There can, I think, be no
argument with the traditionally held view that *abbiamo* derives from
habeāmus via the development of the hiatus vowel to yod (synizesis) with
the subsequent gemination of the stem-final consonant. Wanner (1975)
rightly reminds us, however, that for many verbs the historical path seems
to be via elision of the hiatus vowel (synalife) rather than glide formation.
Thus Latin verbs in *-eō, -iō* regularly come down into Italian as *-o*. Thus:

(14)   *dormiō > dormo*   'I sleep'   *timeō > temo*   'I fear'
         audiō   > odo   'I hear'   *videō > vedo*   'I see'

In particular, it should be noted that there is no gemination:

(15)   *temeat > tema* but *vindemia > vendemmia*

nor palatalization:

(16)   *sentiat > senta* but *absentia > senza*

Hence we should expect the regular reflex of Lat. *dormiāmus* to be **dormamo* and not the attested *dormiamo*. The question therefore arises as to which of these alternative paths of development (synizesis or synalife) we should regard as the normal state of affairs, or whether they are both equally regular but competing sound changes (in the sense of Wang 1969). Evidence from forms where no boundary separates the stem-final consonant from the hiatus vowel suggests that it is synizesis which operates in these cases. Consider the following correspondences:

(17)　*cofeam* > *cuffia*　'bonnet'
　　　caveam > *gabbia*　'cage'
　　　martium > *marzo*　'March'
　　　hordeum > *orzo*　'oats'
　　　calceum > *calcio*　'kick'
　　　fageum > *faggio*　'bean'

We find a similar effect in fixed locutions such as *postea* > *poscia* 'then'. What, then, is the status of elision? Wanner (1975:162) appears to imply that it is to be viewed as a sound change which makes reference to a morphological boundary. We would argue on independent grounds that such changes cannot legitimately be called sound changes (see Vincent 1978), and would suggest instead that the change reflects a spread of a morphologically based generalization. The source of the generalization is to be found in the phonotactics of Latin, which do not permit sequences of the form /ao/. In consequence, a Latin verb form such as *amo* 'I love' can be analysed synchronically as having the underlying structure /am + a + ō/, parallel to *amat* 'he loves' from /am + a + t/, but surfacing as /amō/ via a phonotactically motivated rule (Sommerstein 1974) of vowel deletion. Such a form then provides the basis for a surface generalization (or abduction in the sense of Andersen 1973) that the regular realization of 1st person singular present indicative is attached directly to the stem minus the thematic vowel. Added support for this generalization will be found in the class of historically athematic verbs such as *vendō* 'I sell'. In fact, there is considerable evidence that already in Latin there was oscillation between verbs in *-eō* and in *-ō* (Latin second and third conjugations respectively). We find both *fervēre* and *fervĕre*, *tergēre* and *tergĕre* attested, and the history of many verbs in Italian also requires us to reconstruct a similar conjugation shift. For example, we have Italian *rìdere, rispòndere* with stem stress beside Latin *ridēre, respondēre* with ending stress, and, conversely, Italian *cadère* beside Latin *càdere*. (For further documentation, see Tekavčić 1972, Vol. 2:327ff.)

If elision is indeed the result of a generalization of a paradigmatic pattern, then, of course, it is no accident that its effect is only felt inside the regular verb forms of the language, since it is precisely those which are the product of morphological formation rules. Irregular verb forms as lexical wholes would only secondarily receive an interpretation via those of the formation rules which are relevant, as exemplified above in the case of *potere*, but would not directly be affected by changes in the rules which generate regular forms, since they are not so generated. Synizesis and synalife are certainly therefore competing changes in the history of Italian, but the interesting and important point is that the competition is between a morphologically based paradigm change and a regular sound change, rather than between two sound changes. To focus this point in terms of our opening remarks about the difference between morphologically complex and morphologically simple forms with respect to the process of sound change, it may be said that forms such as *dormiō, temeō* etc. do not undergo synizesis because they are, as it were, dismantled anew by each succeeding generation in terms of the morphological rules which are established in the process of language acquisition. Such changes as they do undergo therefore reflect alteration in these rules rather than in the final forms which are the output of such rules. Our point is well illustrated by comparing the developments of Lat. *capiāmus* 'we take' and *sapiāmus* 'we know', both members of the so-called "mixed" conjugation in Latin. *Capere* remains a regular verb (though shifting to the *-ire* class, whence It. *capire*). It therefore undergoes elision to give **capamu*, which, in due course, becomes *capiamo* when the *-iamo* ending generalizes. The modern reflex of *sapiāmus*, on the other hand, is *sappiamo*, where the geminate testifies to the continued presence of yod throughout its history, and the rest of the present tense of It. *sapere* is certainly irregular enough to predict its lexicalization, viz.:

(18)   *so*   *sappiamo*
         sai   *sapete*
         sa   *sanno*

The alert reader will have observed that our account requires *habeāmus, faciāmus* and similar forms to be lexicalized at an early stage in their development as it is only then that they may undergo the relevant sound changes which lead ultimately to the irregular formations of modern Italian. We have given no account of why just these forms should be plucked out of their regular paradigms in Latin and treated henceforth as lexical wholes. One traditional suggestion (cf. Mańczak 1976) that may be worth following up, especially in view of its recent revival (see Hooper 1978), is that frequency of occurrence may affect the subsequent history of forms. If forms which occur often, particularly at the earliest stage of language acquisition, are stored whole before there is sufficient range of data to permit the extraction of generalizations, then this may be the trigger to lexicalization.[8] Evidence to support this view in the case of *habēre* would be its increasing use as an auxiliary in the new "analytic" perfect and future constructions of Romance. Furthermore, a verb of consistent frequency such as *volo* 'I want' goes from the presumably lexicalized irregular paradigm in the classical language:

(19)   *volō*   *volumus*
       vīs   *vultis*
       vult   *volunt*

to the regular one which must be reconstructed for Vulgar Latin if we are to explain subsequent developments in Romance:

(20)   *voleō*   *volēmus*
       volēs   *volētis*
       volet   *voleunt*

However, already by the earliest Italian we have the emergence of a new set of irregular alternations — largely due to the influence of the yod from the hiatus vowel on the preceding consonant:

(21)   *voglio*   *vogliamo*
       vuo(l)i   *volete*
       vuole   *vogliono*

Again, interestingly, we may compare the palatalization produced in the 1st person plural of *volere* with its absence in *voliamo* from the regular verb *volare* 'to fly' where the suffix is not etymological.

More detailed work on the histories of individual verbs which appear to have undergone lexicalization in this way is urgently needed in order to discover exactly what mechanisms are at work. In the meantime, we conclude by observing that the two problems that were posed at the outset — the appropriateness of polymorphemic forms in exemplifying sound change, and the issue regarding the representation of inflectional morphology within a generative grammar — have found a common solution in the proposal that a grammar be permitted to contain both generative morphological rules and lexical redundancy conditions, and furthermore that the lexicon may contain in some cases only stems, and in others fully-fledged word-forms. In turn, the theoretical machinery is justified by its ability to give a plausible account of the superficially rather puzzling change that Italian *-iamo* presents. We look forward to more research into the balance and interaction of morphological rules and lexical rules, rather than the premature elimination of either.

Notes

1. For an interesting discussion of the same problem from the point of view of reconstruction rather than change, see Jeffers (1976).
2. That Mańczak does intend us to take the Italian as an orthodox, 'lautgesetzlich' reflex of the Latin is clear from his use of the > notation.
3. See Vincent (1972) for details. Wanner (1972) represents an attempt to develop a fairly full system of such rules to handle the irregular verbs of Italian.
4. Naturally, the presentation is greatly oversimplified, but no essential misrepresentation is involved as far as the central issues of this paper are concerned. Particular points of Italian verbal morphology will be expanded on as and when the exposition requires. For a fuller treatment of the descriptive problems posed by the Italian conjugations, see Vincent (in preparation).
5. Wanner (1975) argues that this generalization does not take place all at once, but that the change progresses from conjugation to conjugation and from subjunctive to indicative in a complex chain. The extra details do not add to or detract from our argument, so the simpler account is preferred for clarity of exposition. We may note in passing that this passage of an ending from the subjunctive to the indicative is unusual in the sense that it shows an ending being generalized from the marked category (subjunctive) to the unmarked one (indicative).
6. Note that *avviamo* does exist, but as the 1st pers. pl. of *avviare* 'to start'.
7. Alternatively, separate entries may be limited to each form within the particular subparadigm — e.g. the present tense — which manifests the irregularity. The difference is not crucial to the present argument.
8. The so-called "muzzy" theory of Haber (1975) is suggestive in this direction.

References

Alinei, M.
    1968   *Spogli elettronici dell'italiano delle origini e del Duecento* (The Hague: Mouton).
Andersen, H.
    1973   "Abductive and deductive change", *Language* 49:765–793.
Anderson, S. R.
    1974   *The organization of phonology* (New York/London: Academic).
Bach, E. — R. Harms (eds.)
    1968   *Universals in linguistic theory* (New York: Holt, Rinehart and Winston).
Berko, J.
    1958   "The child's learning of English morphology", *Word* 14:150–177.
Bruck, A. et al. (eds.)
    1974   *Papers from the Parasession on Natural Phonology* (Chicago: Chicago Linguistic Society).

Casagrande, J. — B. Saciuk (eds.)
   1972   *Generative studies in Romance languages* (Rowley, Mass.: Newbury House).
Castellani, A.
   1952   *Nuovi testi fiorentini del Dugento* (Firenze: Sansoni).
Chomsky, N. — M. Halle
   1968   *The sound pattern of English* (New York: Harper & Row).
Christie, W. M. (ed.)
   1976   *Current progress in historical linguistics* (Amsterdam: North-Holland).
Fisiak, J. (ed.)
   1978   *Recent developments in historical phonology* (= *Trends in Linguistics, Studies and monographs* 4) (The Hague: Mouton).
Haber, L.
   1975   "The muzzy theory", *Papers from the regional meeting of the Chicago Linguistic Society* 11:240–256.
Halle, M.
   1973   "Prolegomena to a theory of word formation", *Linguistic Inquiry* 4:3–16.
Hockett, C. F.
   1960   "The origin of speech", *Scientific American* 203:89–96.
Hooper, J. B.
   1978   "Constraints on schwa-deletion in American English", in Fisiak (ed.) 1978:183–208.
Jackendoff, R. J.
   1975   "Morphological and semantic regularities in the lexicon", *Language* 51:639–671.
Jeffers, R. J.
   1976   "Syntactic change and syntactic reconstruction", in Christie (ed.) 1976:1–16.
Kiparsky, P.
   1968   "Linguistic universals and linguistic change", in Bach — Harms (eds.) 1968:171–202.
Klausenburger, J.
   1976   "(De)morphologization in Latin", *Lingua* 40:305–320.
Lightfoot, D.
   1977   "Syntactic change and the autonomy thesis", *Journal of Linguistics* 13:191–216.
Lightner, T.
   1968   "On the use of minor rules in Russian phonology", *Journal of Linguistics* 4:69–72.
MacWhinney, B.
   1975   "Rules, rote and analogy in morphological formations by Hungarian children", *Journal of Child Language* 2:65–77.
Mańczak, W.
   1976   *Fonetica e morfologia storica dell'italiano* (Kraków: Uniwersytet Jagielloński).
Martinet, A.
   1965   *La linguistique synchronique* (Paris: PUF).
Rohlfs, G.
   1968   *Grammatica storica della lingua italiana e dei suoi dialetti*, 2: *Morfologia* (Torino: Einaudi).
Sommerstein, A.
   1974   "On phonotactically motivated rules", *Journal of Linguistics* 10:71–94.
Tekavčić, P.
   1972   *Grammatica storica dell'italiano*, 3 vols. (Bologna: Il Mulino).

Vennemann, T.
  1974   "Words and syllables in natural generative grammar", in Bruck et al. (eds.)
         1974:346–374.
Vincent, N.
  1972   "Minor rules and diphthongization in Italian", Ms.
  1978   "Is sound change teleological?', in Fisiak (ed.) 1978:409–430.
  in preparation   *The morphology and phonology of the Italian verb.*
Wagner, K. H.
  1969   *Generative grammatical studies in the Old English language* (Heidelberg: Julius
         Gross).
Wang, W.
  1969   "Competing changes as a cause of residue", *Language* 45:9–25.
Wanner, D.
  1972   "The derivation of inflectional paradigms in Italian", in Casagrande — Saciuk
         (eds.) 1972:293–318.
  1975   "Die historische Motivierung der Endung *-iamo* im Italienischen", *ZRPh*
         91:153–175.
Wurzel, W. U.
  1970   *Studien zur deutschen Lautstruktur* (= *Studia Grammatica* 8) (Berlin: Akademie).

JERZY WEŁNA

On gender change in linguistic borrowing (Old English)

1 Preliminary remarks

The development of the system of grammatical gender in the history of English has for a long time been in the centre of linguists' interest. As is generally known, some time in Middle English a shift from grammatical to natural gender occurred, and the three-gender system of Old English, which was comprised of masculine, feminine, and neuter, all three marking both animate and inanimate nouns, fell into disuse, being replaced by 'logical gender', where gender distinctions are in principle based on sex.[1] Of course, the stage at which the shift occurred was preceded by one at which grammatical gender began to be confused and gradually obliterated. One of the aims of this study is to present some evidence about how the tendency to simplify grammatical gender distinctions was reflected in the assignment of gender to loan-nouns in Old English.

Another aim of the present writer is to show the reasons for the assignment of gender to particular nouns borrowed during the Old English period; the analysis will be confined only to those substantives which changed their gender on entering Old English. That gender change (and gender preservation) in the process of borrowing are not random processes has been confirmed by a number of studies based on languages with various gender systems (cf., for instance, Aron 1930, Blumer 1890/91, Fisiak 1975, Haden-Joliat 1940, Wełna 1973 and 1976, etc.)

2 Loan-nouns in Old English

Throughout the Old English period, many loanwords, especially those from Latin, but also from Scandinavian, Celtic, Greek and Old French, entered the lexicon of English. It is important to note that Latin, from which most of the borrowings came, possessed a three-gender system based on grammatical gender distinctions. This fact is crucial since it is almost certain that the original grammatical gender was, in many cases, consciously transposed as a feature of the noun undergoing importation. The reason for this seems clear: loanwords from Latin, apart from their earliest stratum, were of a learned character, and those who introduced words of classical origin were fully aware of their grammatical properties, including gender; therefore the presence of nominative case endings, such as -*us* (usually M), -*a* (usually F), and -*um* (N without exceptions) in the nouns being borrowed was not without consequence for gender assignment.

The statistical data concerning preservation or change of gender confirm that grammatical gender was still solidly fixed in the grammar of Old English. From 516 loanwords[2] borrowed by Old English, which are listed in various Old English dictionaries, 357 (69%) preserved the gender of the source language, although there was no overt similarity in the phonetic or graphemic structure of gender-distinctive endings in the donor and the recipient language. On the contrary, the Latin morpheme -*a*, typical of feminine nouns, had its replica in OE -*a*, which marked masculine.

However, when we look closely at the figures concerning preservation of gender we can observe some interesting facts:

1. From 186 masculine nouns borrowed into Old English, 173, i.e. 93%, preserved their original gender.

2. From 216 feminine nouns 145, i.e. 67%, preserved the same gender.

3. From 114 neuter nouns only 39, i.e. 34%, appear with the N gender assignment in Old English.

An obvious tendency to eliminate neuter in the loanwords is evident since, as is seen from the above data, only one-third of them preserved their original gender. Much more stable was feminine lost in only one-third of the nouns, while the losses suffered by masculine were negligible. At this point, however, it is too early to make any generalization, since, while the reasons for gender preservation or change are not explored, the only solution would be that in Old English there existed a masculinizing tendency, which caused this preservation of masculine nouns in a large number of cases. Unless more definite proof were supplied, this view would not be supported by many linguists (cf. Arndt 1973, Fisiak 1975, and others).[3]

3   Gender determiners

When examining Old English loan-nouns preserving the original gender, we can observe some characteristic regularities in the assignment of masculine, feminine or neuter. The following factors must have contributed to the stability of gender in the process of linguistic borrowing[4]:

D1: Sex

This semantic feature makes it possible to assign only two genders, masculine for male beings and feminine for females. In Old English, no foreign nouns marked for sex appear with a contrary-to-sex assignment. Consequently, 98 foreign nouns denoting males and 16 nouns denoting females were, in Old English, assigned masculine and feminine respectively. Because sex specification in the donor language is quite sufficient for preservation of gender, other gender-marking factors, such as synonyms, endings, etc., are irrelevant.

In the search for other semantic and formal determiners of gender it is necessary first to dispose of nouns which owe their gender to D1, which will make further analysis more reliable. Thus, after the exclusion of nouns marked for sex, the number of masculines will decrease to 91 and the number of feminines to 208, while the figure for neuter remains the same, i.e. 114. Other semantic factors are the following:

D2: Cover term

The existence of a general term (cover term) having gender the same as the loanword was found in the case of 13 masculines, 45 feminines and 9 neuters; e.g. L *malva* f. > OE *mealwe* f. 'mallow', because of OE *wyrt* f. 'plant'.[5]

D3: Semantic equivalent

The presence of semantic equivalents of nouns undergoing importation marked for the same gender was found to exist in 53 masculines, 63 feminines and 22 neuters; for instance, L *fons,-tis* m. > OE *font* m. 'spring', because of OE *cwylla* m., *wella* m., both 'spring'.

The following formal factors affect the process of gender assignment:

D4: Some (usually) affixal elements in loanwords associated with Old English suffixes marked for gender, especially those having the structure V(vowel) + *r*, V + *l*, V + *k*, marking masculine; V + *n*, marking feminine, and V + *t* (mainly *-et*), which is typical of neuter (cf. Mossé 1950: §§137–140, Quirk and Wrenn 1957: §172).

Examples: L *caulis* m. > OE *cāwel* m. 'cole', L *culīna* f. > OE *cylen* f. 'kiln', L *tapetum* n. > OE *tæppet* n. 'carpet', altogether in 18 masculines, 8 feminines and 3 neuters.

This determiner influenced relatively few nouns which preserved their gender but, since it was present in addition in 39 masculine nouns and 4 feminine nouns marked for sex, we must consider the presence of the above suffixes as very essential in gender assignment.

D5: The formal resemblance of a borrowed stem or its final element to some native noun-stem in English, with or without similarity in the meaning; e.g. L *almosina* f. > OE *ælmesse* f. 'alms', because of OE *mæsse*

f. 'mass' (hence OE *ælmæsse*); 8 masculines, 11 feminines and 8 neuters.

D6: The similarity of an L_1 inflectional morpheme to some L_2 ending marked for gender (one case only: L *cométa* m. > OE *cométa* m. 'comet'; but cf. also nouns marked for sex: L *pāpa* m. > OE *pāpa* m. 'pope', etc.)

D7: The characteristic endings of Latin (rarely Old Scandinavian) in source forms, i.e. *-us, -a, -um*, marking masculine, feminine, and neuter respectively; e.g. L *discus* m. > OE *disc* m. 'plate, bowl', L *cūpia* f. > OE *cȳf* f. 'vat', L *balsamum* n. > OE *balsam* n. 'balsam'; 50 masculines, 110 feminines, and 27 neuters.

Gender preservation, or, more generally, gender assignment, is thus due to two distinctly different types of identification, here labelled as external and internal. Identification of gender based on sex distinctions takes place when the borrower only identifies the sex of the noun denoting an animate being and transposes its gender into L_2. The same is valid for D7, when gender is identified in L_1 on the basis of foreign inflectional markers, such as *-us* m. or *-a* f., and is then also accepted in L_2. When other determiners are involved, identification is made in terms of L_2, hence it may be labelled as internal. For instance, L *-er-* is at first taken together with the stem, without paying attention to its original gender, and then gender is assigned according to the rules of Old English, where nouns with affixal *-er-* are usually masculine. It is justifiable to say that most nouns whose gender was assigned due to the influence of D7, i.e. through external identification, were introduced by the educated, who knew rules of gender marking in Latin, while the assignment in terms of $D_2 - D_6$ could be made by any L_2 speaker, even without his knowing the grammar of Latin.

4   Reasons for gender change

Change of grammatical gender requires a more complicated procedure for recovering the determiners which contributed to the new gender assignment. When gender remains the same, much can be explained by the influence of sex factors, original endings (D7), or even the tendency to preserve the original gender. Because of the smaller significance of formal criteria and due to the elimination of the sex factor when gender change is involved secondary semantic determiners come to the fore.

The data for change of gender in Old English is as follows[6]:

1. 7% of foreign masculines (13) change their gender: 8 become feminines, and 5 change to neuter.

2. 33% of foreign feminines (71) change their gender to masculine (61) and neuter (10 nouns).

3. 66% of foreign neuters (76) appear either as masculine (43) or as feminine (33 nouns).

From this data some further conclusions concerning the status of the particular genders in Old English may be reached. The most significant fact is the loss of neuter in favour of both masculine and feminine. This may be proof of a relatively strong position being held by feminine in Old English, although most neuters which changed their gender to feminine had, in their Latin plural, an ending in *-a*, which was understood as a mark of feminine (cf. section 7 below, and the Appendix). On the other hand the fact that 64 feminines became masculine also demonstrates the gradual decline of the feminine gender, although this is less striking than the elimination of neuter. The dominating position of the masculine gender is so obvious that it is not necessary to give any further argument to support this claim.

In the following sections of the article our attention will be focused on exploring the reasons for gender assignment of Old English loanwords. To achieve this, the system of semantic and formal determiners arrived at in the analysis of nouns preserving the same gender will be employed. The material is arranged according to the direction of gender change, the most numerous classes being analysed at the beginning.

5   Feminine → Masculine

The most significant group of nouns which appear in Old English with their gender changed is that where foreign feminines take masculine (61 nouns). The replacement of gender in this class was due to both formal and semantic reasons. It is characteristic that 28 nouns showing this type of gender shift had, in Old English, equivalents with the same gender, e.g. L *pars,-tiṣ* f. > OE *part* m., because of OE *dæl* m. 'part, portion', or *ende* m. 'corner, part'. At the same time the following suffixal elements were found in the original nouns: *-el-, -ol-, -ul-*, (cf. OE *-el*, typical of masculine), *-ir-, -er-, -or-, -ur-, -yr* (cf. OE *-ere,* found in masculines), *-end* (cf. OE *-end* m.), *-ic-* (cf. OE *-ic*, usually a masculine suffix). Altogether, such elements appeared in 23 nouns. Relatively numerous was here the occurrence of a cover term, which had the same gender as the noun being borrowed. The most frequent masculine marking D2 in Old English was *stān* m. 'stone'. The gender of the latter could have contributed to the assignment of masculine to the original feminines: OE *cealc* 'chalk', *gimm* 'gem', *ceosel* 'gravel, shingle, sand', *teosel* 'die, small square piece of stone', *ancor* 'anchor' (a stone was used as anchor), *iacinctus* 'jacinth, precious stone'. The noun *bēam* m. 'tree' could have reinforced the masculine gender of OE *fīc* 'fig-tree', *palma* 'palm', *sycomer* 'sycamore'. Masculine was supported by other general terms, such as OE *dæȝ* m. 'day', *sang* m. 'song' (two instances each) and, in single cases, by *crōȝ*, etc. 'vessel', *hwǣte* 'wheat', *drenc* 'drink', *æppel* 'apple', also 'fruit', and *lǣcedōm* 'medicine'.

Only a little less influential was the ending *-a*, appearing in Latin. The force of this morpheme, marking feminine in Latin, was partly neutralized when words equipped with this marker entered Old English. In this language there also existed an *-a* typical of weak masculine nouns. In consequence, 11 feminines from Latin were assigned masculine (e.g. L *letanīa* f. > OE *letanīa* m. 'litany', L *glōria* f. > OE *glōria* m. 'gloria, hymn', L *corōna* f. > OE *corōna* m. 'crown', etc.). The same reason must underlie the assignment of masculine to OIc. *sala* f., which appeared in Old English as *sala* m. 'sale'. The Old English pluralia tantum *expectas* and *reliquias*, both masculine, meaning 'epacts' and 'relics' respectively, were probably borrowed as accusatives, with subsequent false association of the Latin *-as*, marking acc.pl. and OE *-as*, the ending found in nom.acc. of the strong masculine declension.

In a few cases masculine was chosen for a loanword because of the existence in Old English of a D5, i.e. either a word with a structure similar to that of the loanword, or certain word-terminal sequences marking masculine. Such pairs of words were, for instance, OE *pāl* m. (<L *pāla* f. 'spade') and OE *pāl* m. 'pole' (also a borrowing from Latin), OE *ūf* m. (<L *ūva* f.) 'the uvula' and OE *ūf* m. 'owl' (cf. the Old English equivalent of *ūf* 'the uvula', which was *hræcetunge* f.), OE *spelt* m. (<L *spelta* f.) 'corn, spelt' and OE *spelt* m. 'plank', or OE *senep* m. (<L *sinapis*) 'mustard' and OE *henep, cenep*, both masculine nouns.

Finally, cases of external identification must also be mentioned. Although the number of words assuming masculine because of D7 is small (only 9), it seems that the presence of the morpheme *-us* in some Latin feminines could contribute to false identification of this ending as a signal of masculine (L *-us* normally marks masculine in the 2nd and the 4th Latin declensions) and subsequently lead to the masculine assignment of words such as OE *nard* n. (<L *nardus* f.) 'spikenard', *sinoð* m. (<L *synodus* f.) 'synod', or *tapor* m. (<L *papyrus* f.) 'taper', etc.

It is difficult to state convincingly the reasons for the masculine assignment of OE *cyrfet, cyrfæt* m. (<L *cucurbita* f.) 'gourd' (D2 *wryt* f. 'plant', D4 *-et/it-* n., D5 *fæt* n. 'vat')[7]; for OE *flanc* m. (<L **flanca* f.) 'flank, side, half, part' (D3 *sīde* f. 'side', *healf* f. 'half, side, part'; and for OE *ynce* m. (L *uncia* f.) 'inch' (D2 *ȝemet* n. 'measure').[8]

6   Neuter → Masculine

As regards the number of words of this class borrowed by Old English, the neuter > masculine group ranks second and it consists of 43 nouns. However, contrary to the distribution of determiners in the class feminine > masculine, the change of gender from neuter to masculine is primarily due here to formal factors, the masculine assignment being due to suffixal similarity in 27 cases.

The fact that such a high percentage of nouns in this group have shifted their gender to masculine reflects a characteristic feature of word-formation in Latin, where the ending *-um* was very frequently preceded by suffixes with V-plus-*r* or *l*, or by the suffix *-ic*, which resembled the typical masculine suffixes of Old English; cf. OE *mortere* m. (<L *mortārium* n.) 'mortar', *læfel* m. (<L *labellum* n.) 'basin, cup', *cilic* m. (<L *cilicium* n.) 'sackcloth, haircloth'.

When the distinctive suffix marking masculine was absent, semantic determiners, mainly equivalents (D3), were decisive in the choice of that gender (23 nouns). The impact of the synonymous lexical items must have contributed to the masculine assignment of, for instance, OE *weall* m. (<L *vallum* n.), corresponding to OE *wāg* m., *stānheȝe* m. 'wall' or OE *sæcc* m. (<L *saccium* n.) 'sack, bag' and OE *fetels, pusa, pohha*, all masculine, with a meaning very close to that of the loanword.

Much less significant than that in feminine > masculine is the influence of D2, i.e. of cover terms (8 cases, as against 18 in the former class). The general term OE *stān* m. 'stone' could have influenced the shift to M in two nouns: L *crystallum* n. > OE *crystalla* m. 'crystal' and L *marmor* n. > OE *marmor* m. 'marble', also reinforced by D4s, *-al-* and *-or*. Similarly, OE *sang* m. 'song' must have had some influence on the masculine assignment of OE *cantic* m. (<L *canticum* n.) 'canticle'. Other cover terms, such as OE *mēle* m. 'box', *æppel* m. 'apple, fruit', *hwǣte* m. 'wheat' and *dæȝ* m. 'day', contributed to the gender shift in only a few separate cases. It should be noted that some of these determiners were also operative in the feminine > masculine class.

A few nouns may owe their gender change to the fact that the Latin plural form was borrowed. This seems to be the case with OE *cymbala* m. (<L *cymbalum* n.) 'cymbal', which reflects the Latin plural *cymbala*, whose ending was associated with the native morpheme *-a*, marking weak masculine. Also OE *timpana* (< *tympana* n. pl.) 'timbrel', *cristalla* (<L *crystalla* n.pl.) 'crystal' and *ðimiana* (<L *thȳmiāna* n.sg.) 'incense', all masculine, could have obtained their gender through such a false identification. An analogous gender development in L *chrisma* n. > OE *crisma* m. 'chrisom, holy oil' is also caused by false association, the termination *-a* in the Latin word being identified as the native masculine morpheme.

Change of gender due to similarity in the final phonemic (or graphemic) sequences can be illustrated by the masculine assignment of OE *cīsmēl* (<L *chrīsmāle* + *cimelium* n.), caused by the influence of OE *mēle* m., also a cover term, meaning 'box'. Similar reasons must be given in the case of OE *sēam* m. (>Gk. *sagma* n.) 'load' and OE *strið* m. (<OIc. *strið* n.) 'struggle', whose masculine gender could have been due to OE *sēam* m. 'seam' and *strīde* m. 'stride' respectively. This is very probable since the equivalents of the former were either feminine (OE *byrþen*, *hyrd*) or neuter (OE *hlæst*) and most synonyms of the latter noun were as a rule non-masculine; cf. *æscþræc, bat, beadu, tohte* 'fight, battle', all feminine, and *ȝefeoht, ȝewin, orleȝe, wīȝ* 'battle, etc.', all neuter.

The masculine gender of OE *must* (<L *mustum* n.) 'new wine' is puzzling since other nouns denoting wine were neuter. The loanword *wīn* (<L *vinum* n.) 'wine' was neuter, too.[9]

7   Neuter → feminine

This is the third major class of nouns with shifted gender and includes 33 nouns. It also shows a distribution of determiners completely different from that in the two groups discussed earlier. It seems that Latin neuters changing their gender to feminine were in most cases borrowed in their plural form, which was characterized by the ending *-a*, and was thus wrongly associated with feminine.[10] This special treatment of neuters becoming feminines is explained by the fact that most of them were borrowed as collectives, with subsequent change of their original plural meaning to singular; cf. OE *pere* f. (<L *pirum*, pl. *-a* 'pear', OE *butere* f. (<L *butyrum*, pl.*-a*) 'butter', etc. Thus, in the case of these neuters becoming feminines it was external identification which contributed most to feminine assignment (24 instances).

Almost equally important for the choice of the feminine gender was D2, i.e. cover term. The latter may be postulated to have influenced the gender of 22 former neuters, which became feminine in Old English. The most frequent general term was, without any doubt, OE *wyrt* f. 'plant', since no less than 20 Latin neuters denoting plants changed their gender to feminine. It should be emphasized that 38 feminine nouns designating various plants preserved their original gender and only a few changed it (cf. Wełna 1973). On the other hand the tendency to assign feminine to nouns denoting plants is confirmed by a mass shift of neuters to feminines. This can be illustrated by the gender change of L *ervum* n. > OE *earfe* f. 'tares', L *oxymel,-lis* n. > OE *oxumelle* f. 'oxymel', L *zingiber*

n. > OE *ȝinȝiber* f. 'ginger', and many others. In addition, OE *ādl* f. 'disease' seems to have served as cover term for OE *neurism* f. (< L *aneurisma* n.) 'aneurism', and OE *næm* f. 'seizure' for OE *nām* f. (<OIc. *nām* n.) 'legal seizure of property'.

Equivalents could have influenced only 12 of the nouns in this class, and thus they acted only as secondary factors in the process of gender assignment, being in most cases present together with other determiners. Nevertheless, the choice of feminine by OE *stræt* (<L *stratum* n.) 'couch, bed' or by OE *lazu* (< OIc. **lagu*) 'law' was in all probability due to the native feminine equivalents OE *strēowen, rest, bedstōw, strecedness*, etc. 'bed', and OE *ǣ, āsetness* 'law' respectively.

Other determiners are only marginal and isolated: e.g. *-en* (D4) in L *alumen* n. > OE *alifn* f. 'alum', or OE *waru* f. 'ware', which was associated with the Latin termination *-arium*; cf. L *zedoārium* n. > OE *sīdeware* f. 'zedoary'. For other individual cases see the Appendix.

In L *pēsālis* n. > OE *pisle* f. 'warm chamber', the feminine assignment is puzzling because its equivalents and cover terms had different genders. But it is possible that this word was borrowed as *pisale*, a later form of *pēsālis*, with subsequent assignment to the weak feminine declension because of the final *-e*.

8   Feminine → neuter

The change from feminine to neuter is illustrated by only 10 nouns. As neuter was lacking in characteristic formal determiners, semantic indicators seem to have played an essential role in assignment of this gender. In 6 nouns change of gender was probably caused by meaning associations, mainly by equivalents. Thus, the shift from feminine to neuter in L *fenestra* f. > OE *fenester* n. 'window', where the presence of *-er* would rather indicate masculine, was possibly due to the native *ēaȝþȳrel, teolþyrl* 'window', both neuter. Similarly, L *trabs* f. changed to *træf* n. 'tent' because of a range of equivalent nouns, like OE *feldhūs, ȝeteld, seleȝesceot*, all neuter. Altogether, 6 loan-nouns had such equivalents in Old English. The general terms OE *ȝemet* 'measure', *ȝewiht* 'weight', both neuter, could have influenced the new gender assignment of OE *marc* n. (<OIc. *mörk* f.) 'denomination of weight', and the cover term OE *flǣsc* n. 'flesh, body' could have had some influence on the neuter of OE *myrten* (< OF *mort* f.) 'animal corpse'.

The presence of a formal indicator of gender can be assumed in the case of OE *cymed* n. (< L *chamaedrys* f.) 'wall-garmander' and OE *mynet* n. (< L *monēta* f.) 'coin', where *-ed-* and *-ēt-*, usually appearing in Old

English neuters contributed to the selection of the latter gender. The neuter assignment of OE *inwitt* 'deceit, evil, fraud', which reflects L *invidia* f., was due to the replacement of -*vidia* by the similar-looking -*witt* n., with preservation of the gender of the native word.

9 Masculine → feminine

Only a few loan-nouns in Old English (8) show this gender development. In the selection of feminine for masculine, an unusual change of gender because of the strong position of masculine in the earliest English, the femine determiners must have been particularly distinctive. Among those, the most important appears to be D2 (cover term) OE *wyrt* f. 'plant', which probably caused the gender change of L *ebulus* m. 'danewort', *cypressus* m. 'cypress', *humulus* 'hop-plant', entering Old English as *eofole* f., *cypresse* f., *hymele* f. respectively. Semantic equivalents were operative in the assignment of feminine to *læst* (< OIc. *löstr* m.) 'sin, fault', because of the synonymous feminines OE *bealudæd, facendæd, firen, māndæd, scyld, synn, wrōht*, or, in the change of OIr. *clocc* m. > OE *cluc3e* f. 'bell', the latter noun being associated with OE *bell* f. 'bell'. The feminine assignment of OE *læst* could have been reinforced by the presence in Old English of the native *læst* f., with a different meaning ('performance'). In a like manner OE *muscelle* f. (< L *musculus* m.) 'shell-fish, mussel' probably owes its gender to OE *scell* f., which functioned both as D3 (equivalent) and D5 (a formally similar item) in the process of gender assignment.

The only unclear case is the feminine gender of OE *cuopel* (< L *caupulus* m.) 'coble, small ship', whose equivalent, or perhaps cover term, was OE *æsc* m. 'small ship', while the more general cover term was OE *scip* n. 'ship'. In addition, -*ul*- in the Latin source form indicates masculine. The only solution is to postulate the influence of OE *bāt* 'boat', whose gender was both feminine and masculine.

10 Masculine → neuter

Only 5 nouns show the masculine to neuter shift, this being caused mainly by semantic factors: 4 nouns had equivalents in Old English. Thus, OE *bȳ* n. (< OIc. *bȳr* m.) 'dwelling' corresponded in meaning to OE *ærn, flet, 3eset*, all neuter, denoting 'dwelling, house, habitation'; OE *carcærn* n. (< L *carcer* m.) 'prison' was matched by the native *gnornhof* n. 'prison', and OE *market* n. (< L *marcātus* m.) 'market', by OE *cēapung3emōt* 'market, meeting for trade', the latter two also reinforced by the formal determiners: D5 *ærn* 'house, habitation', which replaced the L suffix *-er* in *carcer*, and D4 *-āt-* (< *-et*, a suffix usually used with neuters).

The cover term OE ʒ*emet* n. 'measure' seems to have caused the neuter assignment of OE *mydd* (< L *modius* m.) 'bushel', although the Latin side-form *modium* n. could have been the source of the Old English loanword, with transposition of the original gender.

11 Divergent identification of gender

Divergent identification of gender was very frequent in Old English, where 42 loan-nouns appear with double, and 5 with triple gender. Our attention will concentrate here only on those developments where the original gender of the lending language is replaced by the two other genders.

The 9 nouns which show this type of gender distribution can be classified into three groups, depending on the semantic function and formal structure of the borrowed noun:

a.   Nouns in which the distinction of gender is semantically significant: OE *box* m. 'box-tree', n. 'box'.

b.   Nouns with different final morphemes characteristic of one of the genders, having identical meanings: OE *disma* m. *disme* f. 'musk', *finol* m. *finule* f. 'fennel', *pālent* m. *pālentse* f. 'palace', *syric* m. *serce* f. 'sark, shirt', *meregrota* m. *meregrot* n. 'pebble, pearl'.

c.   Nouns with identical meaning and form: OE *fēfer* m.f. 'fever', *portic* m.f. 'porch', *wīc* f.n. 'dwelling place, house, town, street'.

The double gender of the noun in (a), i.e. of OE *box* m.n. (< L *buxus* f.) is caused by semantic criteria — by D2s, OE *bēam* m. 'tree' and OE *fæt* n. 'receptacle'. The possible false interpretation of the Latin ending *-us* as masculine is only a secondary factor.

The split of gender in words belonging to (b) is of a more complicated nature. In the pairs OE *disma* m. *disme* f. (< L *bisamum* n., pl.-*a*) the feminine gender must be due to the cover term OE *wyrt* f. 'plant', while masculine must have been influenced by formal factors, probably by D6, i.e. L *-a* in the plural preserved as *-a* in *disma* m., an ending typical of the weak declension of the masculine nouns, and D4 *-ul-*, rendered as *-ol* in *finol* m., a suffix favoring masculine. In the pair OE *meregrota* m. *meregrot* n. (< L *margarīta* f.) the masculine form is mainly a reflection of the gender of the cover term *stān* m. 'stone', while neuter is due to the association of L *-grita* with the natuve *grot* n. 'sand, particle', which also showed semantic affinity with the loanword.

The differentiation of gender in OE *pālent* m. *pālentse* f. (< L *palan-*

tium n., pl.-*a*) 'palace' consists mainly in the diverse choice of formal determiners, -*ant* (OE -*ent*), later on associated with OE -*end* m., hence the masculine gender of *palent*, and -*a* of the plural form, identified as marking feminine. It should be emphasized that the meaning of the loanword was paralleled by that of the native *bēorsele* m. and *heall* f., both 'palace, etc.'. Similarly, in the pair *syric* m. *serce* f. (< L *sericum* n., pl.-*a*), masculine is due to -*ic* and feminine to -*a*, this gender split also being reinforced by the gender distinction of other words for 'shirt': OE *ham* m. and *scyrte* f.

In the last group there is no overt formal distinction of the final morphemes, and nouns with different genders are used interchangeably. Consequently, the masculine assignment of OE *fēfer* 'fever' can be easily explained as reflecting the suffixal -*r* of L *febris* f., also supported by the presence of the cover term *bryne* m. 'heat, burning' and the equivalent OE *hriþ* m. 'fever', while the selection of neuter must depend on OE *ādl* n. (also feminine) or on OE *ceald* n. 'coldness, cold'.[11] Nevertheless, absence of feminine assignment is puzzling in view of numerous feminine synonyms, such as *hriðe*, *ʒedrif, byneādl, ridesoht*, etc.

The double gender of OE *portic* m.n. (< L *porticus* f.) reflects different determiners, semantic and formal. Thus, masculine is due, first of all, to formal factors: -*ic*, marking masculine in Old English, and to the false interpretation of L -*us* as a masculine marker. The neuter gender can be explained as being influenced either by the cover term OE *ʒeat* n. 'door', or, more accurately, by the equivalent nouns OE *foredyre* n. 'porch, vestibule', *forehūs* n. 'porch'. Other nouns meaning 'porch' were masculine; cf. OE *forestiʒe, forþtiʒe* 'vestibule, porch'.

OE -*wīc* (< L *vīcus* m.) 'dwelling place, habitation, house, village, street', which is both feminine and neuter because of the two meaning-complexes, 'town' (cf. OE *burh* f. 'town') and 'habitation' (cf. OE *hūs* n., *ærn* n., *bū* n., all 'house, habitation'), shows the influence of semantic determiners only.

12   Concluding remarks

The process of gender assignment of Old English loanwords fully confirms the tendency to eliminate neuter (and, to a lesser degree, feminine) nouns; at the same time the strong position of masculine is unquestionable.[12]

As regards the distribution of loan-nouns in the three gender categories of Old English the following tentative statements can be made:

The change of feminine to masculine was caused mainly by the influence of the Old English semantic equivalents (D3) and association of suffixal elements in the donor language nouns with native masculine suffixes (D4).

The change of neuter to masculine was caused by factors similar to the above, the suffixal association being here, however, stronger than semantic.[13]

The change of neuter to feminine is due both to external identification (D7) and to the impact of Old English cover terms (D2).

In the other three groups (f > n, m > f, m > n), the number of nouns undergoing gender change is relatively small, although prevalence of semantic over formal factors is evident.

Complex gender of loanwords is due to the conflict of semantic and formal determiners.

Appendix

The list below includes loanwords which changed their gender on entering Old English. Semantic determiners are given in all cases; formal determiners, except D5, are marked by symbols. 'L' stands for any variant of Latin.

I   Feminine > masculine

1. L *amūla* > OE *āmel* 'sacred vessel'; D2 *crō₃, sā, mēle* m. 'vessel'; D4; D5 *mēle*.
2. L *amygdala* > OE *āmigdal* 'almond'; D2 *æppel* m. 'fruit'; D4.
3. L *anchora* > OE *ancor* 'anchor'; D3 *stān* 'stone' (used as anchor; cf. Kluge (1957) 'Anker'); D4.
4. L *aspis, -idis* > OE *aspide* 'asp, adder, serpent'; D3 *hringboga* m. 'serpent', *wyrm* m. 'reptile, serpent'.
5. L *astella* > OE *æstel* 'waxed tablet, bookmark'; D4.
6. L *brassica* > OE *brassica* 'colewort, cabbage'; D6.
7. L *bulla* > OE *būl(a)* 'bracelet, necklace, brooch'; D3 *cnæp, dalc, prēon* m. 'brooch'.
8. L *calendae* (pl.) > OE *cālend* 'month, calends'; D3 *mōnaþ* m. 'month', *₃ehealdda₃as* m.pl. 'calends'; D4; [perhaps this word was borrowed as acc.pl. with *-as*, an ending typical of masculines in Old English].
9. L *calx,-cis* > OE *cealc* 'lime, chalk, pebble'; D2 *stān* m. 'stone'; D3 *mealmstān* m. 'chalk, stone', *līm* m. 'lime', *spærstān* m. 'chalk'.

10. L *capa*> OE *(cantel)cāp* 'cope'; D3 *hoppāda* m. 'cope'.

11. L *casella* > OE *ceosel* 'gravel, sand, shingle'; D2 *stān* m. 'stone'; D4.

12. L *casula* > OE *casul* 'overgarment, cloak'; D3 *basing, mentel* m. (borrowing) 'cloak'; D4.

13. L *cella* > OE *cell* 'monastic cell'; D4 (?); [cf. *beclysung, cȳfe* f. 'cell'].

14. L *chronica* > OE *cranic* 'record, chronicle'; D4.

15. L **cocca (< concha)* > OE *(sǣ)cocc* 'cockle, a mollusk'; D3 *weoloc* m. 'cockle'; D5 *cocc* m. 'cock' [a borrowing].

16. L *cucurbita* > OE *cyrfet, -fæt* 'gourd'; D?

17. L *corōna* > OE *corōna* 'crown'; D3 *bēah, cynehelm* m. 'crown'; D6.

18. L *crux,-cis* > OE *crūc* 'cross'; D3 *bēam, galga, Crīstes-mǣl* m.(n.) 'cross'.

19. L *epactae,-as* acc.pl. > OE *epactas* pl. 'epacts'; D2 *daȝas* m.pl. 'days'; D6.

20. L *epistola* > OE *epistol* 'letter'; D4; [cf. OE *ȝewrit* n., *ǣrendbōc*, etc. 'letter', feminines].

21. L *fīcus* > OE *fīc* 'fig, fig-tree'; D2 *æppel* m. 'fruit', *bēam* m. 'tree'; D7.

22. L *flanca* > OE *flanc* 'flank, side, half, part'; D? [cf. OE *sīde, healf* 'side, half', both feminine].

23. L *galla* > OE *ȝealla* 'gall, fretted place on the skin'; D6.

24. L *gemma* > OE *ȝimm* 'gem, jewel'; D2 *stān* m. 'stone'.

25. L *gloria* > OE *gloria* 'gloria, doxology'; D2 *sang* m. 'song'; D3 *lofsang* m. 'gloria'; D6.

26. L *hyacinthus* > OE *iacintus* 'jacinth, precious stone'; D2 *stān* m. 'stone'; D7.

27. L *laurus* > OE *laur, lāwer* 'laurel'; D4; D7.

28. L *letanīa* > OE *letanīa* 'litany'; D7 [cf. OE *hālsungȝebet* n. 'litany'].

29. L *manna* > OE *manna* 'manna'; D3 *fōstraþ, heofonhlāf* m. 'manna' D6 [cf. OE *hwītcorn* n. 'manna'].

30. L *nardus* > OE *nard* 'spikenard, unguent'; D7.

31. L *nota* > OE *nōt* 'mark, note'; D3 *strica* m. 'mark, line'.

32. L *offerenda* > OE *offerenda* 'psalm or anthem sung during the offertory'; D2 *sang* m. 'song'; D3 *lānesang* m. 'offertory, hymn', *lācsang* m. 'offertory'; D6.

33. L *orca* > OE *orc* 'cup, pitcher'; D3 *scenc, stēap* m. 'cup, pitcher'.

34. L *pagella* > OE *pæȝel* 'wine vessel, small measure, pail'; D3 *sā, stoppa* m. 'pail, bucket'; D4.

35. L *pāla* > OE *pæl* 'javelin'; D5 *pāl (pæl)* m. 'pole' [borrowed approximately at the same time].

36. L *palma* > OE *palm*(*a*) 'palm-tree'; D2 *bēam* m. 'tree'; D6.
37. L *panthēra* > OE *palðer* 'panther'; D1 (generalized as male); D4 [but cf. also L *panther,-is* m.].
38. L *papȳrus* > OE *tapor* 'taper, wick of a lamp, candle'; D4; D7.
39. L *papyrus* > OE *paper* 'papyrus'; D3 *dūphamor, eolhsec₃* m. 'papyrus'; D4; D7.
40. L *pars,-tis* > OE *part* 'part'; D3 *dǣl, ende* m. 'part'.
41. L. *pentecoste* (*acc.-en*) > OE *pentecosten* 'pentecost'; D2 *dæ₃* m. 'day'; D3 *Fīfti₃dæ₃* m. 'Pentecosten'.
42. L *rādix,icis* > OE *rædic* 'radish'; D2 *wyrttruma, wyrtwala* m. 'root of a plant'; D4.
43. L *rēgula* > OE *regol* 'rule, canon, pattern'; D4.
44. L *reliquiae* pl. (*acc.pl.-as*) > OE *reliquias* m.pl. 'relics of Saints'; D3 *hāli₃dōm* m. 'reliquiae, relics'; D6.
45. OIc. *sala* > OE *sala* 'sale'; D3 *cēap* m. 'sale' (an earlier borrowing); D6.
46. OIc. *sæng* > OE *sang, song* 'bed'; D3 *sealma* m. 'bed, couch'; D5 *sang, song* m. 'song'.
47. L *scindula* > OE *scindel* 'a shingle'; D4.
48. L *scutella* > OE *scutel* 'dish, platter'; D3 *disc* m. 'platter, dish' (an earlier borrowing); D4.
49. L *secula* > OE *sicol* 'sickle'; D3 *rifter* m. 'sickle'; D4.
50. L *sicera* > OE *sicera* 'intoxicating drink'; D2 *drenc, drinc* m. 'drink'; D4.
51. L *sinapis* > OE *senep* 'mustard'; D5 *-enep* (as in *henep, cenep* m.).
52. L *spelta* > OE *spelt* 'spelt, corn'; D2 *hwǣte* 'wheat', *ry₃e* 'rye', etc., with the masculine gender; D5 *spelt* m. 'plank'.
53. L *sycomorus* > OE *sycomer* 'sycamore'; D2 *bēam* m. 'tree'; D4; D7 [in Vulgar Latin, *sycomorus* became masculine].
54. L *synodus* > OE *sinoð* 'synod, council, meeting'; D7 [this noun shows gender wavering in Old English].
55. L *tessella* > OE *teosel* 'die, small square piece of stone'; D2 *stān* m. 'stone'; D4.
56. L *thiriaca* > OE *tȳriāca* 'a medicine, treacle, remedy'; D2 *lǣcedōm, lǣcecræft* m. 'medicine, remedy'; D6.
57. OIc *topt* > OE *toft* 'house-yard, homestead'; D3 ₃*eard* m. 'yard'.
58. OFr. *tour* > OE *tūr* 'tower, fortress'. ⎱ D3 *scylf* m. 'tower, rock',
59. L *turris* > OE *torr* 'tower, rock, crag'. ⎰ *stūpel* m. 'tower'.
60. L *uncia* > OE *ynce* 'inch'; D?
61. L *ūva* > OE *ūf* 'the uvula'; D5 *ūf* m. 'owl'.

II   Neuter > masculine

1. L *altar(e)* > OE *altar, -er* 'altar'; D3 *glēdstede* m. *wēofod* m.(n.) 'altar'; D4.
2. L *antiphonārium* > OE *antefnere* 'book of antiphons'; D4.
3. L *canticum* > OE *cantic* 'canticle, song'; D2 *sang* m. 'song'; D3 *lofsang* m. 'hymn, canticle'; D4.
4. L *capitulum* > OE *capitol* 'chapter, meeting of ecclesiats'; D3 *hēafodcwide* m. 'chapter'; D4.
5. L *cavellum* > OE *cāwel* 'basket'; D3 *lēap, sprincel, tǣnel, windel* m. 'basket'; D4.
6. L *chrisma* > OE *crisma* 'chrisom, holy oil, chrisom cloth'; D6.
7. L *chrīsmāle (cīmēlium)* > OE *cīsmēl* 'sacramental box'; D2 and D5 *mēle* m. 'box, bowl'.
8. L *cicer* > OE *ciceling* 'chickpea'; D4.
9. L *cilicium* > OE *cilic* 'sackcloth of hair, haircloth'; D4.
10. L *cochlear* > OE *cuculer* 'spoon, spoonful'; D3 *sticca, metesticca* m. 'spoon'; D4.
11. L *crystallum*, pl.-*a* > OE *cristalla* 'crystal'; D2 *stān* m. 'stone'; D6.
12. L *cucurum* > OE *cocer* 'quiver, case, sheath'; D3 *bogefodder* m. 'quiver, case for the bow'; D4.
13. L *cymbalum*, pl.-*a* > OE *cimbala* 'cymbal'; D4; D6.
14. L *fossorium* > OE *fossere* 'spade'; D4.
15. L *hymnārium* > OE *ymnere* 'book of hymns'; D4.
16. L *labellum* > OE *lǣfel* 'spoon, basin, cup, vessel'; D3 *hnæpf, mēle, wearr(hwer)* m. 'cup, bowl, basin' (cf. also OE *cuculer*); D4.
17. L *laser* > OE *lāser* 'tare, wood'; D3 *unwǣstm* m. (f.n.) 'tare, weed'; D4.
18. L *mantellum* > OE *mentel* 'mantle, cloak'; D3 *basing, heden, hwītel, loða, scēata, sciccel(s), wǣfels* m. 'mantle'; D4.
19. L *marmor* > OE *marmor, -ma, -el* 'marble'; D2 *stān* m. 'stone'; D4.
20. L *mortarium* > OE *mortere* 'a mortar'; D4.
21. L *mustum* > OE *must* 'must, new wine'; D?
22. L *organum* > OE *organ* 'canticle, voice'; D2 *sang* m. 'song'; D3 *lofsang* m. 'hymn, canticle'.
23. L *pallium* > OE *pæll* 'cloak, purple garment'; D2? [see *mentel* above]; D3 *acre* m. 'episcopal pallium', *fellerēad* m.(?) 'episcopal pallium'.
24. L *panicum* > OE *panic* 'kind of millet'; D2 [see *spelt* above]; D4.
25. L *persicum* > OE *persic* 'peach'; D2 *æppel* 'fruit'; D4.
26. L *pīlum* > OE *pīl* 'spike, shaft, stake, dart, javelin'; D3 *daroþ, gafeluc* m. 'javelin, spike, shaft, dart'.

27. L *piper* > OE *pipor* 'pepper'; D4.
28. L *psaltērium* > OE *saltere* 'psaltery, psalter'; D4.
29. L *responsōrium* > OE *reps, respons* 'response, a psalm'; D3 *sealm* m. 'psalm' *ʒeʒncwide* m. 'reply'; D4.
30. L *sabbatum* > OE *sabbat* 'the Sabbath'; D2 *dæʒ* m. 'day'; D3 *restedæʒ, symbeldæʒ* m. 'sabbath'.
31. L **saccium* > OE *sæcc* 'sack, bag, sackcloth'; D3 *fētels, pohha, pusa* m. 'sack'.
32. Gk. *sagma* > OE *sēam* 'load, burden'; D3 *hefe* m. 'burden'; D5 *seam* m. 'seam' [borrowed from VL *sauma?*].
33. L *scamellum* > OE *scamol* 'bench, stool'; D3 *hlēda, sess* m. 'bench, seat'; D4.
34. L *scriptum* > OE *scrift* 'absolution; judge, confessor'; D1 *male* (D3 *dōmere, dōmsettend* m. 'judge').
35. L *sēricum* > OE *sioluc* 'silk'; D4.
36. L *sōlārium* > OE *solor* 'upper room, loft'; D3 *upflōr* m.(f.) 'upper chamber'; D4.
37. OIc. *strip* > OE *strip* 'struggle, fight, dispute'; D3 *æscepleʒa* m. *ellen* m.(n.) 'strife, contention'; ?D5 *strīde* m. 'stride'.
38. L *theātrum* > OE *peater* 'theatre'; D3 *wafungstede* m. 'theatre'; D4.
39. L *thymiāma* > OE *pimiama* 'incense'; D3 *rēcels* m. 'incense'; D6.
40. L *tropārium* > OE *tropere* 'service book'; D4.
41. L *tympanum* n., pl-*a* > OE *timpana* 'timbrel'; D3 *glīwbēam* 'timbrel' [cf. also *hylsong* f. 'timbrel'].
42. L *unguen* > OE *ungel* 'fat, tallow, suet'; D3 *rysel* m. 'fat, lard'.
43. L *vallum* > OE *weall* 'wall, dike, rampart'; D3 *wāg, stānheʒe* m. 'wall'.

III   Neuter > feminine

1. L *abrotonum*, pl.-*a* > OE *aprotane* 'southernwood, wormwood'; D2 *wyrt* f. 'plant'; D7.
2. L *alūmen* > OE *ælefn* 'alum' ('sustenance'?); D4 [via Celtic **alīfn?*].
3. L *aneurisma* > OE *neurisn* 'aneurism, kind of paralysis'; D2 *ādl* f.(n.) 'disease'; D7.
4. L *butyrum*, pl.-*a* > OE *butere* 'butter'; D7.
5. L *cærifolium*, pl.-*a* > OE *cerfelle* 'chervil'; D2 *wyrt* f. 'plant'; D7.
6. L *castrum*, pl.-*a* > OE *cæster* 'city, fort, castle, town'; D3 *burh* f. 'town, castle'; D7.
7. L *centaurēum*, pl.-*a* > OE *centaurie* 'centaury'; D2 *wyrt* f. 'plant'; D3 *curmealle, curmille, hyrdewyrt* f. 'centaury'; D7.

8. L *cerasium*, pl.-*a* > OE *cirse* 'cherry'; D2 *wyrt* f. 'plant'; D7 [? from VL *cerasea* (Holthausen)].

9. L *electrum*, pl.-*a* > OE *elehtre* 'lupine'; D2 *wyrt* f. 'plant'; D7.

10. L *ervum*, pl.-*a* > OE *earfe* 'tare'; D2 *wyrt* f. 'plant'; D3 *āte* 'oats, tares', *unwǣstem* f. (m.n.) 'tare'; D7.

11. L *fel* (*terrae*) > OE *fel* (*terre*) 'a plant (centaury?)'; D2 *wyrt* f. 'plant'.

12. L (*inula* +)*helenium* > OE *eolone* 'elacampane'; D2 *wyrt* f. 'plant'; D3 *ehheoloðe, hēahheolode, sperewyrt* f. 'elacampane'; D7.

13. OIc. **lagu* n.pl. > OE *lagu* 'law'; D3 *ǣ* f. 'law', *āsetnes* f. 'institute, law'; D6 [the Old English noun is historical n.pl.].

14. L *līlium*, pl.-*a* > OE *lilie* 'lily'; D2 *wyrt* f. 'plant'; D3 *fleaðe, fleaðowyrt, ēadocce* f. 'water lily', *glōfwyrt* f. 'lily of the valley'; D7.

15. L *marrubium*, pl.-*a* > OE *mārubie* 'horehound'; D2 *wyrt* f. 'plant'; D3 *hārhūne, hūne* f. 'horehound'; D7.

16. OIc. *nām* > OE *nām* 'legal seizure of property'; D2 *nimung, nǣm* f. 'taking'; D5 *nǣm* 'taking'.

17. L *origanum*, pl.-*a* > OE *organe* f. 'marjoram'; D2 *wyrt* f. 'plant'; D3 *cyningeswyrt, wurmille* f. 'wild marjoram'; D7.

18. L *oxymel,-lis* > OE *oxumelle* 'oxymel'; D2 *wyrt* f. 'plant'.

19. L *pēsālis* > OE *pisle* 'warm chamber'; D?

20. L *petrosilium*, pl.-*a* > OE *petersilie* 'parsley'; D2 *wyrt* f. 'plant'; D3 *stānmerce* f. 'parsley'; D7.

21. L *pirum*. pl.-*a* > OE *pere* 'pear'; D2 *wyrt* f. 'plant'; D7.

22. L *pistillum*, pl.-*a* > OE *pilstre* 'pestle'; D3 *stampe, þwēre* f. 'pestle'.

23. L *pisum*, pl.-*a* > OE *peose* 'pea'; D2 *wyrt* f. 'plant'; D7.

24. L *prūnum*, pl.-*a* > OE *plūme* 'plum, plumtree'; D2 *wyrt* f. 'plant'; D7.

25. L *pulegium*, pl.-*a* > OE *polleȝie* 'pennyroyal'; D2 *wyrt* f. 'plant'; D3 *brōþorwyrt, dweorȝwosle, hǣlwyrt* f. 'pennyroyal'; D7.

26. L *pyrethrum*, pl.-*a* > OE *pyretre* 'pellitory, bertram'; D2 *wyrt* f. 'plant'; D7.

27. L *secale* > OE *siȝle* 'rye'; D2 *wyrt* f. 'plant'; D6 [cf., however, *hwǣte* 'wheat', *ryȝe* 'rye', both masculine].

28. L *stratum*, pl.-*a* > OE *strǣt* 'couch, bed'; D3 *bedrest, bedstow, fletrest, rest, strecednes, strēowen* f. 'bed, couch'; D7.

29. L *talentum*, pl.-*a* > OE *talente* 'talent'; D7.

30. L *templum*, pl.-*a* > OE *timple* 'weaver's instrument'; D7.

31. L *tignum*, pl.-*a* > OE *tinn* 'beam, rafter'; D7.

32. L *zedoārium*, pl.-*a* > OE *sīdeware* 'zedoary'; D5 *waru* f. 'ware'; D7.

33. L *zingiber* > OE *ȝinȝiber* 'ginger'; D2 *wyrt* f. 'plant'.

IV   Feminine > neuter

1. L *chamaedrys* > OE *cymed* 'wall-garmander'; D4.
2. L *fenestra* > OE *fenester* 'window'; D3 *ēaʒþȳrel, teolþȳrel* n. 'window' [Toller's Supplement: neuter].
3. L *fīga* > OE *ʒefīgu* (pl.) 'a disease'; ?D2 *ādl* n.(f.) 'disease'.
4. L *historia* > OE *stǣr* 'story, narrative, history'; D3 *spell* n. 'story, narrative, history'.
5. L *invidia* > OE *inwitt* 'deceit, evil, fraud, guile'; D3 *bealu, fācen, yfel* n. 'evil, guile, fraud'; D5 *witt* n. 'wit'.
6. L *monēta* > OE *mynet* 'coin, money'; D4.
7. OFr. *mort* > OE *myrten* 'carrion, flesh of animals'; D2 *flǣsc* n. 'flesh, body'; D3 *ǣs* n. 'carrion, meat', *hrǣw* n.(m.) 'carrion'.
8. OIc. *mörk* > OE *marc* 'denomination of weight'; D2 *ʒemet* n. 'measure', *ʒewiht* n. 'weight'.
9. L *pix,-cis* > OE *pic* 'pitch'; D3 *scipter, sciptearo* n. 'pitch'.
10. L *trabs,-bis* > OE *trǣf* 'tent, pavillion, building'; D3 *ʒeteld* n. 'tent, pavillion', *feldhūs* n. 'tent', *seleʒesceot* n. 'tent, nest'.

V Masculine > feminine

1. L *caupulus* > OE *cuopel* 'small ship'; ?D2 *bāt* f. (m.n.) 'boat, ship'.
2. OIr. *clocc* > OE *clucʒe* 'bell'; D3 *bell(e)* f. 'bell'.
3. L *cypressus* > OE *cypresse* 'cypress'; D2 *wyrt* f. 'plant'; D4.
4. L *ebulus* > OE *eofole* 'danewort, dwarf-elder'; D2 *wyrt* f. 'plant'.
5. L *humulus* > OE *hymele* 'hop-plant'; D2 *wyrt* f. 'plant'.
6. Gk. *krōssós* > OE *crūse* 'cruse, jar, pot, bottle'; D3 *croc* f. 'pot, vessel'.
7. OIc. *löstr* > OE *lǣst* 'fault, sin'; D3 *bealudǣd, fācendǣd, firen, māndǣd, scyld, synn, wrōht* f. 'sin, fault'; D5 *lǣst* f. 'last'.
8. L *mūsculus* > OE *muscelle* 'shell-fish, mussel'; D3 *scell, welocscyll* f. 'shell-fish'; D5 *scell* f. 'shell'.

VI   Masculine > neuter

1. OIc.*bȳr* > OE *bȳ* 'dwelling'; D3 *ærn, flet, ʒeset* n. 'dwelling'.
2. L *carcer* > OE *carcærn* 'prison, jail'; D2 *ærn* n. 'habitation'; D3 *gnornhof* n. 'prison, cell'; D5 *ærn* n. 'dwelling'.

3. L*cruciātus* > OE *crŭcethŭs* 'torture house or chamber'; D2 *hūs* n. 'house'; ?D5 *hūs* n.
4. L *modius* > OE *mydd* 'bushel'; D2 *ʒemet* n. 'measure'.
5. L *marcātus* } OE *market* 'market'; D3 *cēapungʒemōt* n. 'market'; D4

Notes

1. Recent accounts of this shift can be found in, for instance, Baron (1971) and Dekeyser (1975).
2. This figure does not include nouns with double or triple gender, those from parts of speech other than nouns, and proper names, as well as those appearing with some native lexical segment attached to the foreign stem, forming a compound (e.g. L*corōna* > OE *corenbēaʒ* 'crown').
3. The masculinization theory, assuming that in Old and Middle English there was a tendency to change feminine and neuter of inanimates to masculine, is supported, for example, by Clark (1957) and Mustanoja (1960) (cf. Baron 1971). A counter-theory, assuming the existence of a tendency to make the gender of inanimates neuter, was proposed by Ross (1936).
4. The figures concerning the gender preservation in Old English loanwords are drawn from my 1973 dissertation.
5. Actually, 'cover term' is used in this paper as a convenient label: it represents a tendency to assign the same gender to nouns belonging to a common semantic field. Thus the feminine assignment of nouns denoting plants or the masculine assignment of nouns referring to days (cf. OE *mārubie* f. 'horehound' and OE *sabbat* m. 'the Sabbath') need not have been caused by the direct influence of the cover terms *wyrt* f. 'plant' and *dæʒ* m. 'day', but can be due to the tendency to have feminine and masculine respectively in most nouns representing 'plants' or 'days'.
6. Cf. note 2, above.
7. In Old High German this loanword has three-gender assignment; cf. OHG *kurbiz* m.f.n. (Kluge 1957 'Kürbis').
8. Reborrowed later, this noun was assigned feminine; cf. OE *yntse* f. 'ounce'.
9. Kluge (1957) 'Most' suggests L *mustus* (originally an adjective) to be the source form of the corresponding German noun, which is also masculine.
10. Many neuter plurals in *-a* denoting collectives were reanalysed as feminine singular in Late Latin.
11. The neuter assignment of G *Fieber* is explained by Kluge as due to *das Kalt* n. (see 'Fieber' in Kluge 1957).
12. This tendency is seen in both earlier and later periods of Old English. The table below, based on the classification of Old English loanwords from Latin made by Serjeantson (1935), shows that the trend to replace neuter by masculine and feminine, and feminine by masculine is typical of all the strata of these loanwords. The statistical analysis does not include: (a) words which are not nouns; (b) nouns from other parts of speech; (c) nouns whose gender is not specified in the Old English dictionaries; (d) Latin animates; (e) nouns with double or triple gender.

	Total	Gender preserved			Gender changed					
		m	f	n	f > m	n > m	n > f	f > n	m > f	m > n
1st period (up to c.400)	109	19	39	10	15	15	8	2	–	1
		=68(62.4%)			=41(37.6%)					
2nd period (c.450–650)	67	13	19	5	10	6	9	–	4	1
		=37(55.2%)			=30(44.8%)					
3rd period (after 650)	144	25	50	10	25	19	9	2	2	2
		=85(59.0%)			=59(41.0%)					

13. It is important to note that the case most often used in Latin was accusative, whose frequency of appearance in names of inanimates by far exceeded the frequency of the nominative case, at least in the classical period (cf. Winter 1970). Because Latin nouns ending in -*us* m. and -*um* n. used the same accusative ending -*um*, it may have posed some difficulties for the borrowers who were unaware of the nominative form in the identification of the original gender. We can also assume that the educated were in most cases conscious of the original gender and the nominative case of the noun being borrowed. Here we are however dealing only with probabilities, not facts.

References

Arndt, W. W.
  1973 "Nonrandom assignment of loanwords: German noun gender", *Word* 26:244–253.
Aron, A. W.
  1930 "The gender of English loanwords in colloquial American German", *Language Monographs* 7:1–28.
Baron, Naomi
  1971 "A reanalysis of English grammatical gender", *Lingua* 27:113–140.
Blumer, J.
  1890–1891 *Zum Geschlechtswandel der Lehn- und Fremdwörter im Hochdeutschen*, Vol. 1, 2 (Leitmeritz: Anton).
Clark, Cecily
  1957 "Gender in *The Peterborough Chronicle 1070–1154*", *English Studies* 38:109–115.
Dekeyser, Xavier
  1975 "The category of gender in English and some other European languages. A diachronic-contrastive approach", Preprint (Leuven).
Fisiak, Jacek
  1975 "Some remarks concerning the noun gender assignment of loanwords", *Biuletyn Polskiego Towarzystwa Językoznawczego* 33:59–63.
Haden, E. F. — E. A. Joliat
  1940 "Le genre grammatical des substantifs en franco-canadien empruntés à l'anglais", *Publications of the Modern Language Association* 55:839–854.
Mossé Fernand
  1950 *Manuel de l'anglais du moyen âge: Vieil-anglais* (Paris: Aubier).
Mustanoja, T. F.
  1960 *A Middle English syntax. 1: Parts of speech* (Helsinki: Société Philologique).

Quirk, Randolph — C. L. Wrenn
  1958   *An Old English grammar* (London: Methuen).
Ross, Alan S. C.
  1936   "Sex and gender in Lindisfarne gospels", *Journal of English and Germanic Philology* 35:321–330.
Serjeantson, Mary S.
  1935   *A history of foreign words in English* (London: Routledge & Kegan Paul) (1961).
Wełna, Jerzy
  1973   "Linguistic analysis of borrowings in Old English". Unpublished Ph.D. dissertation (University of Poznań).
  1976   "Gender determiners in American English. A study in the grammar of loanwords", *Studia Anglica Posnaniensia* 7:95–108.
Winter, Werner
  1970   "Formal frequency and linguistic change: Some preliminary comments", *Folia Linguistica* 5:55–61.

Dictionaries consulted

Bosworth, J. — T. N. Toller
  1898   *An Anglo-Saxon dictionary* (Oxford: Clarendon Press).
  1921   *Supplement* (by T. N. Toller).
Clark Hall, J. R.
  1966   *A concise Anglo-Saxon dictionary. Fourth edition, with a supplement by H. D. Meritt* (Cambridge: Cambridge UP).
Georges, K. E.
  1913   *Ausführliches lateinisch-deutsches Handwörterbuch*, Vol. 1, 2 (Hannover und Leipzig: Hahnsche Buchhandlung).
Grein, C. T. W.
  1912   *Sprachschatz der angelsächsischen Dichter* (Heidelberg: Winter).
Holthausen, Ferdinand
  1934   *Altenglisches etymologisches Wörterbuch* (Heidelberg: Winter).
Kluge, Friedrich
  1957   *Etymologisches Wörterbuch der deutschen Sprache, 17. Auflage* (Berlin: Walter de Gruyter).
Zoëga, G. T.
  1910   *A concise dictionary of Old Icelandic* (Oxford: U.P.).

WERNER WINTER

Morphological signalling of selection properties: transitiveness in Tocharian B and A verbs

0   It is a characteristic feature of Indo-European languages that selection properties are not necessarily matched by morphological properties of the item triggering the selection. Thus, no overt feature of the genitive, dative, or ablative singular of a Latin consonant-stem noun indicates whether an adjective or a pronoun attached to this noun should be in the masculine/neuter or feminine gender; there is no formal mark of German *Messer* 'knife' which would help a hapless foreigner decide whether to use *der*, *die*, or *das* as the gender-bearing article to go with the noun; there is no outward signal that German *folgen* 'follow' is to be combined with the dative, while *begleiten* 'accompany' requires the accusative.

Selection properties appear to be above all properties of lexical morphemes or of combinations of lexical morphemes with each other or with other material; they are therefore highly likely not to admit useful generalizations, a fact which would seem to contribute substantially to the difficulty of acquiring a good command of a language of the Indo-European group.

It is therefore not surprising that time and again in the history of languages of this group one can observe the effects of attempts to reduce the range of unpredictability found in the inventory of forms in the language. These attempts have the same thrust as that found in the endeavor of young children to employ regularities discovered in the language being learned with forms hitherto not used: One attempts (and sometimes does so successfully) to predict from a grammatical (morphological, phonological) given what its proper complement should be. One bases one's observations on existing patterns; one attempts generalizations and arrives at some proper ones and at some overgeneralizations; and sometimes overgeneralizations will become proper generalizations by the general acceptance of an extended range of pattern validity. Only rarely will the extended range be coextensive with the total language; usually there will be pockets of resistance to a general leveling (for reasons which will not be discussed here), and full predictability will, in natural languages as distinguished from artificial ones, almost never be achieved.

Still, as regularity is so very advantageous (not only does it simplify the encoding process, but it also facilitates decoding, so that in both processes the amount of learning required is drastically reduced), the trend to introduce predictability will always be there, never fully succeeding, but never really checked.

As, at the last Historical Linguistics Conference in Ustronie, I was mildly criticized by one participant for having taken the material for my contribution from such well-known languages as Baltic and Slavic ones, I am going to illustrate my point from two less accessible Indo-European languages; at the same time, I hope to clarify a number of issues in the grammar of these two languages.

1   In the present paper I am going to discuss some parts of the Tocharian verbal system in which selection properties of the verb stem are reflected in morphological features. Some of these features recur in other Indo-European languages; others are the result of Tocharian innovations. I shall proceed in such a way that lists of verbs with common morphological properties will be given first, that next these lists will be extended on strictly morphological grounds, and that then reference will be made to syntactic and/or semantic properties exhibited by the members of each group, introducing at this point certain subgroupings where necessary. An excursus will be added concerning a further large class of Tocharian verbs.

The primary concern of this paper will be with verbs whose simplest stem, as found, i. a., in the mediopassive forms of the subjunctive of A and B and in the infinitive stem of B, ends in Common Tocharian /a/> B/a/, A/ā/. From this class of verbs, we will select those whose present stem is not identical with the subjunctive stem, but shows a suffix CT a > B e, A a or the addition of an -n- preceding CT a. All lists given will contain eight columns:

In the first, the reconstructed Common Tocharian stem is followed by a rendering of its meaning in German and English;

column 2 contains forms of the first subjunctive stem found in the active singular of subjunctive and imperative;

column 3, forms of the second subjunctive stem occurring in all other forms of the subjunctive and imperative, of the optative, the associated verbal adjectives and nouns, and — in B — the infinitive;

column 4, forms of the singular of the active preterite;

column 5, forms of the plural of the active preterite;

column 6, forms of the mediopassive preterite;

column 7, forms of the active present;

column 8, forms of the mediopassive present.

2 Verbs with an attested present stem in B-*e*- A-*a*-

2.1 Without palatalization of the stem-initial consonant (list I)

	1		2	3	4	5	6	7	8
krämpa-	'gestört werden; be perturbed'	B		krämpālyñe	krämpā(sta)		krämpoṣ		krämpetär
kwäla-	'nachlassen; fail'	B		kᵘlätsi	kᵘläc				kᵘletär
		A		kuli(ṣ)					kulatär
lipa-	'übrig bleiben; be left'	B		lipätsi	l(i)pa		lipo		lipeträ
		A					lipo		
lita-	'herabfallen; fall off'	B			lita		litau		litatsi
		A	letaṣ	litälune	lit	lepar			
mänka-	'unterlegen sein; be inferior'	B		mänkämo			mänkau		mänketrä
		A		mänkälune					
märsa-	'vergessen; forget'	B	märsat	marsatsi	marsa	märsäre	märsau		(mä)rseträ
		A			märs	mrasar	märso	<märsneñc>	
mäska-	'sein, sich befinden; be in a place'	B		mäskälläññe	maska				mäsketär
		A							mäskatär
		B						mäskeñca	
mita-	'gehen; go'	B		mīta(ts)y					mitentär
muska-	'verlorengehen; get lost'	B		muskätsi	muska		muskauwa		musketär
		A		muskälune			muskät		
nätswa-	'verhungern; starve' (B *m-*!)	B		mätstsätsi			mätstsor		mätstsentär
		A							nätswatsi
päla-	'erlöschen; fade away'	A		plänträ			plont		platär
pärka-	'aufgehen; rise'	B		pärkälñe	parka	parkar	pärkau		pärkatär
		A			pärkäci		pärko		

stem	1		2	3	4	5	6	7	8
pläṅka-	'zum Verkauf kommen; be put up for sale'	B		pläṅkā(ts)i	pläṅka	pläṅkāre			pläṅ(k)e(trä)
präṅka-	'sich zurückhalten; restrain oneself'	B		(prä)ṅikätsi					präṅketrä
pruka-	'erfüllt sein; be filled'	B		prukälñe		prukare	prukauwa	(pru)ṅketrä	
		A	prokaṣ	prukälune		prokar	pruko		
ritwa-	'verbunden sein; be connected'	B		rittäträ	ritta		rittoṣ		rittetär
		A		ritwälune			ritwo		ritwaträ
sätka-	'sich ausbreiten; spread'	B		sätkälñecci		sätkāre	sätkor		sätkentärne
		A		sätkälune	stäk	satkar	sätko		sätkatär
sika-	'überschwemmt werden; be submerged'	A	sekaṣäṃ				sikont		sikamtär
spänta-	'vertrauen; trust'	B		späntälñe	spänt		späntoṣ		späntetär
		A		späntälune			spänto		
spärka-	'vergehen; perish'	B		spärkälñe	sparkäne		spärkau		spärketrä
		A		spärkälune	spärkäṃ		spärko		
sruka-	'sterben; die'	B	sraukau	srukalñe	sruka	srukām	srukau	sruketrä	
trika-	'verwirrt sein; be confused'	B		trikalyñe (MQ)			trikau	triketär	
		A	trekaṣäṃ		trik		triko	trikatär	
triwa-	'sich vermischen; mix'	B		triwätsi			triwoṣ	triwe(är)	
		A		tr(i)weñci			triwo	triwanträ	
tsälpa-	'hinübergehen; pass away'	B		tsälpätsi	tsälpäwa	tsälpāre	tsälpoṣ		tsälpetär
		A	tsalpaṣ	tsälpälune	tsälp	tsalpar	tsälpos		[tsalpatär]
tsäma-	'wachsen; grow'	B	tsämat	tsmälñe	tsama		tsmo		tsmetär
		A	tsämat	tsmälune	tsäma				[samantär]

tsāra- 'sich trennen; separate'	B	tsrälīe		tsrāwa		tsror	(ts)retär
	A				tsaramäs	tsro	tsratränn
tsāwa- 'sich fügen; attach oneself'	B	tswätär		tsuwa	tswāre	tswauwa	tswetär
	A				tsawar	tswāt	
wätka- 'sich entscheiden; decide'	B	wätkoytär		wätkāwa		wätkau	(wä)kamār
	A	wätkälune	watkāṣäm	wtäk		wätko	
wika- 'schwinden; disappear'	B	wikätsi		wīka			wiketär
	A			wikäm		wikoṣä(ṃ)	wika(trä)
yāwa- 'zuneigen; lean towards'	A	ywälune				ywont	ywatsī
yutka- 'sich sorgen; worry'	A					yutko	yutkatār

2.2 With palatalized stem-initial consonant (list II)

2.2.1 With B -e-, A -a- in the initial syllable

1		2	3	4	5	6	7	8
läwa- 'senden; send'	B	*lāwaṃ*	*lwāl*	*lyuwa*		*lwoṣ*		*lyewetärne*
	A	*lawam*		*lywā*	*lawar*	*lwo*		[*lun(āmäs)*]
nāwa- 'brüllen; roar'	B		*nūwalñe*					*ñewetär*
tsälpa- 'hinübergehen; pass away'	B		*tsälpätsi*	*tsälpāwa*	*tsälpāre*	*tsälpoṣ*		[*tsälpetär*]
	A	*tsalpas*	*tsälpälune*	*tsälp*	*tsalpar*	*tsälpos*		*šälpatär*
tsäma- 'wachsen; grow'	B	*tsämat*	*tsmälne*	*tsama*		*tsmo*		[*tsmetär*]
	A		*tsmälune*	*śmäm*				*šamantär*
tsäṅka- 'sich erheben; rise'	B	*tsäṅkaṃ*	*tsäṅkatsi*	*tsäṅka*		*tsäṅkau*		*tseṅketär*

2.2.2 With B -ä-, A -ä- in the initial syllable

2.2.2.1 Without palatalization outside the present stem (list III)

1		3	8
läwa- 'reiben; rub'	B		*ly(u)wetärä*
	A	*(pä)lwār*	

2.2.2.2 With palatalization outside the present stem (list IV)

1		2	3	4	5	6	7	8
lyuka- 'leuchten; shine'	B			lyukāme				lyuketrä
śura- 'sich sorgen; worry'	A		śurām					śuratär

3 Verbs with an attested present stem in B -na- A -n-ā- (list V)

1		2	3	4	5	6	7	8
kāla- 'führen; lead'	B	kālat	kalatsi	śala	śilārene	klor	[källāṣṣäm]	[källāsträ]
	A		klämär	śäl	kalar	klät	källāṣ	källāmar
kärka- 'rauben; steal'	B		kärkats(i)			kärkäte		kärnātsi
	A							
kärsa- 'wissen; know'	B	kārsaṃ	karsatsi	śarsa	śārsāre	kärsor	kärsanaṃ	kärsanaträ
	A	krasaṣ	kärsātär	śärs	kra(sa)r	kärso	kärsnāṣ	kärsnāträ
kāta- 'streuen; strew'	B	kātaṃ	katoytär	śtasta	śtare	ktäte	katnam	kätnälle
	A				katar	ktoräṣ	knāsäm	knānträ
kātka- 'überschreiten; trespass'	B	katkaṃ	katkatsi	śaika		käikor	käikanaṃ	
	A	katkat	käikälune	kcäk	katkar	käikoräṣ	ktäiŋkātsi	
klänsa- 'liegen; recline'	B	klesaṣ	klisiṣ			kliso	klisnāṣ	
	A							
klupa- 'erlangen; attain'	B	[kallau]	[källäitsi]	kälpäwa	kälpāre	kälpau	[kälpāskau]	[kälpāskemane]
	A		kälpätär			kälpāt		kälpnātär
krästa- 'abschneiden; cut off'	B	[krāstäṃ]	karstatsi	karsta		kārstäte	karsnaṃ	kärsnāträ
	A		kärṣtälune			kärṣät	kärṣnāṣ	kärṣnāntär
kutka- 'verkörpern; embody'	B			śukām		kutkau		kutäiṅkmane
	A					kuk(ā)t		

1		2	3	4	5	6	7	8
kwäsa- 'wehklagen; wail'	B		kwasalñe					kwäsnäträ
läwa- 'senden; send'	B	läwaṃ			lawar	lwoṣ		[lyewetarne]
	A	lawam	lwäl	lyuwa / lyu		lworäṣ		
märsa- 'vergessen; forget'	B	märsat	marsatsi	marsa	märsäre	märsau	märsneñc	[(mä)rseträ]
	A			märs	mrasar	märso		
musa- 'aufheben; lift'	B					musau		musnäträ
	A					musät		musnäträ
näika- 'halten; hold'	B	näikaṃ		ñäika	ñäikärene	näikau	natknaṃ	näiknalle
nuka- 'verschlingen; devour'	B	[naukämne]				nukowä	nuknaṃ	
pärsa- 'besprengen; sprinkle'	B		pärsatsi		pirsäre	pärsäe	parsnän	pärsnälle
	A				prasar	pärsoṣ		
pläska- 'denken; think'	B	pläskaṃ	palskatsi	palska	pälskäre	pälskäte	pälskana(t)	pälskanäträ
	A		pälskälune	pälskä		pälskät	pälts änkäṣ	(pä)ltsänkämäṃ
puka- 'zuteilen; assign'	B	pautkau	putkalñe			putkau	[puttaṅkeṃ]	[puttaṅkälle]
	A	potkam	putkälune			putkorä	putäṅkäṣ	pütäṅkänträ
räma- 'sich verbeugend berühren; touch by bending down'	B		ramoṃ			rämäte	rämnoyeṃ	
	A					rmoräṣ	rämneñc	
räsa- 'recken; stretch'	B	rasaṣ					[rsaṃ]	
	A						räsñä	
räswa- 'herausreißen; pull out'	B	(ra)swar	räswät		rässäre	rsoräṣ	rsunätsi	rsunämäṃ
rita- 'suchen; seek'	B		rïtatsi			ritätai	rinäṛä	
	A		ritälune			rität		
ruka- 'fortbewegen; move'	B	rautkaṃ	rukatsi			rukäte		[ruttaṅkemar]
	A		rukälune		rokar		rutäṅkeñcäm	

säka-	'folgen; follow' (?)	A					skānt		säknāmäṃ
sälka-	'herausziehen; pull out'	B	sälkaṃ	salkatsi			sälkāte		[slaiktär]
sämwa-	'nehmen; take'	A		sumālʷne					sumnātär
sika-	'den Fuss setzen; make a step'	B	saikaṃ					siknaṃ	
täla-	'erheben; lift'	B			(t)lava			tallaṃ	tlanatäri
tärka-	'entlassen; let go'	B	tärkaṃ	tarkatsi	carka	cärkāre	tärkāte	tärkanaṃ	tär(k)nämane
tärka-		A	tarkam	tärkālune	cärk	tarkar	tärkoräṣ	tärnäṣ	tärnamaṃ
truka-	'zuteilen; assign'	B		trukāle					truknälle
tsäka-	'herausziehen; pull out'	A		tskālune		tsakar	tskāt	(t)säknāt	tsäknātär
tsärka-	'brennen, quälen; burn, torment'	B		tsärkalñe				tsarkanoyeñc	tsärkalle
tsita-	'berühren; touch'	A	ptsetā	tsitālune	tsit		tsitoräṣ	tsinātsi	
wänta;	'umhüllen; envelop'	B		wäntālune					
wänta;		A					wäntau / wänto	wäntanañc	
warpa-	'geniessen; enjoy'	B		warpatsi			wärpāte		wärpanatär
warpa-		A		wärpālune			wärpāt		wärpnātär
yäksa-	'umarmen; embrace'	B		yäksātär			yäksau		yäksana(tä)rn(e)
yäksa-		A					yäksat / yäksāt		
yuka-	'besiegen; conquer'	B		yukatsi	yukāne		yukau	[yukṣäṃ]	yuknāl
yuka-		A	yokat				yukoräṣ	yuknäṣ	

4   An inspection of the lists I (in 2.1) and V (in 3) shows some recurring differences between the two sets of forms:

(a)   In the second subjunctive stem (column 3), B forms in list V consistently show an indication of initial accent (/ä/ of the first syllable is spelled ⟨a⟩, not ⟨ä⟩; /a/ of the second is rendered by ⟨a⟩, not ⟨ā⟩), whereas in list I /a/ of the second syllable appears as ⟨ā⟩, not as ⟨a⟩, and /ä/ of the first syllable shows up as ⟨ä⟩ or is deleted altogether — a safe indication of non-initial accent.

(b)   Forms of the first and second active preterite stem in B (columns 4 and 5) and of the first active preterite stem in A (column 4) have palatalized initial consonant in list V, but not in list I.

(c)   Active forms of the subjunctive (column 1; but cf. also column 2) are common in B as far as list V goes; in list I, only two such forms are found, viz., B *mārsat* 'he will forget' and B *sraukau* 'I will die'.

(d)   In the present tense, in list I only mediopassive forms are found (cf. column 8), the lone exception being B *mäskeñca* 'being'; in list V, on the other hand, active present-tense forms abound (cf. column 7), except in such media tantum as B *wärpanatär* 'he enjoys' or B *musnāträ* 'he lifts'.

Obviously, criteria (c) and (d) are less useful as they are based on the absence of certain forms — an argument, if taken by itself, of limited cogency in the case of languages with a moderately-sized corpus.

As for criterion (a), there are three interesting exceptions to be noted: B *märseträ* 'he forgets' is matched by an infinitive B *marsatsi* (and, as noted in (c), by an active subjunctive B *mārsat*); both B *marsatsi* and B *mārsat* point to a membership in list V. The present stem **märs-n-a-* is indeed attested in A *märsneñc*; it seems therefore reasonable to assume that B *märseträ* is an innovation. This conclusion, by the way, appears to be borne out by an extra-Tocharian parallel: Arm. *moṙanam* 'I forget' also is an -*n*-present.

The second exception to (a) in list I, B *srukalñe* 'dying', again is found in a paradigm that also shows a deviation in column 2: B *sraukau* was mentioned in (c). Here, A parallels cannot be cited (the notion 'die' is expressed by a quite different verb); a possible reason for the special behavior of B *sruka*- 'die' will be given later (cf. 6.2.1). The same applies to B *mīta(ts)y* 'go'.

5.   On the basis of the criteria listed in 4, paradigms without attested present stems in B-*e*-, A-*a*-, or B-*na*-, A-*n-ā*- could be assigned to the respective lists.

Thus (list VI),

	1	2	3	4	5	6	7	8
kälska-	'untergehen; perish' B		*kälskälyñ(e)*					
mlutka-	'heraustreten; step outside' B		*mlutkämar*					
tälpa-	'sich purgieren; cleanse oneself internally' B		*tälpäte*					

could be aligned with forms found in list 1, and others (list VII)

	1	2	3	4	5	6	7	8
mälka-	'zusammenlegen; put together' B		*malkatsi*			*mälkänte* *mälkä(nt)*		
	A	*malkam*						
märtka-	'rasieren; shave' B		*markalñe*			*(mä)rtkä(t)e* *märtkänt*		
	A							
näma-	'neigen; bend down' B		*namalñe*			*nmo*		
	A		*nmälune*					
räṅka-	'steigen; climb' B		*raṅkatsi*		*räṅkär(e)*	*räṅkormeṇ*		

with those in list V.

5.1   However, whether one is entitled to conjecture that the present-tense forms of **kälska-, *mlutka-, *tälpa-* should be derived from stems in B-*e*-, A-*a*-, and those of **mälka-, märtka-, näma-* from stems in B-*na*-, A-*n-ā*-, cannot be decided at this point.

There is ample evidence that subjunctive stems in **-a-*, while forming non-present paradigms of the type discussed here, combined with suppletive present-tense stems. Thus we find (list VIII):

(List VIII)

	1		2	3	4	5	6	7	8
kälka-	'gehen; go'	A	*kalkam*	*kälkälune*	*kälk*	*kalkar*	*kälkoräṣ*	[*yäṣ*]	[*ymäṇ*]
sälpa-	'glühen; glow'	B					*sälpau*	[*salpäṇ*]	[*sälpamane*]
		A		*sälpälyi*	*salpa*		*sälp(ont)*	[*salpäṇ*]	[*sälpmäṇ*]

While in these items the absence of palatalization in the initial consonant of column 4 suggests an alignment with list I, criteria (a), (b) and (c) call for an attachment to list V in the following cases (list IX):

	1		2	3	4	5	6	7	8
käska-	'zerstreuen; disperse'	B	*käskat*	*pkaskarñ*			*käskänte*	[*käskanme*]	[*käskäntär*]
klänsa-	'liegen; lie'	B		*klantsalñe*	*klyantsa*			[*kläntsañ*]	[*kläntsañi*]
klätsa-	'bedrohen; threaten'	B	*klätsät*				*(kä)ltsänt(e)*		[*kal,stärme*]
läma-	'sitzen; sit'	B	*lämaṇ*	*lamatsi*	*lyama*	*lymäre*	*lmau*	[*ṣamau*]	[*smemane*]
		A	*laman*	*lmälune*	*lyäm*	*lamar*	*lmo*	[*ṣmäṣ*]	[*smäl*]
mäka-	'laufen; run'	B		*makatsi*			*mkänte*	[*maścer?*]	
pälka-	'sehen; see'	B	*pälkaṇ*	*palkatsi*	*palyka*	*pilykär*	*pälkäte*	[*lkäskau*]	[*lkäskemane*]
		A		*pälkälune*			*pälkät*	[*lkäs*]	[*lkätär*]
pänwa-	'spannen; stretch'	B	*pännaṇ*	*pannatsi*	*piñña*	*panwar*	*pännäte*	[*pañwäṣ*]	[*peññaträ*]
		A					*pänworäṣ*		[*pañwamträ*]
präska-	'sich fürchten; be afraid'	B	*präskau*	*parskam*	*pärska*	*pärskäre*	*pärskau*	[*präskau*]	[*pärskallona*]
		A		*präskäl*	*pärsäk*		*pärsko*		[*praskmär*]
stäma-	'stehen; stand'	B	*stämaṇ*	*stamatsi*	*śama*	*śimäre*	*stmau*	[*klyeñca*]	[*kalträ*]
		A	*ṣtamaṣ*	*ṣtmälune*	*śäm*	*ṣtamar*	*ṣtmo*	[*klyant*]	[*kälytär*]
tsuka-	'trinken; drink'	A	*tsokam*		*śuk*		*tsuko*	[*yoktsi*]	[*yoktsi*]

In some instances, an apparent suppletism may be due to incomplete attestation of two paradigms. Thus, *yuka-* 'conquer', included in list V, has attested present-tense forms only with a stem *yuks-* in B; still, to think that these two stems formed a suppletive paradigm is made unlikely by the fact that for *näma-* 'bend down', again in list V, no present B **nmanaṃ* is attested, while B *namṣäṃ, namstär* is found — but here we find ample indication that B *namṣäṃ* is part of a different, quite regular paradigm: -*s*-present B *namṣäṃ*, Ø-subjunctive B *nmalyñe* (plus intransitive/passive B *nmeträ, ñmetsi*), -*s*-preterite B *nemarneś* (plus intransitive/passive B *nemtsamai*). A parallel to *näma-* is found in *räṅka-* 'climb' — here a present tense B **raṅkṣäṃ* can safely be derived from the attested infinitive form B *raṃktsi* (as seen by Krause 1952:80), but the very fact that B *raṃktsi* is attested precludes the assumption that B **raṅkṣäṃ* should be aligned with B *raṅkatsi*.

There is, then, no evidence that the very common -*s*- present entered into a suppletive relationship with the subjunctive in CT-*a*-. This should make us reluctant to view B *kalṣtärme* as part of one paradigm with B *klātsāt* (list IX), if B *kalṣtärme* and *kältsenträ* were -*s*-presents; but, as rightly seen by Krause (1952:63; 233), they are not — they are otherwise unextended thematic present forms, and these do seem to enter into a paradigmatic relationship wit CT-*a*-stems in the cases of B *maścer* and B *peññaträ*, A *pañwäṣ, pañwamträ* (list IX).

The paradigms of *käska-* and *klänsa-* are suppletive only in a very narrow sense: the present stem, instead of remaining athematic as in list V, has been extended by a*y $^e/_o$-suffix. The older state of affairs is still preserved in the A-derivative of CT *klänsa-, klisā-*: here the third person singular of the active present tense is A *klisnāṣ*.

6 Up to this point, we have looked only at formal properties of the verbs under consideration; as a matter of fact, membership in the various lists has been determined exclusively on the basis of form. When we now raise the question whether all, or at least most, items in a list share also some well-defined syntactic or semantic property, we come up with some very simple observations:

(a)   All verbs in list I are intransitive except for B *märsa-* 'forget'.
(b)   List II is mixed as to transitiveness vs. intransitiveness.
(c)   List III contains only one verb, which is intransitive.
(d)   List IV contains two verbs, both intransitive.
(e)   List V contains mostly transitive verbs; exceptions are *klänsa-* 'lie; sleep' and *kwäsa-* 'wail'.
(f)   List VI comprises three verbs, all intransitive.

(g) List VII is made up of four verbs, all transitive except for *räṅka-* 'climb'.

(h) List VIII contains two intransitive verbs.

(i) Five verbs in list IX are transitive (*käska-* 'disperse', *klätsa-* 'threaten', *pälka-* 'see', *pänwa-* 'stretch', *tsuka-* 'drink'), five are intransitive (*klänsa-* 'lie', *läma-* 'sit', *mäka-* 'run', *präska-* 'be afraid', *stäma-* 'stand').

6.1 B *märsa-* 'forget' can be dismissed as an innovation; see the remarks in section 4. As a result, it can be stated that all verbs with present-tense stem in B-*e*-, A-*a*- and unpalatalized initial are (or were originally) intransitive.

6.2 It is to be noted that *klänsa-* 'lie' occurs twice in lists which contain mostly (as in V) or to a considerable extent (as in IX) transitive verbs. Except for *präska-* 'be afraid of, be frightened by' (constructed with the instrumental and therefore not to be counted as transitive), all other intransitive verbs in list IX can be considered as containing a reference to locomotion. This statement will probably be considered more selfevident if one takes into account that the simplest form of the verbs in question is found in the subjunctive stem, and that therefore the basic meanings should not be 'lie', 'sit', 'run', 'stand', but 'lie down', 'sit down', 'take off running', 'take a standing position'. (From list VII, *räṅka-* should be added here as 'to start climbing'.)

Whether 'movement toward' can be considered fully equivalent to 'transitive' in the present Tocharian context, is a question not easily decided. There are at least two combinations of verb and accusative object that may point in this direction:

The translation of Skt. *gṛhastha* 'householder' into Tocharian B is *ostaṣmeñca*, literally 'house sitter'. While here one might argue that in a compound noun the first part should be interpreted as the mere stem and not as the accusative case (note, however, that the stress shift signalling a compound is not always indicated — cf. B 33 a 5 Š), no such doubt is possible with respect to the rendering of the verb 'meditate, sit in meditation' — B *ompalskoññe lamatsi*, where *ompalskoññe* can only be an accusative case. (In A, the equivalent of B *ompalskoññe*, A *plyaskeṃ* combines with 'sit' in the locative case, cf. A 237 a 2, 294 b 2, 302 b 3, etc.) One might feel tempted to consider B *ompalskoññe* as a combination of a localizing prefix *om-* (<*en-*/$\overline{\text{LABIAL}}$), but descriptively this is not a correct statement (cf. the unambiguous accusative in B 12 a 4).

A derivation from an older quasi-locatival prefix is totally precluded for the fixed phrase B *eś lmau* 'blinded, blind', literally 'the (two) eyes sat (upon?)'. The origin of the — apparently metaphorical — expression can no longer be determined, but the grammatical structure, accusative object + past participle of 'sit', is perfectly clear. Unless one wants to admit an accusative graecus ('regarding the eyes'), one has to take the phrase as prima-facie evidence for a transitive use of 'sit down'.

6.2.1   In section 4, it was stated that B *mīta(ts)y* 'to set out, go' lacked the mark of non-initial accent in the infinitive (actually, the *-ī-* in the first syllable may be taken as an indication of initial accent). We now see that B *mīta(ts)y* agrees in this respect with the suppletive verbs of motion just discussed. Because of the third person plural of the mediopassive present, B *mitentär, mita-* was included in list I. If this decision is right (an alternative exists, but it is not feasible for the verb about to be introduced), we could say that here is an indication that a nonsuppletive verb of motion follows the 'intransitive' pattern (B-*e-*, A-*a-*; list I, etc.) in the present stem, but the 'transitive' one (B-*na-*, A-*n-ā-*; list V, etc.) in the non-present forms — in short, even in non-suppletive stems, there would be a mixed paradigm (or, if one wants it that way, suppletion stricto sensu).

Now, one verb obviously would not suffice to support such a claim as in any way significant. However, there is at least one further item that has to be considered in this context: In section 4, mention was also made of the fact that the B term for 'die' deviates from the pattern regular for list I — it, too, has a present stem in *-e-* (B *sruketrä, srukenträ, srukemāne, srukelle*) matched by *srūka-* (not **srukā-*) in the second subjunctive stem. Here, however, other parts of the paradigm have also been preserved, and we can note that list V, not list I, provides the proper parallels for B *sraukau, sraukaṃ* of the subjunctive singular; as B-*r-* shows no effect of palatalization and blocks palatalization of a preceding consonant, B *srukāwa, sruka, srukām, srukās, srukāre* of the active preterite cannot be directly assigned to either a nonpalatalized or a palatalized set of forms. Since it is very common to use periphrastic terms for 'die', it is perhaps not too rash an assumption to claim that *sruka-* may at least have been classified with verbs of motion by equating 'die' with 'pass away' or the like.(An assumption that *sruka* had this original meaning is less likely as the simple verb *sruk-*, which underlies the derivative B *sruka-* and which is found in A, has the simple meaning 'kill' — cf. A 9 a 1.)

Why should there be a mixed paradigm for verbs of motion? A possible answer seems to be the following: The description 'verb of motion' applies only to the nonpresentic forms — they mean 'move toward state expressed by present stem'; only with the nonpresentic forms could there originally have been the expression of a goal, a local transitivity, as it

were. Therefore, a combination of imperfect plus accusative as in B
297:3.7 *ṣamy ompolskoññe* 'he was sitting in mediation' is best interpreted as based on the analogy of nonpresentic patterns such as found in
B 4 b 7 *lyam ompalskoññe* 'he sat down to meditate'.

Whether B-*e*-, A-*a*- is the regular match in the present tense of verbs of
motion of otherwise list-V-type, cannot be said for sure, though, in our
attested paradigms, there is too much suppletion to make any cogent
assumption about the regular (or regularized) pattern. Still, it would seem
to make sense to consider the possibility that B *raṅkatsi* 'set out to climb'
was matched by a present *räṅketrä**, (or *reṇketrä**, cf. 7.1, 7.2), as
beside *räṅka-* the unextended verb stem *räṅk-* is attested in B *raṃktsi* and
räṅka- was therefore probably not combined with etymologically unrelated material.

7   We are now ready to turn to a discussion of list II

It seems noteworthy that in all cases where present-stem forms exist in
both B and A, there is no full agreement between them. B *tsälpetär* 'is
passing away' and B *tsmetär* 'is in the process of growing' would, if taken
by themselves, have to be placed in list I; for B *tsälpetär*, the remainder of
the paradigm supports this conclusion — in the case of B *tsmetär*, the
second person singular of the active subjunctive, B *tsāmat* (if correctly
identified) provides an argument against it. On the other hand, A *śalpatär*
and A *śamantär* match completely B *lyewetarrne* 'is sending him' and B
ñeweträ 'is roaring' in the vocalism of the first syllable. B *tseṅketär* 'is
rising' has no matching form in A (it should be *śaṅkatär**). In view of this
apparent confusion, it seems appropriate to discuss the verbs in list II
individually or in small groups.

7.1   The A rendering of 'send' is perfectly regular for a transitive verb:
An -*n-ā*- present can be identified in A 349 a 2 (cf. Schmidt 1974:45); the
palatalization of the singular of the active preterite is normal — in short,
the A verb fits list I. The B equivalent also shows the properties of list I
(no form of the second subjunctive stem has come to light, though),
except that the present is irregular. We will hardly hesitate to treat the
conflicting paradigms of *läwa-* as we did those of *märsa-* in section 4
and 6.1: the -*e*- present in B is to be considered an innovation.

One might speculate about the reason for this innovation: Could it be
that in B 'send' was classified with verbs of motion? However, the verb
retained its normal transitive properties, with the affected object remaining the primary one (cf. B 492 a 3 *parso lywāwaś* 'I sent you a letter').

Thus, at best one could call this a semantic realignment without syntactic consequences.

7.2   *tsäṅka-* shows all the characteristics of a verb of motion (palatalization of *ts-* has left no trace in B verbs); as stated above (section 6.2.1), little can be said about the shape the 'regular' present of verbs of motion did take, and whether B *tseṅketär* (and B *lyewetarrne*) are better candidates than B *mitentär* and B *sruketär* cannot be decided off-hand. However, the argument for palatalizing B-*e*-, A-*a*- in the first syllable might just be a little stronger:

As was noted above (section 6.2.1), the basic meaning of *sruka-* must have been 'die'; the alignment with verbs of motion may be quite late. Taken by itself, B *mitentär* also admits of an interpretation as a thematic present — B *mitentär* could be to B *mīta(ts)y* as B *maścer* is to B *makatsi*. Thus, there would be no verb of motion with a present of the type Cä(C)C*e*- left.

On the other hand, if Krause is right (1952:265, but note p. 68) in including B *plyetkemane* 'stepping outside' as a B-*e*- present, there would be further support for an assumption that first-syllable palatalizing B-*e*-, A-*a*- followed by B-*e*-, A-*a*- suffix would be a characteristic of verbs of motion without radical suppletion.

7.3   If so, *tsälpa-* 'pass away, be taken away from this world' and *tsäma-* 'grow' would have been assigned to the verbs of motion class in A, but not in B. Even in A, the assignment would have had only a limited effect on the paradigm — none that is recognizable in the case of *tsälpa-*, while in *tsäma-* the singular of the preterite shows the expected palatalization: A 278 b 2 *śmām knānmune* should not be rendered by 'knowledge came to us' (as suggested by Krause, 1933:2280f.), but by 'knowledge completed its growth with us' — the alleged A **śem* 'it came' does not agree in its vocalism with B *śem* 'he came', and there is no explanation for A-*ā*- in the paradigm of A *käm-* 'come', whereas for 'grow' -*ā*- in the preterite is to be expected.

7.4   One form is left without an explanation — B *ñewetä* 'is roaring' (with a second subjunctive stem matching forms in list V); the preterite B *nawatai* is from a manuscript with inconsistent marking of stressed B/a/ by ⟨ā⟨ — the forms may therefore be taken to represent *nawātai** and thus remain outside the paradigms under consideration here. B *nwalñe* in B 51 b 8 and *sñanwalñeṣṣepi* Pe 1 a 2 are derived not from an extended stem *näwa-*, but from a simple stem *nu-* (attested in Amb b 5 *nuṣt* — Lévi's reading). Thus only the optative B *nuwoytä* in B 236 a 2 and the verbal abstract *nūwalñe* in Amb b 5 are left to attest a list-V-type paradigm for the nonpresent forms of *näwa-* in B (A lacks a reflex of *näwa-* altogether).

Still, the forms with initial accent in the second subjunctive stem deserve to be taken seriously, as they have a striking parallel within the paradigm of a semantically closely related verb: *kwäsa-* 'wail', mentioned as an exception to list V, has a verbal abstract B *kwasalñe*. As the text (B 85 b 5) is strictly of standard Šorčuq type, we cannot but interpret this form as /kwā́sa-/. The meaning of the verb does not point toward transitiveness, but just as with *näwa-*, an affinity with list V is indicated. In the case of *kwäsa-*, this affinity extends to the present stem — here we do have -*na*- forms. However, these in their turn are not unproblematic: In B 88 b 1 *(ku)rār lūwo tu-yäknesa* [read: *tuyknesa*] *kwäsnäträ snai-kärsto* 'thus the eagle is wailing without interruption', one would rather expect to find *kwäsanaträ**, but a variation between B-*ana*- (=/ána/) and B -*nā*- (=/ná/) is not uncommon. B *kwasnāmane* in B 431 a 3 (MQ) may not be more than a misspelling; on the other hand, it could also be a regular present form to be associated with the stem B *kwāsa-* possibly attested in the optative form B *kwāsoyeṃ* (the text in B 110 is too fragmentary to permit strong assertions).

7.5   We thus find that the mixed paradigms encountered in list II have their parallels, so that a limited regularity has to be recognized even here. The regularities are not all-pervasive; therefore, there is reason to believe that we have become witnesses to processes of morphological change.

8   Lists III and IV are too limited in size, and the paradigms establishable are too fragmentary, to enable us to come up with even a reluctant explanation. A *śurām* 'sorrow' must be based on the (second) subjunctive stem, as are other deverbative nouns (cf. A *nākäm* 'blame', A *wākäm* 'difference'), but nowhere in the paradigms discussed in this paper is there an A subjunctive stem with palatial initial to be found. The initial *ś*- defies interpretation — does it correspond to B *ś*- or B *ts*-, and if the latter is the case, is A *śura-* from **ts'äwra-* or from **ts'ärwa-*, and if the latter, is there a connection with B *tsārwa-*, A *tsārwa-* 'be confident'? And if so, how is the semantic gap to be bridged?

9   Without going into very great detail, mention should be made of the fact that the initial accent as a mark of transitiveness, as found in subjunctive-stem forms discussed in this paper, recurs in a very significant component of the Tocharian B verbal system.

The so-called causative in B can be described as having the following general pattern:

(1) Present stem: Initial accent; basic stem extended by -*sk*-suffix
(2) Subjunctive stem: Initial accent; basic stem extended by
        -*sk*-suffix; (1) and (2) coincide in their stems.
(3) Finite preterite forms: Initial accent; verb stem with palatalized
        initial consonant(s) followed by /a/; basic stem
        extended by /a/; if -*sk*-suffix carried over to pret-
        erite, stem extension by /ṣṣa/.
(4) Past participle: Initial accent on reduplication with -*e*- (unless
        subjected to umlaut); initial consonant of stem
        and reduplication palatalized -*sk*-suffix present
        only when also found in finite preterite forms;
        no stem extension by /a/.

In a matrix, the following entries would result:

	initial accent	-*sk*-suffix	-/a/- extension	reduplication
present	+	+	−	−
subjunctive	+	+	−	−
preterite finite	+	∓	+	−
past participle	+	∓	−	+

Even more clearly than the verbal statement, the matrix shows that all causative forms have an initial accent. All causative forms, unless used in the passive, are naturally transitive — the subject of the underlying non-causative verb, be it transitive or intransitive itself, would automatically become the object of a derived causative.

The weight of the signal 'initial accent' becomes even greater when one realizes that it is the only signal that is common to all forms of the causative paradigm. In this respect, the importance of the initial accent is much greater than for verbs of list-V type, where transitiveness is signalled in different ways for different stems: in the present, -*na*- suffix; in the subjunctive, initial accent; in the finite active past, palatalization of the initial consonant; in the mediopassive past (including the participle), no marking whatsoever.

10   This asymmetry between two transitive patterns makes one wonder about the chronology. Initial accent in present and subjunctive of the causative does not recur in A; thus it seems not unlikely to consider it an innovation in B. All forms of the past tense of the causative in A, finite and nonfinite, appear to have initial accent — but this may be due to the general retraction of the accent in A to the first full vowel of a word rather

than to retention of a feature shared with B, the more so as the finite past forms of B and A are not morphologically congruous.

If indeed assumptions concerning the distribution of the word accent made elsewhere are correct (mechanically retracted accent in A vs. B accent free except that it is retracted from morphophonologically final syllable of a word), no use of accent as a marker of transitiveness was possible in A, and in this language only the Common Tocharian signals of transitiveness (-*na*- present, palatalized active preterit at least in the singular) could be utilized. That these should have been rather faithfully retained (replacement of -*na*- by B -*e*-, A -*a*- happens in B, not in A), seems to indicate that the principle of morphological distinction between transitive and intransitive verbs was a viable one in A (as it must have been in Common Tocharian), even if the broad utilization as found in B was impossible to implement in A.

11 Of the two Common Tocharian indicators of transitiveness, one, the initial palatalization of finite preterite forms, cannot be traced back to a specific transitiveness marker in Proto-Indo-European.

On the other hand, there is much to be said for an assumption that -*n*- was associated with transitive present stems prior to the beginnings of Common Tocharian history. When we take Latin verb stems with -*n*- limited to the present (e.g., *cernere* 'detect', *oblinere* 'smear', *pōnere* 'put', *sinere* 'let', *spernere* 'reject', *sternere* 'strew'; *iungere* 'connect', *fingere* 'form', *pingere* 'paint', *stringere* 'pull out'; *frangere* 'break something', *fundere* 'pour out', *relinquere* 'leave behind', *rumpere* 'break something', *vincere* 'conquer'; *findere* 'split', *pangere* 'determine', *pungere* 'stick', *scindere* 'tear to pieces', *tangere* 'touch', *tundere* 'push'; -*cumbere* 'lie down'), we note that all but the last item are transitive verbs. Of 41 verbs with -*nā*-/-*nī*- in the present stem in older Indic texts, only three appear to be intransitives, of 39 verbs in -*no*-/-*nu*-, four or five; of 6 verbs with -*na*- suffix, none; of 5 with -*nva*-, none; of 29 with -*n*- infix, and athematic inflection, none; of 25 with -*n*- infix and thematic inflection, one — a total then of 145 verbs with -*n*- present of which 136 or 137 seem to be transitives.

The situation in Greek is rather similar; thus, in spite of such seemingly contradictory evidence as offered by the -*nan*- verbs in Germanic, one can say (without reopening a discussion that has gone on for a long time, witness, e.g., F. B. J. Kuiper's *Nasalpräsentien*) that the use of -*n*- in the present tense of Tocharian transitive verbs can be traced back to Common Indo-European times.

Whether the presence of such an inherited marker contributed materially to the development of a class of verbs marked partially for transitiveness in Common Tocharian and marked fully so in B, cannot be ascertained: As we note a recurrent tendency toward morphological marking of selection properties in related languages, the development in Tocharian may have been spontaneous, though one would like to believe that the presence of a partial system would always be a stimulant toward the creation of a fully developed regular system (note, e.g., the spread of -*n*- to non-presentic forms of Latin).

Regularization in verbs with -*a*- suffix and in causatives did not affect items in other classes of verbs — e.g., thematic presents in B could, with identical accent patterns, be either transitive or intransitive. This, however, is not surprising: Systematizations have a much better chance of being carried out in open-ended, productive classes than in inherited classes with a limited membership. Such residual phenomena do not detract from the fact that marking for transitiveness had become a prominent feature of the verb system in Tocharian B and, within more narrowly defined limits, of Tocharian A. Whether eventually marking would have become all-pervasive must remain empty speculation as neither language survived beyond the time of the texts on which the present observations have been based.

References

Krause, W.
  1933   Review of *Tocharische Grammatik* by E. Sieg — W. Siegling — W. Schulze, *DLZ* 54:2272–2281.
  1952   *Westtocharische Grammatik* (Heidelberg: Winter).
Kuiper, F. B. J.
  1937   *Die indogermanischen Nasalpräsentia* (Amsterdam: North-Holland).
Schmidt, K. T.
  1974   *Die Gebrauchsweisen des Mediums im Tocharischen* (Göttingen).

WOLFGANG U. WURZEL

Ways of morphologizing phonological rules

0   The borderlines of the extensive field of historical morphology are
quite naturally marked by the phenomenon of formation of morphological regularities on the one hand and the phenomenon of decay of morphological regularities on the other. Both by the development of new
morphological rules and by the elimination of existing morphological
rules morphological systems are changed. Last but not least the historical
transitions between various morphological-syntactic language types such
as the isolative, agglutinative and inflective language type are induced by
the formation or decay of certain types of morphological regularities.
This is why problems of the formation or decay of morphological regularities and their consequences for the morphological system concerned
are in the centre of a theory of morphological change, although such
processes develop on the fringe of the morphological component of the
language system exactly in the sense that here morphological facts and
principles interact either with phonological or with syntactic facts and
principles. From the latter it follows that such problems are relevant not
only for a theory of morphological change. They hold for a field of facts
which show especially clearly how the individual components of the
language system with their different and partly contradictory principles
not only interact but also counteract, which among other things makes up
the specifics of natural language as against all formal constructed language and semiotic systems. The question of how the formation and
decay of morphological rules proceeds within the field of tension among
various components is thus at the same time aimed at essential characteristics of structure and function of the entire language system.

   Below an important partial aspect of this question shall be discussed,
namely the development of phonological rules to morphological rules
within the history of language — in other words: the morphologization of
phonological rules.

1   A question decisive for classifying and assessing the phenomenon of
morphologization, which again and again crops up in the discussion of

these problems either explicitly or implicitly, is that of its cause: For which reasons are phonological rules morphologized at all, what is the 'driving force' in processes of morphologizing?

The answers to these questions are highly different. With all their difference, however, it is largely common to them that either largely phonological or largely morphological causes are quite one-sidedly advanced for morphologization and that the alternative aspect is underrated in its relevance. Cp. a recent controversy: Mayerthaler (1977, esp. p. 116ff.) takes the view that, due to intraphonological developments — the telescoping of rules is treated in great detail — phonological rules lose phonological naturalness, degenerate as it were and for this reason can then be morphologized. This view is discussed by Dressler (1977a:27ff.), who in his turn assumes that, in case of morphologizing, always morphology is the 'driving force'.

Both views represent only half the truth, for even a superficial consideration shows that evidently all processes of morphologization are more or less complex interactions of both phonological and morphological principles and developments. In addition the share of both aspects can apparently be quite different from case to case. For these reasons it is recommendable to be careful about statements on "the" cause of morphologizing and, instead, to analyze and assess cases of morphologizing as different as possible in their specific parameters.

In this sense three cases of morphologizing phonological rules shall be studied in greater detail below and the role of phonological and morphological factors in them.

2   Before studying individual cases, the morphologization of a phonological rule shall be outlined: morphologizing, as we understand it, holds whenever a rule, which so far has held for an operation of permutation, insertion or deletion in a phonological context P, changes in a way that it holds for the same operation (not necessarily only this one) or its inversion[1] in a context of grammatical categories C. A rule, whose original (more or less preserved) function it was to adapt a set of phonetic sequences to human speech organs, takes over the basically new function of formally marking grammatical categories in words.[2] Thus the complete or partial phonetic motivation of the rule is substituted by a semiotic motivation.[3]

In this connection also the question arises of the relationship between morphologization and morphonologization as well as of the delimitation of morphological (MR) and morphonological rules (MPR). In general morphologizations begin as morphonologizations. The introduction of grammatical categorial features into the context of a phonological rule as well as the introduction of other non-phonetic characteristics (features of lexical rules, features of syntactic word classes, morphemic boundaries, etc.) implies a restriction of the phonetic motivation of the rule, a reduction of its phonological naturalness. It is evident that morphonologizing may lead to morphologizing only under certain preconditions. The transition from an MPR with partially grammatical context to an MR can be roughly located where the last remainder of the sequential phonological environment is deleted from the context of the rule. In this way the rule becomes free for categorial marking independently of phonological context conditions.[4]

3.1 Case 1: Morphologization of the "*ir*-rule" in Old High German

In a language state (A), which corresponds to reconstructed Proto-Germanic, the so-called *s*-stems — neuters of the *lambiz 'lamb' type — are roughly inflected as follows:

(A)   N. Sg.   *lamb + iz*   Pl.   *lamb + iz + ō*
      G.   *lamb + iz + aza*   *lamb + iz +om*
      D.   *lamb + iz + ai*   *lamb + iz + omoz*
      A.   *lamb + iz*   *lamb + iz + ō*

(The instrumental, which does not play any role below, is neglected.) The morpheme /iz/ occurs in all forms of the paradigm. Thus it can be identified as a fully intact element of stem formation and is part of the lexical representation of the words concerned which, at this stage of development, has the form ///lamb/$_{R_t}$ir/$_{St}$/$_N$. The occurrence of the morpheme /iz/ is lexically determined.[5]

In the transition to a language state (B), which can be most adequately called Pre-Old High German, the final element /iz/ is decomposed in two steps. To be more exact: There are two phonological changes based on the phonological process of reduction of phonological substance in unstressed syllables. They induce certain resegmentations in lexical units of other inflectional classes and in inflectional rules which are not of interest here. It is decisive that the phonological changes are reflected in the following natural phonological rules (NPR):

(a) $z \rightarrow \emptyset$ / VCV ___ #.
(b) $i \rightarrow \emptyset$ / $\bar{\Sigma}$ ___ #.

At first a [z] is deleted at the end of all bi- and polysyllabic words, then final [i] as well, if preceded by a long syllable. In addition phonological substance is decomposed also in the case-number inflectional morphemes of the *s*-stems and the voiced spirant [z] turns to the sonorant [r].

Due to these developments the discussed paradigm in Pre-Old High German runs as follows:

(B)   N. Sg.   *lamb*   Pl.   *lamb + ir + u*
      G.   *lamb + ir + as*   *lamb + ir + o*
      D.   *lamb + ir + a*   *lamb + ir + um*
      A.   *lamb*   *lamb + ir + u*

The lexical representations in terms of ///lamb/$_{R_i}$ir/$_{S_i}$/$_N$ are preserved after the developments described; however, the occurrence or non-occurrence of the morpheme /ir/ at phonetic level now depends on conditions of phonological context.

The rule (b) does not for long remain an NPR. Due to the shortening of final [ī], new instances of [i] develop in final position, cp. e. g. **gasti* 'guests (N. Pl.)' or *nāmi* 'I/he would take' from **gastī* and **nāmī*. The development of such counterinstances, however, does not lead to the decay of rule (b), for the corresponding paradigms show that the [ī] is phonetically but not phonologically lost. A corresponding shortening rule is introduced into the language system, which follows deletion rule (b). Thus the latter becomes an opaque (non-transparent) rule, i.e. an MPR. Rule (b) has lost in phonological naturalness.

Next the short-syllable words of the *ir*-set such as **blati* 'leaf' which had originally preserved their final [i] join the "surface inflection" of the *lamb* type with N./A. Sg. without ending. They, too, now occur in terms of *blat* etc. As in other inflection classes where forms with [i] and without [i] co-occur, namely in masculine and feminine *i*-stems, there is also a levelling out in favour of the long-syllable [i]-less variant (cp. *gast/*biʒi* 'bite' > *gast/biʒ*, *anst* 'favour'/**stati* 'place' > *anst/stat*), rule (b) is extended in its context:[7]

(b′) $i \rightarrow \emptyset$ / VC __ #.

The cause of this context extension is of morphological nature; there is a levelling out of two subclasses within one class of inflection. The development of the rule from (b) to (b′), however, proceeds according to purely phonological parameters, no morphological conditions being introduced into the rule. The reason for further development of the rule towards morphologizing is therefore not the influence of morphological factors but the repeated decay of phonetic motivation and this is a phonological factor.

Along with further phonological changes and the analogous influence of other inflectional classes the context extension of *i*-elimination finally causes the *i*-stems to be relexicalised according to the principle ///gast/$_{R_t}$i/$_{S_t}$/$_N$>///gast/$_{R_t}$/$_{S_t}$/$_N$ and thus leave the application range of rule (b').

Thus the two phonological rules (a) and (b') hold for the same set of cases and are always applied in common: If the [r] is deleted the [i] is also deleted. They can no longer be identified by the speakers as two separate operations, i.e. individual rules, and telescope to form a uniform MPR (simultaneously realizing the change from [z] to [r]):

(a/b')   *ir* → Ø / VC ___ #.

By telescoping, the phonological naturalness which is weakened anyway in (b') is further restricted, for the elimination of two segments at the same time is certainly less natural than that of one segment. On the other hand it should be noted that in contrast to (b'), MPR (a/b') is no longer opaque, it covers all surface instances of [ir], apart from few exceptions such as *ahir* 'ear (of corn)' and *trestir* 'draff'.[8]

The phonological process of reducing unstressed syllables continues. Final [u] from Proto-Germanic [ō] is deleted. This is the transition to a language state (C), which we want to call Early Old High German. The mentioned change which decomposes the case marker of N./A. Pl. in this and other inflectional classes, along with further reductions of other case markers, leads to the paradigm:

(C)	N. Sg.	*lamb*	P.	*lamb + ir*
	G.	*lamb + ir + es*		*lamb + ir + o*
	D.	*lamb + ir + e*		*lamb + ir + um*
	A.	*lamb*		*lamb + ir*

At this stage of development a decisive change occurs: with the total loss of final [u] the phonological conditions are lost, based on which the alteration of [ir] ~ Ø has functioned so far. In other words: The instances of [ir] in the paradigm can no longer be determined on the basis of phonological parameters. The generation of speakers having to learn the paradigm (C) without the inflectional morpheme /u/ of the N./A. Pl. cannot but acquire the distribution of [ir] in the inflected forms on the basis of given morphological parameters. They learn that the morpheme* /ir/ occurs within the paradigm in the G./D. Sg. and the entire Pl. but not else. This means that they interpretet the morpheme as an inflectional suffix introduced by an inflection rule. In this way there is a simultaneous relexicalisation of words eliminating [ir] from the lexical representation,

///lamb/$_{R_i}$ir/$_{St}$/$_N$ becomes ///lamb/$_{Rt}$/$_{St}$/$_N$. As thus the formal marker of the class has been deleted, the speakers have now to learn in detail for which neutral nouns the rule applies. They are characterised in the lexicon by a special morphological feature [+ *ir*-Inflection]. The inflection rule which, due to the specific conditions of the change discussed here, represents an inversion of the rule (a/b′), has the form:

$$(\text{a/b''}) \quad \emptyset \rightarrow ir \ / \ \left\{ \begin{array}{l} [+\ \text{Plural}] \\ \left[\left\{ \begin{array}{l} +\ \text{Gen} \\ +\ \text{Dat} \end{array} \right\}\right] \end{array} \right\} + [ir\text{-inflect}] \ /_{St}\text{———}/_N.$$

This rule is no longer an MPR. It represents the transition to an MR.

It is easy to see that the inflective paradigm (C) is rather unsystematic from a morphological point of view: The new inflectional morpheme /ir/ occurs not only in the category of Pl., where it takes the function of the only morphological categorial marker in the N./A. It redundantly occurs also in the G./D. Sg. which disturbs the formal uniformity of the Sg. Due to a corresponding morphological change the paradigm is systematised. The transition to language state (D), the Old High German, has been completed:[9]

(D)   N. Sg.   *lamb*   Pl.   *lemb + ir*
       G.   *lamb + es*   *lemb + ir + o*
       D   *lamb + e*   *lemb + ir + um*
       A.   *lamb*   *lemb + ir*

The morpheme /ir/ becomes the uniform plural marker for all cases. Thus it is the first plural marker in the German inflection system which has become independent of case marking. This is clearly expressed by the systematised rule of inflection

$$(\text{a/b''}) \quad \emptyset \rightarrow ir \ / \ \left[\begin{array}{l} +\ \text{Plural} \\ +\ ir\text{-Inflect} \end{array} \right] \ /_{St}\text{———}/_N.$$

In the following centuries and particularly in Early New High German, this morphological rule is extended to many other nouns.

3.2   Case 2:   Morphologization of the Old High German umlaut rule in two masculine classes of inflection

In Early Old High German, which represents language state (A) in this connection, the distribution of umlauted and non-umlauted forms in the masculines of the *i*- and *n*-inflection is as follows:

(A)	(1)	N.	Sg.	*gast*	Pl.	*gesti*	(2)	N.	Sg.	*hano*	Pl.	*hanun*
		G.		*gastes*		*gestio*		G.		*henin*		*hanōno*
		D.		*gaste*		*gestim*		D.		*henin*		*hanön*
		A.		*gast*		*gesti*		A.		*hanun*		*hanun*
		I.		*gestiu*		—		I.		—		—

Quite "lautgesetzlich", there is umlaut in the *i*-stems of the type *gast* 'guest' in the I. Sg. and in the entire Pl., in the *n*-stems of the type *hano* 'cock' in the G./D. Sg. The umlaut rule, at this time still an NPR, accordingly functions purely phonologically. Neglecting details (such as umlaut preventing consonant groups), it can be outlined as:

$$
\text{(c)} \qquad V \rightarrow \ddot{V} \,/\, \underline{\quad} \; C_1 \begin{bmatrix} -\text{ consonant} \\ -\text{ back} \\ +\text{ high} \end{bmatrix}
$$

A (back) vowel changes to the corresponding front one if, separated by one or several consonants, it is followed by an [i] or [j]; cp. the paradigms.

The further development leading to Later Old High German, the language state (B), is characterised by the fact that, by morphological levelling, the umlauted forms disturbing the paradigm — the I. Sg. of masculine *i*-stems and the G./D. Sg. of masculine *n*-stems — are decomposed and substituted by non-umlauted forms. Thus the paradigms *gast* and *hano* change as follows:

(B)	(1)	N.	Sg.	*gast*	Pl.	*gesti*	(2)	N.	Sg.	*hano*	Pl.	*hanun*
		G.		*gastes*		*gestio*		G.		*hanin*		*hanōno*
		D.		*gaste*		*gestim*		D		*hanin*		*hanōn*
		A.		*gast*		*gesti*		A.		*hanun*		*hanun*
		I.		*gastiu*		—		I.		—		—

After the morphological change, a non-umlauted Sg. faces a umlauted Pl. in the paradigm of the type (1), in the type-(2) paradigm umlaut has been entirely lost. This means that the umlaut rule has been restricted by non-phonological features. The mentioned cases are explicitly excluded from umlaut:

$$(c') \ V \rightarrow \ddot{V} \ / \sim \ < \left\{ \begin{array}{c} \left[\begin{array}{c} \overline{+ \ i\text{-Inflect}} \\ + \ \text{Masculine} \\ \underline{- \ \text{Plural}} \end{array} \right] \\ \left[\begin{array}{c} \\ + \ n\text{-Inflect} \end{array} \right] \end{array} \right\} > C_1 \left[\begin{array}{c} - \ \text{conconant} \\ - \ \text{back} \\ + \ \text{high} \end{array} \right]$$

This rule is no longer an NPR but an MPR with non-phonological features, which guarantee the non-application of the rule under certain morphological conditions. Therefore these conditions are negative in their nature ("if not ...") even if, from the formal aspect, they can be formulated in positive terms. After this morphological levelling back vowels ([a] in our examples) may come to stand before [i] or [j] in certain contexts. The phonological naturalness of the rule is restricted but it further has a phonetic motivation: Back vowels, even if no longer all of them, become their front counterparts before [i]/[j].

For the further development of the rule (c') it is decisive that within a phonological change based — as the phonological changes in the discussed Case 1 — on the phonological process of reducing unstressed syllables all short unstressed vowels become [ə]. This also holds for umlaut-effecting [i]. Consequently, in language state (C), Middle High German, *gast* and *hane* are inflected:

(C) (1) N. Sg. *gast*   Pl. *geste*   (2) N. Sg. *hane*   Pl. *hanen*
         G.   *gastes*   *geste*   G.   *hanen*   *hanen*
         D   *gaste*   *gesten*   D.   *hanen*   *hanen*
         A.   *gast*   *geste*   A.   *hanen*   *hanen*

The Instrumental no longer exists as a grammatical category. With unstressed short vowels coinciding in [ə], the phonological environment of the rule (c') is lost and thus its phonetic motivation — the rule has become an MR. It now contains the positive specification of the categories for whose forms it holds, among others, for those of the Plural of masculine *i*-stems. The *n*-stems, however, which no longer alternate between umlauted and non-umlauted forms after levelling, no longer occur in the rule:

$$(c'') \quad V \rightarrow \ddot{V} \ / \left\{ \begin{array}{c} + \ i\text{-Inflect} \\ + \ \text{Masculine} \\ + \ \text{Plural} \end{array} \right\}$$

The non-phonological features no longer prevent the application of the rule but effect its application. Instead of the condition "not in the Singular" there is now the positive condition "in the Plural". As (c) was a phonological modificatory rule, the rule (c″) is a modificatory MR. It has an exclusively semiotic motivation. It is extended to many cases which it did not cover as phonological rule, even today it is still extending its domain within certain morphological classes.

The original phonological umlaut rule (c) caused alternations not only in the two mentioned inflectional classes but also in a number of others. At the loss of conditioning segments it is therefore subject to a number of other morphologizations of our Case 1 type.[10] They will not be studied in detail here. It is essential, however, that the uniform umlaut rule is thus split up into various MRs, which is, as it were, a counterpart of rule telescoping.

3.3   Case 3:   Morphologization of the Old Icelandic *i*-umlaut rule in the present indicative singular of strong verbs

After the occurence of the *i*-umlaut in Proto-Norse the long-syllable strong verbs with umlautable root vowel such as *blōta (n) (Old Icelandic *blóta*) sacrifice are conjugated as follows in the Present Indicative:

(A)   1. Ps. Sg. *blōtu*   Pl. *blōtum*
      2. Ps.   *blǿtiR*   *blōteð*
      3. Ps.   *blǿtiR*   *blōta(n)*

For the language state (A) the distribution of the forms with umlauted and non-umlauted vowels within the paradigm — as *i*-umlaut in general — is determined by a respective phonological rule which at this time most probably still represents an NPR:

(d) $V \rightarrow \ddot{V} /$ $\left. \begin{array}{c} [\overline{}]C_1 \\ \underline{} C_2 \end{array} \right\}$ $\left[\begin{array}{c} - \text{consonant} \\ - \text{back} \\ + \text{high} \end{array} \right]$

Before [i] or [j] of the following syllable, vowels in long syllables are umlauted to the respective front ones.[11]

Probably very early — and therefore when the vowels of final syllables [i] and [u] were still preserved — there is a morphological adjustment of the root vowel of the 1st Pers. Sing. to the forms of the two other Persons of the Singular. The umlaut is extended within the paradigm according to morphological criteria.[12] Thus the transition to language state (B) has been completed. The paradigm now runs as follows:

(B)   1. Sg.   *blǫtu*   Pl. *blōtum*
           2.   *blǫtiR*   *blōteð*
           3.   *blǫtiR*   *blōta(n)*

Due to this morphological change the umlaut rule (d) becomes an MPR,
which functions partially on the basis of positive morphological conditions:

$$(d') \ V \rightarrow \ddot{V} \ / \ \left\{ \begin{array}{c} [\overline{+ \ long}]C_1 \\ \underline{\qquad} C_2 \end{array} \right\} \left\{ \begin{array}{c} / \begin{bmatrix} + \ present \\ - \ plural \\ - \ subjunctive \\ + \ strong \end{bmatrix} X_{/V} \\ \begin{bmatrix} - \ consonant \\ - \ back \\ + \ high \end{bmatrix} \end{array} \right\}$$

This MPR (which is a little difficult to formulate) means that a back vowel
is umlauted in a long syllable if it occurs in the Pres. Indic. Sing. of a strong
verb or if it is followed by a [i]/[j].
    In the next step, the so far umlaut-effecting [i] is eliminated as well as
the final [u] of the 1st Pers Sing. Besides, runic [R] changes to [r] and [ð]
to [þ]. In this language state, Old Icelandic, the verb *blóta* is conjugated in
the Present Indicative as follows:

(C)   1. Sg.   *blǫt*   Pl. *blótum*
           2.   *blǫtr*   *blóteþ*
           3.   *blǫtr*   *blóta.*

With the decay of phonological conditions for umlaut in these cases, the
umlaut is morphologized; the MPR (d') is changed to an MR, the non-
phonological context conditions of the MPR being taken over into the
MR unchanged. As also short-syllable verbs such as *taka* take' which
properly should not have any umlaut, join this type of inflection (*tek, tekr*
instead of **tak, *takr*), the phonological specification in terms of long
syllable is lost from the rule as well:

$$(d'') \quad V \rightarrow \ddot{V} \ / \ \left\{ \begin{array}{c} \vdots \\ \begin{bmatrix} + \ present \\ - \ subjunctive \\ - \ plural \\ + \ strong \end{bmatrix} X_{/V} \\ \vdots \end{array} \right\}$$

Here the umlaut has become a true categorial marker which, in the Pres. Indic. of strong verbs with umlautable vowel, formally distinguishes the Singular from the Plural, similarly as in the Preterite of most strong verbs by means of various ablaut vowels.

The *i*-umlaut rule (d) as well is subject not only to the described morphologization but also to futher morphologizations in other inflectional classes and categories. Again, several MRs correspond to one NPR.

4 For the purpose of confrontation, let us again briefly summarize the essential characteristics of the three described cases of morphologizing phonological rules.

In Case 1 the two NPRs (a) and (b), which decompose the stemforming element /iz/ under certain phonologic conditions, are the starting-point of the development which finally leads to the formation of a new MR. The process starts with the development of counterinstances to rule (b) and thus with its morphonologization in a phonological way. Due to further factors — the extension of the context of rule (b) (which is morphologically conditioned but has only phonological consequences for the rule) and the telescoping of (a) and (b′) into MPR (a/b′), still more phonological naturalness is lost. The new rule (a/b′) however further operates (apart from a few exceptions) in a purely phonologically determinable environment, namely in the context VC __ #. This phonological environment appears quite accidental in the forms of certain grammatical categories in an inflectional class. In this way the absence or presence of [ir] becomes the factual corepresentative of grammatical categories in addition to the categorial markers paroper. We want to call the element [ir] a quasi-marker, that is a linguistic unit which, on the one hand, still has a phonologically determined distribution, but on the other, is already bound to grammatical categories and thus helps to identify them. The final step to morphologizing the *ir*-rule then is a further phonological change, namely the deletion of final short [u]. In this way an essential part of the phonological context is lost, which causes the alternation of [ir] ~ ∅ in the paradigm. This alternation can no longer be determined with phonological means, and the rule (a/b′) loses the rest of its phonetic motivation. As the alternation has so far been implicitly bound to grammatical categories, now the lost phonological conditions can be compensated by explicit reference to the respective categorial features, the element [ir] being willy-nilly interpreted as an inflectional morpheme, i.e. as a true categorial marker. With this re-interpretation the speakers of a new generation adopt an inflectional rule which introduces the inflectional morpheme /ir/ into certain grammatical categories — just as the other inflectional morphemes have been introduced by the other inflectional rules. Thus the new MR (a/b″) is an inversion of (a/b′).[13] As it is no deletion rule but an insertion rule, it has to contain an additional morphological class feature delineating its domain. Due to its way of development, the MR is morphologically un-systematic and is therefore systematized by morphological change in a final step. The result of the entire process is a reasonable, morphologically natural rule of inflection, a rule with purely semiotic motivation. Schematically, this morphologization can be represented as follows:

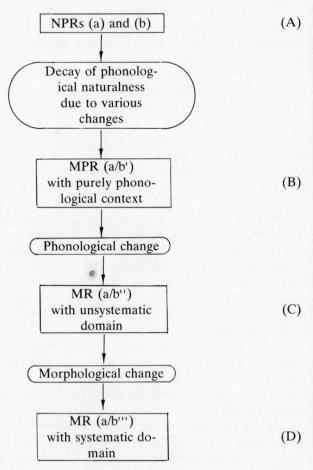

In Case 2 as well an NPR, rule (c), is the historical starting-point for morphologization. The process of the gradual change of the rule to an MR begins with a partial morphological levelling, that is a morphological change: The domain of the umlaut rule is restricted on the basis of non-phonological features; in this process phonological naturalness is lost. The preliminary result is the rule (c'), an MPR, referring explicitly to morphological features. This rule as well, this time in an indirect way, produces a quasi-marker which, in spite of its large phonological conditioning, accompanies grammatical categories. In masculine *i*-stems there is now no umlaut in the Singular but always in the Plural. Due to a phonological change neutralising the conditioning phonological environment the rule becomes an MR for a new generation of speakers, the so far negative (restrictive) morphological specification now appearing in positive form, cp. MR (c″). A systematisation of the rule in the sense of morphological naturalness is no longer necessary in this case, since already by the morphological change at the beginning of the entire process of morphologization the umlaut alternation in the paradigm had been revised according to morphological parameters: no umlaut in the Singular ∼ umlaut in the Plural. For Case 2 thus the following overall picture results:

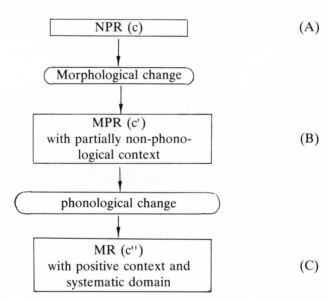

Ad Case 3: Here the starting-point for later morphologization is the rule (d) which has apparently the character of an NPR. As in the preceding case, the process of morphologization is triggered by morphological levelling: The effect of the rule is extended beyond its original, phonologically defined range of application. This is done by introducing additional, non-phonological features into the rule. Thus its phonological naturalness is reduced. At this stage the result is the MPR (d′) whose context conditions are partly phonological, partly morphological. The *i*-umlaut now covering the entire present indicative of strong verbs becomes a quasi-marker. It is at least partly phonologically determined in its occurrence but virtually accompanies a constellation of grammatical categories.[14] Due to phonological changes, the segment [i] still co-conditioning, the alternation between non-umlauted and umlauted vowel is lost. In this way the rule then operates exclusively in its previous morphological environment which is preserved in the same form as at the preceding stage. The transition from the MPR (d′) to MR (d″) has been completed. The resulting MR is already systematic in morphological terms, since — as we have seen — the entire process of morphologization has started with a morphologically motivated redistribution of the two alternants in the paradigm. Case 3 can be outlined as follows:

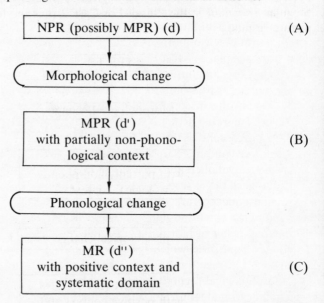

NPR (possibly MPR) (d)   (A)

Morphological change

MPR (d′)
with partially non-phono-   (B)
logical context

Phonological change

MR (d″)
with positive context and   (C)
systematic domain

5   Now what can we state summing up the causes for morphologization in the three cases analysed?

In all three cases the entire process of morphologization consists of (at least) two partial processes, namely the morphonologization of the respective rule (A > B) and its morphologization in the stricter sense (B > C). As has been shown, the reasons for these two developments in the course of morphologization may be of quite different character. Consequently, they have to be distinguished.

In Case 1 there is morphonologization for phonological reasons;

phonological naturalness decays in a phonological way. In the other two cases, however, it is morphological changes that cause morphonologization. In Case 2 the phonologically conditioned non-uniformity of forms in the paradigm (*n*-stems) or in a category (*i*-stems) is eliminated, in Case 3 the phonologically conditioned non-uniformity of forms is directly used in terms of morphology. In both cases morphologization is here realised by introducing morphological context conditions into the rule.

The second step, morphologization proper, is due to phonological change in all three cases, the decay of phonological conditions based on which the alternation had functioned so far.[15] In Case 1 there is also a third partial process, namely the morphological systematisation of the rule.

In all three morphologizations, phonological and morphological factors co-operate. But which of the two aspects has the dominating share, represents the "driving force"? In Cases 2 and 3 this is clearly morphology. Phonological alternations are morphologically regulated, changed with morphological motivation. The morphologically motivated regulation can take place — according to the concrete constellation — in various ways. In Case 2 it consists in the elimination of phonological differentiations obscuring the paradigmatic or categorial connection, in Case 3, however, in the direct utilisation of a phonological differentiation for categorial marking. Roughly summarised: On the one hand, it causes that "the same content" is formally marked in the same way, on the other, that "a different content" is formally marked in a different way.[16] It is evident that these levelling tendencies are based on the principle of analogy. The phonological rule is restricted (Case 2) or extended (Case 3) accordingly. The consequences are different as well which result from the loss of phonological conditions in the so far MPR. The resulting MR in Case 3 is the direct result of morphological regulation. It serves exactly the morphological purpose which caused its development, namely categorial marking. The resulting MR in Case 2, however, is only an indirect result of morphological regulation. Here the regulation served the production of greater formal uniformity in the paradigm. Where this standardization of forms did not cover the entire paradigm, in masculine *i*-stems, instances of alternation were preserved in the paradigm. The MR holds for these cases and marks the respective non-adjusted category of "Plural". The fully levelled paradigms, the *n*-stems, are eliminated from the rule. In Case 3 the morphologized rule thus covers the categories of the paradigm whose forms had been levelled by morphological regulation, in Case 2, however, its complementary class. We want to call the type of morphologization represented by Case 3 "direct morphologically-conditioned morphologization" and the type repre-

sented by Case 2 "indirect morphologically-conditioned morphologization".

In contrast, morphological factors do not play any remarkable role up
to the change of the MPR to an MR in Case 1. The way of both NPRs to a
uniform MR (a/b″) is characterised by the gradual reduction of phonological naturalness in a phonological way up to the final decay of phonological conditions of alternation. As the alternation is implicitly bound to
certain grammatical categories, these can replace the lost phonological
context. Thus the handed-down alternation remains to be practicable. It
is only at this late point of time that morphology comes into play. The
accidentally morphologized — from the aspect of morphology — and
therefore rather unsystematic rule is systematised in a way that the
marker introduced by it clearly marks a grammatical category within the
paradigm. This case is without doubt a phonologically-conditioned morphologization.

Thus the decisive question for the classification undertaken for morphologizations is: Is the explicit connection of an alternation with grammatical categories only the result of the decay of their phonological
conditions or has it existed (in positive or negative form) already before?

In this way we have, without aiming at a near-comprehensive analysis
of the extensive problems as a whole, delimitated three main types of
morphologizations. In conclusion, we want to raise the somewhat
speculative question of which characteristics are common to all possible
morphologizations of phonological rules and try to briefly answer it on
the basis of the insight gained.

At any rate in every (completed) morphologization the sequential
phonological context conditions have to be fully decayed and replaced by
morphological-grammatical ones. The final point of morphologization is
trivially always a morphological rule. But what is its starting-point? In our
three cases it was (most probably) always NPRs. It also stands to reason
that purely phonologically-conditioned processes of morphologization
have to proceed from an NPR; their first step always consists in the
reduction of the phonological naturalness of such a rule. Morphologically
conditioned morphologizations, however, can proceed also from MPRs,
i.e. from rules which no longer function in a purely phonetic way. They
then again reduce their anyway restricted phonological naturalness, morphologizing the respective MPR to a still greater extent.

Thus in such cases the division of the entire process into (at least) a
stage of morphonologization (A > B) and a stage of morphologization
(B > C) would hold. Nevertheless cases are imaginable where an NPR
becomes an MR in one step without preceding morphonologization by
phonological change (A > C). The conditions for such a process are easy

to realize. Similarly for the third stage, systematization, in case of phonological-conditioned morphologizations: It can be missing as well if the distribution of alternants on the categories is morphologically systematic by accident. It becomes clear, however, that a morphologization process contains in all no more than three essential steps (morphonologization, morphologization and systematization).

Last but not least we have seen that two NPRs can coincide in one MR in the course of the morphologizing process and that even the splitting up of a uniform NPR into several MRs with different functions is possible. Here again, no stricter conditions can be formulated.

What is left of common qualities is not too much: morphologizations of phonological rules are developments in the history of language in which the phonological conditions of alternations are replaced by morphological-grammatical conditions and the rules thus changed to MRs; they

— are (directly or indirectly) morphologically or phonologically conditioned,
— have NPRs or MPRs as their starting-points,
— proceed in one, two or three steps,
— lead from one or several phonological rule(s) to one or several MR(s) and
— proceed without or with rule inversion.

Consequently, morphologizations differ with respect to:

(1)   their conditioning (motivation; C),
(2)   the type of their input rule (IR),
(3)   the number of steps in the entire process (S),
(4)   the quantitative relations between input and output rules (QR) and
(5)   the occurrence of rule inversion (RI).

Based on these criteria, a quite plausible typology of morphologizations of phonological rules covering the essence of such developmental processes becomes possible: In all five points there is — as we could see — only a limited number of possibilities which can be represented in terms of the theory of sets as follows:

$(1')$ C $= \{M_{dir}, M_{ind}, P\}$
$(2')$ IR $= \{NPR, MPR\}$
$(3')$ S $= \{1, 2, 3\}$
$(4')$ QR $= \{1R > 1R, 1R > sR, sR > 1R\}$
$(5')$ RI $= \{\sim I, I\}.$

Then a morphologization (M_i) can always be characterized as a quintuple consisting of an element of each of these five sets.[17] For the three cases discussed, thus the following quintuples result:

(Case 1) M_1 = (P; NPR; 3; sR > 1R; I)
(Case 2) M_2 = (M_{ind}; NPR; 2; 1R > sR; ~ I)
(Case 3) M_3 = (M_{dir}; NPR; 2; 1R > sR; ~ I)

According to this classification, there would be a total of 108 different types of morphologizations of phonological rules from purely theoretical aspects. Yet the discussion of our few examples already showed that the various characteristics of morphologizations are not always independent of each other: morphologically-conditioned morphologizations always proceed in two steps, phonologically-conditioned morphologizations always start with NPRs and phonologically-conditioned morphologizations proceed mostly (not necessarily) in three steps etc. The detailed research of such connections will in future certainly lead to new interesting insights.

Notes

1. There is an inversion of a rule e.g. in Case 1 discussed below, cp. there.
2. There is not principally much difference if the categorial marker due to morphologization marks the respective category alone or along with other markers, cp. on the one hand, e.g. German umlaut in *Nagel* — *Nägel* and, on the other, in *Stock* — *Stöcke*.
3. Here such purely conventional morphonological rules are neglected which, although operating on the basis of a phonological context, have no longer any causal relation between phonological context and structural change. Rules of this type have of course no phonetic motivation.
   The change in motivation distinguishes the morphologization of phonological rules from that of syntactic rules which as such have already a semiotic motivation. Morphologization represents here merely a change in the type of means fulfilling the semiotic function.
4. Of course there may be a number of problems in the detailed delimitation between MPRs and MRs, cp. Dressler (1977a, 1977b) and Wurzel (1977).
5. For arguments in favour of the morphological form of complex lexical representations of this type cp. Wurzel (in preparation). The indexes of slants stand for "Root", "Stem" and "Noun" (= word).
6. Thus for instance the phonological representation /nām + ī/ with /ī/ is justified by the fact that the subjunctive marker appears also phonetically as [ī] in all persons except the 1st/3rd pers. sing., cp. Old High German *nāmīs* you would take, *nāmīm* we would take, etc. The conditions are somewhat more complicated in the case of **gasti*: The lexical representation of the word is / / /gast/$_R$i/$_{st}$/$_N$, the n.pl. being formed with /i/ so that the form/gast + i + i/ results which, by a type of monophthongization rule, becomes/gast + ī/.

Forms of the type /nãm + ī/ and /gast + ī/ then lost their vowel length due to the mentioned shortening rule.

It is not without interest that, due to the shortening rule, also the preconditions for restoring the lost categorial marker in the 2nd pers. pret. ind. of long-syllable strong verbs are given: Having the form /i/, it had been lost by the deletion of final *i* so that here "lautgesetzlich" *zugi* 'you pulled' (short syllable) was confronted by **nãm* 'you took' (long syllable). By restoring inflectional forms such as *nãmi* the personal marker /i/ is reinterpreted as /ī/. Due to the shortening rule, it appears phonetically always as [i]. Consequently there is a morphological change by way of resegmenting an inflectional rule.

7. Thus individual non-levelled cases with short root syllable such as *wini* 'friend' and *turi* 'door' or few non-alternating forms such as *furi* 'for', which are actually regular forms from the aspect of language history, take the character of exceptions.

8. Here short-syllable *and* long-syllable words are concerned. For the development of these exceptions partly phonological ("after effect of Verner's law"), partly morphological reasons (levelling within the paradigm) are advanced, cp. Braune (1955: 202) and Paul (1917:24).

9. We do not want to comment on umlaut here which is irrelevant in this connection.

10. Cp. e.g. feminine *i*-stems which became quite "unexpectedly" subject to the loss of umlauting [i]. Here, the root vowel was umlauted "lautgesetzlich" in the G./D.Sg. and in the entire Plural: *anst, enste, enste, anst; enste, enste, ensten, enste*. The disturbing umlaut forms are done away with in a long process virtually covering the entire Middle High German period so that finally also here non-umlauted Singular is confronted by umlauted Plural.

11. Later still other umlaut regularities are added which, along with *i*-elimination and many relatively early levellings, represent a very complicated picture of umlaut conditions in the individual Nordic languages.

12. It is probable that this morphological change has actually occurred in preserved vowels of final syllables but cannot be proved, since runic inscriptions do not contain any forms of the **blǫtu* type.

13. The reason for the inversion of the rule in its morphologizing results from qualities of the morphological structure of Old High German: The form of the N.Sg. throughout represents the lexical representation of nouns and is, in most inflectional classes, at the same time identical with the input of inflectional rules (cp. Wurzel (in preparation)). These inflection rules are all of the additive type, i.e. they mark grammatical categories by introducing inflectional suffixes. There are no subtractive rules (as a morphological *ir*-deletion rule would be) in the Old High German system of declination.

14. It seems inadequate to us to consider the umlaut in the 2nd/3rd Pers.Sing. as a quasi-marker, that of the 1st Pers. Sing., however, as a true categorial marker.

15. The decay of phonological conditions of an alternation can occur in two ways: (a) In the forms covered by the rule so far, the phonological qualities on which it operates are eliminated; the application of the rule is no longer phonologically determined. (b) In forms not covered by the rule so far, phonological qualities develop on which it operates; the non-application of the rule is no longer phonologically determined. The former holds for Cases 2 and 3, the latter for Case 1.

16. What is understood by "same" and "different" mainly depends on the categorial system and its formal distinctions in the individual language.

17. In case essential determinations of morphologizations should be neglected in the present analysis, the *n*-tuple can of course be expanded easily.

References

Braune, Wilhelm
  1955   *Althochdeutsche Grammatik* (8th edition) (Halle: Niemeyer).
Dressler, Wolfgang U.
  1977a "Grundfragen der Morphonologie", *Veröffentlichungen der Kommission für Linguistik und Kommunikationsforschung der österreichischen Akademie der Wissenschaften* 5 (Wien: Verlag der österreichischen Akademie der Wissenschaften).
  1977b "Morphologization of phonological processes (are there distinct morphonological processes?)", *in: Linguistic studies offered to Joseph Greenberg*, edited by Alphonse Juilland (Saratoga: Anma libri), 313–337.
Hirt, Hermann
  1931– *Handbuch des Urgermanischen* (Heidelberg: Winter).
  1934
Krahe, Hans
  1960– *Germanische Sprachwissenschaft* (4th edition) (Berlin: De Gruyter).
  1961
Mayerthaler, Willi
  1977   *Studien zur theoretischen und zur französischen Morphologie* (Tübingen: Niemeyer).
Noreen, Adolf
  1923   *Altisländische und altnorwegische Grammatik* (4th edition) (Halle: Niemeyer).
Paul, Hermann
  1917   *Deutsche Grammatik, Flexionslehre* 2 (Halle: Niemeyer).
Wurzel, Wolfgang U.
  1977   "Zur Stellung der Morphologie im Sprachsystem", *Linguistische Studien, Reihe A* 35:130–165.
  to appear "Zur phonomorphologischen Seite der Lexikonrepräsentation", *Linguistische Studien, Reihe A.*

Index of terms

abductive evolutive innovation, 7, 18
abductive innovation, 7, 8, 11, 14, 16, 18, 19, 25, 44, 45, 393
accomodative innovation, 9, 10
adaptive innovation, 7, 8
analogical change, 159, 161, 162, 164, 176, 178, 179, 244, 287, 308, 338, 359, 375
analogical formation, 178, 179, 180
analogical levelling, 230, 355
analogy, 1, 2, 45, 46, 232, 239, 241, 244, 251, 283, 284, 285, 286, 316, 351, 375, 457

bifurcating change, 2, 11
borrowing, 98, 364, 366, 367, 368, 399

case shift, 136
case reduction, 130, 131, 132, 133
coding, 127
coding change, 300, 308, 312
coding shift, 131, 133, 135
compensation, 275, 276, 278
competing changes, 394
contact change, 12, 360, 364, 365, 368, 369
contact innovation, 11, 12, 13, 14

deductive evolutive innovation, 8, 16
deductive innovation, 7, 8, 14, 15, 16, 26, 45
diachronic correspondence, 7, 45
differentiative integration, 375
drift, 21, 131, 310

evolutive change, 14, 15
evolutive innovation, 7, 14, 175
externally-motivated change, 360, 364

functional motivation, 376

fusion language, 258

gender assignment, 97, 399, 410, 411
gender loss, 100, 366
gender shift, 97, 99, 399, 402, 403, 406, 407, 408, 411
general alternation, 31, 32

historical change, 128, 129, 132, 135, 136, 167, 236, 302
historical syntax, 51

innovation in indexical signata, 27–30
innovation in morphological categories, 20–23
innovation in stem alternations, 30–36
integrating change, 375
interference, 361, 362, 364, 365, 366, 367, 368, 369
interference innovation, 16
internally-motivated change, 359, 360

language acquisition, 157, 158, 159, 160, 163, 166, 178, 367, 394, 395
language contact, 359
lexical conditioning, 252
lexical diffusion, 178, 267
lexicalization, 395
linguistic change, 1, 135, 161, 163, 275, 276, 383, 387

morphological alternation, 35
morphological borrowing, 12
morphological change, 1, 2, 3, 7, 99, 160, 162, 177, 180, 298, 299, 308, 309, 310, 327, 360, 383, 439, 443, 452, 454, 455, 456
morphological conditioning, 252, 456

Index of languages

The index is arranged in accordance with the Latin alphabet. It lists languages, dialects, names of language families and stages of the development of a given language under separate readings. If a given language is referred to in the text by two names, both are included in the index.

Index of names

Gougenheim, G., 146, 156
Goyvaerts, D. L., 138
Grappin, H., 198, 201, 210
Graur, A., 328, 334, 335, 346
Greenberg, J. H., 5, 47, 183
Grein, C. T. W., 420
Grevisse, M., 151, 156
Grimes, J. E., 292, 321
Grossman, R. E., 320, 321
Guberina, P., 196, 210
Guggenheim-Grünberg, F., 258, 271
Gumperz, J. J., 366, 371
Gvozdev, A. N., 47

Haarmann, H., 321
Haas, W., 24, 47, 247, 248
Haber, L., 392, 396, 397
Haden, E. F., 399, 419
Hale, K., 165, 183
Halle, M., 11, 48, 82, 214, 220, 221, 222,
  223, 224, 225, 227, 228, 246, 247, 248,
  385, 386, 397
Hamm, J., 196, 210
Hammerich, I. J., 318, 321
Hankamer, J., 317, 321
Harms, R., 396, 397
Harris, M., 141, 147, 151, 152, 154, 156
Haugen, E., 130, 138
Havránek, B., 380
Heath, J., 56, 69
Helm, K., 263, 270
Hermann, E., 2, 16, 17
Herzog, M. I., 268, 270, 271, 272
Hetzron, R., 352, 358
Hirt, H., 462
Hjelmslev, L., 21, 48, 189, 210, 317
Hoard, J. E., 221, 225, 228, 245, 246, 248
Hock, H. H., 251, 271
Hockett, C. F., 62, 69, 213, 231, 245, 248,
  373, 380, 383, 397
Hofmann, J. B., 306, 308, 321
Hoijer, H., 370
Holmer, N. M., 186
Holthausen, F., 420
Hooper, J. B., 157, 165, 178, 180, 183, 253,
  254, 268, 271, 331, 336, 347, 394, 397
Hope, E., 322
Hraste, M., 196, 210
Hsieh, H.-I., 320, 322
Huntley, D. G., 4, 48, 189, 302, 322

Hurford, J., 267
Hurski, M. I., 121, 122, 124
Hutchinson, L. G., 317, 322
Hyldgaard-Jensen, K., 249
Hymes, D. H., 360, 367, 369, 371

Isačenko, A., 4, 21, 35, 38

Jackendoff, R. J., 386, 392, 397
Jacob, J. M., 186
Jacobi, H., 319, 322
Jacobsen, W. H., Jr., 292, 322
Jakobson, R., 4, 5, 7, 9, 11, 15, 19, 20, 22,
  30, 36, 40, 43, 48, 160, 183, 302, 317,
  318, 322
Jankoŭski, F., 113, 124
Jeffers, R. J., 396, 397
Jēgers, B., 47
Jespersen, O., 137, 138, 157, 178, 183, 239,
  248, 249, 307, 322, 379, 380
Joffe, J. A., 269, 271
Joliat, E. A., 399, 419
Jones, C., 46, 110, 111, 182, 287, 288
Jones, D., 223, 224, 249
Juilland, A., 462

Kachru, B. B., 322
Karskij, E. F., 113, 122, 198, 200, 210
Kastovsky, D., 213, 215, 219, 236, 245,
  247, 248, 249, 316
Katz, J. J., 133, 138
Kaufman, T., 370, 372
Kaye, J., 182
Kedajtene, E. I., 198, 201, 210
Keller, R. E., 271
Keller-Cohen, D., 180
Kenny, J., 170, 183
Kernyc'kyj, I. M., 29, 48, 201, 210
King, R. D., 251, 252, 253, 254, 264, 268,
  271
Kiparsky, P., 136, 138, 271, 387
Kiparsky, V., 22, 29, 31, 48, 267, 397
Klausenburger, J., 165, 183, 384, 397
Klemensiewicz, Z., 31, 33, 34, 48
Klokeid, T. J., 64, 69
Kluge, F., 418, 420
Knobloch, J., 322
Knudsen, T., 130, 139
Komarek, M., 204, 211
Kondrašov, N. A., 193, 211